D1556474

The SAGE
Handbook of

Measurement

The SAGE
Handbook of
Measurement

Edited by
Geoffrey Walford,
Eric Tucker, and
Madhu Viswanathan

Los Angeles | London | New Delhi
Singapore | Washington DC

First published 2010

SAGE Publications Ltd
1 Oliver's Yard
55 City Road
London EC1Y 1SP

SAGE Publications Inc.
2455 Teller Road
Thousand Oaks, California 91320

SAGE Publications India Pvt Ltd
B 1/I 1 Mohan Cooperative Industrial Area
Mathura Road, Post Bag 7
New Delhi 110 044

SAGE Publications Asia-Pacific Pte Ltd
33 Pekin Street #02-01
Far East Square
Singapore 048763

Library of Congress Control Number 2009925933

British Library Cataloguing in Publication data

A catalogue record for this book is available from the British Library

ISBN 978-1-4129-4814-2

Typeset by Glyph International, Bangalore, India
Printed by MPG Books Group, Bodmin, Cornwall
Printed on paper from sustainable resources

Contents

Theorisation of Constructs

Critical and Ethical Perspectives

Sensitive Issues and the Difficult to Measure

Improving the Practice of Measurement

Administrative and Secondary Data and Performance Measurement

List of Contributors

Jamal Abedi is a Professor at the School of Education of the University of California, Davis and a research partner at the National Center for Research on Evaluation, Standards, and Student Testing (CRESST). Abedi's research interests include studies in the area of psychometrics and test and scale developments. His recent works include studies on the validity of assessments, accommodations and classification for English language learners (ELLs), opportunities to learn for ELLs, and measurement of creativity. Abedi is the recipient of the 2003 national Professional Service Award in recognition of his '*Outstanding Contribution Relating Research to Practice*' by the American Educational Research Association. He is also the recipient of the 2008 *Lifetime Achievement Award* by the California Educational Research Association. He holds a Master's and a PhD degree from Vanderbilt University in Psychometrics.

Roger Bakeman (PhD, University of Texas at Austin) is Professor Emeritus of Psychology at Georgia State University, Atlanta, GA, USA. He is the author, with J. M. Gottman, of *Observing interaction: An introduction to sequential analysis* (2nd ed., 1997), and with V. Quera, of *Analyzing Interaction: Sequential Analysis with SDIS and GSEQ* (1995). His interests include observational methodology and sequential analysis of observational data, social development of infants and toddlers, and analysis of behavioral science data generally, especially as related to health psychology. He is a fellow of both the American Psychological Society and the American Psychology Association.

David Bartholomew was born in England in 1931. After undergraduate and postgraduate study at University College London, specializing in statistics, he worked for two years in the operational research branch of the National Coal Board. In 1957, he began his academic career at the University of Keele and then moved to the University College of Wales, Aberystwyth as lecturer, then senior lecturer in statistics. This was followed by appointment to a chair in statistics at the University of Kent in 1967. Six years later he moved to the London School of Economics as Professor of Statistics where he stayed until his retirement in 1996. During his time at the LSE he also served as Pro-Director for three years. He is a Fellow of the British Academy, a Member of the International Statistical Institute, a Fellow of the Institute of Mathematical Statistics and has served as Honorary Secretary, Treasurer and President of the Royal Statistical Society. He has authored, co-authored or edited about 20 books and 120 research papers and articles many of them in the field of social statistics, broadly interpreted.

Martin Bulmer is Emeritus Professor of Sociology at the University of Surrey, UK. From 2000 to 2008 he was director of the ESRC Question Bank, an online resource of social survey questionnaires from major probability surveys which was established to strengthen the academic infrastructure for UK social scientists in relation to survey research [http://surveynet.ac.uk/sqb/qb/]. From 2002 to 2008 he was also director of the ESRC Survey Link Scheme, designed to give UK social scientists an acquaintance with professional social survey data collection. His recent works include edited collections in the Sage Landmarks in Social Research series, *Secondary Analysis of Survey Data* (with P. Sturgis and N. Allum, 2009) and *Questionnaires* (2004). He is the editor of the journal *Ethnic and Racial Studies*, ranked number one in the ISI Ethnic Studies category, 2008. His major books include *The Chicago School of Sociology, Institutionalisation, Diversity and the Rise of Sociological Research* (1985).

Ross Cheit is an Associate Professor of Political Science and Public Policy at Brown University. He has a doctorate in Public Policy and a law degree from the University of California at Berkeley and he attended Williams College as an undergraduate. Professor Cheit is a member of the Rhode Island Ethics Commission and he is working on a book about child sexual abuse in America.

Chi-yue Chiu is a Professor of Psychology at the University of Illinois and a Professor at the Nanyang Business School of the Nanyang Technological University. He is interested in studying cultures as knowledge traditions, and is conducting research on the social, cognitive, and motivational processes that mediate construction and evolution of social consensus. This theoretical perspective has been applied to understand cultural differences and similarities in social justice, conflict resolution, responsibility attribution, and political elections. He is also interested in the dynamic interactions of cultural identification and cultural knowledge traditions, and their implications for cultural competence and intercultural relations.

A. Timothy Church received his PhD in Psychology from the University of Minnesota and is currently a Professor of Counseling Psychology at Washington State University. His research interests include personality and its measurement across cultures, cross-cultural and indigenous psychology, and the integration of trait and cultural psychology perspectives in the study of personality across cultures. His publications on these topics have appeared in the *Journal of Personality and Social Psychology, Journal of Research in Personality, Journal of Personality, European Journal of Personality*, and *Journal of Cross-Cultural Psychology*, among others. He has served on the editorial boards of these and other journals and is a former Associate Editor of the *Journal of Cross-Cultural Psychology*.

Linda Darling-Hammond is Charles E. Ducommun Professor of Education at Stanford University where her research, teaching, and policy work focus on issues of teaching quality, school reform, and educational equity. She is a former president of the American Educational Research Association and member of the National Academy of Education. Among more than 300 publications that she has authored are *Preparing Teachers for a Changing World: What Teachers Should Learn and be Able to Do* (with John Bransford, for the National Academy of Education, winner of the Pomeroy Award from AACTE), *Teaching as the*

Learning Profession: A Handbook of Policy and Practice (with Gary Sykes, recipient of the National Staff Development Council's Outstanding Book Award for 2000), and *The Right to Learn* (recipient of the American Educational Research Association's Outstanding Book Award for 1998).

Aniruddha Das is a Post-Doctoral Fellow at the Center on Aging and NORC, University of Chicago. His current research interests are centered in the social structuration of the life process. Substantive dimensions of interest within this area include sexuality and gender, physical and mental health, and biosocial processes. Secondary interests include the design features of health and associated systems, and their impact on patients and health-care providers. Dr. Das was associated with the 1999–2000 Chinese Health and Family Life Survey, and is currently affiliated with the National Social Life, Health, and Aging Project sponsored by the National Institute of Aging. He has published on various aspects of sexuality, including masturbation, sexual harassment, and sexual practices and problems among the elderly.

Jack Dieckmann is a G. J. Lieberman doctoral fellow at Stanford University. His research is in the area of mathematics education examines the relationship among teaching and learning of mathematics and the mediating role of language, symbols, and other representational tools. Prior to coming to Stanford, Jack worked in educational advocacy in Texas at the Intercultural Development Research Association (IDRA) as a senior education associate in the division of professional development. Formerly a middle and high school math teacher, Jack currently teaches pre-service math teachers at Stanford's Teacher Education Program (STEP).

William W. Eaton, PhD, is the Chair of the Department of Mental Health at the Johns Hopkins School of Public Health. He is the principal investigator of the Baltimore Epidemiologic Catchment Area Study, a population-based longitudinal study of mental health originally recruited in 1981 that has been followed for the past 23 years. He is an expert in study design and measurement of psychopathology, and is the author of *The Sociology of Mental Disorders*.

Howard T. Everson is Senior Fellow at the Center for Advanced Study in Education, Graduate Center, City University of New York, and serves as consulting research scientist to number of organizations, including the American Councils for International Education, the American Institutes for Research, and the National Center for Education and the Economy. Prior to joining the City University, Dr. Everson was a Professor of Psychology and Psychometrics at Fordham University in New York. Professor Everson's research and scholarly interests focus on the intersections of cognitive psychology, instruction, and assessment. He has contributed to developments in educational psychology, psychometrics, and quantitative methods in psychology. Dr. Everson was founding director of the Educational Statistics Services Institute (for NAEP) at the American Institutes for Research. Dr. Everson also served as Vice President and Chief Research Scientist for the College Board, and was a Psychometric Fellow at the Educational Testing Service. Dr. Everson is a Fellow of the American Educational Research Association and the American Psychological Association, a charter member of the American Psychological Society, and past-president of the Division of Educational Psychology (Division 15) of the American Psychological Association.

Stephen Gorard holds the centrally funded Chair in Education Research at the University of Birmingham, UK. His research is focused on issues of equity, especially in educational opportunities and outcomes, and on the effectiveness of educational systems. Recent project topics include widening participation in learning (*Overcoming the barriers to higher education*, Trentham), the role of technology in lifelong learning (*Adult learning in the digital age*, 2006, Routledge), and teacher supply and retention (*Teacher supply: the key issues*, 2006, Continuum). He is particularly interested in the process and quality of research, having recently led the UK ESRC Research Capacity-building Network, and an ESRC Researcher Development Initiative to improve the understanding of randomised controlled trials in social science. He is the author of hundreds of pieces on research methods (and editor of *Quantitative Research in Education*, 2008, Sage).

Edward Haertel is Jacks Family Professor of Education and Associate Dean for Faculty Affairs at Stanford University, where he has been a faculty member since 1980. He is an expert in educational testing and assessment. His research centers on policy uses of achievement test data; the measurement of school learning; statistical issues in testing and accountability systems; and the impact of testing on curriculum and instruction. He has been closely involved in the creation and maintenance of California's school accountability system, and has served on advisory committees for other states and for testing companies. Haertel has served as president of the National Council on Measurement in Education (1998–99), as a member of the National Assessment Governing Board (1997–2003), and as a member of the joint committee for 1999 edition of the Standards for Educational and Psychological Testing (1994–99). He was a Fellow at the Center for Advanced Study in the Behavioral Sciences (1994–95) and is a Fellow of the American Psychological Association and a member of the National Academy of Education.

Martyn Hammersley is Professor of Educational and Social Research at the Open University, UK. His early research was in the sociology of education. Later work has been concerned with the methodological issues surrounding social and educational enquiry. With Paul Atkinson he wrote what has become a standard introductory text on ethnography – *Ethnography: Principles in Practice* (first published in 1983 with the second edition published by Routledge, 1995 and reprinted many times since). Some of the topics he has addressed in recent years include objectivity and partisanship in social research, case study and the nature of causality, the status of discourse analysis as a self-sufficient paradigm, the relationship between research and policymaking, and the concepts of 'systematic review' and 'evidence-based practice'. His most recent books are: *Taking Sides in Social Research* (Routledge, 2000); *Educational Research, Policymaking and Practice* (Paul Chapman, 2002); *Media Bias in Reporting Social Research? The case of reviewing ethnic inequalities in education* (Routledge, 2006); and *Questioning Qualitative Inquiry* (Sage, 2008).

Bill Hillier is Professor of Architectural and Urban Morphology in the University of London, Chairman of the Bartlett School of Graduate Studies and Director of the Space Syntax Laboratory in University College London. As the original pioneer of the methods for the analysis of spatial patterns known as 'space syntax', he is a co-author of *The Social Logic of Space* (Cambridge University Press, 1984, 1990) which presents a general theory of how people relate to space in built environments, *Space is the Machine* (CUP 1996), which reports a substantial body of research built on that theory, and a large number of articles concerned with different aspects of space and how it works. He has also written extensively on other aspects of the theory of architecture, lectures and teaches widely, and maintains an active interest in urban design consultancy projects.

Veronica Nyhan Jones is a Social Development Specialist at the International Finance Corporation, part of the World Bank Group. Working in the Oil, Gas and Mining Department, she advises private extractive clients operating in Africa, Asia, and Latin America on participatory processes and how to improve the local development impacts around their projects. She has also worked for the World Bank Institute building capacity for community driven development in Africa and supporting social cohesion in Eastern Europe. Prior to joining the World Bank in 1997, she worked for the International Youth Foundation and the US Government on crime prevention and health-care reform. She has a master's degree from Harvard University's Kennedy School of Government.

Ujwal Kayande is a Professor of Marketing at the Australian National University. He was previously on the faculty at Penn State University and the Australian Graduate School of Management, Sydney, and has been a visiting faculty at the Wharton School (University of Pennsylvania) and the Indian School of Business. He has a PhD from the University of Alberta, Canada. Ujwal's research interests are in the areas of marketing measurement and models, and marketing strategy. His research has been published in leading business journals, including *Marketing Science, Information Systems Research*, the *Journal of Marketing Research*, the *International Journal of Research in Marketing*, and the *Journal of Retailing*.

Jennifer Klafehn is a doctoral student in industrial and organizational psychology at the University of Illinois at Urbana-Champaign. Her research interests include cross-cultural organizational behavior, cultural intelligence, negotiation, and personality development. Her most recent publication is a chapter in the *Handbook of Cultural Intelligence* focusing on the psychological mechanisms contributing to the development of meta-cognitive cultural intelligence.

Monika Kukar-Kinney is an associate professor of marketing in the Robins School of Business, University of Richmond, Richmond, VA. She completed her PhD in marketing at the Kelley School of Business, Indiana University, in 2003. Her research focuses on compulsive buying, behavioral pricing, retailing, and electronic commerce. Her work has appeared in journals such as the *Journal of the Academy of Marketing Science, Journal of Consumer Research, Journal of Retailing*, and *Journal of Business Research*, among others. She has won an award for the best dissertation proposal in behavioral pricing from the Fordham University Pricing Center (2001), and the best paper award in the Pricing and Retailing Track (2006 Winter American Marketing Association Educators' Conference). Prior to academia, Dr. Kukar-Kinney conducted marketing research for a consulting firm in Slovenia.

Edward O. Laumann is the George Herbert Mead Distinguished Service Professor of Sociology at the University of Chicago. Professor Laumann directed the National Health and Social Life Survey, one of the largest US surveys of sexual attitudes and behaviors since the Kinsey Reports. He was the principal investigator of the 1995–97 Chicago Health and Social Life Survey, and a co-principal investigator of the National Survey of Chinese Sexual Practices. He is currently a co-principal investigator on the National Sexuality, Health, and Aging Project, sponsored by the National Institute of Aging. Professor Laumann is a member of numerous professional associations, including former Chair, Section K of the American Association for the Advancement of Science, the American Sociological Association, the International Academy of Sex Research, and the Society for the Scientific Study of Sex. He has published extensively, authoring numerous scientific articles, books, and abstracts. Some of his book titles include: *Chicago Lawyers: The Structure of the Bar, The Organizational State: Social Choice in National Policy Domains, The Hollow Core: Interest Representation in National Policymaking, The Social Organization of Sexuality, Sex Love and Health*, and *The Sexual Organization of the City*.

Rachel A. Lotan is Director of the Stanford Teacher Education Program and Professor (Teaching) at Stanford University School of Education. Lotan received her PhD in Education (Concentration: Social Sciences in Education) from Stanford University. She also holds master's degrees in Sociology and in Education (Concentration: Second/Foreign Language Teaching and Learning) from Stanford. Her teaching and research focus on aspects of teaching and learning in academically and linguistically diverse classrooms, teacher education, and the sociology of the classroom. Previously, as co-director of the Program for Complex Instruction at Stanford University, she worked on the development, research, and world-wide dissemination of complex instruction, a pedagogical approach to creating equitable classrooms. Her recent publications include two chapters entitled 'Developing language and content knowledge in heterogeneous classrooms' and 'Managing groupwork'.

John J. (Jack) McArdle, PhD, is currently Senior Professor of Psychology at the University of Southern California in Los Angeles, CA USA. From 1984–2005 he was a faculty member at University of Virginia where he taught Quantitative Methods since 1984, and was director of the *Jefferson Psychometric Laboratory*. He teaches classes in topics in psychometrics, multivariate analysis, and structural equation modeling. McArdle is a visiting fellow at the Institute of Human Development at University of California at Berkeley, an adjunct faculty member at the Department of Psychiatry at the University of Hawaii. Since 1989, he has been the lead statistical consultant of the *National Collegiate Athletic Association* (NCAA). McArdle's research has been focused on age-sensitive methods for psychological and educational measurement and longitudinal data analysis including publications in factor analysis, growth curve analysis, and dynamic modeling of adult cognitive abilities. McArdle is the director of the ongoing *National Growth and Change Study* (NGCS), a longitudinal study of cognitive changes over age in the entire USA. McArdle has won the Cattell Award for Distinguished Multivariate Research (1987), was elected President of the Society of Multivariate Experimental Psychology (1993–94), was elected President of the Federation of Behavioral, Psychological, and Cognitive Sciences (1996–99), and was elected as the Secretary of the Council of Scientific Society Presidents (CSSP, 2000–02). McArdle's current NIA research is titled, 'Assessing and Improving Cognitive Measures in the HRS.'

The first phase of this work starts with basic factor analysis of the HRS cognitive measures and expands to dynamic growth curve analyses of the complete longitudinal set of HRS cognitive measures. The second phase is based on factor analysis and prediction modeling of Alzheimer's Disease in the newly available HRS-ADAMS data set. A third phase of this work is based on the creation of several new and improved cognitive measures for possible use in future HRS – these new measures are firmly grounded in contemporary psychometric cognitive tasks but can also be administered over the telephone. A fourth phase of this work is to examine the role various cognitive constructs have in the dynamics of health and economic decisions, including the choice of Medicare choices and prescription drug use.

Briana Mezuk, PhD, is a Robert Wood Johnson Health and Society Scholar at the University of Michigan. She received training in psychiatric epidemiology, study design, biostatistics, and psychometrics from the Department of Mental Health at the Johns Hopkins School of Public Health. From 2002–07 she was the Project Coordinator for the Baltimore Epidemiologic Catchment Area Study, a population-based longitudinal study of mental health in the community, where she assisted in the revision of study instruments to reflect the aging of the cohort and trained interviewers to administer the questionnaire.

Kent B. Monroe (DBA, 1968, Illinois; MBA, 1961, Indiana; B.A., Kalamazoo College) is J.M. Jones Distinguished Professor of Marketing Emeritus, University of Illinois, Urbana-Champaign and is Distinguished Visiting Scholar at the University of Richmond, Richmond, VA. He has authored *Pricing: Making Profitable Decisions*, 3rd ed., McGraw-Hill/Irwin, 2003. His research has been published in the *Journal of Marketing Research, Journal of Consumer Research, Journal of Marketing, Management Science, Journal of the Academy of Marketing Science, Journal of Retailing,* and other journals. He was the editor of the *Journal of Consumer Research*, 1991–93, and of *Pricing Practice and Strategy*, 1993–2003. He is a Fellow of the Decision Sciences Institute, and also the Association for Consumer Research. He received the Pricer of the Year award from the Pricing Institute, April 1999, the Fordham University Pricing Center award for contributions to behavioral pricing research, October 2000, and the Marketing Pioneer Award for lifetime contributions to the development of pricing theory in marketing, Central Illinois Chapter of the American Marketing Association, April 2002. He was the recipient of the 2005 American Marketing Association-McGraw-Hill/Irwin Distinguished Marketing Educator Award and the P. D. Converse Award for contributions to the field of marketing, April 2008.

Sean Mulvenon is a Professor of Educational Statistics and Director of the National Office for Research on Measurement and Evaluation Systems (NORMES) at the University of Arkansas. He has published over 50 manuscripts, one book, and numerous technical reports in addition to having presented over 150 papers at national and international conferences. Since 1998, he has generated over $9 million in research funding as a principal investigator for NORMES studying educational data systems, measurement models associated with school reform, and conducting research on the impact No Child Left Behind (NCLB) legislation. Dr. Mulvenon recently completed a 31-month appointment as a senior adviser to the Deputy Secretary of Education, where he studied NCLB measurement models, developed national data systems, and served on several internal review panels, including evaluation of growth models and policy legislation associated with NCLB.

Xiaoxia Newton is an assistant professor in the division of Policy, Organization, Measurement, and Evaluation (POME), Graduate School of Education, University of California, Berkeley. She comes to POME from Stanford University, where she was a postdoc for the Teachers for a New Era (TNE) research project. She is interested in applying a variety of methodological techniques to address research and evaluation issues in urban school reform, K-12 mathematics education, and teacher learning and professional development, especially from cross-cultural and comparative perspectives.

Josephine Ocloo is Research Associate in Organisational Governance at the Patient Safety and Services Quality Centre (PSSQ) at Kings College, University of London, directed by Professor Naomi Fulop. She is also a UK National Patient Safety Champion for the World Health Organisation.

Remo Ostini is a Research Fellow at the Healthy Communities Research Centre at the University of Queensland in Ipswich, Australia. He taught psychological measurement and the psychology of morality in both Minnesota and Queensland to pay the bills while he pursued his first love – measuring morality. After a brief sojourn discovering the joys and value of pharmacoepidemiology, he now makes himself useful conducting research on participation in community-based chronic illness organizations, workplace health assessments, and health literacy.

David Phillips is Professor of Comparative Education and a Fellow of St. Edmund Hall, University of Oxford. He has written widely on issues in comparative education, with a focus on education in Germany and on educational policy borrowing. He served as Chair of the British Association for International and Comparative Education (BAICE) from 1998 to 2000, on the board of directors of the (US) Comparative and International Education Society (CIES) from 2006 to 2009, and is an Academician of the British Social Sciences Academy and a Fellow of the Royal Historical Society. He was, for 20 years, editor of the *Oxford Review of Education*, is a member of the boards of various journals, and now chairs the editorial board of *Comparative Education*. He edits the on-line journal, *Research in Comparative and International Education* and is series editor of *Oxford Studies in Comparative Education*. His most recent book (with Michele Schweisfurth) is *Comparative and International Education: An Introduction to Theory, Method, and Practice*.

Sandy M. Philipose is a doctoral candidate in Curriculum and Teacher Education at Stanford University. Her research interests generally include teacher education and new teacher support and induction. More specifically, she is interested in understanding the role of preparation and school context in teacher development and practice. During her time at Stanford, Sandy has worked with the Teachers for a New Era project and interned as an Education Pioneer fellow with the research team at the New Teacher Center at the University of California, Santa Cruz. She is also interested in the preparation of language teaching professionals and teaches the world language methods courses in the Stanford Teacher

Education Program. Before coming to Stanford, Sandy worked as high school Spanish teacher in Texas.

Noah Raford is a specialist in evidence-based design of the built environment, with a focus on simulation, measurement, and visualization. His current research focus is on complexity science, resiliency, and decision making under uncertainty, with a special emphasis on climate change and long-term catastrophic risk preparedness. Noah also consults professionally on a range of sustainable urban development projects around the world, with a focus on strategy, forecasting, scenario planning, and policy. He has degrees from Brown University, University College London and the Massachusetts Institute of Technology, and is a researcher at the Complexity Programme, London School of Economics.

Nancy M. Ridgway is a professor at the University of Richmond. Prior to that, she worked at Louisiana State University, the University of Colorado at Boulder and as a visitor at the University of Texas at Austin. She got her BBA, MBA, and PhD degrees from the University of Texas at Austin. She has been published in the *Journal of Consumer Research*, the *Journal of Marketing Research*, the *Journal of Retailing*, the *Journal of the Academy of Marketing Science*, and others. Her teaching expertise lies in consumer behavior and integrated marketing communications. She has also taught marketing management at the MBA level and the history of marketing thought at the PhD level. Her research interests are in the consumer behavior area. She studies such topics as compulsive buying, collecting, hoarding, and search behavior

Marc Riedel is a Professor of Sociology at Southeastern Louisiana University. He is also an Emeritus Professor at Southern Illinois University in both the Criminal Justice and Sociology Departments. He is the author/editor of 10 books, the most recent (with Wayne Welsh) being a second edition of *Criminal Violence: Patterns, Causes, and Prevention*. He is the author of numerous articles which have appeared in the *Annals of the American Academy of Political and Social Science, Journal of Criminal Law and Criminology, Journal of Quantitative Criminology, Journal of Research in Crime and Delinquency*, and *Temple Law Quarterly*. Dr. Riedel received his PhD in Sociology from the University of Pennsylvania in 1972 specializing in Criminology. He holds two MA degrees, one in Sociology and the second in Psychology. Dr. Riedel's undergraduate major was in Biology and Psychology. His research on the death penalty has been cited in two US Supreme Court decisions, *McCleskey v. Kemp* 487 U.S. 279 (1987) and *Pulley v. Harris* 465 U.S. 37 (1984) as well as in *Ross v. Kemp* 756 F.2d 1483 (1985). In 1978, Dr. Riedel was elected to a three-year term on the Executive Counsel of the American Society of Criminology and in 1986 was elected Vice-President of that organization. In 1985, he received the Herbert Bloch Award from the American Society of Criminology for outstanding service to the American Society of Criminology and the Criminology profession.

Norbert Schwarz is Charles Horton Cooley Collegiate Professor of Psychology at the University of Michigan, Professor of Marketing at the Ross School of Business, and Research Professor at the Institute for Social Research. He received a PhD in sociology from the University of Mannheim, Germany (1980) and a 'Habilitation' in psychology from the University of Heidelberg, Germany (1986). Prior to joining the University of Michigan in 1993, he taught psychology at the University of Heidelberg (1981–92) and served as Scientific Director of ZUMA, an interdisciplinary social science research center in Mannheim (1987–92). His research interests focus on human judgment and cognition, including the interplay of feeling and thinking, the socially situated nature of cognition, and the implications of basic cognitive and communicative processes for public opinion, consumer behavior and social science research. For further information and recent publications see http://sitemaker.umich.edu/norbert.schwarz

Elena Soucacou, is an early learning specialist with recent research and clinical experience in working with young children with learning difficulties in various educational settings. Over the past 12 years, Dr. Soucacou has been studying the development of children with diverse educational and behavioral profiles and researching the quality of early education programs and classroom practices. Her first cycle of studies took place in her home country of Greece, where she completed a Bachelor's degree in Psychology at the school of Philosophy, Pedagogy and Psychology of the National University of Athens. Dr. Soucacou completed her master's program in Early Childhood Special Education at Columbia University, and worked in the field of preschool special education in New York for several years. Following her graduate training, Dr. Soucacou undertook her doctoral studies at Oxford University, UK, where she completed a doctoral degree (DPhil) in 2008. Her research focused on quality assessment of classroom practices that support the inclusion of children with disabilities in preschool settings. Her research interests include quality and effectiveness of classroom practices and interventions for preschool children with special education needs, as well as assessment of various aspects of classroom quality in early childhood and special education programs.

Eliza Spang, a Research Associate in Learning Innovations at WestEd, graduated from Stanford University School of Education with a PhD in Curriculum and Teacher Education. While at Stanford, she was a research assistant on several research projects including 'How Does Teacher Education Make a Difference? An Exploration of the Relationship Between Teacher Education, Teacher Practices, and Student Learning', a study sponsored by the Teachers for a New Era initiative. Her research interests are science teacher education, new teacher support/induction programs, and science curriculum development. She is a former high school science teacher and mentor teacher for several beginning teachers.

Kathy Sylva is Professor of Educational Psychology at the University of Oxford, Department of Education. She has carried out many large-scale studies on Early Childhood and on early literacy. A dominant theme throughout her work has been then impact of education and care not only on 'academic knowledge' but on children's problem solving, social skills and dispositions to learn. A related theme in her research is the impact of early intervention on combating social disadvantage. She was specialist Adviser to the House of Commons Select Committee on Education in 2000–01 and again in 2005–09. She was awarded an OBE in 2008 for services to children and families.

Louis Tay is a PhD candidate in industrial/organizational psychology at the University of Illinois at Urbana-Champaign. His major research area is in psychological measurement, and has special research interests in item response theory, latent class modeling, and hierarchical linear modeling.

Ewart A.C. Thomas is a Professor of Psychology at Stanford University, USA. He teaches undergraduate and graduate courses in Statistics and Research Methods. His research interests include the development and application of mathematical and statistical models in many areas, such as, signal detection, motivation, inter-rater reliability, parent-infant interaction, equity, and law as a social science. Thomas has served as Chair of the Psychology Department and, from 1988 to 1993, he served as Dean of the University's School of Humanities and Sciences. In 1989 he received an honorary doctorate from the University of the West Indies, and in 2002 he received a Distinguished Teaching award from the Associated Students of Stanford University (ASSU). From January to June, 2008, he was the Ralph and Claire Landau Visiting Professor of Psychology at The Chinese University of Hong Kong.

Mark Tomlinson is a Senior Research Officer in the Department of Social Policy and Social Work at the University of Oxford and an Associate of Green Templeton College. He specialises in multivariate social statistics and especially in the development of indicators in sociological and economic research. He is author (with Robert Walker) of *Coping with Complexity: Child and adult poverty*, (CPAG, 2009).

Eric Tucker is a Public Policy Research Fellow at Temple University's Institute for the Study of Race and Social Thought in Philadelphia. His research focuses on the development of measurement instruments across the social sciences and on evaluation and performance measurement within public policy and social enterprise. He serves as the Chief Academic Officer and Deputy Director of the National Association for Urban Debate Leagues (www.urbandebate.org), and is working on a comprehensive evaluation of the initiative in 10 cities over a 10-year horizon in collaboration with researchers at the University of Michigan. He is a guest instructor at Brown University in Providence for courses on urban school improvement and social entrepreneurship. Dr. Tucker completed his Doctorate at the University of Oxford with the support of a Marshall Scholarship. His doctoral thesis, which was entitled *Towards a More Rigorous Scientific Approach to Social Measurement: An Empirical and Methodological Enquiry into the Development of Grounded Indicators of Social Capital Formation*, has been published as scholarly articles and a book chapter. He also graduated with distinction from Oxford with a master's of Science in Education Research Methodology from the Department of Educational Studies. He co-authored *Argumentation and Debate: An Educator's Activities Manual* (2004). He also co-wrote *How to Build a Debate Program: An Organizer's Manual* (forthcoming). His next project is *Towards Grounded Indicators: Minimizing Measurement Error Through Social Research* (forthcoming). He holds honors degrees in Public Policy and Africana Studies from Brown University, where he received the Truman Scholarship, Royce Fellowship, and graduated Magna Cum Laude, and Phi Beta Kappa.

Will Tucker is a graduate of Brown University's Alfred A. Taubman Center for Public Policy, and author of *The Effect of Victim Age and Gender on Prosecutors' Willingness to Prosecute Cases of Child Sexual Abuse*. He is the former Assistant Director of Youth

Programs at the Howard R. Swearer Center for Public Service at Brown University and member of the Brown University Steering Committee on Slavery and Justice. A Truman Scholar, he is currently a graduate student at Princeton University's Woodrow Wilson School of Public and International Affairs.

Madhu Viswanathan has been on the faculty at the University of Illinois, Urbana-Champaign, since 1990. His research programs are in two areas; measurement and research methodology, and literacy, poverty, and subsistence marketplace behaviors. He has authored books in both areas: *Measurement Error and Research Design* (Sage, 2005), and *Enabling Consumer and Entrepreneurial Literacy in Subsistence Marketplaces* (Springer, 2008, in alliance with UNESCO). His research program with a methodological orientation on measurement and research design paralleled many years of teaching research at all levels. It culminated in a book directed at the social sciences that provides a most detailed conceptual dissection of measurement error. This work is a striking departure from the existing literature, which emphasizes a statistical orientation without sufficient elucidation of the conceptual meaning of measurement error. His research on subsistence marketplaces takes a micro-level approach to gain bottom-up understanding of life circumstances and buyer, seller, and marketplace behaviors. This perspective aims to enable subsistence marketplaces to move toward being ecologically, economically, and socially sustainable marketplaces. His research is synergized with innovative teaching and social initiatives. He teaches courses on research methods and on sustainable product and market development for subsistence. His research is applied through the *Marketplace Literacy Project* (www.marketplaceliteracy.org), a non-profit organization that he founded and directs.

Geoffrey Walford is Professor of Education Policy and a Fellow of Green Templeton College at the University of Oxford. He has academic degrees from Oxford, Kent, London, and the open universities, and is author of more than 150 academic articles and book chapters. His books include: *Life in Public Schools* (Methuen, 1986), *Restructuring Universities: Politics and power in the management of change* (Croom Helm, 1987), *City Technology College* (Open University Press, 1991, with Henry Miller), *Doing Educational Research* (Routledge, editor, 1991), *Choice and Equity in Education* (Cassell, 1994), *Educational Politics: Pressure groups and faith-based schools* (Avebury, 1995), *Policy, Politics and Education – sponsored grant-maintained schools and religious diversity* (Ashgate, 2000), *Doing Qualitative Educational Research* (Continuum, 2001), *Private Schooling: Tradition and diversity* (Continuum, 2005) and *Markets and Equity in Education* (Continuum, 2006). Within the Department of Education at the University of Oxford he teaches on the MSc in Educational Research Methodology, and supervises doctoral research students. He was Joint Editor of the *British Journal of Educational Studies* from 1999 to 2002, and is Editor the *Oxford Review of Education*. His research foci are the relationships between central government policy and local processes of implementation, private schools, choice of schools, religion based schools, and qualitative research methodology.

Robert Walker is Professor of Social Policy and Fellow of Green Templeton College, University of Oxford. He was formerly Professor of Social Policy at the University Nottingham and before that Professor of Social Policy Research, Loughborough University, where he was Director of the Centre for Research in Social Policy. His 19 books include: *Social Security and Welfare* (2005); *The Welfare We Want* (with Michael Wiseman, 2003); *The Dynamics of Modern Society* (with Lutz Leisering, 1998); and *Poverty Dynamics* (with Karl Ashworth, 1995).

Brian Wansink (PhD Stanford 1990) holds the John S. Dyson Endowed Chair in the Applied Economics and Management Department at Cornell University, where he is Director of the Cornell Food and Brand Lab. Previously, he was a professor at Dartmouth College, the Vrije Universiteit (The Netherlands), the Wharton School at the University of Pennsylvania, the University of Illinois at Urbana-Champaign, INSEAD (France), and he was a visiting scientist at the US Army Research Labs in Natick, MA. From 2007–09, Wansink was Executive Director of the USDA's Center for Nutrition Policy and Promotion, where he was responsible for the 2010 Dietary Guidelines and for promoting the Food Guide Pyramid. In addition to over 100 articles, he was written the books *Mindless Eating* and *Marketing Nutrition* and he co-authored *Asking Questions*, and *Consumer Panels*.

Glenn Williams is Senior Lecturer in Psychology, Nottingham Trent University. He was formerly at the School of Nursing, University of Nottingham as a Lecturer in Behavioural Science. He has also worked in the National Health Service for several years and has been involved with the education and training of health professionals, particularly in the use of quantitative research methods, evidence-based practice and statistics. He has co-authored *An Introduction to Statistics for Nurses* (with John Maltby and Liz Day, 2007) and has published widely in the areas of psychological well-being and health.

Peter W. Williamson is an Assistant Professor of Teacher Education in the Graduate School of Education at the University of San Francisco. Formerly the Director of Stanford's Teachers for a New Era project and an instructor in the Stanford Teacher Education Program, Peter completed his PhD at Stanford in Curriculum and Teacher Education. Before coming to Stanford, Peter taught middle and high school English and journalism in San Francisco Bay Area schools, and worked with advocacy agencies focusing on urban youth. His research interests include the teaching and learning of practice, teacher professional development, teacher effectiveness, urban education, and language acquisition.

Sang Eun Woo received her PhD in industrial/organizational psychology from the University of Illinois at Urbana-Champaign in 2009. She is now an assistant professor at Purdue University. Her research areas include personality, culture, and psychological measurement. Her recent representative publications concern measurement of various psychological constructs including achievement motivation (Personality and Individual Differences), the cognitive and motivational nature of intellectual engagement (Personality and Individual Differences), and engagement in developmental assessment centers (Personnel Psychology).

Michael Woolcock is a Senior Social Scientist with the World Bank's Development Research Group. From 2007–09, he was Professor of Social Science and Development Policy, and Research Director of the Brooks World Poverty Institute, at the University of Manchester. His research draws on a range of disciplinary theories and methods to explore the social dimensions of economic development, in particular the role that social networks play in the survival and mobility strategies of the poor, in managing local conflict, and in shaping the efficacy of legal and political institutions. An Australian national, he has an MA and PhD in sociology from Brown University; in 2002 he was the Von Hugel Visiting Fellow at St. Edmund's College, University of Cambridge, and from 2000–06 he was a (part-time) lecturer in Public Policy at Harvard University's Kennedy School of Government.

Reflections on Social Measurement: How Social Scientists Generate, Modify, and Validate Indicators and Scales

Eric Tucker, Madhu Viswanathan, and
Geoffrey Walford

INTRODUCTION

Our vision – a paradigm shift in measurement

Measurement is at the centre of scientific research and a concern to develop and improve measurement tools unites the social sciences. In this introductory chapter, we describe the thinking that led to this handbook and our proposals for a paradigm shift in measurement. We then discuss some key aspects of the chapters in this handbook that illustrate this vision as it takes shape.

Books on measurement can be broadly classified as either theoretical or practical, either discipline or instrument focused, specialized, advanced, or introductory, and either partially or fully engaged with questions of measurement. Most texts on research present research design and research itself largely as an unproblematic process where careful planning is done in advance, predetermined methods and procedures are followed, and 'results' are the inevitable conclusion. The field of measurement places high priority on the statistical validation of emergent indicators and stepwise adherence to measure development and other processes. Current literature and practice on measurement, we argue, tend to over-emphasize statistical verification and correspondingly de-emphasize issues such as indicator generation and modification, the nature and conceptual meaning of measurement error, and the day-to-day processes involved in developing and using measures (Tucker, Chapter 16, this volume).

Where most texts offer either measurement theory or technical guidance on how to verify that a measure is reliable and valid, in this handbook, we seek to reverse the prescriptive discussion of measurement issues. We seek insights and descriptions from leading scholars in a variety of areas in the social sciences on the measurement-related challenges they have confronted in the course of their work, which often spans many decades. Thus, the goal of this handbook is to examine some of the intangible issues that arise in the practice of measurement in day-to-day social science research. Chapters thus focus on how prominent social scientists design measures, what problems they encounter, and how they overcome these challenges. There is much to be learned by making explicit the too often implicit methodological knowledge accumulated by experienced social scientists with regard to the real-world aspects of measurement that they work to resolve each day.

Our notion of the intangibles of measurement can perhaps best be explained by defining what it is not. The most striking examples of tangible aspects of measurement are the statistical procedures designed to verify the validity and reliability of indicators. The intangibles of measurement relate to how we obtain these numbers to begin with (Viswanathan, 2005). As such, they relate to how complex constructs are defined and delineated; how items are

generated and measures designed to capture such constructs; how a variety of different types of measurement errors creep into the process of measure development requiring a deep conceptual understanding of the nature of such errors; how research methods have to be modified to reduce a variety of types of measurement errors; how challenging contextual factors impinge on the design of measures and methods; how measurement procedures have to be implemented in large-scale data collection in real-world settings with complex socio-political factors; and how an understanding of these intangibles of measurement in turn inform tangible aspects, such as innovative data analyses.

Although experienced researchers are aware of the complexities of actual measurement and what we describe as the intangibles of measurement, descriptions of such issues in the measurement literature are scant. Thus, the experiences of researchers remain implicit, specialized knowledge that a wider audience of researchers do not benefit from. We aim to address a significant gap in the measurement literature which has largely focused on such generic issues as the statistical procedures that need to be applied to data or the steps to be covered in the measure development process. Our vision calls for an emphasis on the conceptual and developmental side of measurement in understanding the processes that lead to the generation of numbers and data, whereas much of the measurement literature to date has largely focused on statistical procedures that need to be applied to numbers generated from measurement. This handbook responds to the call for scholarship on measurement to move beyond foundational, generalized descriptions of how indicators ought to be developed and step-by-step adherence to basic procedures. It seeks to inaugurate an inter-disciplinary conversation that captures the experience and expertise of world-renowned experts on the practical and methodological issues related to measurement issues and the development and validation of instruments.

Good research design and high-quality measurement are inseparable, and, in turn, lead to data that can be properly subjected to statistical verification. Thus, our vision calls for an emphasis on the *process* by which 'numbers are assigned to quantities'. Our central focus is on understanding the conceptual and developmental side of measurement in terms of the nature and meaning of measurement error and its integral role in processes of developing and using measures in great detail. Such conceptual understanding is necessary to generate data for empirical testing and statistical verification, in other words, to generate numbers worthy of statistical verification that actually shed light on phenomena in the social sciences. Our vision refocuses attention on the classical definition of measurement in terms of '*rules* for assigning numbers' whereas the literature on operationalizing constructs has tended to emphasize statistical procedures to the exclusion of other matters. Both the conceptual and the empirical are important, and our contention is that, while the latter has been prioritized across a broad range of disciplinary and methodological conversations in recent decades, the former requires significant attention. An understanding of how numbers should be generated to begin with has important implications for statistical verification procedures as well.

This handbook brings together chapters that explore how methodological decisions about how to develop measures are tied to the context of the research design and to what the researcher ultimately wants to know. The purpose and context of measure development, the properties of the measure, and the social dimensions of administration necessarily shape the final product. Similarly, researchers' own epistemology and research training, as well as their interests and preferences, inform design. This book is thus necessarily multidisciplinary and interdisciplinary in nature. We firmly believe that too many social scientists remain fixed within their disciplines and do not look far enough beyond those disciplines to solve problems and develop new ideas and methods. Measurement is a central feature of all social science research and there is much to be learned through an examination of how these world-renowned specialists have approached measurement issues in their own areas. The chapters are written with a wide audience of social scientists in mind such that readers can benefit from path-breaking work in the wider arena of the social sciences.

This handbook has a number of unique features that stem from our broad vision: it explores how social scientists design measures, what problems they encounter, and how they overcome these challenges; it brings together a blend of renowned scholars who have contributed to their respective fields by developing new ways to measure and understand constructs; it offers multidisciplinary, interdisciplinary, and international perspectives from researchers who are leaders in their fields; it brings together many chapters that share the semi-autobiographical reflections of researchers that illustrate trends, issues, and significant principles in measurement design concretely; it examines the relationship between the theory and practice of measurement and addresses measurement at methodological, procedural, and conceptual levels through accounts of the process of generating indicators and scales; and it advances understanding about the diverse and emergent ways researchers measure the social.

Operationalizing our vision – organization of the handbook

Our vision unfolds through chapters that begin to address a number of questions about the intangibles of measurement: What are the fundamental issues in measurement? How can measurement and research design be improved? How should measures be developed for complex constructs? How should diverse contexts be incorporated into measurement? How does measurement occur in the real world within the complex array of socio-political factors? And what are some critical perspectives of measurement in the social sciences?

The handbook is organized as follows. In *Methods and Data Collection*, authors discuss some of the basic methods used in measurement. Chapters cover topics such as how respondents make sense out of questions, how observational rating scales are developed, linguistic factors affect measurement, lessons learned from measurement, how the objective of the research and purpose of measurement is a central consideration in the procedures used, and what the central issues are in asking questions about sensitive topics. These chapters provide cutting-edge insights for improving measurement and research design.

The range of rich contexts where measures are developed and used in the social sciences takes centre stage in *The Context of Measurement*, an area that is replete with challenges and raises a host of questions. For instance, in the arena of cross-cultural measurement, questions include how the process of measure development, validation, and use incorporate cultural perspectives and how researchers can develop rigorous measures with minimal error when used in diverse cultural and language communities? The chapters in this section address such topics as cross-cultural measurement, measurement

of culture, and international comparisons of educational attainment. The second part of this section expands the focus to include measurement across time and space, where authors consider measurement across the life-course and across urban space.

In *Fundamental Issues in Measurement*, our vision takes shape through such foundational issues such as the meaning and nature of measurement error, emphasizing the conceptual elements of measurement over the statistical. This section emphasizes that measurement error should be understood in great detail in each stage of developing and using measures. The intangibles in developing and using measures and broader perspectives on the assumptions of measurement and the need to enrich measures in the social sciences are discussed. Other such fundamental issues include the need to ground and thereby enrich measures in the context-rich reality that they are designed to capture. The section emphasizes the need to conduct social research to inform the generation, modification and verification of measures. This section also includes some chapters that apply critical lenses to the notion of assigning numbers and measuring phenomena in the social sciences, thus opening up debate beyond normal confines.

In *The Real World Practice of Measurement*, authors reflect upon the complex socio-political factors that impact measurement in the real world. The chapters in this section are characterized by an emphasis on some of the macro-level issues that impinge on measurement; such as the administration of large-scale measurement, interactions with institutions, and so forth. These chapters make clear the interplay between measurement and a host of other issues involved in gathering aggregate-level data in the public arena. Contributors cover real-world challenges including interdisciplinary, multidisciplinary, and mixed-method approaches; managing large-scale and team projects; and administrative and secondary data. The chapters cover a host of issues from the social process in collecting data on child sex abuse to measuring social capital or consumption behaviour.

Summarizing our vision – confronting measurement challenges in the 21st Century

The need for high-quality measurement is increasing with the ever expanding capacity to study a wide range of phenomena through empirical research. Governments, non-governmental entities, and academic and private institutions around the globe are rapidly expanding their commitment to generate, acquire, store, disseminate, and prioritize the use of data. Techno-logical progress in the last century has brought us from pencils and index cards to cutting-edge virtual reality caves. However, as calls for performance measurement and accountability take centre stage in policy making and administrative arenas are fuelled by the increased capacity to produce and store data, there is an accom-panying risk of increasing disconnection between the findings generated and the actual social phenomena they intend to represent. The gap between social real-ity and what the indicator captures is a recurring measurement challenge. The measurement literature, with an overem-phasis on statistical verification, has to shift fundamentally to address the complexity of measurement and confront the significant challenges that lie ahead for social science research.

This handbook presents a vision of measurement approaches and instruments designed for 21st century challenges and capable of capturing the complexity of measurement in the social sciences and the challenges that need to be confronted. Our vision emphasizes the intangibles relating to conceptual and developmental side of measurement through understanding the processes that lead to the generation of numbers and data. We focus on the meaning of measurement error and its integral role in processes of developing and using measures in great detail. Although both the conceptual and the empirical sides of measurement are important, our vision calls for an overdue increase of attention on the former. This handbook consolidates decades of practical experience and insights gained through innovation into a single volume. It serves as an essential sourcebook for researchers in need of inspiration and guidance on their own process of measure development. We hope it will prove to be an essential addition to the bookshelf of researchers across the social sciences.

REFERENCES

Viswanathan, Madhubalan (2005), *Measurement Error and Research Design.* California: Sage Publications.

Methods for Data Collection

How to Get Valid Answers from Survey Questions: What We Learned from Asking about Sexual Behavior and the Measurement of Sexuality

Aniruddha Das and Edward O. Laumann

Social-scientific research on sexuality has only recently picked up steam. One consequence of this late start is that there are, as yet, few standard definitions of sex, standard sets of sexual practices, problems, and attitudes to study, and standard and well-validated ways to query these issues. Social-scientific consensus on these matters is still very much a work in process. Much of the existing scientific experience has come in the context of a few path-breaking nationally representative studies of sexuality, in several of which we were fortunate to have been involved. In the sections below, we describe the 15-year cumulative process of conceptual innovation as well as the trial and error

through which these studies emerged, and the working knowledge resulting from this experience. We hope our account will offer useful insights and analytic strategies to researchers, in bypassing real-world research problems – often idiosyncratic to specific projects – and in innovating their way toward reliable scientific knowledge of complex social phenomena.

THE NATIONAL HEALTH AND SOCIAL LIFE SURVEY

The process began in the late 1980s, with what was to become the 1992 US National Health and Social Life Survey, or NHSLS

(Laumann et al., 1994). The motivation for the study arose in part from the rapid spread of the AIDS epidemic, and the urgent need for reliable information on the social factors involved. In response to the emerging crisis, and repeated calls for reliable data from independent blue-ribbon scientific panels (such as the Institute of Medicine, 1986), a coalition of federal agencies expressed support for a nationally representative survey of adult sexual practices. This coalition included, among others, the National Institute of Child Health and Human Development (NICHD), the Centers for Disease Control (CDC), the National Center for Health Statistics (NCHS), the National Institute on Aging (NIA), and the National Institute of Mental Health (NIMH). Accordingly, in July 1987, NICHD issued a request for proposals (RFP), titled 'Social and Behavioral Aspects of Health and Fertility-Related Behavior' (NICHD-OBS-87-13). This RFP was not for data collection, but for a one-year contract to design a potential survey project – although the team that won the contract would, of course, also be more likely to win the competition to field the survey itself. The NHSLS design team won the design contract, and began work in January 1988.

The contractual nature of the project was intended to facilitate active government participation in, and supervision of, the entire design process and hence the content of the questionnaire itself. While the design team had originally conceptualized the survey as a broad and sociologically informed study of adult human sexuality, subsequent political conflicts forced a narrowing of focus to epidemiological inventories of various sexual practices, especially those directly related to AIDS. Despite this narrowing of focus, the agencies could not secure approval for the heavily modified survey instrument from the first Bush administration, or funding for the study from Congress. In fall 1991, therefore, the design team made the decision to solicit funding from a consortium of major private foundations instead. While this strategy ended politically motivated bowdlerization of the instrument, given the limited funding secured, many items in the original questionnaire – on sexual techniques, foreplay, and sexual attitudes, among other topics – had to be dropped.

These political and financial obstacles were matched by methodological ones. At the time, there were few, if any, guidelines available on the 'proper' way to design a standardized sexuality questionnaire. The famous Kinsey Reports (Kinsey et al., 1948, 1953), then almost four decades old, had relied on a format the NHSLS team was dubious about – flexible, semi-structured interviews conducted by trained interviewers, with question wording and ordering of questions partly at the interviewer's discretion. While Kinsey believed this flexibility would allow an interviewer to tap underlying beliefs or motivations more deeply, it also lowered comparability of responses across interviews. Other, smaller studies were mostly based on convenience samples – i.e., of small sets of self-selected and more motivated respondents – and therefore offered little guidance on how to design measures that would maximize response rates, and minimize reporting error and bias, in a nationally representative probability sample.

As with any social survey, there were two major concerns: first, what to study (theoretically and substantively important factors to query in the questionnaire), and second, how to study it (terminology, definitions, method of asking questions). The next section deals with the first concern, describing the rationale behind the specific contents of the NHSLS instrument.

NHSLS: general organizing principles

With regard to the content of the questionnaire, as noted, the NHSLS was designed to facilitate a general and system-atic investigation of adult human sexuality. However, speculations and investigations of sexuality up to that point, methodolog-ically flawed as they were, had also tended to focus on sexual 'problem areas,' such as premarital sex, adolescent pregnancy, sexual deviance, STDs, and sexual dysfunc-tions. As with methodological guidelines therefore, the NHSLS team was confronted with a complete lack of theoretical insights into the nature of human sexuality in gen-eral, and especially what may be considered 'normal sex.' Two guiding principles were therefore chosen to organize data collection: a network-analytic and a life-course per-spective on human sexuality (Laumann et al., 1989). The central principle of this framework was that once age-related physiological development had been taken into account, much variation remained in the timing and sequence of sexual patterns in an individual's life history. Sexual practices and other life patterns that influence sexuality are, it was argued, timed by cultural and social-structural forces in addition to biological ones.

Life course

Previous research had identified several stages in the life course relevant to the study of sexual patterns. In pre-adulthood, these included the period before puberty as well as early and late adolescence. Early adolescence, for instance, is marked by profound physiological changes – repro-ductive and otherwise. Life course effects during this period are highly correlated with this developmental process. However, even at this stage, sociocultural patterns provide constraints on, and opportunities for, the expression of biologically driven sexual impulses. Moreover, sexual events occurring during these crucial formative years, and their normative status rela-tive to the prevailing social consensus, have lasting effects on adult sexual trajectories (Browning and Laumann, 1997, 2003; Laumann et al., 2003). The questionnaire thus included a range of items on early-life sexual events, such as pre-pubertal sexual contact, and the process through which a respondent first learnt about sexual matters.

In contrast to adolescence, it was argued that once the physiological development process is complete, an individual's stage in the life course becomes less dependent on biological age, and more on personal choices, made under particular sets of social opportunities and constraints. For instance, high-school graduation marks a turning point in the life course, during which an individual's choices can propel them into alternate life trajectories – each marked by different sexual opportunities and behaviors. At any point in adulthood, a person's decision to marry, remain single, or get divorced has larger implications for his/her sexual patterns than age alone. In general, therefore, the NHSLS team hypothesized that adult sexual trajectories are shaped primarily by the presence of a partner. Other transitions, such as the birth of children, shifts in employment status, and incident health problems may contribute secondarily to this dynamic process. These secondary factors were queried in the questionnaire through modules on a respon-dent's fertility history; their employment status and other life course events; and their physical and mental health. Given the primacy of partner-presence, however, the instrument was structured around the size and composition of the respondent's sexual partner network, and changes in this network over time. This dynamic sequence, in turn, was conceptualized in terms of a 'punctuated equilibrium' – with long periods of stasis (when an individual is in a committed relationship, marital or otherwise) broken by transitional periods of intensive partner search (Laumann et al., 1994). Sexual practices, it was argued, would differ during these two periods – both in terms of the meanings they would have for a subject, and the risks involved. It was emphasized that, for many people, this cycle of commitment and search periods tends to be repeated over the life course – with experiences during one cycle informing decisions made during later ones. Information on an individual's partnership- and sexual-trajectories was collected through a 'life history calendar,' described below.

Finally, with respect to the risks involved in sexual behavior (such as pregnancy, STDs, and AIDS), it was argued that, as with other new behavioral patterns (drinking, driving), learning to 'become sexual' under relatively untutored conditions would increase the chances of error-laden actions. Hence, there would be particular windows of vulnerability to sexual risk over the life course, such as in late adolescence and young adulthood. In addition, other periods of status transition – such as enrollment in college or the military, or divorce – could also be accompanied by transient increases in sexual partnerships and risk-taking. Shorter windows of opportunity – such as business trips or vacations – would also be available to individuals in relatively stable and committed relationships, allowing for temporary suspensions of one's normal sexual patterns in favor of sexual experimentation and exploration. Information on this temporal patterning of sexual risk over the life cycle was therefore necessary for designing effective educational or other interventions. The NHSLS instrument was designed

to meet this objective, with modules on a respondent's current risk-exposure (contraception, safe-sex practices, behaviors connected to AIDS), history of exposure (STD history and transfusion or hemophilia exposure), and AIDS knowledge accompanying items on his/her life course during these stages.

Network analysis: the sexual partnership

As noted, the second major organizing principle for the NHSLS was network analysis (Laumann, 2006). The argument was that while sexual practices are age-graded, it is the social strata and network ties individuals find themselves in that provide opportunities for and constraints on sexual events. Some of these systems of stratification emerge early in a person's life, and channel them into particular developmental trajectories. Others are based on ascriptive characteristics like religion or parental socioeconomic status. Still others are determined by decisions made during critical turning points in the life course – such as, the different sexual opportunities and normative constraints faced by a young person who leaves home to go to college, and one who enters a blue-collar occupation while remaining close to friends and family.

From this network perspective, a primary shortcoming of previous sex studies had been the lack of attention to the characteristics of a subject's partners. From a 'macro' perspective, the highly selective nature of sexual pairing – most importantly, through homophily, or the tendency to partner with individuals matching one's own social attributes – may shape the trajectory of sexually driven epidemics such as AIDS (Aral, 1999; Laumann et al., 1993, 1994). In other words, in contrast to epidemiological models of AIDS – which, up to that point, had been based on the notion of random mixture or contact – the NHSLS team argued that the homophily derived departure of social structure from such complete mixture would slow the transmission of the epidemic, as well as insulate some social groups from it altogether. Aggregating information on individual sexual networks would allow for estimation of the contact rates between and within groups (Laumann, 1966, 1973; Laumann and Pappi, 1976; Fararo and Skvoretz, 1986; Laumann et al., 1994; Laumann and Youm, 1999), and thus, the trajectories of disease-diffusion across groups. These trajectories, it was noted, would be affected by the extent of contact, the number of groups, relative group size, the proportion of infectives, and indirect contact between groups at differential risk through third or 'bridging' ties. One of the most important methodological innovations in the NHSLS was thus the inclusion of a systematic accounting frame, to elicit a respondent's egocentric network of sexual contacts over the primary reporting period – the preceding year – as well as the latter's basic demographic attributes (sex, race, highest level of education completed, and how many years older or younger they were than the respondent).

At the individual level, the propensity to engage in risky or other sexual behavior is driven not simply by an individual's psychological traits, but by the transactional nature of partnered sex, the sequence of negotiations involved in any sexual relationship, and the resources – material, social, and symbolic – each party can leverage in these negotiations. Yet another relational source of influence is the subjective meanings of different types of relationships for each party – e.g., a long-term committed versus a short-term pleasure-centric one. For this reason, the NHSLS collected information on a respondent's inventory of

sexual practices in a partner-specific format, for up to two partners in the preceding year. Finally, given that the limited set of indicators for this time window would not capture the full range of risky behaviors, the questionnaire also used a third time frame – the last partnered event – to elicit information on a wider range of sexual practices. As with the partner-network, aggregation of individual-level information on risky behaviors – coupled with demographic information – was also expected to provide an overall picture of the distribution of risk in the general population, social-group differentials in exposure to STDs or AIDS, and social-group contributions to the overall pool of risky behaviors.

Finally, differentials in concurrency – or overlapping sexual partnerships – have been identified as one explanation for variations in HIV or STD prevalence among different social groups. From a biological standpoint, such overlapping partnerships shorten the time between the transmission of infection to a subject from one partner, and the other partner's exposure to the disease. In addition, with serially monogamous relationships, only relationships formed after a subject has been infected result in disease transmission, while ones preceding infection remain protected. With concurrency, in contrast, this temporal buffer against exposure is lost. Finally, in terms of overall network topology, concurrency has an important effect on the 'critical component,' or the number of individuals in the general population that are connected directly or indirectly at a given point in time (Morris et al., 2004). As described in more detail below, the NHSLS was designed to collect information on the timing and sequencing of a respondent's partnerships over the preceding year, as well as on any other sexual relationships their primary or secondary partner may have had over that period.

Thus, from an epidemiological perspective, the patterning of sexual behaviors at the individual level would provide the core physical parameters of disease transmission, while the sociodemographic patterns of sexual contact would provide the social parameters of diffusion. In sum, therefore, network analysis provided the theoretical framework in which these two sets of parameters came together in the NHSLS.

Network analysis: stakeholder relationship

Apart from the dyadic sexual relationship itself, a second network-analytic concept is the social embeddedness of an individual as well as their partnership(s) within broader webs of 'stakeholder' ties – most importantly, with friends and family. Based on a venerable tradition of social network analysis, which has long established the importance of social ties in channeling information, resources, and contacts (Coleman, 1990), it was speculated that stakeholder influence could begin with the first introduction itself. Or, in other words, it was expected that in order to reduce information costs, and maximize the chances of finding a compatible partner, an individual could route the process of search for a mate at least partly through their network of trusted 'alters' – such as close friends and family members. Given the higher stakes, it was felt that such a search strategy would be particularly common among people searching for a marital or other long-term partner. Thus, items were included in the questionnaire, on who – if anyone – introduced a respondent to their primary and secondary partners. To exhaust the range of relevant stakeholder types, for each partner, the response categories included family; mutual friends or acquaintances; co-workers; classmates; neighbors; 'introduced self or partner introduced self;' and 'other.' In addition to this point of initiation, an ongoing relationship's social embeddedness was also hypothesized to affect its chances of survival – if only due to continuing expectations and pressures from its enfolding web of ties. The measure created by the design team to capture this form of embeddedness was the extent to which a partner had gotten to know the respondent's immediate family members, and their close friends.

On a related note, the particular location – or social context – where a person meets a partner may be indicative of the type of partnership they are interested in. Bars, for instance, are a prime meeting ground for individuals interested in less serious, short-term relationships. In contrast, a relationship that begins with a first meeting at a church may from the inception involve greater personal investments – not simply by the respective partners, but also by their family and friends, and other members of a dense congregational network. Encounters at work or at school, while less subject to stakeholder-monitoring than those at church or introductions by family, are also likely to occur within densely interconnected social networks of friends and acquaintances. Based on this sociological conceptualization of the partnering process, the NHSLS questionnaire also included questions on the type of place where a respondent first met their primary or secondary partner, with work, school, church, personal ad, vacation, bar, gym, party, and 'elsewhere' as the response categories.

The sections above described the rationale behind the specific contents of the NHSLS. In the next section, we turn to some decisions about terminology, definitions, and methods of asking questions that allowed this survey to successfully query sensitive sexual topics.

NSHSL questionnaire

Overall structure

Given the sensitive nature of sexual topics, it was particularly important to structure the NHSLS interview so as to allow a subject to comfortably share with a stranger these deeply personal experiences. The interview process was therefore designed to have a narrative flow, i.e., to allow a respondent to tell their story in a natural way even while responding to a standardized and structured instrument. First, therefore, the intent of the interview was made clear to the respondent, including the motivation for the NHSLS, its scientific importance, and its relevance to the national AIDS emergency. Following this, the process began with less sensitive topics, such as demographic information. Two self-administered questionnaires (SAQ) were introduced towards the end of this first section, the first querying personal finances and the second collecting aggregate information on sexual patterns. The interview then proceeded to more sensitive topics, such as major relationships (marriage and cohabitations) and fertility. Only after this background information had been collected – and, presumably, some rapport had developed between respondent and interviewer – was the systematic accounting frame for sexual partners in the preceding year introduced, followed by items on the last partnered sexual encounter. As noted above, information on specific sexual techniques as well as on actions to prevent disease or pregnancy was collected in the context of these specific ties or events. A life history calendar was then used to seek a respondent's sexual history.

In pilot testing, the most sensitive questions in the questionnaire – the ones that made both interviewers and respondents the most uncomfortable – turned out to be those on masturbation. Thus, in the final version of the interview, this set of questions was included in an SAQ, administered immediately after the section on sexual history. This was followed by a face-to-face module on sexual thoughts and fantasies – the frequency and nature of a respondent's sex thoughts, the amount of guilt associated with such thoughts, and sexual fantasies or practices they found appealing.

Next came a set of questions on highly sensitive early life sexual events, including how and from whom a respondent first learnt about sexual matters; the occurrence, timing, and nature of any pre-pubertal sexual contact, the number of people in the individual's personal network who knew of the event(s), and whether and how the experience had affected the adult respondent's life trajectory; the context and details of and reasons for their first partnered sex; and first same-gender sexual experiences. Since the sample was restricted to those aged 18 years and above, information on these early life events was collected retrospectively. This section also introduced the topic of forced sex. Up to this point, all questions had been on mutually voluntary sexual events. The forced sex questions were placed in this section on the assumption that respondents would have become more comfortable with the interview process by this point. The next module queried health and STD-related attitudes and history (including AIDS), followed by generalized sexual attitudes and knowledge. At the end of this long interview, respondents were given another SAQ containing more sensitive questions on lifetime sexual experiences (including paid sex, group sex, drug use, and sexual victimization). Each set of items was thus designed to follow logically from and build on preceding ones.

Definition of sex and sexual dysfunction

Trivial as it may sound, the manner in which the design team bounded the concepts of 'sex' and of a 'sexual partnership' had implications for the prevalence and mechanisms ultimately uncovered by the study. While commonplace definitions of sex have tended to focus on intercourse – specifically, intromission of a penis – this was felt to be too restrictive, excluding, for instance, sex between two women. Similarly, the NHSLS team tried to avoid the traditional focus on orgasmic release, since many sexual interactions may not culminate in either partner's climax. Instead, sex was defined as 'any mutually voluntary activity with another person that involves genital contact and sexual excitement or arousal, that is, feeling really turned on, even if intercourse or orgasm did not occur' (Laumann et al., 1994). To further circumscribe the notion and emphasize the voluntary aspect of the event, the following statements were included: 'Certain activities such as close dancing and kissing without genital contact should NOT be included. Also, this set of questions does NOT refer to occasions where force was used and activity was against someone's will.' (Forced sex was explicitly excluded from this definition for two reasons – first, to avoid emotionally upsetting respondents during this crucial part of the interview; and second, because forced sex belonged at least partly to a different domain.) Designed, therefore, to elicit a broad range of types of partnerships, this definition was placed at the beginning of the module for sexual activity in the preceding year – immediately before the systematic accounting frame for all partners during the period.

An additional definitional question lies with sexual dysfunctions. In the NHSLS, sexual issues were only coded as a problem if they had lasted for 'a period of several months or more' in the preceding year. There has been subsequent criticism of this approach. For instance, Bancroft et al. (2003) have argued that the likelihood of recall bias increases with time frames longer than one month. As Rosen and Laumann (2003) have noted, however, using such short time windows increases the potential for conflation of occasionally experienced or transient sexual problems with the chronic conditions that would reliably indicate an underlying sexual pathology. Hence the emphasis – both in the NHSLS and in the currently ongoing National Social Life, Health, and Aging Project (NSHAP; described in more detail below) – on problems of an extended duration.

Language

In choosing the kind of language in which sensitive sexual questions were to be phrased, the design team consciously chose to avoid highly technical and academic terminology, since it would be less comprehensible to respondents. For instance, terms like 'heterosexual' or 'vaginal intercourse,' while easily understandable for academics and other well-educated individuals, could be less so for respondents from lower socioeconomic strata. One alternative was to use colloquial language or slang, a commonly used mode of reference for sexual matters in the general public. Some previous studies also suggested that allowing a respondent to choose their own preferred terminology would lower reporting bias (Blair et al., 1977; Bradburn et al., 1978; Bradburn and Sudman, 1983). However, this process could also make it difficult for an interviewer to maintain professional distance, and thus counteract the goal of creating a neutral and nonjudgmental atmosphere in which respondents could confide personal experiences. A major advantage of the NHSLS interview format was that the interviewer was a stranger with whom a respondent was unlikely to come into contact with again. Use of colloquial language in the questions, it was felt, could be misperceived by some respondents as receptivity to a more personal relationship (Laumann et al., 1994).

In addition, slang tends to vary highly across social groups – whether individuals of different ages, income or educational levels, or even different parts of the country – and is also more imprecise. As a compromise, the NHSLS team chose to phrase the questions as simply as possible, in Standard English. Thus, for instance, the questionnaire used the term 'oral sex,' in favor of both 'blow job' or 'eating pussy' (slang) and 'fellatio' or 'cunnilingus' (technical/academic). Also, as with sex itself, explicit definitions of particular practices were included in the instrument. For instance, the following statement immediately preceded the first questions on oral sex: 'By oral sex we mean stimulating the genitals with the mouth, that is licking or kissing your partner's genitals or when your partner does this to you.' The analogous statement for vaginal sex was: 'By vaginal intercourse, we mean when a man's penis is inside a woman's vagina.' The question wording was progressively refined based on extensive pilot tests conducted with a broad pool of recruited respondents, and also on detailed feedback from the interview staff.

An additional linguistic device, used only for selected NHSLS items, was borrowed from Kinsey, who argued that many people would be reluctant to admit to certain practices. Hence, responses could be increased by starting from the assumption that a respondent would have engaged in that practice. For instance, asking whether or not a subject had engaged in masturbation in the preceding year would be more likely to lead to denials, while asking how often they had masturbated – including a category for 'never' – would tacitly communicate approval or consent. Similarly, rather than asking whether a respondent had ever engaged in same-gender sex, the NHSLS

used the following phrasing: 'How old were you the first time you had sex with a (same-gender partner)?'

The life history calendar
The basic organizing principle for the elicitation of an individual's partnership history was the division into major (marriages, cohabitations) and minor (non-marital or cohabiting) relationships. First, the following item queried the number of major relationships: 'How many different people have you been married to, or lived with, for a month or more?' The one-month threshold was specifically chosen to include, among short-term relationships, not just one-night stands but also relationships that might have involved a number of sexual encounters, but were nonetheless considered transient. Next, starting with the first major marriage or cohabitation, respondents were asked to list each major partner's first name, initials, or a pseudonym by which they could be consistently identified through the interview process. (More specific identifying information – such as full name, address, or telephone number – was deliberately avoided, to ensure partner anonymity.) In addition, the life history calendar also collected basic demographic information on each major partner – sex, race, educational attainment, age difference with the respondent, as well as the timing of the relationship. Following this enumeration process, more detailed information was collected on the first and the most recent major partner – their employment status during the relationship, religious preference, and how much they and the respondent had enjoyed spending time with each other's family and friends.

A second section of the life history calendar was placed later in the questionnaire, and queried a respondent's sexual career. Based on the logic that major relationships – marriages or cohabitations – would have the greatest impact on the organization of a respondent's sexual network, information on the timing of their minor sexual transactions was collected with reference to these key relationships – i.e., whether the former came before, during, or after the latter. A second reason for this sequencing was to facilitate recall in the reporting of transient, and perhaps easily forgotten, sexual events (Laumann et al., 2004b). Through this life history method, information was collected on up to 28 partnerships after the age of 18. This life history method, wherein major and minor events are used as an organizing principle for data collection, was adapted from demographic studies of pregnancy and fertility histories (Freedman et al., 1988).

Main reporting period: the preceding year

As noted above, the primary reporting period for sexual partners and events was the preceding 12 months. Data from the 1988 US General Social Survey (GSS) – the last available during the design phase of the NHSLS study – had indicated that 80 per cent of the adult population had either one or no partner in the preceding year (Michael et al., 1988). While a non-negligible proportion of this sample did report more than one sexual partnership, very few had had many partners. Thus, it was felt that for most NHSLS respondents, enumerating partners over this short time frame would not impose a cognitive burden.

The module began with the enumeration of sexual partners. The same organizing logic was used as with the respondent's lifetime sexual career. Information on the most recent major partner was collected first, and for each partner, the first name, initials, or a pseudonym was sought in order to ensure consistency of identification throughout the interview process. Next, as noted, a set of items inquired about each partner's basic sociodemographic characteristics, as well as the specifics of the sexual relationship. These latter factors included the first time, as well as the number of times, the respondent had had sex with that partner in the preceding year; and first sexual encounter with them ever. As described above, this merging of a partner-enumeration frame with items on a partner's demographic attributes as well as partner-specific frequency of sexual contact was designed to allow for induction of the network structure of sexual contact – and therefore of disease transmission.

A fundamental assumption with using respondent self-reports as indicators for a partner's characteristics, and one acknowledged by the design team (Laumann et al., 1989), was that measurement error would be small. There had been some support for this conjecture from previous studies. For instance, research on seropositive gay men had found high correlations between respondent and partner self-reports on the type and frequency of sexual behaviors (Coates et al., 1988). Sociological studies of friendship networks had also found similarly high correlations between a respondent's descriptions and their friends' actual attributes (Laumann, 1973). This accuracy was, as may be expected, highest for basic demographic characteristics such as age and religion, and lower for more amorphous attributes, such as a friend's political party preference. This was one reason the NHSLS module on partner attributes queried only demographic factors.

Items on partner-specific sexual practices – asked only for the primary and secondary relationships in the preceding year – followed this section. The primary relationship was defined in terms of marriage or cohabitation – or, in the absence of either, the relationship considered by the respondent to be their most important partnership in the preceding 12 months.

The secondary relationship was the most recent one in the preceding year, other than the primary relationship. Since, as noted, few people had more than two partners in the preceding year, this strategy efficiently covered most of the general population.

Epidemiological evidence available at the time suggested that efficiency of disease transmission varied by type of sexual practice. Hence, partner-specific information was collected on three types of sexual techniques: the frequency of anal intercourse (both receptive and insertive), oral sex, and vaginal sex. Kinsey's technique, of starting from the assumption that a respondent had engaged in an act, was especially useful for anal and oral sex. For instance, rather than asking a respondent whether they had had anal sex, the following question was used: 'When you had sex with (partner's name from the accounting frame), how often did you have anal sex with (partner).' Responses ranged from 1 (always) to 5 (never). The same technique was used for querying associated nonsexual factors, such as having been under drug or alcohol influence during sex – important because they could affect the types of sexual behaviors engaged in, and the level of sexual risk-taking. In contrast, less sensitive questions – such as on condom use – used a simpler yes/no format.

In addition, respondents were also asked about their subjective response to these two partnerships – including how sex with the partner made them feel, and emotional and physical satisfaction in the relationship. These psychosocial factors were especially important for establishing the context of meaning within which particular sexual practices occurred. For instance, anal intercourse in a partnership that made a respondent feel 'scared or afraid' during sex would be substantively different than in one that made them feel

'loved,' or 'thrilled or excited.' Each would be part of a different behavioral repertoire and be driven by a distinct set of intra- and inter-personal 'scripts' (Gagnon and Simon, 1973; Gagnon, 1991), and have divergent implications for a respondent's exposure to AIDS or other STDs. A similar logic applied to a person's reasons for having sex, also included in this module.

Finally, this module also collected information on possible concurrency in partnerships. The epidemiological importance of this information has been described above. The NHSLS did not include any explicit – and sensitive – questions on whether a respondent's own relationships had overlapped. Instead, their concurrency was determined more innocuously, by querying the starting and stopping dates for each partnership. In addition, for both the primary and secondary relationships, respondents were asked whether, to the best of their knowledge, their partner had had other sexual relationships in the preceding year – and if so, whether these other relationships had been concurrent with their own. For each partner, information was also collected on the number of such relationships, as well as the sex of the other partners. This time frame of one year missed, of course, a partner's concurrent relationships preceding that period.

Methods for collecting sensitive information: self-administered questionnaires and hand cards

Two methods allowed for elicitation of sensitive sexual information. First, as noted, four short self-administered forms were used at particular points during the interview. The first and shortest form contained questions on personal and family income, which, for some respondents, were more sensitive than the sexuality items. The second SAQ was a replication of a form that had been included in the preceding four years of the US General Social Survey (GSS), and collected aggregate information on sexual partnerships, paid sex, and extramarital sex. The third was an NHSLS innovation, and used to query masturbatory practices – the most sensitive of all questions in the survey. The fourth, administered at the end of the interview, contained detailed questions on lifetime sexual patterns and AIDS-related behaviors. More extensive use of SAQs was avoided for multiple reasons. First, items in these questionnaires had to be kept simpler in form and language than those asked face-to-face. The burden of comprehension with the former lay completely with respondents – many of whom were not well educated – since the interviewer could not answer any questions about them. Complex skip patterns had to be avoided, since respondents were likely to fill these out incorrectly. For these reasons, the guiding principle of the NHSLS, that sexual practices had to be queried in the context of specific patterns and relationships, could not be well operationalized through SAQs (Laumann et al., 1989). Instead, questions in the SAQs were designed in part to capture aggregate information, with some items providing cross-checks for face-to-face responses. For instance, to check the effectiveness of the life history calendar – at the time a recent methodological advance – in eliciting a person's sexual history, this face-to-face module was immediately followed by the second SAQ, which asked respondents how many female, and separately, male partners they had had since their 18th birthday.

A second set of devices, more extensively used in the survey, were hand cards listing multiple possible responses to a question. These cards had numbers next to the verbal descriptions, and it was these numbers that were used to respond to the questions. The interviewer, who did not have the verbal descriptions on their copy of the interview schedule, recorded the number given and communicated this clearly to the respondent. The procedure was designed to avoid forcing respondents to use sexually explicit language that they might consider inappropriate or unnatural, and was shown to enhance comfort during pilot interviews. There was a noticeable release of respondents' tension when they saw how the process worked. Many respondents explicitly stated in post-interview debriefings that the hand-card strategy made the interview process easier for them (Laumann et al., 1989). For respondents with reading problems, however, the effectiveness of hand cards was obviously limited.

Omitted time frames

Two other major time frames were conceptualized during the design phase of the questionnaire, but were dropped from the final version, due to the financial and other constraints described above (Laumann et al., 1989). The first – the shortest reporting period – was the preceding month. The major purpose for this time window was to collect information on the amount of sexual activity for all respondents, over a period recent enough to minimize the burden of recall. The actual reporting period was to be a two-week window, but that window would be determined by the last time a respondent had had partnered sex in the preceding month, if at all. Basic information on each sexual event as well as detailed information on the most recent encounters was to be collected. The inclusion of a more delimited set of questions on the 'last sexual encounter' partially substituted for this module, although this strategy was less effective in minimizing memory burdens for respondents who had not had sex in the recent past. A second major time frame was the preceding five years. A shortened version of this last module was later to be included in the currently ongoing NSHAP.

In addition to the NHSLS, a second major learning experience in designing sexuality measures came with the 1995–97 Chicago Health and Social Life Survey (CHSLS). In the next section, we describe this process.

THE CHICAGO HEATH AND SOCIAL LIFE SURVEY

The CHSLS was conceived in 1991, during the time when government funding and approval for the NHSLS was stuck in the political limbo described above (Laumann et al., 2004a). The co-principal investigators of the national survey decided at the time that a regular grant proposal to the NICHD, for a community-based sex survey, would evade much of this political maneuvering and delay. In addition, such a local survey could target information that a broad national study such as the NHSLS could not. Sexual partnering, it was argued, is a fundamentally local process. It occurs in the context of specific and locally organized social networks, such as particular church congregations, neighborhood social contexts, or friendship circles. Physical proximity plays a large part in shaping this social arena, as do the local demographic mix, and local cultural rules supporting some types of relationships and sanctioning others. Due in part to the concentration of same-gender (particularly male-male) sexual transactions in cities, American urban areas are also key focal points of AIDS and other STDs. The CHSLS was designed to uncover nuanced information on such local social-constellations. The study had two components, a household survey and a set of interviews with key local informants. In addition to a probability sample of the entire Chicago area, four other separate household surveys were conducted. Each of the latter was representative of a focal Chicago neighborhoods or community area,

with these four over sample neighborhoods specifically selected to enable meaningful comparative analysis.

The questionnaire was designed to complement the NHSLS instrument, with common sexual questions (including number of partners in the preceding year, age at first sex, number of marriages and cohabitations) worded to mirror the NHSLS formats. However, unlike the national survey – which used a paper-and-pencil format – the Chicago study used Computer Assisted Personal Interviews (CAPI), to allow for complex skip patterns as well as self-answered questions. Several new sets of items were added, starting with a respondent's egocentric social network, and the sexual lives of their network partners. To gauge the former, respondents were asked to identify the three adults they spent the most time with in the preceding year, as well as the three with whom they had discussed important matters, with overlap allowed between these two sets of alters. Identifying information (name, initials or pseudonym) was collected for each network member, and their approximate residence. Next, a main goal in the CHSLS was to collect as much information about local sexual patterns as possible, in the context of a standard respondent-driven survey. Items were therefore included on the sexual practices of each identified (and geocoded) network member. Respondents were asked, to the best of their knowledge, how many sexual relationships an alter had had in the preceding year. A series of questions then collected detailed information on the nature of these relationships – whether they were marriages or cohabitations, the gender and sexual orientation of the sexual partners, and whether the alter's partners were all men, all women, or both. Finally, to estimate concurrency, respondents were asked, to the best of their knowledge, whether an alter had every simultaneously been involved with two or more people. Additional questions on the local sexual scene included the number of people in the neighborhood, of those a respondent knew well enough to talk to, who were married, single with and without a partner, gay or lesbian. Finally, items were included on the specific place in the neighborhood respondents went most often to 'hang out,' and which Chicago neighborhood they went to most often to meet prospective partners.

In a second departure from the NHSLS (which queried primary and secondary relationships in the preceding year), the CHSLS also collected detailed information on a respondent's two most recent partnerships. The logic behind this modification was that NHSLS data had already established that, as described above, most people's sexual careers follow a pattern of stable monogamous relationships punctuated by episodes during which sex is more transactional, and relationships short-lived. These transient relationships form a minority of the current partnerships queried in many cross-sectional surveys. Asking people about their two most recent relationships, in contrast, would be more likely to uncover a (current) stable as well as a (past) short-term relationship (Laumann et al., 2004a). As with the NHSLS, it was a self-conscious goal to collect information not simply on sexual practices, but also on the broader relational context within which they acquired meaning. Hence, apart from items on a wide range of sexual practices – many adapted from the national study – the CHSLS also collected information on other, related aspects of a partnership. For instance, an item asked respondents about the sources of conflict in their relationship – with response categories including jealousy, sex, each other's stakeholders (friends, relatives), and household chores, among others. Jealousy, in particular, was probed further.

Items queried how often there had been a quarrel because the respondent thought a partner was paying too much attention to another person – and conversely, because the partner thought they were paying too much attention to someone else. Partly to query the sources of commitment in the relationship, respondents were also asked to imagine how their and, separately, their partners' lives would be different if they separated – i.e., whether particular aspects of their lives (standard of living, social life, overall happiness, sex) would change for the better or worse. Finally, relational equity was probed by asking respondents, considering the investments each had made in the partnership, whether they or the partner had benefited more from it.

The social embeddedness of these two partnerships was also explored in more detail. Respondents were asked whether, during the time they were involved, they and their partner had gotten to know, and gotten along with, each other's parents, as well as whether there was anyone in a partner's immediate network they did not get along with. Spatial information was also collected for these two relationships. For non-cohabiting partners living in the greater Chicago area during the relationship, and from the last five years, respondents were asked to name the neighborhood or suburb of residence. In combination with data on a respondent's own length of residence in their neighborhood, this spatial information allowed for estimation of physical proximity in each partnership.

Additionally, in the social networks module, respondents were asked about the relationships *between* the key (geocoded) alters they had spent time or discussed important matters with in the past year, as well as between these alters and both of their two most recent sexual partners. The goal was to investigate 'network closure' (Burt, 2001; Coleman, 1990),

Table 2.1   Matrix-form questionnaire

	SX*-1	SX-2	SO**-1	SO-2	SO-3	SO-4	SO-5
SX-1	N/A						
SX-2	1	N/A					
SO-1	2	7	N/A				
SO-2	1	2	1	N/A			
SO-3	6	1	1	3	N/A		
SO-4	7	6	4	5	2	N/A	
SO-5	5	5	1	6	2	1	N/A

*Sexual partner.
**Social network alter.

1: Do not know each other
2: Close friends
3: Involved in a sexual relationship with one another (not married)
4: Married to one another
5: Relatives with one another
6: Friends with one another
7: Acquaintances

which had been demonstrated in previous social network studies to facilitate norm enforcement through social sanctions, to facilitate trust between network members, and therefore enhance commitment in a relationship. These complex social patterns were queried through a matrix-form questionnaire (Table 2.1).

Since the relationships were symmetric (a social tie between the most recent sex partner and the first social network alter was the same as the converse tie, between alter 1 and partner 1), only half the matrix was needed. Finally, to investigate the role of stakeholder ties in the formation of each relationship, respondents were also asked whether any of their other key alters knew each partner before they did.

Finally, the CHSLS collected more detailed information on concurrency than the national survey, starting with a respondent's own concurrency. First, similar to the NHSLS, the Chicago survey collected information on the beginning and ending dates of up to five partnerships in the preceding year, allowing for the structure of each respondent's current or recent egocentric sexual network to be estimated. In addition,

a series of concurrency questions were asked in the context of the two most recent partnerships, including whether the respondent had been sexually involved with someone else when initiating sex with the partner; how many other people they had had sex with during the relationship; and separately as a cross-check, whether these two recent partnerships had overlapped. A partner's concurrent relationships were queried through the following question: 'To the best of your knowledge, how many people other than you did (partner) have sex with during the course of your relationship?' It became apparent after the instrument had been fielded, however, that the lack of a time frame for this question created problems, especially when applied to long-term relationships. In contrast to the one-year period for which the national survey collected such information, the CHSLS question wording made it impossible to distinguish concurrent relationships in the distant past with current or recent ones, although each had different implications for a respondent's current exposure to STDs or AIDS (Laumann et al., 2004b).

A final learning experience in the designing of sexuality measures came in the context of the ongoing National Social Life, Health, and Aging Project (NSHAP). The last section of the chapter describes this process.

THE NATIONAL SOCIAL LIFE, HEALTH, AND AGING PROJECT

NSHAP is the first nationally representative study of sexuality, social life, and well-being among the elderly (aged 57 to 85). In addition to health and social factors, as well as 13 biomeasures, the survey also included items on a wide range of sexual topics. Many of these – including questions on sexual practices and attitudes – were adapted from the NHSLS. In a departure from the NHSLS and CHSLS formats, however, NSHAP only collected aggregate information on a respondent's lifetime sexual history. Instead, the focus was on sexual relationships in the preceding five years (Waite et al., 2009). As noted, this five-year window had its origins in the NHSLS design phase, and was dropped from the previous study due to financial and other constraints.

As with lifetime partnership and sexual history in the NHSLS, the five-year module in NSHAP was structured around major relationships. The logic behind this format, to recall, was that using these major partnerships as markers, a respondent could better report on the less serious sexual transactions that either coincided with or occurred between these major relations. In NSHAP, these major partnerships included the current or most recent spouse, cohabiting partner, or a current intimate or romantic partner, as well as either one or two of the next most recent spouses or cohabiting partners – for a maximum of two partners in all. Minor partnerships included up to three of the next most recent relationships within the past five years. For each partnership, information was collected on the timing (month and year) of first sex (except for major partnerships that began more than five years ago) and the most recent sexual event. In addition, a respondent was asked about the gender and relative age of each partner, and whether they expected to have sex with the partner again (Waite et al., 2009). Given the low rate of partner acquisition among elderly adults, this limited set of relationships efficiently covered the total number of sexual contacts for a vast majority of the population. As with the analogous NHSLS and CHSLS modules, the timing information collected allows researchers to estimate the length of each partnership, as well as whether

they were sequentially monogamous or concurrent.

A second departure from the NHSLS was with sexual dysfunctions. As noted, the earlier study had only queried the presence of a problem *per se*, for a duration of several months or more over the preceding year. Subsequently, in 1998, the first International Consensus Development Conference on Female Sexual Dysfunction strongly recommended that a personal distress criterion also be included in the definition (Basson et al., 2000, 2004). A later study by Bancroft et al. (2003) demonstrated, however, that some sexual difficulties may be more strongly correlated with distress about the sexual relationship than with a respondent's negative feelings about their own lack of sexual response. The authors argued that such sexual difficulties (which they term 'sexual problems') may represent adaptive psychosomatic responses to stressful situations, and not medical or physiological 'dysfunctions.' While not disagreeing that the relevance of sexual distress to dysfunction needed to be systematically investigated, Rosen and Laumann (2003) argued that measures of distress have yet to undergo rigorous psychometric tests. In contrast, the broad sexual problems measures in the NHSLS were strongly correlated with well-validated measures of physical and relationship satisfaction, as well as generalized happiness (Laumann et al., 1999). Partly on the basis of these arguments, in 2004, the International Consultation on Erectile Dysfunction recommended a dual definition for each dysfunction – a *per se* definition indicating the presence and/or extent of a sexual problem, and a second definition incorporating the personal distress criterion, to assess the effect of a dysfunction on an individual and on his/her intimate partnerships (Lue et al., 2004). Accordingly, NSHAP queried sexual problems through two measures. The first, mirroring the

NHSLS format, asked about sexual issues experienced for 'several months or more' over the preceding 12 months. In addition, respondents who reported a problem were asked: 'How much did your (problem) bother you?' Response categories for the latter included 'a lot,' 'somewhat,' and 'not at all.' A final innovation in NSHAP was to collect information on a partner's sexual problems over the past year – and how much these problems bothered the respondent. These questions were designed to mirror those on a respondent's own problems.

CONCLUSION

In this chapter, we have presented an account of how measures of different aspects of human sexuality were conceived and operationalized – starting, in the late 1980s, from an almost complete lack of standards and models. It is a process that continues today with NSHAP. In each of the three major studies described above, the respective design-teams deliberately avoided using simple inventories of sexual practices. Instead, the focus was on operationalizing human sexual patterns as inherently socially determined phenomena, meaningful only in the context of specific webs of relationships and the associated normative contexts. We hope our account of this self-consciously theory-driven process will aid researchers in their own operationalizations of complex social realities.

REFERENCES

Aral, S. (1999) 'Sexual network patterns as determinants of STD rates: Paradigm shift in the behavioral epidemiology of STDs made visible', *Sexually Transmitted Diseases*, 26 (5): 262–64.

Bancroft, J., Loftus, J. and Long, J. S. (2003) 'Distress about sex: A national survey of women in heterosexual relationships', *Archives of Sexual Behavior*, 32 (3): 193–208.

Basson, R., Althof, S., Davis, S., Fugl-Meyer, K., Goldstein, I., Leiblum, S. et al. (2004) 'Summary of the recommendations on sexual dysfunctions in women', *Journal of Sexual Medicine*, 1 (1): 24–34.

Basson, R., Berman, J., Burnett, A., Derogatis, L., Ferguson, D., Fourcroy, J. et al. (2000) 'Report of the International Consensus Development Congress on Female Sexual Dysfunction: Definitions and classifications', *Journal of Urology*, 163 (3): 888–93.

Blair, E., Sudman, S., Bradburn, N. M. and Stocking, C. (1977) 'How to ask questions about drinking and sex: Response effects in measuring consumer behavior', *Journal of Marketing Research*, 14 (3): 316–21.

Bradburn, N. M. and Sudman, S. (1983) *Asking Questions: A Practical Guide to Questionnaire Design*. San Francisco: Jossey-Bass.

Bradburn, N. M., Sudman, S., Blair, E. and Stocking, C. (1978) 'Question threat and response bias', *Public Opinion Quarterly*, 42 (2): 221–34.

Browning, C. and Laumann, E. O. (1997) 'Sexual contact between children and adults: A life course perspective', *American Sociological Review*, 62 (4): 540–60.

Browning, C. and Laumann, E. O. (2003) 'The social context of adaptation to childhood sexual maltreatment: A life course perspective', in J. Bancroft (ed.) *Sexual Development in Childhood*. Bloomington: Indiana University Press. pp. 383–404.

Burt, R. S. (2001) 'Structural holes versus network closure as social capital', in N. Lin, K. S. Cook, and R. S. Burt (eds) *Social Capital: Theory and Research*. New York: Aldine. pp. 31–56.

Coates, R. A., Calzavara, L. M., Soskolne, C. L., Read, S. E., Fanning, M. M., Shepherd, F. A. et al. (1988) 'Validity of sexual histories in a prospective study of male sexual contacts of men with AIDS or an AIDS-related condition', *American Journal of Epidemiology*, 128 (4): 719–28.

Coleman, J. S. (1990) *Foundations of Social Theory*. Cambridge, Mass.: Belknap.

Fararo, T. and Skvoretz, J. (1986) 'E-state structuralism: A theoretical method', *American Sociological Review*, 51 (5): 591–602.

Freedman, D., Thornton, A., Camburn, D., Alwin, D. and Young-DeMarco, L. (1988) 'The life history calendar: A technique for collecting retrospective data', *Sociological Methodology*, 18: 37–68.

Gagnon, J. H. (1991) 'The implicit and explicit use of scripts in sex research', in J. Bancroft, C. Davis, and D. Weinstein (eds) *The Annual Review of Sex Research*. Mt. Vernon, Iowa: Society for the Scientific Study of Sex. pp. 1–41.

Gagnon, J. H. and Simon, W. (1973) *Sexual Conduct: The Social Sources of Human Sexuality.* Chicago: Aldine.

Institute of Medicine (1986) *Confronting AIDS: Directions for Public Health, Health Care, and Research.* Washington, D.C.: National Academy Press.

Kinsey, A. C., Pomeroy, W. B. and Martin, C. E. (1948) *Sexual Behavior in the Human Male.* Philadelphia: Saunders.

Kinsey, A. C., Pomeroy, W. B., Martin, C. E. and Gebhard, P. H. (1953) *Sexual Behavior in the Human Female.* Philadelphia: Saunders.

Laumann, E. O. (1966) *Prestige and Association in an Urban Community.* New York: Bobbs-Merrill.

Laumann, E. O. (1973) *Bonds of Pluralism: Form and Substance of Urban Social Networks.* New York: Wiley.

Laumann, E. O. (2006) 'A 45-year retrospective on doing networks', *Connections,* 27 (1): 65–90.

Laumann, E. O., Browning, C., Rijt, A. V. D. and Gatzeva, M. (2003) 'Sexual contact between children and adults: A life-course perspective with special reference to men', in J. Bancroft (ed.) *Sexual Development in Childhood.* Bloomington: Indiana University Press. pp. 293–327.

Laumann, E. O., Ellingson, S., Mahay, J., Paik, A. and Youm, Y. (2004a) *The Sexual Organization of the City.* Chicago: University of Chicago Press.

Laumann, E. O., Gagnon, J. H. and Michael, R. T. (1989) *The National Study of Health and Sexual Behavior.* Chicago: National Opinion Research Center.

Laumann, E. O., Gagnon, J. H., Michael, R. T. and Michaels, S. (1994) *The Social Organization of Sexuality: Sexual Practices in the United States.* Chicago: University of Chicago Press.

Laumann, E. O., Gagnon, J. H., Michael, R. T., Michaels, S. and Schumm, L. P. (1993) 'Monitoring AIDS and other rare population events: A network approach', *Journal of Health and Social Behavior,* 34 (1): 7–22.

Laumann, E. O., Mahay, J., Paik, A. and Youm, Y. (2004b) 'Network data collection and its relevance for the analysis of STDs: The NHSLS and CHSLS', in M. Morris (ed.) *Network Epidemiology: A Handbook for Survey Design and Data Collection.* Oxford: Oxford University Press. pp. 25–41.

Laumann, E. O., Paik, A. and Rosen, R. C. (1999) 'Sexual dysfunction in the United States: Prevalence and predictors', *Journal of the American Medical Association,* 281 (6): 537–44.

Laumann, E. O. and Pappi, F. U. (1976) *Networks and Collective Action.* New York: Academic Press.

Laumann, E. O. and Youm, Y. (1999) 'Race and ethnic group differences in the prevalence of sexually transmitted diseases in the United States: A network explanation', *Sexually Transmitted Diseases,* 26 (5): 250–61.

Lue, T. F., Basson, R., Rosen, R. C., Guiliano, F., Khoury, S. and Montorsi, F. (2004) *Sexual Medicine: Sexual Dysfunction in Men and Women.* Paris: Health Publications.

Michael, R. T., Laumann, E. O., Gagnon, J. H. and Smith, T. W. (1988) 'Number of sex partners and potential risk of sexual exposure to human immunodeficiency virus', *Morbidity and Mortality Weekly Report,* 37 (37): 565–68.

Morris, M., Wawer, M. J., Podhisita, C. and Sewankambo, N. (2004) 'The Thailand and Ugandan sexual network studies', in M. Morris (ed.) *Network Epidemiology: A Handbook for Survey Design and Data Collection.* Oxford and New York: Oxford University Press. pp. 42–57.

Rosen, R. C. and Laumann, E. O. (2003) 'The prevalence of sexual problems in women: How valid are comparisons across studies?', *Archives of Sexual Behavior,* 32 (3): 209–11.

Waite, L. J., Laumann, E. O., Das, A. and Schumm, L. P. (2009, forthcoming) 'Sexuality: Measures of partnerships, practices, attitudes, and problems in the National Social Life, Health and Aging Study', *Journals of Gerontology, Series B.*

3

The SAT®: Design Principles and Innovations of a Quintessential American Social Indicator[1]

Howard T. Everson

INTRODUCTION

Each year, typically in late August, the College Board publishes its report on the SAT® (hereafter the SAT) scores of the US secondary school seniors – some 2.7 million students in all – who plan to go to college in the following academic year. These reports to the nation, which have been published every year since 1972 by the College Board, are reported on by most of the major newspapers in the United States, and changes in SAT score trends are the subject of much commentary and debate among education pundits and social critics across the country. From its early, modest beginning as a college admission test used primarily by a handful of elite colleges and universities in the northeastern United States, the SAT has become an important societal indicator, used not only to gauge the academic strengths of US high-school students, but also as a measure of the quality of neighborhood schools and a driver of housing prices in America's more affluent communities. Though nearly everyone thinks about them at one time or another, few understand what the SAT actually measures and how the scores are derived.

Based on early, somewhat elitist notions of intelligence, the SAT began in the early 20th century by measuring ambitious, often well-heeled, young students' knowledge of the 'canon' – i.e., French, German, Latin, history, mathematics, and the classics. Over time, as we learned more about the psychology of human abilities and how to measure them with more precision, the SAT adapted and changed, becoming along the way a prominent indicator of educational excellence. In my career as the Chief Research Scientist for the College Board I oversaw the research in support of those changes to the SAT. For more than a decade, from 1992 through 2005, I had the good fortune to work with a remarkable group of scholars, some from academe and others from the Educational Testing Service (ETS), the College Board's partner in developing the SAT, to maintain and improve the measurement qualities of this important social indicator. Throughout my tenure at the College Board, I took heed of Campbell's Law: 'The more any quantitative social indicator is used in social decision-making, the more subject it will be to corruption pressures and the more apt it will be to distort the social processes it is intended to monitor' (Campbell, 1975). The SAT was, and is, an important quantitative social indicator. I routinely worried about it becoming corrupted and distorted as the test scores became more widely used. Campbell's admonition helped guide my thinking about how best to maintain the validity and utility of the SAT.

Science instructs us that measurement is central to our understanding of the world. The better we measure, the more our knowledge of the world develops and, in turn, our ways of knowing and measuring improve. Indeed, the history of science offers many illustrative examples. Henry I of England, circa 1100 AD, established the 'yard,' and all the measurement implied today by the term yardstick. As the reigning monarch, Henry I, proclaimed that a yard was the distance from the tip of his nose to the very end of his outstretched thumb. Roughly 600 years later, the French Academy of Sciences introduced a more standard measure of distance, the *meter* or, if you like, the *metre*, and defined it as the distance between two marks on a platinum-iridium bar meant to represent $^1/_{10,000,000}$ of the distance from the equator to the North Pole through Paris. Today the meter – *the* scientific standard of length – is measured by the distance light travels in absolute vacuum in $^1/_{299,792,458}$ of a second. Indeed, as we understand more about nature, the precision of our measures improves. We have witnessed progress in our measures of the physical world. The challenge, as I learned at the College Board, is to continue to improve our social-scientific measurements.

Like other forms of social measurement, the SAT has become a common yardstick for measuring students' academic abilities and the quality of education in the United States. For more than 80 years the College Board has worked to develop and improve the SAT, and during that time has watched its importance as a social metric increase dramatically. In an effort to share some of the measurement and methodological insights gained over time that may be of broader interest to researchers across the social sciences, this chapter provides a sketch of how the SAT has evolved over the years, and speculates on how it may change in the future. The discussion of a social measure, whether it is the SAT or the consumer price index or the gross domestic product, requires placing the measure in a broader social context to better understand how it came about and how it is used today. Thus, I begin by tracing the roots of the College Board and the SAT in the US system of higher education. With this as background, I then go on to describe the research that supports the current uses of the SAT. The chapter concludes with a look ahead, asking what kinds of changes can be expected for the SAT if it is to maintain its role as an important societal metric in the 21st century. My aim is to reflect on the social, practical, and methodological issues related to the design and construction of the SAT, focusing on challenges and changes during the course of the SAT's life and reflecting methodologically on future design and research opportunities.

TRACING THE ARC OF THE SAT: INNOVATIONS AND CHANGE IN RESPONSE TO HISTORICAL SHIFTS IN COLLEGE ADMISSION TESTING

It is clearly the case that historical pressures and processes have influenced the evolution of the SAT. From time to time throughout its history, the College Board introduced changes, sometimes small and incremental and other times large and dramatic, to the SAT. When viewing these changes, it is important to keep in mind the central role of the College Board – an association of secondary schools, colleges, and universities based in New York City – has been to promote the transition from high school to college by creating as system of assessments. In 1901, for example, 973 students took College Board entrance examinations in nine academic subjects – English, French, German, Latin, Greek, history, mathematics, chemistry, and physics. By 1910, the number of students taking the College Board tests had grown nearly fourfold, with 3,731 students taking the subject matter examinations. Unlike today, the admission tests administered in the early part of the 20th century were created within a college preparatory curriculum framework. These were demanding tests that required candidates to submit lengthy essays as part of the examination process. Clearly, the content and measurement practices were not

reflective of the needs of social scientists, but rather were driven more by the demands and expectations of faculty from a small number of highly selective colleges and universities that jealously guarded the postsecondary admission process early in the century.

Following the success of the United States Army's large-scale testing program in World War I, the College Board admission tests, by 1925, came under the influence of the intelligence testing movement associated with Robert M. Yerkes, Henry T. Moore, and Carl C. Brigham – each in his own right a prominent social scientist of the time. Recognizing this growing trend in social scientific (psychological) measurement, the College Board adopted the intelligence testing framework proposed by a blue-ribbon panel of social and behavioral scientists chaired by Carl Brigham, and introduced the Scholastic Aptitude Test (SAT) as the uniform college admission test. This dramatic shift signaled a clear change in the test's framework, moving decidedly away from the curriculum-based achievement measures characteristic of earlier College Board examinations to one steeped in the contemporary views of behavioral scientists.

The first SAT, administered on June 23, 1926 to 8,040 candidates, included nine subtests: seven with verbal content – definitions, classification, artificial language, antonyms, verbal analogies, logical inference, and paragraph reading; and two with mathematical content – arithmetical problems and number series. Similar to the current SAT, the scores were reported on a more precise measurement scale, one that approximated the standard normal curve and with a mean fixed at 500 and a standard deviation of 100. We see with the SAT of 1926 a move toward a much more scientific form of educational and social measurement.

Three short years later, in 1929, again under the direction of Carl Brigham, the SAT was modified to have two separate sections, separately measuring verbal and mathematical aptitudes with scores reported for each section, using differential weights depending on the college(s) receiving the examinees' scores. By the 1930s the SAT was incorporating modern views on measurement scaling and weighting the scores to suit the needs of the users of the SAT. In 1937, the Board's Achievement Tests (today referred to as the SAT-II tests) were introduced and those scores were also reported on a scale with a mean of 500 and standard deviation of 100, giving them the *imprimatur*, through scaling, of the original SAT. Back then, test score reports were sent only to the colleges – students were not privy to their own SAT scores. Indeed, the College Board considered the scores the property of colleges and universities using them. Thus, in the early part of the 20th century, the SAT held no status as a social indicator prior to America's entry into World War II.

About the same time the College Board introduced technology into the SAT with the advent of a machine-scored answer sheets, allowing the test to be made up entirely by efficient and inexpensive multiple-choice question-and-answer formats. A short time later, in June 1941, the scores on every form of the SAT were equated directly to scores on preceding forms to maintain the validity and reliability of the SAT from one administration to the next, and to allow for trend analyses by the colleges and universities. Thus, we see the emergence of a test design-framework that included blending the sciences of intelligence testing, and psychometrics, with early data storage and computing technologies, all in an effort to ensure the quality of the measurement over time. By the end of World War II the framework for the

SAT reflected the prevailing notions of the centrality of verbal and mathematical aptitudes, coupled with the use of multiple-choice formats and norm-referenced scoring to ensure comparability from year to year (Coffman, 1962). More importantly, we see a rapid expansion of access to higher education in the United States and the dawn of an era when trends in SAT scores could be discussed by the *cognoscenti* of American higher education who worried about the dilution of talent as those returning from military service entered postsecondary institutions across the country.

After nearly four decades characterized by continuity and little change, the SAT, during the 1980s, had become something of a social indicator. This became evident when, in 1984, the US Secretary of Education, Terrell Bell, introduced the 'Wall Chart' of educational quality and effectiveness for each state and included the average SAT scores for each state. Educational reform and economic competitiveness were becoming national issues by the end of the of Ronald Reagan's presidency in 1988. The developing educational reform movement, which remains a major policy imperative today, signaled the importance of the SAT as an educational barometer, a social scientific measure growing in cache year after year.

The SAT was modified again in the early 1990s. These changes were in response to calls for reform in education which had begun a decade earlier. Arguably, the most important change was a shift away from the long-held belief that aptitudes for college success were fixed or immutable – a view that was increasingly at odds with Americans' optimistic views of the efficacy of schooling. The SAT once again came under pressure to shift to an assessment framework that included the measurement of verbal and mathematical abilities that developed over time – both in and outside of school. To many, this minor change was a nod in the direction of those who argued that schooling ought to matter when it comes to performance on the SAT, although it remained unclear how exactly those particular cognitive abilities developed and which educational conditions would foster their development.

The verbal section, for example, included measures of critical reading, vocabulary in context, and analogical reasoning. Similarly, the mathematics section of the SAT stressed the application of mathematical concepts and quantitative comparisons, and permitted examinees, for the first time, to use calculators when taking the SAT (Scheuneman and Camara, 2002). The subsections of the test were renamed and the acronym SAT-I was introduced, while direct references to the older name, Scholastic Aptitude Test, were abandoned. The College Board's admission testing program was rebranded and now included the SAT-I Verbal and Mathematics Reasoning Tests and the SAT-II Subject Tests. Moreover, at this time the SAT was re-normed to offset a downward drift in the mean scores that had been taking place since the late 1970s, and to maintain the scaling properties that are essential to the test (see Dorans, 2002 for details). Clearly, by the 1990s we see the SAT score trends, both nationally and by state, as well as by race or ethnicity, contributing to an increasing recognition on the part of the College Board and ETS of the SAT as an important social indicator, one used by a broader, more diverse population of American high-school students. The SAT had been transformed into a social scientific measure with tremendous reach and influence.

Nearly a decade later, in March 2005, the SAT was revised yet again. The SAT had come under growing criticism from a prominent voice in American higher education, Richard C. Atkinson, then President of the University of California – one of America's largest public systems of higher education. Atkinson, a well respected cognitive scientist in his own right, asserted that colleges had become much too reliant on the SAT for admitting students to higher education, and that the SAT – with its long-time focus on abstract reasoning and aptitudes – was much too removed from the high-school curricula to be useful to colleges and universities (Atkinson, 2001). As a social indicator, the SAT was too abstruse, too detached from the high-school curriculum, Atkinson argued. The College Board, in response, moved to strengthen SAT's alignment with curriculum and instructional practices in U.S. high schools and colleges. In doing so, the test developers and social scientists at the College Board and ETS had to address the demand for changes in what the SAT measured, while at the same time ensuring that the scores, the highly communicative SAT score scales, would remain comparable to, and interchangeable with, scores on earlier versions of the SAT. Both change and continuity were required in the measure. From both the social-scientific and the social-policy perspectives, it was essential that the SAT maintain its score trends across years. As a social indicator, the SAT had to remain robust against the pressures of corruption and distortion, to use Campbell's language.

When the SAT was revised in 2005, the test specifications were changed. Analogical reasoning test items were dropped from the verbal section, and a stronger emphasis was placed on the measurement of critical reading skills. More high-school mathematics was added and new item types were included in the mathematics section of the SAT. Perhaps more dramatically, the SAT now included a writing section in which examinees had to draft an essay as part of the test. Thus to remain education-ally relevant the SAT underwent a major renovation (Kobrin and Melican, 2007).

As we have seen, starting in the early 1990s we have witnessed a deliberate movement away from earlier notions of intelligence and aptitude testing, to an SAT that includes a more pronounced emphasis on the idea of developed cognitive abilities, while at the same time trying to remain relevant by responding, or attempting to respond, to the educational reform move-ment in the United States. Thus we see that as our knowledge of how students learn in school increases, the SAT attempts to change accordingly.

It is also the case that the population to which the measurement instrument was applied has also changed relatively rapidly over the past two decades, undoubtedly affecting the SAT as a social indicator. The profile of college-bound students taking the SAT has changed dramatically since it was first administered more than 80 years ago. According to the College Board (see Lawrence et al., 2002), approximately 8,000 students (mostly men, we suspect) took the SAT for the first time in 1926. By 2009, more than 2.7 million high-school students from all over the US and elsewhere took the SAT – more than half were women.

When a test with the social significance of the SAT undergoes changes in content, format specifications, administrative condi-tions, and population, it is essential to assess periodically whether those changes have had a significant effect on the constructs and measurement properties of the scale. Over the years, the College Board and ETS have carried out extensive research to maintain the measurement properties of the SAT, including work on content changes, scale reliability, linking and equat-ing (Dorans et al., 2006), and various forms of validity (Burton and Ramist, 2001; Kobrin and Melican, 2007). Again, this

strategic investment in research has been substantial over recent years, and the current leadership at the College Board, recognizing the prominence of the SAT, has sustained that investment over time.

When it comes to the SAT, much has changed and much remains the same. For the most part, changes in the SAT have been discrete, singular events. Look-ing ahead, we anticipate advances in measurement, psychology, and technol-ogy will continue, and the SAT will be expected to adapt, to keep pace by intro-ducing innovation through a continuous improvement design process. Innovation and improvement will, for example, intro-ducing new multidimensional measurement models, computer-based test administra-tion, and new cognitive and non-cognitive constructs.

TRENDS INFLUENCING THE FUTURE DIRECTIONS FOR THE SAT

On the heels of the recent changes to the SAT, considerations about the future of this iconic measure may have broader significance to social scientists who develop and refine similar kinds of social indicators. The first factor influencing the future direction of the SAT is the mounting pressure from educational reformers who are developing content, performance, and assessment standards for high-school grad-uation. When, for example, in 2001, the President of the University of California, Richard C. Atkinson, proposed dropping the SAT as a requirement for admission to the University of California, he called for a closer alignment between college admis-sion tests and the high-school curriculum. Dr. Atkinson's comments fueled the debate about what college admission tests ought to measure. His remarks raised questions such as: Are admission tests used only to predict grades in the first year of college? More recently, the National Association of College Admission Counseling released a series of recommendations that challenge the fundamental role of the SAT in the college admissions process (NACAC, 2008). The NACAC report suggested strongly that one possible future direction for college admission tests is the development of curriculum-based achievement tests, arguing that a redesigned SAT with an even stronger curricular focus would send a clear message to students that studying in high school is the way to succeed on college admission tests and succeed in college. Should college admission tests provide *all* students with the opportunity to demonstrate their varied academic talents and abilities? Should they signal what colleges and universities want in applicants, thereby driving curricula at the secondary-school level? These questions go to the very heart of the issue of what college admission tests like the SAT should measure and why.

Second, advances in computing and communications technology will influence the content and form of college admission tests in the future. Technological innovations are spurring an ever expanding capacity to generate, acquire, store, and disseminate data, influencing measurement across the social sciences. The computer's potential for presenting test items and tasks using simulations and multimedia will move large-scale testing beyond the constraints of multiple-choice formats, providing design advantages over traditional forms of paper and pencil tests. Coupled with software systems that track and monitor examinee performance during testing, it is not difficult to imagine more informative adaptive testing systems that, in the future, will provide richer and more dynamic forms of assessment (Bennett, 1993, 1998). We see, too, with the recent growth of telecommunications networks,

the possibility of using the internet to deliver tests, thereby providing students and their families with greater access to admission tests and more convenient testing opportunities (Bennett, 1994, 1998).

Third, and perhaps most important, is the influence of cognitive and educational psychology on testing and assessment. Many scholars and theorists working in the area of human learning and intelligence have outlined ways in which educational assessment will benefit and change as the result of emerging research (see, for example, National Research Council, 2000; Snow and Lohman, 1989). The common view of cognitive assessment data, and other forms of social measurements such as surveys and interviews for that matter, is often much too narrow. As Mislevy (2007) put it

> It hides the argument for just what aspects of a performance or a product are recognized and why—an argument that must be made even when the mechanism to effect the evaluation is just identifying whether a multiple-choice response is correct. It narrows the designer's focus to scoring items rather than scrutinizing performance for clues about what students know or can do in what kinds of situations (p. 466).

Richer analyses of existing tests will, no doubt, improve our understanding of what they measure and why. Moreover, like other areas of scientific inquiry, research in these areas is likely to lead to the use of new and different measures, as well as improved precision of measurement in existing areas. Even research not directly related to the test's underlying construct, such as inquiries into intended uses of the test scores or the social consequences of using a particular measure, might inform researchers attempting to generate new items, refine measurement approaches, and thereby improve the social scientific character of the measurement instrument themselves.

To remain relevant in the future, succeeding generations of the SAT must incorporate advances in psychology, measurement science, and technology. Change and innovation in college admission tests will progress very slowly if driven solely by the swirl of politics and the anti-measurement positions of foes of standardized testing. Evolving the SAT to meet future needs calls for a test design-framework built on the principles of cognitive theory, modern measurement science, and a commitment to technology-based design and delivery systems that promote innovation without sacrificing access and equity. This background theme of a *principled design* framework, one that deliberately attempts to integrate new perspectives in cognitive psychology, as well as advances in measurement theory and technology, to create a conceptual framework for the design of an assessment (Mislevy et al., 2002), in my view, could move the SAT from its current task-based focus to an assessment system better positioned to incorporate advances in measurement (Everson, 2000).

A design framework for the SAT[2]

As noted above, maintaining the SAT's relevance in the college admission process depends largely on the framework that guides innovation in the future. The underlying contention, again, is that explicating the test design-framework for the SAT makes continuous improvement sustainable and provides opportunities to introduce a new generation of college admission tests without the disruption that often accompanies sweeping technological change. The need for a design framework is motivated by progress in four areas related to testing and assessment – cognitive psychology, learning theory applied to

academic disciplines, psychometric modeling, and information technology (Almond et al., 2002). We ensure improved measurement now and in the future by designing and developing tests that conform to the principles that we will refer to as evidence-centered assessment design – i.e., that define the decisions made based on test results and then work backwards to develop the tasks, delivery mechanisms, scoring procedures, and feedback mechanisms (Almond et al., 2002). A design framework, for example, provides test developers with a common language for discussing the knowledge, skills, and abilities measured by the SAT, and why they are essential to success in college and beyond. These discussions, one could argue, help create consensus about the role and value of the SAT, sharpen the focus on its measurement goals and, along the way, demystify what the SAT measures and why it measures those constructs and not others. Thus, as our understanding of what the SAT measures is increased, test scores have more meaning and a richer body of information is available to schools, colleges, and universities. Higher-education policies and the role of standardized testing benefit from improved measurement as well. And perhaps more importantly, we are better positioned to evaluate students' abilities and potentialities, and to make changes to the SAT in the future.

The measurement implications of networks of assessments

As computing technology has transformed itself – and the worlds of business, science, and education change along with it – computers have moved from numerical calculators to data processing machines to interacting networks of intelligent information retrieval, control, and delivery systems. In this world of networks and information webs it is easy to imagine a future where the best schools, teachers, and courses are available to *all* students (Bennett, 1998; Everson, 1998). This scenario suggests that tests and assessments designed with a single, narrow focus – such as summative forms of assessment – may be unnecessary in the future.

In some sense the future is already here. Distance learning opportunities are more widely available. Computer-based adaptive tests, i.e., assessments in which the examinee is presented with different test questions or tasks matched to their ability or skill levels, are in widespread use with the College Board's Accuplacer® tests as well as with the Graduate Record Examination® (GRE®), Graduate Management Admission Test® (GMAT®), the Test of English as a Foreign Language® (TOEFL®), and others. In these instances and others, computers construct the tests, present the items adaptively, score the responses, and generate reports and analyses. The potential of computer-based testing can be pushed further, and more intelligent forms of assessment are possible, even likely (Bennett, 2001, 2002). More than a decade ago Bennett (1993) framed the future of intelligent assessment this way.

> Intelligent assessment is conceived of as an integration of three research lines, each dealing with cognitive performance from a different perspective: constructed-response testing, artificial intelligence, and model-based measurement ... These tasks will be scored by automated routines that emulate the behavior of an expert, providing a rating on a partial credit scale for summative purposes as well as a qualitative description designed to impart instructionally useful information. The driving mechanisms underlying these tasks and their scoring are cognitively grounded measurement models that may dictate what the characteristics of items should be, which items from a large pool should be administered, how item responses should be combined to make more general inferences, and how uncertainty should be handled (p. 99).

This convergence of computer-based testing with advanced networks makes possible new forms of college admission tests. These might include, for example, assessments containing more complex items and tasks, or tests with the ability to seamlessly branch across content areas and domains, as well as assessments with modular components that can be added or removed to suit particular inferential purposes. This merging of cognitive psychology and measurement theory with computer-based technologies also makes likely the introduction of new test delivery systems like video games and other hand-held methods, remote scoring of constructed responses, and more powerful means for summarizing and communicating test performance. These advances in information technologies, no doubt, will provide platforms for the next generation of the college admission tests. If Bennett (1998) is right, these new technologies will be the prime mover of innovation in educational testing. Bennett makes a strong argument for a future-oriented design framework for the SAT that accommodates technological advances, improved measurement, and breakthroughs in the learning sciences. These technologies, moreover, will likely influence other forms of social measurement – including political polling methods and other survey methodologies.

Model-based measurement

Similar to many instruments and indicators, the SAT is evolving in response to innovations related to the measurement model underlying the design of the instrument. The SAT, and tests like it, have been based on classical measurement principles. The dominant goal of the so-called classical psychometric approach to measurement was to estimate an examinee's relative position on a scale that measures a latent variable, e.g., an aptitude for verbal or mathematical reasoning. The classical test model was developed largely to permit inferences about how much knowledge, aptitude, or ability an individual possesses in a normative sense. In the case of the SAT, the latent variable space includes both verbal and mathematical reasoning. In general, this measurement model has proved useful for inferences related to selection and classification. This classic psychometric approach, however, is much less helpful for making prescriptive instructional decisions or for diagnosing learning or achievement deficiencies – an oft-stated measurement goal of many new assessments (Nichols et al., 1995; Leighton and Gierl, 2007).

With the emergence of the cognitive perspective in the learning sciences, the emphasis shifts from measures of how much a student has learned, or where they rank on a continuum of achievement, to a focus on the importance of how knowledge is organized, and how students reorganize that knowledge to represent and solve problems. Thus, educational measures like the SAT now need to tell us more about *what* students know and what they can do – i.e., frame problems, develop multiple solution strategies, and evaluate the feasibility of those solutions. Indeed, this theoretical shift underscores the need for measurement models that distinguish learners in terms of their knowledge states, cognitive process abilities, and strategies for solving problems (National Research Council, 2000). This work will likely influence the measurement models used in other forms of social indicators. We are seeing this happening, for example, in the health-related fields where there is a need to improve the measurement in patient-reported outcomes measures (McDowell and Newell, 1996; Streiner and Norman, 2008), as well

as in the human resource arena where measures of job satisfaction and employee fitness are needed (Embretson and Reise, 2000).

In response to the challenge articulated by the National Research Council's Committee on the Foundations of Assessment (NRC, 2001), a number of new and promising psychometric approaches with a decidedly cognitive flavor are in development. These include, for example, latent trait models, statistical pattern classification methods, and causal probabilistic networks. While these measurement models may rank students along a proficiency scale, their intent is to build on detailed task analyses and cognitively rich representations of how knowledge is structured by learning in school to produce assessments that inform instruction in ways that are diagnostic as well as prescriptive (Leighton and Gierl, 2007).

Many of these newer models attempt to provide descriptions of the students' knowledge or ability structures, as well as the cognitive processes presumed to underlie performance on single test items or tasks, or sets of tasks. Thus, if successfully developed and adapted, they hold promise not only for tests like the SAT, but also for dynamically linking assessment and instruction (Everson, 1995).

New test items and tasks will be needed to capture the complex models of reasoning, problem solving, and strategic thinking that are emerging from the learning sciences. It is not likely that traditional item characteristics, such as item difficulty or person ability, will be of much use for assessments that are theory-based. As Embretson (1996) suggests 'applying cognitive principles to the design of test items requires analyzing how item stimulus content influences the cognitive processes, strategies, and knowledge structures that are involved in item solving' (p. 29). Test items and tasks that go beyond the four- or five-option multiple-choice format will be required. Innovations in technology and theory will enable the development of a variety of constructed-response formats and simulations to support the evaluation of a broader range of abilities. As any young school kid can tell you, it is not difficult to imagine that computer-based simulations that capitalize on multimedia have a good deal of potential for future assessments.

Together, these relatively new psychometric models all take the important step of attempting to integrate cognitive psychology and model-based measurement. Indeed, they are seen as intelligent forms of assessment (Bennett, 1993), and as efforts that synthesize methods and techniques from three vital research areas, artificial intelligence and expert systems, modern psychometrics, and cognitive psychology – i.e., smart tests. To be useful in a theory-based test design framework a number of issues will have to be resolved. More work, for example, is needed on the painstaking task analyses that fore-shadow cognitive-model development in various academic domains like mathematical problem-solving or language learning. As measurement science and computer technologies advance so, too, does our ability to gather and incorporate evidence from other cognitively rich constructs – such as metacognitive abilities, problem-solving strategies, prior knowledge, and response mode preferences. These various forms and combinations of evidence could be incorporated into a design framework for assessment in the SAT.

The generation and emergence of new measures

Students' developed abilities in, for example, verbal reasoning, reading comprehension, writing, and mathematical problem solving may be assessed in the future with test items and tasks that are based on more firmly established theoretical foundations. Achievement tests reflect what students know and can do in specific subject areas. Assessments of cognitive abilities, on the other hand, are not the same as subject-matter achievements. They are often more general, and together with measures of achievement may provide more comprehensive diagnoses of academic potential. This view of educational achievement stresses not only knowledge as the product of learning, but also knowledge as a means to more advanced levels of learning. Indeed, the potential exists for an SAT that provides cognitive profiles of developed abilities not only in the traditional verbal and mathematical domains but also in the subject-specific domains, such as writing and reading comprehension, which provide direct connections to classroom learning. By incorporating this view of learning in its framework, the SAT's relevance to educational reform is strengthened. Furthermore, as mentioned earlier, as calls for measurement instruments more closely aligned with classroom learning grow louder, the SAT will have to focus on developing new measures that embrace standards for the highest of measurement quality: validity, reliability, utility, consistency, integration, prediction, and explanation. These are some the challenges faced by those who seek to develop new measure across the social sciences. These demands, for example, will have to be faced by those creating indices of quality of life, job fitness, and policy development, to name but a few.

In this section I outline a representative set of constructs that holds promise for improving our ability to predict success in higher education and, therefore, add value to the SAT. The constructs currently in the research and development pipeline fall into three broad categories: (1) the more or less traditional achievement areas, such as writing; (2) measures of strategic learning ability, and (3) theory-based measures of intellective competence, such as practical and creative intelligences. Collectively, these research efforts are aimed at improving the precision of the SAT as a measure of developed abilities. Here is a snapshot of some of those efforts.

Writing ability

'Writing is thinking on paper' says William Zinsser in his short, but wonderful book *Writing to Learn* (Zinsser, 1988). Striking a similar note, the *National Writing Project* introduced its 2001 annual report by declaring 'Writing is pivotal to learning and to success in and beyond school.' That writing is central to success in college is not in dispute. As we noted earlier, the revisions to the SAT introduced in 2005 include a separate measure of writing ability. As researchers working in this domain are quick to point out, narrating a story, revising a memo, or reporting on current events all come under the general heading of writing, and all differ with respect to the knowledge, skills, and abilities they draw upon. Thus, the designers of future SATs will have to address the question of whether writing is a unitary construct and, if not, how best to measure this important skill. If, indeed, writing is thinking on paper as Zinsser suggests and, if writing is central to learning in school and in college, then continuing to include a measure of writing on the SAT fits within the design framework of a college admission test and adds to the overall utility of the SAT with respect to both predictive and consequential validity. Suffice it to say, there are also a number of more or less traditional achievement areas, such as language learning, literacy, historical analysis, and scientific inquiry, that have merit attention from the measurement community.

Strategic learning skills

Research on the border between cognitive psychology and educational measurement is yielding promising methods for assessing students' understanding of their ability to learn. Recent work in the general area of self-regulated learning and problem solving (Tobias and Everson, 2002; Weinstein and Palmer, 1990; Zimmerman, 1995; Zimmerman and Schunk, 2001), for example, adds to the body of evidence suggesting that successful students are strategic learners. According to this view, strategic learners are able to take responsibility for their own learning by setting realistic learning goals and using knowledge about themselves as learners as part of their approach to learning. Strategic learners, apparently, use a variety of cognitive processes, e.g., the metacognitive skills and abilities of planning, monitoring and modifying their learning strategies, to achieve their educational objectives.

There is an emerging body of research that suggests self-regulated learners are more efficient and effective learners (Hacker, Dunlosky, and Grissmer, 2009; Tobias and Everson, 2002; Zimmerman and Schunk, 2001). This research makes clear, for example, that students who have developed the abilities to analyze, plan, execute, and evaluate academic tasks outperform their less capable counterparts in a variety of academic settings – giving them a decided advantage in the classroom.

Given the importance of self-regulated learning and study strategies, a number of self-report type measures have been developed to assess individual differences in strategic learning and study skills. The *Learning and Study Strategies Inventory®*, the LASSI® (Weinstein et al., 1987), is perhaps the most widely used instrument. The LASSI is a self-report instrument consisting of 76 items organized into 10 subscales measuring students' attitudes toward learning, motivation for academic achievement, time-management skills, test anxiety, ability to concentrate, information processing, the ability to select main ideas in text, the use of study aids, frequency of self testing, and the use of test strategies. The LASSI requires students to estimate the degree to which a statement is indicative of their learning experiences by making a selection from 1 (Not at all like me) to 5 (Very much like me). Test scores are reported by subscale and feedback to students usually comes from teachers and guidance counselors. The LASSI has been adapted for use in both high-school and college settings.

Curious about the construct of learning strategies and how they might predict students' academic achievement, we conducted research to estimate the influence of students' LASSI scores on measures of academic achievement, i.e., on college admission test scores (the preliminary SAT) and high-school grade point average. We sampled 1,645 students from 11 US high schools and collected their LASSI scores, their high-school grade point averages, and their PSAT/NMSQT® test scores. The students were either 10th or 11th graders at the time of testing, and about 45 per cent of them were girls.[3]

We conducted a series of regression analyses of the type used typically to predict students' grade point averages (GPA) using their PSAT/NMSQT verbal and math scores, and their LASSI scores. Generally, we were interested in estimating how much the LASSI scores improved our ability to predict students' GPAs, once the effects of their pre-SAT scores were controlled statistically. Surprisingly, we found that the LASSI – as a measure of strategic learning ability – improved our predictions of academic achievement by 11 per cent overall. Earlier work by Ackerman and Heggestad (1997), suggests that

measures of individuals' *typical* cognitive performance – such as self-reports like the LASSI – may be used along with *maximal-performance* cognitive-skills measures (e.g., the PSAT/NMSQT or the SAT-I) to increase validity of admission and selection decisions. The results of our study using the LASSI are promising results and tend to support the positions reached by Ackerman and others. Thus, I suspect work to improve the measurement qualities of self-reports like the LASSI will continue, and may find their way into the SAT in the future.

New views of human intelligence

In collaboration with Robert J. Sternberg and his colleagues (Sternberg, R. J., and Rainbow Project Collaborators, 2005) at the Tufts University *Center for the Psychology of Abilities, Competencies, and Expertise* (the PACE Center), the College Board has been developing new measures based on more advanced understanding of the psychology of human abilities and how they develop. The goal is to better identify a broader range of student abilities and thereby prepare a more diverse population of students for success in college. Because abilities beyond conventional verbal and mathematical reasoning abilities are required for success in and out of college, including a broader spectrum of abilities should, in theory, help refine the measurement quality of the SAT. Research suggests, for example, that other abilities, including creative and practical intellective competencies, are also important to school and life success. The theory animating these new forms of assessment is rooted in Sternberg's (1985, 1988) triarchic theory of human intelligence.

In collaboration with the College Board, researchers at the PACE Center have developed prototype tests to measure these abilities, as well as achievements – creative work, leadership roles, etc. – based on these abilities. These new measures are currently in the early stages of research and development and are undergoing pilot testing. These prototypes, and the data generated from the initial field studies, will remain in the research and development pipeline for a few more years undergoing further testing and refinement before they can be introduced as part of the admission testing battery sponsored by the College Board.

Other non-cognitive measures

In addition to research on learning and study strategies and the development efforts based on new views of intelligence, the College Board's research and development efforts also focus on non-cognitive measures, as well (Camara and Kimmel, 2005). For example, initial work is underway to develop a biographical inventory of past experiences and (or) accomplishments, and a situational judgment inventory that, together, may add to the prediction of college success. In general, this work borrows from current theories of job performance and looks at the domain of college performance through this lens. More specifically, if the domain of college-success skills is broader than the traditional measures of academic achievement, then we may find evidence for the value of non-cognitive predictors such as social skills, interests, and personality useful for predicting college performance. Though these measures are in the very early stages of development, the data gathered thus far suggest that they may be useful for predicting first year grade point averages, as well as students' self-assessments of their academic ability, while having relatively low correlations with SAT scores and other more traditional measures of academic ability. These non-cognitive measures, generally, may provide college admission committees and others with information that goes beyond what we can measure using the SAT – leadership

qualities, a gauge of a student's academic self-esteem, and a measure of how well a student would handle the everyday problems of college life. Their potential for preparing and connecting students to college, and ensuring their success in college, is promising.

CONCLUSION

This is an exciting time for the SAT. Change and innovation are in the air. The research and development programs presented in this paper, I believe, have promise for creating a strong theoretical foundation for the next generation of the SATs. The design framework outlined here suggests a shifting view of testing and assessment, and depicts a future for large-scale assessment that addresses the many, often competing, demands and driving forces in education and society.

Clearly, an ambitious program of research will be required to make the next generation of the SAT useful not only for selection and prediction, but also for placement and diagnosis as the design framework implies. The College Board, no doubt, will continue its investment in research and deveopment in a number of promising areas, including (1) developing new measurement constructs that go beyond verbal and mathematical reasoning, e.g., critical reading, problem solving, and metacognition; (2) designing new item types and response formats; (3) developing psychometric models for multidimensional scales and cognitive diagnosis, and (4) communicating examinee performances in ways that inform the teaching and learning process.

Reform and innovation appear to be everywhere in education – particularly when it comes to large-scale assessment. Portfolios, standards-based assessment design, performance assessments, and computer adaptive test methods are just some of what we see when we look across the landscape. Technological innovation, as was noted earlier, will transform not only how we test but what we test. Networks of closely aligned tests are easily imagined. It is clear, too, that rapidly advancing scientific areas like the brain sciences, artificial intelligence, and the psychology of learning will influence testing by reshaping the conceptual basis of teaching and learning. The challenge for organizations like the College Board and the Educational Testing Service is to learn from these innovations, and incorporate what is new and helpful while, at the same time, holding fast to the traditional strengths of key social indicators like the SAT. As other large-scale national and international surveys and assessments grow or emerge, and here I am thinking of the kinds of surveys sponsored by the Organization for Economic Co-operation and Development (OECD), the social scientists responsible for developing them will face similar challenges. They, too, may find themselves guided well by revisiting Campbell's Law.

NOTES

1 Portions of this chapter are drawn from an earlier paper, 'Innovation and change in the SAT: A design framework for future college admission tests', which appeared as a chapter in R. Zwick (ed.), *Rethinking the SAT: The Future of Standardized Testing in University Admissions*, NY: Routledge Falmer, 2004. pp. 75–91.

2 A more detailed discussion of the measurement models presented here can be found in Everson, H. T. (1998). 'A theory-based framework for future college admissions test,' in S. Messick (ed.) *Assessment in higher education: Issues of access, quality, student development and public policy*. NJ: Erlbaum. pp. 113–32.

3 For a complete description of the LASSI and how we studied its structure and its predictive validity, see Everson, H., Weinstein, C. E., and Laitusis, V. (2000). *Strategic learning abilities as predictors of academic achievement*. A paper presented at the annual meeting of the American Educational Research Association, New Orleans, LA.

REFERENCES

Ackerman, P. L. and Heggestad, E. D. (1997) 'Intelligence, personality, and interests: Evidence of overlapping traits', *Psychological Bulletin*, 121 (3): 219–45.

Almond, R. G., Steinberg, L. S. and Mislevy, R. J. (2002) 'Enhancing the design and delivery of assessment systems: A four process architecture', *Journal of Technology, Learning, and Assessment*, 1 (1). Available from http://www.jtla.org.

Atkinson, R. (2001) 'Standardized tests and access to American universities'. The 2001 Robert H. Atwell Distinguished Lecture, delivered at the annual meeting of the American Council on Education, Washington, DC.

Bennett, R. E. (1993) 'Toward intelligent assessment: An integration of constructed-response testing, artificial intelligence, and model-based measurement', in N. Frederiksen, R. J. Mislevy and I. Bejar (eds) *Test theory for a new generation of tests*. Hillsdale, NJ: Erlbaum. pp. 99–131.

Bennett, R. E. (1994) 'The role of technology in creating assessments that increase participation in post-compulsory education'. Paper presented at the annual meeting of the International Association for Educational Measurement, Montreal, Canada.

Bennett, R. E. (1998) *Reinventing assessment: Speculation on the future of large-scale educational testing*. Princeton, NJ: Policy Information Center, Educational Testing Service. Available from http://www.edt.org./research/pic/bennett.html.

Bennett, R. E. (2001) 'How the Internet will help large-scale assessment reinvent itself', *Education Policy Analysis Archives*, 9 (5). Available from http://epaa.asu./epaa/v9n5.html.

Bennett, R. E. (2002) 'Inexorable and inevitable: The continuing story of technology and assessment', *Journal of Technology, Learning, and Assessment*, 1 (1). Available from http://www.jtla.org.

Burton, N. and Ramist, L. (2001) *Predicting success in college: SAT studies of classes graduating since 1980*. College Board Research Report No. 2001–2. NY: The College Board.

Camara, W. and Kimmel, E. (eds.) (2005) *Choosing students: Higher education admission tools for the 21st century*. Mahwah, NJ: Erlbaum Associates.

Campbell, D. T. (1975) 'Assessing the impact of planned social change', in G. M. Lyond (ed.) *Social Research and Public Policies: The Dartmouth/OECD Conference*. Hanover, NH, Public Affairs Center, Dartmouth College.

Coffman, W. E. (1962) 'The scholastic aptitude test, 1926–1962'. Paper presented to the Committee of Examiners on Aptitude Testing, Princeton, NJ: Educational Testing Service.

Dorans, N. J. (2002) *The recentering of SAT scales and its effects on score distributions and score interpretations.* College Board Research Report No. 2002–11. NY: The College Board.

Dorans, N. J., Cahn, M., Jiang, Y. and Liu, J. (2006) *Score equity assessment of transition from SAT I verbal to SAT math: Gender* (SR-2006-63). Unpublished statistical report. Princeton, NJ: Educational Testing Service.

Embretson, S. E. (1996) 'Cognitive design principles and the successful performer: A study on spatial ability', *Journal of Educational Measurement*, 33 (1): 29–39.

Embretson, S. E. and Reise, S. P. (2000) *Item response theory for psychologists.* London: Erlbaum Associates.

Everson, H. T. (1995) 'Modeling the student in intelligent tutoring systems: The promise of a new psychometrics', *Instructional Science*, 23 (5): 433–52.

Everson, H. T. (1998) 'A theory-based framework for future college admission test', in S. Messick (ed.) *Assessment in higher education: Issues of access, quality, student development and public policy.* NJ: Erlbaum. pp. 113–32.

Everson, H. (2000) 'A principled design framework for admission tests: An affirmative research agenda', *Psychology, Public Policy, and Law*, 6 (1): 112–20.

Everson, H. T., Weinstein, C. E. and Laitusis, V. (2000) *Strategic learning abilities as predictors of academic achievement.* Paper presented at the Winter Meeting of the Data Analysis Research Network of the National Collegiate Athletic Association, San Francisco, CA.

Hacker, D., Dunlosky, J. and Graesser, A. C. (2009) Handbook of metacognition in education. NY: Routlege.

Kobrin, J. and Melican, G. (2007) *Comparability of scores on the new and prior versions of the SAT reasoning tests.* College Board Research Note RN-31. NY: The College Board.

Lawrence, I., Rigol, G. W., Van Essen, T. and Jackson, C. A. (2002) *A historical perspective on the SAT 1926–2001.* College Board Report No. 2002–7. NY: The College Board.

Leighton, J. P. and Gierl, M. J. (2007) *Cognitive diagnostic assessment for education.* New York: Cambridge University Press.

McDowell, J. and Newell, C. (1996) *Measuring health: A guide to rating scales and questionnaires,* (2nd edition). Oxford: Oxford University Press.

Mislevy, R. J. (2007) 'Comments on Lissitz and Samuelsen: Validity by design', *Educational Researcher*, 36 (8): 463–69.

Mislevy, R. J., Steinberg, L. S., Almond, R. G. and Haertel, G. D. (2002) *Leveraging points for improving educational assessments.* Paper presented

at the annual meeting of the American Educational Research Association, New Orleans, LA.

National Association for College Admission Counseling. (2008) *Report of the commission on the use of standardized tests in undergraduate admission.* Arlington, VA.

National Research Council (2001) *Knowing what students know: The science and design of educational assessment.* Committee on the Foundations of Assessment. J. Pellegrino, N. Chudowsky, and R. Glaser (eds) Division of Behavioral and Social Sciences and Education, Washington, DC: National Academy Press.

Nichols, P. D., Chipman, S. and Brennan, R. (eds.) (1995) *Cognitively diagnostic assessment.* Hillsdale, NJ: Erlbaum.

Scheuneman, J. and Camara, W. (2002) *Calculator use and the SAT-I Math.* College Board Research Note #16. New York: College Board.

Snow, R. E. and Lohman, D. F. (1989) 'Implications of cognitive psychology for educational measurement', in R. L. Linn (ed.), *Educational Measurement* (3rd edition). New York: Macmillan. pp. 263–332.

Sternberg, R. J. (1985) *Beyond IQ: A triarchic theory of human abilities.* New York: Cambridge.

Sternberg, R. J. (1988) *The triarchic mind: A new theory of intelligence.* New York: Viking.

Sternberg, R. J., and Rainbow Project Collaborators (2005). Augmenting the SAT through assessments of analytical, practical and creative skills. In W. Camara and E. Kimmel (eds.) *Choosing students: Higher education admission tools for the 21st century* (pp. 159–176). Mahwah, NJ: Erlbaum Associates.

Streiner, D. L. and Norman, G. R. (2008) NY: Oxford University Press.

Tobias, S. and Everson, H. T. (2002) *Knowing what you know, and what you don't know.* College Board Report (2002–04). New York: College Board.

Weinstein, C. E. and Palmer, D. R. (1990) *LASSI-HS: Learning and Study Strategies Inventory-High School Version.* Clearwater, FL: H and H Publishing.

Weinstein, C. E. Palmer, D. R. and Schulte, A. C. (1987) *Learning and Study Strategies Inventory (LASSI): User's Manual.* Clearwater, FL: H and H Publishing.

Zimmerman, B. J. (1995) 'Self-regulation involves more than metacognition: A social cognitive perspective', *Educational Psychologist*, 30 (4): 217–22.

Zimmerman, B. J. and Schunk, D. H. (2001) *Self-regulated learning and academic achievement.* Mahwah, NJ: Erlbuam.

Zinsser, W. (1988) *Writing to learn.* New York: Harp.

Zwick, R. (ed.) (2004) Rethinking the SAT: The Future of Standardized Testing in University Admissions, NY: Routlege Falmer.

4

Measurement as Cooperative Communication: What Research Participants Learn from Questionnaires

Norbert Schwarz

As a perusal of the measures included in this handbook illustrates measurement in the social and behavioral sciences is dominated by self-report. Whether we are interested in personality characteristics, public opinion, dietary habits, purchase intentions, or the nation's unemployment rate, we are likely to rely on the answers that research participants provide in response to a set of questions administered in a standardized format. When data are collected in personal interviews, interviewers are trained to read the questions verbatim and to provide standardized explanations, if any, should the respondent ask for clarification; when data are collected in a self-administered format, opportunities to ask for clarifications are usually not provided. In either case, participants are expected to provide their answers in a pre-defined format, by checking a number on a rating scale or by endorsing one of several response alternatives presented to them. Standardization is introduced to avoid idiosyncratic variation in the questions asked, presumably ensuring that all participants respond to the same question (see Fowler and Mangione, 1990, for a discussion). Unfortunately, however, participants' interpretation of the question may differ from the meaning the researcher had in mind. Standardization increases the risk of such discrepancies by precluding the mutual negotiation of meaning that characterizes communication in everyday life.

This chapter addresses how research participants make sense of the questions asked by going beyond their literal meaning, relying on contextual information to infer what they are expected to report on. It is organized as follows: Drawing on Paul Grice's (1975, 1978) logic of conversation, the first section introduces the tacit assumptions that govern the conduct of conversation in daily life. These assumptions license listeners' reliance on the context of a speaker's utterance to infer its intended meaning. Bringing these assumptions to the research situation, participants make extensive use of the context in which a question is presented to infer what the researcher wants to know. Moreover, the researcher's contributions to the standardized research conversation include apparently 'formal' characteristics of the questionnaire, like its visual layout or the format of the response scales, and respondents draw on these characteristics in inferring the intended meaning of the question. As a result, the same question may acquire different meanings in different contexts and minor changes in questionnaire layout or the format of response alternatives are sufficient to elicit unintended meaning shifts. The second section illustrates these pragmatic inference processes with selected research examples and highlights that the observed context effects are part and parcel of normal conversational conduct. Unfortunately, researchers who routinely observe the rules of cooperative conversational conduct in their everyday communications often fail to do so when they design a questionnaire, resulting in numerous 'surprises' that may well have been anticipated. The final section discusses the implications of a conversational perspective for the conceptualization of 'response artifacts' and provides some advice on pretest methods that are suited to reduce pragmatic surprises in research conversations.

THE LOGIC OF CONVERSATION

To understand the meaning of an utterance, listeners have to go beyond the semantic meaning of the words to infer what the speaker intended to convey. As Clark and Schober (1992: 15) observed, it is a 'common misperception that language use has primarily to do with words and what they mean. It doesn't. It has primarily to do with people and what they mean. It is essentially about speakers' intentions'. To determine the intended meaning listeners rely on a set of tacit assumptions that have been described by Paul Grice (1975, 1978), a philosopher of language. These assumptions can be expressed in the form of four deceptively simple maxims, which jointly comprise a general cooperative principle of conversation.

A maxim of manner asks speakers to make their contribution such that it can be understood by their audience. To do so, speakers need to avoid ambiguity and wordiness. Moreover, they have to take the characteristics of their audience into account, designing their utterance in a way that the audience can figure out what they mean – and speakers are reasonably good at doing so (Krauss and Fussel, 1991). At the heart of this process are speakers' assumptions about the information that they share with recipients, that is, the common ground (Schiffer, 1972; Stalnaker, 1978). Listeners, in turn, assume that the speaker observes this maxim and interpret the speaker's utterance against what they assume to constitute the common ground (e.g., Clark et al., 1983; Fussel and Krauss, 1989). Moreover, each successful contribution to the conversation extends the common ground of the participants, reflecting that 'in orderly discourse, common ground is cumulative' (Clark and Schober, 1992: 19).

This cumulative nature of the common ground reflects, in part, the operation of a maxim of relation that enjoins speakers to make all contributions relevant to the aims of the ongoing conversation. This maxim entitles listeners to use the context of an utterance to disambiguate its meaning by making bridging inferences (Clark, 1977). Moreover, this maxim implies that speakers are unlikely to assume that a contribution to a conversation is irrelevant to its goal, unless it is marked as such. As an example, suppose A asks, 'Where is Bill?' and B responds, 'There's a yellow VW outside Sue's home' (Levinson, 1983: 102). If taken literally, B's contribution fails to answer A's question, thus violating (at least) the maxim of relation and the maxim of quantity (to be addressed below) When reading the exchange, however, we are unlikely to consider B's contribution an inappropriate change of topic. Instead, we infer that Bill probably has a yellow VW and that the location of the yellow VW may suggest Bill is at Sue's home. These inferences, and the ease with which readers draw them, reflect the implicit assumption that B is a cooperative communicator whose contribution is relevant to A's question. As Sperber and Wilson (1986: vi) put it, 'communicated information comes with a guarantee of relevance' and if in doubt, it is the listener's task to determine the intended meaning of the utterance by referring to the common ground or by asking for clarification.

A maxim of quantity requires speakers to make their contribution as informative as is required, but not more so. That is, speakers should respect the established, or assumed, common ground by providing the information that the recipient needs, without reiterating information that the recipient already has or may take for granted anyway (Clark and Haviland, 1977). If Mary lives in Middletown, Kansas, she may plausibly answer a question about where she lives with 'In the US'. when asked in Paris,

but not when asked in New York; may say 'In Middletown' when asked in Kansas, and may offer '28 Main Street' when asked in Middletown, tailoring the level of detail to questioner's likely interest and knowledge. Despite observing the maxim of quantity in daily life, we rarely take its implications into account when designing questionnaires. Finally, a maxim of quality enjoins speakers not to say anything they believe to be false or lack adequate evidence for.

As Grice (1975) emphasized, these maxims apply most directly to situations in which participants attempt to exchange information to get things done, whereas conversations that are characterized by other goals, such as entertaining one another, are less likely to follow these rules (see Higgins, 1981). In general, research participants are likely to perceive the research situation as a task-oriented setting in which participants attempt to exchange information as accurately as possible, thus rendering the assumptions underlying task oriented conversations highly relevant.

Implications for research settings

Whereas speakers and addressees collaborate in unconstrained natural conversations to establish the intended meaning of an utterance, their opportunity to do so is severely limited in standardized research settings. To begin with, the standardization of instructions and of the questions asked does not allow researchers to tailor their utterances to specific participants or to take a given participant's preceding answers into account. Moreover, when research participants ask for clarification, they may often not receive additional information and a well-trained interviewer may respond, 'Whatever it means to you'. In other cases, as when a respondent is asked to complete a self-administered questionnaire, there may also be nobody who can be asked for clarification. As a result, a mutual negotiation of intended meaning is largely precluded. Nevertheless, participants will attempt to cooperate by determining the intended meaning of the researcher's contributions to the constrained conversation. To do so, they will need to rely even more on the tacit assumptions that govern the conduct of conversation in daily life than they would under less constrained conditions. Unfortunately, however, they are bound to miss one crucial point: Whereas the researcher is likely to comply with conversational maxims in almost any conversation he or she conducts outside of a research setting, the researcher is much less likely to do so in the research setting itself. A considerable body of research suggests that this misunderstanding is at the heart of many apparent biases, shortcomings and artifacts that have been observed in psychological experiments and survey measurement (for reviews see Bless et al., 1993; Clark and Schober, 1992; Hilton, 1995; Schwarz, 1994, 1996; Strack, 1994).

THE RESEARCHER'S CONTRIBUTIONS: WHAT PARTICIPANTS LEARN FROM QUESTIONNAIRES

Survey researchers have long been aware that minor variations in the wording of a question or the design of a questionnaire may strongly affect the obtained responses (see Payne, 1951; Schuman and Presser, 1981; Sudman and Bradburn, 1974), leading researchers to wonder how meaningful the obtained answers are. While the observed contextual influences have often been considered 'artifacts' of survey measurement, a conversational perspective suggests that they merely reflect the fact that participants bring the tacit assumptions of everyday conversations to the

research situation. Facing an ambiguous question or an otherwise difficult task, they draw on contextual information presented in the questionnaire to arrive at a meaningful interpretation. In doing so, they assume that the contributions of the researcher are relevant to the task at hand, as the examples in this section illustrate.

Researcher's affiliation

In natural conversations, we take our knowledge about the speaker into account when we interpret his or her utterances. Few of us fail to notice that the question 'Can you read this?' has a different pragmatic meaning when posed by our ophthalmologist or the traffic police. The same logic applies to research situations, where the researcher's affiliation may provide important clues about the intended meaning of a question. For example, Norenzayan and Schwarz (1999) asked respondents to explain a case of workplace homicide, described in a newspaper clipping. The otherwise identical questionnaire was either printed on the letterhead of an 'Institute for Personality Research' or on the letterhead of an 'Institute for Social Research'. As expected, respondents' open-ended explanations entailed a greater emphasis on personality variables or on social-contextual variables, depending on whether they thought the researcher was a personality psychologist or a social scientist. Similarly, Galesic and Tourangeau (2007) presented otherwise identical questions about work place behavior as part of an alleged 'Sexual Harassment Survey' conducted for Women Against Sexual Harassment or as part of an alleged 'Work Atmosphere Survey' conducted for a Work Environment Institute. Their respondents perceived the same behaviors as more likely to represent sexual harassment when they were presented as part of a sexual harassment survey – after all, why else would they have been included? Moreover, once considered sexual harassment, they also rated these behaviors as more bothersome and reported that they experienced them with higher frequency.

Such findings highlight that participants take the researchers' likely epistemic interest into account to provide an answer that is relevant to the goals of the ongoing conversation, much as they would be expected in daily life. Unfortunately, the researchers themselves are often insensitive to the information that their institutional affiliation or the title of their study may convey.

Preceding questions

In natural conversations, we are also expected to take a speaker's preceding utterances into account when we interpret later ones and failure to do so quickly undermines a meaningful exchange. Yet in research settings, we would often prefer respondents to answer each question in isolation and consider the emergence of any order effects highly undesirable. Our participants, however, have no reason to assume that the usual rules of conversational conduct do not apply and do their best to make sense of the questions asked by drawing on the context in which they are presented.

As an extreme case, consider questions about highly obscure or even completely fictitious issues, such as the 'Agricultural Trade Act of 1978' (e.g., Bishop et al., 1986; Schuman and Presser, 1981). In a typical study, some 30 per cent of the respondents of a representative sample are likely to report an opinion on these issues, despite the fact that they can hardly know anything about it. One possible interpretation holds that the 'fear of appearing uninformed' induces 'many respondents to conjure up opinions

even when they had not given the particular issue any thought prior to the interview' (Erikson et al., 1988: 44), casting serious doubt on the meaningfulness of survey responses. A conversational perspective, however, suggests a different interpretation. The sheer fact that a question about an issue is asked conveys that the issue exists or else the question would violate each and every maxim of conversational conduct. Having no reason to assume that the researcher would ask a perfectly meaningless question (or even get funded to do so), respondents will draw on contextual information to arrive at a plausible interpretation. Once they have inferred a likely meaning, thus transforming the fictitious issue into one that makes sense in the context of the interview, they may have no difficulty reporting a subjectively meaningful opinion.

To test this possibility, Strack and colleagues (1991, Experiment 1) asked German college students about their attitude toward the introduction of an 'educational contribution' allegedly discussed in state parliament. For some participants, this question was preceded by a question about the average tuition fees that students have to pay at US universities (in contrast to Germany, where university education is free), whereas others had to estimate how much money Swedish students receive from their government as financial support. At the end of the study, participants were asked what the 'educational contribution' implied. As expected, they inferred that students would receive money when the fictitious issue was preceded by the Swedish support question, but that students would have to pay money when it was preceded by the American tuition question. Not surprisingly, they favored the introduction of an 'educational contribution' in the former case, but opposed it in the latter case.

Open versus closed question formats

Respondents also rely on contextual information when the question is less obviously ambiguous than in the above case. As Grice (1975) emphasized, answering any question requires more than an understanding of the semantic meaning of the words – it requires a pragmatic understanding of the speaker's intended meaning: What is it, that the questioner wants to know? Suppose, for example, that you are asked to report what you have done today. Most likely, you would not include in your report that you took a shower, then dressed, and so on. However, if these activities were included in a list of response alternatives, you would probably endorse them. This thought experiment reflects a familiar set of findings from the survey methodology literature (see Schwarz and Hippler, 1991, for a review): Any given opinion or behavior is less likely to be volunteered in an open-response format than to be endorsed in a closed response format, if presented. On the other hand, opinions or behaviors that are omitted from the set of response alternatives in a closed format are unlikely to be reported at all, even if an 'other' category is explicitly offered, which respondents in general rarely use. Several processes contribute to this reliable pattern.

Most importantly, respondents are unlikely to spontaneously report, in an open-answer format, information that seems self-evident or irrelevant. In refraining from these responses they follow the conversational maxim that an utterance should be informative and should provide the information that the recipient is interested in. This results in an underreporting of presumably self-evident information that is eliminated by closed-response formats, where the explicit presentation of the proper response alternative indicates the investigator's interest in this information. Similarly, a generic 'other' response provides little information and would be considered inadequate as an answer in most conversations; hence, it is rarely checked. In addition, the response alternatives may remind respondents of options that they may otherwise not have considered.

The numeric values of rating scales

When constructing a rating scale, researchers typically pay attention to the verbal end anchors used and to the number of scale points presented (see Dawes and Smith, 1985, for a review). Having settled for a seven-point rating scale, for example, they are less likely to worry whether those seven points should be represented by unnumbered boxes, by numbers ranging from 1 to 7, or by numbers ranging from −3 to +3. However, the specific numerical values used may again change the inferred meaning of the question, strongly affecting the obtained responses.

For example, Schwarz et al. (1991a, Experiment 1) asked a representative sample of German adults, 'How successful would you say you have been in life?' This question was accompanied by an 11-point rating scale, with the endpoints labeled 'not at all successful' and 'extremely successful'. In one condition, the numeric values of the rating scale ranged from 0 ('not at all successful') to 10 ('extremely successful'), whereas in the other condition they ranged from −5 ('not at all successful') to +5 ('extremely successful'). The results showed a pronounced impact of the numeric values used. Whereas 34 per cent of the respondents endorsed a value between 0 and 5 on the 0 to 10 scale, only 13 per cent endorsed one of the formally equivalent values between −5 and 0 on the −5 to +5 scale.

As subsequent experiments showed (Schwarz et al., 1991a), respondents draw on the numeric values of the rating scale to interpret the verbal anchor 'not at all successful' – does this term refer to the absence of noteworthy success or to the presence of explicit failure? When the numeric values of the scale run from 0 to 10, respondents assume that the researcher has a unipolar dimension in mind, where different values reflect different degrees of the same attribute. Conversely, when the numeric values run from −5 to +5 they infer that the researcher has a bipolar dimension in mind, where one endpoint (−5) refers to the opposite of the other (+5). Accordingly, 'not at all successful' refers to the mere absence of success when combined with the numeric value '0', but to the presence of failure when combined with the numeric value '−5'.

Such differential question interpretations can also affect participants' later judgments on related issues. For example, Haddock and Carrick (1999) observed that UK citizens rated the British Prime Minister Tony Blair as more honest, intelligent, caring, and friendly when the numeric values of the rating scale ranged from −5 to +5 rather than from 0 to 10. These shifts again indicate that the scale anchor 'not at all honest' refers to the absence of remarkable honesty in a unipolar format, but to the presence of dishonesty in a bipolar format. More important, once respondents made these trait ratings, they used them as input into the next judgment. Those who rated Blair's personality along the −5 to +5 scale, subsequently arrived at a more favorable overall assessment of Tony Blair. Accordingly, the numeric values of rating scales may not only influence respondents' interpretation of a specific question, with corresponding shifts in ratings, but may also affect subsequent judgments to which those ratings are relevant.

Finally, respondents' use of numeric values in making sense of verbal labels is not restricted to variations that include or omit negative numbers. For example, Schwarz and colleagues (1998) asked undergraduates how often they engaged in a variety of low-frequency activities. In all conditions, the 11-point rating scale ranged from 'rarely' to 'often'. However, 'rarely' was combined with the numeric value 0 or 1. As expected, respondents interpreted 'rarely' to mean 'never' when combined with 0, but to mean 'a low frequency' when combined with 1. As a result, they provided higher mean frequency ratings along the 0 to 10 ($M = 2.8$) than the 1 to 11 scale ($M = 1.9$; scale recoded to 0 to 10).

Frequency scales

Research participants are often asked to report the frequency with which they engage in a behavior by checking the appropriate value from a set of frequency response alternatives provided to them (see Table 4.1 for an example). Again, the range of response alternatives may serve as a source of information for respondents (see Schwarz, 1999, for a review). In general, respondents assume that researchers construct a meaningful scale that reflects appropriate knowledge about the distribution of the behavior. Accordingly, values in the middle range of the scale are assumed to reflect the 'average' or 'typical' behavior, whereas the extremes of the scale are assumed to correspond to the extremes of the distribution. These assumptions influence respondents' interpretation of the question, their behavioral reports, and related judgments.

Question interpretation

Suppose, for example, that respondents are asked to indicate how frequently they were 'really irritated' recently. To give

Table 4.1   Reported daily TV consumption as a function of response alternatives

Low-frequency alternatives (hours)	Responses (%)	High-frequency alternatives (hours)	Responses (%)
< 0.5	7.4	< 2.5	62.5
0.5–1	17.7	2.5–3	23.4
1–1.5	26.5	3–3.5	7.8
1.5–2	14.7	3.5–4	4.7
2–2.5	17.7	4–4.5	1.6
> 2.5	16.2	> 4.5	0.0

Note. N = 132. Adapted from Schwarz et al. (1985). Reprinted by permission.

an informative answer, they must decide what the researcher means by 'really irritated': does the term refer to major or minor irritations? When the scale presents high-frequency response alternatives participants may infer that the researcher is interested in relatively frequent events, whereas low-frequency response alternatives presumably indicate an interest in rare events. Given that major irritations are less frequent than minor ones, the range of frequency values may therefore indirectly specify the kind of irritations the researcher has in mind. Empirically, this is the case.

Schwarz et al. (1988) asked participants to report how frequently they were 'really irritated' along a high-frequency scale ranging from 'several times daily' to 'less than once a week' or along a low-frequency scale ranging from 'several times a year' to 'less than once every three months'. Subsequently, participants reported a typical example of irritation. As expected, their examples were more extreme when the preceding question presented a low- rather than high-frequency scale, indicating that they drew on the frequency scale to determine the intended meaning of the question. Accordingly, identical question stems in combination with different frequency scales result in different interpretations, and hence assess different experiences (see Schwarz, 1999, for a review).

Frequency estimates

Even if the behavior under investigation is reasonably well defined the range of response alternatives may strongly affect respondents' frequency estimates. Mundane behaviors of a high frequency, such as watching TV for example, are not represented in memory as distinct episodes; instead, the individual episodes blend into generic representations that lack time and space markers (see Belli, 1998, for a discussion). Accordingly, respondents cannot recall and count relevant episodes but have to resort to various estimation and inference strategies to arrive at a plausible answer (for more detailed treatments see Brown, 2002; Schwarz and Oyserman, 2001). One of these strategies draws on the range of the frequency scale as a frame of reference, resulting in higher frequency estimates along scales that present high rather than low-frequency response alternatives.

For example, only 16.2 percent of a sample of German consumers reported watching TV for more than 2.5 hours a day when presented with the low-frequency scale shown in Table 4.1, whereas 37.5 percent did so when presented with the high-frequency scale (Schwarz et al., 1985). Similar results have been obtained for a wide range of different behaviors, including health behaviors (e.g., Schwarz and Scheuring, 1992), sexual behaviors (e.g., Tourangeau and Smith, 1996), and consumer behaviors (e.g., Menon et al., 1995). More demanding estimation tasks increase the degree to which scale values affect participants' personal frequency estimates (e.g., Bless et al., 1992) and the less concrete information people have in memory, the more they rely on the scale when making their judgments (e.g., Schwarz and Bienias, 1990). In contrast, the impact of response alternatives is weak or absent when the question pertains to highly regular behaviors, for which respondents can draw on rate-of-occurrence information (e.g., 'once a week'; Menon, 1994; Menon et al., 1995).

Because different behaviors are differentially memorable for different groups of respondents, the numeric values of frequency scales not only bias respondents' average reports but also affect the observed differences between behaviors or social groups. For example, Knäuper et al. (2004) observed that the frequency range of the response scale affected older respondents more than younger respondents when the question pertained to mundane behaviors, such as buying a birthday present; yet older respondents were less affected than younger respondents when the question pertained to the frequency of physical symptoms, which older people monitor more closely, resulting in better memory representations (see Ji et al., 2000, for similar observations in cross-cultural comparisons). Unfortunately, any differential effect of response scales on different groups of respondents can undermine meaningful group comparisons.

Comparative judgments

In addition, the frequency range of the response alternatives has been found to affect subsequent comparative judgments. Given the assumption that the scale reflects the distribution of the behavior, checking a response alternative is the same as locating one's own position in the distribution. Accordingly, respondents extract comparison information from their own location on the response scale and use this information in making subsequent comparative judgments.

For example, checking 2h on the low-frequency scale shown in Table 4.1 implies that a respondent's TV consumption is above average, whereas checking the same value on the high-frequency scale implies that their TV consumption is below average. As a result, respondents in the Schwarz et al. (1985) studies reported that TV plays a more important role in their leisure time (Experiment 1), and described themselves as less satisfied with the variety of things they do in their leisure time (Experiment 2), when they had to report their TV consumption on the low rather than the high-frequency scale. Moreover, these frame-of-reference effects are not limited to respondents themselves, but influence the users of their reports as well. For example, in a study by Schwarz et al. (1991b, Experiment 2) experienced medical doctors considered having the same physical symptom twice a week to reflect a more severe medical condition when 'twice a week' was a high rather than a low-response alternative on the symptoms checklist presented to them.

Reference periods

Similarly, Winkielman et al. (1998) observed that the length of the reference period can profoundly affect question interpretation. In their studies, respondents were either asked how frequently they had been angry 'last week' or 'last year'. Again, they inferred that the researcher is interested in more frequent and less severe episodes of anger when the question pertained to one week rather than one year, and their examples reflected this differential question interpretation.

On theoretical grounds, one may further expect that formal features of question-naires, like the values of a frequency scale or the length of a reference period, seem more relevant when they are unique to the question asked rather than shared by many heterogeneous questions. In the latter case, respondents may conclude that this is the format used for all questions, rendering it less informative for the intended meaning of any given one. Empirically, this is the case. For example, using the same reference period for several substantively unrelated questions attenuates its influence on question interpretation relative to conditions where each question is associated with a unique reference period (Igou et al., 2002).

Conclusions

As this selective review indicates, question comprehension is not about words – it is about speaker meaning. To infer the speaker's intended meaning, respondents pay close attention to contextual information, bringing the tacit assumptions that govern conversations in daily life to the research situation (Grice, 1975; Schwarz, 1996). That their responses are systematically affected by minor features of the research instrument highlights how closely participants attend to the specifics at hand in their quest to provide informative answers. Unfortunately, these efforts are rarely appreciated by the researcher, who considers such features substantively irrelevant and treats their influence as an undesirable artifact. Nor are researchers likely to note these influences in most studies, where control conditions with different question formats are missing. Even regular pretests of a new instrument are unlikely to identify these problems because respondents will rarely complain that the question is meaningless and will instead do their work to provide a plausible answer.

Instead, these problems are best addressed by using cognitive interviewing procedures at the questionnaire development stage, as addressed in the final section of this chapter.

MAKING ONE'S ANSWER INFORMATIVE: QUESTION REPETITION AND MEANING CHANGE

The preceding examples illustrated how research participants draw on conversational maxims in interpreting the researcher's contributions. Not surprisingly, they also heed the maxims that underlie their conversational conduct in daily life when they design their own answer to the researcher's questions. Adhering to the maxim of quantity, they observe the common ground and try to provide information that is new to the researcher, rather than information they have already given earlier – or information the researcher may take for granted anyway. Unfortunately, the researcher may not always appreciate their attempt to avoid redundancy.

Redundant questions and children's cognitive skills

As an example, consider the well-known conservation task introduced by Piaget (1952). In a typical study, a child is shown two rows of objects, equal in number and aligned in one-to-one correspondence. When asked, 'Is there more here or more here, or are both the same number?' the child usually answers that both rows are the same. Next, the experimenter rearranges the objects in one of the rows, pulling them further apart to extend the length of the row. Following this transformation, the previously asked question is repeated. Many young children now respond that there are more objects in the longer row, suggesting that they have not yet mastered number conservation.

However, from a conversational perspective one may wonder why a speaker would ask the same question twice within a very short time, unless he or she inquired about some new aspect? And what would that new aspect most likely be? The child has already reported that the number is the same and the questioner obviously knows that he or she did not change the number of objects in the row. So perhaps the questioner repeats the same question because he wants to know which row 'looks bigger' after the transformation? To test this possibility, McGarrigle and Donaldson (1974) changed the standard procedure by introducing a 'naughty teddy bear' who tried to 'spoil the game' by rearranging the objects, increasing the length of one row. In this case, 50 out of 80 children showed number conservation by assuring the experimenter that the rows are the same and that 'naughty teddy' hasn't taken any objects; yet only 13 out of the *same* 80 children showed number conservation when the experimenter herself manipulated the length of the row and hence knew the answer to the numerosity question (see Dockrell et al., 1980; Light et al., 1979; Rose and Blank, 1974, for conceptual replications).

This conversational interpretation of 'incorrect' conservation responses raises the question of why older children perform better than younger children under standard conditions? What is it that develops with increasing age? Probably the answer lies, in part, in children's increasing experience that adults may ask questions to which they already know the answer.

Partially redundant questions and adults' life-satisfaction

In the preceding example, children changed their interpretation of a previously answered question when it was repeated, apparently assuming that the repetition cannot be a request for the same information. Similar changes in question interpretation have been observed when two questions are only partially redundant. In this case, research participants typically assume that the second question refers to aspects that have not yet been addressed in the first question, resulting in a unique pattern of question order effects (Schwarz et al., 1991c; Strack et al., 1988).

Schwarz et al. (1991c) asked survey respondents to report their marital satisfaction as well as their general life-satisfaction and varied the order in which the two questions were presented. As shown in the first column of Table 4.2, the answers to both questions correlated $r = 0.32$ when the general life-satisfaction question preceded the more specific marital satisfaction question. Reversing the question order, however, increased the correlation to $r = 0.67$. This reflects that answering the marital satisfaction question increased the accessibility of marriage related information in memory. The quality of one's marriage clearly bears on the overall quality of one's life and respondents considered this information when they evaluated their life as a whole. This interpretation is supported by a correlation of $r = 0.61$ when a reworded version of the general question explicitly asked respondents to take their marriage into account. These differences were also reflected in respondents' mean reports of general life-satisfaction. Happily married respondents reported higher, and unhappily married respondents lower, general life-satisfaction when the preceding question brought their marriage to mind than when the general question was asked first.

In a third condition, however, Schwarz and colleagues deliberately evoked the conversational norm of non-redundancy. To do so, they introduced both questions with

Table 4.2   Correlation of relationship satisfaction and life-satisfaction as a function of question order and conversational context

	Number of specific questions	
	One	Three
Condition:		
General-specific	0.32*	0.32*
Specific-general	0.67*	0.46*
Specific-general with joint lead-in	0.18	0.48*
Specific-general, explicit inclusion	0.61*	0.53*
Specific-general, explicit exclusion	0.20	0.11

Note. $N = 50$ per cell, except for 'Specific-general with joint lead-in', $N = 56$. Correlations marked by an asterisk differ from chance, $p < 0.05$. Adapted from Schwarz et al. (1991c). Reprinted by permission.

a joint lead-in that read, 'We now have two questions about your life. The first pertains to your marital satisfaction and the second to your general life-satisfaction'. Under this condition, the same question order that resulted in $r = 0.67$ without a joint lead-in, now produced a low and nonsignificant correlation or $r = 0.18$. This suggests that respondents deliberately ignored information that they had already provided in response to a specific question when making a subsequent general judgment. Apparently, they interpreted the general question as if it were worded, 'Aside from your marriage, which you already told us about, how satisfied are you with other aspects of your life?' Consistent with this interpretation, a correlation of $r = 0.20$ was obtained when the general question was reworded in this way. Again, these differences were also reflected in respondents' mean reports of general life-satisfaction. When respondents were induced to disregard previously considered information about their marriage, unhappily married respondents reported higher general life-satisfaction, and happily married respondents reported lower life-satisfaction, than when the conversational norm of nonredundancy was not evoked. Thus, contrast effects were obtained when a joint lead-in elicited the exclusion of previously

provided information, whereas assimilation effects were obtained without a joint lead-in (see Schwarz and Bless, 2007, for a more detailed discussion of the processes underlying assimilation and contrast effects).

Note, however, that the pragmatic implications of the norm of nonredundancy may change when several specific questions precede a more general one. Suppose, for example, that respondents are asked to report on their job satisfaction, their leisure time satisfaction, and their marital satisfaction before a general life-satisfaction question is presented. In this case, they may interpret the general question in two different ways. On the one hand, they may assume that it is a request to consider still other aspects of their life, much as if it were worded, 'Aside of what you already told us'. On the other hand, they may interpret the general question as a request to integrate the previously reported aspects into an overall judgment, much as if it were worded, 'Taking these aspects together ...' Note that this interpretational ambiguity does not arise if only one specific question is asked, as in the above example. In that case, an interpretation of the general question in the sense of 'taking all aspects together' would make little sense because only one aspect was addressed, thus rendering this interpretation of the general question completely redundant with the specific one. If several specific questions are asked, however, both interpretations are viable. In this case, an integrative judgment is informative because it does provide 'new' information about the relative importance of the respective domains. Moreover, 'summing up' at the end of a series of related thoughts is acceptable conversational practice, whereas there is little to sum up if only one thought was offered.

To explore these possibilities, other respondents of the Schwarz et al. (1991c) study were asked three specific questions, pertaining to their leisure time satisfaction, their job satisfaction, and, finally, their marital satisfaction. As shown in the second column of Table 4.2, the correlation between marital satisfaction and life-satisfaction increased from $r = 0.32$ to $r = 0.46$ when answering the specific questions first brought information about one's marriage to mind. However, this increase was less pronounced than when the marital satisfaction question was the only specific question that preceded the general one ($r = 0.67$), reflecting that the three specific question brought a more varied set of information to mind. More importantly, introducing the three specific and the general question by a joint lead-in did *not* reduce the emerging correlation, $r = 0.48$. This indicates that respondents adopted a 'Taking-all-aspects-together' interpretation of the general question if it was preceded by three, rather than one, specific questions. This interpretation is further supported by a correlation of $r = 0.53$ when the general question was reworded to request an integrative judgment, and a correlation of $r = 0.11$ when the reworded question required the consideration of other aspects of one's life.

In combination, these findings further illustrate that the interpretation of an identically worded question may change as a function of conversational variables,

resulting in markedly different responses. Moreover, the emerging differences are not restricted to the means or margins of the response distribution, as social scientists have frequently assumed. Rather, context variables may result in different correlational patterns, thus violating the assumption that context effects would be restricted to differences in the means, whereas the relationship between variables would be 'form resistant' (Schuman and Duncan, 1974; Stouffer and DeVinney, 1949). Obviously, we would draw very different substantive conclusions about the contribution of marital satisfaction to overall life-satisfaction, depending on the order in which these questions are presented and the perceived conversational context evoked by their introduction.

CONCLUSION

The reviewed research indicates that participants bring the tacit assumptions that govern the conduct of conversation in daily life to the research situation. They assume that the researcher is a cooperative communicator, whose contributions are informative, relevant, and clear – and when the researcher does not live up to these ideals, they draw on contextual information to determine the likely pragmatic meaning of the researcher's utterances. In fact, they have little choice but doing so, given that the standardized nature of the research interaction does not allow for a mutual negotiation of meaning (Strack and Schwarz, 1992). This perspective has important implications for the analysis of 'artifacts' in social science measurement.

Artifacts and social facts

Following Orne's (1962, 1969) seminal discussion of demand characteristics, work on the nature of artifacts in social measurement has been guided by the assumption that participants are motivated to look for cues in the research situation that provide them with the researcher's hypothesis. Depending on their motivation to play the role of a 'good subject', they may then react in line with the suspected hypothesis. Accordingly, most research in this tradition focused on participants' motivation rather than on the process by which participants extract information from the research procedures used. In contrast, a conversational analysis suggests that we do not need to make special assumptions about motivations that may be germane to research situations. Instead, a conversational analysis holds that participants' behavior in experiments and survey interviews is guided by the *same* assumptions and motivations that govern the conduct of conversation in any other setting (see Schwarz, 1996, for a more detailed discussion) The key difference between conversations in research settings and everyday settings is merely that the researcher is less likely to comply with conversational rules when designing a questionnaire. Our participants have no reason to assume so and treat every aspect of the questionnaire – from the wording of the question to the numeric values of the rating scale – as a contribution that is informative and relevant to the goal of the ongoing conversation. From this perspective, the problem is not that our research participants behave in unusual ways once they enact the role of subject; the problem is that we are likely to behave in unusual ways once we enact the role of researcher, while our participants have no reason to suspect this is the case.

Recommendations

The most important recommendations resulting from the reviewed findings are straightforward. First, participants bring the tacit assumptions of everyday communication to the research situation – and so should researchers. By not observing basic aspects of regular conversational conduct, researchers contribute to unintended pragmatic interpretations of their utterances. Second, there is nothing 'purely formal' or 'probably irrelevant' in questionnaire design. Every feature of the questionnaire can serve as contextual information and researchers are well advised to ask themselves what their participants may infer from the features of the question and the context in which it is presented. Third, one efficient way to explore participants' interpretations of the questions asked is the use of cognitive interviewing techniques at the pretest stage (for reviews see Willis, 2005, and the contributions in Schwarz and Sudman, 1996). Most widely used are verbal protocols, in the form of concurrent or retrospective think-aloud procedures, and requests to paraphrase the question (see DeMaio and Rothgeb, 1996, for commonly employed combinations of methods) Suitable cognitive pretests can be conducted with a relatively small number of respondents and provide the best available safeguard against later surprises. Finally researchers need to keep in mind that what needs to be standardized to ensure comparable answers is question meaning, not question wording (see Suchman and Jordan, 1990). In an influential series of studies, Schober and Conrad provided compelling evidence that a liberalization of the traditional standardization requirement increases the likelihood that respondents understand the question as intended, improving the quality of the obtained data (see Schober and Conrad, 2002, for a review). While this holds promise for face-to-face interviews, it does little to improve comprehension in self-administered modes of data collection, where nobody is present with whom the intended meaning of a question can be established.

REFERENCES

Belli, R. F. (1998) 'The structure of autobiographical memory and the event history calendar: Potential improvements in the quality of retrospective reports in surveys', *Memory*, 6: 383–406.

Bishop, G. F., Oldendick, R. W. and Tuchfarber, R. J. (1986) 'Opinions on fictitious issues: The pressure to answer survey questions', *Public Opinion Quarterly*, 50: 240–50.

Bless, H., Bohner, G., Hild, T. and Schwarz, N. (1992) 'Asking difficult questions: Task complexity increases the impact of response alternatives', *European Journal of Social Psychology*, 22: 309–12.

Bless, H., Strack, F. and Schwarz, N. (1993) 'The informative functions of research procedures: Bias and the logic of conversation', *European Journal of Social Psychology*, 23: 149–65.

Brown, N. R. (2002) 'Encoding, representing, and estimating event frequencies: Multiple strategy perspective', in P. Sedlmeier and T. Betsch (eds), *Etc.: Frequency processing and cognition*. New York: Oxford University Press. pp. 37–54.

Clark, H. H. (1977) 'Inferences in comprehension', in D. La Berge and S. Samuels, (eds), *Basic processes in reading: Perception and comprehension*. Hillsdale, NJ: Erlbaum. pp. 243–63.

Clark, H. H. and Haviland, S. E. (1977) 'Comprehension and the given-new contract', in R. O. Freedle (ed.), *Discourse production and comprehension*. Hillsdale, NJ: Erlbaum. pp. 1–40.

Clark, H. H. and Schober, M. F. (1992) 'Asking questions and influencing answers', in J. M. Tanur (ed.), *Questions about questions*. New York: Russell Sage. pp. 15–48.

Clark, H. H., Schreuder, R. and Buttrick, S. (1983) 'Common ground and the understanding of demonstrative reference', *Journal of Verbal Learning and Verbal Behavior*, 22: 245–58.

Dawes, R. M. and T. Smith (1985) 'Attitude and opinion measurement', in G. Lindzey and E. Aronson (eds), *Handbook of social psychology*. New York: Random House. Vol. 2, pp. 509–66.

DeMaio, T. J. and Rothgeb, J. M. (1996) 'Cognitive interviewing techniques: In the lab and in the field', in N. Schwarz and S. Sudman (eds), *Answering questions: Methodology for determining cognitive and communicative processes in survey research*. San Francisco: Jossey-Bass Publishers. pp. 177–95.

Dockrell, J., Neilson, I. and Campbell, R. (1980) 'Conservation accidents revisited', *International Journal of Behavioral Development*, 3: 423–39.

Erikson, R. S., Luttberg, N. R. and Tedin, K.T. (1988) *American public opinion*. 3rd edition. New York: Macmillan.

Fowler, F. J. and Mangione, T. W. (1990) *Standardized survey interviewing: Minimizing interviewer related error*. Newbury Park, CA: Sage.

Fussel, S. R. and Krauss, R. M. (1989) 'The effects of intended audience on message production and comprehension: Reference in a common ground framework', *Journal of Experimental Social Psychology*, 25: 203–19.

Galesic, M. and Tourangeau, R. (2007) 'What is sexual harassment? It depends on who asks!' *Applied Cognitive Psychology*, 21: 189–202.

Grice, H. P. (1975) 'Logic and conversation', in P. Cole and J. L. Morgan (eds), *Syntax and semantics, 3: Speech acts*. New York: Academic Press. pp. 41–58.

Grice, H. P. (1978) 'Further notes on logic and conversation', in P. Cole (ed.), *Syntax and semantics, 9: Pragmatics*. New York: Academic Press. pp. 113–28.

Haddock, G. and Carrick, R. (1999) 'How to make a politician more likeable and effective: Framing political judgments through the numeric values of a rating scale', *Social Cognition*, 17: 298–311.

Higgins, E. T. (1981) 'The "communication game": Implications for social cognition and communication', in E. T. Higgins, M. P. Zanna and C. P. Herman (eds), *Social cognition: The Ontario Symposium*. Hillsdale, NJ: Erlbaum. Vol. 1, pp. 343–92.

Hilton, D. J. (1995) 'The social context of reasoning: Conversational inference and rational judgment', *Psychological Bulletin*, 118: 248–71.

Igou, E. R., Bless, H. and Schwarz, N. (2002) 'Making sense of standardized survey questions: The influence of reference periods and their repetition', *Communication Monographs*, 69: 179–87.

Ji, L., Schwarz, N. and Nisbett, R. E. (2000) 'Culture, autobiographical memory, and behavioral frequency reports: Measurement issues in cross-cultural studies', *Personality and Social Psychology Bulletin*, 26: 586–94.

Knäuper, B., Schwarz, N. and Park, D. C. (2004) 'Frequency reports across age groups: Differential effects of frequency scales', *Journal of Official Statistics*, 20: 91–96.

Krauss, R. M. and Fussel, S. R. (1991) 'Perspective-taking in communication: Representations of others' knowledge in reference', *Social Cognition*, 9: 2–24.

Levinson, S. C. (1983) *Pragmatics*. Cambridge, UK: Cambridge University Press.

Light, P., Buckingham, N. and Robbins, A. H. (1979) 'The conservation task as an interactional setting', *British Journal of Educational Psychology*, 49: 304–10.

McGarrigle, J. and Donaldson, M. (1974) 'Conservation accidents', *Cognition*, 3: 341–50.

Menon, G. (1994) 'Judgments of behavioral frequencies: Memory search and retrieval strategies', in N. Schwarz and S. Sudman (eds), *Autobiographical memory and the validity of retrospective reports*. New York: Springer Verlag. pp. 161–72.

Menon, G., Raghubir, P. and Schwarz, N. (1995) 'Behavioral frequency judgments: An accessibility-diagnosticity framework', *Journal of Consumer Research*, 22: 212–28.

Norenzayan, A. and Schwarz, N. (1999) 'Telling what they want to know: Participants tailor causal attributions to researchers' interests', *European Journal of Social Psychology*, 29: 1011–20.

Orne, M. T. (1962) 'On the social psychology of the psychological experiment: With particular reference to demand characteristics and their implications', *American Psychologist*, 17: 776–83.

Orne, M. T. (1969) 'Demand characteristics and the concept of quasi-controls', in R. Rosenthal and R. L. Rosnow (eds), *Artifact in behavioral research*. New York: Academic Press.

Payne, S. L. (1951) *The art of asking questions*. Princeton: Princeton University Press.

Piaget, J. (1952) *The child's conception of number*. London: Routledge and Kegan Paul.

Rose, S. A. and Blank, M. (1974) 'The potency of context in children's cognition: An illustration through conservation', *Child Development*, 45: 499–502.

Schiffer, S. (1972) *Meaning*. Oxford, UK: Clarendon Press.

Schober, M. F. and Conrad, F. G. (2002) 'A collaborative view of standardized survey interviews', in D. Maynard, H. Houtkoop-Steenstra, N. C. Schaeffer and J. van der Zouwen (eds), *Standardization and tacit knowledge: Interaction and practice in the survey interview*. New York: John Wiley and Sons. pp. 67–94.

Schuman, H. and Duncan, O. D. (1974) 'Questions about attitude survey questions', in H. L. Costner (ed.), *Sociological methodology*. San Francisco, CA: Jossey-Bass. pp. 232–51.

Schuman, H. and Presser, S. (1981) *Questions and answers in attitude surveys*. New York: Academic Press.

Schwarz, N. (1994) 'Judgment in a social context: Biases, shortcomings, and the logic of conversation', in M. Zanna (ed.), *Advances in experimental social psychology*. San Diego, CA: Academic Press. Vol. 26, pp. 123–62.

Schwarz, N. (1996) *Cognition and communication: Judgmental biases, research methods and the logic of conversation*. Hillsdale, NJ: Erlbaum.

Schwarz, N. (1999) 'Frequency reports of physical symptoms and health behaviors: How the questionnaire determines the results', in D.C. Park, R.W. Morrell and K. Shifren (eds), *Processing medical information in aging patients: Cognitive and human factors perspectives*. Mahaw, NJ: Erlbaum. pp. 93–108.

Schwarz, N. and Bienias, J. (1990) 'What mediates the impact of response alternatives on frequency reports of mundane behaviors?' *Applied Cognitive Psychology*, 4: 61–72.

Schwarz, N. and Bless, H. (2007) 'Mental construal processes: The inclusion/exclusion model', in D. A. Stapel and J. Suls (eds), *Assimilation and contrast in social psychology*. Philadelphia, PA: Psychology Press. pp. 119–41.

Schwarz, N., Bless, H., Bohner, G., Harlacher, U. and Kellenbenz, M. (1991b) 'Response scales as frames of reference: The impact of frequency range on diagnostic judgment', *Applied Cognitive Psychology*, 5: 37–50.

Schwarz, N., Grayson, C. E. and Knäuper, B. (1998) 'Formal features of rating scales and the interpretation of question meaning', *International Journal of Public Opinion Research*, 10: 177–83.

Schwarz, N. and Hippler, H. J. (1991) 'Response alternatives: The impact of their choice and ordering', in P. Biemer, R. Groves, N. Mathiowetz and S. Sudman (eds), *Measurement error in surveys*. Chichester, UK: Wiley. pp. 41–56.

Schwarz, N., Hippler, H. J., Deutsch, B. and Strack, F. (1985) 'Response scales: Effects of category range on reported behavior and subsequent judgments', *Public Opinion Quarterly*, 49: 388–95.

Schwarz, N., Knäuper, B., Hippler, H. J., Noelle-Neumann, E. and Clark, F. (1991a) 'Rating scales: Numeric values may change the meaning of scale labels', *Public Opinion Quarterly*, 55: 570–82.

Schwarz, N. and Oyserman, D. (2001) 'Asking questions about behavior: Cognition, communication and questionnaire construction', *American Journal of Evaluation*, 22: 127–60.

Schwarz, N. and Scheuring, B. (1992) 'Selbstberichtete Verhaltens- und Symptomhäufigkeiten: Was Befragte aus Anwortvorgaben des Fragebogens lernen. [Frequency-reports of psychosomatic symptoms: What respondents learn from response alternatives.]' *Zeitschrift für Klinische Psychologie*, 22: 197–208.

Schwarz, N., Strack, F. and Mai, H. P. (1991c) 'Assimilation and contrast effects in part-whole question sequences: A conversational logic analysis', *Public Opinion Quarterly*, 55: 3–23.

Schwarz, N., Strack, F., Müller, G. and Chassein, B. (1988) 'The range of response alternatives may determine the meaning of the question: Further evidence on informative functions of response alternatives', *Social Cognition*, 6: 107–17.

Schwarz, N. and Sudman, S. (1996) *Answering questions: Methodology for determining cognitive and communicative processes in survey research*. San Francisco, CA: Jossey-Bass.

Siegal, M., Waters, L. J. and Dinwiddy, L. S. (1988) 'Misleading children: Causal attributions for inconsistency under repeated questioning', *Journal of Experimental Child Psychology*, 45: 438–56.

Sperber, D. and Wilson, D. (1986) *Relevance: Communication and cognition*. Cambridge, MA: Harvard University Press.

Stalnaker, R. C. (1978) 'Assertion', in P. Cole (ed.), *Syntax and semantics, Vol. 9: Pragmatics*. New York: Academic Press. pp. 315–32.

Stouffer, S. A. and DeVinney, L. C. (1949) 'How personal adjustment varied in the army – by background characteristics of the soldiers', in S. A. Stouffer, E. A. Suchman, L. C. DeVinney, S. A. Star and R. M. Williams (eds), *The American soldier: Adjustment during army life*. Princeton, NJ: Princeton University Press.

Strack, F. (1994) 'Response processes in social judgment', in R. S. Wyer and T. K. Srull (eds), *Handbook of social cognition*. 2nd edition. Hillsdale, NJ: Erlbaum. Vol. 1, pp. 287–322.

Strack, F., Martin, L. L. and Schwarz, N. (1988) 'Priming and communication: The social determinants of information use in judgments of life-satisfaction', *European Journal of Social Psychology*, 18: 429–42.

Strack, F. and Schwarz, N. (1992) 'Communicative influences in standardized question situations: The case of implicit collaboration', in G. Semin and K. Fiedler (eds), *Language and social cognition*. London: Sage. pp. 173–93.

Strack, F., Schwarz, N. and Wänke, M. (1991) 'Semantic and pragmatic aspects of context effects in social and psychological research', *Social Cognition*, 9: 111–25.

Suchman, L. and Jordan, B. (1990) 'Interactional troubles in face-to-face interviews', *Journal of the American Statistical Association*, 85: 232–41.

Sudman, S. and Bradburn, N. M. (1974) *Response effects in surveys: A review and synthesis*. Chicago: Aldine.

Tourangeau, R. and Smith, T. (1996) 'Asking sensitive questions: The impact of data collection, question format, and question context', *Public Opinion Quarterly*, 60: 275–304.

Willis, G. (2005) *Cognitive interviewing: A tool for improving questionnaire design*. Thousand Oaks, CA: Sage Publications.

Winkielman, P., Knäuper, B. and Schwarz, N. (1998) 'Looking back at anger: Reference periods change the interpretation of emotion frequency questions', *Journal of Personality and Social Psychology*, 75: 719–28.

5

Developing Observation Instruments and Arriving at Inter-rater Reliability for a Range of Contexts and Raters: The Early Childhood Environment Rating Scales

Elena Soucacou and Kathy Sylva

INTRODUCTION

In this chapter we focus on the practice of measuring what are often called 'difficult to measure' concepts. In the field of early childhood, those who attempt to measure concepts such as the quality of classroom environments engage in a rather challenging task. Constructs such as 'global' or 'overall' classroom quality have long been in the centre of debate with regards to both their definitions and measurement. As one can easily understand, difficulties in defining

which conceptual domains are included in such constructs also pose real challenges in any attempt to create an 'objective' measure of them. Two observation rating scales are used to describe the process of generating the content and structure of the measures as well as testing the resultant instruments. The autobiographical accounts of these methodological processes aim to shed light onto what is often not included in many introductory 'how to create a rating scale' texts. This chapter thus reflects upon the methodological considerations that informed the generation of subscales and items, the factors that influenced the decisions that were made in each case, and the ways that the authors dealt with various difficult measurement problems.

The chapter begins by examining the debate about measuring a contested concept such as classroom quality. This is followed by a rationale for assessing quality in early childhood settings using structured observation measures, rather than other approaches. The example of one of the most widely used and researched instruments for assessing quality in early childhood settings is presented and critically discussed. The chapter continues with a rationale for developing new 'situation-specific' observation rating scales to assess quality. The two ratings scales are presented and are described across the phases involved in their development. Within each phase, the authors provide their insights on the methodological issues, concerns and challenges that were involved in generating, modifying, and validating new indicators to assess quality. The chapter ends with a critical reflection on the 'lessons learned' from these attempts to ensure reliable and valid measurement of quality in early childhood classrooms. The hope is that these reflections on the process of generating and refining a new measurement instrument for classroom quality will shed light on methodological concerns regarding measure development more broadly.

THE DEBATE ABOUT MEASURING A CONTESTED CONCEPT

The debate about quality of early childhood provision: a synopsis

The debate on measurement of quality in early childhood settings, as is the case with measuring social constructs more generally, is founded in the different views that surround its definition. Questions such as 'Is there anything like *overall quality* of a classroom?' and if so, 'What does it involve?' abound in the literature of early childhood classroom research. Views are often split into two ends of a continuum on which quality is seen from a wholly subjective, values-based concept on one end to a highly objective and therefore easily operationalised construct on the other (Moss and Pence, 1994; Perlman et al., 2004; Siraj-Blatchford and Wong, 1999).

Within a 'relativist' approach, quality is generally considered to be a socially-constructed concept, wholly subjective in nature and dependent on the values, beliefs, and goals of many stakeholders such as parents, politicians, school administrators, researchers, children and citizens within different social, cultural and political contexts (Moss and Pence, 1994; Woodhead, 1998). According to this approach, the perspectives and views of the many stakeholders should be considered in any attempt to evaluate quality. In the case of early childhood programmes, quality can be determined not only from certain aspects of a programme's environment, but also in terms of the child's perceived experiences or parents' satisfaction (Katz, 1993).

For example, it is possible that a programme which rates highly in structural aspects, such as staff–child ratio, may be considered poor quality if an assessment of the children's experiences revealed an unfriendly, unsupportive, or non-stimulating environment (Katz, 1993). Within a relativist approach, therefore, quality is reflective of the experiences and perspectives of multiple parties (Katz, 1993; Moss and Pence, 1994; Woodhead, 1998). Another characteristic of the relative nature of quality is its dependence on cultural and social context. For example, certain aspects of quality considered appropriate and of high standards in the UK and the US, including small class size and low adult–child ratios, are valued differently in other countries. In the case of Reggio Emilia, a widely recognised preschool programme in Italy, the above aspects of quality are often applied in ways that violate US and UK acceptable standards (Siraj-Blatchford and Wong, 1999). What such examples show is that how we value different aspects of early childhood environments shapes the way we define and evaluate their quality. Certain researchers and practitioners will place a relatively greater influence on the notion of the phenomena as a social construct, dependent on the subjective experience of participants and the context shaping the experience.

At the other end, an 'objective' approach suggests that the quality of classroom environments can best be understood as a set of objective and measurable characteristics. Specifically, quality might best be perceived as an objective reality consisting of agreed criteria measured in standardised ways with the ability to generalise across contexts (Siraj-Blatchford, 1999). In existing literature, objective definitions of quality are often based on the most common aspects that have been shown to predict children's learning, such as physical environment/resources, curriculum/learning experiences, teaching strategies, staffing, planning, assessment and record keeping, relationships and interactions, parental and community partnership and management.

For example, in the High Scope study – a longitudinal study which assessed overall quality of preschool programmes and its effects on children's progress from preschool age into adulthood – classroom quality was defined in terms of a child-centred curriculum, well-trained staff, and sustained parental involvement

(Schweinhart et al., 1993). Such generalised criteria are usually precisely defined, and measured through a variety of available standardised instruments. In another example, the authors of an observation rating scale designed to assess the quality of early childhood environments have conceptualised quality as 'classroom level variables that presumably produce benefits for children's development. These include practices related to the quality of the interactions teachers have with children; the management of time and activities; and the quality of instruction and feedback to students (e.g. how the teacher facilitates children's engagement and learning)' (La Paro et al., 2004: 412).

Applying research-based, objective criteria to assess quality in early childhood environments has two main advantages: First, it allows researchers and practitioners to make comparisons between different types of provisions and second, it enables the identification of poor standards that require improvement (Siraj-Blatchford and Wong, 1999). For example, measurable environmental features of early childhood classrooms have been used to compare programmes in Germany and the US (Tietze and Cryer, 2004). A major criticism of this approach is that the ecological validity of applying universal quality standards within or across cultures can be problematic. Classrooms in Germany may embrace different views on quality than classrooms in the US. However, in their study, Tietze and Cryer (2004) addressed this problem by consulting German researchers and adjusting their measures to accurately reflect differing cultural values and practices.

A more balanced approach suggests that quality may involve both objective *and* subjective elements (Siraj-Blatchford and Wong, 1999; Woodhead, 1998). Woodhead (1998) argued that 'Quality is relative but not arbitrary' (p. 7). He proposed a framework in which two elements are essential to the conceptualisation and assessment of quality of early childhood environments: (1) The contribution of established research and knowledge of universal aspects of child development; and (2) The consideration of contextual variations within developmental theories and philosophies which reflect individual, family, societal and cultural differences. Therefore, common characteristics of quality may exist but these cannot be understood and evaluated independently of the ecological contexts in which they belong (Woodhead, 1998).

From the above perspectives, it can be seen that researchers, practitioners, and policy makers have tried to understand quality in terms of what it includes as well as in terms of its effects; or in other words, in terms of 'what it does' for various stakeholders. However, as considerable debate exists within such understandings, debate also surrounds the ways that quality ought to be assessed.

According to a highly relativist approach, measuring the overall quality of an early childhood programme, with a set of quality indicators, through a structured observation instrument would assume that there is 'an explicit model of what constitutes good provision' (Statham and Brophy, 1992: 145), and such an assumption would not be endorsed among relativists.

A problem, however, with taking the relativist paradigm to its logical conclusion is that although it emphasises the multidimensional nature of the construct of quality, it does not allow the development of a functional tool for practitioners seeking to improve their practice, inspection teams looking for clearly articulated standards, researchers seeking to understand the early childcare provision at a national level, or parents needing help in identifying suitable programmes for their children. In other words, the merits of developing standardised measurement instruments to assess quality are manifold, and the relativist perspective tends to discount them.

On the other side, approaches which have defined classroom quality of early childhood programmes through sets of concrete, seemingly 'objective' indicators have also generated discussion regarding what practices or behaviours should be included in, as well as, whose views or progress they should be evaluated against. For example, traditionally, a significant body of research (Odom, 2000; Rafferty et al., 2003) assessing the quality of classroom environments focused on the effects of programmatic elements on children's academic and social outcomes, as measured by standardised tests and measures. Many researchers, however, have stressed the need to expand the assessment of outcomes for children to include additional measures, such as child-related goals (e.g. impact of classroom quality on student membership, development of friendships) as well as outcomes involving the family and the community in which children participate (Odom, 2000; Rafferty et al., 2003). Discussions about how to operationalise quality have frequently turned to empirical research to justify positions regarding which dimensions of the construct merit inclusion.

After considering the many differing perspectives which, so far, have inhibited the development of a common definition and approach to assessment of quality, Munton et al. (1995) have come to ask 'What might replace the quest for a universally applicable definition of quality?' (p. 12). The authors propose a deconstruction of available definitions of quality in order for different stakeholders to identify common elements across their definitions and to acknowledge the different purposes served by different definitions. They suggest the need for an accepted conceptual framework within which definitions of quality can be considered (Munton et al., 1995).

Perhaps it is within a framework that allows multiple definitions to be operationalised, different methodologies to be used for their measurement, and expanded outcomes to be considered, that quality might best be understood. Within such a framework, assessment of quality is not seen as a hierarchical structure, with one approach representing the 'gold standard' for evaluation. Instead, the various questions asked from the point of view of multiple stakeholders, and the different purposes of assessment would give way to the most appropriate conceptual and operational definition of quality and most suitable method for its assessment. Of course, the application of such a framework can be a real challenge in the policy world, where one set of standards is often needed to determine 'high' quality settings. Yet, within research it is of critical importance, as the plurality of investigations through the use of diverse methodologies has the potential power to enhance our understanding of quality and how to measure it.

ASSESSMENT OF CLASSROOM QUALITY

Why is it important to assess classroom quality?

Developing valid measurement instruments for classroom quality is linked to broader questions regarding the value of such assessment. In recent years, there has been a great interest among parents, teachers, researchers, and policy makers in assessing classroom quality in early years settings. (Friedman and Amadeo, 1999). Such interest resulted from: (a) the increased use

of non-parental childcare in many western countries and (b) the recognition of the important relationship between quality of early childhood classroom environments and children's development.

Findings from early childhood research have shown that children's progress across diverse areas of development is associated with the quality of early childhood programmes (Burchinal et al., 2000; Gallagher and Lambert, 2006; Peisner-Feinberg et al., 2001; Sylva et al., 2004). Children who attended high-quality early years settings have better developmental profiles later on in life compared to those attending lower quality settings, and these profiles include cognitive attainment and social-behaviour adjustment. On this basis, a wide range of assessment approaches and methods have been developed and used to evaluate quality of early childhood classrooms. Some of the most prominent assessment methods involve the use of structured observation methods.

Assessment of classroom quality through observation methods

Ways to assess classroom environments can be broadly classified into those involving direct observation of the environment and those that do not involve direct observation, such as survey methods or document reviews. Such approaches are very often used in combination in research, as each has strengths and weaknesses (Moser and Kalton, 2003). A major advantage of observation over self-report approaches to measurement is that observational methods allow researchers to directly look at how people behave or how things look and, therefore, to generate authentic information about the nature of the phenomena that are being observed (Robson, 2002).

In classroom research, direct observation of a teacher's actual performance is often a preferred method of assessment. Rather than relying on teachers' reports of the quality of their practice, direct structured observation allows the evaluator to observe a range of events and behaviours as they naturally take place within the context of the daily activities and classroom routines (Bryman, 2001). However, despite its advantages as a measurement methodology, direct observation can be time consuming and often requires extensive training and practice in order for the evaluator to design and use various observational procedures appropriately (Wolery, 1989).

Observation rating scales

Structured observation methods to assess classroom quality include the use of checklists, structured coding schedules (e.g. time and event sampling) and rating scales. A main strength of an observation rating scale is that rather than assessing just whether a behaviour takes place or not, such as in the case of checklists, it enables a measurement of the extent to which a behaviour takes place (Bentzen, 2000). This is particularly useful in the case of measurement of classroom quality. A rating scale comprised of indicators, which take the form of well-defined behaviours, may enable not only the measurement of the intensity or frequency of a behaviour (e.g. how often a teacher asks questions) but also the measurement of more qualitative dimensions of a classroom practice (e.g. *how* the teacher asks a question). However, within this possible advantage lies a general disadvantage of rating scales, that is, the need to develop precise operational definitions of the constructs to be measured. Such a task can often be time consuming (Netemeyer et al., 2003). Also, certain constructs, such as those involving higher levels of abstraction (e.g. expression of affect) can be particularly difficult to define, allowing for a greater degree of inference and subjective

interpretation when ratings are assigned (Bentzen, 2000; Viswanathan, 2005).

Rating scales have been widely used for the assessment of early childhood classroom environments. Such measures give overall, as well as specific, ratings of the quality of a classroom. They consist of a number of items, usually categorised within several broader dimensions of classroom quality, which represent subscales of the main rating scale (Karp, 1996). The following section presents a review of selected observation measures used to assess various aspects of classroom quality in early childhood settings. Conducting this review was a stage in the development of our own measurement instruments.

Existing observation measures of quality of early childhood environments

There are many structured observation measures that have been designed and used for quality assessment of early childhood environments. Observation measures have been classified according to their focus into those that assess: (a) global or overall quality of an early childhood setting; and (b) specific dimensions of classroom quality in a particular setting. The term global (or overall) quality of the classroom environment characterises measures which look at many different dimensions of quality, usually including aspects such as the physical setting, curriculum, caregiver–child interactions, health, safety, schedule of routines and activities. Such measures provide a total score to be calculated which represents the overall level of quality for a certain setting (Aytch et al., 2004; Perlman, et al., 2004).

Examples of measures of overall quality are the Early Childhood Environment Rating Scale (Harms et al., 1998; Perlman, et al., 2004), the Early Childhood Environment Rating Scale: Extension (ECERS-E);

(Sylva et al., 2003), the Classroom Assessment Scoring System (CLASS); (Pianta et al., 2004) and the Assessment Profile for Early Childhood Programs (Abbott-Shim and Sibley, 1998). Other measures focus on specific dimensions of quality. For example, the Caregiver Interaction Scale (CIS) (Arnett, 1989) focuses on the quality of social interactions that take place between staff and children in the setting (Aytch et al., 1999; Perlman et al., 2004).

ECERS-R: TURNING 'QUALITATIVE' JUDGEMENTS INTO QUANTITATIVE RATINGS

One of the most widely used scales designed to rate the quality of preschool environments is the Early Childhood Environment Rating Scale (Harms et al., 1998; Perlman et al., 2004). First published in 1982 and revised in 1998, the measurement instrument comprehensively assesses the quality of early childhood settings. Using a 7-point Likert-type scale (1 representing 'inadequate practice' and 7 'excellent practice'), the ECERS-R provides an overall rating of quality, but also allows ratings of subscales measuring broad domains of quality in early childhood environments (Harms et al., 1998). Items are organised in seven subscales, each including a set of descriptors that enable assessors to make quantitative judgements about classroom practices. Assessment of items requires direct systematic observation of adult and child behaviours alongside materials and facilities. A smaller number of items are evaluated through interview and review of a programme's records and documents. The authors recommend that at least one block of three hours should be set aside for observation of non-staff members, but suggest that observations of more than three hours are preferable.

The seven subscales are: space and furnishings, personal care routines, language-reasoning, activities, interaction, programme structure and parents and staff (Harms et al., 1998). Validity was assessed through the use of an expert review-panel who rated the importance of items. Using two sets of field tests, inter-rater reliability showed high levels of agreement (.92 Pearson product moment and .86 Spearman rank order). Internal consistency of the scale was also calculated at the subscale and total scale levels with a total internal consistency of .92 (Harms et al., 1998; Sakai et al., 2003).

The ECERS-R was designed to be used as both a research instrument and as a tool for improvement. It has been widely used in large-scale childcare quality research in many countries, including the US and Europe and has suggested a relationship between ratings on the scale and developmental outcomes for preschool children (Aytch et al., 1999; Perlman et al., 2004; Sylva et al., 1999).

An essential strength of ECERS-R is that indicators within items take the form of descriptions of classroom practices and behaviours that might be considered 'qualitative' in nature. For example, one of the indicators included in the item 'Using language to develop reasoning skills' is 'Staff encourage children to reason throughout the day, using actual events and experiences as a basis for concept development (e.g. children learn sequence by talking about their experiences in the daily routine or recalling the sequence of a cooking project)' (Harms et al., 1998: 37). Descriptors such as this are usually supported by examples and further 'notes for clarification', making possible consistent and reliable scoring. This is an important strength because the comprehensiveness of indicators lessens the need for high inference judgments while providing adequate information for reliable assessment. Thus the detailed specification of what is meant by terms such as 'encourage children to reason' turns what at first glance may appear a qualitative judgment into a quantitative score.

Criticisms concerning the development and use of the ECERS scales tend to be of two kinds: conceptual and technical. Conceptual criticisms focus on the idea of 'overall quality', and question the appropriateness of using a single measure to assess it. Supporters of such criticisms often argue that if there is not an agreed model of what constitutes good provision, the idea of operationalising quality through a rating scale may be problematic (Statham and Brophy, 1992: 145). This line of criticism also involves arguments that oppose the idea of having a set of standards that can apply to various settings, as contextual differences might create different environments in which quality can differentially be defined by the values, beliefs and characteristics within each context.

The second line of criticism is less concerned with the overall concept of quality and more concerned with its measurement. When taking this stance, criticisms involve details related to how rating scales are developed, tested or administered. For example, a group of researchers have raised concerns about the psychometric properties of the ECERS-R by examining the factor structure of the scale. Some studies which applied factor analysis on the scale's subscales and items revealed that the measure does not measure seven distinct factors as asserted by the developers of the measure (Perlman et al., 2004; Sakai et al., 2003; Scarr et al., 1994). Two studies have shown that the ECERS-R measures one single factor, a global quality. This finding together with observed high inter-item and inter-subscale correlations have suggested that the scale could be reduced to a single quality factor including fewer items (Perlman et al., 2004; Scarr et al., 1994).

WHY NEW RATING SCALES?

The following two sections describe two approaches for developing and validating observation measures. Two examples of rating scales to assess quality of classroom practice are provided. The nature of the concepts that they measure and the purpose for which they were designed led to shared and also distinct experiences in the ways in which the rating scales were structured (e.g. creation of dimensions) as well as in the ways indicators were generated. As a consequence, each example involved a unique set of issues and challenges related to reliable and valid measurement. They are described below.

EXAMPLE 1) THE DEVELOPMENT OF THE ECERS-E TO ASSESS IN-DEPTH CURRICULAR PROVISION

Rationale for a measure of centre quality

In 1996 a team of researchers[1] at the Institute of Education, University of London was funded by the British government to study 'the Effective Provision of Preschool Education', a research programme that later became known as EPPE (Sylva et al., 2004). Their initial aim was to study the major influences on the development of children between the ages of three and seven, i.e., between entry to preschool around three years of age and the completion of the first stage of the National Curriculum (called Key Stage 1) when they were seven years old. Additional funding from the government later extended the age range to 16 years old. The project was ambitious, not in the least because it aimed to disentangle the effects on children's development of preschool education (in centre-based early education and care) from the influences of family and community. The study followed an 'educational effectiveness' design (Sammons, 1999).

More than 2,800 children were recruited to the study at entry to preschool and they were all assessed for cognition, language, and social behaviour. An additional group of 300+ 'home children' without preschool experience was recruited to serve as a comparison group. Using value-added approaches and multi-level modelling, a developmental trajectory for each child was created (Sammons et al., 2008b, a). In addition, information about preschool and home learning experiences enabled the creation of statistical models that were used to assess the effects of preschool experience on children's developmental outcomes after taking into account child and family demographic characteristics (such as gender and parental education). At first, the research plans centred on the children's developmental trajectories and the influence of family factors and attendance at preschools on these trajectories. By 1997 the research team decided that they needed to study the educational processes inside each preschool centre to provide a full description on vital *educational* influences on development. They decided to measure the quality of the learning environment when the children were in preschool in order to study its effects when children were older. The EPPE researchers needed a measurement instrument that was robust and relevant to English curriculum policy and practice.

After considering the international research literature, the research team decided to administer the ECERS-R (Harms et al., 1998) in each centre along with the Caregiver Interaction Scale (CIS, Arnett, 1989). However, after studying the items on the ECERS-R and the CIS, and consulting with an advisory group of early childhood professionals, the research team decided that the ECERS-R was not sufficiently focused on educational processes to provide a robust measure of the kinds of *educational* practices in England that might have an effect on the development of children in their sample. The EPPE researchers began work on an 'extension' to the ECERS-R that would be sensitive to the kinds of learning opportunities that would lead to the developmental outcomes specified in the UK government curriculum. The curricular extension to the ECERS-R, now known as the ECERS-E, was developed to supplement the ECERS-R whose scales and indicators were based on ideas of 'Developmentally Appropriate Practice' current in the US and other western countries during the 1980s. The English curriculum was based on the concept of emerging literacy and numeracy and was detailed in terms of cognitive development relevant to early childhood practice.

Developmental process

Phase one: exploratory research
The EPPE team believed that the ECERS-R was broad in its range of domains of practice, and they thought that its seven-point format for scoring was practical and easy to communicate. Their exploratory research for the new instrument was confined to listing the domains of practice that were not covered by the ECERS-R in sufficient depth to accommodate the English preschool curriculum. For example, the quality of educational provision that supports the emergence of literacy, numeracy and scientific thinking was not sufficiently detailed for the ambitious English curriculum. The authors created three subscales, one

for each cognitive domain in the English curriculum (communication, language and literacy, numeracy, knowledge and understanding of the world) and a fourth subscale to assess the extent to which the first three are implemented with respect to children of different genders, cultural/ethnic groups, and varying levels of ability.

The English curriculum was revised in 2000 and then again in 2008. It has three remaining areas of development (aside from the three included in the ECERS-E): creative development; physical development; and personal, social and emotional development. These non-cognitive domains were considered to be already covered adequately by the ECERS-R scale and, therefore, the team decided to focus on the cognitive domains of development and rely on the ECERS-R for the others. From the very beginning the ECERS-E was intended to supplement the ECERS-R and not to replace it (Sylva et al., 2008).

Phase two: conceptualisation

In creating items and subscales, the authors of the ECERS-E turned to the rich literature on the kinds of learning opportunities that underpin cognitive development in young children, especially those involving interactions with adults. They were inspired by the research on ways that adults 'scaffold' learning in young children (Rogoff, 1999), 'extend' their language (Wood et al., 1976), and cater to their individual needs. The literature led to a conceptualisation of the support for learning and development that an early childhood centre might offer. The conceptualisation was based on the research literature in developmental psychology and also in early childhood. An example of the literature used in creating the 'literacy' subscale is described below.

Whitehurst and Lonigan (1998) put forward the following definition: 'skills, knowledge and attitudes that are presumed to be developmental pre-cursors to reading and writing'. Other researchers have also endorsed similar conceptualisations (Sulzby and Teale, 1991). Included in the many studies of emergent literacy is the consideration of the *social environments* that support the emergence of literacy, including shared book reading and especially discussion about the text. In this view of emergent literacy, the eventual acquisition of reading is conceptualised as a developmental continuum, with origins early in the life of the child. This is in sharp contrast to considering reading as an all-or-none phenomenon that begins when children start school (Storch and Whitehurst, 2001; Whitehurst and Lonigan, 1998). Within the concept of emergent literacy, there is no clear demarcation between reading and pre-reading, with literacy related behaviours 'emerging' well before entry to school and supported by many different kinds of interactions and texts. Thus, there is a continuum of literacy acquisition that includes all of the preschool period. The origins of the skills needed to read and write can be found in the interactions that take place in the home and in the preschool setting, especially in children's exposure to interactions in social contexts with print (e.g. book reading, 'environmental print').

The construct of emergent literacy includes children's conceptual knowledge about literacy as well as their procedural knowledge about reading and writing. Here, children's 'pretend reading' and 'invented writing' are important pre-cursors to reading and the formal writing that take place later in the school years (Mason and Stewart, 1990; Senechal et al., 2001). The authors of the ECERS-E had a vast literature on emergent literacy (and a smaller literature on emergent numeracy and science) to aid them in constructing indicators of the enabling environment that would support children's emergent literacy in the preschool setting.

Phase three: item generation

Items were generated that might 'pick up' the kinds of supportive and educational processes found in the theoretical and research literature. Four subscales were sketched out and developers tried them out informally in settings. Immediately a problem made itself apparent.

The ECERS-R had been designed to focus on activities and behaviours that occur frequently and are thus easy to score in a half-day visit. The biggest problem with designing items for specific curricular areas, such as mathematics, was to find ways to score an item where the essential information might not be observed in a one day visit. Many maths and science activities do not take place daily and the developers of the scale encountered a sampling problem. How could the scorer 'give credit' for activities that were part of the weekly plan but not seen on the day of the visit? The ECERS-R did not rely heavily on document review or on a review of the planning sheets of the staff. The new ECERS-E had to get information through consulting planning documents (P), by examining children's records for evidence about practices (R), and by examining displays around the room, e.g., photographs of yesterday's science activities (D). This was made possible by the large emphasis in English practice on planning for the year, the term, the week and the day and it made the job of the observer much easier than it would have been in countries with a less developed planning tradition.

The ECERS-R authors made major contributions to the new scale. Debby Cryer visited London during the early stages of the EPPE project where she contributed ideas and criticisms to the new scales.

The book *Active Learning for Fours* (Cryer et al., 1996) was recommended as a useful resource for item-generation. The authors of both the ECERS-R and the ECERS-E scales exchanged ideas at international conferences and engaged in regular correspondence about items, subscales and analyses. Such discussions with the more experienced American team helped the developers of the new scale to avoid some common pitfalls in designing instruments. An example of this was their sound guidance on the construction of indicators for a score of 1 on the scales.

Phase four: expert review

In this phase the new instrument was shared with colleagues on the EPPE team (Edward Melhuish and Pam Sammons), and with the regional research officers (Anne Dobson, Isabella Hughes, Marjorie Jeavons, Margaret Kehoe, Katie Lewis, Maria Morahan and Sharon Sadler). Next, advice was sought from EPPE's professional Consultative Committee; this included tutors responsible for training preschool staff, several leaders of innovative preschool centres and finally several officers of professional early childhood societies. They all made suggestions, but there was no pro-forma for them to complete or formal 'feedback' forms. Colleagues informally gave suggestions for additions and amendments, and some trialled the items and subscales in their own settings, a great boon to the developers.

Phase five: piloting

The ECERS-E was piloted in five settings. This was a rather informal exercise to test the items and discover whether one full-day, including consulting of non-observed evidence would be sufficient to assess activities that did not take place everyday. The ECERS-E probes more deeply into curricular areas than the ECERS-R and the developers worried that the half day needed for the ECERS-R might not be long enough to complete the ECERS-E. The fears on this front were confirmed at pilot phase and it was decided that a full day would be needed to assess details of curriculum implementation.

Phase six: validation and psychometrics
The ECERS-E was validated in several ways but it is important to note that the main validity exercise took place after using the instrument in 141 settings (Sylva et al., 1999).

First construct validity was looked at in comparison with ECERS-R scores. Because the ECERS-E was considered a supplement to the ECERS-R, the two instruments were used together on one day in 141 settings. This allowed correlation between the total scores on both instruments. The ECERS-R and the ECERS-E correlated 0.77, showing that the two instruments are highly related to one another, but not completely. A perfect correlation of $r = 1.00$ would have meant that the two scales measured the same thing, whereas a non-significant correlation, for example $r = .11$, would have suggested that what the ECERS-E was measuring an entirely different construct. The high correlation between the two quality measures validates the new ECERS-E as a 'quality' instrument but shows that it measures some different aspects of quality (i.e. curricular quality).

Second, Predictive validity was looked at against developmental progress made by children attending centres of varying quality. The predictive validation was undertaken in a statistical exercise using the ECERS-E to predict children's developmental progress over a range of measures between the ages of three and five years. This provided robust evidence that the subscales (but mostly the total score) were related to children's developmental progress in cognitive as well as social-behavioural outcomes (Sylva et al., 2006).

Third, factor structure and internal consistency were examined. Factor analysis conducted on the ECERS-E in 141 centres (Sylva et al., 1999) indicated the presence of two factors that accounted for about 50 per cent of the total variance in the scores. The first factor was called 'curriculum areas' and the second, 'diversity'. These factors are relatively coherent and show that the ECERS-E has a curricular focus as well as a focus on provision within the setting which takes into account children of different cultures, genders, and ability levels.

Cronbach's alpha was calculated for each factor; it was high for factor 1 (0.84) but only moderate for factor 2 (0.64). Since internal consistency is high only for the first factor, this indicates that more factor analyses on the ECERS-E are needed in order to support the factor structure provided by the EPPE study (Sylva et al., 1999).

Fourth, inter-rater reliability was examined. Inter-rater reliability on the ECERS-E was calculated from 25 randomly chosen centres, with one 'gold standard' coder observing on the same day as five different researchers (each responsible for five settings) within one region. The reliability coefficients were calculated separately for separate regions, both percentages of exact agreement between the raters and also weighted Kappa gold efficiency. The percentages of inter-rater agreement ranged from 88.4 to 97.6 and the Kappas ranged from 0.83 to 0.97, indicating very high levels of agreement between raters.

Phase seven: revision
After the EPPE fieldwork in 141 settings, the authors decided not to change the

structure of the instrument but to transfer the 'informal' rules for scoring (which had been 'word of mouth' between researchers) into more formal statements printed in the manual. The initial research version of the ECERS-E included a few 'notes for clarification' but the field researchers telephoned and e-mailed each other often during the administration of the instrument. EPPE researchers and academic colleagues were asked to help the authors make clear what was meant by items. Mathers and colleagues (2007) had used the scales extensively in professional development work collecting evidence on users' experiences and what worked or did not work in the manual text. A re-printing of the ECERS-E scales in 2007 allowed the authors to include additional guidance on how to use the scales efficiently and accurately, e.g., what 'many' or 'most' meant in practice. So, the ECERS-E has gone through several revisions, none of which changed the structure or definition of the items but all aimed at clarifying how to score in local circumstances. Thus, the validated instrument remains but further experience by researchers or those involved in professional development have been used to clarify scoring.

Limitations of the development process

The ECERS-E has proved to be a robust research instrument, validated in several UK studies and currently being validated in Germany (Kluczniok and Sechtig, 2008) through a prediction study of children's learning outcomes. The development of the ECERS-E proceeded at great pace because of the need to 'get into the field' for the purpose of a large research study. Although the ECERS-E was not researched for months and months before its initial field trial in 141 settings, it had the benefit of the authors' extensive experience in research and practice. This interdisciplinary

team knew they were taking the risk of an instrument that might end up being neither valid nor practical, but the time pressures of the research grant required a short item generation and pilot phase, with much longer phases devoted to training the field workers, and to establishing reliability and validity. In other words, the 'nuts and bolts' of field-testing and implementation were given careful attention, but the actual design phase was truncated. Indeed, much of the design rested on the combined expertise of the authors, their experience in a diverse range of preschool settings, their in-depth knowledge of the pedagogical literature, as well as research in developmental psychology, and their first hand access to the developers of the ECERS-R. Thus, for practical as well as scholarly reasons they were able to construct subscales and items to measure some aspects of quality that reliably predicted children's developmental outcomes.

EXAMPLE 2) THE INCLUSIVE CLASSROOM PROFILE (ICP): A NEW CONCEPT IN MEASUREMENT?

Rationale for a measure of 'inclusive classroom quality'

The development of the ICP (Soucacou, 2007) stemmed from a concern about the adequacy of existing measures to assess those aspects of classroom practice that specifically pertain to the quality of support provided to children with disabilities included in mainstream preschool settings. Many researchers have argued that measures which have traditionally been used to assess quality in early childhood classrooms might not be not sufficient in assessing those dimensions of classroom quality that support the diverse needs of children with disabilities. For example,

Wolery and colleagues (2000), have endorsed this argument and have suggested that 'young children with disabilities can experience low-quality in classes that are otherwise rated as being of high quality' (p. 3).

Building on this rationale, a research study was set up to investigate quality indicators of classroom practices that specifically support the individualised needs of children with disabilities in inclusive settings. Such practices were conceptualised in general as 'inclusive classroom practices' and once identified, the aim was to measure their quality on a seven-point rating scale.

However, at the beginning of this investigation, a great challenge emerged: how to define the concept 'inclusive classroom practices' and which practices would be included in the rating scale. Such a challenge stemmed from the fact that there is no consensus in the literature about what classroom practices can be considered as 'inclusive' or what classroom practices are considered effective in supporting the needs of children with disabilities in mainstream settings.

Therefore, in the case of the Inclusive Classroom Profile (ICP), the nature of the concept required two important steps in the development of the measure. These were: (1) exploratory research and; (2) conceptualisation of the construct. These were the first two of a total of six phases that comprised the development process of the scale and they are described below:

Development process

Phase one: exploratory research
As previously mentioned, the abstract and complex nature of the construct 'inclusive classroom practices' suggested the need to explore the concept within the context of preschool inclusion in the UK. Therefore,

initial research in inclusive classrooms examined the range of children's experiences and adults' efforts to support children with special needs throughout daily classroom activities and routines.

Data was collected in four inclusive preschool settings in Oxfordshire, UK. For sample recruitment purposes, *inclusive* was defined as any classroom serving at least one child with identified special educational needs (SEN) in the two to five years age range. Children were identified with SEN according to the school's identification process. In all cases this process followed the Code of Practice (DfES, 2001), a policy document on SEN provided to all schools by the UK government for consideration. Data was collected through: (1) classroom observations, (2) reflective diary, (3) semi-structured interviews with teaching staff and (4) consultation with experts. Parallel to this process, the context of preschool inclusion in the UK was investigated through a review of the literature.

Findings of this exploratory phase revealed a range of children's experiences and adult practices that must be considered in understanding quality. These data were used to develop a conceptual definition that demonstrated how quality of inclusive classroom practices was being understood and what it involved. The purpose of this second phase is described below.

Phase two: conceptualisation
A *conceptual* definition tends to describe the construct in ways that it can be understood and distinguished from other related constructs (Viswanathan, 2005). It differs from an operational definition, which describes the construct in ways that it can be reliably and accurately measured. This distinction between conceptualising and operationalising constructs is important because the former is a necessary step

before attempting the latter (Viswanathan, 2005). Concepts, and especially those that are more abstract in nature, should be well investigated and understood before attempting to measure them. People often use the same concepts but mean different things when referring to them. Therefore, in this phase, it was important to clearly explicate what type of classroom practices were to be included and in the construct's domain, as well as what type of practices would not be included.

To conceptualise the specific practices that would comprise the construct's domain as 'inclusive', data from the exploratory research were integrated with literature reviews. Specifically, this process involved synthesizing the findings from the exploratory research to identify a set of important, common goals for children with disabilities participating in inclusive classrooms. Thinking of common goals for the children with SEN enabled the conceptualisation of specific classroom practices that could support those goals.

An important step in defining the construct of 'inclusive classroom practices' was conceptualising it terms of what would not be included its domain. Such a step involved determining the level of specificity of the domain; that is, considering how specific classroom practices would be thought of. In the ICP, classroom practices were conceptualised as general in nature rather than specific interventions. Moreover, right from the start it was decided that classroom practices related to specific academic areas, such as literacy, numeracy and science, would not be measured in the scale. The clarification of a set of excluding characteristics of the construct to be measured facilitated the development of a comprehensive conceptual definition for the main construct. A detailed description of the conceptualisation process can be found in (Soucacou, 2007).

Phase three: item generation

The aim of this phase was to turn the identified classroom practices into measurable quality indicators that would 'fill' the scale's 11 items. Indicators were created following an *'emergent item generation approach'*. In this approach, instead of pre-defining a set of items and then creating indicators for each of them, one item would guide the generation other items based on data (classroom observations and related literature) relevant to the item. For example, one of the categories of classroom practices that had been identified in phase II was 'adult–child social interactions'. Data on several aspects of communication involved in the quality of adult–child interactions, gradually led to the generation of another item that assessed particular elements of the social-communication between adults and children. Therefore, the item 'adult–child social interactions' measured dimensions, such as the frequency and reciprocity of social interactions, whereas the item 'support for social-communication' included indicators that measured the extent to which adults support children's communication with adults and peers.

Moreover, the 'emergent item generation approach' included four procedures: (1) generating and selecting indicators; (2) determining dimensions of indicators (3) establishing evidence criteria for indicators and (4) mapping the gradual incline of indicators on a 7-point scale.

Generating and selecting indicators involved taking a category example of classroom practice and delineating its domain by listing all possible descriptive behaviours that indicate or explicate the practice. Ideas were generated through various types of literature (e.g. reviews, experimental studies and recommended practices), classroom observations, discussions with teachers and consultation with professionals. From the above list, descriptive behaviours/indicators were selected through hypothesis testing and comparison with other items, and then were operationalised by applying a set of criteria that enabled observable measurement.

Determining dimensions of indicators to be measured was important. For example, if an item assessed the quality of social interactions between adults and children, it was necessary to decide if the item would measure the frequency, intensity, or nature of observable behaviours.

Once the dimensions of the behaviours to be assessed were decided, the next step was to determine a set of criteria for reliable and accurate scoring of indicators. Such criteria took the form of specific frequency values and particular examples of behaviours and were listed in the *clarification notes* section of each item page. For example, when assessing the frequency of a particular behaviour, the clarifications notes would list the number of times that the behaviour would need to be observed in order to get credit.

Mapping the gradual incline of quality indicators on a 7-point scale involved defining first the lowest degree of quality (1) as practices that are considered harmful or highly inappropriate, defining the highest degree of quality (7) as practices that are thought to promote inclusion while nurturing individualisation, and arranging intermediate indicators to ensure a gradual incline.

Issues and challenges involved in generating items

There were two main challenges involved in generating items for the ICP. The first challenge was measuring the 'difficult to measure' items. These included classroom practices which can not be easily observed in the classroom on a daily basis, as well as behaviours which by nature are more difficult to quantify (e.g. affect, excitement, etc.). The ICP is an observation rating scale and as such, indicators are assessed predominately through observation. Therefore, the challenge was to find ways reliably to measure such indicators.

To enable reliable measurement of behaviours which cannot easily be observed on a daily basis (e.g. conflict between children), the following two courses of action were taken when creating indicators: (1) Identification of items focused on behaviours which indirectly measured the intended concept, through observable behaviours. For example, to assess the ways in which adults facilitate conflict resolution in classroom, indicators included classroom practices such as reminding children of classroom and behaviour rules. These proactive behaviours can be observed more easily on a daily basis and are thought to assess adult involvement in children's conflict indirectly. (2) In a few cases where certain behaviours could not be assessed through observation at all, indicators were assessed through interviewing staff. Interview questions were structured and specific criteria were applied in order to score the responses.

The second challenge was creating indicators which could apply to a group of children with special education needs while enabling individualisation. As each child demonstrates unique needs, it is possible that a classroom practice rated as 'excellent' for one child might be 'inadequate' for another child. To tackle this problem, indicators took the form of general descriptions of classroom practices that could apply to a group of children. Such descriptions were then followed by detailed examples of the different ways in which a classroom practice could be performed for different children. Creating rich examples and descriptions of the different ways that classroom practices can be manifested in different situations was of critical importance in order to preserve the validity of measurement.

Phase four: expert review

To assess the content and structure of the ICP, the scale was submitted to five expert reviewers. Reviewers scored the importance of each item on a 1–5 point rating scale. They also completed an open ended questionnaire on which they provided feedback with regards to the balance of items, omission of items, clarity of indicators, and gradual incline of indicators on the scale.

Findings revealed that most reviewers assessed most items as highly important and provided positive feedback on the content and structure of the scale. A detailed description of findings can be found in Soucacou (2007).

However, despite a general common agreement about the importance of items, findings revealed a lack of consensus among reviewers with regards to omission of items and overall the operationalisation of many indicators. For example, reviewers had different ideas as to what was missing in the scale and what could be included.

Lack of consensus among reviewers required particular attention as it related to issues of validity and reliability of the developed scale. One possible interpretation might be that the concept was not clearly defined when the scale was submitted for review and that greater consensus among reviewers would have been reached if it was clearer what was and was not included in the definition of 'inclusive classroom practices'.

However, it is also possible that measurement of the main construct assessed in the ICP is far more complex. The construct, 'inclusive classroom practices', is abstract, value-driven, and includes many dimensions that lack consensus in the research. Therefore, debates are usual in research and policy circles, and the evidence for what counts as a high quality inclusive classroom practice is inconclusive. As a consequence, it is possible that reviewers with diverse backgrounds and interests are likely to give a range of suggestions and opinions that are dissimilar in some cases.

In the case of ICP where the main concept under measurement is not clearly defined in the literature, disagreement on the dimensions of quality might not necessarily mean that the instrument is not measuring the construct that it was set up to measure. As there is not a common definition of quality of inclusive classroom practice, the construct might involve different dimensions, and such a reality challenges the assessment of construct validity. This stage revealed that in situations where a rating scale, such as the ICP, attempts to measure concepts that are new or debated in the literature, it might be necessary to create a comprehensive conceptual definition *before* proceeding to an expert review of the measure's content and structure.

Phase five: piloting

The scale was piloted in five early childhood inclusive classrooms in Oxfordshire, UK. Through purposive sampling, five settings were selected to represent a range of environments varying in number of children with disabilities, type and severity of disabilities, and type of early years setting.

To meet the above aims, the rating scale was administered once in each classroom for a period of three hours. In addition to scoring the items of the scale, classroom observation notes were recorded throughout the three-hour period. These included notes on the function of indicators, as well as notes on various classroom characteristics, such as number of children with special needs served in the classroom, role of adults working with individual children (e.g. learning support assistants), and type of specialised support provided to children (e.g. therapy, equipment, specific interventions, etc).

Following the piloting of the ICP, three types of revisions were made. The first type involved omissions and additions of indicators in order to assess the construct more adequately. The second type involved merging indicators or items which appeared to be measuring similar aspects of the construct. For example, 'adaptations of space and furniture' and 'adaptations of materials' were merged forming one item 'adaptation of space and materials/equipment.' The third type of revision involved rephrasing certain indicators to clarify their content, as well as adding examples and clarification notes to facilitate scoring.

Phase six: validation

Following the piloting of the rating scale, the measure was field tested in order to investigate its psychometric properties and examine dimensions of reliability and validity. The newly developed measure was field tested in 45 early childhood classrooms in England, which included at least one child with special education needs.

Specifically, this study aimed at assessing evidence for the scale's (1) internal consistency reliability, (2) factor structure, (3) inter-rater reliability and (4) construct validity (correlations with other measures). The methods for field testing the rating scale included the use of structured observation and structured interviews. Data analysis was undertaken through formal reliability and validity tests. These included assessment of the scale's internal consistency (using Cronbach's Alpha statistic), inter-rater reliability (using weighted Cohen's Kappa scores), and assessment of the scale's factor structure (through Confirmation Factor Analysis).

Construct validity was examined by correlating the scale with three additional measures that were designed to assess dimensions of classroom quality. These were: (1) The Early Childhood Environment Rating Scale (ECERS-R); (2) The Early Childhood Environment Rating Scale: Extension (ECERS-E) and (3) The Caregiver Interaction Scale (CIS).

A hypothesis was that the ICP would correlate more positively with measures that were conceptually more similar to the new instrument, while it would be less strongly correlated with measures that are not supposed to measure similar constructs to the ICP. A positive moderately high correlation was found between the ICP and the ECERS-R scales ($r = .625, p < .0005$) The pattern of moderately high and low correlations with measures such as the ECERS-R, CIS, and ECERS-E provided some initial evidence of convergent and divergent validity of the new measure. Full results of the validation study for the ICP are reported elsewhere (Soucacou, 2007). Overall, results have shown that the ICP has good inter-rater reliability at the item level (mean weighted kappa $= 0.79$), is internally consistent ($\alpha = 0.79$) and shows a good factor structure following confirmatory factor analysis ($\chi^2 = 35.164$, $df = 35$, $p = .460$, CMIN/$df = 1.005$, RMSEA $= .010$, NNFI $= .998$ and CFI $= .998$).

Limitations of the development process

The study for developing the ICP had several limitations:

1 *Characteristics and size of the study's sample.* All settings used for the development and validation of the rating scale were purposively selected to include diverse characteristics, but these may not make them representative of most preschool inclusive settings in England. Therefore, this group of settings cannot be generalised to other contexts. Further studies using larger samples with varied characteristics can strengthen the ICP's external validity.

2   *Observer bias.* Throughout the validation study, the main researcher administered all quality assessment instruments; that is, the newly developed measure as well as the other rating scales that were used for construct validity. Therefore, as the aim of administering multiple measures was to assess their inter-correlation, it is possible that 'expectancy' effects influenced the measurements.

3   *Limited inter-rater reliability.* To assess inter-rater reliability of the newly developed measure, the main researcher trained a second rater who administered the scale along with the main researcher on 10 settings. Overall, the mean inter-rater agreement at the item level was found to be 'excellent' according to recommended guidelines (Robson, 2002). However, inter-rater reliability was limited to just one other person and a small number of settings. Therefore, results need to be triangulated with additional raters and should be replicated with a larger sample of settings in order to test these results against a variety of observations.

REFLECTION AND CONCLUSION

This chapter focused on the development of structured observation rating scales to assess aspects of classroom quality in early childhood settings. At the start of this chapter, attention was given to the debate about quality in early childhood programmes and classrooms. This was particularly important to acknowledge, as the challenges in defining quality in early childhood environments inevitably pose significant challenges in any attempt to measure aspects of quality.

The examples of two observation rating scales that were designed to assess two different aspects of quality in early years settings were used throughout this chapter in order to shed light onto the various measurement issues such as domain specificity, and communities of practice. Although the two rating scales (ICP and ECERS-E) included many different procedures throughout the development

process, these two measures also faced some common challenges and measurement issues that influenced the ways in which they were developed. These are presented in themes below.

Selecting and specifying domains for assessment that 'cover' the construct

A common issue that concerned both measures at the beginning of measure construction involved what is often termed 'domain specification'. In the case of the ECERS-E, as well as the ICP, it was found necessary throughout the conceptualisation phase to define which domains of classroom practice would be measured on the quality instrument. In the case of the ECERS-E, the authors did not seek to 'cover' the full spectrum of quality in early childhood classrooms because of the availability of a broader, more global instrument, the ECERS-R. They wished to supplement this instrument, which assesses domains such as space and furnishings, greeting and departures, provision for parents and staff, with subscales that focus on specific curriculum areas, such as literacy, numeracy and science. Because the ECERS-E was to be used in conjunction with the ECERS-R, it was possible for its authors to concentrate specifically on the more academic aspects of the curriculum, including the way it was implemented to meet the needs of children of different gender, cultural/ethnic group, and ability levels. Therefore, from the very beginning, the ECERS-E was set to measure preschool activities and facilities likely to support 'emergent' understanding that, for the most part, were well defined in the research literature.

In contrast, the ICP aimed to measure a concept for which considerable debate surrounded its definition and meaning. As a consequence, the ICP required exhaustive exploratory research in order to conceptualise the concept under measurement. Such exploratory research was needed in order to understand the concept better and create a conceptual definition for it. Understanding what the domain 'inclusive classroom practices' would cover (i.e. which classroom practices could be conceptualised as 'inclusive') required an integration of empirical and conceptual examination. A purely conceptual examination (e.g. review of available literature) was not adequate as there was little agreement on this matter and various interpretations were offered in the literature.

In light of this context, it was important to observe and interact with real practice in order to achieve a better understanding of the day to day manifestation of practices, which in the literature have been thought to support children's inclusion in their school setting. This was not as necessary in the case of ECERS-E, where there was greater understanding of the domains to be assessed.

What these examples show is that the nature of the concept and the purpose for which a scale is created might require distinct procedures right from the start of the development process. Also, the context of educational policies and the status of available research to ground indicators are factors that each drives the ways in which a measure might be created.

Interestingly, although literature on scale development emphasises the need to establish clarity of what it is to be measured and how one arrives to such conceptualisation (Viswanathan, 2005), fewer published studies that involve the development of new measures provide a clear conceptual definition of the construct to be measured. Such lack of guidance from other studies often challenged the development process of the ICP.

With respect to research design, the lack of a clear conceptual definition of the construct being measured in a reported study might result in measurement error which, in turn, might weaken inferences made about the concept (Viswanathan, 2005). In many summated rating scales, measurement of the main concept is made by adding up items and creating a composite score. However, if a construct is not clearly delineated, interpretations of the composite score and therefore inferences about the construct might not always reflect what was *actually* measured but rather what it was *desired* or *intended* to be measured. Such measurement error might be particularly evident when studies compare composite scores of constructs derived by different instruments which assume they are measuring the same constructs when, in reality, these involve very different domains and are operationalised in dissimilar ways.

Balance between indicators of general and specific relevance

In developing indicators of inclusive classroom practices for the ICP, the integration of the notion of 'individualisation' posed a significant challenge in the overall measurement of quality of 'inclusive classroom practice'. This challenge involved the ability to create quality indicators that apply to a group of children with SEN inclusively while enabling individualisation.

Operationalisation of such indicators can be particularly challenging. How can an indicator of a broad teaching approach also capture the extent to which adult support promotes children's individual needs and strengths? This dilemma was addressed by creating indicators which are broad enough to apply to a group of children but which also include a list of rich examples and guidelines that demonstrate the different ways that a certain teaching strategy can be applied with various children, in different situations.

The need for broadening the scope of indicators was mainly revealed during piloting, when certain indicators narrowly operationalised were found to be associated with systematic measurement error. For example, in the ICP, an indicator required adults to encourage children to engage in pretend play. However, in several pilot classrooms there were children so impaired that such practice might have not been developmentally appropriate. In this example, systematic measurement error would have occurred if raters consistently underscored teachers for not performing a practice that might have not been appropriate if a child had not mastered symbolic representation.

Therefore, such indicators were modified based on feedback by experts and pilot observations. Modifications focused on broadening the scope of indicators while providing many examples of diverse manifestation of classroom practices. Future development of this instrument may involve the creation of a manual that would further guide observers to differentially rate indicators of practices which aim to support the diverse needs of children with special education needs in the classroom.

Differentiated use of quality indicators for research and practice

A common question about the development of measures that aim to assess quality of early childhood programmes is whether the quality indicators outlined in such instruments can be used not only for research purposes but also as practice guides in professional development. There are various views on this issue. To date, the majority of existing instruments have also been used in quality improvement by teachers, administrators or external evaluators. Instruments such as the ECERS-R and the ECERS-E are examples of measures that have been used in program improvement and self-assessment.

The research base of quality indicators included in such instruments, the simplicity of the descriptors and the ease with which one can implement and score these instruments have constituted them appropriate measures for quality improvement initiatives. However, the extent to which such measures can be used for professional development might depend on the how far the items 'capture' that which is important in practice. To better understand the use of items and indicators for teacher development, one needs to consider the way indicators are developed in the first place. Because reliable scoring of rating scales requires behaviours to be observed in a short period of time, creators of these scales often select behaviours or practices that can be readily observed in a brief time rather than those that occur infrequently. These are chosen if they are indicative of other practices of interest that may be less easily observed. Therefore, when attempting to create a rating scale, the question in mind is often 'What practices, teacher behaviours, and classroom elements *that can easily be observed* are most indicative of the practices that make up the construct to be measured?'. Therefore, according to this consideration, in many of these instruments, quality indicators, as their name signifies, are just examples of practices which are *indicative* of other practices that are not necessarily outlined in the instrument. In other words, the limited set of items selected for inclusion in many of these scales are the 'tip of the iceberg'; they are readily observable while other equally important practices are not included because they are difficult to measure through direct observation.

As one can understand, these indicators reflect clusters of observable practices and therefore, treating them as complete practice guides for teacher development might not be appropriate. Moreover, the operationalisation of many indicators (how the indicator is worded in order to be reliably observed and scored) is again often based on the need for reliable evaluation. For example, one indicator might read 'adults ask at least three questions to the children about their personal experiences'. Such an indicator might have been purposefully created to enable inter-rater reliability among evaluators in a short period of observation time. However, using this example as it is for teacher development might be highly inappropriate as it is a rather narrow operationalisation of a classroom practice that involves other parameters which are not listed on the scale, but that would be important to know and use in teacher training.

What these examples suggest is that where quality rating scales are used to enhance practice, the use of such instruments requires careful examination, as indicators have often been developed and operationalised in specific ways in order to reflect accurate and reliable measurement and therefore should not be treated as complete practice guides. Additional research is needed to examine how items and quality indicators included in such measures can be used for teacher training purposes.

Balancing technical rigour with practical or political concerns

A concern related to technical rigour versus practicality can be seen in the ECERS-E subscales. The ECERS-E items factor analysed into two factors, and not four, despite the fact that the measure is structured into four subscales. The authors took the view that the four domains (literacy, numeracy, science and diversity) made more 'sense' to practitioners and policy makers, because

of their place in the English curriculum, despite the fact that factor analysis only yielded two factors. This was a deliberate decision in which 'commonsense' practical concerns to link to the English national curriculum trumped technical advice. For this reason the total score is considered more valid for research purposes.

Community of practice

All measurement tools benefit from informal exchange amongst those who devise, implement and critique them. In the development of the ECERS-E, the authors of the ECERS-R were generous in giving suggestions and criticism. In 1993 the ECERS-E authors initiated an annual international workshop at which authors of similar environmental rating scales (e.g. ECERS-R, ECERS-E, ITERS, SACERS) met to present their ongoing work. This highly supportive and often technical forum has provided an informal impetus for critique and extension. Each year, researchers who have published papers using the scales are invited to present their work, as well as to provide constructive feedback on the work of others. Such dialogue has three benefits: First, it creates a climate for constructive criticism and improvement of the scales; second, it keeps the instruments 'alive' and promotes their use; third, the cross cultural exchange promotes a shared understanding of assessment methods and interpretations across nations and cultures. These lively meetings take place in North America, Europe, and South America and provide opportunity for those working specifically within a region to learn about the ECERS 'family' of instruments, as well as to contribute to its development. Practical as well as technical critique contributes to revisions, new forms of analysis, fresh interpretations and innovative applications.

NOTE

1 Kathy Sylva, Edward Melhuish, Pam Sammons, Iram Siraj-Blatchford and Brenda Taggart.

ACKNOWLEDGEMENTS

We are very grateful to Brenda Taggart and Iram Siraj-Blatchford for their insightful comments on early drafts; the chapter is much improved because of their feedback and their deep understanding of measurement tools.

REFERENCES

Abbott-Shim, M. and Sibley, A. (1998) *Assessment Profile for Early Childhood Programs* (Research Edition). Altanta: Quality Assist.

Arnett, J. (1989) 'Caregivers in day care centers: Does training matter?' *Journal of Applied Developmental Psychology*, 10 (4): 541–52.

Aytch, L. S., Castro, D. C. and Selz-Campbell, L. (2004) 'Early Intervention Services Assessment Scale (EISAS). Conceptualization and development of a program quality self-assessment instrument', *Infants and Young Children*, 17 (3): 236–46.

Aytch, L. S., Cryer, D., Bailey, D. B. and Selz, L. (1999) 'Defining and assessing quality in early intervention programs for infants and toddlers with disabilities and their families: challenges and unresolved issues', *Early education and development*, 10 (1): 8–23.

Bentzen, W. R. (2000) *Seeing young children. A guide to observing and recording behavior*. 4th edition. Albany, NY: Delmar.

Bryman, A. (2001) *Social research methods*. Oxford: Oxford University Press.

Burchinal, M. R., Roberts, J. E., Riggins, R., Zeisel, S. A., Neebe, E. and Bryant, D. (2000) 'Relating quality of center-based child care to early cognitive and language development longitudinally', *Child Development*, 71 (2): 339–57.

Cryer, D., Harms, T. and Ray, A. R. (1996) *Active learning for fours*. London: Addison Wesley.

DfES (2001) *Special educational needs: Code of practice*. London: DfES.

Friedman, S. L. and Amadeo, J. A. (1999) 'The child-care environment: Conceptualizations, assessments and issues', in S. Friedman, L. and T. Wachs, D. (eds) *Measuring environment across the lifespan*. Washington, DC: American Psychological Association. pp. 127–65.

Gallagher, P. A. and Lambert, R. G. (2006) 'Classroom quality, concentration of children with special needs and child outcomes in Head Start', *Exceptional Children*, 73 (1): 31–53.

Harms, T., Clifford, R. M. and Cryer, D. (1998) *Early Childhood Environment Rating Scale*. Revised edition. New York: Teacher's College Press.

Karp, J. M. (1996) 'Assessing environments', in M. McLean, D. B. Bailey and M. Wolery (eds) *Assessing infants and preschoolers with special needs*. 2nd edition. New Jersey: Prentice-Hall, Inc. pp. 234–67.

Katz, L. (1993) Five Perspectives on Quality in Early Childhood Programs (Vol. Catalog 208). Available from http://ceep.crc.uiuc.edu/eecearchive/books/fivepers.html

Kluczniok, K. and Sechtig, J. (2008) *Measurement of global and domain-specific quality in German preschools: Data from BiKS-3-8*. Paper presented at the ECERS International Workshop.

La Paro, K., Pianta, R. C. and Stuhlman, M. (2004) 'The classroom assessment scoring system', *The Elementary School Journal*, 104 (5): 409–26.

Mason, J. M. and Stewart, J. P. (1990) 'Emergent literacy assessment for instructional use in kindergarten', in L. M. Morrow and J. K. Smith (eds) *Assessment for instruction in early literacy*. Englewood Cliffs, NJ: Prentice-Hall.

Mathers, S., Linskey, F., Seddon, J. and Sylva, K. (2007) 'Using quality rating scales for professional development: Experiences from the UK', *International Journal of Early Years Education*, 15 (3): 261–74.

Moser, C. A. and Kalton, G. (2003) *Survey methods in social investigation*. 2nd edition. Aldershot: Dartmouth Publishing.

Moss, P. and Pence, A. R. (1994) *Valuing quality in early childhood services : New approaches to defining quality*. London: Paul Chapman.

Munton, A. G., Mooney, A. and Rowland, L. (1995) 'Deconstructing quality: A conceptual framework for the new paradigm in day care provision for the under eights', *Early Child Development and Care*, 114: 11–23.

Netemeyer, R. G., Bearden, W. O. and Sharma, S. (2003) *Scaling procedures. Issues and applications*. Thousand Oaks, CA: Sage.

Odom, S. L. (2000) 'Preschool inclusion: What we know and where we go from here', *Topics in Early Childhood Special Education*, 20 (1): 20–27.

Peisner-Feinberg, E. S., Burchinal, M. R., Clifford, R. M., Culkin, M. L., Howes, C., Kagan, S., L. et al. (2001) 'The relation of preschool child care quality to children's cognitive and social developmental trajectories through second grade', *Child Development*, 72 (5): 1534–53.

Perlman, M., Zellman, G. L. and Vi-Nhuan, L. (2004) 'Examining the psychometric properties of the Early Childhood Environment Rating Scale (ECERS-R)', *Early Childhood Research Quarterly*, 19: 398–412.

Pianta, R., La Paro, K. and Hamre, B. (2004) *Classroom Assessment Scoring System (CLASS). Unpublished Measure.* Charlottesville, VA: University of Virginia.

Rafferty, Y., Piscitelli, V. and Boettcher, C. (2003) 'The impact of inclusion on language development and social competence among preschoolers with disabilities', *Exceptional Children*, 69: 467–79.

Robson, C. (2002) *Real world research: A resource for social scientists and practitioner-researchers.* 2nd edition. Oxford: Blackwell.

Rogoff, B. (1999) 'Thinking and learning in a social context', in J. Lave (ed.), *Everyday cognition: Development in social context.* Cambridge, MA: Harvard University Press. pp. 1–8.

Sakai, L. M., Whitebook, M., Wishard, A. and Howes, C. (2003) 'Evaluating the Early Childhood Environment Rating Scale (ECERS): Assessing differences between the first and revised edition', *Early Childhood Research Quarterly*, 18: 427–45.

Sammons, P. (1999) *School effectiveness: Coming of age in the 21st century.* Lisse: Swets and Zeitlinger.

Sammons, P., Sylva, K., Melhuish, E., Siraj-Blatchford, I., Taggart, B. and Hunt, S. (2008b) *Effective Pre-school and Primary Education 3–11 Project (EPPE 3–11). Influences on children's attainment and progress in key stage 2: Cognitive outcomes in year 6. Research report No. DCSF-RR048* Nottingham: DCSF Publications.

Sammons, P., Sylva, K., Siraj-Blatchford, I., Taggart, B., Smees, R. and Melhuish, E. (2008a) *Effective Pre-school and Primary Education 3–11 Project (EPPE 3–11). Influences on pupils' self-perceptions in primary school: Enjoyment of school, anxiety and isolation, and self-image in year 5.* London: Institute of Education, University of London.

Scarr, S., Eisenberg, M. and Deater-Deckard, K. (1994) 'Measurement of quality in child care centers', *Early Childhood Research Quarterly*, 9: 131–51.

Schweinhart, L. J., Barnes, H. and Weikart, D. P. (1993) *Significant benefits: The high scope perry pre-school study through age 27.* Ypsilanty, Michigan: High Scope.

Senechal, M., Lefevre, J.-A., Smith-Chant, B. L. and Colton, K. V. (2001) 'On refining theoretical models of emergent literacy: The role of empirical evidence', *Journal of School Psychology*, 39: 439–60.

Siraj-Blatchford, I. (1999) 'Early childhood pedagogy: Practice, principles and research', in P. Mortimore (ed.) *Understanding pedagogy and its impact on learning.* London: Paul Chapman. pp. 20–45.

Siraj-Blatchford, I. and Wong, Y.-l. (1999) 'Defining and evaluating "quality" of early childhood education in an international context: Dilemmas and possibilities', *Early Years*, 20 (1): 7–18.

Soucacou, E. P. (2007) *Assessment of classroom quality in inclusive preschool settings: Development and validation of a new observation of a new observation measure.* Unpublished Thesis. Department of Education, University of Oxford.

Statham, J. and Brophy, J. (1992) 'Using the early childhood environment rating scale in playgroups', *Educational Research*, 34 (2): 141–48.

Storch, S. A. and Whitehurst, G. J. (2001) 'The role of family and home in the literacy development of children from low-income backgrounds', *New Directions For Child and Adolescent Development*, 92: 53–71.

Sulzby, E. and Teale, W. (1991) 'Emergent literacy', in R. Barr, M. Kamil, P. Mosenthal and P. D. Pearson (eds) *Handbook of reading research* (Vol. 2). New York: Longman.

Sylva, K., Melhuish, E., Sammons, P., Siraj-Blatchford, I. and Taggart, B. (2004) *The effective provision of pre-school education (EPPE) project. Technical paper 12. The final report: Effective pre-school education.* London: Institute of Education, University of London.

Sylva, K., Melhuish, E., Sammons, P., Siraj-Blatchford, I. and Taggart, B. (2008) *Effective preschool and primary education 3–11 project (EPPE 3–11). Final report from the primary phase: Pre-school, school and family influences on children's development during key stage 2 (age 7–11).* Nottingham: DCSF Publications.

Sylva, K., Sammons, P., Melhuish, E., Siraj-Blatchford, I. and Taggart, B. (1999) *The Effective provision of pre-school education (EPPE) project. Technical Paper 1-An introduction to the EPPE project.*

Sylva, K., Siraj-Blatchford, I. and Taggart, B. (2003) *Assessing quality in the early years : Early Childhood Environment Rating Scale: Extension (ECERS-E). Four curricular subscales.* Stoke on Trent, UK: Trentham.

Sylva, K., Siraj-Blatchford, I., Taggart, B., Sammons, P., Melhuish, E., Elliot, K. et al. (2006) 'Capturing quality in early childhood through environmental rating scales', *Early Childhood Research Quarterly*, 21: 76–92.

Tietze, W. and Cryer, D. (2004) 'Comparisons of observed process quality in German and American infant /toddler programs', *International Journal of Early Years Education*, 12 (1): 43–62.

Viswanathan, M. (2005) *Measurement error and research design*. Thousand Oaks, CA: Sage.

Whitehurst, G. J. and Lonigan, C. J. (1998) 'Child development and emergent literacy', *Child Development*, 69: 848–72.

Wolery, M. (1989) 'Using direct observation in assessment', in D. B. Bailey and M. Wolery (eds) *Assessing infants and preschoolers with handicaps*. Columbus, OH: Merrill. pp. 64–95.

Wolery, M., Pauca, T., Brashers, M. S. and Grant, S. (2000) *Quality of inclusive experiences measure*. Chapel Hill, NC: Frank Porter Graham Child Development Center, University of North Carolina at Chapel Hill.

Wood, D. J., Bruner, J. S. and Ross, G. (1976) 'The role of tutoring in problem solving', *Journal of Child Psychology and Psychiatry*, 17: 89–100.

Woodhead, M. (1998) *In search of the rainbow: pathways to quality in large scale programmes for young disadvantaged children*. The Hague: Bernard Van Leer Foundation.

6

Studying Teacher Effectiveness: The Challenges of Developing Valid Measures

Linda Darling-Hammond,
Jack Dieckmann, Ed Haertel,
Rachel Lotan, Xiaoxia Newton,
Sandy Philipose, Eliza Spang,
Ewart Thomas, and Peter Williamson

INTRODUCTION

Recent research has suggested that teacher effects on student learning are sizable, sometimes enough to match or overcome the effects of socioeconomic status (Clotfelter et al., 2007; Rivkin et al., 2001; Wright et al., 1997). A growing body of evidence confirming the importance of teachers has led to studies that seek to measure and predict teacher-effectiveness through value-added methods for examining student achievement gains, and through various observation instruments, surveys, and performance assessments that examine teacher practices.

Although many of the knotty issues associated with measures of teaching effects have as yet received little systematic treatment in the literature, the policy world has been moving rapidly to incorporate new measures of effectiveness into personnel policies as the basis for teacher evaluation, recognition, and compensation decisions. Programs of teacher preparation and professional development are seeking to establish their influences on teacher practices and teaching outcomes.

And researchers are seeking to understand how what teachers do is related to what their students learn. As both researchers and policy makers increasingly seek to incorporate various methods for measuring teacher effectiveness into their efforts, it is important to investigate the tacit judgments and dilemmas embedded in these measures, including diverse conceptions of teaching and assumptions about the sources of variation in student outcomes associated with particular teachers or teaching practices.

This chapter describes how we have sought to develop measures for assessing teacher effectiveness and to evaluate their validity by triangulating the findings we have derived using multiple methods of measurement and analysis. These methods include assessments of the value-added test score gains of students assigned to specific teachers in a set of local schools, as well as classroom observations of a sample of teachers identified either as being unusually 'effective' or as being less effective through these value-added student achievement analyses. We used evidence from these analyses and from pilot studies embedded in a larger study to examine what value-added analyses of student test score gains may – and may not – reveal about the construct called 'teacher effectiveness.' We also examined what observable dimensions of teaching practice may be important for supporting student learning in the classroom.

This measurement challenge is relevant to researchers across the social sciences for at least two reasons. First, the issue of measuring teacher effectiveness, though not entirely new to researchers, has taken on important implications for policy and practice that require greater attention to the operationalization of this construct and the consequences these may have for what happens in the real world: for example,

how teachers are trained and evaluated, what behaviors are encouraged in classrooms, and even how personnel judgments are made. These concerns for construct validation and measurement are increasingly prominent in other fields as well, with the growing use of indicators throughout our society to manage areas of social, economic, and professional activity.

In addition, the task of instrumentation is made complex – as it is in other fields – by the fact that there are many policy and social contexts which influence how the construct functions, and the design of the new instrument interacts with these social forces. Because many of these have been studied and are relatively known quantities, it is possible, and we believe imperative, to examine these interactions explicitly in the development of instruments and measures.

This chapter gives us the opportunity to discuss many of the practical and methodological issues related to the construction of measurement instruments in an area – the development and assessment of teacher effectiveness – where we have spent considerable time studying both policy and practice. We have sought to discover, develop, and provisionally verify the integrity of a new instrument through the systematic collection and analysis of data that pertains to this construct.

In these analyses, we go beyond most approaches for examining concurrent and consequential validity by using both sets of measures to query the integrity of the other and to develop more fine-grained analytical approaches that are then further tested. Because of the nature of our data set, we are also able to consider, in a highly textured fashion, the influences of school contexts on students' and teachers' performance. The result, we believe, is a set of important insights about the meaning of teacher 'effects' as measured by student achievement growth and about the construction of observation protocols that can validly measure teacher practices. In the course of this discussion, we reflect on many of the conflicts, compromises, and ambiguities that are inherent within the instrument development and piloting process.

Background of the study

Through the Carnegie Corporation's Teachers for a New Era (TNE) project, Stanford researchers launched a study of student value-added achievement gains in relation to teachers' preparation and teaching contexts. This study draws upon a database linking teacher and student data – including three years of student demographic data, course data, and state end-of-course test scores – in a set of five participating high-schools. Researchers used several different statistical models to develop value-added measures of teacher 'effectiveness,' and developed observation instruments to be used to examine the practices of a subset of teachers identified as highly effective or less effective.

As part of this work, we piloted early versions of our observation instruments in conjunction with value-added student achievement analyses in summer-school classrooms, using pre- and post-assessments of student learning based on the summer-school curriculum in several content areas. This opportunity allowed us to examine how our observation instruments captured teaching practices across multiple subject area domains, using value-added achievement data for students as an anchor for examining whether the instruments appeared to be capturing aspects of teaching related to differential effectiveness in supporting student learning gains. The pilot work led us to substantially revise our

observation instruments to better capture dimensions of teaching that were not captured by the initial instruments. These were aspects our expert observers, trained practitioners who had expertise in each content area, noticed were important for student engagement and understanding – and were associated with larger gains in student achievement on the pre- and post-assessments. As we describe later, many of these were aspects of content-specific pedagogy not assessed in the first version of the instruments.

After we revised our protocols from the pilot study, we were ready to use them in the broader study. We identified teachers from our value-added analyses of student achievement who seemed especially effective or ineffective to use for selecting a sample for further observation. In the course of these analyses, we further discovered that our value-added measures of teacher effectiveness varied substantially based on the statistical model that we used (with or without specific student demographic controls and school fixed effects), the specific course the teacher was teaching, and the year we examined, as we had two years of value-added data for each teacher. This provoked concern about what these ratings of teacher 'effectiveness' were actually measuring, and occasioned further analysis of the teaching conditions that were associated with these ratings. (Another part of the study involved surveys of the full teacher sample, which gave further information about their preparation, professional learning opportunities, teaching context, and self-reported practices. For this chapter, however, we report only on our statistical models and observational data.)

Ultimately, we selected for observation teachers who had fairly stable ratings across the different models, appearing either to be highly effective or less effective, relative to the full sample of teachers. Researchers assigned to conduct observations did not know how the teachers they observed were categorized, so they would not be influenced by their expectations in this regard. When we conducted the final analyses, we found that the observation protocols better captured dimensions of teaching associated with value-added measures of teacher effectiveness. However, we also identified further aspects of the observation instrument that did not fully capture teachers' practices as they seemed related to student understanding, engagement, and performance. Just as in the pilot study, we identified additional areas for refinement in the protocols, based on our observations of teaching in the field, which led to yet another round of revisions in these instruments.

In the following sections, we discuss our analytical process, initial findings, and our reasoning as we sought to understand and document teacher effects on student learning. We aim to illustrate how concurrent validation processes can stimulate refinement of measures. We also discuss how our efforts to contribute to the field's understanding of how to assess teaching can shed light on measurement issues in the social sciences more broadly.

USING VALUE-ADDED MODELING TO ASSESS TEACHER EFFECTIVENESS

Efforts to assess teacher effectiveness have increasingly sought to use value-added models (hereafter referred to as VAM) to look at student achievement gains associated with specific teachers. By measuring test score gains with a range of statistical controls, these methods seek to isolate the effect of teachers from other powerful factors, such as students' demographic and socioeconomic characteristics, school or neighborhood environments, and

the nonrandom assignment of students to classrooms and schools.

Despite its appealing conceptual and methodological premises, researchers have identified many concerns with value-added methods. (For a review, see Braun, 2005.) These include the stability of teacher effects across time – a topic that has long been of interest to researchers (e.g., Brophy, 1973; Doyle, 1977; Rosenshine, 1970); differences in teacher ratings associated with ways in which student achievement is measured (Lockwood et al., 2007: 47); disagreements and the appropriateness and effects of including student background variables as covariates in the models (McCaffrey et al., 2003); and concerns about whether it is possible to disentangle the influences of student characteristics, former teachers, and school contexts from what is thought to be the individual 'teacher effect' (Braun, 2005). Although many researchers seek to handle the school-level problem by including school-fixed effects in the model, some (e.g., McCaffrey et al., 2004) have pointed out that additional empirical investigation is needed to examine whether including school-fixed effect changes the inferences about teacher effectiveness. We explored all of these issues in our efforts to model teacher effectiveness.

Data and methods

Our sample included about 250 secondary teachers of mathematics, science, history/social studies, and English language arts (ELA) and their approximately 3,500 pupils in a set of five schools. We base our measurement of 'value added' on the variation in pupils' test scores on the California Standards Tests (CST), controlling for previous test scores, rather than on variation in year-to-year test score gains, because the CST is not vertically scaled and, therefore, does not yield interpretable gain scores. We use ordinary least square (OLS) regression analyses to predict pupils' standardized scores after taking into consideration the prior year's achievement (standardized CST scores in the same subject area), as well as key demographic background variables (i.e., race/ethnicity, gender, free/reduced lunch status, English-language learner status, and parent education). Some analyses include school-fixed effects. A teacher's effectiveness is then conceptualized as the residual difference between the average actual scores and the average predicted scores for all students assigned to that teacher. This measure of teacher effectiveness has the advantage of transparency and of being based on test scores rather than on the less reliable gain scores. Further, the residual difference between actual and predicted scores is conceptually similar to estimates of the teacher fixed effect in VAM regression models with or without controls for previous test scores.

Data analysis

We investigated empirically whether teacher 'effectiveness' rankings were consistent across different models and different courses for teachers who taught more than one type of course, and across two years for teachers for whom we had three waves of pupil test scores. Focusing on math and ELA and for 2006 and 2007, these OLS analyses generated four residual (or difference) scores for each student (see Table 6.1).

These residual scores for each student were aggregated to the class or teacher level. Based on the aggregated residual scores, teachers were assigned 'effectiveness' rankings for each of the OLS models, and several types of descriptive and correlational analyses were conducted. These analyses included: (1) Spearman rho correlations among teacher ranks using different models, (2) Pearson correlations between different teachers' ranks and their classroom student composition (e.g., mean parent education level, proportions of English language learners or low-income students), (3) Pearson correlations between the differences in teacher ranks using different models and classroom student composition, and (4) changes in teacher ranks depending on the model, year, and course taught. Finally, for math and ELA teachers who taught the same sets of courses within the same school, a series of analysis of variance (ANOVA) was conducted to test for the interaction between teacher and course in influencing rankings.

Findings

Results indicated that teacher ranks varied considerably across models, courses, and years, with most teachers' ranks shifting by at least one decile across models and at least two deciles across courses and years (see Table 6.2). Some teachers' rankings changed as much as 8 or 9 deciles across courses or years.

Table 6.1 List of ordinary least square (OLS) regression models

OLS Models	Predictors
Model 1 (M1)	Prior achievement only
Model 2 (M2)	Prior achievement plus student characteristics
Model 3 (M3)	Model 1 plus school fixed effects
Model 4 (M4)	Model 2 plus school fixed effects

Table 6.2 Per cent of teachers whose effectiveness rankings change

	By 1 decile or more	By 2 deciles or more	By 3 deciles or more
Across models*	56–80	12–33	0–14
Across courses*	85–100	54–92	39–54
Across years*	74–93	45–63	19–41

* The range reflects results for the four different statistical models.

Factors related to teacher ranking instability

The instability of measurement instruments is a challenge across the social sciences. In this study, results suggested that the teacher rankings generated by these four models as well as differences in these rankings were significantly related to student characteristics, such as racial/ethnic background, poverty, parents' educational level, and student English language status, even when the models producing the residual scores already included such variables as controls.

To illustrate how student characteristics can impact teacher rankings drastically, Figure 6.1 displays the student characteristics associated with a mid-career English language arts teacher in one of the sampled large comprehensive high schools, whose ranking changed across two years from the bottom decile (1) to the top decile (10). In the first year, this teacher was teaching a course in which 58 per cent of students were English language learners, 75 per cent were Latino, and 42 per cent

were eligible for free or reduced price lunch. In the second year, by contrast, only 4 per cent of the students were classified as English language learners and the proportions who were Latino and low-income were about half as much as the year before. The parent education level was also significantly higher in year two, with the average parent having at least some college education as compared to the average parent education of year one students having less than a high-school education. Thus, in this instance, the following student demographic factors appeared relevant to the instability of the measurement tool: (1) race/ethnicity, (2) English language status, (3) poverty, and (4) parents' educational level.

Similarly, for both math and ELA teachers who taught more than one type of course, we found that correlations between teacher ranks across courses were rather weak, and were non-significant across all models. When we ran analyses of variance (ANOVA) for 16 sets of teachers who

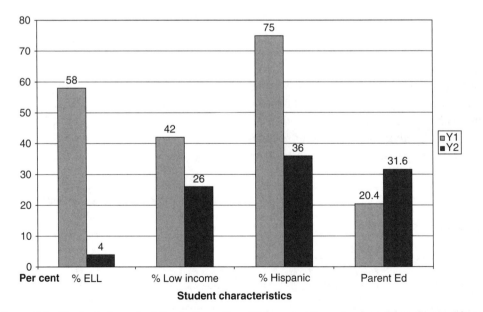

Figure 6.1   Student characteristics in Years 1 and 2 for a teacher whose ranking changed from the 1st to the 10th decile.

taught the same set of math or ELA courses within the same school (in all cases to a high-tracked group and a lower-tracked group), we found that, controlling for students' prior achievement, the course taught was more often a significant predictor of student achievement (11 times) than the teacher (3 times). In addition, the teacher by course interaction was significant in three analyses. Our ANOVA findings suggested that the 'teacher effect' was often less strong as a predictor of student achievement gains than the 'course effect.' Furthermore, the analyses suggested that teachers' rankings were higher for courses with 'high-track' students than for untracked classes. For example, Figure 6.2 shows rankings for three English teachers from the same large comprehensive high school when they taught the same pairs of courses, one designed for higher level students (with teacher ranks falling in the 7th–9th deciles) and the other for lower-achieving students (with teacher ranks in the 1st–3rd deciles).

These examples and our general findings highlight the challenge inherent in developing a measurement model or tool that adequately captures teacher effectiveness, when teacher effectiveness itself is a variable with high levels of instability across contexts (i.e., types of courses, types of students, and year) as well as statistical models that make different assumptions about what exogenous influences should be controlled. Further, the contexts of instability are themselves highly relevant to the notion of teacher effectiveness.

There are several ways to think about the implications of our empirical findings. Conceptually and theoretically, we might need to broaden our definition of teacher effectiveness from a generic perspective to a differentiated perspective acknowledging that teacher effectiveness is context specific rather than context free. Several researchers in the UK (e.g., Campbell et al., 2004) have argued for developing a differentiated model for assessing teacher effectivess

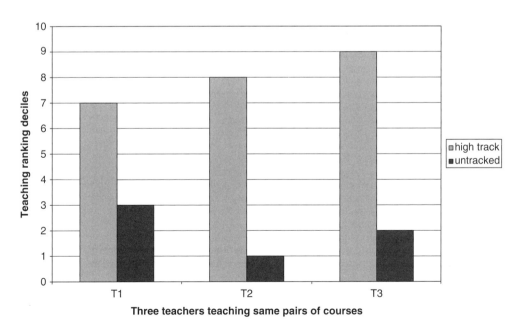

Figure 6.2   Teacher rankings by courses.

which considers that teachers might be more effective teaching some students than others. Our empirical investigation lends some support to this line of thinking on teacher effectiveness.

On the other hand, it is also possible that a teacher's effects are less well-measured by existing standardized tests for some student populations than others. For example, in California, where we conducted these studies, new immigrant students who have less than one year of English-language learning opportunity have to take the same tests in English as other students, with none of the language modifications and few of the accommodations generally permitted in other states. In addition, tests geared narrowly to grade-level standards may not measure the gains that students exhibit who begin the year far below (or for that matter above) grade level, as the areas and extent of their actual learning growth may not be measured on the test. This might be particularly true for students with exceptional needs, as well as new immigrants entering with little formal education, or others who have fallen behind academically. Thus, a teacher who has a large population of such students in her classroom may appear less effective than she in fact is.

Practically, the notion that the contexts of teaching (which are contributory factors to the instability of teacher effectiveness measures) are an integral part of, or relevant to, the concept of teacher effectiveness has important implications for policy and practice. For instance, policies advocating the use of high-stake test scores to hold teachers accountable for student learning may need to take the contexts of teaching and the characteristics of students into consideration. They may also need to consider the development and use of adaptive student tests that measure a broader range of learning gains, and that

do so validly for special populations of students.

Our observations that judgments of teacher effectiveness differed based on the model used, as well as class and year examined – and that student characteristics appear to play a role in these variations – helped guide our selection of teachers for in-depth observations and interviews. We eliminated high-tracked or selective classes from our teacher observations so as to minimize the confound between teacher quality and tracking. Instead, we selected teachers who taught diverse learners and, wherever possible, selected teachers with stable ratings across courses and years. We also stockpiled a long list of important questions to pursue at a later time regarding the meaning of these kinds of value-added assessments of teachers, which appear to be influenced by teaching contexts as well as by the intrinsic traits of individual teachers.

DEVELOPING OBSERVATION INSTRUMENTS TO EXAMINE TEACHER EFFECTS

As a first step in developing an observation instrument for examining teaching effects, our team compared 10 existing observation protocols to determine which elements of practice consistently appeared and which were uniquely captured by specific instruments. We identified the strengths of specific protocols, and evaluated what additional elements would be needed to align specific protocols with our conception of teaching, which was informed by professional standards – i.e., the California Standards for the Teaching Profession (CCTC, 1997) and those of the National Board for Professional Teaching Standards (1999) – and by research on teaching (see, in particular, Darling-Hammond and Bransford, 2005).

Instrument development process

We aimed to create an observation instrument that could capture both subject-specific pedagogy and teachers' capacities to serve the needs of diverse learners. This process led us to decide upon three thematic areas of importance: classroom environment, subject-specific pedagogical practices, and academic language development (especially for English language learners). Of these, we found that other researchers had done significant work on measuring the classroom interactions and some generic instructional strategies within that environment, but there was less work on assessing content pedagogical practices at the secondary level and even less on supporting language development.

Classroom environment

As a foundation for developing a new observation instrument, we drew upon what we perceived to be the strengths of the Classroom Assessment Scoring System (CLASS) Secondary developed by Pianta et al. (2006). The original elementary version of the CLASS protocol on which the Secondary version was built has been validated in over 3,000 classrooms at the pre-kindergarten and elementary school levels (Pianta, 2006, Pianta et al., 2002). These studies found that the quality of student-teacher interactions predicts social and academic outcomes. The CLASS focuses on capturing both the social organization and instructional formats of the classroom, defining the construct of 'classroom quality' along four dimensions with sub-indicators, which are outlined in Table 6.3.

Observers were trained in the use of the CLASS instrument and used it in pilot observations to understand its strengths and limitations for our purposes. As a result of these pilots, we decided to adapt the protocol by opting for a modified approach to the observation process and an analytic rather than holistic scoring procedure. We also added domains to capture subject-specific practices and teaching practices for academic language. Each of these adaptations is discussed below.

The CLASS protocol calls for an observation cycle in which researchers observe and take unstructured notes for 20 minutes, followed by a 10-minute period when the researcher uses her notes to score the teacher on a range of indicators in each of the four domains described above. The scores are then averaged to provide a single score for the entire observation period. In the pilot study, we chose instead to have researchers provide one score for each item based on what they observed during an entire class period. This procedural decision was intended to reflect the trajectory of a typical lesson cycle in a secondary content classroom, where teachers might emphasize the rationale and goals of activities in

Table 6.3 Dimensions of CLASS

Emotional support	Instructional support
○ Positive climate	○ Procedures and skills
○ Negative climate	○ Content understanding
○ Teacher sensitivity	○ Analysis and problem solving
○ Regard for adolescent perspectives	○ Quality of feedback
Classroom organization	Student outcomes
○ Behavior management	○ Student Engagement
○ Productivity	
○ Instructional learning formats	

the first 20 minutes of class rather than throughout the course of the class. We chose to score each item in the domain separately rather than provide a holistic score for the domain to see what might be gained or lost by scoring analytically rather than holistically. This allowed us to better examine the validity and utility of specific items for describing teaching in terms related to teacher effectiveness.

Subject-specific pedagogical practices

We elaborated the CLASS protocol by adding a domain to describe discipline-specific teaching practices for secondary teachers, since the CLASS's evaluation of instructional practice is generic, and does not focus explicitly on content pedagogy, which research suggests is an important predictor of teacher effectiveness (Ball, 1991; Grossman and Schoenfeld, 2005; Shulman, 1986; Wilson et al., 1987). In our review of other instruments, we found several that focused on subject-specific practices for teachers, particularly in math and science. We determined that the Observation Scoring Guide of the Mosaic II Project developed by the RAND Corporation (2004), one of the larger observational studies to link teacher practice to student outcomes, contained a robust set of indicators, capturing elements of practice for mathematics and science (each assessed separately) that have been found to be related to teacher effectiveness in a number of studies. For example, key indicators for mathematics on the MOSAIC II instrument include: encouraging students to generate multiple solutions; using a variety of pictures, graphs, diagrams, and other representations; and using manipulatives. Where necessary, we added additional indicators to more fully represent the teaching standards that anchored our conception of teaching. These included observation indicators that paralleled items used in our survey of

self-reported practices, which was also content specific.

Based on the templates we developed for math and science, we developed analogous subject-specific pedagogical indicators in English/Language Arts and History-Social Science. In creating the instrument, we also sought a balance between discipline-specific and cross-cutting dimensions of teaching, and instantiated certain generalized aspects of teaching in each content area. For example, aspects of developing disciplinary discourse were represented in each protocol, using indicators specific to the subject area. In some cases, although indicators might look similar or identical, we understood that it would take an informed disciplinary eye to assign the rating/score. For instance, an indicator of 'sequencing,' which assesses how well the teacher organizes tasks and concepts in a logical fashion to help students develop skills, requires observers to have a grasp of disciplinary curriculum and connections between specific concepts in order to evaluate the teacher's practice. Our protocol, therefore, required observers to use their disciplinary knowledge while observing.

Our protocol's requirement that observers be expert teachers in the discipline stands in contrast with the implicit assumption of some other instruments that individuals with or without education or content area backgrounds can observe a teacher using a generic protocol. In our research team, we found significant variation in both inference and scoring on content specific items when we observed classrooms outside our respective disciplines. This adds support to our belief that content knowledge influences what is captured in observations of teaching. It also confirms a point frequently made about observation tools in the social sciences: that the observer themself is part of the instrumentation.

Academic language development

In the course of piloting and refining this measurement tool, we discerned the desirability of adding a domain to assess a dimension of teaching practice that we deemed significant: academic language development. The decision to refine the scale to include this new dimension was informed by extant research and our own expertise and understanding of the policy and social context. Given state and national shifts in student demographics and the importance of access to content for English language learners, as well as access to academic language in the disciplines for all learners, we believe that a comprehensive view of the classroom needs to account for the complexity of academic language development (Echevarria et al., 2003).

To examine this domain of teaching, we looked to the Sheltered Instruction Observation Protocol (SIOP) produced by the Center for Research on Education, Diversity and Excellence (CREDE) (Echevarria et al., 2003). This is the leading observational protocol for content area teachers who teach English language learners and one of the few language instruments that has shown a relationship between teachers' scores and learning gains of their language-minority students in English proficiency (Guarino et al., 2001).

To assess teacher practices regarding language development, we included a select group of SIOP items in our protocol. These items were as follows: clearly defined language objectives, ample opportunities to clarify key concepts in first/native language, activities integrating all language skills, and adaptation of content to differing levels of student language proficiency. Our decision about dimensions of practice to include was guided by the literature and expert knowledge of members of our team regarding language acquisition and the teaching of new English learners, as well

as the results of our pilots. The items we selected were, in our view, the most relevant to the disciplinary teaching contexts we sought to study at the secondary level.

Context and procedures for the pilot study

As described above, the measurement instrument we developed was comprised of items from several existing, validated approaches to measuring aspects of teacher quality. A small-scale, five-week summer school program in July and August of 2007 provided an opportunity to pilot the observation of this instrument. The program was designed for rising sixth, seventh, and eight graders in a local school district. Sixteen teachers participated in the study, six men and ten women, four from each of four main content areas: English, History, Math, and Science. The participating teachers represented both teachers who worked for the district and educators who were affiliated with a local teacher preparation program. As such, we felt the summer school session provided a targeted, feasible, and appropriate context to pilot the instrument.

Further, the pre- and post-tests administered as a component of the program provided an opportunity to examine the alignment of the instrument with outcomes within particular disciplines and for specific teachers, allowing us to both validate the scale preliminarily and assess the ability of particular items to capture aspects of teacher quality. Each teacher administered a pre-assessment in the first week and a half of the summer school program, and a post-assessment during the last week of the program. These assessments were designed specifically to assess the summer school curriculum content.

Researchers observed each teacher for a 90-minute period three times over the course of the summer. Researchers also conducted pre- and post-observation interviews with each observation. Questions guiding the pre-observation interviews focused on teachers' goals for the lesson that day and the classroom context (e.g., number of English language learners, students with special education accommodations), as well as predictions regarding possible challenges that they anticipated during the lesson. The post-observation interviews included questions asking teachers to reflect on the lesson and, if necessary, to clarify any questions regarding what had come up for the researcher during the observations.

During observations, researchers took extensive field notes. Most teachers wore a digital microphone during the lessons which captured teachers' interactions with individual students. Since groupwork was a common feature in many of the classrooms, audio recordings helped create a more complete picture of student-teacher interactions outside of whole class instruction. Following each observation and interview cycle, the researcher listened to the digital recording of the lesson (if available), filled in field notes, and scored each lesson based on the protocol.

The piloting process thus generated multiple forms of data from repeated, in-depth observation and interviews that compared the instrument (itself developed from existing, well-established measures) with achievement outcomes. The detailed picture of teacher quality generated from this rich pilot data set allowed us to evaluate how well the instrument conformed to our own theoretical and experience-based expectations, to understand the context and alternative interpretations of the teaching activities (from what was learned in teacher interviews and observed in our more extensive field notes), and to assess the degree to which aspects of the measure were correlated with outcomes.

Data analysis

Student learning gain scores were calculated using the pre- and post-assessment scores of students who completed both assessments. We used gain scores in order to simplify the analysis of this small-scale study. Our tentative assessment of teachers' 'effectiveness' based on these gain scores was one source of data for grounding our analysis of our observation instrument. Limitations with pilot data, a perennial concern, encouraged us to treat these findings as tentative hypotheses, rather than strong conclusions. These limitations included the brevity of the summer school program, the small sample, and our awareness that many factors influence student learning and its measurement, including the extent to which our measures are aligned with the curriculum that was taught. In some subject matter areas, changes in the curriculum after summer school started made this alignment less close than in others.

Using student gain scores, observation protocol scores, field notes, and audio and video data, we examined whether the kinds of practices captured by the instruments seemed to be related to differences in teacher effectiveness and then, which of these practices seemed to be most salient. We also shared our reflections about the utility of our data recording strategies, what we learned from the observations and interviews, and how we might adapt the observation instrument for the future use in a larger study. By explicitly digesting the pilot experience of our team with regard to these methodological concerns, we helped refine and codify the research protocol for our emerging instrument and to resolve differential experience from different raters.

What we learned: a case from math

Because of the close fit between curriculum as enacted and the assessments in mathematics (supporting strong content alignment and validity), we use our analysis of the mathematics teachers to highlight the kinds of issues that emerged across the content areas. For the pre- and post-assessment, the four mathematics teachers used an authentic task from the MARS (Mathematics Assessment Resource Service) battery designed to assess students' understanding of pattern, function, algebraic notation, and mathematical explanations. These ideas were at the core of the five-week curriculum designed by one of the teachers and used, with minor modifications, by all teachers in the sample. The curriculum aimed to orient students with different mathematical backgrounds and interests toward an active problem-solving approach and to help students use an array of strategies as appropriate. Students practiced attacking problems in groups and working collaboratively with peers and teachers, with pre-service teachers serving as tutors. The constancy of curriculum materials and approaches to problem-solving allowed for a reasonable comparison of learning outcomes across teachers.

Scored on a five-point rubric, there was a substantial divergence of gain scores for students across the four teachers in the sample, ranging from 0.20 in Ms. Miller's class to 1.17 in Mr. Jones's class (all names are pseudonyms). When comparing student gain scores and observation protocol scores, the ratings on our protocol for the first three teachers (Jones, Tyler, and Abraham) aligned with their average gain scores. Ms. Miller was an anomaly, as she consistently scored highly on the protocol we used, especially on the content pedagogical measures, but her students' gain scores were lower than the other teachers' students. This provoked a further analysis of our protocol and how it evaluated practice given what we observed about her decisions in the classroom.

Using our observation field notes – which extended beyond the protocol – and our interview data, we identified aspects of Ms. Miller's teaching practices that differed from the other teachers and seemed associated with lower levels of learning for her students. As one example, we noted that Ms. Miller provided challenging tasks, and she was explicit about wanting students to reason through the problems, but she offered little assistance in helping students learn how to tackle these tasks. In contrast to other teachers, Miller did not give students any direct mathematical tools (formulas, conventions, heuristics, etc.), nor did she model or describe cognitive strategies for problem solving. Instead, she required students mostly to 'invent methods.'

What seemed to be missing from Ms. Miller's practice was explicit modeling and strategy instruction on the mathematical practices that she was trying to foster. Based on how students proceeded through the tasks, it seemed that this was completely new intellectual territory for them. Consequently, the level of stress they experienced from the ambiguity of the novel problems and the deferment of assistance left many students feeling unable to complete the tasks. The observation protocol did not allow us to code the extent of scaffolding and support the teacher provided the students. Based on this finding, we generated an observation protocol item designed to capture an important distinction between invoking a mathematical practice versus teaching and developing it explicitly. We also added indicators of explicit scaffolding to the protocols for other subject areas, and as we describe below, we later found these indicators to be associated with measured effectiveness in the broader study.

We also noted across the content areas that our observation protocols did not allow us to record how different teachers attended differently to marginal students' needs, as the

CLASS protocol is specifically designed to capture the 'typical student's experience,' and we had maintained that aspect of the protocol as we built our instrument. And while the protocols allowed us to record whether teachers used hands-on activities, they did not capture the quality of the tasks or whether the lesson activities were aligned with the learning goals and the assessments. These things appeared to matter to student understanding and engagement, and to the teachers' measured effectiveness. In these ways, our observations called our attention to dimensions of teaching related to content and pedagogical issues as well as more general classroom and interpersonal concerns.

Changes in the protocol

The pilot process provided insight as we subsequently revised the protocol and sought to address concerns that were raised through the analysis of the pilot data. We used our extended observations and further research on the assessment of teaching practice to expand our observation protocols to incorporate elements that were not coded in the original protocols – especially the *extent* of instructional scaffolding and the *appropriateness* of tasks, representations, and supports for teaching the concepts under study to the students in the class. The new version of the protocol included a shorter version of the CLASS protocol, excluding items that proved to be less visible or significant in secondary classrooms, and we added a series of new domains created to capture the features of teaching that seemed to be missed by the initial protocol. These changes are reflected in the domains and items listed in Table 6.4.[1]

Use of the protocol in the larger study

After achieving 85 per cent inter-rater reliability on the revised protocol by observing and coding videos of high-school instruction as a team, we used the protocol in the larger study. Four teachers were selected in each of three content areas: mathematics, science and English Language Arts, who were identified as 'highly' or less effective according to our value-added analysis of test scores, with the added limitation that teachers were selected only if classes they taught were hetero-geneously grouped 9th or 10th courses, rather than upper level or 'high tracked' courses. Observations were 'blind' in that observers did not know the classification of the teachers they observed until after all of the observations were completed and fully scored.

Interestingly, it became more difficult in two of the content areas to observe teachers classified as less effective, because these teachers often refused to participate in the study or were removed from consideration by the school principal. This occurred despite the fact that there was no explicit designation or knowledge on the part of researchers, principals, or teachers about the classifications of teachers to be observed. As in other fields of study that often carry non-neutral normative perceptions (e.g., the study of homelessness, poverty, or other social challenges), this suggests the degree to which certain phenomena, in this instance, teaching effectiveness, can be difficult to measure across the entire continuum because self-consciousness may limit access to subjects.

Thus, because we also needed to select teachers who were still in the same school and still teaching 9th or 10th grade untracked classes in the year after the student data were collected and analyzed, *and* we prioritized teachers with more than one year of data to correct for instability of effectiveness rankings, we needed to select teachers in two cases who were closer to the middle of the distribution of effectiveness

Table 6.4 Additional domains of observation protocol

Domain: Curriculum goals	**Domain: Classroom discourse**
Clear purpose	Classroom discourse/discussion
Focus on standards	Frequency of feedback loops
Links to prior knowledge	Quality of feedback
Links to personal experience	Peer feedback
Connection between prior understanding and new concepts	Academic press
	Nature of oral participation
Domain: Instructional supports	**Domain: Attention to learners' needs**
Explicit strategy instruction	Recognizing and addressing student misconceptions
Guided practice	Differentiated support
Pacing	Student choice appropriate to task
Sequencing	Academic language use
	Academic language development
Domain: Assessment	**Domain: Content pedagogy**
Checking understanding	Content knowledge
Availability of models	Depth/accuracy of representations
Quality dimensions	Example/analogies/extensions/connections
Student use of assessment for learning	
Use of assessment for planning	
Link of assessment and learning goals	
Domain: Discipline-specific practices	**Domain: Intellectual challenge**
Explicit teaching of key disciplinary concepts (Math, Science)	Intellectual demand of task
Standards of evidence (E/LA, Math, Science)	Nature of task
Attention to discipline-based practices (Math, Science)	Level of questioning strategies
Connecting discipline-based practices to content (Science, Math)	**Domain: Planning for language support**
	Comprehensible input
	Differentiated materials
	Grouping strategies
	Assessment
	Graphic organizers

scores, rather than in the bottom tail of the distribution.

In contrast to our procedure in the summer, we observed each teacher three times during a three- to five-day span to capture the coherence of a lesson cycle and interviewed each one at the beginning and end of the series of observations. From the pilot, we had noted that some practices or domains of teacher practice are not always visible at the level of the individual lesson (assessment, for example), and we decided to score those domains based on the series of lessons and interview data.

Regarding the interview protocol from the pilot study, we added a question asking about the teacher's planning process and degree of autonomy in planning. We wanted to gather data about curricular constraints and mandates under which teachers might be working. In some cases schools were under state improvement programs, and teachers had limited choice regarding instructional materials. We needed to understand how these and other contextual factors might influence the inferences we could draw from our measures. For example, judgments about the quality and appropriateness of curriculum goals and materials might not reflect a teacher's own professional judgment in instances where curricular decision making is constrained. While this might not change the inference drawn about the effectiveness of the *teaching* observed, it might limit inferences about traits inherent to the individual *teacher*.

Findings regarding the validity of the new protocols

We present data from the mathematics classes we observed to illustrate how we established concurrent validity, linking valued-added effectiveness scores (highly effective and less effective) with the ratings on our observation protocol (on scale of 1 to 7, with seven being the highest). Across our statistical models, the four teachers we observed were classified as follows, based on their student achievement data:

- Math Teacher A – highly effective
- Math Teacher B – highly effective
- Math Teacher C – somewhat effective
- Math Teacher D – less effective

Figures 6.3–6.5 demonstrate the results of the domain-level comparison across the four teachers in the math sample. As is visible in the graphs, Teachers A and B, designated as the most effective based on their student achievement gains

scored highest on both the CLASS items we used in the study (Figure 6.3) and on the disciplinary-specific items that we developed (Figures 6.4 and 6.5). Teacher C (designated as somewhat effective) scored more highly than Teacher D, (selected as low on the effectiveness rankings) on all but one dimension – curricular goals – where the two were rated almost identically, and where there was little difference across the four teachers.

A closer look at the data indicates that ratings in some domains showed much smaller differences across teachers than others. For example, most observed classrooms had relatively positive climates and were productive in the sense that students had tasks to work on, and most students sustained their engagement. We did find that teachers managed student behavior in very different ways, with the two highly effective teachers scoring well above the other two, and we saw a much higher rating on 'negative climate' (as well as a somewhat lower rating for 'positive climate') for the least effective teacher (see Figure 6.3). Small differences were also apparent on ratings for curricular

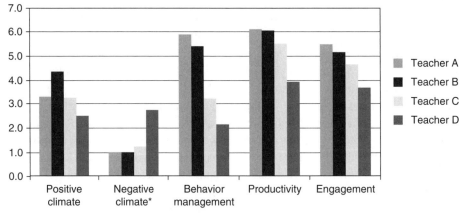

* = This item is scored in reverse.

Figure 6.3 Math teacher's ratings by CLASS domains.

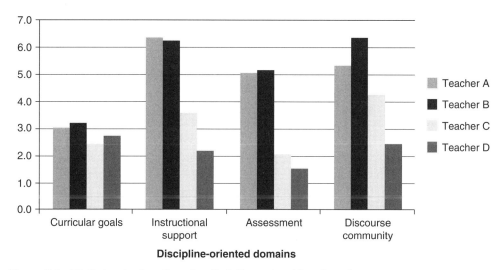

Figure 6.4 Math teacher's ratings by disciplinary teaching domains.

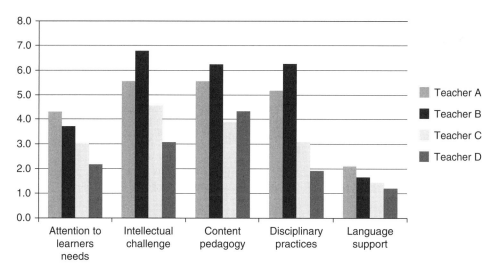

Figure 6.5 Math teacher's ratings by disciplinary teaching domains (continued).

goals (Figure 6.4) for both math and science teachers, but not English teachers. There was little variation in 'language support' across teachers in all content areas (see Figure 6.5). Given our small sample size, we did not draw any hard conclusions from these differences, but noted them as issues to explore further at a later time with larger samples, to evaluate whether some aspects of practice may be more strongly associated with overall effectiveness than others.

We noted that many of the discipline-specific domains also captured large differences in teacher practices consistent with their value-added scores. In particular, instructional support, assessment practices, the degree of intellectual challenge, and disciplinary practices strongly distinguished among the teachers (see Figures 6.4 and 6.5). For example, the highly-effective teachers consistently engaged the students in mathematical sense-making activities, provided opportunities to explore and formalize mathematical patterns, continually assessed students' understanding through questioning, conversation, and observations. These features were consistently less present in less-effective teachers' classrooms.

In looking for domains that were associated with differential ratings of effectiveness across content areas, we found that in this small study, teacher variation in some domains was not as wide as it was in math. In addition to possible inadequacies in specific items and descriptors, part of this discrepancy may be due to contextual factors. For example, in one school where we studied several teachers, we found that Science teachers co-planned extensively, making their practice more similar on our measures for the teacher who was highly effective and one who was less effective according to the student achievement data. In this instance, knowing how the context of piloting influenced the differentials on particular domains enhanced our ability to interpret specific findings. Nonetheless, the direction of the ratings was appropriate in all of the cases we studied, even when the size of the differential was smaller.

Further review of our interview data, field notes and observation ratings allowed us, once again, to probe and interpret the data more fully, reinforcing our sense that generating multiple forms of data during the piloting phase can give researchers a more comprehensive and illuminating perspective on the validity of the measurement instrument. Although we were successful in establishing a substantial degree of concurrent validity

(associating value-added teacher effectiveness with observation-based ratings of teaching practices), we once again noted that some teaching practices of highly effective teachers were not fully captured by our instrument. For example, the two highly effective math teachers were skillful at systematically highlighting important mathematics from students' board work and presentations, regardless of whether the answer was correct or not. They consistently made their students' thinking visible and the object of discussion. In contrast, the two less-effective teachers tended to be satisfied with correct answers.

Our future work will include developing items to capture this aspect of mathematics teaching, analysing how it might manifest in other content areas, and ascertaining whether it is observed in teachers deemed highly effective by value-added analyses. Through an iterative, ongoing approach to research, we thus aim to identify and account for potential threats to validity and reliability, and refine the instrument accordingly. We have also identified ways to improve implementation of the protocol to better reflect those teaching dimensions that appear to be related to teachers' effectiveness. For example, in our study, we observed a series of connected lessons, but only within one week at one point in the year. Stability and representativeness of practice could be better verified by observing multiple series of such connected lessons throughout the year.

CONCLUSION

This study provided an opportunity to explore the possibilities and limitations of value-added methods of examining teacher effectiveness and to develop methods for observing teaching practice that may be associated with teacher effectiveness. We approached the development of both sets of measures with an eye toward evaluating empirically, in an iterative fashion, what distinctive approaches can reveal about teacher influences on student learning. By cross-referencing our findings across multiple, complementary methods, we were able to refine our understanding of how both teaching practices and contexts influence student outcomes.

One result was a greater appreciation of the importance of examining the stability and interpretation of data from value-added models, carefully querying inferences about 'teacher effects,' and examining the inter-actions of 'effectiveness' ratings with student and classroom characteristics. Another result was the construction of observation and interview protocols for examining teacher practices that take into account evidence of both content pedagogical practices and student learning outcomes when deciding what to look at in classrooms. This strategy integrates theoretical frameworks for constructing observation instruments with practical insights grounded in the real work of teachers with very diverse learners in contemporary classrooms.

NOTE

1 See Appendix

REFERENCES

Ball, D. L. (1991) 'Research on teaching mathematics: Making subject matter knowledge part of the equation', in J. Brophy (ed.), *Advances in research on teaching: Vol. 2, Teachers' subject matter knowledge and classroom instruction*. Greenwich, CT: JAI Press. pp. 1–48.

Braun, H. I. (2005) *Using student progress to evaluate teachers: A primer on value-added models*. ETS Policy Information Center. Available online, www.ets.org/research/pic.

Brophy, J. E. (1973) 'Stability of teacher effectiveness', *American Educational Research Journal*, 10 (3): 245–52.

California Commission on Teaching Credentialing, California Department of Education. (1997) *California Standards for the Teaching Profession*. Sacramento, CA: California Commission on Teacher Credentialing and California Department of Education.

Campbell, J., Kyriakides, L., Muijs, D. and Robinson, W. (2004) *Assessing teacher effectiveness: Developing a differentiated model*. London: RoutledgeFalmer.

Clotfelter, C. T., Ladd, H. F. and Vigdor, J. L. (2007) *Teacher credentials and student achievement in high school: A cross-subject analysis with student fixed effects*. Washington, DC: National Bureau of Economic Research Working Paper 13617.

Darling-Hammond, L. and Bransford, J. (eds) (2005) *Preparing teachers for a changing world: What teachers should learn and be able to do*. San Francisco: Jossey-Bass.

Doyle, W. (1977) 'Paradigms for research on teacher effectiveness', *Review of Research in Education*, 5 (1): 163–98.

Echevarria, J., Vogt, M. and Short, D. (2003) *Making Content comprehensible for english language learners*. New York: Allyn and Bacon.

Grossman, P. and Schoenfeld, A. (2005) 'Teaching Subject Matter', in L. Darling-Hammond and J. Bransford (eds) *Preparing teachers for a changing world: What teachers should learn and be able to do*. San Francisco: Jossey-Bass. pp. 301–31.

Guarino, A. J., Echevarria, J., Short, D., Schick, J. E., Forbes, S. and Rueda, R. (2001) 'The sheltered instruction observation protocol', *Journal of Research in Education*, 11 (1): 138–140.

Lockwood, J. R., McCaffrey, D. F., Hamilton, L.S., Stetcher, B., Le, V. N. and Martinez, J. F. (2007) 'The sensitivity of value-added teacher effect estimates to different mathematics achievement measures', *Journal of Educational Measurement*, 44 (1): 47–67.

McCaffrey, D., Lockwood, J., Koretz, D. and Hamilton, L. (2003) *Evaluating value-added models for teacher accountability*. Santa Monica, CA: RAND.

McCaffrey, D., Lockwood, J., Koretz, D. and Hamilton, L. (2004) 'Models for value-added modeling of teacher effects', *Journal of Educational and Behavioral Statistics*, 29: 67–101.

National Board for Professional Teaching Standards. (1999) *What teachers should know and be able to do*. Washington, DC: NBPTS.

Pianta, R. C. (2006) 'Teacher-child relationships and early literacy', in D. Dickinson and S. Newman (eds),

Handbook of early literacy research, Vol. II. New York: The Guilford Press. pp. 149–62.

Pianta, R. C., Hamre, B. K., Haynes, N. J., Mintz, S. L. and La Paro, K. M. (2006) *Classroom Assessment Scoring System (CLASS).* Middle/Secondary Version Pilot. University of Virginia, Charlottesville.

Pianta, R. C., La Paro, K. M., Payne, C., Cox, M. J. and Bradley, R. (2002) 'The relation of kindergarten classroom environment to teacher, family, and school characteristics and child outcomes', *Elementary School Journal,* 102 (3): 225–38.

Rivkin, S. G., Hanushek, E. A. and Kain, J. F. (2001) Teachers, schools, and academic achievement. Working Paper No. 6691, National Bureau of Economic Research.

Rosenshine, B. (1970) 'The stability of teacher effects upon student achievement', *Review of Educational Research,* 40 (5): 647–62.

Shulman, L. (1986) 'Those who understand: Knowledge growth in teaching', *Educational Researcher,* 15 (2): 4–14.

Wilson, S. M., Shulman, L. S. and Richert, A. E. (1987) '150 different ways of knowing: Representations of knowledge in teaching', in J. Calderhead (ed.), *Exploring teachers' thinking.* London: Cassell. pp. 104–24.

Wright, S. P., Horn, S. P. and Sanders, W. L. (1997) 'Teacher and classroom context effects on student achievement: Implications for teacher evaluation', *Journal of Personnel Evaluation in Education,* 11 (1): 57–67.

7

Identifying Consumers' Compulsive Buying Tendencies: Lessons Learned for Measuring Consumer-Related Phenomena

Kent B. Monroe, Nancy M. Ridgway, and Monika Kukar-Kinney

This chapter discusses the measurement-related methodological insights gained when developing an expanded conceptualization and new measure of consumers' tendencies to buy compulsively. This new measure includes dimensions of both obsessive-compulsive and impulse-control disorders. By including dimensions of obsessive-compulsive disorder and excluding income-dependent or consequences of compulsive buying, we develop a measure that has both a strong theoretical foundation and important psychometric properties.

Throughout the chapter, we discuss the unique issues involved in measuring this and other consumer-related phenomena, seeking to share methodological lessons relevant to measure development across the social sciences. We begin by providing some in-depth background on compulsive buying behavior.

It has been over 20 years since the problem of compulsive buying behavior was introduced to the consumer research literature (Faber et al., 1987). This pioneering research has generated considerable interest in this troubling issue in consumer behavior. A recent study estimated that 5.8 per cent of US consumers were compulsive buyers (Koran et al., 2006). However, other researchers believe that this estimate is too low and that there is an increasing tendency by consumers to buy compulsively (Manolis and Roberts, 2008; Muller and de Zwaan, 2004). The continuous stream of research articles, books, television documentaries, and websites addressing compulsive buying and the problems it creates indicates that the issue continues to be relevant (e.g., Chaker 2003; McElroy 1994; Mellan and Christie 1997; *www.stoppingovershopping.com*). Therefore, it is important to develop a valid and easy-to-use measure of the tendency of consumers to be compulsive buyers.

Researchers have offered various definitions of compulsive buying (emphasis added): *'chronic repetitive purchasing'* (O'Guinn and Faber, 1989: 155); *'impulsive and/or compulsive buying of unneeded objects'* (Ninan et al., 2000: 362); and *'excessive or poorly controlled preoccupations, urges or behaviors regarding ... spending'* (Black, 2001: 17). These excerpts contain dimensions of both obsessive-compulsive behaviors (i.e., preoccupation with buying, repetitive buying) as well as lack of impulse control (i.e., the lack of control over the urge or impulse to buy). Given this, compulsive buying is defined as a consumer's tendency to be preoccupied with buying that is revealed through repetitive buying and a lack of impulse control over buying (Ridgway et al., 2008). Although several existing scales purport to measure 'compulsive buying', only one scale includes items that tap the obsessive-compulsive dimension (i.e., preoccupation with and repetitive buying) while excluding the impulsive dimension (Monahan et al., 1996). All other scales focus solely on buying stemming from impulse-control problems (Christenson et al., 1994; Edwards, 1993; Faber and O'Guinn, 1992; Lejoyeux et al., 1997; Valence et al., 1988). Consequently, despite the nomenclature, no existing compulsive buying scale includes items measuring both dimensions within the same scale.

To be classified as a psychiatric disorder, a behavioral problem or disorder must result in harm to the individual or others (*Diagnostic and Statistical Manual of Mental Disorders* 2000-IV-TR, the standard reference text for psychiatric diagnoses, APA, 2000). For this reason, diagnostic scales (which result in a yes or no conclusion) often include the consequent harm within the measure itself. However, from the perspective of construct validity, compulsive buying tendency and the consequent effects of such behavior should be measured separately (DeVillis, 2003; Tian et al., 2001). Moreover, public concern with compulsive buying is not limited to people previously identified with a psychiatric disorder. Indeed, there is a widespread belief that there are many consumers who, although not identified psychiatrically as suffering from a buying disorder, nevertheless, may be compulsive buyers (Chaker, 2003). For example, if their financial resources are ample, their compulsive buying may not result in serious financial consequences and they may not seek psychiatric care. Due to their dependence on financial consequences and income-related items, previous scales cannot identify these compulsive buyers. Therefore, we measure only obsessive-compulsive and impulse-control tendencies in the scale and separately measure multiple adverse consequences of compulsive buying, including financial, emotional, and behavioral.

In this chapter, drawing on an emerging theory from the psychiatric literature, we describe the development of a new scale measuring compulsive buying. We present the motivation for developing the scale, the theory underlying the scale and three studies using different samples to establish the validity of the scale. We describe the process used to validate the scale with actual and self-reported consumer purchase data. The advantages of this compulsive buying measure are that it: (1) does not require a previous diagnosis of a psychiatric disorder as do some previous scales, (2) excludes consequences (e.g., financial or other harm) of the behavior from the scale itself, and (3) excludes items that may be related to a consumer's income level from the scale. A challenge facing measurement development in the social sciences is to ensure the scale itself corresponds with the construct's conceptual definition, and does not include extraneous dimensions or factors. By reflecting on how we developed a scale with these characteristics, we provide more general insights into this particular measurement challenge.

THEORETICAL FOUNDATION OF THE COMPULSIVE BUYING SCALE

An important beginning point in scale development is surveying the theoretical literature relating to the construct of interest. Drawing on the underlying theory helps to develop conceptual clarity and separate out the antecedents and consequences of the phenomenon. However, theory, like knowledge in general, is not static and over time the underlying theory may change in several ways. In the case of the present research, many researchers today believe that compulsive buying should be considered as exhibiting elements of both obsessive-compulsive and impulse-control disorders, calling this theory *obsessive-compulsive spectrum disorder* (Hollander

and Allen, 2006; Hollander and Dell'Osso, 2005; McElroy et al., 1994). Our definition and measure of compulsive buying are based on this emerging theoretical foundation. Previously, compulsive buying ironically had been considered an impulse-control disorder, which is classified in psychiatry as a separate disorder from obsessive-compulsive disorder (Black, 1996; Faber and O'Guinn, 1992).

An impulse-control disorder (ICD) is characterized by an inability to control impulses to perform behaviors that result in temporary pleasure. On the other hand, an obsessive-compulsive disorder (OCD) is an anxiety disorder, with obsessions (preoccupations) and compulsions (behavior) that are an attempt to relieve anxiety (Hollander and Allen, 2006). These impulses and anxieties lead one to perform a behavior repetitively, consume large amounts of time, and interfere with one's everyday functioning (McElroy, 1994). The rationale for classifying compulsive buying as an obsessive-compulsive spectrum disorder is that, like OCD, the consumers' thoughts are preoccupied with buying and repetitive buying behavior is performed to reduce anxiety. Moreover, like ICD, these consumers lack control over the urge to buy. Both disorders involve an urge to perform an act followed by a loss of control over the urge (Hollander and Dell'Osso, 2005). We draw on this theoretical rationale to first develop the conceptual definition of compulsive buying, and second, its measure. From a measurement perspective, it is critical that the construct is clearly defined and that its definition is firmly grounded in theory, reflecting the true meaning of the construct. In addition, there needs to be a close correspondence between the construct definition and the measurement items (sometimes called the auxiliary theory).

It is also important to draw on available empirical evidence supporting the theoretical perspective concerning the construct. Indeed, there is evidence supporting the idea that compulsive buying should be considered as an obsessive-compulsive spectrum disorder. McElroy (1994) found that 80 per cent of her previously identified compulsive buyers also had anxiety disorders (OCD) and 40 per cent had impulse-control disorders. Also, Christenson et al. (1994) found that 67 per cent of compulsive buyers were diagnosed with OCD and 96 per cent were diagnosed with ICD. This overlap between the two disorders provides empirical support for the proposed theoretical definition of compulsive buying as containing elements of both OCD and ICD.

Based on the theoretical rationale and the empirical evidence presented above, it is our belief that characteristics of both disorders should be included in the conceptualization and measurement of compulsive buying. Thus, our definition and measurement of compulsive buying includes the extent that consumers' buying behaviors are caused by an urge and are repetitive (characteristic of OCD) and lack impulse control (characteristic of ICD). A similar clinical example of another disorder that could be placed along the obsessive-compulsive spectrum is kleptomania, or repetitive (OCD characteristic) and uncontrollable (ICD characteristic) stealing of items not needed for personal use (Grant, 2006).

DEVELOPING THE COMPULSIVE BUYING SCALE

As mentioned previously, scale development needs to be informed by a review of extant theory and research. Given the theoretical background and emerging evidence supporting the idea that compulsive buying includes characteristics of both OCD and ICD, we then reviewed previous research on obsessive-compulsive disorders, impulsive-control disorders, compulsive buying, and impulsive buying. Developing a measure of compulsive buying tendency required that we also had a firm grounding in the various underlying research domains, not only within consumer research, but also in the basic related disciplines. With this foundation, we began to specify the dimensions of compulsive buying.

Compulsive buying dimensions

Researchers agree that compulsive buyers have an obsession or preoccupation with buying and a compulsion that leads them to engage in repetitive buying (Faber and O'Guinn, 1992; Hirschman, 1992). Similarly, we expected compulsive buyers to exhibit this *obsessive-compulsive dimension* by buying both more frequently and in larger amounts than average buyers. In terms of the lack of impulse control, the urge to buy may lead consumers to retail outlets where a wide array of products encourages them to assuage this urge regardless of need for a product. Repeating this behavior to regulate arousal as well as the element of making frequent unplanned and unneeded purchases of products is included in the *impulsive buying dimension*.

Item selection

The next step in developing a scale is to generate a large pool of candidate items for inclusion in the scale. A comprehensive, systematic review of the literature can guide this item generation, and subsequently, item selection. In our research, a pool of 121 potential items designed to measure either the compulsive or impulsive buying dimensions was developed based on a review of over 300 research articles, over 100 popular press articles, and during the course of brainstorming exercises using the construct definition and its two dimensions. An item pool is a rich source from which a scale emerges (DeVillis, 2003). There should be a large set of items with a certain degree of redundancy. Redundancy is important as it facilitates developing items that are internally consistent. Internally consistent or reliable measures are a necessary condition for construct validity.

We considered either all items or only partial statements from all the existing scales of compulsive buying. Next, we reviewed key phrases related to shopping and buying from the popular press articles, such as 'Are you a shopaholic?' and 'Shop until you drop'. We brainstormed how to develop clear and simple statements based on these phrases to include in our measure (e.g., 'Others might consider me a "shopaholic"'). Then each of these 121 items was carefully examined and judged as to whether it either reflected one of the dimensions of compulsive buying or was an overall indicator of compulsive buying tendency. The goal of developing a construct-valid scale required that the selected items capture the concept only and not any precursors or consequences of compulsive buying. The initial list was narrowed to 15 items using these criteria while also eliminating items that were double-barreled, ambiguous, or had other wording problems (e.g., shopping instead of buying). To ensure consistency, items were converted so that each was measured using a seven-point Likert-type or frequency scale.

Initial test and scale refinement

After an initial construct measure is developed, scale refinement and modification can be achieved through a range of methodological techniques, requiring attention and rigor. We used both exploratory and confirmatory factor analysis. Specifically, for extra course credit, 352 undergraduate students (54 per cent female, average age 21) completed a survey that included the 15 compulsive buying items. Additional variables (frequency of buying clothing and accessories, average amount spent per shopping trip) were also measured.

Principal component exploratory factor analysis with oblique rotation (Promax) was used on the 15 compulsive buying items first. Exploratory factor analysis is used to investigate potential dimensionality of the construct without specifying the number of factors or dimensions, and usually represents a preliminary step in the development of a construct measure. It allows for all items to be related to all factors (Viswanathan, 2005). When performing exploratory factor analysis, we chose oblique rotation because we expected the construct dimensions (factors) to be correlated. Items were retained if they loaded .50 or more on an individual factor or dimension, did not load .50 or more on more than one factor, and their item-to-total correlation in reliability analysis exceeded .40 (Hair et al., 1998; Viswanathan, 2005). Using these criteria, six items were eliminated. The remaining nine items all loaded on the two hypothesized factors, together explaining 69 per cent of the total variance (see Table 7.1).

To correctly specify the latent variable measurement model, we carefully inspected the construct definition and the proposed construct dimensions to determine whether the dimensions were reflective or formative measures of compulsive buying (Diamantopoulos and Winklhofer, 2001). For reflective measures, the direction of causality is from the underlying latent construct to its measures, which are considered manifestations of the construct (Jarvis et al., 2003). On the other hand, for formative (or composite) dimensions, the direction of

Table 7.1   Nine items retained from the exploratory factor analysis in student sample

Dimensions of compulsive buying	Preoccupation with buying	Impulsive buying
Obsessive-compulsive buying		
My closet has unopened shopping bags in it.	.72	.05
Others might consider me a 'shopaholic'.	.63	.19
I buy something for myself almost everyday.	.91	−.06
Much of my life centers around buying things.	.91	−.06
Impulsive buying		
Buy things I don't need.*	−.09	.82
Buy things I did not plan to buy.*	.02	.82
Buy things without thinking.*	.11	.80
Am a bit reckless about what I buy.*	.05	.84
I consider myself an impulse purchaser.	.01	.84

Note: All items were measured on a 7-point Likert scale, anchored at 1 = strongly disagree, and 7 = strongly agree, except the items denoted by *, which were responses to a question 'How often do you. . .?' and were measured on a 7-point scale, anchored at 1 = never, and 7 = very often.

causality is from dimension to construct. Unlike the reflective model, formative measures all have an impact on (or cause) the construct (Jarvis et al., 2003). After careful examination of the two compulsive buying dimensions, we concluded that obsessive-compulsive buying behaviors and impulse-control buying behaviors are manifestations (i.e., revealed behaviors) of the underlying compulsive buying tendency; hence, they should be considered as reflective measures. The two dimensions were also highly correlated ($\rho = .77$).

After specifying the latent measurement model, confirmatory factor analysis was used on the remaining nine items to confirm the dimensionality of the construct. In contrast to exploratory factor analysis, the confirmatory factor model is constructed in advance with the number of latent variables or factors set by the analyst (Bollen, 1989). Individual items are then constrained to load on a single factor (Viswanathan, 2005). Since our exploratory factor analysis indicated a two-factor solution, this two-factor model was next transferred into the confirmatory analysis model. An additional three items were removed because of large error covariances with other items or because

their error terms loaded significantly on multiple dimensions (Bollen, 1989). Six items remained in the final set, and all dimensions exhibited item and construct reliabilities above the recommended levels (Bagozzi and Yi, 1988). Table 7.2 displays the final items and their standardized factor loadings. Construct reliabilities for the individual dimensions as well as correlations among the two dimensions are shown below the table. Coefficient alpha for the scale was .84. The confirmatory model showed a good fit with the data ($\chi^2 (8) = 11$, $p > .10$; NFI $= .99$, IFI $= 1.00$, CFI $= 1.00$, RMSEA $= .03$). The standardized factor loadings of these dimensions on the second order factor, compulsive buying tendency, are .99 for the obsessive-compulsive buying dimension and .78 for the impulse-control dimension.

VALIDATING THE NEW COMPULSIVE BUYING SCALE

Once a set of items has been identified and selected, researchers turn their attention to the challenge of rigorously verifying the validity of the scale. The scale was

Table 7.2 Six items retained from the confirmatory factor analysis

Dimensions of compulsive buying	Standardized item loading (students)	Standardized item loading (staff)	Standardized item loading (Internet)
Obsessive-Compulsive Buying; $\alpha = .75$ (.77) [.78] in Study 1 (2) [3]	.69	.50	.61
My closet has unopened shopping bags in it.	.77	.88	.83
Others might consider me a 'shopaholic'.	.71	.83	.79
Much of my life centers around buying things.			
Impulsive buying; $\alpha = .80$ (.78) [.84] in Study 1 (2) [3]			
Buy things I don't need.*	.70	.75	.83
Buy things I did not plan to buy.*	.81	.77	.82
I consider myself an impulse purchaser.	.76	.69	.70

Note: All items were measured on a 7-point Likert scale, anchored at 1 = strongly disagree, and 7 = strongly agree, except the items denoted by *, which were responses to a question 'How often do you . . .?' and were measured on a 7-point scale, anchored at 1 = never, and 7 = very often.

Correlation between the two dimensions is .77 (.60) [.72] in student sample (staff) [internet].

Overall reliability (α) for the scale as a whole is .84 (.81) [.84] in student sample 1 (staff) [internet].

developed using a relatively homogeneous sample of undergraduate students who were primarily enrolled in business. The next step was to validate the scale using a more heterogeneous sample with respect to age, education level and household income. In addition, we sought people who would have a broader set of buying experiences. This widening of the population from which to draw a sample is also a first step to achieve external validity of the scale. External validity refers to the degree to which the measure can be applied and the research findings generalized to other populations, settings, and times.

To validate the new scale, 1,200 university staff members from a large Midwestern university were randomly selected and sent a survey through campus mail containing the compulsive buying scale along with other measures needed to validate the scale. This predominantly female population was chosen because prior research suggested that the majority of compulsive buyers were women. After two-and-a-half weeks, a reminder e-mail message was sent to the entire sample. A total of 555 surveys were returned, for a response rate of 46 per cent. Among the respondents, 92.7 per cent were

female, average age was 47 years (age range 20–77 years), average household income was $55,000, 61.5 per cent were married, 20 per cent had a high-school diploma, 42 per cent had attended college, while 27 per cent had received a college degree. Thus, as anticipated, the obtained sample was substantially more heterogeneous than the original sample on which the scale was developed. Each participant was paid $10 as an incentive to participate and enhance the response rate. An additional benefit of providing a monetary reward for participation is an increased involvement by the respondents. To maintain confidentiality respondents separately returned a form indicating that they had completed the questionnaire. As soon as respondents indicated that they had returned the completed survey to the mail drop, the monetary compensation was sent to them. This quick response to their action encouraged others who had not yet responded to return their questionnaires.

The scale was evaluated by examining the factor loadings obtained in confirmatory factor analysis and comparing them to those achieved in the student sample and to the established cutoff criteria. All item loadings were at or above .50 and were comparable in magnitude to those in the student sample. Correlations between the two compulsive buying scale dimensions and their reliabilities were also similar (see below Table 7.2). The fit indices confirm a good model fit (χ^2 (8) $= 37.86$, $p < .01$; NFI $= .97$, IFI $= .97$, CFI $= .97$, RMSEA $= .08$). The standardized factor loadings of the two dimensions were similar to those achieved previously (.73 for the obsessive-compulsive and .82 for impulse-control dimension), as were the internal consistency reliabilities of the scale as a whole and of the individual dimensions (Table 7.2). This analysis confirms that the psychometric properties of the scale remained at the appropriate levels when the measure was tested on a different sample, and provides support for the validity of the scale.

To further validate the scale as a whole, a composite index (compulsive buying index or CBI) was formed by summing the individual scores for the six items (Carver, 1989). The average value for the compulsive buying index was 15.39 and *SD* $= 6.44$ (possible value range 6–42; actual range 6–40), and the median value was 14. Women had a higher compulsive buying tendency than men; $\rho = .10, p < .05$). Compulsive buying tendency decreased with age; $\rho = -.17$, $p < .01$ and was inversely related to education; $\rho = -.11$, $p < .05$. An important finding was that income did not correlate with the compulsive buying index ($\rho = -.03$, $p > .10$), suggesting that compulsive buying tendency is independent of income.

Non-response error

Non-response error can thwart efforts to establish the validity of a new scale and undermine efforts to minimize measurement error. Non-response error refers to initial differences in those consumers who choose to respond to the survey and those who decide not to participate (Fowler, 2002; Mangione, 1997, 2004). If such differences exist, the obtained sample and the results may not be representative of the population from which the sample has been drawn. However, a problem arises because the survey data from non-respondents do not exist. Thus, it is impossible to directly compare the two groups of consumers to assess any differences. To address this problem, researchers have traditionally compared early and late survey respondents to assess whether any differences exist between these two groups, and extrapolated their findings to the non-respondent group to determine whether non-response error is a likely problem (Armstrong and Overton, 1977). To account for the threat of non-response error in the present research, everyone who responded to our survey before the reminder e-mail message was classified as an early respondent (91 per cent). People who returned the survey after the reminder message were categorized as late respondents (nine per cent). The sample demographic characteristics as well as the compulsive buying scale and its correlates were evaluated across both sets of respondents. The early and late respondents did not differ relative to their compulsive buying tendency or any other variables used to assess the validity of the scale (*p*-values $> .05$), indicating that non-response error was not a likely threat. Nevertheless, researchers must still be careful that the mechanisms used to improve response rates do not skew the results, so that a representative sample can be obtained.

Common method variance

Common method variance, another threat to the validity of the scale, is a measurement error that results from a consumer's tendency to answer questions incorrectly, either deliberately or non-consciously (Malhotra et al., 2007; Podsakoff et al., 2003). Researchers define common method variance bias as the inflation (or deflation) in the true correlation among observable variables in a study. Typically, this type of measurement error may occur when the data on these variables are collected using a cross-sectional survey. That is, respondents are answering questions on both dependent and independent variables at the same time. Thus, it is possible that respondents' answers are knowingly or unknowingly influenced by other questions or answers. The presence of common method variance can create difficulty in understanding the phenomenon being studied as it alters the true correlations between the variables. Social desirability bias is one of the important potential sources of this problem.

Social desirability bias refers to consumers answering untruthfully in order to present themselves in a more favorable light. Because compulsive buying is a sensitive issue, the scale may be subject to socially desirable responses. To check and control for social desirability bias, we used the 33-item Crowne and Marlowe (1960) social-desirability scale. The correlation between social desirability and compulsive buying was significant ($\rho = -.21$, $p < .01$). That is, the more likely a respondent answered in a socially approved way, the less likely she would report compulsive buying tendencies. To correct for possible underestimation of compulsive buying, we used social desirability as a control variable in our analyses. Given the nature of compulsive buying, a negative relationship between compulsive buying and the tendency to respond in a socially approved way was theoretically expected and confirmed. Consequently, in this case, social desirability could serve as another

indicator of nomological validity, which is discussed next.

Nomological validity

In designing and validating new scales, researchers should design tests to check for nomological validity. A construct measure is said to have nomological validity if it correlates with other constructs in a theoretically predicted manner. To assess nomological validity, a theoretical net of antecedents and consequences of the construct of interest is usually developed, and the relationships between them and the central construct are evaluated. The ease of identifying the precursors and the potential consequences of a concept vary, but the advantages of doing so for scale quality are manifold. Empirically showing the relationships between compulsive buying and its antecedents and consequents demonstrates the compatibility of the scale with existing knowledge about this important consumer phenomenon.

To assess the nomological validity of the compulsive buying scale, we investigated the relationship of compulsive buying with previously identified precursors and consequences of compulsive buying. Previous research has identified a positive link between compulsive buying and precursors such as materialism (Faber and O'Guinn, 1992; Manolis and Roberts, 2008), depression and stress/anxiety disorders (Aboujaoude et al., 2003; Black, 1997), and negative feelings about oneself or one's life (Aboujaoude et al., 2003; Dahl et al., 2003). Researchers have also found a negative relationship between compulsive buying and self-esteem (Dittmar, 2004). Our measure of compulsive buying is significantly correlated with these precursors as expected (see Table 7.3).

Potential consequences of compulsive buying include: (1) having short-term

Table 7.3   Construct validity tests: University staff sample

Validity test	No. items	Mean	SD	Reliability	Correlation with compulsive buying index
Response bias:					
Socially desirable response scale	33	.63	.14	.74	−.21***
Convergent validity:					
Clinical screener (reverse scored)	7	−1.99	1.66	.80	.62***
Discriminant validity:					
OCD	30	2.93	.67	.82	.29***
Nomological validity:					
1. Traits and states					
Materialism	9	2.81	1.17	.86	.51***
Self-esteem	10	5.70	1.03	.89	−.08*
Negative feelings	3	1.98	1.30	.81	.65***
Depression [a]	7	.39	.47	.89	.21***
Anxiety [a]	7	.27	.35	.72	.31***
Stress [a]	7	.70	.51	.83	.26***
2. Consequences					
Positive feelings	3	3.46	1.59	.82	.59***
Hiding behavior	3	1.72	1.20	.82	.59***
Returning items	1	2.65	1.31	NA	.13***
Family arguments	1	1.38	.92	NA	.44***
Credit cards paid in full each month	1	1.08	1.51	NA	−.11**
Credit cards within $100 of limit	1	.42	1.02	NA	.10**
3. Self-reported buying behavior					
Frequency of buying [b]	1	1.54	.75	NA	.37***
$ amount spent per buying occasion	1	68.18	56.47	NA	.09**
Demographics:					
Age	1	47.30	10.28	NA	−.17***
Income	1	3.27	1.21	NA	−.03
Education	1	3.33	1.03	NA	−.11**

Note: *** $= p < .001$; ** $= p < .01$; * $= p < .05$.

[a] These constructs were measured on a 0–3 scale.

[b] Frequency of buying was measured on a 1–5 scale, where 1 = less than once a month, 2 = about once a month, 3 = about once in two weeks, 4 = about once a week, and 5 = more than once a week.

All correlation tests were performed controlling for social desirability bias (except for reported correlation with the social desirability; first row).

positive feelings or a 'high' associated with buying (Aboujaoude et al., 2003; Chaker, 2003; Dittmar and Drury, 2000), (2) feeling remorseful or guilty and hiding buying behavior or purchases from others (Christenson et al., 1994), (3) making frequent returns of purchased items (Hassay and Smith, 1996), (4) engaging in family arguments about buying (Pirog and Roberts, 2007), and (5) experiencing financial difficulties because of buying, such as credit card debt (Faber and O'Guinn, 1992). As expected, positive feelings associated with buying ($\rho = .59$, $p < .01$), hiding behavior ($\rho = .60$, $p < .01$), frequency of returning purchases ($\rho = .13$, $p < .01$), and frequency of family arguments related to buying ($\rho = .44$, $p < .01$) all exhibited positive relationships with compulsive buying. Among the financial consequences of compulsive buying, the number of credit cards paid in full each month was negatively correlated with the compulsive buying index ($\rho = -.11$, $p < .01$), while the number of credit cards within \$100 of their limit exhibited a positive correlation with the compulsive buying index ($\rho = .10$, $p < .05$), as expected. Both the precursors and the potential consequences of compulsive buying correlated with the compulsive buying index as theoretically predicted, providing evidence for the nomological validity of the scale.

Discriminant validity

Establishing the discriminant validity of a new measurement tool is a methodological priority with implications for the utility of the scale. The new measure needs to be able to differentiate between different, but related constructs. Thus, a newly developed measure of a specific construct should not be highly correlated with a different measure of a similar, but conceptually distinct construct. To assess the discriminant validity of the compulsive buying measure, the relationship between compulsive buying tendency and obsessive-compulsive disorder (OCD) was examined. The two constructs are similar in that they both contain the compulsive component, and hence, should be positively correlated (Scherhorn et al., 1990). However, since the constructs are not measuring identical tendencies, this correlation should not be high. The correlation between the compulsive buying index and OCD (Maudsley Obsessive-Compulsive Inventory; Hodgson and Rachman, 1977) was positive and significantly less than one ($\rho = .29$, $p < .01$), indicating that the two constructs are related, but conceptually distinct.

Convergent validity

Another important form of construct validity or the degree to which a new measure is indeed measuring what it is purporting to measure (and only that), is convergent validity. To achieve convergent validity, a newly developed measure must be highly correlated with a different measure of the same underlying construct. To assess convergent validity of the compulsive buying scale, we compared it with the most frequently used compulsive buying measure in consumer research, the clinical screener (Faber and O'Guinn, 1992). Since both scales are purporting to measure compulsive buying, we would expect them to show high correlation. We reverse scored the clinical screener and, as expected, the correlation between the two scales was positive, $\rho = .62$, $p < .01$ (95 per cent confidence interval .59–.65), providing evidence of convergent validity of the two scales.

Classification into compulsive and non-compulsive buyers

One goal of developing the new compulsive buying scale was to be able to classify consumers as to whether they have a tendency to be compulsive or non-compulsive buyers. To assess the ability of this new scale to identify consumers with a tendency to be compulsive buyers, we needed to determine an appropriate cutoff point between the compulsive and non-compulsive buyer groups. To do this, we examined the relationship between the compulsive buying index and the most important nomological correlates of compulsive buying: negative feelings, hiding purchases, arguing with family about buying, and self-reported frequency of buying.

The key criterion used to determine the cutoff point was that the compulsive buying group needed to show a substantially higher tendency to experience the stated feelings and behaviors relative to the non-compulsive group. Thus, we were looking for a sharp break or an elbow in the

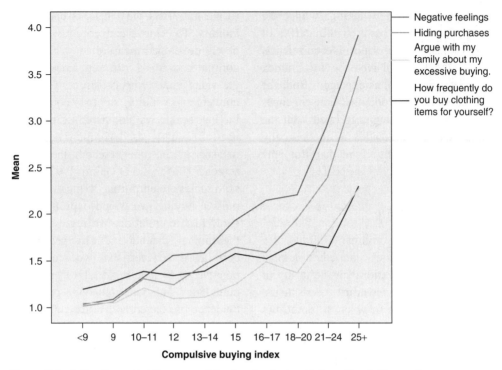

Figure 7.1   Inflection point for compulsive buying index: University staff sample.

Note: Based on their compulsive buying index, the respondents were divided into 10 groups that were about equal in size. The values of the compulsive buying index for each of the ten groups are shown on the X-axis. The last group (Compulsive Buying Index $\geq$ 25) represents the compulsive buyers.

relationship, where the rate of increase in these behaviors and feelings would accelerate as the compulsive buying index increased. As shown in Figure 7.1, the value of these variables dramatically increases when the compulsive buying index reaches 25. Indeed, for some variables, the inflection point occurs even before the index reaches 25. Interestingly, and in support of the value 25, a cutoff point of 25 or greater on the index also represents a natural divider between those respondents who on average agree with the statements and those people who are neutral or disagree with the compulsive buying statements. Thus, in addition to denoting the inflection point in the graph, it has an intuitive interpretation. Following the analysis, we classified all respondents who scored 25 or more on the compulsive buying index as compulsive buyers. Respondents with a score of 24 or less were classified as non-compulsive buyers. We found that 8.9 per cent of the university staff sample fit into the compulsive buying category using the compulsive buying index.

VALIDATING THE COMPULSIVE BUYING INDEX WITH PURCHASE DATA

Being able to calibrate a new scale using another sample of respondents to correlate it with actual behavior is an important validation step. We were fortunate to be able to validate the new scale using actual purchase data. Thus, we conducted a third data collection using a national consumer sample of respondents from 42 states. To evaluate the scale's performance in predicting consumer buying behavior, we obtained both actual and self-reported consumer purchase data. Matching these purchase data with the consumers' responses to the questions from the compulsive buying scale allowed us to show that the new measure correlates with both actual and self-reported purchase behavior.

An e-mail message was sent to a sample of 1,294 customers of an internet women's clothing retailer. From this set, 309 people completed the survey, a response rate of 23.9 per cent. In the sample, 98.5 per cent of respondents were women, 63 per cent were married, the average age was 53 years (range 28–75 years), and average household income was $82,000. The survey contained questions about general shopping and buying behavior on the internet and at bricks-and-mortar stores, the compulsive buying scale, questions about individual consumer characteristics, and demographic questions. As an incentive, the respondents had a choice of receiving $10 or free shipping on their next order to the internet retailer (value up to $24.95). Reliabilities and factor loadings were similar to the previous two studies and are provided in Table 7.2. The mean value of the compulsive buying index was 17.13 ($SD = 7.27$) with a median of 16 and range of 6–42.

Steps to preserve confidentiality

In research where individual participants' names could be identified and linked with information that they provide, a concerted effort must be made to protect the participants. To preserve the confidentiality and commercial value of the internet retailer's customer e-mail address list and actual purchase records as well as the privacy of the respondents' answers to the internet survey questions, we developed and implemented IRB approved procedures. First, once the relevant purchase history (2001–04 period) had been compiled by customer and categorized by analytical variables, the purchase history documents were returned to the retailer, as this was a single use opportunity. Second, once the respondents had completed the internet survey and returned it to the independent organization's server, they then sent a separate e-mail message to the researchers indicating that they had completed the survey and selecting their preferred method of compensation for completing the survey. Third, matching the purchase data with the respondents' completed surveys was accomplished by using the e-mail addresses that were common to the two datasets. All other personal information about the respondents was provided by the respondents themselves. After the data had been matched, customers' e-mail addresses were removed from the combined dataset, so that no identifying information for any respondents was present in further analysis.

Validation of the scale with self-reported spending

The next step in validation of the new measure of compulsive buying tendencies was to evaluate the agreement between the measured compulsive buying tendencies and the consumers' self-reported spending and frequency of buying. Specifically, respondents reported how much on average they spent at their top five retail stores and their top five internet stores per month (in dollars) for clothing and accessories for themselves as well as how frequently (per month) they bought from each of these stores. To validate the compulsive buying measure with respondents' self-reports of buying behavior, partial correlations between the two were examined after controlling for social desirability bias. As expected, the higher the respondents' compulsive buying index, the more frequently they bought clothing and accessories on the internet ($\rho_{internet} = .19, p < .01$) and from the retail stores ($\rho_{retail} = .24, p < .01$). Moreover, the average monthly amount spent at the top five retail ($\rho_{retail} = .14, p < .01$) and top five internet stores ($\rho_{internet} = .19, p < .01$) increased significantly with increases in the compulsive buying index.

Next, consumers were divided into compulsive and non-compulsive buyer categories, using the cutoff value of 25 or greater for the index. Using this cutoff, 49 respondents (or 16 per cent) were classified as compulsive buyers. Using the general linear model and controlling for social desirability bias, compulsive buyers reported buying more frequently per month from both internet and retail stores than non-compulsive buyers ($M_{compulsive/internet} = 3.69, M_{non-compulsive/internet} = 2.31, F_{1,296} = 4.44, p < .05, r = .12; M_{compulsive/retail} = 4.82, M_{non-compulsive/retail} = 1.57, F_{1,296} = 23.68, p < .01, r = .27$). Compulsive buyers also spent more money on their purchases ($M_{compulsive/internet} = \$284, M_{non-compulsive/internet} = \$182, F_{1,292} = 3.94, p < .05, r = .12; M_{compulsive/retail} = \$318, M_{non-compulsive/retail} = \$169, F_{1,296} = 9.08, p < .01, r = .17$). This analysis offers further support for the selected cutoff point.

Validation of the scale with actual spending data

The next step was to validate the new measure of compulsive buying with consumer actual spending data. Actual spending data provide a unique way of validation as they offer a different and objective source of data as compared to consumers' self-reports of buying. Using data collected through two different sources allows us to minimize

potential common-method bias that could occur when collecting data on dependent and independent variables using the same questionnaire. While highly beneficial, this practice is unusual in consumer research, as scale development researchers traditionally rely on a single source of consumer data (e.g., consumer self-reports). We obtained actual customer purchase data for the period 2001–04 from the internet retailer and matched the purchase data with the survey data. Because some of the respondents had purchased only once from the retailer during 2004, we limited our analysis to those respondents who had purchased at least twice from the retailer over the four-year period. The resulting sample size of this matched data set was 177 respondents.

Table 7.4 shows that as compulsive buying tendency increases, so does actual spending: total amount spent at the surveyed Internet retailer ($\rho = .19, p < .01$), total number (i.e., frequency) of purchases ($\rho = .18, p < .01$), total number of purchases over $100 ($\rho = .18, p < .01$), and the highest amount spent on any purchase ($\rho = .17, p < .05$). Thus, we were able to validate the compulsive buying index with actual consumer purchase data. Moreover, examining the correlations between actual purchase data at this retailer and self-reported Internet spending shows that as the self-reported internet spending increases, so does the actual: total spending ($\rho = .24, p < .01$), total number of purchases ($\rho = .24, p < .01$), total number of purchases over $100 ($\rho = .36, p < .01$) and the highest amount on any purchase ($\rho = .12, p < .10$).

Validation of the cutoff point for classifying compulsive buyers

As the final validation step, we sought to verify the appropriateness of the

Table 7.4   Correlations for actual and self-reported purchase data: Internet sample

N = 177	Compulsive buying index	Actual total $ amount	Actual total # of purchases	Actual # of purchases over $100	Actual highest amount	Self-reported internet spending	Self-reported internet frequency	Self-reported retail spending	Self-reported retail frequency
Compulsive buying index	1								
Actual total $ amount	.19***	1							
Actual total # of purchases	.18***	.92***	1						
Actual # of purchases over $100	.18***	.91***	.88***	1					
Actual highest amount of purchase	.17**	.69***	.44***	.59***	1				
Self-reported internet spending	.24***	.24***	.24***	.36***	.12*	1			
Self-reported Internet frequency	.19***	−.01	.03	.05	−.05	.50***	1		
Self-reported retail spending	.20***	.00	.02	.10	−.02	.51***	.29***	1	
Self-reported retail frequency	.27***	−.03	.00	.00	−.09	.27***	.56***	.46***	1

Note: The table shows partial correlations obtained after controlling for social desirability bias.

*** = $p < .01$, ** = $p < .05$, * = $p < .10$

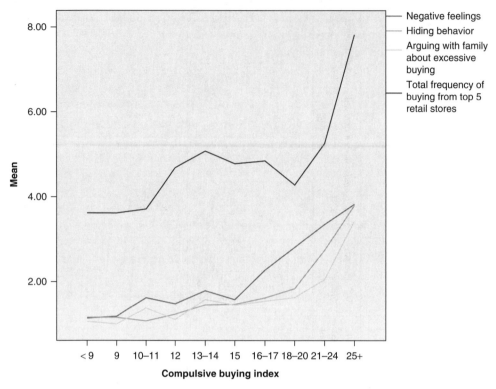

Figure 7.2   Inflection point for compulsive buying index: Internet sample.

compulsive buying index cutoff point used to separate compulsive and non-compulsive buyers. Figure 7.2 shows the relationships of the same variables (negative feelings, hiding behavior, arguing with family about buying, and frequency of buying) with the compulsive buying index for the internet customers' sample. Figure 7.2 demonstrates that the value of these variables again jumps up when the compulsive buying index reaches 25. For some variables, the inflection point occurs even earlier, confirming that the cutoff point of 25 is appropriate.

DISCUSSION AND CONCLUSION

This chapter illustrates the steps followed in conceptualizing, developing, and validating a new measure of compulsive buying. We discussed the steps with regards to a specific consumer phenomenon, compulsive buying; however, the addressed measurement issues are widely applicable to a broad set of consumer-related phenomena. We summarize the key points for measuring consumer-related phenomena below.

Defining the construct

The first step of the measurement process is to develop a construct definition. Before the construct can be defined, potential construct dimensions need to be also identified. This development of the construct definition and its dimensions should be primarily theory-based, but it can also be further informed by empirical insights. Care should be taken that the construct is not defined in terms of its antecedents or consequences. For another example, see the scale measuring consumers' need for uniqueness (Tian et al., 2001).

Item generation

Once the construct is clearly defined, a pool of possible measurement items needs to developed. This development should be based on the construct definition. Researchers are advised to carefully examine previously published research on the topic, as it may provide a rich source of potential items as well as ideas for new items. Modifications of these items may be needed based on the new construct definition and to address any shortcomings of the existing items. Related popular press articles may represent another source of ideas for new items. Key words or phrases related to the construct of interest can be identified, and brainstorming exercises focused on generating statements containing these key phrases can be conducted. For another example of this step in scale development, see Richins and Dawson (1992).

Need for exploratory and confirmatory factor analysis

Once the set of measurement items has been developed, exploratory factor analysis allows for an initial exploration of the construct's dimensionality based on these items, usually using the initial data sample. The items satisfying the pre-set conditions (e.g., no cross-loadings on two factors, etc.), should be next used in a confirmatory analysis model to confirm that these items indeed correspond with the proposed factors as predicted. Confirmatory analysis can be performed on the initial sample, but it also

has to be followed up with an additional sample (or samples).

Validity testing

The outcome of confirmatory factor analysis, i.e., the final set of items, is next subjected to rigorous testing and multiple types of validity analysis to evaluate the psychometric characteristics and establish validity of the measure. External validity is shown by testing the measure on different populations (samples), contexts, and times. Construct validity is shown by establishing the construct's discriminant and convergent validity. Another type of validity that should be evaluated is nomological validity. Eliminating or controlling for presence of any error, such as non-response and response errors (e.g., common method variance, social desirability bias, etc.) further helps establish validity. A valuable and unique approach to validation employed in this research is validation of the measure with actual behavioral (purchase, in this case) data. Another example of careful validity testing of a new measure can be found in Bearden et al. (1989).

Determining cutoff points

Depending on the purpose for which a new measure should be used, the researcher also may need to determine the appropriate form in which to use the scale. The goal in the present research was to develop a measure that could be used both to identify the strength of the consumers' compulsive buying tendency by using the scale in a continuous form and to classify the consumers into compulsive and non-compulsive buyers by using the scale in a bivariate (i.e., yes or no) form. To determine the cutoff point to be used for classification purposes with bivariate measures, multiple factors should be considered, such as the expected functional form of the relationship between the underlying construct and other factors (e.g., looking for an inflection point 'elbow' in the correlations), and the interpretability and the substantive meaningfulness of the value chosen for the cutoff point.

Conclusion

Although this chapter has focused on the development of a scale to measure one type of consumer-related phenomenon, this detailed description of the process can and should be applied to other constructs of consumer behavior. Developing and validating a measurement scale requires careful attention to many methodological details. Moreover, the validation process should go beyond demonstrating construct validity (i.e., discriminant and convergent validity) by also determining the scale's applicability to multiple settings, times, and contexts. Too often, failure to show that the scale's psychometric properties are relatively invariant to the context or the sample of respondents leads to less than satisfactory application of the scale in future research endeavors.

REFERENCES

Aboujaoude, E., Gamel, N. and Koran, L. (2003) 'A 1-year naturalistic follow-up of patients with compulsive shopping disorder', *Journal of Clinical Psychiatry*, 64 (8): 946–50.

American Psychiatric Association (2000) *Diagnostic and Statistical Manual of Mental Disorders*, 4th edition, Washington, DC: APA.

Armstrong, S. J. and Overton, T. S. (1977) 'Estimating non-response bias in mail surveys', *Journal of Marketing Research*, 14 (3): 396–402.

Bagozzi, R. P. and Yi, Y. (1988) 'On the evaluation of structural equation models', *Journal of the Academy of Marketing Science*, 16 (1): 74–97.

Bearden, W. O., Netemeyer, R. G. and Teel, J. E. (1989) 'Measurement of consumer susceptibility to interpersonal influence', *Journal of Consumer Research*, 15 (March): 472–80.

Black, D. (1996) 'Compulsive buying: A review', *Journal of Clinical Psychiatry*, 57 (8): 50–5.

Black, D. (1997) 'Urge to splurge', *The American Journal of Psychiatry*, 154 (11): 1629–30.

Black, D. (2001) 'Compulsive buying disorder: Definition, assessment, epidemiology and clinical management', *CNS Drugs*, 15 (1): 17–27.

Bollen, K. A. (1989) *Structural Equations with Latent Variables*, New York: John Wiley & Sons.

Carver, C. S. (1989) 'How should multifaceted personality factors be tested? Issues illustrated by self-monitoring, attributional style, and hardiness', *Journal of Personality and Social Psychology*, 56 (April): 577–85.

Chaker, A. M. (2003) 'Hello, I'm a shopaholic! There's a move afoot to make compulsive shopping a diagnosable mental disorder, but should it be?' *The Wall Street Journal*, (January 14): F–1.

Christenson, G., Faber, R., de Zwaan, M., Raymond, N., Specker, S., Ekern, M. et al. (1994) 'Compulsive buying: descriptive characteristics and psychiatry comorbidity', *Journal of Clinical Psychiatry*, 55 (1): 5–11.

Crowne, D. P. and Marlowe, D. (1960) 'A new scale of social desirability independent of psychopathology', *Journal of Consulting Psychology*, 24 (4): 349–54.

Dahl, D., Honea, H. and Manchanda, R. (2003) 'The nature of self-reported guilt in consumption contexts', *Marketing Letters*, 14 (3): 159–71.

DeVillis, R. F. (2003) *Scale Development: Theory and Applications, Second Edition*, Thousand Oaks, CA: Sage Publications.

Diamantopoulos, A. and Winklhofer, H. M. (2001) 'Index construction with formative indicators: An alternative to scale development', *Journal of Marketing Research*, 38 (May): 269–77.

Dittmar, H. (2004) 'Understanding and diagnosing compulsive buying', in R. Coombs, (ed.), *Handbook of Addictive Disorders: A Practical Guide to Diagnosis and Treatment*, New York: Wiley. pp. 411–50.

Dittmar, H. and Drury, J. (2000) 'Self-image – is it in the bag? A qualitative comparison between "ordinary" and "excessive" consumers', *Journal of Economic Psychology*, 21 (2): 109–42.

Edwards, E. A. (1993) 'Development of a new scale for measuring compulsive buying behavior', *Financial Counseling and Planning*, 4 (1): 67–84.

Faber, R. J. and O'Guinn, T. C. (1992) 'A clinical screener for compulsive buying', *Journal of Consumer Research*, 19 (December): 459–69.

Faber, R. J., O'Guinn, T. C. and Krych, R. (1987) 'Compulsive consumption,' in M. Wallendorf and P. Anderson, (eds), *Advances in Consumer Research*. Vol. 14, Provo, UT: Association for Consumer Research. pp. 132–35.

Fowler, F. J. Jr. (2002) *Survey Research Methods, Third Edition*, Thousand Oaks, CA: Sage Publications.

Grant, J. E. (2006) 'Understanding and treating kleptomania: New models and new treatments', *Israel Journal of Psychiatry and Related Sciences*, 43 (2): 81–87.

Hair, J. F., Anderson, R. E., Tatham, R. L. and Black, W. C. (1998) *Multivariate Data Analysis, Fifth Edition*, Upper Saddle River, NJ: Prentice Hall.

Hassay, D. N. and Smith, M. C. (1996) 'Compulsive buying: An examination of the consumption motive', *Psychology and Marketing*, 13 (December): 741–52.

Hirschman, E. (1992) 'The consciousness of addiction: Toward a general theory of compulsive consumption', *Journal of Consumer Research*, 19 (September): 155–72.

Hodgson, R. J. and Rachman, S. (1977) 'Obsessional-compulsive complaints', *Behaviour Research and Therapy*, 15 (5): 389–95.

Hollander, E. and Allen, A. (2006) 'Is compulsive buying a real disorder, and is it really compulsive', *American Journal of Psychiatry*, 163 (10): 1670–72.

Hollander, E. and Dell'Osso, B. (2005) 'New developments in an evolving field', *Psychiatric Times*, 22 (8): 17.

Jarvis, C. B., MacKenzie, S. B. and Podsakoff, P. M. (2003) 'A critical review of construct indicators and measurement model misspecification in marketing and consumer behavior research', *Journal of Consumer Research*, 30 (2): 199–218.

Koran, L., Faber, R. J., Aboujaoude, E., Large, M. D. and Serpe, R. T. (2006) 'Estimated prevalence of compulsive buying behavior in the United States', *American Journal of Psychiatry*, 163 (1): 1806–12.

Lejoyeux, M., Tassain, V., Solomon, J. and Ades, J. (1997) 'Study of compulsive buying in depressed patients', *Journal of Clinical Psychiatry*, 58 (4): 169–73.

Malhotra, N. K., Ashutosh P. and Kim, S. S. (2007) 'Bias breakdown', *Marketing Research*, 19 (1): 24–29.

Mangione, T. W. (1997) 'Mail surveys', in L. Bickman and D. J. Rog, (eds), *Handbook of Applied Social Research Methods*, Thousand Oaks, CA: Sage Publications. pp. 399–428.

Mangione, T. W. (2004) *Mail Surveys: Improving the Quality*, Thousand Oaks, CA: Sage Publications.

Manolis, C. and Roberts, J. A. (2008) 'Compulsive buying: Does it matter how it is measured?' *Journal of Economic Psychology*, 29 (August): 555–76.

McElroy, S. (1994) 'Compulsive buying: A report of 20 cases', *The Journal of the American Medical Association*, 272 (11): 835.

McElroy, S., Phillips, K. and Keck, P. (1994) 'Obsessive compulsive spectrum disorder', *Journal of Clinical Psychiatry*, 55 (10): 33–53.

Mellan, O. and Christie, S. (1997) *Overcoming Overspending: A Winning Plan for Spenders and Their Partners*, New York: Walker and Company.

Monahan, P., Black, D. W. and Gabel, J. (1996) 'Reliability and validity of a scale to measure change in persons with compulsive buying', *Psychiatry Research*, 64 (1): 59–67.

Muller, A. and de Zwaan, M. (2004) 'Current status of psychotherapy research on pathological buying', *Verhaltenstherapie*, 14 (2): 112–19.

Ninan, P. T., McElroy, S., Kane, C., Knight, B., Casuto, L., Rose, S. et al. (2000) 'Placebo-controlled study of fluvoxamine in the treatment of patients with compulsive buying', *Journal of Clinical Psychopharmacology*, 30 (3): 362–66.

O'Guinn, T. C. and Faber, R. J. (1989) 'Compulsive buying: A phenomenological exploration', *Journal of Consumer Research*, 16 (September): 147–57.

Podsakoff, P. M., MacKenzie, S. A., Lee, J. Y. and Podsakoff, N. P. (2003) 'Common method biases in behavioral research: A critical review of the literature and recommended remedies', *Journal of Applied Psychology*, 88 (5): 879–903.

Pirog, S. F. and Roberts, J. A. (2007) 'Personality and credit card misuse among college students: The mediating role of impulsiveness', *The Journal of Marketing Theory and Practice*, 15 (1): 65–77.

Richins, M. L. and Dawson, S. (1992) 'A consumer values orientation for materialism and its measurement: Scale development and validation', *Journal of Consumer Research*, 19 (December): 303–16.

Ridgway, N. M., Kukar-Kinney, M. and Monroe, K. B. (2008) 'An expanded conceptualization and a new measure of compulsive buying', *Journal of Consumer Research*, 35 (December): 622–39.

Rosenberg, M. (1965) *Society and the Adolescent Self-Image*, Princeton, NJ: Princeton University Press.

Scherhorn, G., Reisch, L. A. and Raab, G. (1990) 'Addictive buying in West Germany: An empirical study', *Journal of Consumer Policy*, 13 (December): 699–705.

Tian, K. T., Bearden, W. O. and Hunter, G. L. (2001) 'Consumers' need for uniqueness: Scale development and validation', *Journal of Consumer Research*, 28 (June): 50–66.

Valence, G., d'Astous, A. and Fortier, L. (1988) 'Compulsive buying: Concept and measurement', *Journal of Consumer Policy*, 11 (4): 419–33.

Viswanathan, M. (2005) *Measurement Error and Research Design*, Thousand Oaks, CA: Sage Publications.

www.stoppingovershopping, website of A. L. Benson to aid compulsive buyers.

The Context of Measurement

8

Linguistic Factors in the Assessment of English Language Learners

Jamal Abedi

INTRODUCTION

Assessment plays a consequential role in the academic life of English language learners (ELLs). It affects their classification, curriculum planning, instruction, promotion, and graduation. Therefore, it is imperative that we carefully examine the content and psychometric properties of these assessments for ELL students. Unnecessary linguistic complexity in content-based test items may be a source of *construct-irrelevant variance* and may threaten the validity of assessment for ELL students. Research suggests that ELL students may not possess language capabilities sufficient enough to demonstrate their content knowledge (such as math and science) in English. Therefore, assessments that are developed for native speakers of English may not produce valid outcomes for ELL students.

To provide fair and valid assessment for all students, and for ELL students in particular, the effect of language unrelated to content-based assessments must be considered and controlled.

This chapter explicates the impact of language factors on the assessment of ELL students. Common linguistic features, which induce unnecessary language barriers, are described and modifications for mitigating their negative impact on the performance of ELL students are recommended.

THE ROLE OF ASSESSMENT IN ELL STUDENTS' ACADEMIC CAREERS

Providing reliable and valid assessments is of the utmost importance for English language learner (ELL) students. These students are assessed in two different yet quite related areas: (1) their level of English proficiency, and (2) their level of content knowledge in areas such as math, science, and social sciences as well as English language arts. Assessments in both of these areas wield great influence on their academic careers, as the results of these tests may impact curriculum planning, placement, instruction, and eventually even graduation. ELL students who are inaccurately assessed may be misclassified with respect to their level of English proficiency and, as a result, may receive inappropriate instruction. They may even be misclassified as students with learning disabilities, which may greatly impact their academic career (see, for example, Abedi, 2006a; Artiles et al., 2005). Therefore, assessment outcomes based on questionable measures may cause detrimental academic consequences for these students.

THE IMPACT OF LANGUAGE FACTORS ON THE ASSESSMENT OF ELL STUDENTS

Research findings clearly show a major performance gap between ELL and non-ELL students in all content areas – particularly those areas with high language demands. Such a performance gap decreases substantially as language demand of the assessment decreases (see, for example, Abedi, 2006b, Solano-Flores and Trumbull, 2003). For example, studies indicate that ELL students perform far below their native English speaking peers in reading as there is a high level of language demand, but the performance gap decreases (or even disappears) in math computation where the level of language demand is minimal (Abedi, 2006b; Abedi, 2002). Therefore, it is clear that the performance gap between

ELL and non-ELL students in content-based assessments is due – at least in part – to the complex linguistic structure of the assessment. The complex linguistic structure in content-based assessments that may lead to a performance gap may be unnecessary and quite unrelated to the construct being measured.

Abedi et al. (1997) demonstrated that item length as a major factor in measurement could impact performance of ELL students. They found that the longer the test items (stem and/or distractors, in the case of multiple-choice items) the more difficulty ELL students have with the items. To illustrate the impact of item length, we use the language of a released test item from the study (Abedi et al., 1997).

Point O is the center of the circle above. Line segment AC is a diameter of the circle. Line segment BC does not pass through the center of the circle. Which of the following is true?

A. AC is longer than BC.
B. BC is longer than AC.
C. AC and BC are the same length.
D. BC is twice as long as OA.
E. The lengths of AC and BC change, depending on how this piece of paper is turned.

In this example, the correct response is option A. The three remaining options serve as distractors in this item. As it can be seen in this example, distractor E is longer than the other three distractors. Based on research findings summarized above, ELL students may have difficulty with this distractor and as a result they may select it less than the other three distractors. However, the classical test theory assumes that all distractors perform similarly and receive about a third of incorrect responses (in case of a four-choice item). The classical test theory, therefore, introduces its correction for a guessing formula based on the assumption that: (1) the incorrect responses are distributed equally across the possible distractors, and (2) this pattern of response is the same across different subgroups of students taking the test – which may not be true for ELL students (see, Abedi et al., 2008). Minimizing linguistic complexity improves the validity of these assessments as long as the content of the assessments is not altered.

Research shows that the assessment outcomes for ELL students, particularly those at the lower end of the English proficiency spectrum, suffer from lower reliability and validity (Abedi et al., 2003a). According to Allen and Yen (1979), a test is reliable if it produces consistent measurements; it is valid if it measures the construct that it is designed to assess. Unnecessary linguistic complexity as a source of construct-irrelevant variance may seriously undermine the validity of assessment for ELL students and as a source of measurement error it may impact the reliability of assessments for ELL students. The impact of language factors on the psychometric characteristics of assessments is elaborated below and features of linguistic complexity that may affect ELL students' understanding of test items are discussed along with recommendations for ameliorating linguistic bias in assessment items.

LANGUAGE AS A SOURCE OF MEASUREMENT ERROR IN ASSESSMENTS

'Reliability refers to the consistency of measurement; that is, how consistent test scores or other assessment results are from one measurement to another' (Linn and Gronlund, 1995: 81). Reliability is directly impacted by measurement error. There are many sources of measurement error that would affect reliability of test scores such as problems in test format, unclear test instructions and problems with test administration and scoring. These sources of measurement error directly or indirectly affect the validity of assessment as well, since reliability puts a limit on the validity of assessment (see, Allen and Yen, 1979; Thorndike, 2005: 191, 192). Unnecessary linguistic complexity of assessment is a major source of measurement error which systematically affects the reliability of assessments for ELL students.

To see the impact of linguistic complexity on the assessment of ELLs, one must compare the reliability of assessments for items that are linguistically complex with the less linguistically complex items. Unfortunately, techniques for estimating reliability under classical test theory may not provide accurate information since these techniques may not be quite sensitive to the impact of linguistic complexity as an additional source of measurement error because this theory assumes all the sources of measurement error are random effects and does not account for any systematic sources of error (such as a linguistic complexity).

Language factors may differentially impact performance of subgroups of students such as ELLs. Therefore, the internal consistency approach may not provide accurate measures of reliability of test items when those items are linguistically complex. The main limitation of the internal consistency approach in classical test theory is the assumption of uni-dimensionality. That is, the internal consistency approach can only be applied to assessments that measure a single concept or construct (see, for example, Abedi, 1996; Cortina, 1993). However, unnecessary linguistic complexity may introduce another dimension into the assessment, making the assessment multi-dimensional. To illustrate this point, item-level data from a standardized achievement test (Stanford 9) were analyzed at different grade levels (Abedi et al., 2003b).

Internal consistency coefficients (Cronbach's alpha) of the Stanford 9 test data were compared across ELL categories (ELL versus non-ELL) (Cronbach et al., 1972). The results of data analyses indicated that the gap in the reliability and validity coefficients among these two groups decreased as the level of language demand of the assessment was reduced. The reliability coefficients (alpha) for non-ELL students ranged from .805 for science and social science to .898 for math. Among ELL students, however, alpha coefficients differed considerably across the content areas (see Table 8.1). In math, where language factors might not have as great an influence on performance, the alpha coefficient for ELL (.802) was only slightly lower than the alpha for non-ELL students (.898). However, in English

language arts, science, and social science, the gap on alpha between non-ELL and ELL students was large. Averaging across English language arts, science, and social science results, the alpha for non-ELL was .808 as compared to an average alpha of .603 for ELL students. Thus, as elaborated earlier, language factors introduce a source of measurement error negatively affecting ELL students' test outcomes, while their impact on students who are native or fluent speakers of English is limited. As the level of linguistic complexity in science and social science tests decreased, the gap in the reliability coefficient was substantially reduced (for a more detailed description, see Abedi, 2006b; Abedi et al., 2003b).

LANGUAGE AS A SOURCE OF CONSTRUCT-IRRELEVANT VARIANCE

Language factors that introduce sources of construct-irrelevant variance (Messick, 1994) may also threaten the validity of the test. The *Standards for Educational and Psychological Testing* (American Educational Research Association [AERA], American Psychological

Table 8.1 Site 2 Stanford 9 sub-scale reliabilities (alpha), Grade 9

Sub-scale (items)	Non-ELL	LEP	Difference in alpha
Reading, $N =$	181,202	52,720	
Vocabulary (30)	.835	.666	0.169
Reading comp (54)	.916	.833	0.083
Average reliability	.876	.750	0.126
Math, $N =$	183,262	54,815	
Total (48)	.898	.802	0.096
Language, $N =$	180,743	52,863	
Mechanics (24)	.803	.686	0.117
Expression (24)	.812	.680	0.132
Average reliability	.813	.683	0.130
Science, $N =$	144,821	40,255	
Total (40)	.805	.597	0.208
Social Science, $N =$	181,078	53,925	
Total (40)	.805	.530	0.275

Association [APA], and National Council on Measurement in Education [NCME], 1999) caution:

> Test use with individuals who have not sufficiently acquired the language of the test may introduce construct irrelevant components to the testing process. In such instances, test results may not reflect accurately the qualities and competencies intended to be measured. [Therefore] special attention to issues related to language and culture may be needed when developing, administering, scoring, and interpreting test scores and making decisions based on test scores (p. 91).
>
> Complex language in the content-based assessment for non-native speakers of English reduces the validity of inferences drawn about students' content-based knowledge. (Sandoval and Durán, 1998; Messick, 1994)
>
> With respect to the distortion of task performance, some aspects of the task may require skills or other attributes having nothing to do with the focal constructs in question, so that limitations in performing construct-irrelevant skills might prevent some students from demonstrating the focal competencies. (Messick, 1994: 14)

To examine the possible differences in the validity of standardized achievement tests between non-ELL and ELL students, a multiple-group, confirmatory factor analysis model was used in a study by Abedi et al. (2003a). Test items were grouped in a smaller subset of items called *item parcels*. These item parcels were then used as measured variables in a factor analysis model where common variance (degree of association) between these parcels were identified and were labeled as *latent variable*. The results of the analyses indicated that the correlations of item parcels with the latent factors were consistently lower for ELL students than they were for non-ELL students. This finding was true for all parcels regardless of which grade or which sample of the population was tested. For example, among 9th grade ELL students, the correlation

for the four reading parcels ranged from .719 to .779, across the two samples. In comparison, among non-ELL students, the correlations for the four reading parcels were slightly higher, ranging from .832 to .858, across the two samples. The item parcel correlations were also larger for non-ELL students than for ELL students in math and science. Again these results were consistent across the different samples (See Abedi et al., 2003a, for a detailed description of the study; see also Kane, 2006, for a discussion of criterion-related validity).

The correlations between the latent factors (math and science contents) were also larger for non-ELL students than they were for ELL students. This gap in latent factor correlations between non-ELL and ELL students was especially large in test items with higher language-demands. For example, for grade nine, the correlation between latent factors for math and reading for non-ELL students was .782 compared to just .645 for ELL students. When comparing the latent factor correlations between reading and science from the same population, the correlation was still larger for non-ELL students (.837) than for ELL students (.806), but the gap between the correlations was smaller. This was likely due to language-demand differences. Multiple group structural models were run to test whether the differences between non-ELL and ELL students mentioned above were significant. There were significant differences for all constraints tested at the .05 nominal level.

The data presented above clearly suggest that ELL students perform far behind their non-ELL peers. Studies have shown that the distortion caused by construct irrelevant or 'nuisance' variables, such as linguistic biases, may mainly be responsible for such performance gaps (Abedi, 2006b).

AVOIDING UNNECESSARY LINGUISTIC COMPLEXITY IN THE ASSESSMENT OF ELL STUDENTS

In order to accurately demonstrate their knowledge within content areas, students must comprehend what the items are asking and understand the response choices. Unfamiliar vocabulary and complex text structures increase language demands making comprehension difficult, particularly for ELL students. While standardized achievement tests attempt to measure students' knowledge of specific content areas, an analyses of mathematics and science subsections of the Test of Achievement and Proficiency (TAP) conducted by Imbens-Bailey and Castellon-Wellington (1999), revealed that two-thirds of the items include vocabulary that was uncommon or used in an atypical manner. They also found that one-third of the items included syntactic structures that are evaluated as complex or unusual in their construction (Imbens-Bailey and Castellon-Wellington, 1999).

It must be emphasized at this point that linguistic complexity in general, not only vocabulary and grammar, impacts performance of ELL students. For example, Abedi and colleagues (1997) presented 48 linguistic features that affected performance of ELL students in content-based assessments such as math and science. They grouped these 48 linguistic features into 14 categories and showed that all of these features influenced ELL performance. Similarly, Abedi and Lord (2001), Abedi et al. (2000), Abedi (2006a), Kiplinger et al. (2000), and Maihoff (2002) reached the same conclusion that many linguistic features negatively impact ELL performance.

Although it has been indicated that cultural background may have a substantial impact on performance, linguistic complexity of assessments affects students' performance regardless of cultural background. Several randomized field trial studies on the impact of linguistic factors on the assessment of ELL students included different groups of students with different linguistic and cultural backgrounds and found that, regardless of cultural and linguistic differences, the linguistic complexity of assessment impacted the performance of all non-native English speakers at relatively the same rate (see, for example, Abedi et al., 2003a; Celce-Murcia et al., 1995).

To minimize the impact of language factors on ELL students' performance outcomes, one may reduce the level of unnecessary (non-essential) linguistic complexity of the assessment – that is, complexity unrelated to the construct being assessed – and then examine the impact of such reduction of linguistic complexity on student performance. If the hypothesis that reducing linguistic complexity on assessment provides clearer interpretations of student performance is supported, then improvements on the outcome of assessments can be observed by using less linguistically complex test items. This process is referred to as *linguistic modification*.

The concept of linguistic modification applies to areas in which content other than language is being assessed (e.g., math, science, and social sciences) since the language construct may be unrelated to the purpose of assessment. However, the judgment of whether language is related or unrelated to the target of assessment is arguable. Some researchers determine whether language is related or unrelated based on the judgment of content experts. For example, Abedi et al. (1997) presented both the original and the linguistically modified version of the math test used in their study to two math, content experts independently. The math-content experts were asked to compare the original test item with its modified version and make a judgment as whether or not the content was altered in the process of linguistic modification. They both provided some minor suggestions but generally agreed that the math content in the items had not been altered.

There is a difference between language that is an essential part of the content of the question and language that makes the question incomprehensible to many students, particularly to ELLs. While it is important to understand and value the richness of language in an assessment system; it is also important to make sure that students with limited English proficiency and other students with similar language needs not be penalized for their lack of English proficiency in areas where the target of assessment is *not* language. Though we understand the views of some language modification critics in not 'dumbing down' assessment questions by simplifying the language, we also recognize the distinction between necessary and unnecessary linguistic complexity. Content assessment specialists should make these distinctions when creating test items.

SOURCES OF LINGUISTIC COMPLEXITY AFFECTING COMPREHENSION

Research has identified several linguistic features that appear to contribute to the difficulty of comprehending text (Abedi et al., 1997; Abedi, 2006b, 2007; Shaftel et al., 2006). These features may slow the reader down, increase the likelihood of misinterpretation, or add to the reader's cognitive load thus interfering with concurrent tasks. Indexes of language difficulty include unfamiliar (or less commonly used) vocabulary, complex grammatical structures, and styles of discourse that include extra material,

abstractions, and passive voice (Abedi et al., 1997). In order to better understand the need for linguistic modification, some of these linguistic features are discussed in detail below. The following examples are used for illustration purposes and not from released test items.

Vocabulary

Unfamiliar words/idioms
Some words, word pairs, or groups of words unfamiliar to ELLs might be used in a test item. They are unnecessary if they are not essential to the concept being tested. Idioms are words, phrases, or sentences that cannot be understood literally. Many proverbs, slang phrases, phrasal verbs, and common sayings cannot be decoded by ELLs because they are not literal. See the following:

Circle the **clumps** of eggs in the illustration.
In the last **census**, 80% of the households had one or more wage-earners.
In the story, **who is in charge** when the parents are gone?
James bought a used car from his uncle for $5,000, but he **put nothing down**. If his loan is for 24 months, how much will his payments be?

False cognates
False cognates are words which are similar in form or sound in two different languages, but have two completely different meanings.

In the story, how does Mack **dote** on his wife? (*la dote* in Spanish means dowry)
Examine the **pie** chart below to answer questions 4-8. (*pie* in Spanish means foot)

Grammar/syntax

Long phrases in questions
Complex question types might have an opening phrase or clause that either replaces or postpones the question word.

At which of the following times should Ed feed the parking meter?
Of the following bar graphs, which represents the data?

Complex sentences

A complex sentence contains a main clause and one or more subordinating (dependent) clauses. Subordinating (dependent) words include *because, when, after, although, if,* and *since*. (More on *if* under Conditional Clauses.)

Because she wants to stay in touch, Peggy frequently writes and phones her sister.
Brad is an excellent basketball player **although he is only 5′ 6″ tall**.

Compound sentences

A compound sentence consists of two or more clauses of equal importance. A coordinating conjunction (*and, or, but, so, for, yet, nor*) often connects the two clauses. Sometimes a conjunctive adverb (*however, therefore, moreover, nevertheless, as a result, accordingly*) combines the two ideas or begins a new sentence.

Jordan said that he ate more pizza than Ella, **but** she said they both ate the same amount.
We were hungry; **however**, there was no time to heat up the pizza.

Logical connectors: conditional/adverbial clauses

Logical connectors are adverbial expressions which allow a listener/reader to infer connections between two structures. They mainly include dependent words (subordinating conjunctions – see above).

Adverbial clauses:

When the barber was finished with the haircut, he took the customer's money.
Mother cooked dinner **while the children played outside**.

Conditional clauses:

As long as you bring your own bedding, you can stay with us.
Given that *a* is a positive number, what is −*a*?

Unfamiliar tenses

Unfamiliar tenses include perfect tenses and modal auxiliaries; they are among the most difficult structures ELLs must interpret (Adams, 1990).

Perfect tenses use a helping verb and a past participle: *had gone, will have gone*:

She **had been waiting** three hours when he arrived. (Past perfect progressive)

Modals are used to interject perspective or more subjectivity, which introduces potentiality versus the concreteness of present tense of the simple past tense:

What length other than the original estimate **could have been** the actual length of this dinosaur?

Perfect tense plus modal:

If Shirley **had won** three more marbles, **could** she **have beaten** Rodney in the game?

Long noun phrases

Nouns sometimes work together to form one concept, such as a *pie chart* or *bar graph*. Sometimes adjectives and nouns work together to create meaning: *high school diploma, income tax return*. To further complicate interpretation, strings of adjectives and nouns create subjects and objects: *freshwater pond, long-term investment, new word processing program*.

Of the **following number pairs**, which is the dimension of a **100-square-foot room**?

To become **next year's tennis team captain**, how many votes will Sandra need?

Relative clauses

A relative clause is an embedded clause which provides additional information about the subject or object it follows. Words which lead a relative clause include *that*, *who*, and *which*. Often *that* is omitted from a relative clause. When possible, relative clauses should be removed or recast.

A bag **that contains 25 marbles**. *versus* One bag has 25 marbles.
The algebra teacher, **who is new this year**, is very strict. *versus* The new algebra teacher is very strict.

Prepositional phrases

Prepositional phrases work as adjectives or adverbs to modify nouns, pronouns, verbs, adverbs, or adjectives. When they occur before question words, between the subject and the verb, or in strings, they can be especially confusing to English language learners.

Which of the following is the best approximation **of the area of the shaded rectangle in the figure above** if the shaded square represents one unit of area?
Before the beginning of the race in the park, the runners warmed up by stretching.

Comparative construction

Comparisons are made using *greater than*, *less than*, *n times as much as*, *as ... as* – as well as by using certain verbs. Even though structures such these are useful and widespread in mathematical discourse, studies have shown that comparative structures are difficult for students to comprehend.

Jesse saw **more** mountains **than** he'd ever seen.
Who has **more** marbles **than** Carlos? Who has the most?

Style of discourse

Long problem statements/unnecessary expository material

When the problem context set-up is long, ELL students do not perform as well. Limit the story line to the essentials; however, don't reduce math items to bare computation.

Abstract (versus concrete) presentation of problem

Respondents show better performance when test items are presented in concrete rather than abstract terms. Information presented in narrative structures tends to be understood and remembered better than information presented in expository text.

The **weights** of two objects **were measured**. *versus* The clerk **weighed** two suitcases.

Passive voice

In active voice, the subject is the one performing an action. In passive voice, the one receiving the action is in the subject position. Often the 'actor' is not stated.

He **was given** a ticket. *versus* The officer **gave him** a ticket.

Complex arrangement of parts of speech

At times the traditional subject-verb-object word order of English may be altered for expressing focus and emphasis. Passive voice is only one example.

John I **can understand**; the others just confuse me. (*object*-subject-**verb**)
Ambitious she **must have been**, or she wouldn't have come. (*adj*-subject-**verb**)

Negation

Several types of negative forms are confusing to English language learners.

Not all the workers at the factory are male versus
     Both males and females work at the factory.
All the workers at the factory are not male versus
     Both males and females work at the factory.

LINGUISTIC MODIFICATIONS TO REDUCE LANGUAGE DEMANDS

The process of identifying the potentially problematic linguistic features in test items must be based on the judgment of content and linguistic experts and the actual characteristics of test items. The process can also be informed by research literature (see, for example, Abedi, 2006a; Abedi et al., 1997) and knowledge of the type of linguistic features likely to cause problems for ELLs. Finally, the linguistic features that were introduced above can guide the process of linguistic modification.

To illustrate the process of identifying the potentially problematic linguistic features in assessment, a summary of linguistic modification implemented in a previously mentioned study (Abedi et al., 1997) will be presented. A test with 69 NAEP math items for 8th grade students were used to demonstrate the linguistic modification approach. Each of the 69 items was read and the mathematical operations attempted. Items in which the language was considered potentially difficult for students to understand were flagged and analyzed; linguistic features likely to contribute to the difficulty were identified and categorized. Simplified forms of linguistically complex items were drafted in order to make these items easier for students to understand. From this set of features, only the most salient and frequent language problems were selected for investigation in the field study.

Changes were made to the language of the original NAEP items in the following categories: (1) familiarity/frequency of non-math vocabulary, (2) voice of the verb phrase, (3) length of nominals (noun phrases), (4) conditional clauses, (5) relative clauses, (6) question phrases, and abstract or impersonal presentations. Changes in each of these areas that were done in the study are described and illustrated below (for a more detailed description of these changes, see Abedi et al., 1997; Abedi and Lord, 2001).

Familiarity/frequency of non-math vocabulary

Potentially unfamiliar, low-frequency lexical items were replaced with more familiar, higher frequency lexical items.

Original: *A certain reference file contains approximately six billion facts.*
Revision: *Mack's company sold six billion pencils.*

The concepts of 'company' and 'pencils' are more familiar to ELL students, and are encountered more frequently, than 'certain reference file.' If a student does not understand all the words in a test item, they may not understand what the question is asking and may be unable to respond to it. A task places greater demands on a student if his attention is divided between employing math problem-solving strategies and coping with difficult vocabulary and unfamiliar content (Gathercole and Baddeley, 1993).

In revising the items, estimates of familiarity/frequency of vocabulary were made based on established word frequency sources as well as judgment from linguistic experts of the students' familiarity with the words and concepts. For example, *The American Heritage Word Frequency Book* (Carroll et al., 1971), based upon 5 million words from textbooks and library materials for Grades 3–9, and the *Frequency Analysis of English Usage: Lexicon and*

Grammar (Francis and Kucera, 1982), based on the 1 million-word Brown University Corpus, listed the word 'company' as occurring more frequently than 'reference' or 'file.'

Voice of verb phrase

Verbs in the passive voice were replaced with verbs in the active voice.

Original: *A sample of 25 was selected.*
Revision: *He selected a sample of 25.*

Passive constructions occur less frequently than active constructions in English (Biber, 1988; Celce-Murcia and Larsen-Freeman, 1983). Children learning English as a second language have more difficulty understanding passive verb forms than active verb forms (Bever, 1970, deVilliers and deVilliers, 1973).

Length of nominals

In processing longer and novel nominal compounds, people use lexical information as well as knowledge of the world and the context to rule out implausible readings. A student with a limited English vocabulary may encounter difficulty with the long nominals.

The number of pre-nominal modifiers in a noun phrase was reduced, as in the example below:

Original: *last year's class vice president*
Revision: *vice president*

Postmodifiers can be similarly ambiguous. Adding more modifiers multiplies the possibilities for ambiguity.

In a noun phrase followed by two prepositional phrase modifiers, such as: '*the man in the car from Mexico*,' (the man may be from Mexico, or the car may be from Mexico).

Conditional clauses

Some conditional *if* clauses were replaced with separate sentences. In some instances the order of the *if* clause and the main clause was reversed.

Original: *If two batteries in the sample were found to be dead.*
Revision: *He found three broken pencils in the box.*

In this item, in addition to removing the conditional clause, unfamiliar vocabulary (dead batteries) was replaced with familiar vocabulary (broken pencils).

Separate sentences, rather than subordinate *if* clauses, may be easier for some students to understand (Spanos et al., 1988). Some languages do not allow sentences with the conditional clause in last position (Haiman, 1985). Consequently, sentences with the conditional clause last may cause difficulty for some non-native speakers (such as 'I won't go *if it is raining*').

Relative clauses

While sometimes the number of sentences in the revised item is increased, the number of clauses per sentence is reduced. Shorter sentences with lower information density levels are more easily processed by students. Some relative clauses are removed or recast.

Original: *Reports, each containing 64 sheets of paper, are required.*
Revised: *He needs 64 sheets of paper for each report.*

In this example, the original version contains information in a relative clause, whereas the revised item contains the same information in a simple sentence.

Complex question phrases

Some question structures were changed from complex question phrases to simple question words.

Original: *At which of the following times …?*
Revision: *When …?*

In the first example, the complex question phrase in the original version was replaced with a single question word in the revision. The single-word structure is simpler syntactically, and the placement of the question word at the beginning of the sentence gives it greater salience. The longer question phrases occur with lower frequency, and low-frequency expressions will in general be harder to read and understand (Adams, 1990).

Concrete versus abstract or impersonal presentations

In some instances, an abstract presentation mode was made more concrete.

Original: *The weights of three objects were compared using a pan balance. Two comparisons were made …*
Revision: *Sandra weighed three objects using a pan balance. She made two comparisons …*

In this example, the problem statement was made more story-like by the introduction of 'Sandra.' Abstract or non-situated items may employ the passive voice, but not all passive constructions are abstract or non-situated; abstract/impersonal presentations may also employ modals or generic nominals, for example. A problem expressed in concrete terms may be easier for students to understand than an abstract problem statement (see, for instance, Lemke, 1986).

SUMMARY OF LINGUISTIC MODIFICATION RESEARCH

By reducing the impact of language barriers on content-based assessments, the validity and reliability of the assessment can be improved, resulting in fairer assessments for all students (see Abedi and Lord, 2001; Abedi et al., 2000; Kiplinger et al., 2000; Maihoff, 2002; Hansen and Mislevy, 2004). When math test items were modified to reduce the level of linguistic complexity over 80 per cent of middle-school students who were interviewed (including native speakers of English) preferred the linguistically modified over the original English version of the test items (see Abedi et al., 1997). They indicated that those linguistically modified items are 'more clear' and they 'get to the point'. Research also shows that minor changes in the wording of content-related test items can raise student performance (Abedi and Lord, 2001; Abedi et al., 2000; Abedi et al., 1997; Cummins et al., 1988; De Corte et al., 1985; Durán, 1999; Hudson, 1983; Riley et al., 1983). For example, rewording a verbal problem can make semantic relations more explicit, without affecting the underlying semantic and content structure; thus, the reader is more likely to construct a proper problem representation and to solve the problem correctly.

Findings from the analyses of many national and state studies clearly show the impact of language on the assessment outcomes for ELL students. For example, the results of analyses of NAEP extant data (Abedi et al., 1997) suggested that ELL students had difficulty with the test items that were longer and were linguistically complex. The study also found that ELL students exhibited a substantially higher number of omitted/not-reached test items, since it took them a much longer time to read and understand assessment questions.

Based on the findings of these studies, the concept of linguistic modification approach was introduced. In one study, researchers identified 48 linguistic features that may affect ELL students' performance and grouped them into 14 general categories (Abedi et al., 1997). The impact of these linguistic features on the performance of ELL students in content-based areas (math and science) was then examined.

The effects of some of these linguistic features on a sample of 1,031 8th grade students in Southern California were examined (Abedi and Lord, 2001). In this study, the math items for Grade 8 students were modified to reduce the complexity of sentence structures (see guidelines for conducting 'Linguistic Modifications to Reduce Language Demands' section in Appendix 8.1) and to replace potentially unfamiliar vocabulary with more familiar words without changing the content-related terminologies (i.e., mathematical terms were not changed). The results showed significant improvement in the scores of ELL students and also non-ELLs in low- and average-level mathematics classes, but changes did not affect scores of higher performing non-ELL students. Among the linguistic features that appeared to contribute most to the differences between ELL and non-ELL were low-frequency vocabulary and passive voice verb constructions. These features increased the linguistic complexity of the text and made the assessment more linguistically challenging for ELL students.

Note: this study occurred before the one previously described therefore, it may not be accurate to state that the 1998 study cross-validated it. Perhaps stating the reverse would work. The outcome of the above study cross-validated an earlier study in which Abedi et al. (1998) examined the impact of linguistic modification on the mathematics performance of English learners and non-English learners on a sample of 1,394 8th graders in schools with a high enrolment of Spanish speakers. Results confirmed findings of the earlier studies and showed that modification of the language in the test items contributed to improved performance on 49 per cent of the items; the ELL students generally scored higher on shorter, less linguistically complex problem statements. The results of this study also suggested that lower performing native speakers of English also benefited from the linguistic modification of assessment. As indicated earlier, math-content experts compared the original and the linguistically modified test items and indicated that the math content was not altered by the process of linguistic modification of items (Abedi et al., 1997).

Other studies were conducted to obtain cross-validation evidence on the contribution of the linguistic modification approach, as compared to other accommodations, in improving the validity of assessments for ELL students. A study (Abedi et al., 2000) on a sample of 946 eighth graders found that among four different accommodation strategies for ELL students (such as extended time, use of an English dictionary and a glossary of linguistically complex terms unrelated to the math content), only the linguistically modified English form narrowed the score gap between English learners and other students.

The effectiveness of the language modification approach in reducing the performance gap between ELL and non-ELL students was the focus of another study (Abedi et al., 2003). This study examined 1,594 eighth-grade students using items from the National Assessment of Educational Progress (NAEP) and the Third International Math and Science Study (TIMSS). Students were given a customized English dictionary (words were selected directly from test items), a bilingual glossary, a linguistically modified test version, or the standard test items. Only the linguistically modified version improved the ELL students' scores without affecting the non-ELL students' scores.

The results of the studies presented above are consistent with the findings of others suggesting that linguistic modification of assessment items provides a more valid and effective alternative to the conventional testing approach. Maihoff (2002) found linguistic modification of content-based test items to be a valid and effective accommodation for ELL students. Moreover, in response to critics concerned about reducing the quality of assessment, a study by Kiplinger and colleagues (2000) found linguistic modification of math items helped improve the performance of ELL students in math without affecting the performance of non-ELL students. Rivera and Stansfield (2001) compared ELL performance on regular and linguistically modified fourth and sixth grade science items. Although the small sample size in the Rivera and Stansfield study did not show significant differences in scores, the study did demonstrate that linguistic modification did not affect the scores of English-proficient students, indicating that linguistic modification is not a threat to score comparability.

In sum, the research evidence shows linguistic complexity as a major source of measurement error in the assessment results for ELL students. Research findings also suggest that reducing the level of unnecessary linguistic complexity of assessments may help improve assessment validity and reliability for these students. Consequently, improvement of the assessment validity and reliability can be linked to reducing unnecessary linguistic complexity of assessment. Some argue that reducing the complexity level of academic content may change

the construct being taught and assessed; therefore, the complex linguistic structures that are related to the content of assessment and instruction must be distinguished from the unnecessary linguistic complexity of the text in both assessment and instruction.

SUMMARY AND DISCUSSION

This chapter discusses the impact of language factors on the assessment of English language learners, introduces the concept of linguistic modification of test items, provides research support for this concept, and offers practical guidelines to improve assessment for ELL students.

Research findings (Abedi and Lord, 2001; Abedi et al., 2000), illuminate a substantial performance gap between ELLs and their native English-speaking peers. While there is no evidence to suggest any difference between ELL and non-ELL students on their ability to learn, these academic performance differences are alarming. Unnecessary linguistic complexity of test items as a source of construct-irrelevant variance threatens the reliability and validity of assessment for ELLs. Research-based evidence suggests that the lower performance of ELL students is mainly due to the impact of language factors on the instruction and assessment of these students. It is extremely challenging for ELL students to be instructed and assessed in a language that they are not quite proficient in and are striving to learn. To provide a valid and fair assessment for all students, it is imperative to bring this issue to the attention of the education and measurement community – particularly to test developers and test item writers.

Research that was cited in this chapter explicated the serious impact that unnecessary linguistic complexity of test items that may have on content-based assessments. Language that is an essential part of the question content was differentiated from language that makes the question incomprehensible to many students, particularly English language learners. Although there is great value in the richness of language in an assessment system, it is critical that students with limited English proficiency and other students with similar language needs not be penalized for their lack of English proficiency in areas where the target of assessment is *not* language. Views of critics arguing against reducing the quality of assessment questions by simplifying the language are warranted; however, it is also important to recognize the distinction between necessary and unnecessary linguistic complexity. Content assessment specialists should take heed of these distinctions when creating test items.

It was demonstrated that the linguistic modification of test items improves the quality of assessment for ELL students without altering the construct being measured, thereby providing valid assessment outcomes for ELL students. Findings of the studies cited in this chapter clearly suggest that the performance of non-ELL students tested under linguistically modified assessments is not different than their performance under the original version. These findings provide assurances that linguistic modification of an assessment used as an accommodation for ELL students does not compromise the validity of assessment for these students.

In the proposal for linguistic modification of assessments, past research findings were used to inform practical suggestions in addressing language issues in assessments. Since past research has consistently found the linguistic modification approach to control for sources of assessment validity threats, the hope is that this chapter will encourage test item writers develop more valid assessments for every student to assure that no students will be left behind (NCLB, 2002).

ACKNOWLEDGEMENTS

The author acknowledges the contribution of several people in this work. Rita Pope contributed substantially with comments and assistance in structuring and revising the paper. Shannon Cannon provided valuable comments and suggestions during the revision process. The author would also like to acknowledge Dr. Robert Bayley for his input.

REFERENCES

Abedi, J. (1996) 'The interrater/test reliability system (ITRS)', *Multivariate Behavioral Research*, 31(4): 409–17.

Abedi, J. (2002) 'Standardized achievement tests and English language learners: Psychometrics Issues', *Educational Assessment*, 8(3): 231–57.

Abedi, J. (2006a) 'Psychometric issues in the ELL assessment and special education eligibility', *Teacher's College Record*, 108 (11): 2282–303.

Abedi, J. (2006b) 'Language issues in item-development', in S. M. Downing and T. M. Haladyna (eds.), *Handbook of test development*. New Jersey: Lawrence Erlbaum Associates. pp. 377–98.

Abedi, J. (2007) 'Utilizing accommodations in the assessment of English language learners', in N. H. Hornberger (ed.), *Encyclopedia of language and education: Vol. 7: Language testing and assessment*. Heidelberg, Germany: Springer. pp. 341–7.

Abedi, J., Courtney, M. and Leon, S. (2003a) *Effectiveness and validity of accommodations for English language learners in large-scale assessment* (CSE Tech. Rep. No. 608). Los Angeles: University of California: Center for the Study of Evaluation/National Center for Research on Evaluation, Standards, and Student Testing.

Abedi, J., Leon, S. and Kao, J. C. (2008) *Examining differential distractor functioning in reading assessments for students with disabilities* (CSE Tech. Report 743). Los Angeles: University of California: Center for the

Study of Evaluation/National Center for Research on Evaluation, Standards, and Student Testing.

Abedi, J., Leon, S. and Mirocha, J. (2003b) *Impact of student language background on content-based performance: Analyses of extant data* (CSE Tech. Rep. No. 603). Los Angeles: University of California, National Center for Research on Evaluation, Standards, and Student Testing.

Abedi, J. and Lord, C. (2001) 'The language factor in mathematics tests', *Applied Measurement in Education*, 14 (3): 219–34.

Abedi, J., Lord, C. and Hofstetter, C. (1998) *Impact of selected background variables on students' NAEP math performance* (CSE Tech. Rep. No. 478). Los Angeles: University of California, National Center for Research on Evaluation, Standards, and Student Testing.

Abedi, J., Lord, C., Hofstetter, C. and Baker, E. (2000) 'Impact of accommodation strategies on English language learners' test performance', *Educational Measurement: Issues and Practice*, 19 (3): 16–26.

Abedi, J., Lord, C. and Plummer, J. (1997) *Language background as a variable in NAEP mathematics performance* (CSE Tech. Rep. No. 429). Los Angeles: University of California, National Center for Research on Evaluation, Standards, and Student Testing.

Adams, M. J. (1990) *Beginning to read: Thinking and learning about print*. Cambridge, MA: MIT Press.

Allen, M. J. and Yen, W. M. (1979) *Introduction to measurement theory*. Monterey, CA: Brooks/Cole.

American Educational Research Association, American Psychological Association, and National Council on Measurement in Education (1999) *Standards for educational and psychological testing*. Washington, DC: American Educational Research Association.

Artiles, A. J., Rueda, R., Salazar, J. and Higareda, I. (2005) 'Within-group diversity in minority disproportionate representation: English language learners in urban school districts', *Exceptional Children*, 71: 283–300.

Bever, T. (1970) 'The cognitive basis for linguistic structure', in J. R. Hayes (ed.), *Cognition and the development of language*. New York: John Wiley. pp. 279–353.

Biber, D. (1988) *Variation across speech and writing*. New York: Cambridge University Press.

Caroll, J. B., Davies, P. and Richman, B. (1971) *The American Heritage word frequency book*. Boston: Houghton Mifflin.

Celce-Murcia, M., Dornyei, Z. and Thurrell, S. (1995) 'Communicative competence: A pedagogically motivated model with content specifications', *Issues in Applied Linguistics*, 6 (2): 5–35.

Celce-Murcia, M. and Larsen-Freeman, D. (1983) *The grammar book: An ESL/EFL teacher's book*. Rowley, MA: Newbury House.

Cortina, J. M. (1993) 'What is coefficient alpha? An examination of theory and applications', *Journal of Applied Psychology*, 78 (1): 98–104.

Cronbach, L. J., Gleser, G. C., Nanda, H. and Rajaratnam, N. (1972) *The dependability of behavioral measurements: Theory of generalizability for scores and profiles*. New York: John Wiley.

Cummins, D. D., Kintsch, W., Reusser, K. and Weimer, R. (1988) 'The role of understanding in solving word problems', *Cognitive Psychology*, 20: 405–38.

De Corte, E., Verschaffel, L. and DeWin, L. (1985) 'Influence of rewording verbal problems on children's problem representations and solutions', *Journal of Educational Psychology*, 77 (4): 460–70.

deVilliers J. and deVilliers, P. (1973) 'Development of the use of word order in comprehension', *Journal of Psychological Research*, 2: 331–41.

Durán, R. P. (1999) 'Directions in assessment of linguistic minorities', in S. Messick (ed.), *Assessment in higher education: Issues in access, quality, student development, and public policy*. Hillsdale, NJ: Erlbaum. pp. 193–202.

Francis, W. N. and Kucera, H. (1982) *Frequency analysis of English usage: Lexicon and grammar*. Boston: Houghton Mifflin.

Gathercole, S. E. and Baddeley, A. D. (1993) *Working memory and language*. Hillsdale, NJ: Erlbaum.

Haiman, J. (1985) *Natural syntax: Iconicity and erosion*. New York: Cambridge University Press.

Hanson, E. G. and Mislevy, R. (2004) *Towards a unified validity framework for ensuring access to assessments by individuals with disabilities and English language learners*. Paper presented at the annual meeting of the National Council on Measurement in Education, San Diego, CA.

Hudson, T. (1983) 'Correspondences and numerical differences between disjoint sets', *Child Development*, 54: 84–90.

Imbens-Bailey, A. and Castellon-Wellington, M. (1999) *Linguistic demands of test items used to assess ELL students*. Paper presented at the annual conference of the National Center for Research on Evaluation, Standards, and Student Testing, Los Angeles, CA.

Kane, M. T. (2006) 'Validation', in R. L. Brennan (ed.), *Educational Measurement*. 4th edition. Westport, CT: Praeger Publisher. pp. 17–64.

Kiplinger, V. L., Haug, C. A. and Abedi, J. (2000) *Measuring math – not reading – on a math assessment: A language accommodations study* of English language learners and other special populations. Presented at the annual meeting of the American Educational Research Association, New Orleans, LA.

Lemke, J. L. (1986) *Using language in classrooms.* Victoria, Australia: Deakin University Press.

Linn, R. L. and Gronlund, N. E. (1995) *Measurement and Assessment in Teaching.* 7th edition. Englewood Cliffs, NJ: Merrill/Prentice Hall.

Maihoff, N. A. (2002) *Using Delaware data in making decisions regarding the education of LEP students.* Paper presented at the Council of Chief State School Officers 32nd Annual National Conference on Large-Scale Assessment, Palm Desert, CA.

Messick, S. (1994) 'The interplay of evidence and consequences in the validation of performance assessments', *Educational Researcher,* 23 (2): 13–23.

No Child Left Behind Act (2001) Public Law No. 107-110, 115 Stat. 1425 (2002).

Riley, M. S., Greeno, J. G. and Heller, J. I. (1983) 'Development of children's problem-solving ability in arithmetic', in H. P. Ginsburg (ed.), *The development of mathematical thinking.* New York: Academic Press. pp. 153–96.

Rivera, C. and Stansfield, C. W. (2001) *The effects of linguistic simplification of science test items on performance of limited english proficient and mono-lingual english-speaking students.* Paper presented at the Annual Meeting of the American Educational Research Association, Seattle, Washington.

Sandoval, J. and Durán, R. (1998) 'Language', in J. Sandoval, C. Frisby, K. Geisinger, J. Scheuneman, and J. Grenier (eds), *Test interpretation and diversity: Achieving equity in assessment.* Washington, DC: American Psychological Association. pp. 181–212.

Shaftel, J., Belton-Kocher, E., Glasnapp, D. and Poggio, J. (2006) 'The impact of language characteristics in mathematics test items on the performance of English language learners and students with disabilities', *Educational Assessment,* 11 (2): 105–126.

Solano-Flores, G. and Trumbull, E. (2003) 'Examining language in context: The need for new research and practice paradigms in the testing of English-language learners', *Educational Researcher,* 32(2): 3–13.

Spanos, G., Rhodes, N. C., Dale, T. C. and Crandall, J. (1988) 'Linguistic features of mathematical problem solving: Insights and applications', in R. R. Cocking and J. P. Mestre (eds), *Linguistic and cultural influences on learning mathematics.* Hillsdale, NJ: Erlbaum. pp. 221–40.

Thorndike, R. M. (2005) *Measurement and evaluation in psychology and education.* New Jersey: Pearson, Merrill.

APPENDIX 8.1: GUIDELINES FOR PERFORMING LINGUISTIC MODIFICATION OF CONTENT-BASED TEST ITEMS

Items with no linguistic complexity.

- Familiar or frequently used words; word length generally shorter.
- Short sentences and limited prepositional phrases.
- Concrete item(s) and a narrative structure.
- No complex conditional or adverbial clauses.
- No passive voice or abstract or impersonal presentations.

Items with a minimal level of linguistic complexity.

- Familiar or frequently used words; short to moderate word length.
- Moderate sentence length with a few prepositional phrases.
- Concrete item(s).
- No subordinate, conditional, or adverbial clauses.
- No passive voice or abstract or impersonal presentations.

Items with a moderate level of linguistic complexity.

- Unfamiliar or seldom used words.
- Long sentence(s).
- Abstract concept(s).
- Complex sentence/conditional tense/adverbial clause(s).
- A few passive voice or abstract or impersonal presentations.

Items with a high level of linguistic complexity.

- Relatively unfamiliar or seldom used words.
- Long or complex sentence(s).
- Abstract item(s).
- Difficult subordinate, conditional, or adverbial clause(s).
- Passive voice/ abstract or impersonal presentations.

Items with a maximum level of linguistic complexity.

- Highly unfamiliar or seldom used words.
- Very long or complex sentence(s).
- Abstract item(s).
- Very difficult subordinate, conditional, or adverbial clause(s).
- Many passive voice and abstract or impersonal presentations.

APPENDIX 8.2: CHAPTER QUESTIONS

1. How can the effects of language as a source of measurement error be controlled?
2. What are the principles underlying the linguistic modification approach? How is it performed?
3. How does linguistic modification improve assessment for ELL students?

REVIEW EXERCISES

In order to understand better the process of linguistic modification, we have provided sample test items with linguistic complexity for you to practice. To follow is a set of six math items. The first three items are from the 1992 National Assessment of Educational Progress for Grade 8 students and the last three items are from the current state assessments that are released for public use. We used the two sets of items from two generations of test items to show that current research on the impact of linguistic modification influenced item writing practice by major test publishers in the U.S. such as Educational Testing Service (ETS), CTB/McGraw-Hill, Pearson, etc. The last two items therefore are less linguistically complex and more accessible to ELL students. For this exercise, try to do the following:

Modify the items to remove unnecessary linguistic complexity of the items. For these exercises, you need to make sure that the language related to math content is retained. Linguistically modified versions for each of these items have been provided following the original items. We strongly suggest preparing your own modified version of the items, and then reviewing the suggested modifications for clarification.

1. To assure retaining of content-related language in a formal assessment, you need to consult with math and linguistic content experts.
2. Use the guidelines provided in Appendix 8.1 to judge the level of linguistic complexity of items.
3. To further your understanding, you may consider conducting a small-scale study in which you randomly assign the original and revised test items to a group of about 100 eighth grade students (four classes) and then compare their performance across the original and revised versions of the test.

Original test items

Puppy's age	Puppy's weight
1 month	10 lbs.
2 months	15 lbs.
3 months	19 lbs.
4 months	22 lbs.
5 months	?

1. John records the weight of this puppy every month in a chart like the one shown above. If the pattern of the puppy's weight gain continues, how many pounds will the puppy weigh at 5 months?
    A. 30
    B. 27
    C. 25
    D. 24

2. The length of a dinosaur was reported to have been 80 feet (rounded to the nearest 10 feet). What length other than 80 feet could have been the actual length of this dinosaur?
    Answer: _____ feet

3. What is the greatest number of 30-cent apples that can be purchased with $5.00?
    A. 6
    B. 15
    C. 16
    D. 17
    E. 20

4. Tammy scored 52 out of 57 possible points on a quiz. Which of the following is closest to the per cent of the total number of points that Tammy scored?
    A. 0.91
    B. 1.10
    C. 52
    D. 91
    E. 95

5. A new pipeline is being constructed to re-route its oil flow around the exterior of a national wildlife preserve. The plan showing the old pipeline and the new route is shown below.

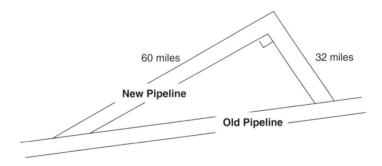

60 miles — New Pipeline

32 miles

Old Pipeline

    About how many extra miles will the oil flow once the new route is established?
    A. 24
    B. 68
    C. 92
    D. 160

6. Abelardo wants to create several different 7-character screen names. He wants to use arrangements of the first 3 letters of his first name (abe), *followed by* arrangements of 4 digits in 1984, the year of his birth. How many different screen names can he create in this way?
    A. 72
    B. 144
    C. 288
    D. 576

Linguistically modified test items

Puppy's age	Puppy's weight
1 month	10 lbs.
2 months	15 lbs.
3 months	19 lbs.
4 months	22 lbs.
5 months	?

1. Mike weighs his puppy every month. He writes how much weight his puppy gains each month. Look at the pattern. How much will the puppy weigh when it is 5 months old?
   A. 30
   B. 27
   C. 25
   D. 24

   In item 1, the following linguistic modifications were made: changed the name to a more decodeable name, sequenced events chronologically, and removed conditional phrase.

2. Pat estimated the height of a building to be 80 feet, rounded to the nearest 10 feet. The height of the building may be 80 feet tall. It may also be _____ feet tall.
   In item 2, the following linguistic modifications were made: changed the format of the item to narrative, provided a cloze answer format to be more concrete, changed passive voice to active voice, and changed sentence structure.

3. Kate wants to buy some apples. She has $5.00. Each apple costs 30 cents. How many apples can Kate buy?
   A. 6
   B. 15
   C. 16
   D. 17
   E. 20

   In item 3, the following linguistic modifications were made: changed the format of the item to narrative, sequenced events chronologically, and changed sentence structure.

4. Tammy scored 52 out of 57 possible points on a quiz. What per cent did she answer correctly?
   A. 0.91
   B. 1.10
   C. 52
   D. 91
   E. 95

   In item 4, the following linguistic modifications were made: removed string of adjectives, and changed sentence structure.

5. Anna can use two routes to drive to her parents' house. How much farther is Route 2 than Route 1?
   A. 24
   B. 68
   C. 92
   D. 160

   In item 5, the following linguistic modifications were made: changed the format of the item to narrative, used more common vocabulary, and changed sentence structure.

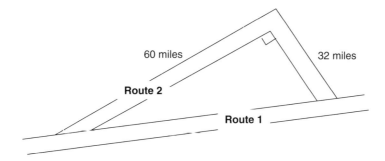

6. Abel wants to create many different codes with 3 letters and 4 numbers in each code. He wants to use different combinations of the first 3 letters of his name (abe) *followed by* different combinations of the 4 numbers in his birth year (1984). How many different codes can Abel make?
   A. 72
   B. 144
   C. 288
   D. 57

In item 6, the following linguistic modifications were made: exchanged to an easier to de-code name, broke out information into discrete sentences, removed unnecessary adjectives, andchanged sentence structure. Changed potential false cognate (*creer* in Spanish means to believe) in the active question.

9

Measurement Issues in Cross-cultural Research

A. Timothy Church

Cross-cultural research is thriving in the behavioral and social sciences (e.g., Matsumoto and Yoo, 2006; Smith et al., 2006). Cross-cultural studies test the generalizability of theories and constructs and provide a natural experimental 'treatment' for studying the influence of culture and ecology on behavior. Cross-cultural studies can also aim to reduce ethnocentrism in science and practice by broadening perspectives on value and belief systems and patterns of behavior. Conversely, mono-cultural research can lead to 'a sense of 'culture-blindness' whereby observed findings in one's own culture are assumed to be universal' (Heine and Norenzayan, 2006: 254).

Cross-cultural researchers must address the usual measurement issues, including selection and definition of constructs, representativeness of items, instrument format, reliability, and validity. However, these issues are complicated further when measures are applied cross-culturally, and additional concerns – in particular, the conceptual and measurement equivalence of instruments – are largely unique to cross-cultural research. In this chapter, I address (a) alternative theoretical perspectives in cross-cultural research and their implications for measurement; (b) the specific conceptual and measurement issues confronting cross-cultural researchers; (c) the advantages and disadvantages of imported (*imposed-etic*) and indigenous (*emic*) measures; and (d) issues in the measurement of culture. I draw primarily on cross-cultural research in psychology, but the issues are relevant to other social sciences as well.

ALTERNATIVE THEORETICAL PERSPECTIVES

It is useful to distinguish cross-cultural, cultural, and indigenous perspectives in cross-cultural research, although the distinctions are fuzzy (Triandis, 2000; Yang, 2000). Typical features of the cross-cultural approach include (a) comparisons of multiple cultures with the goal of identifying cross-cultural universals or culture-specifics amidst these universals; and (b) treatment of culture, or quantitative variables indexing culture and ecology, as variables 'outside' the individual, which can be used to predict individual attributes or behaviors. Cross-cultural researchers tend to measure attributes in a relatively context-free manner with traditional psychometric scales or inventories. Prominent examples in psychology include efforts to identify and assess universal dimensions of personality (McCrae and Allik, 2002), values (Schwartz, 1992), beliefs (Leung et al., 2002), and emotions (Yik et al., 2002). A typical approach is to 'transport,' with varying levels of adaptation, constructs and measures to new cultural contexts to compare their structure, mean levels, and correlates (i.e., nomological networks). Concomitant with the focus on cross-national comparisons is sensitivity to issues of conceptual and measurement equivalence.

Whereas cross-cultural psychologists tend to treat culture and psychological attributes as relatively distinct, cultural psychologists emphasize their 'mutually constitutive' and deeply intertwined nature (e.g., Cross and Markus, 1999; Greenfield, 1997; Heine, 2001). Conceptions of the person and self are viewed as socially constructed (i.e., produced through the shared cognition and experience of members of particular cultures) and hence variable across cultures. As a result, the existence of universal dimensions of individual differences that can be measured in a context-free or equivalent manner across cultures is questioned.

Cultural psychology perspectives have a number of significant implications for measurement across cultures. One is a degree of skepticism about the meaning of traditional inventory assessments. Shweder (1991) argued that scores obtained on such inventories 'lend illusory support to the mistaken belief that individual differences can be described in a language consisting of context-free global traits, factors, or dimensions' (pp. 275–6). In general, traditional inventory assessments provide a descriptive, nomothetic, and molar description of personal attributes, whereas many cultural psychologists prefer the 'thick,' holistic, and contextualized descriptions provided by more qualitative assessment methods (Marsella et al., 2000; Miller, 1997). Nomothetic measures, which assess dimensions assumed to be relevant for all individuals, may facilitate comparisons of individuals and cultures, but idiographic methods may lead to a richer understanding of individual lives and psychological dynamics.

The extent of measurement error to which an instrument is susceptible may vary across cultures. For example, cultural psychologists have suggested that traditional rating scales and inventories may be less reliable and valid in collectivistic cultures, as compared to individualistic cultures, because introspecting about one's attributes is a less natural task, and self-concepts are less clear, in collectivistic cultures (Campbell et al., 1996; Markus and Kitayama, 1998). Measures of internal attributes may also predict behavior less well in collectivistic cultures, where behavior may be more determined by social roles, relationships, and norms (Markus and Kitayama, 1998; Triandis, 1995). Finally, cultural psychologists have noted that the items in personality inventories are typically general, with minimal specification of situational context. Although general items may transfer better across cultures, they are less representative, contextual, and lifelike, possibly reducing content validity. General items also require an intuitive aggregation of one's behavior across situations that respondents in collectivistic cultures may find difficult if behavior is indeed more context-specific in these cultures (Marsella et al., 2000).

Rather than trait attributes, cultural psychologists have focused on measuring aspects of self-concept. In anthropology, conceptions of self have been assessed primarily through ethnographic methods (e.g., Marsella et al., 1985), whereas psychologists have most often used the Twenty Statements Test (TST), in which respondents complete the statement 'Who am I' up to 20 times. Cultural psychologists have expected respondents to generate more dispositional attributes (e.g., traits, aspirations, preferences) in individualistic cultures and more social identities (e.g., relationships, roles, statuses) in collectivistic cultures (del Prado et al., 2007). Other constructivist methods such as free-descriptions (e.g., Kohnstamm et al., 1998) and personal narratives or life stories (Howard, 1991) are also consistent with cultural psychology perspectives, because they emphasize the construction of meaning by individuals and cultures and can provide idiographic information that is embedded in cultural contexts (Church, 2001). Nonetheless, cultural psychologists have also applied traditional psychometric scales to measure individual-differences dimensions thought to mediate cultural differences in self-processes, such as self-construals (Singelis, 1994), holistic thinking (Choi et al., 2003), and dialecticism (i.e., tolerance for holding apparently contradictory beliefs; Spencer-Rodgers et al., 2004).

The merits of applying measurement instruments across cultures is contested. For example, efforts to measure intelligence across cultures illustrate the different perspectives of cross-cultural and cultural psychologists. Some cross-cultural psychologists believe that Western intelligence tests can be meaningfully applied in diverse cultures if adequately translated, adapted, and tested for cross-cultural equivalence (e.g., Sternberg, 2004; van de Vijver, 2002, 2003). For example, the Wechsler Intelligence Scale for Children (WISC-III) has been translated into numerous languages (Georgas et al., 2003) and culture-comparative studies continue to be conducted (e.g., Lynn and Vanhanen, 2006; Rindermann, 2007; van de Vijver, 1997, 2002). However, cultural psychologists are deeply skeptical about the cross-cultural validity of such assessments. For example, Greenfield (1997) has argued that cognitive ability tests presuppose a particular cultural framework that is not universally shared. Cultures differ in their conceptions of intelligence, the cognitive processes that are valued, the meaning of particular items and procedures, and communication conventions that are relevant to testing (e.g., the acceptability of decontextualized, impersonal communications). From a cultural psychology perspective, cross-cultural comparisons can only be made, if at all, after an investigation of each culture on its own terms.

The relevance and application of social science concepts outside their culture of origin has also been debated. In particular, indigenous social scientists emphasize the need to formulate theory, concepts, and measures that reflect indigenous cultural contexts (Church and Katigbak, 2002; Kim et al., 2006). For example, indigenous psychologists have focused on identification and elaboration of psychological constructs thought to be particularly salient or unique to single cultures, such as Japanese *amae* (Yamaguchi and Ariizumi, 2006), Korean *cheong* (Choi et al., 1993), and Filipino *kapwa* (Enriquez, 1994). Indigenous psychologists generally endorse relativistic rather than universalistic perspectives, and utilize an *emic* (culture-specific) approach to test construction. Standard psychometric scales and inventories are often constructed, but with culture-specific content (e.g., Cheung and Leung, 1998; Guanzon-Lapeña et al., 1998; Ortiz et al., 2006).

EQUIVALENCE AND BIAS IN CROSS-CULTURAL MEASUREMENT

Types of bias

A number of biases can detract from the equivalence or comparability of constructs and measures across cultures. Van de Vijver and Leung (1997) differentiated *construct*, *method*, and *item bias*. *Construct bias* occurs when the definitions of the construct only partially overlap across cultures (i.e., lack *construct* or *conceptual equivalence*). For example, the concept of achievement motivation may be more socially oriented – emphasizing group goals and family achievement – in collectivistic cultures, as compared to the Western conception, which emphasizes individualistic striving for personal goals (Yu, 1996). Similarly, much of the controversy surrounding the cross-cultural assessment of intelligence involves concerns about conceptual equivalence. For example, in many African and Asian cultures, lay people's conceptions of intelligence include cognitive aspects and also social skills or competence (Church et al., 1985; Serpell, 2000; Sternberg, 2004).

Method bias can take three forms: (a) *sample bias* (e.g., cultural samples are non-equivalent on confounding variables); (b) *instrument bias* (e.g., lack of familiarity with item formats); and (c) *administration bias* (e.g., communication problems between the assessor and assessee). Finally, *item bias* or *differential item*

functioning (DIF) occurs when individuals with the same level or amount of a trait, but from different cultural groups, exhibit a different probability of answering the item in the keyed direction. DIF could result from non-equivalent translation of items, or inclusion of items that are less relevant in certain cultures.

The inverse of bias is equivalence or invariance. A number of researchers have delineated types or levels of equivalence (e.g., Hui and Triandis, 1985; Marsella et al., 2000; Steenkamp and Baumgartner, 1998; Vandenberg and Lance, 2000). Here we distinguish conceptual, linguistic, and measurement equivalence, with measurement equivalence broken down further into configural, metric, and scalar invariance.

Conceptual equivalence

Conceptual equivalence is the absence of construct bias, and thus refers to the degree of overlap between the conceptual definitions of a construct across cultures. To demonstrate conceptual equivalence, researchers must show that concept definitions and behavioral indicators of constructs are the same or very similar across cultures. For example, researchers can conduct interviews or questionnaire studies in which cultural informants are asked to define the construct of interest and its behavioral indicators (e.g., Church and Katigbak, 1989). Most frequently, researchers conduct exploratory or confirmatory factor analyses to determine whether the items used to measure a construct define the same 'structure' or dimensions across cultures. Indirect evidence for conceptual equivalence can be obtained by comparing the nomological network of relationships with other variables in each culture, although differences in these networks might also reflect valid differences in predictive relationships.

Linguistic equivalence

Linguistic equivalence refers to the accuracy of instrument translations. Translation can involve writing items that are easier to translate, translation using one of the available methods, and follow-up analyses to check the quality of the translation. A number of authors have offered guidelines for writing items that will be translated (e.g., using simple sentences, active voice, avoiding metaphors and colloquialisms, avoiding negations) (e.g., Brislin, 1986; Marín and Marín, 1991). Ideally, instruments are developed simultaneously in each language so that items can be modified (i.e., *decentered*) to make them easier to translate with equivalent meaning.

Among the alternative methods of translation (see Brislin, 1986; Marín and Marín, 1991), back translation is generally considered superior and is the only method that provides a monolingual researcher with a means to evaluate linguistic equivalence. The source language version is translated into the target language by one bilingual, a second bilingual independently translates the target language version back into the source language, and the original and back translated source versions are compared for meaning differences. Supplemental steps are recommended, including a check of the target version by a local language expert to verify grammatical accuracy and the familiarity and naturalness of the language used. In our experience, the simple declaration in journal articles that the back translation method was used belies the time-consuming and challenging nature of the process, which often requires refined judgments about whether apparent meaning differences are significant or trivial. In addition, some items may not be culturally-relevant and the researcher must decide whether to abandon or replace them with alternative content.

A variety of methods are also available to evaluate the quality of a translation, including pretesting with cultural informants, bilingual test-retest methods, and statistical analyses of *differential item functioning* (DIF). In the bilingual test–retest method, bilinguals complete the instrument in two languages. Significant cross-language discrepancies in item or scale means suggest translation problems, as do cross-language scale correlations that are less than about .80 (e.g., Mallinckrodt and Wang, 2004; Wiebe and Penley, 2006). Analyses of differential item functioning using item response theory methods provide a stringent test of translation equivalence but require large sample sizes and greater statistical expertise (e.g., Bontempo, 1993; Ellis, 1995; Ellis and Mead, 2000).

Another language issue arises when participants are reasonably bilingual and could respond to an instrument in a non-native or second-language, thereby avoiding translation. However, aside from language proficiency issues, research indicates that the language of assessment often affects the results (e.g., Bond and Yang, 1982; Church et al., 1988; Ralston et al., 1995; Ramírez-Esparza et al., 2004; Watkins and Gerong, 1999). Several hypotheses have been offered to explain the language differences in these studies. The *cross-cultural accommodation* hypothesis – which predicts that respondents will endorse items in the direction valued by their native culture to a greater extent when responding in their native language – has garnered the most support, but findings are by no means definitive. Ramírez-Esparza et al. (2004) offered a conceptually equivalent hypothesis in terms of the *cultural frame switching* of bilinguals. This hypothesis predicts that bilinguals undergo a cultural frame switch when they change from one language to another, leading them to describe their attributes in a manner that is more similar to the cultural samples that speak the given language. The important point for cross-cultural researchers is that the language of measurement can make a difference. In cross-national studies, use of native or primary languages is probably preferable in most cases, because researchers will generally be interested in assessing conceptions and attributes that are salient in the underlying cultures.

Measurement equivalence

Different levels of measurement equivalence or invariance need to be demonstrated depending on the research questions addressed. Although terminology in this area varies, the terminology used by Vandenberg and Lance (2000), among others, is useful because it corresponds well with the confirmatory factor analysis (CFA) framework that is frequently used to test levels of invariance. *Configural invariance* (invariance of form, weak factor invariance) is exhibited when the same number of latent constructs or factors, and the same pattern of salient and non-salient loadings, defines the structure of the instrument across cultures. The magnitude of the salient factor loadings need not be invariant. Configural invariance is directly relevant to conceptual equivalence because it implies that the latent construct(s) have the same meaning (i.e., number of dimensions and observed indicators) across cultures.

In CFA, the regression slopes (i.e., factor loadings) of the items define the metric of the measurement, as they indicate the amount of change in the observed item responses due to a unit change in the latent construct. Accordingly, *metric invariance* (or strong factorial invariance) is present when the factor loadings can be constrained to be equal across cultures without significant loss of model fit. Metric invariance implies equivalent

scale *intervals* across cultures, but cross-cultural comparisons of the absolute level of scores may still not be meaningful. Equivalent scale intervals facilitate comparisons of the nomological networks of the construct across cultures (Steenkamp and Baumgartner, 1998). Finally, to compare the *absolute* level of scores across cultures requires *scalar invariance*, a more stringent level in which the item intercepts can also be constrained to be equal across cultures without significant loss of model fit. Scalar invariance can be tested using mean and covariance structures analyses (MACS), an extension of CFA. Vandenberg and Lance (2000) offer a recommended sequence of tests within a CFA framework for these levels of measurement invariance. Configural invariance is a prerequisite for tests of metric invariance, which, in turn, is a prerequisite for tests of scalar invariance.

Finally, it is likely that partial rather than full metric and scalar invariance will be obtained in most cross-cultural studies (Byrne et al., 1989). Researchers differ in their views regarding the proportion of items that need to demonstrate invariance to allow meaningful cross-cultural comparisons (e.g., Steenkamp and Baumgartner, 1998; Vandenberg and Lance, 2000). Ideally, the majority of items will exhibit invariant factor loadings and intercepts, so that estimates of cultural means will be based on many cross-culturally comparable items (Steenkamp and Baumgartner, 1998).

Although CFA is generally viewed as the most comprehensive method for testing measurement invariance, some CFA applications can be problematic and cumbersome. Aside from occasional model identification problems and improper solutions, χ^2 tests of overall fit and χ^2 difference tests comparing nested models are sensitive to sample size and often reject reasonably good models. As a result, various quantitative indices have been developed to evaluate model fit, although interpretative guidelines are somewhat subjective and still evolving (Vandenberg and Lance, 2000). A more common problem is the very stringent nature of CFA. To attain good model fit, proposed models need to account for most of the covariation among the measured variables (unlike in exploratory factor analysis, where factor solutions that account for 40–50 per cent of the variance are common). When there are many items, or simple structure is limited (e.g., secondary loadings are needed), a priori theoretical models are unlikely to explain enough of the covariation among the measured variables to exhibit good model fit (Church and Burke, 1994). If the researcher is more interested in the latent constructs than the loadings of specific items, one strategy is to form item parcels or subscales comprised of multiple items (Kishton and Widaman, 1994; Labouvie and Ruetsch, 1995). We have used this strategy in a number of studies and found that measurement models with poor fit at the item level typically exhibit good model fit when the items are combined into a few item parcels, and the need for post-hoc model respecifications is also reduced or eliminated (e.g., Church et al., 2006). Several authors have discussed the pros and cons of item parceling and strategies for combining items into parcels (e.g., Kishton and Widaman, 1994; Little et al., 2002).

An alternative CFA strategy is to use prior results from an exploratory factor analysis to specify, in cross-validation samples, a greater number of anticipated factor loadings (including secondary loadings) in a priori CFA models (e.g., Caprara et al., 2000; Church and Burke, 1994; Katigbak et al., 1996). Alternatively, McCrae and colleagues (1996) proposed the use of exploratory factor analysis followed by targeted (Procrustes) rotations

to a hypothesized or normative structure. Although targeted rotations have limitations, they have been the method of choice in studies examining the cross-cultural replicability of the Five Factor Model (FFM), as assessed by the Revised NEO Personality Inventory (McCrae and Allik, 2002).

Finally, if the researcher is primarily interested in investigating scalar invariance, then *differential item functioning* (DIF) methods are particularly relevant. DIF methods based on item response theory are generally viewed as the most theoretically cogent (Camilli and Shepard, 1994; Embretson and Reise, 2000; Reise and Henson, 2003). Item response theory (Hambleton et al., 1991; Lord, 1980) postulates that the conditional probability of individuals giving the keyed ('correct') response to an item, given their level on the underlying latent trait, can be described by a monotonically increasing function called an item characteristic curve (ICC). The exact form of the ICC depends on the particular mathematical formula (e.g., logistic, normal ogive) used to generate the S-shaped curve and the number of item parameters estimated. In two-parameter models, an item discrimination parameter provides an index of how well the item differentiates individuals along the latent trait continuum and an item difficulty parameter provides an index of the likelihood of the item being endorsed in the keyed direction. In some applications (e.g., intelligence and achievement testing) a third, 'guessing' or chance-level, parameter is estimated and indexes the probability of a keyed response for someone with extremely low levels of the latent trait.

In item response theory, an item is said to exhibit DIF, that is, to lack scalar equivalence, when two cultures' ICCs for the item differ by more than sampling error. DIF can be tested statistically in a variety of ways, including tests of (a) the differences between the two cultures' item parameters once they have been transformed to the same metric (e.g., Lord, 1980); (b) the areas between the two cultures' ICCs (Raju, 1990); and (c) the comparative fit of models that constrain the two cultures' parameters to be equal versus models that allow the two cultures' parameters to be freely estimated. DIF analyses become more complex when polytomous items with multiple response options (e.g., Likert scales) are investigated (e.g., Embretson and Reise, 2000).

IRT-based DIF methods have been applied to measures of a variety of constructs, including intelligence (Ellis, 1990), personality traits (Huang et al., 1997; Johnson et al., 2008; Waller et al., 2000), home environment (Bingenheimer et al., 2005), and individualism-collectivism (Bontempo, 1993). They have also been used to investigate linguistic (translation) equivalence at the item-level (Ellis et al., 1989). Overall, however, DIF analyses have been underutilized as a method to investigate scalar equivalence (Reise and Henson, 2003). One reason is that large sample sizes (e.g., 500 or more) are typically recommended in order to obtain good parameter estimates (Stark et al., 2006). In addition, DIF methods are more complex than analogous CFA methods. For detailed comparisons of CFA and IRT-based DIF analyses, see Stark et al. (2006), Raju et al. (2002), Reise et al. (1993), and Meade and Lautenschlager (2004).

Finally, whether conducted with IRT or CFA methods, there is a paradox in DIF studies. On the one hand, the researcher may wish to demonstrate the absence of DIF to enable cross-cultural comparisons. On the other hand, the presence of DIF items may be of special interest to the researcher seeking to identify cultural differences in the relevance (i.e., item discrimination differences) or prevalence (i.e., item difficulty

differences) of the behavioral exemplars of constructs (e.g., see Church et al., 2007; Huang et al., 1997).

In psychology, the issues of scalar equivalence have taken on increased importance with the renewed efforts to draw conclusions about cultural differences in mean trait levels by comparing aggregate personality profiles across cultures (McCrae, 2002; Schmitt et al., 2007). Some data suggest that these aggregate personality profiles are meaningful – for example, they exhibit geographical patterning and cultural-level correlates (Allik and McCrae, 2004; Hofstede and McCrae, 2004; Schmitt et al., 2007). However, concerns about measurement inequalities and other method biases remain (see Church, 2008, for a discussion). McCrae et al. (2005) suggested that item-level DIF may cancel out at the scale level, and DIF researchers have recently described methods for investigating this possibility (e.g., Ellis and Mead, 2000; Waller et al., 2000). Waller et al. (2000) found substantial DIF (38 per cent of the items) but little differential test functioning (DTF) in an investigation of MMPI factor scales. In contrast, Ellis and Mead (2000) found that about three-fourths of the scales in a Spanish translation of the 16PF questionnaire showed significant DTF.

Some researchers (e.g., van de Vijver and Poortinga, 2002) have suggested that an additional step should be taken before mean profiles on inventories can be compared across cultures. Researchers should show that the factor structure exhibited at the individual level replicates at the cultural level (i.e., in a factor analysis of the cultural means for the relevant items). If not, the constructs do not retain their meaning at the cultural level and one would not be able to interpret the cultural mean differences in terms of the individual-level constructs (e.g., see Van Hemert et al., 2002). Muthén (1994) described multi-level

CFA procedures for comparing individual- and cultural-level factor structures, and van de Vijver and Poortinga (2002) described an analogous multi-level procedure based on exploratory factor analysis.

It is also important to note that even in the absence of DIF, other forms of bias, for example, response styles and reference group effects (see next section) can impact item and scale scores uniformly and thus go undetected by DIF analyses. In addition, factors outside the test can impact items in a uniform manner and go undetected by DIF analyses. For example, cultural mean differences on intelligence and achievement tests are known to correlate highly with differences in national affluence, amount and quality of schooling, and previous exposure to similar test materials (Lynn and Mikk, 2007; Rindermann, 2007; van de Vijver, 1997, 2002), so conclusions about inherent cultural differences in intelligence are risky.

RESPONSE STYLES, REFERENCE GROUP EFFECTS, AND ITEM WORDING OR FORMAT

Response styles refer to systematic tendencies to respond to items on some basis unrelated to the content or attribute the instrument is designed to measure. Cultural differences in response styles are a significant issue in cross-cultural research, because they can confound conclusions about cultural differences in substantive constructs. A variety of response styles have been identified and include the following: (a) acquiescence, or the tendency to agree (or disagree) with items regardless of the content; (b) extreme response style (ERS), or the tendency to use more extreme rating points on Likert-type rating scales; (c) neutral, midpoint, or moderacy bias, or the tendency to overuse the neutral or middle points on a scale; (d) social desirability, or the tendency to respond in a manner that is socially desirable or acceptable; and (e) ambivalent responding, or the tendency to endorse items referring to opposite attributes (e.g., both high and low self-esteem items, or both positive and negative emotions). Related conceptually to socially desirable responding, but typically assessed differently, is the concept of self-enhancement, which refers to the tendency to describe one's attributes in an overly positive manner (e.g., as being better than most others). Although there is some controversy over how best to measure self-enhancement (Sedikides et al., 2007), Heine and Hamamura (2007) concluded that Asians exhibit less self-enhancement tendencies than North Americans.

A variety of theoretical explanations have been offered to account for cultural differences in various response styles (e.g., see Baumgartner and Steenkamp, 2001: Table 1; Grimm and Church, 1999). Two of the more intriguing explanations have been offered by cultural psychologists. First, cultural differences in self-enhancement are typically explained in terms of self-construals (Markus and Kitayama, 1991). In individualistic cultures, where independent self-construals are predominant, personal attributes are more important for identity than in collectivistic cultures, so there is greater motivation to provide self-enhanced evaluations of one's attributes. Second, a tendency for East Asians to exhibit greater ambivalent response style has been attributed to East Asian dialecticism, which leads East Asians to be more inclined than people in Western cultures to acknowledge and accept psychological contradictions (Hamamura et al., 2008; Spencer-Rodgers et al., 2004).

Although some tentative patterns have emerged in cross-cultural comparisons of response styles, most comparisons have involved only two or three cultural groups, reducing confidence in the results (e.g., Chen et al., 1995; Hamamura et al., 2008; see Grimm and Church, 1999, for a review). More definitive findings will probably come from large-scale multinational studies. For example, in a 19-country investigation, Johnson et al. (2005) found that ERS was positively associated with Hofstede's (2001) power distance (acceptance of unequal power in society) and masculinity (valuing achievement, assertiveness, and material success) dimensions, while acquiescence bias was negatively associated with individualism, uncertainty avoidance (valuing of beliefs and institutions that provide certainty and conformity), power distance, and masculinity. The ERS results were largely consistent with the researchers' expectation that ERS would be associated with respondents' motivation to achieve clarity and decisiveness, rather than ambiguity and modesty. In a similar study, Smith (2004) reported substantial correlations between acquiescence bias and a number of cultural dimensions and concluded that acquiescence is not so much an artifact to be controlled, but 'a nation-level reflection of the individual communication styles and patterns of intergroup relations that prevail within certain specifiable cultural contexts' (p. 60). Smith's (2004) conclusion presents a dilemma for cross-cultural researchers, because it raises questions about whether they should try to control for response styles, or if doing so will eliminate valid substantive variance.

Reference group effects can also confound cross-cultural comparisons. Drawing on social comparison theory, Heine et al. (2002) argued that when respondents rate their attributes on standard Likert-type scales, they need to judge their attributes in reference to similar others. Because respondents in different cultures will be comparing themselves to different reference groups,

cross-cultural comparisons are confounded. Indeed, Heine et al. (2002) found that the common view that North Americans are more independent and less interdependent than Japanese was better supported when North American and Japanese respondents were explicitly asked to rate themselves relative to the other cultural group, as compared to when they rated themselves in the more typical situation with no explicit reference group. The extent to which reference group effects are a problem has generated controversy (Ashton, 2007; McCrae et al., 2007; Perugini and Richetin, 2007). A strong version of the effect (i.e., respondents rate themselves largely in reference to cultural norms) seems difficult to reconcile with the substantial mean differences found between cultures for some constructs, because it would presumably result in similar mean levels of scores in all cultures (McCrae et al., 2007). However, a weaker version (i.e., respondents' ratings are influenced by comparisons with those with whom they typically interact) seems plausible and could impact the size of country-level differences (Ashton, 2007).

Many of these response style or reference-group effects can interact with item wording or format. One significant problem is the behavior of reverse-keyed items across cultures. Test construction guidelines often call for inclusion of a balance of positively-keyed and reverse-keyed items, in large part to offset the effects of acquiescence bias. However, cross-cultural researchers have rarely emphasized this guideline because items involving negations are confusing to respondents in some languages and respondents in some cultures are hesitant to disagree with items (Smith, 2004). Prominent measures of self-construals (Singelis, 1994; Kashima and Hardie, 2000) and individualism-collectivism (Singelis et al., 1995; Triandis, 1995) contain few if any reverse-keyed items.

Even in Western studies, there is evidence that reverse-keyed items contribute less than positively keyed items to scale reliability and validity, and contain less trait variance (Schriesheim and Eisenbach, 1995; Schriesheim and Hill, 1981). The problem of reverse-keyed items is even more salient in cross-cultural studies, because research suggests that some cultural groups interpret positively keyed and reverse-keyed items differently, and not as bipolar opposites (Bagozzi et al., 1999; Hamamura et al., 2008; Kitayama et al., 2000; Lai and Yue, 2000; Schimmack et al., 2005; Scollon et al., 2005; Spencer-Rodgers et al., 2004). Thus, when positively and negatively keyed items are scored as a single bipolar scale, internal consistency reliability and correlations with external variables can be adversely affected (Wong et al., 2003).

Some researchers view the lack of bipolarity in opposite-keyed items as a methodological artifact (Marsh, 1996; McPherson and Mohr, 2005), while others have interpreted these findings in substantive terms. For example, the weak bipolarity of self-esteem and affect items in Asian samples has been attributed to East Asian dialecticism, which is thought to make East Asians (a) 'more able and willing than Westerners to store incompatible and contradictory information about the self in their self-concepts' (Choi and Choi, 2002: 1516), and (b) less likely to view emotions of opposite valence as incompatible with each other (Bagozzi et al., 1999; Kitayama et al., 2000). Hamamura et al. (2008) found that cultural differences in ambivalent responding were completely mediated by cultural differences in dialectical thinking, suggesting that ambivalent responding is not a method artifact. Spencer-Rodgers et al. (2004) went further, arguing that it is important to assess positive and negative self-esteem dimensions as separate unipolar dimensions to give East Asians the opportunity to exhibit their dialectical tendency to endorse both positive and negative aspects of themselves.

Some researchers deal with the issue of response styles by controlling them statistically. Many have applied within-subject standardization (ipsatization) to eliminate individual differences in the level and sometimes variability of ratings provided on Likert-type scales (Hofstede, 2001; Leung and Bond, 1989; Schwartz, 1994; Smith et al., 2002). See Hofstee et al. (1998) for a discussion of alternative methods. Alternatively, response styles can be treated as method factors in structural equations analyses (e.g., Cheung and Rensvold, 2000; Watson, 1992). In our own research, we have had mixed experiences using within-subject standardization to control for response styles. In some studies, results obtained with ipsatized data were more interpretable or consistent with theory (e.g., Church et al., 2008, 1998; Imperio et al., 2008). In other studies, however, we have concluded that ipsatization overcontrolled response styles and eliminated valid content variance. Given this state of affairs, researchers might consider analyzing their data both with and without controlling response styles and reporting whether it makes any difference.

It may be preferable to try to preclude response style effects by using alternative item formats. Marsh (1996) suggested eliminating negatively keyed items, because their disadvantages may offset their advantages, or including a few negative items to break up response patterns, but not scoring them. Other researchers have advocated paired-comparison or forced-choice items (Heine et al., 2002; Oishi et al., 2005). Indeed, Oishi et al. (2005) found that expected cultural differences in values between Americans and Japanese were better supported using a paired-comparison method than Likert scale ratings. To obtain an interval level of measurement, McPherson and Mohr (2005) suggested a bipolar format in which respondents indicate their position on a multi-point response scale between a positively and negatively keyed example of each item. A disadvantage of these bipolar or paired-comparison methods, however, is that they only enable assessment of the *relative* preference of two alternatives (e.g., individualism versus collectivism). This is not ideal if the two tendencies can, in fact, coexist in varying degrees in all individuals (Triandis, 1995). Wong et al. (2003) found better measurement equivalence and convergent validity of a materialistic values measure using an interrogative format with bipolar anchors than with traditional Likert statements. Scenario methods, which describe a short scenario and a limited number of alternative responses, have been used with success by some researchers (Peng et al., 1997; Triandis and Gelfand, 1998). For example, Peng et al. (1997) found that a scenario measure of values converged better with cultural experts' judgments of differences between Chinese and Americans than did ranking and rating methods.

The above considerations highlight the importance – even more so than in mono-cultural studies – of applying multiple measurement methods in cross-cultural research because of the limitations associated with each method. For example, if self-report methods are particularly susceptible to response bias differences across cultures, supplementing self-ratings with observer-ratings will be informative, and methods other than self-report (e.g., experimental methods, behavioral observations) can also be included, where feasible. Similarly, self-report measures of cultural dimensions such as individualism-collectivism can be augmented by true culture-level indicators (e.g., the percentage of people living

alone or the percentage of households with grandparents in them; Vandello and Cohen, 1999).

IMPORTED VERSUS INDIGENOUS MEASURES

Measurement across cultures can proceed using imported (imposed-etic) or indigenous (emic) measures. Several considerations are relevant in deciding which type of measure to use, including efficiency, constructs assessed, item content, universals versus culture-specifics, ease of cross-cultural comparisons, and contributions toward indigenous and universal social sciences (Church, 2001). Regarding efficiency, it may be more expedient to translate and, if necessary, adapt existing measures for use in a new culture, rather than develop indigenous measures. Further, training and resources for the development of indigenous measures may be limited in some cultural contexts. On the other hand, adaptation of imported tests may be less expedient than presumed if researchers conduct the studies and analyses needed to evaluate measurement equivalence. Regarding the constructs assessed, imported measures assess constructs of interest to the researcher and are often associated with extensive theory and research. On the other hand, the conceptual equivalence of imported constructs needs to be demonstrated and the researcher is more likely to identify culture-specific constructs using indigenous approaches.

Regarding item content, even when imported instruments measure universal constructs, some proportion of the items may not tap relevant indicators of the construct in new cultural contexts, and salient culture-specific indicators may be missed, reducing content validity. Regarding universals and culture-specifics, researchers interested in universals often favor imported measures, but their use may bias the results in the direction of cross-cultural comparability. For example, personality inventories with different dimensions have replicated equally well across cultures, demonstrating that imported inventories impose their embedded structure to some extent in new cultural contexts (Church, 2000). Researchers interested in culture-specifics favor indigenous measures. At the same time, the case for universal dimensions is particularly strong if these dimensions emerge independently in different cultures with indigenous instruments. Indigenous and imported dimensions can be related using a combined emic-etic approach (e.g., Benet-Martínez and Waller, 1997; Katigbak et al., 2002).

Regarding the ease of cross-cultural comparisons, the use of imported instruments facilitates direct cross-cultural comparisons, assuming that scalar equivalence can be demonstrated. In contrast, scores on indigenous measures are not directly comparable across cultures, although using item response theory methods, latent trait scores can be compared across cultures using sets of items that only partially overlap across cultures (Hambleton et al., 1991). Finally, regarding contributions toward indigenous and universal social sciences, it is shortsighted to uncritically reject imported theories, constructs, and methods. Nonetheless, the emergence of indigenous and less ethnocentric social sciences will probably be facilitated by decreased reliance on the importation of Western theories, constructs, and measures and increased emphasis on indigenous theory, constructs, and methods. Indeed, it can be argued that the emergence of more comprehensive and universal social sciences will result from the integration of indigenous social sciences that are initially derived with some degree of independence.

Although the etic-emic distinction is useful, it is more precise to delineate a continuum of levels of test adaptation or indigenization (see Table 9.1). For convenience, researchers occasionally avoid translation issues by administering imported tests in a non-native or second language (level 1 in Table 9.1; e.g., Huang et al., 1997). However, issues associated with language proficiency and language effects in data collection are then relevant. Most frequently, researchers translate existing measures as is (level 2) or with some degree of item adaptation (level 3). The psychometric and measurement equivalence analyses that comprise level 4 have become more common, but it is still easy to locate cross-cultural studies in which such analyses are minimal or non-existent. Level 5 involves content-indigenization, in which imported (e.g., Western) constructs are retained but measured with some proportion of locally developed items. For example, many of the personality inventories developed around the world contain local or culture-relevant items, but do not feel very culture-specific because they measure constructs that are familiar to Western psychologists (e.g., Schmit et al., 2002; Taylor and Boeyens, 1991; van Leest, 1997; Yanai et al., 1987). This approach is unlikely to reveal culture-specific dimensions if they exist.

Some researchers have used more completely indigenous approaches, with local items written to measure local constructs (level 6). Indigenous test construction follows the usual steps in instrument construction, but a key feature is the use of native languages, cultural informants, or local social science literatures to identify indigenous constructs and culture-relevant items (Church and Katigbak, 1988). Native languages can provide a particularly rich source of indigenous concepts, and a strong case can be made for their

Table 9.1 Levels of test adaptation and indigenization

Imposed-etic	1. Administration of an imported test in a non-native or second language.
	2. Administration of an imported test in literal translation without item adaptations.
Indigenization from without (i.e., outside the culture studied); culture as target	3. Items modified, where necessary, to be more relevant to the new culture
	4. Psychometric investigations of cross-cultural applicability and equivalence (e.g., local norm development; analyses of reliability, dimensional structure, validity, differential item functioning; differential response styles).
	5. Indigenous items/content developed to assess constructs identified in (primarily Western) psychological literature (content indigenization).
Indigenization from within (i.e., inside the culture studied); culture as source; emic	6. Indigenous constructs identified and assessed with indigenous items/content.
	7. Consideration or incorporation of more culturally relevant response formats and administration procedures (format indigenization).
	8. Consideration of appropriateness of item content, response formats, administration procedures for diverse indigenous subpopulations (e.g., less Westernized or educated individuals).
	9. Investigation of the reliability and construct validity of indigenous measures, including studies using indigenous criteria.

Note: Indigenization-from-without versus indigenization-from-within and culture-as-target versus culture-as-source terminology used by Enriquez (1994). Content versus format indigenization terminology used by Sahoo (1993). Imposed-etic versus emic terminology used by Berry (1969), among others.

From 'Personality measurement in cross-cultural perspective,' by A.T. Church, 2001, *Journal of Personality*, 69: 984. Copyright Blackwell Publishers. Adapted with permission.

representativeness and comprehensiveness if a fairly complete search for concepts is implemented, for example, by culling all relevant concepts or terms from a native language dictionary (Church et al., 1998, 1999; Saucier and Goldberg, 2001). In psychology, researchers in Mexico, the Philippines, and Chinese countries have been especially active in the development of indigenous measures, although combined etic-emic studies – which relate to indigenous and imported measures – do not provide much evidence for clearly culture-specific dimensions. Rather, they typically reveal more subtle differences in the salience or cultural flavor of particular dimensions (Katigbak et al., 1996, 2002; Ortiz et al., 2006; see, however, Cheung et al., 2001; Wang et al., 2005). An important question for social science researchers will be determining the extent to which indigenous constructs identified in various cultures exhibit universal versus unique cultural features.

Developers of indigenous measures also have the option of indigenizing the format of their instruments, which involves adapting traditional response formats and administration procedures, or developing new, more culturally relevant procedures (i.e., level 7). For example, in our development on cognitive ability subtests for rural Philippine children we employed both content- and format-indigenization (levels 5 and 7). We used tasks from Western intelligence tests such as vocabulary, information, concept formation, and picture construction (Church et al., 1985). However, all content was relevant to the barrio setting and gathered using participant observation, interviews with key informants, and questionnaire responses from high-school classes about barrio objects, words, events, and so forth. Format indigenization was illustrated by our adaptation of administration procedures for some of the verbal subtests, which involved systematic follow-up prompts (and partial credit) to elicit responses from children who were reserved, but not less able. Scores on these subtests were validated against indigenous criteria such as school performance and parents' ratings of the children's 'adaptive competencies' in the barrio setting (Church et al. 1985).

Another level of indigenization involves systematic studies of the applicability of indigenous measures for less educated indigenous subpopulations (level 8). An example in psychology was provided by the developers of the *Panukat ng Ugali at Pagkatao* (Measure of Behavior and Personality) in the Philippines (see Guanzon-Lapeña et al., 1998), who investigated the feasibility of administering the instrument to rural respondents, many of whom were not literate. The inventory was administered orally to small groups and interviewer assistants helped record the oral responses of respondents who could not do so themselves. The benefits and desirability of indigenizing response formats and administrative procedures in measurement have not yet been fully explored.

A final level of indigenization involves validating indigenous inventories against culture-relevant criteria (level 9). For example, Zhang and Bond (1998) found that measures of indigenous Chinese dimensions, in particular Harmony and Ren Qing, predicted filial piety beyond the prediction provided by Western personality dimensions. Similarly, we have found that indigenous Filipino scales and Western inventories predict societally relevant behaviors and attitudes about equally well in the Philippines, but that the indigenous dimensions added incremental prediction (Katigbak et al., 2002).

In summary, a range of levels or approaches to content and format indigenization of instruments can be employed by social scientists. Clearly, as noted earlier, there are trade-offs for the researcher in applying existing (imported) instruments in essentially the same form across cultural contexts versus employing instruments obtained using various levels or degrees of indigenization. Ultimately, the measurement approach adopted by researchers will depend on their goals (e.g., universals versus culture-specifics) and the research questions to be addressed.

MEASURING CULTURE AND THE LEVELS OF ANALYSIS ISSUE

To study the impact of culture, we must measure it. Two general approaches have been used. Less commonly, researchers have identified true culture- or nation-level indicators in such domains as ecology (e.g., temperature), education (e.g., school enrollment levels), economics (e.g., Gross National Product per capita), mass communications (e.g., radios per 1,000 inhabitants), and population (e.g., rate of population increase) (e.g., Georgas and Berry, 1995). This approach is consistent with an ecocultural model, which postulates systematic links between ecological and sociopolitical contexts and individual behavior (Georgas et al., 2004). As Georgas et al. (2004) have argued, if one wishes to link ecological and other culture-level variables to individual behavior, one must actually incorporate true culture-level variables, rather than simply aggregating individual-level data to the cultural level. A disadvantage of this approach is that the variables used to assess ecology or culture are typically rather distal from the individual-level behaviors they are trying to predict, so the variables that mediate between these ecocultural variables and individual behavior still need to be explicated. Also, if we conceive of culture as largely involving shared values, beliefs, and behaviors (e.g., Smith et al., 2006), these nation-level variables seem to measure ecological environment more than 'culture' per se.

Accordingly, the most common method used to measure culture has been to assess values and beliefs at the level of individuals, and then to aggregate (average) these individual-level scores over a large (and ideally representative) sample in each culture or nation. How these aggregated means are computed relates to the 'levels of analysis' issue in cross-cultural research (Smith et al., 2006). In discussing this issue, Smith et al. (2006) made a useful distinction between *citizen means* and *nation-level means* in deriving aggregate scores for cultural samples. To derive citizen means it is first necessary to demonstrate reasonable metric and scalar equivalence at the individual level across cultures, for example, by applying multigroup CFA or MACS to the items. The scale scores of individual participants are then computed in the normal manner and averaged across individuals within each culture. The result is a single average score (i.e., citizen mean) for each scale in each culture at the individual or psychological level of analysis.

Alternatively, a nation-level mean can be derived by first computing the national average for each item separately, then conducting a factor analysis on these item means across nations. The nation-level mean for each culture can be computed as the mean of the national averages across the items defining the derived 'ecological factors' (or by using the ecological factor scores themselves). The sample size for the factor analysis is the number of cultures. Whereas the citizen means depict the average participant within each of the nations,

the nation-level means represent the cultural or ecological level and summarize the national or cultural context within which individuals are located (Smith et al., 2006). Typically, the citizen means will not be equal to the nation-level means. In addition, the dimensional structure of the measure need not be the same at the individual and cultural levels because the relationships among values or beliefs may be different at the two levels.

For example, Schwartz (1992, 1994) identified ten value types at the individual level of analysis (Stimulation, Self-direction, Security, Conformity, Tradition, Achievement, Power, Universalism, Benevolence, and Hedonism), but seven value types at the ecological or cultural level (Intellectual Autonomy, Affective Autonomy, Embeddedness, Hierarchy, Egalitarianism, Mastery, and Harmony). An illustration of how specific values can be related differently at the individual and cultural level was provided by the specific values of *humble* and *authority*. At the individual level, the two values are negatively correlated, indicating that individuals who value humility tend not to value authority. However, at the cultural level, both values were associated with the Hierarchy value type, indicating that cultures with a preponderance of individuals who value authority also tend to have individuals who value humility, presumably because the different individuals relate to each other through a system of hierarchical roles (Smith et al., 2006). Similar results were obtained by Leung et al. and Bond and colleagues (Leung et al., 2002; Bond et al., 2004) in their measure of cultural dimensions based on beliefs or social axioms. At the individual level of analysis, they identified five factors (Social Cynicism, Social Complexity, Reward for Application, Religiosity, and Fate Control), but only the Social Cynicism factor replicated well at the nation-level, while the other four individual-level factors merged into a single Dynamic Externality factor. Such results indicate that social scientists cannot assume that constructs or dimensions identified at the cultural level – which differentiate cultures – also apply at the individual level (i.e., differentiate individuals), or that the relationships between constructs will be same at the cultural and individual levels of analysis.

Importantly, whether the researcher measures and compares citizen means or nation-level means depends on the level of analysis of the researcher's hypotheses. As Smith et al. (2006) noted, 'citizen means lend themselves to the types of comparisons that are most relevant to psychological theories, which mostly refer to individuals, not to larger entities' (p. 51), whereas nation-level means 'describe the contexts within which individuals are socialized' (p. 54) and are best related to other culture-level indices. Smith et al. (2006) emphasized that relationships among variables should always be investigated at the relevant level of analysis, using measures appropriate for that level. Attempts to infer relationships among constructs at the nation-level based on their structure at the individual level have been referred to as the *ecological fallacy*, whereas attempts to infer individual-level relationships from nation-level relationships have been labeled the *reverse ecological fallacy*.

A number of researchers have developed measures to assess dimensions of culture at the individual level (sample means thus represent citizen means). Most of these measures assess individualism-collectivism or self-construals (Singelis, 1994; Triandis and Gelfand, 1998) and an extensive literature exists on the individual-level correlates of individualism-collectivism (for reviews, see Oyserman et al., 2002; Triandis, 1995). Other individual-level measures

assess values (Schwartz, 1992), beliefs (Leung et al., 2002), and aspects of Asian dialecticism (Choi et al., 2003; Choi et al., 2007; Spencer-Rodgers et al., 2004). In addition to examining the individual-level correlates of these constructs, researchers often hope to demonstrate that these constructs mediate or account for cultural differences in various behavioral phenomena (e.g., Choi et al., 2003).

Recently, self-report measures of individualism-collectivism have undergone extensive scrutiny (Bond, 2002; Fiske, 2002; Kitayama, 2002), as have measures of self-construals (Breshnahan et al., 2005; Gudykunst and Lee, 2003). In addition, the measures of Asian dialecticism are fairly new and validity evidence is presently limited. Several researchers have suggested that the concept of individualism may be too broad and distal from behavior to have much explanatory power. Contributing significantly to the reevaluation of individualism-collectivism and self-construal measures is the frequent finding of unexpected cultural mean differences on the scales (Matsumoto, 1999; Oyserman et al., 2002). And, of course, these measures are subject to the same problems of measurement equivalence, response styles, and reference group effects discussed earlier (Heine and Norenzayan, 2006; Matsumoto and Yoo, 2006). Heine and Norenzayan (2006) argue that these problems reduce the utility of such measures in mediational designs.

Some critics have noted more fundamental limitations of these self-report instruments as measures of culture. For example, many aspects of culture may be too inaccessible to awareness or self-reflection to be measured using self-report (e.g., Heine and Norenzayan, 2006). Such measures also tend to suggest that culture is a static entity rather than a dynamic system of meanings, practices, and mental processes. For example, Hermans and Kempen (1998) criticized the tendency to treat culture as geographically localized and in terms of static dichotomies such as individualism versus collectivism, independence versus interdependence, and Western versus non-Western. These authors pointed out the increasing hybridization and dynamic interconnectedness of cultures, and the considerable heterogeneity and multiplicity of cultural meanings and practices within nations. However, because researchers have not yet determined how to measure these dynamic aspects of cultures, they have been forced to rely on measures that provide relatively static representations of the predominant tendencies (e.g., values and beliefs) that differentiate particular national groups or subgroups.

Some critics have proposed that self-report measures of cultural dimensions be abandoned in favor of methods such as participant observation, experience sampling of ongoing behavior, implicit measures, experimental designs, or true ecological or culture-level variables (Bond, 2002; Fiske, 2002; Heine and Norenzayan, 2006; Kitayama, 2002). Other researchers continue to believe, however, that self-report measures can be valid and useful (e.g., Gudykunst and Lee, 2003; Oyserman et al., 2002; Schimmack et al., 2005). For example, Schimmack et al. (2005) demonstrated greater convergent validity for individualism-collectivism measures when response styles were statistically controlled. Others have suggested that researchers should focus on measuring more specific components of individualism-collectivism (Noguchi, 2007; Oyserman et al., 2002).

CONCLUDING REMARKS

As evident from this review, cross-cultural researchers have gone a long way toward delineating conceptual and methodological issues and methods that are relevant in measurement across cultures. However, many issues remain unresolved. Below, I list some of the outstanding issues that require additional attention:

1. The alternative theoretical perspectives on measurement across cultures probably complement each other, so it will be useful to incorporate measures from multiple perspectives in cross-cultural research designs (e.g., see Church, 2001: 997–9).

2. The types of bias that can confound cross-cultural measurements are well known. These include various construct, method, and item biases. However, the impact of these biases under various conditions is not well-established. In particular, more research is needed on response styles and reference-group effects. Researchers that are unaware of these biases may draw faulty conclusions, while all researchers need more definitive methods for addressing these biases.

3. Valid measurement across cultures will require that cross-cultural researchers keep abreast of ongoing developments in the statistical methods used to test measurement equivalence (e.g., confirmatory factor analysis, IRT-based DIF methods, multi-level analyses) or that they collaborate with researchers who have this expertise. For example, hierarchical linear modeling, with its ability to simultaneously test hypotheses at both the individual and cultural levels of analyses, will likely become increasingly important (e.g., Oishi et al., 2004; van de Vijver et al., 2008).

4. Growing disenchantment with the validity of traditional Likert rating scales in cross-cultural research is a fairly recent development. Research is needed to evaluate the effectiveness of the alternative methods being suggested by some researchers.

5. Measures have not been developed for many of the culture-specific constructs described by indigenous social scientists. Such measures would be useful in investigating the cultural uniqueness and incremental validity of indigenous dimensions relative to imported measures.

6. Alternative measures of cultural dimensions need to be explored, including methods that go beyond self-report.

With the increasing globalization of science and society, cross-cultural research will likely continue to grow in importance, as will the need to successfully address some of the unresolved measurement issues.

REFERENCES

Allik, J. and McCrae, R. R. (2004) 'Toward a geography of personality traits: Patterns of profiles across 36 cultures', *Journal of Cross-Cultural Psychology*, 35: 13–28.

Ashton, M. C. (2007) 'Self-reports and stereotypes: A comment on McCrae et al.', *European Journal of Personality*, 21: 983–6.

Bagozzi, R. P., Wong, N. and Yi, Y. (1999) 'The role of culture and gender in the relationship between positive and negative affect', *Cognition and Emotion*, 13: 641–72.

Baumgartner, H. and Steenkamp, J.-B. E. M. (2001) 'Response styles in marketing research: A cross-national investigation', *Journal of Marketing Research*, 38: 143–56.

Benet-Martínez, V. and Waller, N. G. (1997) 'Further evidence for the cross-cultural generality of the Big Seven factor model: Indigenous and imported Spanish personality constructs', *Journal of Personality*, 65: 567–98.

Berry, J. W. (1969) 'On cross-cultural comparability', *International Journal of Psychology*, 4: 119–28.

Bingenheimer, J. B., Raudenbush, S. W., Leventhal, T. and Brooks-Gunn, J. (2005) 'Measurement equivalence and differential item functioning in family psychology', *Journal of Family Psychology*, 19: 441–55.

Bond, M. H. (2002) 'Reclaiming the individual from Hofstede's ecological analysis—A 20-year odyssey: Comment on Oyserman et al.', (2002) *Psychological Bulletin*, 128: 73–7.

Bond, M. H., Leung, K., Au, A., Tong, K.-K., de Carrasquel, S. R., Murakami, F., et al. (2004). 'Culture-level dimensions of social axioms and their correlates across 41 cultures', *Journal of Cross-Cultural Psychology*, 35: 548–70.

Bond, M. H. and Yang, K.-S. (1982) 'Ethnic affirmation versus cross-cultural accommodation: The variable impact of questionnaire language on Chinese bilinguals in Hong Kong', *Journal of Cross-Cultural Psychology*, 13: 169–85.

Bontempo, R. (1993) 'Translation fidelity of psychological scales: An item response theory analysis of an individualism-collectivism scale', *Journal of Cross-Cultural Psychology*, 24: 149–66.

Breshnahan, M. J., Levine, T. R., Shearman, S. M., Lee, S. Y., Park, C.-Y. and Kiyomiya, T. (2005) 'A multimethod multitrait validity assessment of self-construal in Japan, Korea, and the United States', *Human Communication Research*, 31: 33–59.

Brislin, R. W. (1986) 'The wording and translation of research instruments', in W. J. Lonner and J. W. Berry (eds), *Field methods in cross-cultural research.* Beverly Hills, CA: Sage. pp. 137–164.

Byrne, B. M., Shavelson, R. J. and Muthén, B. (1989) 'Testing for the equivalence of factor covariance and mean structures: The issue of partial measurement invariance', *Psychological Bulletin*, 105: 456–66.

Camilli, G. and Shepard, L. A. (1994) *Methods for identifying biased test items* (Vol. 4). Thousand Oaks, CA: Sage.

Campbell, J. D., Trapnell, P. D., Heine, S. J., Katz, I. M., Lavallee, L. F. and Lehman, D. R. (1996) 'Self-concept clarity: Measurement, personality correlates, and cultural boundaries', *Journal of Personality and Social Psychology*, 70: 141–56.

Caprara, G. V., Barbaranelli, C., Bermúdez, J., Maslach, C. and Ruch, W. (2000) 'Multivariate methods for the comparison of factor structures in cross-cultural research: An illustration with the Big Five Questionnaire', *Journal of Cross-Cultural Psychology*, 31: 437–64.

Chen, C., Lee, S.-Y. and Stevenson, H. W. (1995) 'Response style and cross-cultural comparisons of rating scales among East Asian and North American students', *Psychological Science*, 6: 170–5.

Cheung, F. M., and Leung, K. (1998) 'Indigenous personality measures: Chinese examples', *Journal of Cross-Cultural Psychology*, 29: 233–48.

Cheung, F. M., Leung, K., Zhang, J. X., Sun, H. F., Gan, Y. Q., Song, W. Z., et al. (2001) 'Indigenous Chinese personality constructs: Is the Five Factor Model complete?' *Journal of Cross-Cultural Psychology*, 32: 407–33.

Cheung, G. W. and Rensvold, R. B. (2000) 'Assessing extreme and acquiescence response sets in cross-cultural research using structural equations modeling', *Journal of Cross-Cultural Psychology*, 31: 187–212.

Choi, I. and Choi, Y. (2002) 'Culture and self-concept flexibility', *Personality and Social Psychology Bulletin*, 28: 1508–17.

Choi, I., Dalal, R., Kim-Prieto, C. and Park, H. (2003) 'Culture and judgment of causal relevance', *Journal of Personality and Social Psychology*, 84: 46–59.

Choi, I., Koo, M. and Choi, J. A. (2007) 'Individual differences in analytic versus holistic thinking', *Personality and Social Psychology Bulletin*, 33: 691–705.

Choi, S.-C., Kim, U. and Choi, S.-H. (1993) 'Indigenous analysis of collective representations: A Korean perspective', in U. Kim and J. W. Berry (eds), *Indigenous psychologies: Research and experience in cultural context*. Newbury Park, CA: Sage. pp. 193–210.

Church, A. T. (2000) 'Culture and personality: Toward an integrated cultural trait psychology', *Journal of Personality*, 68: 651–703.

Church, A. T. (2001) 'Personality measurement in cross-cultural perspective', *Journal of Personality*, 69:979–1006.

Church, A. T. (2008) 'Current controversies in the study of personality across cultures', *Social and Personality Psychology Compass*. 2: 1930–51.

Church, A. T., Anderson-Harumi, C. A., del Prado, A. M., Curtis, G. J., Tanaka-Matsumi, J., Valdez-Medina, J. L., et al. (2008) 'Culture, cross-role consistency, and adjustment: Testing trait and cultural psychology perspectives', *Journal of Personality and Social Psychology*, 95: 739–55.

Church, A. T. and Burke, P. J. (1994) 'Exploratory and confirmatory tests of the Big Five and Tellegen's three- and four-dimensional models', *Journal of Personality and Social Psychology*, 66: 93–114.

Church, A. T. and Katigbak, M. S. (1988) 'The emic strategy in the identification and assessment of personality dimensions in a non-western culture', *Journal of Cross-Cultural Psychology*, 19: 140–63.

Church, A. T. and Katigbak, M. S. (1989) 'Internal, external, and self-report structure of personality in a non-western culture: An investigation of cross-language and cross-cultural generalizability', *Journal of Personality and Social Psychology*, 57: 857–72.

Church, A. T. and Katigbak, M. S. (2002) 'Indigenization of psychology in the Philippines', *International Journal of Psychology*, 37: 129–48.

Church, A. T., Katigbak, M. S. and Almario-Velazco, G. (1985) 'Psychometric intelligence and adaptive competence in rural Philippine children', *Intelligence*, 9: 317–40.

Church, A. T., Katigbak, M. S. and Castañeda, I. (1988) 'The effects of language of data collection on derived conceptions of healthy personality with Filipino bilinguals', *Journal of Cross-Cultural Psychology*, 19: 178–92.

Church, A. T., Katigbak, M. S., del Prado, A. M., Valdez-Medina, J. L., Miramontes, L. G. and Ortiz, F. A. (2006) 'A cross-cultural study of trait self-enhancement, explanatory variables, and adjustment', *Journal of Research in Personality*, 40: 1169–1201.

Church, A. T., Katigbak, M. S., Miramontes, L. G., del Prado, A. M. and Cabrera, H. F. (2007) 'Culture and the behavioral manifestations of traits: An application of the act frequency approach', *European Journal of Personality*, 21: 389–417.

Church, A. T., Katigbak, M. S. and Reyes, J. A. S. (1998) 'Further exploration of Filipino personality structure using the lexical approach: Do the big five or big seven dimensions emerge?' *European Journal of Personality*, 12: 249–69.

Church, A. T., Katigbak, M. S., Reyes, J. A. S. and Jensen, S. M. (1999) 'The structure of affect in a non-Western culture: Evidence for cross-cultural comparability', *Journal of Personality*, 67: 503–32.

Cross, S. E. and Markus, H. R. (1999) 'The cultural constitution of personality', in L. A. Pervin and O. P. John (eds), *Handbook of personality: Theory and research*, 2nd edition. New York: Guilford. pp. 378–96.

del Prado, A. M., Church, A. T., Katigbak, M. S., Miramontes, L. G., Whitty, M. T. and Curtis, G. J. (2007) 'Culture, method, and the content of self-concepts: Testing trait, individual—self-primacy, and cultural psychology perspectives', *Journal of Research in Personality*, 41: 1119–60.

Ellis, B. B. (1990) 'Assessing intelligence cross-nationally: A case for differential item functioning', *Intelligence*, 14: 61–78.

Ellis, B. B. (1995) 'A partial test of Hulin's psychometric theory of measurement equivalence in translated tests', *European Journal of Psychological Assessment*, 11: 184–93.

Ellis, B. B. and Mead, A. D. (2000) 'Assessment of the measurement equivalence of a Spanish translation of the 16PF Questionnaire', *Educational and Psychological Measurement*, 60: 787–807.

Ellis, B. B., Minsel, B. and Becker, P. (1989) 'Evaluation of attitude survey translations: An investigation using item response theory', *International Journal of Psychology*, 24: 665–84.

Embretson, S. E. and Reise, S. P. (2000) *Item response theory for psychologists*. Mahwah, NJ: Lawrence Erlbaum.

Enriquez, V. G. (1994) *From colonial to liberation psychology: The Philippine experience*. Manila, Philippines: De La Salle University Press.

Fiske, A. P. (2002) 'Using individualism and collectivism to compare cultures—A critique of the validity and measurement of the constructs: Comment on Oyserman et al. (2002)', *Psychological Bulletin*, 128: 78–88.

Georgas, J. and Berry, J. W. (1995) 'An ecocultural taxonomy for cross-cultural psychology', *Cross-Cultural Research*, 29: 121–57.

Georgas, J., van de Vijver, F. J. R. and Berry, J. W. (2004) 'The ecocultural framework, ecosocial indices, and psychological variables in cross-cultural research', *Journal of Cross-Cultural Psychology*, 35: 74–96.

Georgas, J., Weiss, L. G., van de Vijver, F. J. R. and Saklofske, D. H. (2003) *Culture and children's intelligence: Cross-cultural analysis of the WISC-III.* Amsterdam: Academic Press.

Greenfield, P. M. (1997) 'You can't take it with you: Why ability assessments don't cross cultures', *American Psychologist*, 52: 1115–24.

Grimm, S. D. and Church, A. T. (1999) 'A cross-cultural study of response biases in personality measures', *Journal of Research in Personality*, 33: 415–41.

Guanzon-Lapeña, M. A., Church, A. T., Carlota, A. J. and Katigbak, M. S. (1998) 'Indigenous personality measures: Philippine examples', *Journal of Cross-Cultural Psychology*, 29: 249–70.

Gudykunst, W. B. and Lee, C. M. (2003) 'Assessing the validity of self-construal scales: A response to Levine et al.', *Human Communication Research*, 29: 253–74.

Hamamura, T., Heine, S. J. and Paulhus, D. L. (2008) 'Cultural differences in response style: The role of dialectical thinking', *Personality and Individual Differences*, 44: 932–42.

Hambleton, R. K., Swaminathan, H. and Rogers, H. J. (1991) *Fundamentals of item response theory.* Newbury Park, CA: Sage.

Heine, S. J. (2001) 'Self as a cultural product: An examination of East Asian and North American selves', *Journal of Personality*, 69: 880–906.

Heine, S. J. and Hamamura, T. (2007) 'In search of East Asian self-enhancement', *Personality and Social Psychology Review*, 11: 1–24.

Heine, S. J., Lehman, D. R., Peng, K. and Greenholtz, J. (2002) 'What's wrong with cross-cultural comparisons of subjective Likert scales?: The reference-group effect', *Journal of Personality and Social Psychology*, 82: 903–18.

Heine, S. J. and Norenzayan, A. (2006) 'Toward a psychological science for a cultural species', *Perspectives on Psychological Science*, 1: 251–69.

Hermans, H. J. M. and Kempen, H. J. G. (1998) 'Moving cultures: The perilous problems of cultural dichotomies in a globalizing society' *American Psychologist*, 53: 1111–20.

Hofstede, G. (2001) *Culture's consequences: Comparing values, behaviors, institutions, and organizations across cultures.* 2nd edition. Thousand Oaks, CA: Sage Publications.

Hofstede, G. and McCrae, R. R. (2004) 'Personality and culture revisited: Linking traits and dimensions of culture', *Cross-Cultural Research*, 38: 52–88.

Hofstee, W. K. B., Ten Berge, J. M. F. and Hendriks, A. A. J. (1998) 'How to score questionnaires', *Personality and Individual Differences*, 25: 897–909.

Howard, G. S. (1991) 'Culture tales: A narrative approach to thinking, cross-cultural psychology, and psychotherapy', *American Psychologist*, 46: 187–97.

Huang, C. D., Church, A. T. and Katigbak, M. S. (1997) 'Identifying cultural differences in items and traits: Differential item functioning in the NEO Personality Inventory', *Journal of Cross-Cultural Psychology*, 28: 192–218.

Hui, C. H. and Triandis, H. C. (1985) 'Measurement in cross-cultural psychology: A review and comparison of strategies', *Journal of Cross-Cultural Psychology*, 16: 131–52.

Imperio, S. M., Church, A. T., Katigbak, M. S. and Reyes, J. A. (2008) 'Lexical studies of Filipino person descriptors: Adding personality-relevant social and physical attributes', *European Journal of Personality*, 22: 291–321.

Johnson, T., Kulesa, P., Cho, Y. I. and Shavitt, S. (2005) 'The relation between culture and response styles: Evidence from 19 countries', *Journal of Cross-Cultural Psychology*, 36: 264–77.

Johnson, W., Spinath, F., Krueger, R. F., Angleitner, A. and Riemann, R. (2008) 'Personality in Germany and Minnesota: An IRT-based comparison of MPQ self-reports', *Journal of Personality*, 76: 665–706.

Kashima, E. S. and Hardie, E. A. (2000) 'The development and validation of the Relational, Individual, and Collective self-aspects (RIC) Scale', *Asian Journal of Social Psychology*, 3: 19–48.

Katigbak, M. S., Church, A. T. and Akamine, T. X. (1996) 'Cross-cultural generalizability of personality dimensions: Relating indigenous and imported dimensions in two cultures', *Journal of Personality and Social Psychology*, 70: 99–114.

Katigbak, M. S., Church, A. T., Guanzon-Lapeña, M. A., Carlota, A. J. and del Pilar, G. H. (2002) 'Are indigenous personality dimensions culture specific? Philippine inventories and the five-factor model', *Journal of Personality and Social Psychology*, 82: 89–101.

Kim, U., Yang, K.-S. and Hwang, K.-K. (eds). (2006) *Indigenous and cultural psychology: Understanding people in context.* New York: Springer.

Kishton, J. M. and Widaman, K. F. (1994) 'Unidimensional versus domain representative parceling of questionnaire items: An empirical example', *Educational and Psychological Measurement*, 54: 757–65.

Kitayama, S. (2002) 'Culture and basic psychological processes—Toward a system view of culture: Comment on Oyserman et al. (2002).' *Psychological Bulletin*, 128: 89–96.

Kitayama, S., Markus, H. R. and Kurokawa, M. (2000) 'Culture, emotion, and well-being: Good feelings in Japan and the United States', *Cognition and Emotion*, 14: 93–124.

Kohnstamm, G. A., Halverson, C. F., Jr., Mervielde, I. and Havill, V. L. (1998) *Parental descriptions of child personality: Developmental antecedents of the Big Five?* Mahwah, NJ: Lawrence Erlbaum.

Labouvie, E. and Ruetsch, C. (1995) 'Testing for equivalence of measurement scales: Simple structure and metric invariance reconsidered', *Multivariate Behavioral Research*, 30: 63–76.

Lai, J. C. L. and Yue, X. (2000) 'Measuring optimism in Hong Kong and mainland Chinese with the revised Life Orientation Test', *Personality and Individual Differences*, 28: 781–96.

Leung, K. and Bond, M. H. (1989) 'On the empirical identification of dimensions for cross-cultural comparisons', *Journal of Cross-Cultural Psychology*, 20: 133–52.

Leung, K., Bond, M. H., de Carrasquel, S. R., Muñoz, C., Hernandez, M. and Murakami, F. (2002) 'Social axioms: The search for universal dimensions of beliefs about how the world functions', *Journal of Cross-Cultural Psychology*, 33: 286–302.

Little, T. D., Cunningham, W. A., Shahar, G. and Widaman, K. F. (2002) 'To parcel or not to parcel: Exploring the question, weighing the merits', *Structural Equation Modeling*, 9: 151–73.

Lord, F. M. (1980) *Applications of item response theory to practical testing problems*. Hillsdale, NJ: Lawrence Erlbaum.

Lynn, R. and Mikk, J. (2007) 'National differences in intelligence and educational attainment', *Intelligence*, 35: 115–21.

Lynn, R. and Vanhanen, T. (2006) *IQ and global inequality*. Athens, GA: Washington Summit Books.

Mallinckrodt, B. and Wang, C. C. (2004) 'Quantitative methods for verifying semantic equivalence of translated research instruments: A Chinese version of the experiences in close relationships scale', *Journal of Counseling Psychology*, 51: 368–79.

Marín, G. and Marín, B. V. (1991) *Research with Hispanic populations*. Newbury Park, CA: Sage.

Markus, H. R. and Kitayama, S. (1991) 'Culture and the self: Implications for cognition, emotion, and motivation', *Psychological Review*, 98: 224–53.

Markus, H. R. and Kitayama, S. (1998) 'The cultural psychology of personality', *Journal of Cross-Cultural Psychology*, 29: 63–87.

Marsella, A. J., De Vos, G. A. and Hsu, F. L. K. (eds) (1985) *Culture and self*. London: Tavistok.

Marsella, A. J., Dubanoski, J., Hamada, W. C. and Morse, H. (2000) 'The measurement of personality across cultures', *American Behavioral Scientist*, 44: 41–62.

Marsh, H. W. (1996) 'Positive and negative global self-esteem: A substantively meaningful distinction or artifactors?' *Journal of Personality and Social Psychology*, 70: 810–19.

Matsumoto, D. (1999) 'Culture and self: An empirical assessment of Markus and Kitayama's theory of independent and interdependent self-construal', *Asian Journal of Social Psychology*, 2: 289–310.

Matsumoto, D. and Yoo, S. H. (2006) 'Toward a new generation of cross-cultural research', *Perspectives on Psychological Science*, 1: 234–50.

McCrae, R. R. (2002) 'NEO-PI-R data from 36 cultures: Further intercultural comparisons', in R. R. McCrae, and J. Allik (eds), *The five-factor model of personality across cultures*. New York: Kluwer Academic/Plenum. pp. 105–25.

McCrae, R. R. and Allik, J. (2002) *The five-factor model of personality across cultures*. New York: Kluwer Academic/Plenum.

McCrae, R. R., Terracciano, A. and 79 Members of the Personality Profiles of Cultures Project (2005) 'Personality profiles of cultures: Aggregate personality traits', *Journal of Personality and Social Psychology*, 89: 407–25.

McCrae, R. R., Terracciano, A., Realo, A. and Allik, J. (2007) 'On the validity of culture-level personality and stereotype scores', *European Journal of Personality*, 21: 987–91.

McCrae, R. R., Zonderman, A. B., Costa, P. T., Bond, M. H. and Paunonen, S. V. (1996) 'Evaluating replicability of factors in the Revised NEO Personality Inventory: Confirmatory factor analysis versus Procrustes rotation', *Journal of Personality and Social Psychology*, 70: 552–66.

McPherson, J. and Mohr, P. (2005) 'The role of item extremity in the emergence of keying-related factors: An exploration with the Life Orientation Test', *Psychological Methods*, 10: 120–31.

Meade, A. W. and Lautenschlager, G. J. (2004) 'A comparison of item response theory and confirmatory factor analytic methodologies for establishing measurement equivalence/invariance', *Organizational Research Methods*, 7: 361–88.

Miller, J. (1997) 'The interdependence of interpretive ethnographic and quantitative psychological methodologies in cultural psychology', *Ethos*, 25: 164–76.

Muthén, B. O. (1994) 'Multilevel covariance structure analysis', *Sociological Methods and Research*, 22: 376–98.

Noguchi, K. (2007) 'Examination of the content of individualism/collectivism scales in cultural comparisons of the USA and Japan', *Asian Journal of Social Psychology*, 10: 131–44.

Oishi, S., Diener, E., Scollon, C. N. and Biswas-Diener, R. (2004) 'Cross situational consistency of affective experiences across cultures', *Journal of Personality and Social Psychology*, 86: 460–72.

Oishi, S., Hahn, J., Schimmack, U., Radhakrishan, P., Dzokoto, V. and Ahadi, S. (2005) 'The measurement of values across cultures: A pairwise comparison approach', *Journal of Research in Personality*, 39: 299–305.

Ortiz, F. A., Church, A. T., Vargas-Flores, J. D., Ibáñez-Reyes, J., Flores-Galaz, M., Iuit-Briceño, J. I., et al. (2006) 'Are indigenous personality dimensions culture-specific? Mexican inventories and the five-factor model', *Journal of Research in Personality*, 41: 618–49.

Oyserman, D., Coon, H. M. and Kemmelmeier, M. (2002a) 'Rethinking individualism and collectivism: Evaluation of theoretical assumptions and meta-analyses', *Psychological Bulletin*, 128: 3–72.

Oyserman, D., Kemmelmeier, M. and Coon, H. M. (2002b) 'Cultural psychology, a new look: Reply to Bond (2002), Fiske (2002), Kitayama (2002), and Miller (2002)', *Psychological Bulletin*, 128: 110–17.

Peng, K., Nisbett, R. E. and Wong, N. Y. (1997) 'Validity problems comparing values across cultures and possible solutions', *Psychological Methods*, 2: 329–44.

Perugini, M. and Richetin, J. (2007) 'In the land of the blind, the one-eyed man is king', *European Journal of Personality*, 21: 977–81.

Raju, N. S. (1990) 'Determining the significance of estimated signed and unsigned areas between two item response functions', *Applied Psychological Measurement*, 14: 197–207.

Raju, N. S., Laffitte, L. J. and Byrne, B. M. (2002) 'Measurement equivalence: A comparison of methods based on confirmatory factor analysis and item response theory', *Journal of Applied Psychology*, 87: 517–29.

Ralston, D. A., Cunniff, M. K. and Gustafson, D. J. (1995) 'Cultural accommodation: The effect of language on the responses of bilingual Hong Kong Chinese managers', *Journal of Cross-Cultural Psychology*, 26: 714–27.

Ramírez-Esparza, N., Gosling, S. D., Benet-Martínez, V., Potter, J. P. and Pennebaker, J. W. (2004) 'Do bilinguals have two personalities? A special case

of cultural frame switching', *Journal of Research in Personality*, 40: 99–120.

Reise, S. P. and Henson, J. M. (2003) 'A discussion of modern versus traditional psychometrics as applied to personality assessment scales', *Journal of Personality Assessment*, 81: 93–103.

Reise, S. P., Widaman, K. F. and Pugh, R. H. (1993) 'Confirmatory factor analysis and item response theory: Two approaches for exploring measurement invariance', *Psychological Bulletin*, 114: 552–66.

Rindermann, H. (2007) 'The g-factor of international cognitive ability comparisons: The homogeneity of results in PISA, TIMSS, PIRLS and IQ-tests across nations', *European Journal of Personality*, 21: 667–706.

Sahoo, F. M. (1993) 'Indigenization of psychological measurements: Parameters and operationalization', *Psychology and Developing Societies*, 5: 1–13.

Saucier, G. and Goldberg, L. R. (2001) 'Lexical studies of indigenous personality factors: Premises, products, and prospects', *Journal of Personality*, 69: 847–79.

Schimmack, U., Oishi, S. and Diener, E. (2005) 'Individualism: A valid and important dimension of cultural differences between nations', *Personality and Social Psychology Review*, 9: 17–31.

Schmit, M. J., Kihm, J. A. and Robie, C. (2002) 'The Global Personality Inventory (GPI)', in B. de Raad and M. Perugini (eds), *Big Five assessment*. Seattle, WA: Hogrefe and Huber. pp. 195–236.

Schmitt, D. P., Allik, J., McCrae, R. R., Benet-Martínez, V., Alcalay, L., Ault, L., et al. (2007) 'The geographic distribution of big five personality traits: Patterns and profiles of human self-description across 56 nations', *Journal of Cross-Cultural Psychology*, 38: 173–212.

Schriesheim, C. A. and Eisenbach, R. J. (1995) 'An exploratory and confirmatory factor-analytic investigation of item wording effects on the obtained factor structures of survey questionnaire measures', *Journal of Management*, 21: 1177–93.

Schriesheim, C. A. and Hill, K. D. (1981) 'Controlling acquiescence response bias by item reversals: The effect on questionnaire validity', *Educational and Psychological Measurement*, 41: 1101–14.

Schwartz, S. H. (1992) 'Universals in the content and structure of values: Theoretical advances and empirical tests in 20 countries', in M. P. Zanna (ed.), *Advances in experimental social psychology Vol. 25.* Orlando, FL: Academic. pp. 1–65.

Schwartz, S. H. (1994) 'Beyond individualism and collectivism: New cultural dimensions of values', in U. Kim, H. C. Triandis, C. Kağitçibaşi, S. C. Choi and G. Yoon (eds), *Individualism and collectivism: Theory, method and applications.* Thousand Oaks, CA: Sage. pp. 85–119.

Scollon, C. N., Diener, E., Oishi, S. and Biswas-Diener, R. (2005) 'An experience sampling and cross-cultural investigation of the relation between pleasant and unpleasant affect', *Cognition and Emotion*, 19: 27–52.

Sedikides, C., Gaertner, L. and Vevea, J. L. (2007) 'Evaluating the evidence for pancultural self-enhancement', *Asian Journal of Social Psychology*, 10: 201–3.

Serpell, R. (2000) 'Intelligence and culture', in R. J. Sternberg (ed.), *Handbook of intelligence*. New York: Cambridge University Press. pp. 549–77.

Shweder, R. A. (1991) *Thinking through culture: Expeditions in cultural psychology*. Cambridge, MA: Harvard University Press.

Singelis, T. M. (1994) 'The measurement of independent and interdependent self-construals', *Personality and Social Psychology Bulletin*, 20: 580–91.

Singelis, T. M., Triandis, H. C., Bhawuk, D. and Gelfand, M. (1995) 'Horizontal and vertical dimensions of individualism and collectivism: A theoretical and measurement refinement', *Cross-Cultural Research*, 29: 240–75.

Smith, P. B. (2004) 'Acquiescent response bias as an aspect of cultural communication style', *Journal of Cross-Cultural Psychology*, 35: 50–61.

Smith, P. B., Bond, M. H. and Kağitçibaşi, C. (2006) *Understanding social psychology across cultures*. London: Sage Publications.

Smith, P. B., Peterson, M. F., Schwartz, S. H., et al. (2002) 'Cultural values, sources of guidance and their relevance to managerial behavior: A 47-nation study', *Journal of Cross-Cultural Psychology*, 33: 188–208.

Spencer-Rodgers, J., Peng, K., Wang, L. and Hou, Y. (2004) 'Dialectical self-esteem and East-West differences in psychological well-being', *Personality and Social Psychology Bulletin*, 30: 1416–32.

Stark, S., Chernyshenko, O. S. and Drasgow, F. (2006) 'Detecting differential item functioning with confirmatory factor analysis and item response theory: Toward a unified strategy', *Journal of Applied Psychology*, 91: 1292–1306.

Steenkamp, J.-B. E. M. and Baumgartner, H. (1998) 'Assessing measurement invariance in cross-national consumer research', *Journal of Consumer Research*, 25: 78–90.

Sternberg, R. J. (2004) 'Culture and intelligence', *American Psychologist*, 59: 325–38.

Taylor, T. R. and Boeyens, J. C. (1991) 'The comparability of scores of Blacks and Whites on the South African Personality Questionnaire: An exploratory study', *South African Journal of Psychology*, 21: 1–11.

Triandis, H. C. (1995) *Individualism and collectivism*. Boulder, CO: Westview Press.

Triandis, H. C. (2000) 'Dialectics between cultural and cross-cultural psychology', *Asian Journal of Social Psychology*, 3: 185–95.

Triandis, H. C., and Gelfand, M. J. (1998) 'Converging measurement of horizontal and vertical individualism and collectivism', *Journal of Personality and Social Psychology*, 74: 118–28.

van de Vijver, F. J. (1997) 'Meta-analysis of cross-cultural comparisons of cognitive test performance', *Journal of Cross-Cultural Psychology*, 28: 678–709.

van de Vijver, F. J. (2002) 'Inductive reasoning in Zambia, Turkey, and the Netherlands: Establishing cross-cultural equivalence', *Intelligence*, 30: 313–51.

van de Vijver, F. J. R. (2003) 'Principles of adaptation of intelligence tests to other cultures', in J. Georgas, L. G. Weiss, F. J. R. van de Vijver and D. H. Saklofske (eds), *Culture and children's intelligence: Cross-cultural analysis of the WISC-III*. Amsterdam: Academic Press. pp. 255–63.

van de Vijver, F. J. and Leung, K. (1997) *Methods and data analysis for cross-cultural research*. Thousand Oaks, CA: Sage.

van de Vijver, F. J. and Poortinga, Y. H. (2002) 'Structural equivalence in multilevel research', *Journal of Cross-Cultural Psychology*, 33: 141–56.

van de Vijver, F. J. R., Van Hemert, D. A. and Poortinga, Y. H. (2008) *Multilevel analysis of individuals and cultures*. Mahwah, NJ: Lawrence Erlbaum Associates.

Van Hemert, D. A., van de Vijver, F. J., Poortinga, Y. H. and Georgas, J. (2002) 'Structural and functional equivalence of the Eysenck Personality Questionnaire within and between countries', *Personality and Individual Differences*, 33: 1229–49.

van Leest, P. F. (1997) 'Bias and equivalence research in the Netherlands', *European Review of Applied Psychology*, 47: 319–29.

Vandello, J. A. and Cohen, D. (1999) 'Patterns of individualism and collectivism across the United States', *Journal of Personality and Social Psychology*, 77: 279–92.

Vandenberg, R. J. and Lance, C. E. (2000) 'A review and synthesis of the measurement invariance literature: Suggestions, practices, and recommendations for organizational research', *Organizational Research Methods*, 3: 4–70.

Waller, N. G., Thompson, J. S. and Wenk, E. (2000) 'Using IRT to separate measurement bias from true group differences on homogeneous and heterogeneous scales: An illustration with the MMPI', *Psychological Methods*, 5: 125–46.

Wang, D., Cui, H. and Zhou, F. (2005) 'Measuring the personality of Chinese: QZPS versus NEO PI-R', *Asian Journal of Social Psychology*, 8: 97–122.

Watkins, D. and Gerong, A. (1999) 'Language of response and the spontaneous self-concept: A test of the cultural accommodation hypothesis', *Journal of Cross-Cultural Psychology*, 30: 115–21.

Watson, D. (1992) 'Correcting for acquiescent response bias in the absence of a balanced scale', *Sociological Methods and Research*, 21: 52–88.

Wiebe, J. S. and Penley, J. A. (2006) 'A psychometric comparison of the Beck Depression Inventory-II in English and Spanish', *Psychological Assessment*, 17: 481–85.

Wong, N., Rindfleisch, A. and Burroughs, J. E. (2003) 'Do reverse-worded items confound measures in cross-cultural consumer research? The case of the Material Values Scale', *Journal of Consumer Research*, 30: 72–91.

Yamaguchi, S. and Ariizumi, Y. (2006) 'Close interpersonal relationships among Japanese: *Amae* as distinguished from attachment and dependence', in U. Kim, K.-S. Yang and K.-K. Hwang (eds), *Indigenous and cultural psychology: Understanding people in context*. New York: Springer. pp. 163–74.

Yanai, Y. H., Kashiwagi, S. and Kokusho, R. (1987) 'Construction of a new personality inventory by means of factor analysis based on Promax rotation', *Japanese Journal of Psychology*, 58: 158–65.

Yang, K.-S. (2000) 'Monocultural and cross-cultural indigenous approaches: The royal road to the development of a balanced global psychology', *Asian Journal of Social Psychology*, 3: 241–63.

Yik, M. S. M., Russell, J. A., Ahn, C.-K., Dols, J. M. F. and Suzuki, N. (2002) 'Relating the five-factor model of personality to a circumplex model of affect: A five language study', in R. R. McCrae and J. Allik (eds), *The five-factor model of personality across cultures*. New York: Kluwer Academic/Plenum. pp. 79–104.

Yu, A. B. (1996) 'Ultimate life concerns, self, and Chinese achievement motivation', in M. H. Bond (ed.), *The handbook of Chinese psychology*. Hong Kong: Oxford University Press. pp. 227–46.

Zhang, J. X. and Bond, M. H. (1998) 'Personality and filial piety among college students in two Chinese societies: The added value of indigenous constructs', *Journal of Cross-Cultural Psychology*, 29: 402–17.

10

Conceptualizing and Measuring Culture: Problems and Solutions

Louis Tay, Sang Eun Woo,
Jennifer Klafehn, and Chi-yue Chiu[1]

Recent advances in the cultural sciences have uncovered marked cultural differences in cognition, motivation, emotion, and behaviors (see Chiu and Hong, 2006, 2007). Meanwhile, these discoveries have prompted investigators to question some entrenched assumptions in the field (Breugelmans et al., in press). For example, opinions are heavily divided among major theories on the nature of culture and its measurement. We contend that new measurement models and data analytic techniques can shed new light on these debates.

In the present chapter, we present several examples to illustrate how recent advances in measurement and data modeling can contribute to an informed resolution of three key debates on the nature of culture. First, is culture a coherent meaning system with a deep structure and organized by such themes as individualism or collectivism (Greenfield, 2000; Hofstede, 1980; McCrae, 2004; Triandis, 1995), or is it a network of domain-specific symbolic elements with loose inter connections (Chiu and Hong, 2007; Dutton and Heath, in press; Kashima, 2009; Matsumoto, 1999; Poortinga, 2003; Oyserman et al., 2002; Shore, 2002)? Second, are culturally typical responses reflections of shared pre-stored and enduring personality or knowledge structures, or are they situation-dependent responses evoked in a shared environment (Oyserman and Lee, 2008)? Third, do cultures differ primarily in their relative positions on a handful of pan-cultural dimensions, or do cultures differ qualitatively from each other? Is it possible to study cross-cultural differences in such a way that successfully resolves the tension between the generality and specificity of psychological constructs as they occur within and across cultures? More specifically, can researchers quantitatively arrange or classify cultures according to culture-universal scales, while simultaneously analyzing them from a qualitative, idiosyncratic perspective? These inter-related issues pertain to the coherence, malleability, and commensurability of cultures, respectively. A common key to their successful resolution rests on the development of new measurement models and their implementation in statistical modeling of cultures.

Because these measurement models and their implementation in data analysis are relatively new in the cultural sciences, we will illustrate the basic principles of these models as they apply to cultural research. Each of the following sections addresses one of the three issues described above. In each section, we will begin with a brief review of the debate in the field, propose new techniques for measuring and modeling cultures that can potentially help resolve the debate, and wherever possible, illustrate techniques with brief descriptions of research examples. We will restrict our discussion of the measurement models to their conceptual foundation and applications in cultural research. A detailed description of the statistical foundation of these models is included in Appendix A. We want to emphasize that the focus of the current chapter is not on the techniques for measuring cultures. Instead, our focus is on the application of advanced statistical models to address thorny issues in the conceptualization of culture. As an overview, the Table in Appendix B summarizes how the statistical models discussed in the present chapter address the three conceptual issues described above.

DEBATE 1: IS CULTURE A COHERENT MEANING SYSTEM OR A NETWORK OF DOMAIN-SPECIFIC SYMBOLIC ELEMENTS?

The debate between 'culture-as-system' versus 'culture-as-elements' has a long history in the social sciences (Dutton and Heath, in press). Many scholars, especially those from the anthropological tradition (e.g., Bloch, 2000), have conceptualized culture as a coherent system of meanings. According to this view, it is possible to use broad cultural dimensions (e.g., individualism–collectivism; Hofstede, 1980) to capture essential differences across countries. These broad dimensions organize cultural differences along narrower, domain-specific dimensions, resulting in consistent cultural differences across various situations (e.g., Greenfield, 2000; Hofstede, 1980; McCrae, 2004; Triandis, 1995). For instance, many differences between Eastern and Western cultures in self-perception (unrealistic optimism), causal attribution (dispositional versus situational attribution), feelings (e.g., life satisfaction), and behaviors (e.g., conformity) have been assumed to be reflections of higher levels of individualism in Western cultures and higher level of collectivism in Eastern cultures (see Lehman et al., 2004).

An alternative view is that culture represents a network of narrower, domain-specific symbolic elements (Breugelmans et al., in press; Chiu and Hong, 2007; Dutton and Heath, in press; Kashima, 2009; Oyserman et al., 2002; Shore, 2002). Hence, cultural differences in one domain may not cohere with cultural differences in a seemingly related domain. For instance, a culture high in political individualism may be low in religious individualism (Ho and Chiu, 1994).

From this perspective, cultures should be understood as a network of loosely interconnected domain-specific symbolic elements (e.g., beliefs about the malleability of the world, perceived occupational mobility). These narrower elements are causally connected to specific behaviors in the same domain. For example, delegated deterrence is a narrow construct in the domain of social control. It refers to the idea of punishing group members not because they are deemed collectively responsible for a wrongdoing but simply because they are in an advantageous position to identify, monitor, and control the individual responsible for the wrongdoing. The greater endorsement of this idea in Asian (versus North American) societies explains Asians' (versus North Americans') greater tendency to hold the collective responsible for the wrongdoing of an individual (Chao et al., 2008). In contrast, although global (domain-general) constructs, such as individualism–collectivism, are useful constructs for making sense of seemingly related cultural differences, they do not explain these differences (Kashima, 2009). Apparently, these are two conceptually incompatible perspectives.

Solution: Bifactor models of cultural constructs

We argue that the uneasiness between these two perspectives can be reduced by simultaneously modeling both broad and narrow psychological constructs in cross-cultural investigations. In previous research, cultural dimensions were typically studied as either broad *or* narrow constructs. To enable direct comparison of broad- and narrow-level differences across cultures, investigators need to model both theoretically relevant global factor *and* domain-specific facets. The relative contributions of global and domain-specific constructs can then be assessed with bifactor models (see below). Applying this method, investigators

can assess the coherence among domain-specific constructs, and at the same time compare the magnitudes of cross-cultural differences at different levels of specificity or abstraction.

Because the measures of broad and narrow cultural constructs may have different measurement errors, directly comparing the explanatory power of broad and narrow cultural constructs is difficult and can lead to misleading conclusions. This is not an issue in bifactor models because in these models, magnitudes of cross-cultural differences in broad and narrow constructs are corrected for measurement error. In the next two sections, we will introduce bifactor models and use the example of individualism–collectivism to illustrate how they can be implemented to address the 'system versus element' debate in culture.

Bifactor models

Two types of measurement models can be constructed to simultaneously model broad constructs as well as domain-specific constructs influencing observed behaviors (e.g., responses to questionnaire items): bifactor models and hierarchical factor models. Figure 10.1 illustrates what a typical bifactor model and second-order factor model (a specific case of hierarchical factor models) look like. In second-order factor models, observed behaviors are organized into domain-specific latent factors (e.g., different facets of individualism–collectivism), which in turn are organized into a higher-order global factor (e.g., individualism–collectivism).

As illustrated in Figure 10.1, in bifactor models, items can be organized *simultaneously* into several domain-specific factors and a global domain-general factor. Unlike second-order factor models, in bifactor models, the domain-specific facets are not nested within the global factor. That is, bifactor models carry fewer statistical

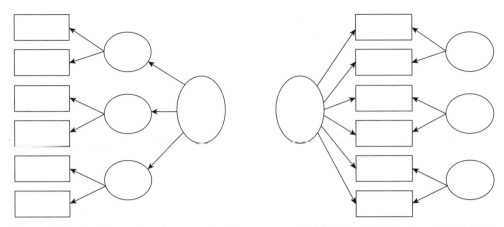

Figure 10.1   An illustration of a second-order factor model (left) and a bifactor model (right).

constraints than do second-order factor models. In fact, conceptually, second-order factor models are special, more restricted forms of bifactor models.

Bifactor models originated from psychometric research on intelligence (e.g., Carroll, 1993; Gustafsson and Balke, 1993; Holzinger and Swineford, 1937; Spearman, 1904), and have subsequently been applied to a number of other content areas such as personality (Woo et al., 2008), psychopathology (Krueger et al., 2007, and health outcomes (Chen et al., 2006; Reise et al., 2007). While hierarchical factor models seem to be more widely used in various domains of psychology (e.g., DeYoung et al., 2002; Hills and Argyle, 2002; Judge et al., 2002; Marsh et al., 2002), recent studies suggest that bifactor models have a few advantages over second-order factor models. For example, bifactor models tend to yield better model-data fit than second-order models because they carry fewer statistical constraints.

More importantly, bifactor models are useful for resolving the culture-as-system versus culture-as-elements debate because in these models, domain-specific factors are not nested within the domain-general factor.

Hence, bifactor models allow investigators to examine the influences of domain-specific and global factors independent of each other. That is, with these models, researchers can examine how much a global factor influences the observed behaviors above and beyond domain-specific factors. In addition, these models also allow researchers to examine the unique influences of domain-specific factors on the observed behaviors, independent of the influence of the global factor.

Illustration: The case of individualism–collectivism

In this section, we first illustrate how a bifactor structure can be constructed for the global dimension and multiple specific facets of individualism–collectivism. Next, we describe how factors at different levels of abstraction can be compared across different nations (or cultural groups) by implementing the bifactor model.

When Oyserman and colleagues (2002) meta-analyzed cross-national differences in individualism–collectivism, they encountered a fundamental measurement problem: There was no single standard or commonly used measure of individualism–collectivism. Based on a thorough review and content analysis of 27 existing scales, they identified seven facets of individualism (Independence, Goals, Competence, Uniqueness, Privacy, Self-knowing, and Direct communication) and eight facets of collectivism (Relatedness, Belongingness, Duty, Harmony, Advice seeking, Context, Hierarchy, and Group).

In Figure 10.2, we represent the seven individualism facets in a bifactor model of individualism and the eight collectivism facets in a bifactor model of collectivism. After a bifactor model has been constructed, other models can be specified and compared to it. For example, to determine whether the global dimension of individualism has explanatory power above and beyond the domain-specific facets of individualism, we can compare the bifactor model of individualism depicted in Figure 10.2 with

an alternative model without the global factor of individualism. If the alternative model (the one without the global factor) provides a good fit *and* fits as well as the bifactor model, then we do not need the global construct of individualism to explain the observed behaviors. In this case, culture is best understood as a loose network of domain-specific constructs.

Bifactor models also allow researchers to examine cross-cultural differences in global and domain-specific factors of individualism–collectivism. This can be accomplished by carrying out latent mean analysis. If there are consistent latent mean differences at both the global and specific levels of individualism–collectivism, this finding would support the culture-as-system position. That is, cultural variations in individualism and collectivism explain cultural differences in a diverse set of

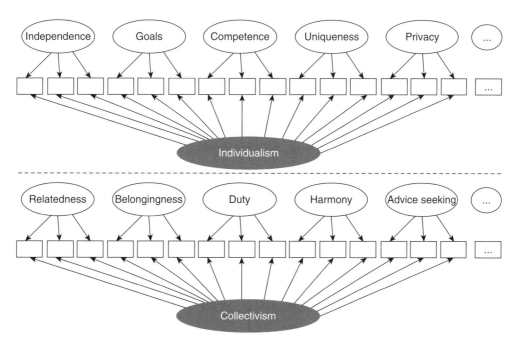

Figure 10.2   An illustration of bifactor models for Individualism (top panel) and collectivism (bottom panel).

observed behaviors. On the contrary, if cross-cultural differences exist at the level of domain-specific constructs (e.g., independence, relatedness, goals, etc.) only and not at the global level of individualism–collectivism, this evidence would weaken the culture-as-system position and support the idea that culture is a network of loosely connected shared meanings.

The proposed modeling technique has been applied to analyze existing cross-cultural data. As an example, in a study on culture and the psychological structure of Openness to Experience (Woo et al., 2008), we collected data from 262 college students in the US and 299 college students in Mainland China. Using the proposed technique, we found a barely discernible cross-cultural difference in the general factor of Openness to Experience. However, we found substantial cultural differences in several more specific factors of Openness such as Intellectual Efficiency, Curiosity, Aesthetics, and Tolerance. Interestingly, the directions of these differences were not consistent across factors, with Chinese students scoring higher on Aesthetics and Tolerance and US students scoring higher on Intellectual Efficiency and Curiosity. These results suggest that the different facets of Openness are not organized coherently into a single general factor of Openness in Chinese and American cultures. Instead, Intellectual Efficiency and Curiosity may be organized under one higher-order factor (namely, Intellectual Openness), while Tolerance and Aesthetics may be organized under another higher-order factor (namely, Cultural Openness or Sophistication).

In short, one important debate in cultural research centers around the issue of whether culture is better conceptualized as a coherent meaning system with several central themes or as a network of loosely connected ideas. We argue that bifactor models of cultural differences can help to generate useful empirical data to settle this debate.

DEBATE 2: CULTURE AS ENDURING TRAITS OR EMERGENT BEHAVIORS

Another important debate in cultural research concerns the malleability of culture: Does culture consist of enduring shared traits that are temporally stable, or is it a constellation of emergent behaviors evoked and maintained by a shared environment?

Cultural scientists study the *dynamic interdependence* between an individual's psychological world and the sociocultural context (Markus and Hamedani, 2007). From this view, the psychological and cultural are mutually constitutive of one another; both require and interact with each other, resulting in ongoing transformations. To understand the nature of these interactions, cultural studies have led to 'rich descriptions of complex theoretical models of culture and self that predict and explain cultural differences' (Matsumoto and Yoo, 2006: 236). Many of these descriptions emphasize the malleability of culturally conditioned behavioral patterns.

However, most measurement models of culture, which assume the presence of culturally invariant dimensions and focus on evaluation of cultures on these dimensions, have not caught up with the rich theorizations in culture and psychology. Instead, many of these measurement models, which are primarily concerned with measurement invariance across groups, tend to promote the idea that culture consists of static shared traits organized around a handful of universal trait dimensions.

The measurement models described above are limited in their ability to address the dynamic interplay of culture and psychology *across time*. We propose supplementing these models with a temporal analysis of culture and psychology because such analyses can help to answer the question of whether culture consists of enduring collective traits or emergent, situation-dependent behavioral patterns. A temporal analysis will also allow investigators to understand the magnitude and the nature of cultural change. To facilitate such temporal analysis, we propose a measurement framework that models changes in different types of psychological constructs across time.

Measurement invariance across groups

Cultural studies have laid the groundwork for examining interdependencies between the sociocultural and psychological systems by linking cultural constructs to individual psychology. Oftentimes, observed psychological differences between cultural groups are attributed to the influences of cultural constructs. For example, differences in self-concepts (psychological dimensions) such as independent or interdependent self-construals (Markus and Kitayama, 1991) have been attributed to differences in individualism–collectivism (cultural dimensions; Hofstede, 1984) at the cultural level (see Matsumoto and Yoo, 2006).

An assumption in this analysis is that cultures differ along some pancultural dimensions (e.g., individualism–collectivism). Factor analytic techniques have been widely used to identify and position cultural groups along these dimensions. For example, to determine meaningful dimensions of cultural variability, Hofstede (2001) conducted a country-level factor analysis based on work-related values data from 72 countries. Five important cultural dimensions were identified in this landmark

work: individualism–collectivism, power–distance, uncertainty–avoidance, masculinity and long- versus short-term orientation. In a parallel effort to understand the structure of different psychological constructs, factor analysis has been conducted on self-esteem (Shevlin et al., 1995), self-construals (Singelis, 1994), and personality (Digman, 1990; McCrae and Costa, 1987), among many others.

Despite these advances, cultural research has not incorporated dynamic aspects of culture and psychology into its measurement models. One contributing factor is that the common methodological approach focuses on group comparisons rather than comparisons across time. In part, researchers are more acquainted with testing for cross-group measurement invariance than for within-group measurement invariance.

Although testing cross-group and within-group measurement invariance are statistically similar, their aims are vastly different. The goal of cross-group comparisons is to document between-group psychological differences (e.g., in self-conceptions) and to link these differences to the theoretically pertinent cultural dimensions (e.g., individualism–collectivism). For cross-group comparisons to be meaningful, the psychological dimensions compared must be invariant. To this end, measurement invariance is the prescribed hurdle. A major conceptual difference between within-group and cross-group measurement models is that within-group measurement models model data from the individuals over time, whereas cross-group models compare different groups of individuals within a specified time frame. See Appendix A for the differences in within-group and cross-group model specifications.

In contrast, when modeling dynamic interplay, we expect continuity, but also anticipate change across time. In fact, change is of the greatest interest – how do psychological constructs change with respect to culture over time? Answering this question requires longitudinal assessment of psychological constructs within a cultural group and careful analysis of systematic change (or the lack of it) across time.

Solution: Within-group measurement invariance

The concept of change has had a long history in cultural research. While this idea has been pursued and expanded in various forms (e.g., cultural evolution; Dutton and Heath, in press), we have chosen to focus on (1) the velocity of change for different psychological variables, and (2) whether the change represents a shift in magnitude or a shift in meaning.

Our decision to focus on these two aspects of change is in part inspired by a recent meta-analysis on the psychological consequences of culture priming (Oyserman and Lee, 2008). Generally speaking, culture priming studies entail presenting culture-laden concepts in ostensibly unrelated tasks. These concepts, in turn, cue associated cognitive contents and/or procedures (Higgins and Bargh, 1987; Hong and Chiu, 2001; Hong et al., 2000). With regard to cognitive contents, conceptual priming activates a nexus of interrelated concepts, such as self-concepts and values, which then serve as a lens for processing subsequent information. With respect to cognitive procedures, culture primes activate their attendant mindsets and their associated cognitive styles, like attributions, whose effects are spilled over to subsequent tasks (Oyserman and Lee, 2008).

The magnitude of the culture priming effect reflects how readily individuals will change their habitual way of responding to the situation depending on what cultural

cues are present in the environment. Thus, the effect size of culture priming can provide an indirect way of assessing the change velocity of a certain psychological variable in response to changes in the cultural environment.

In this connection, it is important to note that in their review of studies priming individualism–collectivism, Oyserman and Lee (2007) found that the sizes of culture priming effects vary across the dependent psychological variables assessed in the studies, with small effect sizes for values and self-concepts and larger effect sizes for cognition. One explanation for the effect size differences is that self-concepts and values are more trait-like and less malleable compared to the more situation-dependent variables such as appraisals and attributions.

An unanswered question in the culture priming literature inspires our interest in examining whether time-dependent shifts in psychological variables represent quantitative or qualitative shifts. In their analysis of the culture priming effects on self-concept, Oyserman et al. (2002) stated that 'an open question is whether cultural differences in IND (individualism) and COL (collectivism) have the most influence by affecting what is chronically salient about one's self-concept or by affecting how the self-concept is structured' (p. 32). That is, culture priming can increase the salience of certain aspects of self-concept, resulting in a mean level (quantitative) change in the endorsement of these aspects of self-concept. Alternatively, culture priming can also alter the structure of self-concept. More broadly, culture can effect a quantitative or qualitative change in a psychological construct over time.

In summary, to understand culture's impact on psychology, we need to document both the nature and velocity of psychological change in response to an evolving cultural environment. In the next section, to foster full understanding and accurate assessment of what and how much changes can occur, we propose to delineate the different types of change using the gamma, beta and alpha change framework (Golembiewski et al., 1976).

A measurement framework for modeling psychological change and stability

Gamma change refers to a reconceptualization or a change in the meaning of a construct, such that over time, the psychological measure represents different or differentiated constructs in the minds of the individuals (Golembiewski et al., 1976). In this case, cultural experiences may produce a change in the dimensionality of psychological constructs. For example, when Americans are asked to complete the Chinese Personality Assessment Inventory (CPAI; Cheung et al., 1996, 2001), the interpersonal relatedness (IR) items may not have consistent loadings on the IR factor, because the IR factor is unique to Chinese samples. In line with this possibility, Cheung and colleagues (2001) reported that while the IR dimension holds for Chinese samples, IR items are scattered across dimensions of the Five Factor Model (FFM) for a multiethnic Hawaiian sample. However, for American migrants to China, as their experiences of interacting with the Chinese locals increase, these American migrants may develop an understanding of the relationship orientation. Consequently, the ideas underlying IR (e.g., avoidance of conflict, adherence to norms and traditions) have a coherent organization, resulting in a restructuring of personality. Evaluating these American migrants on the CPAI later after they have established themselves in China should yield a detectable change

in factor structure, such that IR items will hold together as a distinct factor. Statistically, this qualitative change is reflected in differences in factor structure over time.

Beta change occurs when individuals change their subjective metric of the scale over time. That is, the change in scale scores from one time to the next is not due to changes in the behaviors defining the construct, but due to changes in the perceived centrality of the component behaviors defining the construct (Golembiewski et al., 1976). Individuals can redefine a construct by assigning different weights to the connotations of that construct. From a factor analytic perspective, this change is reflected in a re-ordering of factor loadings such that low-loading items at an initial time point are weighted as high-loading items at the next time point, indicating that the perceived centrality of the items to the construct have changed. However, the construct does not fractionate or merge with another construct. Beta change is demonstrated statistically through changes of the factor loadings and indicator thresholds over time, but the pattern of zero and nonzero factor loadings remains the same.[2]

Alpha change is an absolute change that corresponds to quantitative differences in scores across time periods along the same underlying construct. Such change reflects purely quantitative shifts (Golembiewski et al., 1976). In the case of alpha change, culture changes the cultural group's average standing on a psychological continuum (e.g., the degree to which individuals hold on to a particular belief, self-construal or cognitive style). This change is shown by a change in factor scores, with factor loadings and indicator thresholds remaining constant over time.

Extrapolating from Oyserman and Lee's (2008) meta-analysis results, in the relatively short run, we would expect greater cultural change on situation-dependent psychological constructs such as emotions, behaviors, and cognitions. Also, because culture provides a lens for subjective appraisal and interpretations of situations, qualitative changes (i.e., gamma and beta change) may be observed more frequently on situation-dependent emotions, behaviors, and cognitions. In contrast, trait-like constructs are divorced from specific situations and tap into generalized cross-situational (and even cross-cultural) tendencies. Accordingly, for these trait-like constructs, less construct malleability and hence very little gamma and beta changes are expected, although some alpha change is possible.

Within a cultural group, an individual's behaviors may change not only because of cultural change, but also because of other factors (e.g., developmental changes). Thus, aside from modeling different kinds of group-level changes in situation-dependent or trait-like constructs individually in response to cultural change, investigators may also seek to model the prediction coefficients (i.e., structural coefficients) between constructs across time at the individual level under a common framework. There are two main advantages in doing so: first, one can compare the consistency of the constructs across time at the individual level, controlling for measurement error (Sturman et al., 2005). That is, the prediction coefficients focus conceptually on whether the relative rankings of individuals' latent scores within the cultural group remain the same over time. Consistency is distinct from gamma, beta and alpha changes because it reflects change at the individual level (i.e., rank-order consistency), whereas gamma, beta, and alpha changes are qualitative or quantitative changes at the aggregate (group) level; such aggregated changes may not be systematic across individuals.

A second advantage in examining prediction coefficients (i.e., structural coefficients) is that we can model whether trait-like constructs concomitantly influence state-like constructs (or vice versa) along with cultural influence. This framework captures the extent to which individual traits moderate cultural influence. For example, individuals higher on self-esteem may be more immune from cultural influence.

Figure 10.3 illustrates a possible model of the consistency and cross-influences of the different construct types. The horizontal arrows indicate consistency of the construct. Because we expect the consistency of trait-like constructs to be higher than situation-dependent constructs, we use thicker arrows to denote trait-like consistency. Cross-influences are shown by the cross-arrows. Along with cultural influence, trait-like constructs are more likely to affect situation-dependent constructs than the other way around. If individual traits moderate the influence of culture on situation-dependent constructs, we would expect the arrow leading from the trait-like construct at time 1 to significantly predict the situation-dependent construct at time 2. Simply stated, an individual's standing on the trait construct influences his or her standing on the situation-dependent construct; thus, not all situation-dependent changes are due to cultural influence. These predictions await systematic verifications in future research, and within-group measurement invariance provides a statistical tool for testing these predictions.

A key to the issue of whether culture consists of enduring collective traits or situation-dependent constructs is whether cultural constructs would display systematic change over time as culture evolves. Although we do not have the empirical evidence to resolve this issue, we believe that culture consists of a mixture of relatively

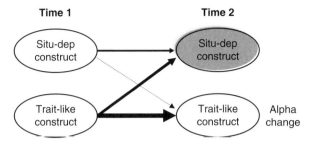

Figure 10.3 Paths of dynamic change in trait-like and situation-dependent constructs over time. Parallel arrows and cross-arrows depict consistency and cross-influence respectively. Thicker arrows could indicate higher consistency or greater influence from Time 1 to Time 2. Dotted arrows indicate weaker pathways.

change-resistant trait-like constructs and change-sensitive situation-dependent constructs. In this section, we propose a common measurement framework for tracking the velocity and nature of change in a variety of psychological constructs. Hopefully, this framework can be applied to resolve this important debate in the cultural science.

DEBATE 3: IS CULTURE A HOMOGENEOUS ENTITY?

Culture: universalism versus relativism

Cross-cultural comparisons, defined here as mean-level evaluations of psychological constructs across different countries, have become the gold standard for psychologists interested in assessing 'cultural' differences between groups. For example, should an investigator assume that German and Chinese people differ substantially from one another on a particular construct (e.g., Conscientiousness), he or she would collect the necessary data from both sources, aggregate participants' responses across each country, and perform a test of significance to determine whether the two groups do, in fact, differ.

This approach to cross-cultural measurement is often referred to as the 'universalistic' or 'absolutist' approach, such that various psychological dimensions are assumed to operate universally across cultures, much in the same way physiological mechanisms operate universally across members of the same species. This assumption of universality allows researchers to quantitatively categorize and compare cultures along the same continuum (e.g., individualism–collectivism, Hofstede, 1980; independent-interdependent self-construal, Markus and Kitayama, 1991). Likewise, if members of one culture are assumed to interpret a psychological construct in the same way as members of another culture, conclusions regarding the extent to which those cultures are similar or different can be drawn quite reliably by using comparison studies akin to the example mentioned above.

Though its interpretation is both straightforward and facilitative, the universalistic approach to cross-cultural measurement is severely limited by its assumption of invariant, common cultural dimensions. In essence, the idea that cultures share a common understanding of psychological constructs hinders one's ability to detect the presence of 'real' cultural differences occurring at the qualitative level.

Contrary to the universalistic approach, relativistic cross-cultural psychology views cultures as qualitatively distinct from one another. In other words, the way in which individuals come to understand and interpret the world around them differs from one culture to the next. Likewise, each culture is assumed to have certain non-represented, or 'indigenous', factors that are qualitatively independent from those of other cultures. For example, recent studies have identified culturally unique personality factors (e.g., Interpersonal Relatedness, Cheung et al., 2001) that are independent of the dimensions constituting the more popular, Western-based Five-Factor Model of personality. Similarly, many terms that exist within one culture are often untranslatable, sometimes even nonexistent, in another culture. The Chinese word 'guanxi', for instance, is most commonly used in business settings to describe a kind of social capital between two individuals. To date, there is no known English translation for 'guanxi', a discrepancy most likely stemming from the differences between Western and Chinese business practices (Zhu et al., 2007).

Of course, the problem with assuming that all cultures interpret psychological constructs in their own unique way is that it is virtually impossible to make cross-cultural comparisons of any kind. Even if two cultures share something considered to be psychologically fundamental, the lack of a common dimension or scale between those cultures prevents us from drawing reliable conclusions about how they relate to one another. Along a similar vein, the assumption that all cultures are inherently different tends to create an alienated view of the world in which we live (Chiu and Hong, 2005; Chiu et al., 2008). In other words, emphasizing the ways in which cultures are distinct and unique, rather than shared and common, serves only to widen the gap

between members of different cultures who, despite their background, may otherwise be quite similar to one another.

Such a conundrum ultimately raises the question: Is it possible to study cross-cultural differences in such a way that successfully resolves the tension between the generality and specificity of psychological constructs as they occur within and across cultures? More specifically, can researchers quantitatively arrange or classify cultures according to culture-universal scales, while simultaneously analyzing them from a qualitative, idiosyncratic perspective? Perhaps the biggest obstacle to answering these questions is in defining the theoretical boundary separating the culture-common from the culture-unique (Poortinga and van Hemert, 2001). That is, at what point along the psychological continuum does a construct cease to behave idiosyncratically for one culture and start behaving normatively for all cultures?

One possible solution to this problem is to use a 'bottom-up' approach in the identification of cultural factors. Rather than classifying individuals from the top down (i.e., according to pre-defined demographic groups, such as nationality, ethnicity, religion, etc.), cultural groups are created 'organically' from individuals' responses to cultural/psychological scales. The resulting cultural groups can then be examined on various demographic variables or any other psychological trends the researcher may deem of interest.

Factor analytic approach

When conducting cross-cultural studies using a 'top-down' analytic approach, researchers have traditionally relied on data-reduction techniques to identify the various factors upon which cultural groups can be based. One of the most popular techniques of this kind is MACS analysis, or, as it is more commonly implemented and termed, multi-group confirmatory factor analysis (CFA). Because multi-group CFA approaches can be subsumed under MACS, we will use the terms interchangeably (see Appendix A for details).

In MACS/CFA approaches, cultural groupings are predefined according to some observed demographic variable. For example, country groupings are frequently used as proxies for culture. If the estimated and constrained parameters satisfy the measurement invariance conditions, then the groups are comparable.

The MACS/CFA approach, however, carries with it several limitations. First, the MACS/CFA approach assumes that the defined groupings are from two separate subpopulations. Nevertheless, there may be more commonalities among individuals around the world than there are country-differences. Having a large proportion of individuals with similar response patterns across countries occludes differences on factor structure and means since these individuals are driving the correlations and aggregate scores. Interesting results from smaller sub-populations that are often stereotypical of say, Chinese or American cultures, may not appear.

Second, demographic partitioning may not be the most effective way of partitioning the variance. Empirically, there exist up to four or five times more within-country variation than between-country variation on a variety of psychological characteristics (cf. Poortinga and van Hemert, 2001). This implies that there may be a more effective way of partitioning differences on the construct of interest. In short, it is still an untested assumption that cultural divides align with demographic lines.

Third, MACS/CFA requires measurement invariance to ensure construct comparability of both groups. Measurement invariance is much like the methodological

counterpart to the assumption of universality: it assumes that cultures are homogenous not only in how they view the world, but also in the way they respond to psychological stimuli. Poortinga and van Hemert (2001: 1037) noted that 'in culture-comparative research, personality is conceptualized as a multi-dimensional space. It is almost axiomatic that the basic structure of this space is culturally invariant or universal'. Non-invariance is commonly dealt with by allowing for partial invariance, parceling of items, or removing items from the analysis altogether. There is commonly no explanation for why some items exhibit non-invariance.

Solution: latent class analysis

Given these limitations, how, then, can researchers attempt to measure and analyze cultural variation? We propose that a potential solution to this problem may be found via the use of latent class (LC) analysis techniques (Lazarsfeld, 1950; Masters, 1985). In LC approaches, it is possible to empirically determine whether a common grouping exists across countries. This is done by maximally partitioning differences on the pattern of responses. In this case, we obtain groups that respond differently to the administered scale. Alternatively, one can extend LC models to include latent factors and obtain groupings that maximize the differences of item difficulties and/or loadings on the construct of interest (see Rost, 1990; Maij-de Meij, Kelderman & van der Flier, 2008). Here, we have groupings in which the same measurement model holds (see Appendix A for details). Hence, there is intra-group homogeneity and inter-group heterogeneity: individuals within groups view the construct in a similar way, but individuals between groups view the construct in qualitatively different ways (e.g., Hernandez et al., 2004).

Cultural differences in regulatory focus: An illustrative example

In a recent study, we used LC analysis to examine a five-item promotion regulatory focus scale (Higgins, et al., 2001) administered to 328 Chinese and 272 US students. Promotion focus refers to a chronic eagerness to ensure the presence of positives (gains) and to ensure against the absence of positives (non-gains). Promotion-focused individuals are primarily concerned with maximizing positive outcomes; they eagerly pursue gains or successes. Focusing on accomplishments, achievements, and the pursuit of ideals, they are oriented towards fulfilling their hopes and aspirations, and they scrutinize their social world for information that bears on the pursuit of success. Promotion focus is believed to be more prevalent in North American and East Asian societies (Higgins, 2008; Lalwani et al., 2009). Promotion is assessed using the Regulatory Focus Questionnaire (Higgins et al., 2001). The promotion focus scale is composed of 5 items (e.g., 'I feel like I have made progress toward being successful in my life'). The items were measured on a five-point scale, with higher scores indicating higher promotion focus. The respondents in our study indicate on a five-point scale the extent to which they agreed with each item.

Our research goal was to obtain the best set of latent classes to represent the data. If a homogeneous promotion focus style exists within each country, participants from a particular country would be categorized in a latent class distinct from one another. In this instance, two latent classes can be expected – one predominantly consisting of Chinese participants and another of US participants. Since these latent classes would largely consist of individuals from only one of two countries, they are idiosyncratic classes.

In contrast, if Chinese and US participants have the same understanding and level of endorsement of promotion focus, the proportions of individuals within latent classes would be evenly spread across countries. Unlike idiosyncratic classes, normative or culture-independent classes demonstrate that regulatory focus styles are equally distributed across countries. One should note that it is possible to find both normative and idiographic classes in the same dataset such that some latent classes have proportionately more members from a particular country, while another would have an even spread.

A secondary aim of the analysis was to examine the response styles of participants. Some research has shown that Japanese and Chinese students are more likely to use the mid-point of a scale while Americans tend to use extreme points of a scale (Chen et al., 1995). However, these differences in response styles are confounded with the level of a construct when using mean level comparisons across countries.

Using LC modeling, we treated the five response options on each item as nominal categories, using the software Latent GOLD 4.0 (Vermunt and Magidson, 2000). In effect, we can obtain groupings that maximize the differences in how they respond to different options. The results showed that the best fitting latent class model was a discrete factor model (DFactor) consisting of 2 factors with 2 levels each.[3] In short, we identified four latent classes (two factors × two levels) through latent class analysis of the participants' responses to the five promotion focus items.

From the upper panel in Figure 10.4, DFactor 1 shows that individuals in level 2 have higher probabilities of endorsing options 1 to 3 as compared to 4 and 5. Thus, DFactor 1 shows the extent to which individuals respond higher or lower on the scale. In contrast, the lower panel in

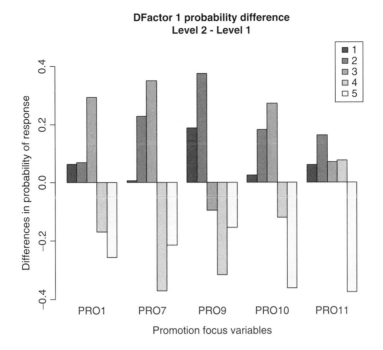

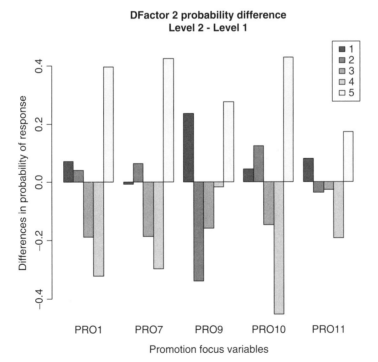

Figure 10.4   Results of latent class analysis of responses to the five-item promotion-focused scale. The upper (lower) panel illustrates the nature of Factor 1 (Factor 2). Both factors consist of two levels. The vertical axis represents the difference between the two levels of the factor in the probability of choosing a particular scale value (1–5) on each item.

Table 10.1   Interpretation and distribution of Chinese and US Participants in the four latent classes

Class	1	2	3	4
Class Size (Percentage of participants in the class)	.49	.11	.33	.07
DFactor 1: Level of regulatory focus	High	High	Low	Low
DFactor 2: Response style or preferred scale value	Moderate	End-point	Moderate	End-point
Proportion of participants who were Chinese in this latent class	0.44	0.12	**0.79**	**0.80**
Proportion of participants who were Americans in this latent class	0.56	**0.88**	0.21	0.20

Figure 10.4 shows that DFactor 2 appears to be a response style factor. It divides individuals into end-point responders (level 2) and mid-point responders (level 1). Because these factors are orthogonal, we can examine the proportions of individuals based on combinations of factors and levels (4 latent classes in all) as seen in Table 10.1.

Table 10.1 shows that there are four classes of individuals who respond to the regulatory focus promotion items. About half of the participants fall into the first latent class, representing a middling response style and generally high regulatory focus. Importantly, we see that the proportions of Chinese and Americans who fall within the first latent class are similar (.44 to .56, respectively). Hence, this class may be regarded as a normative class. On the other hand, latent class 2, which consists of individuals who use end-point responding and are high on regulatory focus, is idiosyncratic to USA (.88 Americans). Finally, latent classes 3 and 4 are individuals with low regulatory focus, which is commonly associated with Chinese participants (about .80 Chinese). However, there are differences in response styles between these two classes.

From this analysis, we see that simply assuming that Chinese or Americans are homogeneous within their country can be misleading. A substantial number of participants are similar on their regulatory focus and response styles across countries. A MACS/CFA approach of pre-determining cultural groups based on demography hinders researchers from examining how groups of individuals are similar and different on a construct of interest.

These results illustrate the incremental utility of applying latent class analysis to modeling cross-cultural data. First, the results are consistent with the contention that promotion focus is more prevalent in American culture than in Chinese culture (Higgins, 2008). Among the end-point users with high level of promotion focus, 88 percent were Americans. Among the end-point users with low level of promotion focus, 80 percent were Chinese. However, it is also important to point out that the end-point users made up only 18 percent of the participants in the current sample. About 50 percent of the participants in the sample (evenly distributed between Americans and Chinese) had a similar preference for choosing the mid-point and similarly high levels of promotions focus. In short, cross-cultural differences were obtained primarily among the end-point users – participants with strong preference for or aversion toward promotion focus, although most participants did not have strong preference for or aversion toward promotion focus.

The results are also consistent with the previous finding that Chinese (versus Americans) are more likely to choose the mid-point on the rating scale (Chen et al., 1995): 47.6 percent of Chinese participants fell into the two moderate response classes, compared to 34.4 percent of American participants. Again, latent class analysis reveals a more nuanced cultural difference: Whereas American participants tended to give more moderately high ratings than moderately low ratings, Chinese participants were equally likely to give moderately high and moderately low ratings.

Returning to the debate on the commensurability of cultures, our results show that there are culturally unique response patterns in both American and Chinese cultures. However, there are also striking cultural similarities – the majority class in both American and Chinese samples consists of individuals with moderate preference for promotion focus. In short, cultures may differ both quantitatively and qualitatively, and the LC approach provides a powerful statistical tool for documenting and modeling both types of cultural differences.

CONCLUSION

Cultural research has experienced exponential growth in the last two decades. The rapid expansion of the cultural sciences has stimulated many divided views on the very nature of culture. Three major debates in the field concern the coherence, malleability, and commensurability of cultures. Resolution of these issues is critical to the sustainable growth of the cultural sciences. The measurement models that most cultural researchers are acquainted with are useful for evaluating between-group measurement equivalence on measures of psychological variables. These models have played an important role in revealing important psychological

differences between cultures. However, these models have limited applicability in addressing the debates on the nature of culture.

In this chapter, we have argued that recent innovations in psychological measurement can be applied to examine the coherence, malleability, and commensurability of cultures. Although it will still be a very long way before definitive conclusions can be reached on the nature of culture, we hope that the measurement models and their implementations we introduced in this chapter will shorten the distance by providing cultural scientists with more exact quantitative tools to directly address the debates with pertinent cross-cultural data.

Although we have focused primarily on issues related to cross-cultural comparisons, our analysis and the proposed solutions can be applied to other comparative research as well, including research comparing gender, age and racial groups. Furthermore, conceptual issues that have engaged cross-cultural psychologists have also engaged researchers in other behavioral science disciplines. For example, personality researchers have debated whether human personality consists of global traits or domain-specific constructs, how temporarily stable one's personality is, and whether situational variability can overwhelm the influence of global traits (John et al., 2008). Similarly, social psychologists have debated whether social attitudes are domain-specific or domain-general and whether social attitudes are pre-stored knowledge structures or ad hoc constructions in response to emergent properties in the social context (Schwarz, 2007). The issues are at the heart of personality and social psychology. We hope that the methods proposed in this chapter can help provide new answers to these issues.

NOTES

1 The authors made equal contribution to this chapter. The order of authorship is determined by a random process.

2 It is possible to test for item reliabilities (i.e., residual variances), but such test *may* not be essential for demonstrating beta change because conceptually it deals with familiarity of scoring formats (see Cheung and Rensvold, 2002).

3 Analogically, the discrete factor model is similar to a factor model except that it consists of discrete levels rather than a continuum. In this case, there are two orthogonal, discrete factors that best represent the groupings.

REFERENCES

Bentler, P. M. (1990) 'Comparative fit indexes in structural models', *Psychological Bulletin*, 107: 238–46.

Bentler, P. M. and Bonett, D. G. (1980) 'Significance tests and goodness of fit in the analysis of covariance structures', *Psychological Bulletin*, 88: 588–606.

Bloch, M. (2000) 'A well-disposed social anthropologist's problems with memes', in R. Aunger (ed.), *Darwinizing culture*. Oxford: Oxford University Press. pp. 189–204.

Breugelmans, S. M., Chasiotics, A., and van de Vijver, F. (in press) 'Fundamental questions of cross–cultural psychology', in S. M. Breugelmans, A. Chasiotics and F. van de Vijver (eds) *Fundamental questions of cross-cultural psychology*. Cambridge, UK: Cambridge University Press.

Carroll, J. B. (1993) *Human cognitive abilities: A survey of factor-analytical studies*. New York: Cambridge University Press.

Chao, M. M., Zhang, Z-X. and Chiu, C-y. (2008) 'Personal and collective culpability judgment: A functional analysis of East Asian-North American differences', *Journal of Cross-Cultural Psychology*, 39: 730–44.

Chen, C., Lee, S-y. and Stevenson, H. W. (1995) 'Response style and cross-cultural comparisons of ratings scales among East Asian and North American students', *Psychological Science*, 6: 170–5.

Chen, F. F., West. S. G. and Sousa, K. H. (2006) 'A comparison of bifactor and second-order models of quality of life', *Multivariate Behavioral Research*, 41: 189–225.

Cheung, F. M., Leung, K., Fan, R. M., Song, W. Z., Zhang, J. X. and Zhang, J. P. (1996) 'Development of the Chinese Personality Assessment Inventory', *Journal of Cross-Cultural Psychology*, 27: 181–99.

Cheung, F. M., Leung, K., Zhang, J. X., Sun, H. F., Gan, Y. Q., Song, W. Z., et al. (2001) 'Indigenous Chinese personality constructs: Is the Five Factor Model complete?' *Journal of Cross-Cultural Psychology*, 32: 407–33.

Cheung, G. W. and Rensvold, R. W. (2002) 'Evaluating goodness-of-fit indexes for testing measurement invariance', *Structural Equation Modeling*, 9: 233–55.

Chiu, C-y. and Hong, Y-y. (2005) 'Cultural competence: Dynamic processes', in A. Elliot and C. S. Dweck (eds), *Handbook of motivation and competence*. New York: Guilford. pp. 489–505.

Chiu, C-y. and Hong, Y-y. (2006) *The social psychology of culture*. New York: Psychology Press.

Chiu, C-y. and Hong, Y-y. (2007) 'Cultural processes: Basic principles', in E. T. Higgins, and A. E. Kruglanski (eds), *Social psychology: Handbook of basic principles*. New York: Guilford. pp. 785–809.

Chiu, C-y., Kim, Y-H. and Wan, W. N. (2008) 'Personality: Cross-cultural perspectives', in G. J. Boyle, G. Matthews and D. H. Salofske (eds), *Handbook of personality theory and assessment. Vol. 1: Personality theory and testing*. London: Sage. pp. 124–44.

Clogg, C. C. (1995) 'Latent class models', in G. Arminger, C. C. Clogg and M. E. Sobel (eds), *Handbook of statistical modeling for the social and behavioral sciences*. New York: Plenum. pp. 311–59.

DeYoung, C. G., Peterson, J. B. and Higgins, D. M. (2002) 'Higher-order factors of the Big Five predict conformity: Are there neuroses of health?' *Personality and Individual Differences*, 33: 533–52.

Digman, J. M. (1990) 'Personality structure: Emergence of the five-factor model', *Annual Review of Psychology*, 41: 417–40.

Dutton, Y. C. and Heath, C. (in press) 'Cultural evolution: Why are some cultural variants more successful than others?' In M. Schaller, S. J. Heine, T. Yamagishi, and T. Kameda (eds), *Evolution, culture, and the human mind*. Mahwah, NJ: Lawrence Erlbaum.

Golembiewski, R., Billingsley, K. and Yeager, S. (1976) 'Measuring change and persistence in human affairs: Types of change generated by OD designs', *Journal of Applied Behavioral Science*, 12: 133–57.

Greenfield, P. M. (2000) 'Three approaches to the psychology of culture: Where do they come from? Where can they go?' *Asian Journal of Social Psychology*, 3: 223–40.

Gustafsson, J. and Balke, G. (1993) 'General and specific abilities as predictors of school achievement', *Multivariate Behavioral Research*, 28: 407–34.

Heinen, T. (1996) *Latent class and discrete latent trait models: Similarities and differences*. Thousand Oaks, CA: Sage.

Hernandez, A., Drasgow, F., and Gonzalez-Roma, V. (2004) 'Investigating the functioning of a middle category by means of a mixed-measurement model', *Journal of Applied Psychology*, 89: 687–99.

Higgins, E. T. (2008) 'Culture and personality: Variability across universal motives as the missing link', *Social and Personality Psychology Compass*, 2: 608–34.

Higgins, E. T. and Bargh, J. A. (1987) 'Social cognition and social perception', *Annual Review of Psychology*, 38: 369–425.

Higgins, E. T., Friedman, R. S., Harlow, R. E., Idson, L. C., Ayduk, O. N. and Taylor, A. (2001) 'Achievement orientations from subjective histories of success: Promotion pride versus prevention pride', *European Journal of Social Psychology*, 31: 3–23.

Hills, P. and Argyle, M. (2002) 'The oxford happiness questionnaire: A compact scale for the measurement of psychological well-being', *Personality and Individual Differences*, 33: 1071–82.

Ho, D. Y. F. and Chiu, C-y. (1994) 'Component ideas of individualism, collectivism, and social organization: An application in the study of Chinese culture', in U. Kim, H. C. Triandis, C. Kagitcibasi, G. Choi and G. Yoon (eds), *Individualism and collectivism: Theory, method and applications*. Thousand Oaks, CA: Sage. pp. 137–56.

Hofstede, G. (1980) *Culture's consequences*. Thousand Oaks, CA: Sage.

Hofstede, G. (1984) *Culture's consequences* (Abridged edition). Thousand Oaks, CA: Sage.

Hofstede, G. H. (2001) *Culture's consequences: Comparing values, behaviors, institutions and organizations across nations*. 2nd edition. Thousand Oaks, CA: Sage Publications.

Holzinger, K. J. and Swineford, F. (1937) 'The bi-factor method', *Psychometrika*, 2: 41–54.

Hong, Y-y. and Chiu, C-y. (2001) 'Toward a paradigm shift: From cultural differences in social cognition to social cognitive mediation of cultural differences', *Social Cognition*, 19: 118–96.

Hong, Y-y., Morris, M., Chiu, C-y. and Benet, V. (2000) 'Multicultural minds: A dynamic constructivist approach to culture and cognition', *American Psychologist*, 55: 709–20.

John, O. P., Robins, R. W. and Pervin, L. A. (2008) *Handbook of personality: Theory and research*. 3rd edition. New York: Guilford.

Judge, T. A., Erez, A., Bono, J. E. and Thoresen, C. J. (2002) 'Are measures of self-esteem, neuroticism, locus of control, and generalized self–efficacy indicators of a common core construct?' *Journal of Personality and Social Psychology*, 83: 693–710.

Kashima, Y. (2009) 'Culture comparison and culture priming: A critical analysis', in R. S. Wyer, Jr., C-y. Chiu, and Y-y. Hong (eds), *Understanding culture: Theory, research and application*. New York: Psychology Press. pp. 53–77.

Krueger, R. F., Markon, K. E., Patrick, C. J., Benning. S. D. and Kramer, M. (2007) 'Linking antisocial behavior, substance use, and personality: An integrative quantitative model of the adult externalizing spectrum', *Journal of Abnormal Psychology*, 116: 645–66.

Lalwani, A. K., Shrum, L. J. and Chiu, C-y. (2009) 'Motivated response styles: The role of cultural values, regulatory focus, and self–consciousness in socially desirable responding', *Journal of Personality and Social Psychology*, 96: 870–82.

Lazarsfeld, P. F. (1950) 'The logical and mathematical foundation of latent structure analysis and the interpretation and mathematical foundation of latent structure analysis', in S. A. Stouffer (ed.), *Measurement and prediction*. Princeton, NJ: Princeton University Press. pp. 362–472.

Lehman, D., Chiu, C-y. and Schaller, M. (2004) 'Psychology and culture', *Annual Review of Psychology*, 55: 689–714.

Maij-de Meij, A. M., Kelderman, H. and van der Flier, H. (2008). Fitting a mixture item response theory model to personality questionnaire data: Characterizing latent classes and investigating possibilities for improving prediction. *Applied Psychological Measurement*, 32, 611–631.

Markus, H. R., and Hamedani, M. G. (2007) 'Sociocultural psychology: The dynamic interdependence among self systems and social systems', in S. Kitayama and D. Cohen (eds), *Handbook of cultural psychology*. New York: Guilford Press. pp. 3–39.

Markus, H. R. and Kitayama, S. (1991) 'Culture and the self: Implications for cognition, emotion, and motivation', *Psychological Review*, 98: 224–53.

Marsh, H. W., Ellis, L. and Craven, R. G. (2002) 'How do preschool children feel about themselves? Unravelling measurement and multidimensional self-concept structure', *Developmental Psychology*, 38: 376–93.

Masters, G. N. (1985) 'A comparison of latent trait and latent class analysis of Likert-type data', *Psychometrika*, 50: 69–82.

Matsumoto, D. (1999) 'Culture and self: An empirical assessment of Markus and Kitayama's theory of independent and interdependent self-construals', *Asian Journal of Social Psychology*, 2: 289–310.

Matsumoto, D. and Yoo, S. H. (2006) 'Toward a new generation of cross-cultural research', *Perspectives on Psychological Science*, 1: 234–50.

McCrae, R. R. (2004) 'Human nature and culture: A trait perspective', *Journal of Research in Personality*, 38: 3–14.

McCrae, R. R. and Costa, J. P. T. (1987) 'Validation of the five-factor model of personality across instruments and observers', *Journal of Personality and Social Psychology*, 52: 81–90.

Oyserman, D., Coon, H. M. and Kemmelmeier, M. (2002) 'Rethinking individualism and collectivism: Evaluation of theoretical assumptions and meta-analyses', *Psychological Bulletin*, 128: 3–72.

Oyserman, D. and Lee, S. W. S. (2007) 'Priming "culture"', in S. Kitayama and D. Cohen (eds), *Handbook of cultural psychology*. New York: Guilford Press. pp. 255–79.

Oyserman, D. and Lee, S. W. S. (2008) 'Does culture influence what and how we think? Effects of priming individualism and collectivism', *Psychological Bulletin*, 134: 311–42.

Ployhart, R. E., and Oswald, F. L. (2004) 'Application of mean and covariance structures analysis: Integrating correlational and experimental approaches', *Organizational Research Methods*, 7: 27–65.

Poortinga, Y. H. (2003) 'Coherence of culture and generalizability of data: Two questionable assumptions in cross-cultural psychology', in V. Murphy-Berman and J. J. Berman (eds), *Cross-cultural differences in perspectives on the self: Nebraska symposium on motivation (Vol. 49)*, Lincoln, NE: University of Nebraska Press. pp. 257–305.

Poortinga, Y. H. and van Hemert, D. A. (2001) 'Personality and culture: Demarcating between the common and the unique', *Journal of Personality*, 69(6): 1033–60.

Raju, N. S., Laffitte, L. J. and Byrne, B. M. (2002) 'Measurement equivalence: A comparison of methods based on confirmatory factor analysis and item response theory', *Journal of Applied Psychology*, 87: 517–29.

Reise, S. P., Morizot, J. and Hays, R. D. (2007) 'The role of the bifactor model in resolving dimensionality issues in health outcomes measures', *Quality of Life Research*, 16: 19–31.

Rost, J. (1990) 'Rasch model in latent classes: An integration of two approaches to item analysis', *Applied Psychological Measurement*, 14: 271–282.

Rozin, P. (2003) 'Five potential principles for understanding cultural differences in relation to individual differences', *Journal of Research in Personality*, 37: 273–83.

Schwarz, N. (2007) 'Attitude construction: Evaluation in context', *Social Cognition*, 25: 638–56.

Shevlin, M. E., Bunting, B. P. and Lewis, C. A. (1995) 'Confirmatory factor analysis of the Rosenberg self-esteem scale', *Psychological Reports*, 76: 707–10.

Shore, B. (2002) 'Taking culture seriously', *Human Development*, 45: 226–8.

Singelis, T. (1994) 'The measurement of independent and interdependent self-construals', *Personality and Social Psychology Bulletin*, 20: 580–91.

Sörbom, D. (1974) 'A general method for studying differences in factor means and factor structure between groups', *British Journal of Mathematical and Statistical Psychology*, 27: 229–39.

Spearman, C. (1904) ' "General intelligence", objectively determined and measured', *American Journal of Psychology*, 15: 201–93.

Stark, S., Chernyshenko, O. S. and Drasgow, F. (2006) Detecting differential item functioning with confirmatory factor analysis and item response theory: Toward a unified strategy', *Journal of Applied Psychology*, 91: 1292–1306.

Sturman, M. C., Cheramie, R. A. and Cashen, L. H. (2005) 'The impact of job complexity and performance measurement on the temporal consistency, stability, and test-retest reliability of employee job performance ratings', *Journal of Applied Psychology*, 90: 269–83.

Triandis, H. C. (1995) *Individualism and collectivism*. Boulder, CO: Westview Press.

van de Vijver, F. J. R. (2001) 'Research methods', in D. Matsumoto (ed.), *Handbook of culture and psychology*. Oxford: Oxford University Press. pp. 77–97.

van de Vijver, F. J. R. and Leung, K. (2001) 'Personality in cultural context: Methodological issues', *Journal of Personality*, 69: 1007–31.

Vandenberg, R. J. and Lance, C. E. (2000) A review and synthesis of the measurement invariance literature: Suggestions, practices, and recommendations for organizational research', *Organizational Research Methods*, 3: 4–70.

Vermunt, J. and Magidson, J. (2000) *Latent GOLD 4.0 User Manual*. Belmont, MA: Statistical Innovations.

Woo, S.E., Zhang, Z., Chiu, C-y. and Chernyshenko, O.S. (2008) 'A six-faceted measure of Openness: Measurement invariance across three cultures', in F. Oswald, and T. Rench, (Co-chairs), *Face it: The Predictive Validity of Personality Facets*. Symposium conducted at the 23rd Annual Meeting of the Society for Industrial and Organizational Psychology, San Francisco, CA.

Zhu, Y., McKenna, B. and Sun, Z. (2007) 'Negotiating with Chinese: Success of initial meetings is the key', *Cross-Cultural Management: An International Journal*, 14: 354–64.

APPENDIX A
MACS, CFA, AND LCA: TECHNICAL NOTES

I. Means and covariance structure (MACS) analysis and confirmatory factor analysis (CFA)

Mean and covariance structures analysis (MACS; Ployhart and Oswald, 2004; Sörbom, 1974; Vandenberg and Lance, 2000) is a statistical method for examining the pattern of means and covariances across groups or within groups (i.e., across time). It allows for the comparison of cross-cultural difference scores or within-group difference scores that are corrected for measurement error. Additionally, we can ensure cross-cultural or cross-time comparability via measurement equivalence (see Matsumoto and Yoo, 2006; van de Vijver, 2001; van de Vijver and Leung, 2001). Measurement equivalence of a construct demonstrates that the observed variables defining the construct relate in the same manner to one another across different groups of individuals or across time. Hence, the operational definition of the construct is sufficiently consistent across these situations for one to compare the construct scores.

Confirmatory factor analysis (CFA) can be subsumed under the MACS framework. In a single-group CFA, the aim is to examine the factor structure of variables in a scale. In a multi-group CFA, the factor structures are compared in the same manner in MACS. Notably, some researchers use

the multi-group CFA approach to ensure measurement equivalence, but do not go on to compare latent mean scores as in MACS. Instead, they use observed mean scores instead.

I.1 Between-group MACS with bifactor models

Measurement equivalence is typically tested through implementing multi-group MACS or multi-group confirmatory factor analysis (Cheung and Rensvold, 2002; Raju et al., 2002; Vandenburg and Lance, 2000) In this instance, the covariance matrices and mean vectors for two cultural groups are compared to see if there is configural, metric, scalar, and construct equivalence.

Model 1: Configural invariance [Same pattern of fixed (at zero) and free factor loadings across groups]
Model 2: Metric invariance [Factor loadings constrained to be equal]
Model 3: Scalar invariance [Indicator intercepts constrained to be equal]

Configural invariance is achieved when the same pattern of fixed (at zero) and free factor loadings apply across groups. This initial model has to fit well so that further nested submodels can be compared to it (Stark et al., 2006). Metric equivalence adds the additional requirement of equal factor loadings Λ_x across groups, as seen in the measurement model,

$$x = \tau_x + \Lambda_x \xi + \delta \qquad (10.1)$$

The equality of factor loading matrices suggests that the constructs are manifested in the same way across groups with the same degree of the item-construct relationships. Scalar invariance requires indicator intercepts τ_x to be equal. Note that it is possible to test for the equality of measurement errors δ or residual variances across groups, which suggests that the qualities of items as measures of underlying constructs (i.e., internal consistency) are the same across groups. However, there is a controversy over whether this step is necessary (see Stark et al., 2006).

Model 4: Latent mean invariance [Latent means of constructs constrained to be equal]

After ascertaining measurement invariance, we can test for whether the latent means are equal across groups, with all the aforementioned conditions of measurement invariance being satisfied. In order to estimate the mean differences in latent variables, the latent means of one of the groups has to be fixed at zero. The estimated latent mean for the other group then represents the mean difference in the construct between the two groups.

I.2 Within-group MACS

To elaborate on the within-group MACS model, two measurement models, as seen in equations (10.1) and (10.2) can be specified for the time 1 and time 2 construct respectively:

$$y = \tau_y + \Lambda_y \eta + \varepsilon \qquad (10.2)$$

The terms in the time 2 measurement model, $y, \tau_y, \Lambda_y, \eta$, and ε are defined analogously as the time 1 measurement model. Importantly, for within-group MACS, because the same individuals are assessed at both time points, it is usually necessary to allow the error terms δ_i and ε_i for each observed indicator i to correlate across time (Ployhart and Oswald, 2004). Without modeling these correlations, a poor model-data fit is frequently obtained.

Where one is interested in examining gamma, beta, and alpha change in multiple

constructs, the analysis should be conducted for each construct in turn.

Gamma change

Here, gamma change is evaluated as with the configural invariance model, Model 1. Hence, the same pattern of fixed (at zero) and free factor loadings at both time 1 and time 2 constructs are specified. If this baseline model does not fit, there is evidence of gamma change.

Beta change

After which, we can proceed to Model 2, where factor loadings for time 1 and time 2 constructs are constrained as equal, with the both latent means at time 1 and time 2 fixed at zero for identification purposes. A significant decrement in fit from Model 1 to Model 2 indicates beta change. Finally, τ_x and τ_y can be constrained as identical, while freeing the latent mean at time 2. A substantial decrement in fit from Model 2 to Model 3 indicates a change in indicator intercepts, which is indicative of beta change.

Alpha change

Changes in latent means can be examined by constraining both the latent means at time 1 and time 2 to be equivalent. A significant decrement in fit from Model 3 to Model 4 indicates alpha change.

I.3 Model comparisons and model-data fit

To determine whether constraints in each model yield a significant decrease in fit, there are several possibilities. One can use the ΔCFI as the criterion, which has been found to be most robust and independent of both model complexity and sample size (Cheung and Rensvold, 2002). Results from Cheung and Rensvold's (2002) simulation study suggest that ΔCFI

value higher than .010 should be considered as a significant drop in fit. Alternatively, one can compare the adjusted chi-square differences between nested models (F. Drasgow, personal communication, October 2008). One problem with using the ordinary chi-square statistic is its sensitivity to sample size because

$$\chi^2 = (N{-}1)F[\mathbf{S}, \Sigma(\hat{\theta})] \qquad (10.3)$$

where N is the sample size, and $F[\mathbf{S}, \Sigma(\hat{\theta})]$ is the minimized fit function. From the above equation, N directly affects the size of the chi-square, and the consequent differences between model chi-squares. Thus, differences in model chi-squares may result simply from having a large sample size. Instead we propose an adjustment of chi-square to a fixed sample size. The expected value of a noncentral chi-square is equal to its df plus N times its noncentrality parameter d,

$$E(\chi^2) = df + N\delta \qquad (10.4)$$

Then, an estimate of the noncentrality parameter is

$$\hat{\delta} = (\chi^2 - df)/N \qquad (10.5)$$

An observed χ^2 can be adjusted to a common sample size of, say, $N = 250$, by

$$\chi^2_{adj} = [df + 250(\chi^2 - df)/N] \quad (10.6)$$

Differences between nested models can be evaluated using the change in adjusted chi-squares $\Delta\chi^2_{adj}$ to the change in degrees of freedom Δdf. Significant changes show the nested model is not equivalent.

Aside from comparing $\Delta\chi^2_{adj}$ to evaluate model differences, other fit indices can be used to assess global model-data fit: These include the non-normed fit index (NNFI; also known as the Tucker-Lewis index) and

the comparative fit index (CFI) (Bentler, 1990; Bentler and Bonett, 1980) where values of above 0.95 generally indicate good fit. Also, the root mean squared error of approximation (RMSEA) can be examined to see if its value is smaller than .08. Similarly, the standardized root mean square residual (SRMR) should have a value less than .08 indicating good fit. A host of other local fit indices can also be examined to determine where the source of misfit occurs.

II. Latent class modeling

A traditional latent-class model (Lazarsfeld, 1950; Masters, 1985) can be implemented in the form of

$$f(\underset{\sim}{y_i}) = \sum_{x=1}^{K} P(x) \prod_{t=1}^{T} f(y_{it}|x) \qquad (10.7)$$

where the marginal probability density corresponding to an individual response pattern $f(\underset{\sim}{y_i})$ is assumed to depend on (a) the mixing weights, which refers to the probability of an individual being in a specific latent class $P(x)$ ($x = 1, \ldots, K$), and (b) the mixture of densities $f(y_{it}|x)$, which refers to the conditional probabilities of an individual response to item t given a latent class x. According to the model, all variation in responding is captured by the underlying latent classes, resulting in independent conditional probabilities $\prod_{t=1}^{T} f(y_{it}|x)$ across T items. Substantively, the mixture of densities shows that individual responses patterns come from a mixture of qualitatively different regulatory focus groups. The mixing weights illustrate that the proportions of these groups are different.

Unlike the traditional latent class models, which assume a single nominal latent variable, the discrete latent trait model (DFactor) allows for more than one latent variable $(x_1, x_2, \ldots, x_L)$, and the K categories within each latent trait x is assumed to be ordered (Heinen, 1996). The latent trait here is essentially a discretized version of the latent continuum assumed in item response theory (IRT). For two discrete latent traits, the mathematical equation is given by

$$f(\underset{\sim}{y_i}) = \sum_{x=1}^{K_1} \sum_{x_2=1}^{K_2} P(x_1, x_2) \prod_{t=1}^{T} f(y_{it}|x_1, x_2)$$

(10.8)

Now, the response patterns depend on two different latent traits (x_1 and x_2) and their respective levels. The main statistical advantage is that this model is more parsimonious as compared to the traditional latent class models. Another advantage is that in the 2 latent trait DFactor model, each latent trait can possibly represent response style and the degree of regulatory focus as shown in the illustration. This model can be implemented in the software Latent GOLD 4.0 (Vermunt and Magidson, 2000).

Extensions to the latent class model can include latent traits. This is also known as a mixed-measurement model (Rost, 1990), where one estimates the latent classes and factor analytic parameters (e.g., item loadings) simultaneously. Hence, each latent class has a different measurement model (see Hernandez et al., 2004).

APPENDIX B

	Debate		
	Coherence: Culture as a coherent meaning system versus a network of domain-specific symbolic elements	**Malleability: Culture as enduring traits or emergent behaviors**	**Commensurability between cultures and homogeneity of culture**
The defining modeling/ measurement issues	What drives differences in observed behaviors across cultures: Global factors or domain-specific factors?	Do cultural experiences cause qualitative or quantitative change in psychological constructs across time?	How can country-specific and nonspecific cultural constructs be identified? How can between- and within-country differences be assessed simultaneously?
Current approach	Second order factor model	Not available	Between-group measurement invariance
Problems with the current approach	Does not address the debate because domain-specific factors nested within global factors hence it impossible to assess the independent effects of the two types of factors		Presupposes invariant universal cultural dimensions along which countries or groups differ. Hence, differences obtained are strictly quantitative not qualitative. Having a large proportion of individuals that are similar across countries or groups can occlude interesting effects from smaller sub-populations. It is still an untested assumption that cultural boundaries align with demographic boundaries. There are problems in comparing groups when there is no measurement invariance. Forcibly dropping non-invariant items may result in loss of information on how groups differ
Suggested alternatives	Bifactor model	Within-group mean and covariance structures (MACS) analysis; alpha, beta, and gamma change	Latent Class modeling; mixture-measurement modeling
Advantages of the suggested alternatives	Simultaneous modeling of broad and domain-specific constructs allows independent assessment of effect of each type of factor	Allows examination of the types of changes (qualitative or quantitative) that occur across time. Simultaneous modeling of different types of constructs to determine how they are related across time; specifically, looking at construct consistency or cross-construct influence	Cultural groups are empirically obtained. Hence, one can identify the demographic variables that explain the most variance in cultural groupings. Permits identification of common classes of individuals across countries and idiosyncratic classes of individuals
Further readings	Carroll, 1993; Woo et al., 2008	Golembiewski et al., 1976; Vandenberg and Lance, 2000; Ployhart and Oswald, 2004	Clogg, 1995; Rost, 1990

11

International Comparisons of Educational Attainment: Purposes, Processes, and Problems

David Phillips

This chapter will describe – in the context of some of the more important attempts at international studies of achievement – the problems and challenges that beset both large- and small-scale international surveys. Comparativists have been at the forefront of developments in this significant area of educational inquiry and in particular bring to it an understanding of context that is critical if survey results are to be properly understood and acted upon. Much of the technical expertise required in the construction and administration of the tests that form the basis of surveys of pupil achievement comes from specialists who are not primarily involved in policy analysis or pedagogy; and such specialists do not always have the detailed knowledge of other

education systems and their histories and traditions that those working in comparative and international education bring. In what follows I shall attempt to look at the main issues that surround international comparisons of pupil attainment from the perspective of the comparativist rather than that of the expert on testing and assessment.

In the introduction to his book *Studies in Comparative Education*, Isaac Kandel, one of the founding fathers of the field, wrote of what he saw as the impossibility of making various kinds of comparison in education 'until the raw material, the statistics, becomes more uniform and comparable'. 'Comparative studies of the quality of education', he asserted, may be possible in time, but not before the instruments of measurement have been made more perfect and reliable than they are at present, or when aims of education in different countries are more nearly alike, or finally, when tests have been developed which can measure more accurately the results of education rather than of instruction in fundamentals of subject-matter. (Kandel, n.d., p.xi)

That was written in 1933, and it moves a few steps on from the view of an earlier comparativist, writing in 1902, that 'it is impossible to measure comprehensively any system of national education in terms of another': 'These systems cannot be arranged in order of merit. The finer elements, the more ethical and spiritual factors in national culture, defy the balance of the analyst and the scalpel of the anatomist; they are susceptible to no quantitative tests' (Hughes, 1902: 387).

Over a century later perceptions could not be more different, and we can now at least be confident that we have at our disposal – as Kandel had anticipated – a range of sophisticated means with which the task of international comparison is at least made rather easier. This is to be welcomed. The huge resource now available to us as a result of the surveys of recent years has transformed our ability to make comparisons and reach judgements on how education systems are performing.

The desire to measure quality and to 'arrange in order of merit' is now of course very powerful and driven by varying political imperatives. Governments want to know where they stand in terms of educational performance in relation to their competitors, and they wish to do so for reasons ranging from celebration of supposed policy successes to denigration of their predecessors' achievements or self-flagellation *pour encourager*.

And there is a general desire – beyond the motives of governments – to discover differences in ability and performance across nations, to explain them, and to contemplate reform as a result. One of the more surprising literary revelations of 2008 was George Steiner's unfulfilled wish – so he says – to write a book on comparative education. He describes in *My Unwritten Books* how he would construct a novel and idiosyncratic curriculum, but how he would be interested too to run an 'international literacy and "general knowledge" Olympiad' with common tests, essays, and oral examinations:

Could a sixth former from a British school be matched against a pupil in the *première* of a French *lycée* and a boy or girl in the *Matura*-class of a German or Austrian *Gymnasium*? Conceivably, this could be managed at an élite level. Where less selective, less 'academic' secondary education is enlisted, the obstacles to reciprocal concordance may be insurmountable. (Steiner, 2008: 120–1)

Achieving 'reciprocal concordance' – a nice term – is indeed fraught with obstacles. How can we realistically compare what young people in different parts of the world know/can do/have achieved in subjects ranging from mathematics and science, through mother tongue competence, to foreign languages and citizenship?

THE INTERNATIONAL ASSOCIATION FOR THE EVALUATION OF EDUCATIONAL ACHIEVEMENT

In the late 1950s serious work began on the international evaluation of young people's educational achievement by what was to become known as IEA (the International Association for the Evaluation of Educational Achievement). IEA achieved status as a legal entity in 1967, with important national research institutions becoming members of the organisation. (Postlethwaite, 1985)

Arthur W. Foshay and colleagues (1962) undertook a pilot study investigation of 13-year-old children in 12 countries during the period 1959–1961. Some 9,918 pupils were tested in reading comprehension, mathematics, science, and geography. The countries included were Belgium, England, Finland, France, the Federal Republic of Germany, Israel, Poland, Scotland, Sweden, Switzerland, the United States, and Yugoslavia. A report on the study was published in 1962 and initiated a long and important series of IEA studies covering a range of different subject areas. There have been more than 20 IEA surveys since the 1962 report and their impact on policy discussion around the world has been profound. Among them are an early project (1962–1966) on home and school factors affecting achievement in mathematics and studies of science, reading comprehension, literacy, first foreign languages, and civic education (1966–1975), and significant investigations of mathematics and science, including the Trends in International Mathematics and Science Survey (TIMSS) and widely discussed projects on citizenship education. (Phillips and Schweisfurth, 2007)

The 1962 study aimed to move research in comparative education from 'cultural analysis' to a predominantly empirical approach, as Foshay puts it in his chapter on the background and procedures of the research. (1962: 7) The purposes of the exploratory study were:

1   To see whether some indications of the intellectual functioning behind responses to short-answer tests could be deduced from an examination of the patterning of such responses from many countries.
2   To discover the possibilities and the difficulties attending a large-scale international study. (pp. 7–8)

This was very much in the tradition of a pilot study, and its design was such that it produced challenges that have remained of significance in subsequent surveys. It did not include 'a strictly random sample of the school population of the stated age in each country' (Pidgeon, 1962: 58) but instead a representative sample. It tackled the problems involved with administering tests in eight languages, but despite the fact that 'a translated test is … a different test' (Pidgeon, 1962) the researchers did not feel that the scores had been unduly affected by the translation process. The tests could not all be administered at the same time. Some test items had to be changed. (Foshay, 1962: 11). The test items used were mostly taken from existing tests in five of the countries involved (Foshay, 1962: 10) and so were not written specifically for the study. The sample sizes covered a huge range: 300 for Switzerland; 1,732 for Israel (Foshay, 1962: 11). We shall return to some of these issues below.

Since it was felt that this carefully designed project 'showed that it was possible to conduct meaningful research of this kind' (Postlethwaite, 1985: 2645), it was decided to initiate the series of attainment studies that has established IEA as a principal player in the field of international testing. IEA describes the aims and importance of its work as follows:

[IEA's] primary purpose is to conduct large-scale comparative studies of educational achievement, with the aim of gaining a more in-depth understanding of the effects of policies and practices within and across systems of education

[…]

IEA studies are an important data source for those working to enhance students' learning at the international, national and local levels. By reporting on a wide range of topics and subject matters, the studies contribute to a deep understanding of educational processes within individual countries, and across a broad international context. In addition, the cycle of studies provides countries with an opportunity to measure progress in educational achievement in mathematics, science and reading comprehension. The cycle of studies also enables monitoring of changes in the implementation of educational policy and identification of new issues relevant to reform efforts. (IEA Mission Statement, http://www.iea.nl/iea/hq/ http://www.iea.nl/iea/hq/ (19.09.2003))

Two IEA studies can serve as examples of strategies and problems in the conduct of large-scale international surveys: TIMSS (1996); and the Civic Education Project (1999).

TIMSS is IEA's most ambitious project to date. It involves both quantitative and qualitative case studies and covers an investigation of attainment in mathematics and science of fourth and eighth grade pupils in some 40 countries (the French- and Flemish-speaking parts of Belgium are treated separately), a comparison of curricula and textbooks, and video-recorded analyses of mathematics lessons, as well as ethnographic studies, in Germany, Japan, and the United States. The result is a particularly rich collection of data which can be used to make sophisticated between- and within-country comparisons. The TIMSS investigation has continued with TIMSS 2007, thus providing four surveys at four-year intervals over a period of 12 years (1995, 1999, 2003, and 2007).

The technical data reveal a few problems which indicate something of the fragility of even such highly organised surveys as TIMMS:

- data for Argentina, Indonesia, and Italy were not included since those countries had been unable to fulfil various IEA requirements;
- the normally high-performing German state of Baden-Württemberg was not included in the German data;
- Israel and Kuwait were not involved in the 7th grade tests;

- The Latvian sample only included Latvian-speaking schools;
- Mexico decided not to make its results available;
- The Philippines was left out as a result of lack of information about the sample. (*Education Journal* International Supplement, February 1997, p.23)

IEA no longer allows non-publication of data, but data on individual countries' performance can clearly still be excluded as a result of data collection problems or failure to comply with other conditions required for participation. The absence of data for Baden-Württemberg in the German sample is a serious flaw.

The Civic Education Project involved 28 countries and was self-consciously ambitious in scope. Despite the problems evident in reaching agreement about the issues of importance in civic education among so many nations,[1] the principal researchers concluded that it was nevertheless possible to identify common ground and to determine viable ways of testing knowledge in this complex area:

IEA researchers working in a collaborative process demonstrated that there is a core of agreement across democratic societies regarding important topics in civic education. They showed that it is possible to construct a meaningful, reliable, and valid international test of student knowledge about fundamental democratic principles and processes, as well as a survey of concepts of citizenship, attitudes, and civic-related activities. (Torney-Purta et al., 2001b: 3)

The population which the study wished to test was defined as:

all students enrolled on a full time basis in that grade in which most students aged 14.00 to 14.11 {years; months} are found at the time of testing. Time of testing is the first week of the 8th month of the school year. (Torney-Purta et al., 2001a: 33)

The report on the study mentions some divergence from this expectation that demonstrates how the reality can differ from the planned approach in such surveys:

- in most countries pupils were in grade 8, in nine they were in grade 9; in Switzerland some were in grade 8, others in grade 9;
- Hong Kong and the Russian Federation had a sample whose average age was above 15 and so did not meet the age/grade stipulations;
- in Belgium and Chile the proportion of 13-year-olds was larger than that of 14-year-olds.
- two German *Länder* declined to take part, and another would not allow *Gymnasium* pupils to be tested;
- ten countries did not reach a required 75 per cent participation rate. (Torney-Purta et al., 2001a: 33–5)
- the school sample sizes were in the range 112–183; the pupil sample sizes ranged from 2,076 to 5,688; in the case of Cyprus two classes from each of the total number (61) of schools were tested.

The extent to which this kind of divergence matters – probably not much in this particular instance – is difficult to assess, but such differences at least raise the question: 'What is a 14-year-old?' Media reporting will almost certainly speak of the survey as if all pupils were aged 14 and were in grade 8.

This particular IEA study generated much interest, especially in the context of discussion in England and elsewhere about the forms which education for citizenship might take.

THE OECD AND PISA

The IEA studies have made, and continue to make, a significant impact on how educational standards are perceived. They have been headline news in both the educational press and national newspapers as commentators seize on comparative listings to celebrate success or – more often – to condemn failure. But they have now been somewhat overshadowed by an important initiative of the Organisation for Economic

Co-operation and Development (OECD). The OECD's PISA (Programme for International Student Assessment) surveys have become one of the most influential factors in terms of impact on educational policymakers throughout the developed world. In Germany the term 'PISA-Schock' has been invented to describe the effects of PISA results on the educational psyche of the nation. There have even been television quiz programmes and popular test-yourself publications which have used the term.

PISA differs from previous international surveys of attainment in that it aims to test the application of knowledge, rather than just knowledge *per se*. It is careful to talk of reading, mathematical, and scientific *literacy* – that is, 'students' ability to reflect actively on their knowledge and experience and to address issues that will be relevant to their own future lives' (OECD, n.d.). The first round of PISA focused principally on reading and included 265,000 pupils in 32 countries (in addition to OECD countries, Brazil, China, Latvia, and the Russian Federation decided to participate). PISA 2003 focused mainly on mathematics and again sampled over a quarter of a million pupils, this time in an additional 11 countries. The chief focus of PISA 2006 was on science, now with some 4,000,000 pupils taking part in 57 countries. (Alongside the main focus in each case, tests were also conducted in the other two subjects.)

In a press notice the OECD highlighted the findings which resulted from the first round of PISA.

- Finland is the top performing country in … reading literacy among 15-year-olds.
- On average, 10 per cent of 15-year olds in the world's most developed countries have top-level reading literacy skills.
- At the other end of the scale, an average of 6 per cent of 15-year-olds – and in some countries more than twice that proportion – fall below level 1, PISA's lowest level of reading proficiency.

- Japan and Korea are the top performers in mathematical and scientific literacy.
- High overall performance can go hand in hand with an equitable distribution of results.
- In many countries, boys are falling far behind in reading literacy.
- In about half of the countries surveyed, boys perform better than girls in mathematical literacy.
- About half of 15-year-olds consider mathematics important in a general sense.
- Students show wide differences in their general engagement with school, including big variations in attitudes to reading and even more so in mathematics.
- Higher average spending per student tends to be associated with higher average performance [... but does not guarantee it].
- Students from privileged social backgrounds tend to perform better, but differences are less pronounced in some countries than in others.
- Results vary widely across schools.
- There is no single factor that explains why some schools or countries have better results but there are some school policies and practices that tend to be associated with success (OECD, 2001b: 1–2).

This summary list from the OECD indicates the diversity of the findings that emerge from the PISA surveys. They range from 'league table' placements (Finland top in reading literacy; Japan and Korea top in mathematics and science), through general trends (boys falling behind in reading literacy; better performance from those with privileged social backgrounds), to ventures into causation (higher average spending on education; particular school policies and practices). PISA 2006 marked the completion of the first cycle of the OECD's assessment programme; the second cycle involves investigations in 2009 (reading), 2012 (mathematics) and 2015 (science).

OTHER INTERNATIONAL STUDIES

There are other studies of relevance which must be briefly mentioned. Since 1991 UNESCO has produced its biennial *World Education Report* which provides statistical data and commentary on a range of factors of interest when comparing countries' educational performance. The OECD's sophisticated annually produced 'performance indicator' series *Education at a Glance* is an exhaustive compilation of data that provides a wealth of information designed to assist in assessing how educational systems are performing in the OECD countries.

The Southern and Eastern Africa Consortium for Monitoring Educational Quality (SACMEQ) is a collaborative initiative involving UNESCO's Institute for International Educational Planning (IIEP) and the ministries of education of Botswana, Kenya, Lesotho, Malawi, Mauritius, Mozambique, Namibia, Seychelles, South Africa, Swaziland, Tanzania (Mainland), Tanzania (Zanzibar), Uganda, Zambia, and Zimbabwe. It began work in 1995 and has produced surveys of educational quality firstly involving seven ministries (SACMEQ I, 1995–1999) and later 14 (SACMEQ II, 2000–2003). (www.sacmeq.org)

Its particular strength lies in its difference from other organisations conducting surveys:

> SACMEQ differs from other studies in that it has created a systematic strategy for consulting with governments and policy-makers in order to identify concerns and the research questions they wish to have answered, It is these research questions obtained from senior decision-makers in ministries of education that form the basis of the SACMEQ studies. (Grisay and Griffin, 2006: 78)

There are of course particular problems with surveys in developing countries. The factors which make inclusion in international surveys difficult for many developing nations include:

> shortage of classroom teaching and learning aids; very large classroom sizes; underqualified

or unqualified teachers; poor health among learners; and a prevalence of illiteracy among parents. Even the logistics of conducting a rigorous data collection in contexts with poor infrastructures would contribute to undermining the reliability and comparability of such a survey. (Phillips and Schweisfurth, 2007: 126)

The Educational Testing Service (ETS) of the United States, which has considerable experience and expertise in national assessment through its National Assessment of Educational Progress (NAEP) has also conducted international surveys within its International Assessment of Educational Progress (IAEP) which has involved studies of mathematics and science.

PIRLS (Programme in International Reading Literacy Study) is an IEA project that measures trends in the reading achievement of fourth grade pupils at five-year intervals (2001, 2006 so far).

Among the many significant small-scale comparative studies we might mention are those of Alexander (2000, returned to below) and Prais and Wagner (1985). The Prais and Wagner study, which enjoyed very wide coverage in England and attracted the attention of politicians, attempted to compare standards in England and Germany by postulating rough equivalences of curricula and examinations and is particularly interesting for the way in which one of its tentative findings has been misquoted. On the basis of their tentative comparisons the authors reported that 'attainments in mathematics by those in the lower half of the ability range in England *appear* to lag by the equivalent of *about* two years' schooling behind the corresponding section of pupils in Germany' (Prais and Wagner, 1985: 68, present author's emphasis). Note the authors' careful insertion of 'appear' and 'about'. But this finding was soon quoted in terms of *all* British pupils being *generally* two years behind German pupils. Such is the danger of misinterpretation.

This particular dilemma, the use and misuse of comparative studies of attainment, leads us to consider some of the problems that surround international surveys.

PROBLEMS

'League tables' and reporting

Large-scale surveys of attainment result in vast amounts of statistical data which can be presented in a variety of ways. Inevitably presentations take the form of rankings, in which it can be shown – as, for example, in the TIMSS scores for mathematics and science in grades 7 and 8 – that Singapore came 'top' and South Africa 'bottom'. The 'league table' approach suits the media very well and results in wide graphic coverage of the results, but the analogy with football scores that gives rise to use of the term does a disservice to the complexities of the data produced in what are very sophisticated studies. Between-country differences in scores might be very small; a whole country's scores might be affected by an underperforming region; sampling – despite the research design requirements – might skew results through omission. With different countries participating in studies over time, the position of a given country in rankings can vary as a result of other countries not participating: the effect might then be to judge that the country concerned has performed less well even if the scores have remained constant. The reverse can also be true, giving the impression of increased performance levels. In sum, 'rankings in themselves tell us nothing about the many factors that may underlie differences between countries in performance' (Greaney and Kellaghan, 2008: 73–4).

League tables in the footballing sense are the result of clear-cut decisions about success and failure. Rankings in international comparative surveys disguise fine nuances in performance to an extent that can be very misleading to uninformed observers.

The full picture of results for a given country only emerges when the data are looked at in far more detail than the league table approach allows. PISA, for example, reveals performance data for the individual *Länder* (federal states) of Germany which permit within-country analyses to be undertaken. (Baumert et al., 2002) The OECD also provides special briefing notes on individual countries. Those for PISA 2006 for the United Kingdom include the following among the 'key results':

> *15-year olds in the United Kingdom achieve a mean score of 515 score points in science, on a scale that has an OECD average of 500 score points and for which two thirds of the OECD student population perform between 400 and 600 score points.*
>
> [...]
>
> Korea, Germany, Czech Republic, Switzerland, Austria, Belgium, Ireland, cannot be distinguished from the United Kingdom's performance with statistical significance.
>
> *In relative terms, the United Kingdom ranks 9th among the 30 OECD countries, but the confidence interval extends from the 8th to the 12th rank.* (OECD 2007c: 2)

Similar country reports are produced by TIMSS. We can also access country data for the IEA Civic Education Study (Baldi et al., 2001).

The data are used too by researchers to make comparisons which are beyond the scope of the normal reporting of results. Two examples, using PISA data, are Xu's analysis of sibship size and educational achievement and Ma's study of within-school gender gaps, both reported in the *Comparative Education Review* (2008). There are very many others.

But all too often the results are reported and interpreted in stark summative and political terms: 'The clear message is that the Pisa [sic] study is right: Britain now seems to have an education system that is often not much better than bog standard, despite the amount of taxpayers' money spent on it' (Grimston, 2007: 16). Jaworski and Phillips (1999) listed some sensational headlines from reporting of a variety of international comparative research in the 1980s and 1990s:

> As each new piece of evidence about standards is published, both the serious and the popular press reinforce the public's perception of falling standards with headlines that seek to outvie each other for immediate impact: 'Why England is to be found sitting in the dunce's corner' (*The Independent*, 15 January 1987); 'Muddle + indifference = a nation that can't add up' (*Independent on Sunday*, 5 November 1995); 'British pupils and a maths disaster'; 'Weakness in numbers' (*The Times*, 19 January 1996); 'A lesson in sums from the French' (*The Mail on Sunday*, 4 February 1996); Are we failing by numbers?' (*The Times*, 15 November 1996); 'English pupils "years behind"' (*The Times Educational Supplement*, 19 January 1996). (p. 7)

It will ever be thus. And so it becomes the task of the comparativist to delve deep into the data to provide a proper commentary on the results. Respected analysts like Neville Postlethwaite and Harvey Goldstein provide not only expert analysis of methodological problems but are also competent to unpick the complex statistical data to reveal problems or to counter criticism. Jürgen Baumert fulfils a similar role in Germany and internationally.

In sum: 'Rankings in themselves tell us nothing about the many factors that may underlie differences between countries in performance' (Greaney and Kellaghan, 2008: 73–4).

Outcomes and processes

With some exceptions – notable among them the detailed video study that was part of TIMSS – large-scale international studies focus largely on outcomes rather than the processes that have led to them. Those processes become part of the considerations of causation and are often left to other analysts to examine or speculate about. But for the educationist – and especially for the comparativist – processes are the key element. This means that a fundamental question must be: To what extent is it of use to know that country x is ranked higher than countries y and z in a list based on measured performance averages? As in so many areas in comparative studies, context is of vital importance – and context implies approaches to, and the conditions of, teaching and learning that are interestingly different from country to country and, indeed, within countries. What is more, other measures might be as significant as measured performance outcomes: the perceived happiness of pupils, for example; or the development of social and other skills that do not show up in listings based on test scores.

Causation/Explanation

Recently those in charge of large-scale surveys of attainment have been venturing opinions on causation. Previously reasons as to why results are as they are have in the main been left to other commentators to deduce. One view of current PISA researchers seems to be, for example, that a common system of schooling (without rigid differentiation at secondary level) tends to produce higher scores. This explanation in particular has resulted in much agony among educationists in Germany, where dual or tripartite structures exist in all *Länder*, with the prestigious *Gymnasium* providing an elite academic education, the *Realschule* catering for a huge range of middle ability with a significant technical bent, and the *Hauptschule* offering a

basic education for those intending to join the workforce at an early opportunity. Vocational training, which is compulsory up to the age of 18 and highly advanced in Germany compared to other nations, builds on the curricula of the schools below *Gymnasium* level. (Advances in attainment as a result of vocational training are not of course apparent in surveys which focus on 14–16-year-olds.) The *Gesamtschule* (comprehensive school) has not found favour in most of the *Länder* and has never replaced a differentiated system, existing instead alongside other forms of secondary school.

In the course of a radio programme in the mid-1980s (at a time of considerable debate in England that was to lead up to the 1988 Education Reform Act) Neville Postlethwaite listed homework and teacher salaries as important contributing factors in the measured success of education systems:

> Homework is important at all levels …, the more homework in general, the more the children will learn, and if homework is given and not marked, that is still better than not having homework. If the homework is given and is marked and *used* …, this is very beneficial.
>
> [...]
>
> Where the teachers are relatively well paid compared with the average civil servant in a country, then the students tend to have higher [achievement] scores.

[Finland, incidentally, a country that has performed spectacularly well in all three rounds of PISA to date, does not pay its teachers especially high salaries compared with other usually high performing countries or even with the average for OECD countries (2005 figures, OECD, 2007d, Table D3.1: 396).]

Additional factors, not surprisingly, were thought to be continuous examination of the curriculum, the task-orientation of teachers and their insistence on and expectation of high standards and discipline (BBC, 1986).

A later discussion in which Postlethwaite was involved produced a checklist of features of education systems in Continental Europe that might account for higher performance levels compared to the UK. Most of the factors listed had to do with the structure of those systems:

- teaching groups of roughly similar abilities, grade repetition;
- different pathways with academic, technical or vocational goals;
- access to pathways through (parental) choice
- progression along pathways dependent on performance
- existence of 'bridging' and transfer mechanisms;
- crucial end of year mark (on which the grade progression decision is based) depends on all subjects a pupil is studying;
- existence of a range of school leaving diplomas associated with employment opportunities;
- labour market demands clear standards which depend on success at school (Halsey et al., 1991: 22–3).

Explanations for a country's success in international surveys of attainment are often a matter of speculation rather than hard evidence. Correlation is not causation. Policy makers need to be wary of jumping to quick and far-reaching conclusions as a result of averaged test scores presented alongside socio-economic data.

Let us take the example of Germany again. Germany had not previously been an underperforming country in large-scale surveys, and so the shock of the results from the first round of PISA was understandable. But – and this is not to diminish the general desire for educational reform in Germany – a wholesale rethink of approaches to education could potentially undermine what the country has always been good at, namely, imparting knowledge. German schools have a good record of ensuring that children learn what they are taught, and this knowledge is reflected in tests (those of IEA, for example) that require a demonstration of what has been learnt. PISA specifically tests the application of knowledge and reveals that German schoolchildren in the target age range fall short of their counterparts in many other advanced nations. It could be, however, that emphasis on the application of knowledge comes a little later in Germany, during the vocationally oriented stage of schooling. While it is desirable that the application of knowledge should not be neglected, caution should be exercised before concluding that previous approaches to teaching have been seriously flawed.

Impact

In the aftermath of the 'PISA-Shock' the German Chancellor, Angela Merkel, decided to make education a central pillar of the 2008 election campaign: 'Public concern about Germany's state education system has risen markedly in recent years. The country has slipped in international rankings of schools, its universities – once a model for the world – no longer figure in the upper echelons of international league tables' (Benoit, 2008: 6).

Analyses of the effects of TIMSS on policy makers in the participating countries reveals a huge variety of consequent activity, including parliamentary debate, the setting-up of taskforces and committees, new curricula, teacher professional development initiatives, and the development of new teaching materials. Among other things, PISA has, according to Greaney and Kellaghan:

- cast doubt on the value of extensive use of computers [...];
- highlighted the fact that level of national expenditure on education is not associated with achievement [...];

- prompted general policy debate on education (Germany);

[...]

- emphasized the complexity of the relationship between socio-economic status and reading achievement across countries;
- underscored the link between achievement and school types and curriculum tracking within schools;

[...]

- stressed the need for intensive language and reading programs for foreign-born students to help boost achievement (Switzerland). (2008: 68–70)

Pedagogy

Comparative pedagogy is a neglected field, the subject of a plea by Claire Planel (2008) for its inclusion as an element in teacher training courses:

> Comparative pedagogy, the area of comparative education that deals with understanding the cultural context of teaching and learning, should be included in teacher training as it is held to be relevant to all teachers [...] It is suggested that comparative pedagogy could develop teachers' intercultural competence, that it could equip teachers for pluricultural classrooms and that it could increase teachers' professional understanding and practice in general. Further research is needed to explore how an understanding of comparative pedagogy could affect teacher performance. (Planel, 2008: 396)

What actually happens in the classroom is often far removed from the matters investigated in international surveys of attainment. The TIMSS video study forms an important exception. Mathematics lessons in Germany, Japan, and the United States were filmed and analysed, and a subsequent video recording was made widely available as a teaching aid. Some 231 classrooms were used and constituted a random subsample of the TIMSS sample (100 in Germany, 50 in Japan, 81 in the United States) (Stigler and Hiebert, 1999).

Also of considerable importance is Alexander's groundbreaking comparative study of pedagogy in France, Russia, India, the United States, and England (2000). This huge achievement involves, in more than 640 pages, profound coverage of what actually happens in primary education in the five countries. Based on his detailed background knowledge of the histories and traditions of the systems and schools in question, Alexander probes into teaching styles, lesson structure and form, classroom organisation, tasks and activities, routines, rules and rituals, interaction, time and pace, and learning discourse. The result is one of the most thorough comparative studies of schooling ever undertaken. In particular the very existence of this account draws attention to what is lacking in large-scale international surveys of attainment – namely, coverage of the processes that lead to the measured outcomes that the surveys produce.

Without considerable in-depth analysis of classroom teaching of the kind that Alexander's exhaustive survey exemplifies, there is a danger that simplistic conclusions about pedagogy will be reached. Greaney and Kellaghan warn: 'Because the relative effect of variables depends on the context in which they are embedded, practices associated with high achievement in one country cannot be assumed to show a similar relationship in another' (2008: 71). Comparativists are of course all too aware of the centrality of context when it comes to the interpretation of educational phenomena in different countries.

INTERROGATING THE DATA

Several prominent analysts (among them Goldstein, 1995, 1996; Greaney and

Kellaghan, 2008; Keys, 1996; Mclean, 1996; Postlethwaite, 1999a, b, 2006; Prais et al., 2000; Purves et al., 1989; Tabberer and Le Métais, 1997) have provided detailed accounts of ways in which data from large-scale international surveys of student attainment might be assessed. The following is an attempt at a selective checklist of basic questions which can be used to interrogate the data, it takes into account the points frequently raised in the accounts of these and other commentators.

Purpose

*   What is the purpose of any particular large-scale international survey? Are the principal questions clearly formulated? Can they be properly operationalised?

Clearly there should be aims beyond the mere reporting of scores. As with studies on a much smaller scale, the research questions should be transparent and should inform the methods used throughout the investigation. There is a danger that some studies might lose sight of the starting point through the accumulation of too many disparate data: this can lead to a naïve reliance on corollation on the part of those trying to deduce causation.

Postlethwaite is very clear on the need to define both national and cross-national purposes in international studies. And he argues that *general* aims should generate *specific* aims which break down into operational questions using 'dummy tables' that will produce answers to the general questions: 'A study that does not have such operational aims does not really know where it is headed' (1999b: 12).

Sampling

*   What is the population to be tested? Is the sample representative? Which pupils are to be included and excluded? Is there a proper basis for

comparing like with like between countries? What are the defining age parameters of the sample? Can such a sample be used over time?

Getting sampling right is clearly essential but in practice difficult (see, for example, the exchange between Prais (2003, 2004) and Adams (2003) on sampling in the first round of PISA, where Prais criticised the sampling and in particular the response rates for England.) And we have seen above that in TIMSS and in the IEA Civic Education Project there were important departures from what had been planned in terms of the sample investigated.

Samples might not be properly comparable for a variety of reasons:

> Differences in performance might arise because countries differ in the extent to which categories of students are removed from mainstream classes and so may be excluded from an assessment (for example, students in special programs or students in schools in which the language of instruction differs from the language of the assessment). The problem is most obvious where (a) age of enrolling in schools, (b) retention, and (c) dropout rates differ from one country to another and is particularly relevant in studies in which industrial and developing countries participate. (Greaney and Kellaghan, 2008: 71–2)

Goldstein points out (1996: 63) that some age groups tend to be neglected in international surveys (ages 5–8 and 11–12 particularly) and that the school year or grade is often the determining factor in sampling, despite the fact that grade promotion policy varies from country to country and even in some cases from school to school.

One of the potential values of series of international comparative surveys is that they can inform us about developments over time. And so we need to be sure that similar samples are capable of being used in successive surveys, so that the basis for comparison remains stable.

Test construction

- On what basis have the tests been constructed? Has there been thorough analysis of national curricula? Is any country favoured or disadvantaged through the particular choice of test items? Are the tests so devised as to produce a full range of results?

It is of course difficult to devise tests that measure the outcomes of curricula that inevitably differ very widely and that are assessed in various ways in different countries. Finding common ground is a complex process, requiring much expert knowledge and close analysis of appropriate documentation in many languages. Some countries might feel that the tests as finally agreed will not adequately reflect the knowledge and skills its school population is expected to achieve as a result of its curricula. Greaney and Kellaghan make a point about national tests that highlights the problems of international test construction:

> We would expect an achievement test that is based on the content of a national curriculum to provide a more valid measure of curriculum mastery than one that was designed to serve as a common denominator of the curricula offered in 30 to 40 countries. For example, a national curriculum authority and the designers of an international assessment might assign quite different weights of importance to a skill such as drawing inferences from a text. A national assessment, as opposed to an international assessment, can also test curricular aspects that are unique to individual countries. (2008: 70–1)

Greaney and Kellaghan also consider the fact that some subjects are easier to assess internationally than others. Mathematics is often taken to be the most straightforward subject to investigate internationally, since – though this is disputed (see Jaworski and Phillips, 1999: 11–12) – it is said to be culture-free and to constitute a universal language in itself. Science, on the other

hand, is much more complex, being taught in different ways to different age groups in different countries.

Language and cultural issues

- Are procedures in place to ensure that tests administered in different languages are actually testing the same thing? Has all ambiguity been eliminated? Are there cultural differences that should be taken into consideration?

The writing of tests has to start somewhere and usually in only one language. There is then the question of how to produce the tests in a variety of languages that do not contain significant differences as a result of translation problems. A common technique is to use what is termed 'back translation', i.e. a text is translated from language A to language B and then separately retranslated into language A to test for inaccuracy, ambiguity, etc. Even this has its problems, as Goldstein has observed:

> Even where there is a good match between the original and back-translated version, the target version will not necessarily be an appropriate translation. This might occur, for example, because a single source word can have several translations in the target language, each of which would be back-translated into the original source word, yet each target language word can nevertheless have a somewhat different meaning. (1996: 67)

Resources might not even allow for the process of back translation. McLean reports in connection with IEA that 'two translations were one too many for a number of countries' and so 'a single translation, carefully checked by bilingual educators, often had to suffice' (1996: 203).

Simple instructions like 'find x' or 'expand' in mathematics tests might not work in other languages or even in other English-speaking contexts,[2] since usage and expectation in the classroom will vary. Bonnet et al. describe a range of difficulties in terms of lexical, grammatical, syntactic, stylistic, and cultural equivalences (2001: 18–20).

Analysis

- Is the analysis undertaken by researchers with knowledge of educational issues and not by statisticians or economists alone? Are correlations used with caution and not glibly taken to prove causation? Are the scores sufficiently disaggregated, or is too much reliance placed on aggregated scores? Are the data presented in an accessible form? Is there a technical report which presents the modus operandi of the analysis? Are there separate country reports? Is information available to show regional (in-country) differences?

There must of course be proper analysis that does not misinterpret the data. Studies nowadays are of such a high level of professional attention to detail that there is little danger of crass fundamental error. Nevertheless, the data are subjected to ever closer scrutiny by educationists and others with appropriate expertise. Much of the discussion takes place in the pages of the specialist journals, and so some criticism might not be widely reported.

There is a debate about the use of aggregated and disaggregated scales. Harvey Goldstein argues forcefully against the use of aggregated scales which assume that there can be one trend-describing score that can be used to compare performance over time for two reasons: first that a lot of interest lies in specific areas within each subject tested and second that aggregated scores '[reflect] the weightings of the topic items chosen by the test constructors' (1996: 72–4).

Much reliance is placed on executive summaries of results, since policy makers and others do not have time to read bulky reports (PISA 2006 is published in two parts, at a total of nearly 700 pages). We need to be sure that the summaries properly reflect the findings in the main report(s). Experts with statistical knowledge need access to the raw data so that checks can be made on the presentation and analysis of results.

Contention

As with much widely reported research that relies on huge data banks, international surveys of pupil achievement are often contentious. Many of the criticisms that are made have been mentioned above. One particular exchange concerning the results from the first round of PISA will illustrate the detailed methodological issues that can form the basis of disagreement.

As mentioned in passing above, Sig Prais of the London-based National Institute of Economic and Social Research produced a number of criticisms of PISA in a journal article published in 2003. He expressed surprise at the apparent disparity between the results for the United Kingdom from the 1999 IEA survey and those from the first round of PISA. The pupils involved were assumed to be from the same cohort, namely those born in 1984, though of course the IEA and PISA surveys – as we have seen above – were testing quite different things. However, Prais found the improvement in performance remarkable and, if correct, likely to vindicate the government's recent policies aimed at improving standards: 'Educational policy makers […] can therefore now both celebrate and relax; and overall policy priorities might properly be shifted (less of taxpayers' money to education …)' (Prais, 2003: 140).

His detailed criticism – against the background of the apparent narrowing of the gap in performance of pupils in the UK and Switzerland – involved concerns about the type of questions set, differences in the age group in the IEA and PISA surveys, the execution of the PISA tests and consequently the reliability of the results, especially with regard to the representativeness of the participating schools and that of the pupils in each of the schools. Further, he had a range of technical questions about the complex processing of the test scores (Prais, 2003).

Raymond J. Adams responded to Prais's criticisms on behalf of the OECD. (Adams, 2003) He argued that the TIMSS and PISA surveys were not 'statistically linked' and therefore not comparable, and he questioned Prais's assertions about the nature of the education system of Switzerland. He then defended PISA in terms of Prais's 'five major concerns', listed as:

- the nature of the mathematics questions;
- differences between TIMSS and PISA in target population definitions;
- the representativeness of the UK's sample of schools;
- the representativeness of the UK's sample of students in schools;
- the scaling and data processing errors. (Adams, 2003: 378)

In a spirited rejoinder Prais argued (Prais, 2004) that there was then agreement about 'five main factors that contribute importantly to the differences of PISA and of previous surveys' and he reiterated his argument that substantial changes in PISA's objectives and methods were necessary (2004: 572).

In such exchanges it is difficult for the non-expert to make judgements without detailed knowledge of the complex statistical data involved and of the methodological decision making that underpins surveys such as PISA. But Prais highlights in his critique a number of issues from which lessons can be learnt.

1   When surveys, even if they test rather different aspects of achievement, show marked difference in the performance of particular countries, it is

right to ask questions about the nature of the tests and what they are designed to show.
2   It is vital to be alert to all aspects of sampling (of both schools and pupils within schools) and to check particularly for representativeness and for changes over time which affect the comparability of successive surveys.
3   Experts will wish to subject the data processing to minute detailed analysis and to rework the data to reveal findings which might not be contained in the reports.

CONCLUSION

In November 1885 Matthew Arnold (who was a school inspector for most of his life) was approached by the then Education Department in London to undertake an investigation of elementary education in Germany, Switzerland, and France. Included in his brief was an instruction to compare standards:

> My Lords are anxious to ascertain the quality of the education furnished in the Elementary Schools – particularly in the case of children between 10 and 14. For this purpose, it will be necessary that you should request some Masters and Mistresses to set a certain number of papers in writing and especially Arithmetic, so that a comparison may be instituted between the results obtained in the foreign schools with the results obtained in English schools. It will, or course, be necessary to state the ages of children whose papers are to be examined and compared: These specimens – worked in the foreign schools – will form a most important part of your inquiry.[3]

This request for what Margaret Thatcher in rather different circumstances wanted to be 'simple tests to show what pupils knew' (1993: 593) reminds us of the basic purpose of international tests – to ascertain how children of a given age in country x are performing in basic subjects compared to children in countries y and z.

In his foreword to the report of Foshay et al. (1962: 5) Saul Robinsohn called that study 'an unusual addition to the literature of education' and foresaw future benefits from such surveys for both empirical research and comparative education:

> The results … suggest that both empirical educational research and comparative education can gain new dimensions, the one by extending its range over various educational systems, the other by including empirical methods among its instruments.

He continued:

> [The results] offer real encouragement for believing that such researches can, in the future, lead to more significant results and begin to supply what Anderson has lamented as 'the major missing link in comparative education', which in his view is crippled especially by the scarcity of information about the outcomes or products of educational systems.

Robinsohn's vision of 'new dimensions' has certainly proved to be the case, and it is now inconceivable that there will not in future be a flow of information from international studies of attainment that will continue to provide evidence for policy makers and others. But the data will need to be continually interrogated on the general lines that Postlethwaite and others suggest and specifically in terms of the statistical detail which only experts can properly unpack in the pages of specialist journals. All too often reporting will focus on aggregated scores. And all too often the public perception of findings will be what the newspapers and other popular media have presented in the form of league tables, because that is what aggregated scores lead to.

What will continue to be needed in parallel to sophisticated surveys like PISA is research on pedagogy, on what teachers do to produce results – and that requires different kinds of investigation and analysis on a larger scale than has usually been possible. The rewards of such investigation

for the development of schooling generally would be very great.

NOTES

1 Australia, Belgium (French-speaking), Bulgaria, Chile, Colombia, Cyprus, Czech Republic, Denmark, England, Estonia, Finland, Germany, Greece, Hong Kong, Hungary, Italy, Latvia, Lithuania, Norway, Poland, Portugal, Romania, Russian Federation, Slovak Republic, Slovenia, Sweden, Switzerland, United States.

2 It is said that when asked to 'find x' in one mathematics test in England a child drew in an arrow pointing at x in the diagram in question and wrote 'here it is'.

3 National Archives Ed36/1. Letter to Matthew Arnold dated 3 November 1885.

REFERENCES

Adams, R. J. (2003) 'Response to "Cautions on OECD's Recent Educational Survey (PISA)"', *Oxford Review of Education*, 29 (3): 377–89.

Alexander, R. (2000) *Culture and Pedagogy. International Comparisons in Primary Education*. Oxford: Blackwell.

Baldi, S., Perie, M., Skidmore, D., Greenberg, E., Hahn, C. and Nelson, D. (2001) *What Democracy Means to Ninth-Graders: US Results from the International IEA Civic Education Study*. Washington DC: US Department of Education.

Baumert, J., Artelt, C., Klieme, E., Neubrand, M., Prenzel, M., Schiefele, U., Schneider, W., Tillmann, K.-J. and Weiss, M. (2002) (eds) *PISA 2000: Die Länder der Bundesrepublik Deurschland im Vergleich*. Opladen: Laske and Budrich.

Baumert, J. and Lehmann, R. (1997) *TIMSS – Mathematisch-naturwissenschaftlicher Unterricht im internationalen Vergleich. Deskriptive Befunde*. Opladen: Laske and Budrich.

BBC (1986) 'International Assignment: Educational Standards', Radio 4, 12 July.

Benoit, B. (2008) 'Merkel puts poll focus on education', *The Financial Times*, 13 June.

Bonnet, G., Braxmeyer, N., Horner, S., Lappalainen, H.-P., Levasseur, J., Nardi, E. et al. (2001) *The Use of National Reading Tests for International Comparisons: ways of Overcoming Cultural Bias*. Paris: Ministère de l'Education Nationale.

Foshay, A. W., Thorndike, R. L., Hotyat, F., Pidgeon, D. A. and Walker, D. A. (1962) *Educational Achievements of Thirteen-Year-Olds in Twelve Countries.* Hamburg: UNESCO Institute for Education.

Goldstein, H. (1995) *Interpreting International Comparisons of Student Achievement.* Paris: UNESCO.

Goldstein, H. (1996) 'International Comparisons of Student Achievement', in A. Little and A. Wolf (eds) *Assessment in Transition: Learning, Monitoring and Selection in International Perspective.* Oxford: Elsevier. pp. 58–87.

Goldstein, H. and Lewis, T. (eds) (1996) *Assessment: Problems, Developments and Statistical Issues.* Chichester: John Wiley.

Greaney, V. and Kellaghan, T. (2008) *Assessing National Achievement Levels in Education.* Washington, DC: The World Bank.

Grimston, J. (2007) 'The three Rs – really rotten results?' *The Sunday Times*, 9 December, p.16.

Grisay, A. and Griffin, P. (2006) 'What Are the Main Cross-national Studies?' in K. N. Ross and I. J. Genevois (eds) *Cross-National Studies of the Quality of Education. Planning Their Design and Managing Their Impact.* Paris: UNESCO/IIEP. pp. 67–103.

Halsey, A. H., Postlethwaite, N., Prais, S. J., Smithers, A. and Steedman H. (1991) *Every Child in Britain.* London: Channel 4 Television.

Hughes, R. E. (n.d.) [1902]: *The Making of Citizens. A Study in Comparative Education.* London and Felling-on-Tyne: Walter Scott Publishing.

Husén, T. and Postlethwaite, T. N. (1985) *The International Encyclopedia of Education. Research and Studies.* Oxford: Pergamon Press.

Jaworski, B. and Phillips, D. (1999) (eds) *Comparing Standards Internationally. Research and Practice in Mathematics and Beyond.* Wallingford: Symposium.

International Assignment: Educational Standards (1986), broadcast, BBC Radio 4, 12 July.

International Supplement (1997), *Education Journal*, February, pp.19–25.

Kandel, I. L. (n.d.) (1933): *Studies in Comparative Education.* London: Harrap.

Keys, W. (1996) 'What do International Comparisons or Achievement Really Tell us?' National Foundation for Educational research Annual General Meeting and Conference, 10 December.

Little, A. and Wolf, A. (1996) (eds) *Assessment in Transition: Learning, Monitoring and Selection in International Perspective.* Oxford: Elsevier.

Ma, Xin (2008) 'Within-school Gender Gaps in Reading, Mathematics, and Science Literacy', *Comparative Education Review*, 52 (3): 437–60.

McLean, L. D. (1996) 'Large-scale Assessment Programmes in Different Countries and International Comparisons', in H. Goldstein and T. Lewis (eds)

Assessment: Problems, Developments and Statistical Issues. Chichester: John Wiley. pp.189–207.

OECD (n.d.) *OECD Programme for International Student Assessment.* Paris: OECD.

OECD (2001a) *Knowledge and Skills for Life. First Results from PISA 2000.* Paris: OECD.

OECD (2001b) 'OECD PISA Study Provides International Comparative Data on Schooling Outcomes', *OECD Current Issues*, Paris, 4 December.

OECD (2004) *Learning for Tomorrow's World. First Results from PISA 2002.* Paris: OECD.

OECD (2007) *PISA 2006: Science Competencies for Tomorrow's World, Volume 1: Analysis.* Paris: OECD.

OECD (2007a) *PISA 2006: Volume 2: Data/Données.* Paris: OECD.

OECD (2007b) *Education at a Glance 2007. OECD Indicators.* Paris: OECD.

OECD (2007c) *OECD Briefing Note for the United Kingdom.* Paris: OECD.

OECD (2007d) *Education at a Glance 2007: OECD Indicators.* Paris: OECD.

Phillips, D. and Schweisfurth, M. (2007) *Comparative and International Education. An Introduction to Theory, Method, and Practice.* London: Continuum.

Pidgeon, D. A. (1962) 'A Comparative Study of the Dispersions of Test Scores', in A. W. Foshay, R. L. Thorndike, F. Hotyat, D. A. Pidgeon and D. A. Walker (eds) *Educational Achievements of Thirteen-Year-Olds in Twelve Countries.* Hamburg: UNESCO Institute for Education. pp. 57–62.

Planel, C. (2008) 'The Rise and Fall of Comparative Education in Teacher Training: Should it Rise Again as Comparative Pedagogy?' *Compare*, 38 (4): 385–99.

Postlethwaite, T. N. (1985) 'International Association for the Evaluation of Educational Achievement (IEA)', in T. Husén, and T. N. Postlethwaite *The International Encyclopedia of Education. Research and Studies.* Oxford: Pergamon Press. pp. 2645–46.

Postlethwaite, T. N. (1999a) 'Overview of Issues in International Achievement Studies', in B. Jaworski and D. Phillips (eds) *Comparing Standards Internationally. Research and Practice in Mathematics and Beyond.* Wallingford: Symposium. pp. 23–60.

Postlethwaite, T. N. (1999b) *International Studies of Educational Achievement: Methodological Issues.* Hong Kong: Comparative Education Research Centre.

Postlethwaite, T. N. (2006) 'What is a "Good" Cross-National Study?' in K. N. Ross and I. J. Genevois (eds) *Cross-National Studies of the Quality of Education. Planning Their Design and Managing Their Impact.* Paris: UNESCO/IIEP. pp. 105–20.

Prais, S. J. (2003) 'Cautions on OECD's Recent Educational Survey (PISA)', *Oxford Review of Education*, 29 (2): 139–63.

Prais, S. J. (2004) 'Cautions on OECD's Recent Educational Survey (PISA) Rejoinder to OECD's Response', *Oxford Review of Education*, 30 (4): 569–73.

Prais, S., St John Brooks, C., Woodhead, C. et al. (2000) *Comparing Standards. The Report of the Poltiteia Education Commission*. London: Politeia.

Prais, S. J. and Wagner, K. (1985) 'Schooling Standards in England and Germany: Some Summary Comparisons Bearing on Economic Performance', *National Institute Economic Review*, No.112 (May): 53–76.

Purves, A. C. (ed.) (1989) *International Comparisons and Educational Reform*, Alexandria, Virginia: Association for Supervision and Curriculum Development.

Ross, K. N. and Genevois, I. J. (2006) (eds) *Cross-National Studies of the Quality of Education. Planning Their Design and Managing Their Impact*. Paris: UNESCO/IIEP.

Steiner, G. (2008) *My Unwritten Books*. London: Weidenfeld and Nicolson.

Stigler, J. W. and Hiebert, J. (1999) 'Understanding and Improving Classroom Mathematics Instruction: An Overview of the TIMSS Video Study', in B. Jaworski and D. Phillips (eds) *Comparing Standards Internationally. Research and Practice in Mathematics and Beyond*. Wallingford: Symposium. pp. 119–33.

Tabberer, R. and Le Métais, J. (1997) 'Looking Behind International Comparisons', *Education Journal*, (February): 20.

Thatcher, Margaret (1993) *The Downing Street Years*. London: Harper Collins.

Torney-Purta, J., Lehmann, R., Oswald, H. and Schutz, W. (2001a) *Citizenship and Education in Twenty-Eight Countries: Civic Knowledge and Engagement at Age Fourteen*. Delft: IEA.

Torney-Purta, J., Lehmann, R., Oswald, H. and Schutz, W. (2001b) *Citizenship and Education in Twenty-Eight Countries: Civic Knowledge and Engagement at Age Fourteen. Executive Summary*. Delft: IEA.

UNESCO (1991) *World Education Report 1991*. Paris: UNESCO.

Xu, J. (2008) 'Sibship Size and Educational Achievement: The Role of Welfare Regimes Cross-Nationally', *Comparative Education Review*, 52 (3): 413–36.

12

Reflections on Measuring Behavior: Time and the Grid

Roger Bakeman

Observing the behavior of others is an ancient activity. Hardly unique, it is an activity we share with all the other animals. Talking about behavior may be more uniquely human. We may not know how humans first came to speak, but we can imagine that observations about the behavior of others figured prominently in the early conversations of our hunter-gatherer progenitors.

Another ancient activity involves measurement, an activity whose importance grew as humans formed more permanent settlements and engaged in settled agriculture. Measurement is usually understood as the act of assigning names or numbers to things. Is this a propitious day or not? Who owns the most animals in my village? How many days before I should plant? How much wheat and wine in my storehouse?

The systematic measurement of behavior builds on these early roots but is a much more recent activity. It is associated with the rise of self-conscious behavioral science during the industrial age, primarily in the 19th and 20th centuries. Now, as increasingly we are moving into what many call the post-industrial, information age, possibilities for the systematic measurement of behavior are dramatically expanding.

In this chapter I describe how my views on measuring behavior have developed and changed in the years since 1973 when I earned my doctorate. I emphasize not only contemporary ideas and practices that were important to me, but also a few relatively simple but very powerful organizing ideas. These ideas, or organizing concepts, appear so early in human history that they sometimes seem to be features of the natural world, although they remain human mental constructions. I have in mind two in particular: our organization of time along a single dimension into hours, minutes, and seconds; and our imposition of a grid – a two-dimensional Euclidean or Cartesian space – on all sorts of phenomena. My emphasis on time lines and grids here is meant to be a bit playful – and I will not complicate it further by considerations of three-dimensional space or four-dimensional Einsteinian space-time continuums – but it can also be useful, as I hope to demonstrate

A third organizing concept involves the scale of measurement. It embodies ancient distinctions but was given modern form by S. S. Stevens (1946). As almost all of us know, he identified three types of measurement: categorical or *nominal measurement* requires no more than assigning names to entities of interest where the names have no natural order, *ordinal measurement* requires ordering or ranking those entities, and *interval-scale measurement* involves assigning numbers such that an additional number at any point on the scale involves the same amount of whatever is measured. These three distinctions are key for any discussion of measuring behavior, although as you know Stevens additionally distinguished between interval scales for which zero was arbitrary like degrees Celsius, and ratio scales for which zero indicated truly none of the quantity measured like kilograms.

Interval-scaled variables are often referred to as *continuous*, presumably to distinguish them from discrete nominal categories, but this has always struck me a bit muddled. Interval-scaled variables can be both discrete, for example when anything from eggs to camels is counted, or continuous, for example when time is measured with varying degrees of precision. This simply reflects the usual mathematical distinction between integers and real numbers. I mention this now because viewing time discretely and not continuously is especially useful when measuring behavior, as I discuss later.

Measurement of anything requires a measuring instrument, that is, some kind of apparatus. Like clocks, thermometers, and rulers, such instruments are often physical. In contrast, instruments for measuring behavior are often, at least in part, conceptual. I identify three primary components. First, like the lens of an eye or a camera, is the coding scheme or schemes. A coding scheme consists of a list of names for the behaviors of interest, where the names or codes indicate the behaviors on which we ask our observers to focus. Thus a coding scheme – just like Steven's three- or four-category scheme for scales – is more a conceptual than a physical matter. Second, like the retina of an eye or the image sensor of a digital camera or video recorder, is the apparatus and format for recording the primary data, that is, for capturing the data as initially collected. But such raw data, like primary sense experience, may be too overwhelming or confusing to be immediately useful. Thus, like subsequent processing of visual signals in the optic nerve and brain, or distilling of information from the image sensor in a digital camera to a memory device, a third component involves representing. By representing – literally, re-presenting – I mean data reduction, that is, transforming the data-as-collected into a form more useful for subsequent analysis. This component often receives scant attention, but can be critical to the success of an investigation.

Five sections follow. The first three sections consider each of these components of behavioral measurement – coding, recording, and representing – in turn, and distill what I think I have learned about systematic behavioral observation in the past 35 years. Other observational methods are possible of course, for example, those that produce historical or journalistic or more personal narratives or that distill themes from such narratives, as in qualitative research. In contrast, systematic observation is unabashedly quantitative research, which is to say it is about measurement. It is defined not only by its measuring instruments, the coding schemes and recording and representation methods already mentioned, but also by attention to whether independent observers agree in their measurements. Thus the fourth section considers recent advances in gauging observer reliability. Finally, I consider how the ongoing digital revolution has already changed, and will continue to change, what we can do. Throughout I emphasize our debt to history and indicate how time lines and grids help organize our thinking and our work.

CODING SCHEMES: THE INITIAL LENS

When I first became interested in measuring behavior in the 1970s, almost all my models came from researchers interested in the behavior of animals or human infants and young children. This is hardly surprising. Animals and young children are not very good at telling us what they think. They cannot fill out a questionnaire or take a test. Observational methods were then, and continue to be, an important method for studying nonverbal behavior and the behavior of nonverbal organisms. I was a graduate student in a social psychology program at a time when the field was criticized for studying unnatural behavior in tightly controlled laboratories. Thus observational methods had the additional appeal of being able to study behavior in relatively natural contexts. Indeed, for my dissertation research I studied the work and social behavior of marine scientists living in a space-station-like habitat 50 feet below the surface of Coral Bay in the Virgin Islands. Third, I was interested in

process, not just product, with how events unfold sequentially in time – and this is an enterprise for which observational methods are especially well-suited.

Observational research begins with a coding scheme or schemes. As noted earlier, a coding scheme is like a lens; it focuses observer attention. In its simplest form, a coding scheme is simply a list of names or categories that the investigator believes important. For example, simplifying somewhat, for my dissertation research one scheme categorized a scientist's activity as either doing scientific work, at leisure, eating, habitat-maintenance, self-maintenance, or asleep. A similar scheme for infants could include the infant states of quiet alert, fussy, crying, rapid-eye movement sleep, and deep sleep (Wolff, 1966). Another would be the play states of unoccupied, onlooker, solitary, parallel, associative, and cooperative play applied to preschoolers by Parten (1932).

Each of these coding schemes consists of a set of mutually exclusive and exhaustive (ME&E) codes. This is a desirable and easily achieved attribute of coding schemes, one that usually simplifies subsequent recording and analysis. Of course any list of codes can be made mutually exclusive by defining combinations. For example, if the list consisted of two codes, infant gazes at mother and mother gazes at infant, adding a third code, mutual gaze, would result in a mutually exclusive set. And any list of codes can be made exhaustive by simply adding a final code, none of the above. Another solution is to define multiple ME&E sets. For the current example, two ME&E sets, each with two codes, would be defined: mother gazes at infant or not, and infant gazes at mother or not. In this case, mutual gaze, instead of being an explicit code, could be determined later analytically. As the reader can see, this strategy (each set coding presence and absence) could be applied to a list of any number of co-occurring codes.

In addition to assuring that each coding scheme consists of a set of ME&E codes, there are other good reasons for defining several different schemes. Coders can make several passes, attending just to the codes in one scheme on each pass, which simplifies their work; or independent coders can be assigned to different schemes, which gives greater credibility to any patterns we detect later between codes in different sets. I do not want to minimize the effort and hard work usually required to develop effective coding schemes – many hours of looking, thinking, defining, arguing, modifying, and refining can be involved – but if the result is well-structured, that is, consists of several sets of ME&E codes each of which characterizes a coherent dimension of interest, then subsequent recording, representing, and analysis is almost always greatly facilitated.

In my work with Gottman (Bakeman and Gottman, 1986, 1997), I suggested that coding schemes could be placed on an ordered continuum, with one end anchored by physically based schemes and the other by socially based ones (see also Viswanathan, 2005). At the risk of offending the philosophically inclined, more physically based codes reflect attributes that are easily seen while more socially based codes require some inference. An example of a physically based code might be infant crying, whereas an example of a more socially based code might be child engaged in cooperative play.

To understand why I made this distinction, it is helpful to remember the time in which I was working. Ethology was enjoying considerable prestige. Indeed, the year I earned my doctorate (1973) the ethologists Lorenz, Tinbergen, and von Frish won a Nobel prize for their discoveries in individual and social behavior patterns.

A year earlier, Tinbergen's student, Nick Blurton Jones (1972), attempted to define a human ethology, and a few years later, Paul Ekman published an influential and anatomically based coding scheme for human facial patterns (Ekman and Friesen, 1978). When studying a species, ethologists begin by defining an ethogram, which is a list of the discrete behaviors available to that species, defined descriptively without reference to purpose, and which are believed to be exhaustive; Ekman likewise defined codes that were regarded as biologically based. The spirit of the times did not favor codes like disgust, joy, and contempt, but instead favored the presumed objectivity of physically based codes, codes that were regarded as more suitable for scientific endeavor.

Today, the fires of logical positivism seemingly extinguished, and almost 50 years since Chomsky published his review of Skinner's *Verbal Behavior* (1959), researchers may feel little need to apologize for coding schemes that seem more socially than physically based. This distinction may matter most when selecting and training observers. Do we regard them as detectors of things 'really' there? Or more as cultural informants, able through experience to 'see' the distinctions embodied in our coding schemes? In our perhaps more pragmatic age, what matters most about coding schemes may be whether we can train observers to be reliable, a matter to which I return later.

RECORDING: ITS ABOUT TIME

Earlier I suggested that coding schemes constitute one component of our behavior measuring apparatus, and that a recording component comes next. However, another key component should be mentioned, the human observer. Observational measurement, in the first instance, is the act of assigning codes to events. This nominal measurement does not happen automatically, but is performed by human coders. There is no simple display to read as with a thermometer, and although computer scientists are attempting to automate the process, for the foreseeable future, a human coder – one might say, perceiver – will likely remain an essential part of the apparatus. Some limited success has been achieved with automatic computer detection of Ekman-like facial action patterns (Cohn and Kanade, 2007), but the more socially based codes become, the more elusive any kind of computer automation seems.

Along with observing and measuring, recording is likewise an ancient human activity. It is associated with clay and stylus in Sumeria, with papyrus and pen in Egypt, and, thanks to the development of paper by the Chinese in the second century, with paper and pencil by generations of modern researchers. When I first became interested in measuring behavior at the beginning of the computer age, paper and pencil methods were still the rule. As I noted in Bakeman and Gottman (1986, 1997), pencil and paper feel good in the hand; they possess a satisfying physicality, rarely malfunction, and do not need batteries. The paper I have in mind is the sort of ruled tablet found in schoolrooms and laboratories everywhere. With the addition of vertical lines, it becomes a grid, a format which lends itself readily to recording observational data, as the work of countless generations of researchers demonstrates.

When Quera and I first attempted to define standard formats for observational data in the early 1990s, we were influenced, in part, by the pencil-and-paper inspired recording formats in use at the time. The result was the *Sequential Data Interchange*

Standard or SDIS format (Bakeman and Quera, 1992). The two simplest data types we defined, and the ones most tied to pencil-and-paper recording, were *event sequential data* and *interval sequential data*. Event sequential data is useful only under somewhat limited circumstances. It assumes that the investigator has defined a single set of ME&E codes, is interested only in how often those events occur and how those events are sequenced, and is not interested in how long individual events last or what proportion of the total observation time is devoted to each kind of event. A recording form for such data using infant states is shown in Figure 12.1 along with its SDIS representation. Each line represents a successive event. By definition, events cannot co-occur; that is, the observer can record one and only one check per line.

Interval sequential data is somewhat more flexible. It allows for the co-occurrence of events and provides approximate estimates of how often events occur and what proportion of time is devoted to each kind of event. In origin, it is perhaps more influenced by the ubiquitous lined-paper tablet than is event sequential data. Each line represents a successive arbitrary interval,

| Subject ID _____   Observer _____ |
| Start time _____   Stop time _____   Date _____ |

event	alert	fussy	cry	REM	sleep
1		X			
2	X				
3			X		
4					X
5				X	
...					

State; <Infant 32> fussy alert cry sleep REM /

Figure 12.1   Event sequential data: an example of a recording form along with the SDIS representation for the data recorded.

for example, 15 seconds. The observer then notes which if any of the events occurred within each interval. A recording form for infant states and two maternal codes (touch and vocalize; regarded as two sets since they can co-occur) is given in Figure 12.2 along with its SDIS representation.

The interval sequential recording method (sometimes called time sampling) has both advantages and partisans. Perhaps its chief advantage is cost; it requires only pencil, paper, and some simple timing device to demarcate intervals. One major disadvantage is the approximate nature of its summary statistics: Frequencies are underestimated (a check can indicate more than one occurrence in an interval) and proportions are overestimated (a check does not mean the event occupied the entire interval). Another disadvantage is the way interval sequential data can muddle sequences (which of several events checked for an interval came first?). There are possible fixes to these problems, but none seem completely satisfactory. As a result,

I tend to regard both simple event recording and interval recording as a bit archaic and of limited use, and recommend whenever feasible another data type instead.

A third SDIS type we call *timed-event sequential data*, and it is the most flexible of the three. Either pencil and paper or more automatic, electronic recording methods can be used with all three, but when defining timed-event sequential data (and the closely related *state sequential data* type) we had electronic recording specifically in mind. When an event occurs, its onset time is recorded. When codes belong to ME&E sets, offset times need not be recorded because the onset of a code implies the offset of any previous code from the same set (offset times need not be recorded for momentary codes either, that is, for codes whose frequency of occurrence and not duration is of interest). A timed-event SDIS representation for the events given in Figure 12.2, assuming that each interval in fact represents a single second and that times are rounded to the nearest second, is

Subject ID _____ Observer ____ _____ Date _____							
	Infant code					**Mother code**	
interval	**alert**	**fussy**	**cry**	**REM**	**sleep**	**touch**	**voc**
1		X					
2		X					X
3	X						X
4			X				X
5			X			X	
6			X			X	
7			X			X	X
8					X	X	X
9					X		X
10				X			
...							
Interval; <Infant 32> fussy, fussy voc, alert voc, cry voc, cry touch *2, cry touch voc, sleep touch voc, sleep voc, REM /							

Figure 12.2   Interval sequential data: an example of a recording form along with the SDIS representation for the data recorded.

```
Timed-event (alert fussy cry REM sleep) touch voc;
<Infant 32>
  fussy,1–  alert,3–  cry,4–  sleep,8–  REM,10– &
  voc,2–5  touch,5–9  voc,7–10, 11/
```

Figure 12.3   Timed-event sequential data: an SDIS representation for the data shown in Figure 12.2 assuming each interval is one second.

given in Figure 12.3. The ampersand (and) indicates separate streams, and is useful for separating codes from different ME&E sets so that offset times need not be entered explicitly.

Earlier I stated that the recording component of our apparatus was about time, which I meant in more than one sense. Perhaps most obviously, the recording of observational data takes time, often lots of time. Also, the behavior we observe unfolds sequentially in time. Information about event frequency, duration, proportion of total time, and sequencing is most completely preserved for timed-event sequential data, which is why I recommend this data type whenever feasible. Later I will discuss how easy it is to record such data in our digital world, but first I want to explain why I find it useful to view time discretely.

The way we structure time is an ancient human invention. We can thank the Sumerians for introducing 60-second minutes, 60-minute hours, and 24-hour days, a convention so universal we sometimes forget it is a human construction and not a feature of the natural world. Usually we think of time as continuous and assume that any stretch of time can be divided into ever smaller pieces of a second. This may be fine theoretically, but limited as we are by the precision of our timing devices, we could say that, practically, time is always discrete. A clock that displays only seconds lets us structure time as successive one

second intervals. Likewise, a clock that gives time only to the nearest tenth of a second, lets us structure time as successive one-tenth of a second intervals. Similarly, a video recording that contains 25 or almost 30 frames per second (per PAL or NTSC, the European and US standards, respectively) permits accuracy to something greater than a tenth of a second but not accuracy to a hundredth of a second.

Unless research questions require greater accuracy, and unless appropriate specialized recording equipment is being used, I recommend that times used in behavioral research be rounded to the nearest second or tenth of a second – no matter how many digits after the decimal point whatever equipment or computer program we use may print. For the sorts of behavioral events considered by most researchers, greater precision seems neither required nor appropriate.

The advantages of a discrete view of time primarily occur when representing and analyzing observational data, as I discuss shortly, but it can help us avoid confusion when recording observational data as well. This may seem a fairly precious and arcane matter, but consider the SDIS representation in Figure 12.3. *Fussy* begins in second 1 and, since no offset time was given, implicitly ends with the onset of alert in second 3. Thus *fussy* lasts two seconds. Similarly *voc* begins in second 2 and ends in second 5, a duration of three seconds as the interval representation in Figure 12.2

makes clear. The discrete view reminds us that offset times are exclusive, not inclusive. Per the discrete-interval view, if the onset of *touch* is five seconds and its offset nine seconds, then *touch* begins at second 5, meaning the beginning of the interval, and continues up to but not through second 9, that is, through the end of second 8. All of this might be self-evident and not in the least confusing if language usage were more precise, but, at least in US English usage, *to* and *through* are often used interchangeably. Here, per the Oxford English Dictionary, *to* means 'in the direction of, towards' (p. 163), whereas through means 'from one end ... to the other or opposite end' (p. 10; Simpson and Weiner, 1989); thus, for example, the phrase, three- to six-year olds, excludes six-year-olds whereas the phrase, three- through six-year olds, does not.

REPRESENTING: IMPOSING THE GRID

Data require organization, and well-organized and structured data can facilitate analysis. When collecting observational data initially, observer ease and accuracy are of primary importance. Therefore, it makes sense to design data collection procedures that work well for our observers; but analysis can be facilitated by how those data are represented subsequently. This is considerably less true for event and interval sequential data than for the timed-event sequential data I just described.

An ancient organizing device is the grid, which was applied to cities from the time of the very first Sumerian and Hittite settlements, and subsequently to such cities as Beijing, the 19th century extension of Barcelona, and Manhattan. We have already shown its application to event and interval sequential data in Figures 12.1 and 12.2. Indeed, for such data a grid can be used as a data collection form, as we have

4. Subject ID _____		
Observer _____		
Date _____		
event	**onset**	**offset**
fussy	1	3
voc	2	5
alert	3	4
cry	4	8
touch	5	9
voc	7	10
sleep	8	10
REM	10	11
...		

Figure 12.4   Timed-event sequential data: an example of a recording form. Time is given in seconds.

previously noted. A grid could also be used to collect timed-event sequential data, as shown in Figure 12.4 – and in fact the organization of Figure 12.4 is very close to what some computer programs that are designed to automate observational data collection produce. But Figure 12.4 grid is less useful for analysis than the event and interval grids of Figures 12.1 and 12.2.

To explain why, it is helpful to consider the various kinds of units that are used in an observational research study. Such units are of two kinds, those that pertain to the design of the study and those that pertain to its data. Observational researchers, even as they lavish time on careful coding of behavior, are thinking about their subsequent data analysis, analysis that will be guided by the study's design. Thus it is important at the outset to specify the *basic sampling units*—these are the individual participants, parent-child dyads, families, or other groups; called cases in SPSS or subjects in older literature – and the *research factors* that constitute the design. Such factors are usually described as *between-subjects* (e.g., gender with two levels, male and female) or *within-subjects* (subjects observed more than once, e.g., at two, three, and four years of age). When repeated measures exist, *analytic units*, each identified with a repeated measure, are nested within sampling units. In observational research terms, each analytic unit in the case of repeated measures or each basic sampling unit otherwise, represents an observational *session*, that is, a sequence of coded events for which continuity can generally be assumed (although either planned or unplanned breaks might occur). Statistics and indices derived from the coded data for an observational session constitute scores; scores from the various subjects and sessions are then organized by any between- and within-subjects factors and are analyzed subsequently using conventional statistical techniques, as guided by the design of the study. For readers of this chapter, this should be familiar ground.

Other kinds of units pertain to the observational data within a session. For the nominal measurement of data recording, the key unit is the entity to which codes are assigned. For event sequential data, this unit is an event. For interval sequential data, it is an interval. And for timed-event sequential data, it is again an event. However, to serve generalization and for ease of analysis (and not incidentally for ease of computer programming), when it comes to data representation, we want to preserve a universal grid for all data types. We accomplished this in the computer program, the Generalized Sequential Querier (GSEQ), that Quera and I developed (Bakeman and Quera, 1995), and it has served us well. For both event and interval sequential data, rows represent different codes and columns represent the recording units – events and intervals, respectively. However, for timed-event sequential data, whereas the recording units are events, the representational units – the columns in the universal data grid – are units of time as defined by the precision used; for example, these are seconds when times are measured to the nearest second. Figure 12.5 represents a universal data grid for timed-event data. The grids for event and interval data are the same, only the column label is changed.

Three advantages are noteworthy. First, representing observational data as a grid where each row represents a code and columns represent successive events, intervals, or time units makes the application of standard frequency or contingency table statistics easy. Here is a simple example. Assume timed-event recording to the nearest second. We define a 2×2 contingency table (another grid) like that given in Figure 12.6, that is, each successive one second time interval is cross classified by whether or not it is coded for infant cry and for maternal touch. For this

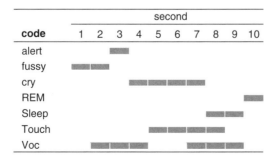

Figure 12.5 Timed-event sequential data: an example of a time plot representation.

	touch	no touch	
cry	100	80	180
no cry	140	280	420
	240	360	600

p (cry) = .30
p (touch) = .40
p (touch/cry) = .56

Odds ratio = 1.25/0.5 = 2.5

Figure 12.6 Determining the association between infant cry and maternal touch: an example of a 2 × 2 table tallying one-second time units and its associated odds ratio.

example, although the probability that an interval would be coded touch was .40, the probability that an interval would by coded touch given it was coded cry was .56 (i.e., 100/180). This suggests that this mother was more likely to touch her infant when her infant was crying. The odds ratio, a simple descriptive statistic that I think is underused by psychologists, makes the point clearly. The odds of touch to no touch when this infant was crying were 1.25 to 1 (100/80) whereas the odds of touch to no touch when this infant was not crying were or 0.5 to 1 (140/280). Thus the odds ratio was 2.5 (1.25/0.5), that is, this mother was 2.5 times more likely to touch her infant when crying than when not. Odds ratios could then be computed for each session in a given study and analyzed as any other score using standard statistical techniques (after log transforming to improve its distribution).

Second, the grid representation makes data modification easy and easy to understand. New codes (i.e., rows in the grid) can be defined and formed from existing codes using standard logical operations. This can be very useful. For example, you could use the OR operator to define a new code,

awake, that occurs whenever alert, fussy, or cry is coded. Or, you could use the AND operator to code only those seconds when the mother is both touching and vocalizing to her infant (GSEQ allows other logical operations as well). Even more useful is GSEQ's ability to form new codes that are tied to onsets, offsets, and occurrences of existing codes. For example, a new code might identify just the second when an infant cry begins, the three seconds before the cry begins, or a stretch of time that includes all seconds coded for cry as well as three seconds before and after. Such new codes can then be used to label the rows and columns of 2 × 2 contingency tables like the one shown in Figure 12.6; again statistics derived from such tables would serve as scores in subsequent analyses.

Here is an example. Deborah Deckner and colleagues (2003) wanted to know whether mothers and infants matched each other's rhythmic vocalizations. She coded onset and offset times for such vocalizations for 30 mother–infant pairs, observed for 20-minute sessions when infants were 18 and 24 months of age. To determine whether infants responded to mothers, she defined two new codes: one, a window of opportunity, coded the five seconds at the start of a mother vocalization, while the other coded just the onset second of an infant vocalization. An odds ratio greater than 1 indicated that an infant was more likely to begin a rhythmic vocalization during the first five seconds of a maternal rhythmic vocalization than at other times. A similar strategy was used to determine whether mothers responded to infants, and session scores were analyzed with a standard one-between (male or female), one-within (18 or 24 months) analysis of variance. She found that mothers matched their infants but more so for female infants, and that only 24-month-old females matched their mothers. This strategy, which makes use of GSEQ's ability to flexibly create new codes from existing ones, strikes me as a productive and promising way to study behavioral contingency generally.

Third, the discrete time-unit view of timed-event sequential data solves some, but not all, problems in gauging observer agreement, a matter to which I now turn.

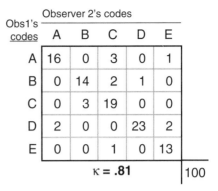

Figure 12.7   Observer agreement: an example of an agreement matrix and its associated kappa; the example assumes entities were independently coded by two observers using a coding scheme that consisted of five mutually exclusive and exhaustive codes.

OBSERVER AGREEMENT: THE SINE QUA NON

Observer agreement is often regarded as the sine qua non of observational measurement. Without it, we are left with nothing more than individual narratives. Of course, a suitable level of agreement between two independent observers does not guarantee perfect accuracy – two observers might share similar deviant views of the world – but it is widely regarded as indicative of acceptable measurement. If the records of two observers recorded independently do not agree, the accuracy of any scores derived from these records is dubious: Modification of the coding scheme, further observer training, or both are required. On the other hand, when observers' records substantially agree, we infer that our observers are adequately trained and that scores derived from those records will be reliable.

Probably the most frequently used statistic of observer agreement is Cohen's kappa (1960). The classic Cohen's kappa characterizes agreement with respect to a set of ME&E codes while correcting for chance agreement. It assumes that things – demarcated entities – are presented to a pair of observers, each of whom independently assigns a code to each entity. Observer agreement is displayed in an agreement matrix, sometimes called a confusion matrix (another grid). Each pair

of observer decisions is tallied in this K by K table, where K is the number of codes in the set. For example, assuming five codes and 100 entities coded, the agreement matrix might be like that shown in Figure 12.7. In this case, the two observers generally agreed (i.e., most tallies were on the diagonal); the most frequent confusion – when Observer 1 coded A but Observer 2 coded C – occurred just three times. Kappa is computed by dividing chance-corrected observed agreement (i.e., the probability of observed agreement minus the probability of agreement expected by chance) by the maximum agreement not due to chance (i.e., 1 minus the probability of agreement expected by chance; Bakeman and Gottman, 1997): $\kappa = (P_{obs} - P_{exp})/(1 - P_{exp})$. For this example, the value of kappa was .81, a value Fleiss (1981) characterized as excellent (Fleiss characterized values .40–.60 as fair, .60–.75 as good, and over .75 as excellent).

Now here is the problem. Cohen's kappa assumes that pairs of coders make decisions when presented with a discrete entity so that the number of tallies represents the number of paired-coding decisions made.

This decision-making model fits interval sequential data but it fits event sequential data only when events are presented to coders as already demarcated discrete units, for example, as turns of talk in a transcript. And it does not really fit timed-event sequential data at all. Almost always, when recording either events or timed-events – that is, when the recording unit is the event – observers are asked to first segment the stream of behavior into events (i.e., detect the seams between events) and then code those segments. Due to errors of omission and commission – one observer detects events the other misses – usually the two observer's records will contain different numbers of events and exactly how the records align is not always obvious. And when alignment is uncertain, how events should be paired and tallied in the agreement matrix is unclear.

This is a classic problem in observational research (Bakeman and Gottman, 1986, 1997). With respect to event sequential data, Bakeman and Gottman wrote that, especially when agreement is not high, alignment is difficult and cannot be accomplished without subjective judgment. However, recently Quera and colleagues (Quera et al., 2007) have developed an algorithm that determines the *optimal global alignment* between two event sequences. Our algorithm is adopted from sequence alignment and comparison techniques that are routinely used by molecular biologists (Needleman and Wunsch, 1970). The task is to find an optimal alignment. The Needleman–Wunsch algorithm belongs to a broad class of methods known as *dynamic programming*, in which the solution for a specific sub-problem can be derived from the solution for another sub-problem immediately preceding it. It can be demonstrated that the method guarantees an optimal solution, that is, it finds the alignment with the highest possible number of agreements

between sequences (Sankoff and Kruskal, 1999: 48) without being exhaustive, that is, it does not need to explore the almost astronomical number of all possible alignments (Galisson, 2000).

The way the algorithm works is relatively complex, but a simple example can at least show what results. Assume the two event sequences (S_1 and S_2) shown in Figure 12.8. The first observer coded 10 events and the second 11, but the optimal alignment shows 12. The seven agreements are indicated with vertical bars and the two actual disagreements with two dots (i.e., a colon), but there were three additional errors: Observer 1 missed two events that Observer 2 coded (indicated with a hyphen in the top alignment line) and Observer 2 missed 1 event that Observer 1 coded (indicated with a hyphen in the bottom alignment line). The alignment then lets us tally paired observer decisions (using nil to indicate a missed event) and compute kappa, with two qualifications. First, because observers cannot both code nil, the resulting agreement matrix contains a logical (or structural) zero; as a consequence, the expected frequencies required by the kappa computation cannot be estimated with the usual formula for kappa but require an iterative proportional fitting (IPF) algorithm instead (e.g., see Bakeman and Robinson, 1994). Second, because Cohen's assumptions are not met we should not call this a Cohen's kappa; it might better be called an event-based dynamic programming kappa instead.

With respect to timed-event sequential data, my colleagues and I have proposed two solutions to the problem posed by the lack of fit with the classic Cohen model. The first solution depends on the discrete view of time I discussed earlier; it is the one presented in my work with Gotttman (Bakeman and Gottman, 1986, 1997) and implemented in earlier versions of the GSEQ program. Assuming a discrete view of time and a code-time grid like the one shown in Figure 12.5, agreement between successive pairs of time units is tallied, as in Figure 12.7, and kappa computed. However, because this kappa is based on tallying time units, it should be called a time-unit kappa.

One variant of time-unit kappa, also implemented in GSEQ, is called a time-unit kappa with tolerance. Assuming a time unit of a second, the exact second-by-second agreement of time-unit kappa can seem overly stringent (Hollenbeck, 1978). Imagine, for example, we defined a tolerance of two seconds, and then examined each successive time unit for the first observer, tallying an agreement when there was a match with any time unit for the second observer that fell within the stated

tolerance (e.g., a two-second tolerance defines a five-second window, two units before and two after the current time unit). The effect would be to move some tallies from off-diagonal to on-diagonal cells, thus giving credit for near misses and increasing the magnitude of kappa. I think this is often a more realistic index of agreement than time-unit kappa without tolerance, and that its off-diagonal tallies may more sharply indicate disagreements requiring further observer attention and training.

Still, one aspect of time-unit kappa, with or without tolerance, has always concerned me. With the classic Cohen model, the number of tallies represents the number of decisions coders make, whereas with time-unit kappa the number of tallies represents the length of the session; for example, when time units are seconds, a five-minute session generates 5 times 60 or 300 tallies. When recording timed-event sequential data, observers are continuously looking for the seams between events, but how often they are making decisions is arguable, probably unknowable. One decision per seam seems too few – the observers are continuously alert – but one per time unit seems too many. Moreover, the number of tallies is affected by the precision of the time unit chosen—although multiplying all cells in an agreement matrix by the same factor does not affect the value of kappa (Bakeman and Gottman, 1984, 1997).

One solution is to somehow align the events in timed-event sequences, similar to the alignment just described for event sequences. This probably underestimates the number of decisions observers actually make, but the number of tallies is closer to the number of events coded. An event matching algorithm, based on an algorithm described by Haccou and Meelis (1992), was implemented in The Observer Version 5.0 (Jansen et al., 2003;

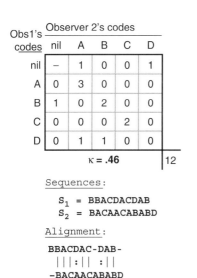

Figure 12.8 Alignment of two event sequences per a dynamic programming algorithm, and the resulting agreement matrix and kappa. For alignment, vertical bars indicate exact agreement, two dots disagreements, and hyphens events coded by one observer but not the other.

Noldus Information Technology, 2003; www.noldus.com) and a similar algorithm was implemented in Version 8.4.4 of INTERACT (P. T. Mangold, personal communication, November 14, 2007; C. Spies, personal communication, February 1, 2008; www.mangold-international.com). In the process of examining how the event-based kappas produced by these two commercially available programs compare with time-unit kappa, Quera pointed out how the dynamic programming kappa we had developed for event sequential data could easily be extended to timed-event sequential data as well, as we explain in a recent article (Bakeman et al., 2009).

The dynamic programming algorithm we developed for timed-event sequences is available in Version 5.0 of GSEQ. It is conceptually similar to the dynamic programming algorithm described earlier, but is adapted to consider information about onset times of events. Like our earlier algorithm, it permits errors of omission and commission, which not all event-based algorithms do. Based on simulations we ran, it does not give dramatically different values than the algorithms in either INTERACT or The Observer, but it does seem more mathematical in conception and with a deeper base in the literature.

Based on the simulations we ran, we would recommend that for timed-event sequential data investigators report values for both a time-unit kappa and an event-based kappa; their range likely captures the 'true' value of kappa. Similarly, we would recommend that investigators provide observers with agreement matrixes for both a time-unit and an event-based kappa. Each provides somewhat different but valuable information about disagreements as observers strive to improve their agreement.

THE DIGITAL FUTURE

Finally, and very briefly, let me comment on the digital future, even though this may be a bit risky. For my dissertation research we used punched cards – a medium that not everybody would even recognize today. Video cameras were expensive and electronic storage devices were largely custom built, expensive, and cranky. The tape for the first video recorder I used for research was three-quarters of an inch wide, and we were thrilled with devices that added a time code to the screen and combined more than one image. Electronically recorded SMPTE time codes were complex and required specialized equipment. We were happy when tape recorders did not mangle our tape. Today tape is rapidly disappearing as a recording medium. Video recording devices are relatively inexpensive, and digital files increasingly standard. Time codes no longer seem so electronically mysterious as in the SMPTE era and monitors are becoming both bigger and cheaper. Huge volumes of data no longer intimidate, as data mining techniques and computer programs like Quera's (2008) random projection program for the visual exploration of similarities within and between sequences demonstrates.

Here is what I would like to be able to do. I would like to be able to select any session from my corpus and play and replay it, jumping immediately to any point in the session. I would like my coders be able to play and replay those sessions, backward and forward, slower and faster, even frame by frame if necessary. I would like codes to be stored automatically in data files whenever coders depress keys. More, I would like coders to be able to depress a key when they think an event has begun, and then only after the event has ended decide what kind of event it was. If more than one recording was made, perhaps from different angles, I want to be able to watch all of those different images simultaneously, appropriately synchronized. I want the coders work to be displayed on the screen so that they can easily edit it, correcting any mistakes. I want to click on an event or events I have already coded, and have that event or those events replayed. Finally, I want the computer to provide me instantly with time plots like Figure 12.5, showing how a session was coded; and I would like instant summary statistics as well.

This is not fantasy, but a description of capabilities already available in two of the better known commercially available computer programs for recording and analyzing digital multimedia files, Mangold International's INTERACT and Noldus Information Technology's The Observer. These programs are not inexpensive, which can be a concern for those without adequate funding. I hear rumors of freeware being developed, but I know that software developed for a particular laboratory may not generalize as well to others as software, like that developed by the commercial leaders, that was intended for general use in the first place. Quera's and my GSEQ will not solve the problem; although available for free it is intended for data analysis and not data collection. Still, here is my prediction: Within the next five years a viable and free, probably open-source product will provide the capabilities that I just described at a price all can afford. Video recorders and digital files are the new pencil and paper.

CONCLUSION

It is a truism of science that we can only measure what we see, and that what we can see often changes dramatically when new tools become available. The microscope and telescope, which were developed in The Netherlands around the turn of the 17th century, are two prominent examples. With respect to measuring behavior, we might add, we can measure better what we can see repeatedly, an option that did not exist before tools for recording moving images – first film, then video tape, now digital files – were available. Scientists are understandingly eager to exploit these new possibilities, especially when new technologies are relatively inexpensive and convenient. With respect to measuring behavior, the video technology of the 1960s and 1970s was a breakthrough. Prior possibilities had been time-consuming live observation and expensive and demanding film, whereas video cameras and tape recorders seemed within even graduate student grasp. What might be called an explosion in the use of video-based observational methods occurred.

This explosion has followed a perhaps predictable trajectory. Perhaps because we now could, huge volumes of data were often assembled – and were at times even referred to as a burden: How to analyze so much data? At the same time, perhaps enhanced by the remnants of logical positivism and the influence of ethology I mentioned earlier, often inductive methods of data analysis were emphasized, as though if only enough data were collected, understanding would somehow emerge, for example, from the thousands of transitional probabilities generated by hundreds of codes. With time, however, emphasis has shifted from what the tool can do to the questions we can ask, from volumes of data to the derivation of targeted scores (e.g., selecting indicators for particular contingencies, such as GSEQ computes), from the raw empiricism of multiple descriptive statistics to more theoretically guided hypothesis-testing analyses.

Multiple approaches have merits, but in general I think emphasizing less the tool and more what it can do is a reasonable progression. We are now at the beginning of a second explosion, this time digital. Earlier I discussed coding (as defined by the coding schemes used), recording (the initial capture of coded data), and representing (data reduction, e.g., computing contingency scores). Because digital methods make recording less arduous, I would like to say almost transparent, and because we have experience in effective data reduction (and the computer programs to do it), I think the present progression will not be stopped or reversed, but only enhanced by the digital explosion in which we now find ourselves.

REFERENCES

Bakeman, R. and Gottman, J. M. (1986) *Observing interaction: An introduction to sequential analysis.* New York: Cambridge University Press.

Bakeman, R. and Gottman, J. M. (1997) *Observing interaction: An introduction to sequential analysis.* 2nd edition. New York: Cambridge University Press.

Bakeman, R. and Quera, V. (1992) 'SDIS: A sequential data interchange standard', *Behavior Research Methods, Instruments, and Computers*, 24: 554–9.

Bakeman, R. and Quera, V. (1995) *Analyzing interaction: Sequential analysis with SDIS and GSEQ.* New York: Cambridge University Press.

Bakeman, R., Quera, V. and Gnisci, A. (2009) 'Observer agreement for timed-event sequential data: A comparison of time-based and event-based algorithms', *Behavior Research Methods*, 41: 137–47.

Bakeman, R. and Robinson, B. F. (1994) *Understanding log-linear analysis with ILOG: An interactive approach.* Hillsdale, NJ: Lawrence Erlbaum Associates.

Blurton Jones, N. (1972) *Ethological studies of child behavior.* New York: Cambridge University Press.

Chomsky, N. (1959) 'Review of verbal behavior, by B. F. Skinner', *Language*, 35: 26–57.

Cohen, J. A. (1960) 'A coefficient of agreement for nominal scales', *Educational and Psychological Measurement*, 20: 37–46.

Cohn, J. F. and Kanade, T. (2007) 'Automated facial image analysis for measurement of emotion expression', in J. A. Coan and J. B. Allen (eds), *The handbook of emotion elicitation and assessment.* New York: Oxford. pp. 222–38.

Deckner, D. F., Adamson, L. B. and Bakeman, R. (2003) 'Rhythm in mother-toddler interactions', *Infancy*, 4: 201–17.

Eckman, P. W. and Friesen, W. (1978) *Manual for the facial action coding system.* Palo Alto, CA: Consulting Psychologist Press.

Fleiss, J. L. (1981) *Statistical methods for rates and proportions.* New York: Wiley.

Galisson, F. (2000) *Introduction to computational sequence analysis.* Tutorial, ISMB 2000, 8th International Conference on Intelligent Systems for Molecular Biology, San Diego, CA. (Online: www.iscb.org/ismb2000/tutorial_pdf/galisson4.pdf)

Haccou, P. and Meelis, E. (1992) *Statistical analysis of behavioural data: An approach based on time-structured models.* Oxford: Oxford University Press.

Hollenbeck, A. R. (1978) 'Problems of reliability in observational data', in G. P. Sackett (ed.), *Observing behavior* (Vol. 2, *Data collection and analysis methods*). Baltimore: University Park Press. pp. 79–88.

Jansen, R. G., Wiertz, L. F., Meyer, E. S. and Noldus, L. P. J. J. (2003) 'Reliability analysis of observational data: Problems, solutions, and software implementation', *Behavior Research Methods, Instruments, and Computers*, 35: 391–99.

Needleman, S. B. and Wunsch, C. D. (1970) 'A general method applicable to the search for similarities in the amino acid sequence of two proteins', *Journal of Molecular Biology*, 48: 443–53.

Noldus Information Technology. (2003) *The Observer: Professional system for collection, analysis, presentation and management of observational data. Reference Manual, Version 5.0.* Wageningen, The Netherlands: Author.

Parten, M. B. (1932) 'Social participation among preschool children', *Journal of Abnormal and Social Psychology*, 27: 243–369.

Quera, V. (2008) 'RAP: A computer program for exploring similarities in behavior sequences using random projections', *Behavior Research Methods*, 40: 21–32.

Quera, V., Bakeman, R. and Gnisci, A. (2007) 'Observer agreement for event sequences: Methods and software for sequence alignment and reliability estimates', *Behavior Research Methods*, 39: 39–49.

Sankoff, D., and Kruskal, J. (eds). (1999) *Time warps, string edits, and macromolecules: The theory and practice of sequence comparison*. 2nd edition. Stanford, CA: CSLI Publications.

Simpson, J. A. and Weiner, E. S. C. (1989). *The Oxford English dictionary* (Vol. 38, 2nd edition). Oxford, UK: Clarendon Press.

Stevens, S. S. (1946) 'On the theory of scales of measurement', *Science*, 103: 677–80.

Viswanathan, M. (2005) *Measurement error and research design*. Newbury Park: Sage Publications.

Wolff, P. (1966) 'The causes, controls, and organization of the neonate', *Psychological Issues*, 5: (whole No. 17).

13

Approaches to Measuring Multi-dimension Constructs across the Life Course: Operationalizing Depression over the Lifespan

Briana Mezuk and William W. Eaton

INTRODUCTION

Depression syndrome is a state of disordered affect or mood that has been the subject of empirical and philosophical inquiries for centuries (Jackson, 1990). Symptoms of depression include persistent (e.g., lasting two weeks or longer) feelings of sadness (dysphoria), lost interest or pleasure in things or activities normally found enjoyable (anhedonia), somatic complaints (e.g., sleep disturbances, appetite or weight changes, fatigue, psychomotor agitation or retardation), cognitive difficulties (trouble thinking or concentrating), and preoccupation with feelings of guilt or death and dying, including suicidal ideation.

Depression is one of the most common psychiatric conditions, with an estimated 8–16 per cent of the US adult population experiencing a major depression episode (MDE) at some point in their lives (Kessler et al., 2003; Narrow et al., 2002). However, the conceptualization and assessment of depression changes over the lifespan, and these transformations have implications for the longitudinal study of precursors, course, and outcomes of depressive disorders. It is important for investigators to conceptualize and interpret psychiatric epidemiologic research within a developmental framework in order to understand how early-, middle-, and late-life risk factors interact with each other and how the consequences of depression change with age. The measurement of depression over the lifespan must also be understood within the context of cultural and social group factors which may influence the expression of depressive symptomology. For example, depression syndrome is approximately twice as common among women as among men, and although some have argued for a biological or physiological basis for this difference, there is also strong evidence that expression of distress and psychopathology is gendered (McPherson and Armstrong, 2006) and that the measurement of distress should reflect this. While this chapter will not focus on the heterogeneity that such social and cultural factors may introduce into the measurement of psychopathology, there are several excellent reviews of these issues that interested readers may want to explore (Aneshensel et al., 1983; Lincoln et al., 2007; McPherson and Armstrong, 2006; Whaley and Geller, 2003). Finally, it is recognized that some of the issues commented on here may have more or less relevance to other psychiatric diagnoses (e.g., conditions characterized by limited insight such as psychosis) and measurement modalities.

One of the hallmarks of measurement of psychopathology in the population, as it is currently practiced, is the reliance on fully structured instruments administered by trained lay interviewers (or, in some cases, self-administered by the respondent). Previously, epidemiologists and other population health researchers had relied on either mental health admissions or utilization data combined with information gathered from key informants (the 'first generation'

of psychiatric epidemiology, which ended before World War II), or through clinical interviews or review of lay interviews by psychiatrists (the 'second generation,' which lasted from World War II until the publication of the *DSM-III* in 1980) (Dohrenwend and Dohrenwend, 1982). In contrast, the third generation of measurement in psychiatric epidemiology (which began with the publication of the *DSM-III* and continues to the present day) has been marked by the use of fully structured measurement instruments, many of which are designed to mimic the type of questions that psychiatrists ask during clinical interviews (discussed in more detail below).

This chapter is focused on measurement of depression syndrome over the lifespan, and in particular methodological insights to be gleaned from the assessment strategies used by the multisite National Institute of Mental Health (NIMH) Epidemiologic Catchment Area Project and the longitudinal follow-ups conducted by the Baltimore site, from 1981 to 2005. At the time, the five-site 1981 NIMH Epidemiologic Catchment Area (ECA) Project (Baltimore, MD; Durham, NC; New Haven, CT; Los Angeles, CA; and St. Louis, MO) represented the largest survey of mental health in the community conducted in the United States (*Psychiatric disorders in America: The epidemiologic catchment area study*, 1990). The development of the ECA project paralleled the publication of the third edition of the *Diagnostic and Statistical Manual of Mental Disorders* (*DSM-III*) by the American Psychiatric Association in 1980. The *DSM-III* dramatically altered the conceptualization and assessment of mental illness and embodied a shift to improve the reliability of psychiatric phenomena. The baseline ECA interviews in 1981 and the publication of the *DSM-III* marked a new age of psychiatric epidemiology, both in clinical settings and the general population (Dohrenwend and Dohrenwend, 1982).

The instrument developed to assess psychopathology for this project – and the main topic of this chapter – is the Diagnostic Interview Schedule (DIS). This instrument essentially operationalized the *DSM-III* diagnostic criteria for several forms of psychopathology, including mood conditions such as depression, anxiety disorders such as phobias and panic, and substance abuse and dependency (Robins, 1989). The DIS is one of the most characterized measures of depression used today (Eaton et al., 2007a), and analyses using this measure have provided a more thorough understanding of the evolution of depression in the population (Eaton et al., 1997, 2008). The underlying theme of this chapter is to link fundamental questions regarding the measurement of depression, including methodologic assumptions of assessments, reliability and validity of diagnostic criteria, and case definition, to epidemiologic findings concerning the varying expression, predictors, and consequences of depression over the lifespan.

OVERVIEW OF DIAGNOSTIC VERSUS DIMENSIONAL MEASUREMENT APPROACHES TO DEPRESSION

One of the most fundamental issues concerning the measurement of psychopathology in the population is the model of the underlying construct. Indeed, as is the case certainly with constructs across the social sciences, the conceptualization and measurement of depression are inseparable (Kraemer, 2007; Regier, 2007). Depression, like many forms of psychological distress, is commonly measured as both a *dimension* of affect and as a *clinical syndrome* (Andrews et al., 2007). The dimensional approach conceptualizes depression as a collection of symptoms that constitute a gradient of depressive affect. In contrast, the syndromic approach frames depression as a group of signs and symptoms that are functionally and hierarchically related to one another and which collectively characterize the condition, which is either present or absent (dichotomous). This categorical approach can be further conceptualized as comprising what Haslam (2003) calls 'fuzzy' diagnostic entities in which depressive symptoms are viewed as a continuum but membership in a particular diagnostic category can be non-arbitrarily assigned based on symptom thresholds or severity (e.g., below, above and at a threshold level of symptomology) thus producing three categories of diagnosis (absent, present, and equivocal) (Haslam, 2003). The costs and benefits of this quasi-dimensional categorical approach have been discussed by others (Andrews et al., 2007; Kraemer, 2007), and therefore this chapter will focus on the contrasts between dimensional and dichotomous constructs of depression, which are the ones most often employed in epidemiologic and clinical research.

Depression symptom scales, such as the Centers for Epidemiologic Studies – Depression (CES-D) scale, generally consist of a checklist of symptoms which are then summed to produce an overall depression 'score' (Eaton et al., 2004). These scales include items on both the essential (e.g., dysphoria or anhedonia) and associated (i.e., appetite change, sleep disturbances) symptoms of depression, as well as symptoms that are not directly derived from the diagnostic criteria, such as feelings of hopefulness and happiness. The symptom scores are summed additively, meaning that the items are treated as interchangeable (i.e., dysphoria is treated the same as fatigue). Such symptom checklists intrinsically measure depression as a dimension (i.e., a continuous construct ranging from zero to all possible symptoms) and are therefore not intended to measure a syndrome. Scales often do not include probe items to determine if the endorsed symptoms are attributable to causes other than depression (i.e., appetite disturbances are common in depression, but may also be due to physical illness or use of medications) and may not include items on duration of symptoms or associated levels of distress. As Murphy (2002) has emphasized, this additive approach to scoring symptoms means that a person can score above a designated threshold of depressive symptoms (i.e., a cut-off of 16 or above is commonly used for the CES-D to indicate 'clinical depression') without having to endorse the essential symptoms of depression – dysphoria or anhedonia (Murphy, 2002). Higher scores on symptom scales are therefore highly correlated with depression syndrome, but when a 'diagnostic' cut-off or threshold is applied to the summed score they introduce more heterogeneity into what it means to be a 'case' relative to syndromic measures (Eaton et al., 2004). In contrast, diagnostic measures of depression (also often referred to as schedules) conceptualize depression as a syndrome and utilize algorithms to ensure that the essential features of the disorder as outlined in the *Diagnostic and Statistical Manual of Mental Disorders* are present in order to classify a person as a 'case' (e.g., expressing symptomology in a distinct pattern which is deemed to warrant clinical attention). There is a hierarchy of items and they are not just summed additively to produce the diagnosis). Schedules have a greater level of precision in that they often include probes to determine alternate causes, duration, and associated levels of distress or impairment for each symptom. They take considerably longer to complete than symptom scales (especially compared to prolific 'short-form' scales), but the group

classified as 'cases' are more homogenous in regards to their symptom profiles than a group identified by a threshold cut-off from a symptom scale. Both schedules and scales have only moderate concordance with semi-structured clinical instruments administered by a mental health professional such as the Schedules for Clinical Assessment in Neuropsychiatry (SCAN) or the Structured Clinical Interview for DSM (SCID) (Eaton et al., 2000, 2007a). Fully-structured instruments such as the Diagnostic Interview Schedule tend to have high specificity and low sensitivity relative to these clinical measures, meaning that few persons are incorrectly classified as 'depressed' when they are not (false positives), but many are misclassified as 'not-depressed' when they in fact are (Eaton et al., 2007a). As is often the case across psychological measurement and diagnosis, it is important to note that there is no 'gold standard' of diagnostic validity with which to compare against for psychiatric conditions (that is, current diagnostic criteria are understood to be reliable, but not necessarily valid), although consensus clinical assessments by psychiatrists using all available information are commonly used as the 'lead (Longitudinal, Expert, All Data) standard' for such evaluations (Farone and Tsuang, 1994). Many other constructs commonly assessed by self-report in survey research, such as social support and functional impairment, also lack an accepted standard against which to assess sensitivity and specificity. The implications of the lack of a gold standard for assessment of depression over the lifespan in the general population are discussed in more detail below.

There are numerous factors that impact on the ability to measure psychopathology: choice of modality (i.e., clinical assessment, semi or fully structured interview); mode of data collection (i.e., in-person, self-administered, telephone, informant); concerns about respondent burden (i.e., duration of assessment, items related to personal thoughts and feelings); and insight (i.e., young children and cognitively impaired adults). This chapter will address some of these aspects related to the administration of DIS, although evaluating the relative trade-offs associated with these components of psychiatric epidemiologic research in general is beyond the scope of this chapter (See Murphy, Textbook in psychiatric epidemiology, 2002 for a comprehensive review).

DSM-III AND THE 1981 NIMH EPIDEMIOLOGIC CATCHMENT AREA PROJECT

The institutional and popular support for NIMH Epidemiologic Catchment Area Project was motivated by Rosalynn Carter's 1977 commission to assess the state of knowledge regarding the prevalence, distribution, and service needs of mental health conditions in the United States. The findings from this commission revealed that very little was known about these basic epidemiologic characteristics, and existing data simply could not provide the answers (*Psychiatric disorders in America: The epidemiologic catchment area* study, 1990). The deinstitutionalization movement of the 1960s and 1970s mandated that assessments of mental health focus on the general population and not just in the hospitals, and researchers were required to develop new instruments and employ novel survey techniques to meet this need. The development of the NIMH ECA Project and its instrument the Diagnostic Interview Schedule (DIS) has been discussed in detail by Lee Robins and colleagues in the monograph *Psychiatric Disorders in America*, published in 1990, as well as

several peer-reviewed articles (Helzer and Robins, 1988; Regier et al., 1984; Robins, 1989), and we will defer to these texts the description and motivation for the ECA project overall. However, we will emphasize some particular qualities of the ECA project and the DIS that are relevant to the discussion of the experience at the Baltimore site.

Table 13.1 displays the nine symptom groups of *DSM-III* major depressive episode (MDE). The cardinal symptoms of major depression are dysphoria (feelings of sadness) and anhedonia (lost interest or pleasure). At least one of these two symptoms, plus symptoms in four or more of the remaining eight symptom *groups* (e.g., appetite/weight, sleep, psychomotor, cognitive, fatigue, guilt, lost interest in sex, preoccupation with death or thoughts of suicide), must be present for the *DSM-III* diagnosis of MDE. The DIS is updated with each new edition of the *DSM*, and although the criteria for MDE have evolved somewhat since the *DSM-III* (see the footnote of Table 13.1), the main symptom groups have remained the same. It is important to note that regardless of the specific diagnostic system in place at the time, the issues discussed here remain directly relevant measurement of depression over the lifespan.

Measurement advances of the Diagnostic Interview Schedule

The DIS embodied several advances in measurement of psychiatric disorder, particularly depression. Foremost, the items for each psychiatric condition were linked to a diagnostic algorithm that was designed to mimic the process a psychiatrist would go through to determine whether or not a person was a 'case' of any particular disorder. In practice, this meant that after respondents were asked about specific

Table 13.1   Diagnostic interview schedule items used to describe a major depressive episode

Symptom group	Corresponding diagnostic interview schedule version III items*
Dysphoria/ anhedonia	In your lifetime, have you ever had two weeks or more during which you felt sad, blue, depressed or when you lost all interest and pleasure in things that you usually cared about or enjoyed?
Appetite/ weight	In your lifetime, have you ever had a period of two weeks or longer when you **lost your appetite**?
	Have you ever **lost weight** without trying to, as much as two pounds a week for several weeks?
	Have you ever had a period when your eating increased so much you **gained** as much as two pounds a week for several weeks?
Sleep	Have you ever had a period of two weeks or more when you had **trouble falling asleep**, staying asleep, or waking up too early?
	Have you ever had a period of two weeks or longer when you were **sleeping too much**?
Fatigue	Has there ever been a period lasting two weeks or more when you felt **tired out** all the time?
Slow/restless	Has there ever been a period of two weeks or more when you talked or moved more **slowly** than is usual for you?
	Has there ever been a period of two weeks or more when you had to **be moving all the time** – that is, you couldn't sit still and paced up and down?
Lost interest	Was there ever a period of several weeks when your interest in **sex** was a lot **less** than usual?
Worthless	Has there ever been a period of two weeks or more when you felt **worthless**, sinful, or guilty?
Trouble thinking	Has there ever been a period of two weeks or more when you had a lot more **trouble concentrating** than is normal for you?
	Have you ever had a period of two weeks or more when your **thoughts** came much **slower** than usual or seemed mixed up?
Thoughts of death	Has there ever been a period of two weeks or more when you thought a lot about **death** – either your own, someone else's or death in general?
	Has there ever been a period of two weeks or more when you felt like you **wanted to die**?
	Have you ever felt so low you **thought** of committing **suicide**?
	Have you ever attempted **suicide**?

*These items reflect the diagnostic criteria for Major Depressive Episode from the DSM-III. The DSM was updated in 1987 (DSM-III-Revised) and 1994 (DSM-IV) to include additional symptoms, and each time the DIS was updated to reflect these changes.

The DSM-IV and its corresponding version of the DIS includes the following modification to the items listed above:

Dysphoria: In your lifetime, have you ever had **two weeks or more** when nearly every day you felt sad, blue depressed?

The DSM-IV and its corresponding version of the DIS includes the following 11 additions to the items listed above:

Appetite/weight: Has there ever been at least two weeks when you had an increase in appetite?

Sleep: Have you ever had two weeks or more when nearly every morning, you would **wake up at least 2 hours before you wanted to**? Have you ever had two weeks or longer when nearly every day you were **sleeping too much**?

Fatigue: Did you ever have two weeks or more when you **felt very bad when you got up but better later in the day**?

Slow/restless: Have you ever had a period of weeks of **feeling fidgety or restless** more than half the time?

Lost interest: Has there ever been two weeks or longer when you lost all interest in things like work or hobbies or things you usually liked to do for fun? Has there ever been a week or more when you wanted to **stay away from people**, not mix with them?

Worthless: Has there ever been a week or longer when you **felt** that **you were not as good as other people** or inferior? Has there ever been a week or longer when you **had so little self-confidence** that you wouldn't try to have your say about anything? Have you ever had two weeks or longer when you **lost the ability to enjoy** having **good things** happen to you, like winning something or being praised or complimented?

Trouble thinking: Have you ever had two weeks or more when nearly every day you were **unable to make up your mind** about things you ordinarily have no trouble deciding about?

symptoms, these questions were followed by inquiries about the severity of the symptom, whether alternate causes (e.g., use of drugs or alcohol or physical illness/injury) might explain the symptom, whether the symptoms occurred together, and whether that clustering of symptoms was prolonged or acute (see the DIS Probe Flow Chart, Figure 13.1). The timing of the first onset and last experience of each symptom are also recorded.

The ECA implementation of the DIS is distinct from other fully structured diagnostic measures of depression, such as the Composite International Diagnostic Interview Schedule (CIDI) (Robins et al., 1988), in that all items were asked of all respondents, regardless of 'case' status – that is, even if it became clear during the course of the interview that a respondent could no longer meet diagnostic criteria. For example, in order to meet *DSM* criteria for major depressive episode, respondents *must* endorse feelings of dysphoria or anhedonia (the cardinal symptoms of the syndrome), regardless of their responses to the other symptom items. Because of the requirement that the cardinal symptoms are present for case identification, some instruments like the CIDI employ them as 'screening' questions in the interview and only ask the items for the associated symptoms if the screening items are endorsed. This screening process is done to reduce respondent burden by avoiding asking items that will not impact on case status. However, the trade-off of using screening items is that the distribution and patterning of the associated depression symptoms – independent of the cardinal symptoms – cannot be estimated. The 'item-independence' employed by the depression module of the DIS in the ECA permitted estimates of the prevalence of each symptom, regardless of case status, and allow for a finer assessment how case status derived from survey measures like

the DIS *differs* from case status derived from psychiatric interviews (which utilize clinical judgment and generally do not mandate that particular items are endorsed for the clinician to inquire about other symptoms). For example, analyses comparing the *total* number of depression symptom groups endorsed across the DIS and the SCAN have provided a more nuanced understanding of the sources of measurement error in self-report assessments (Eaton et al., 2000).

Depression syndrome in the population

The discussion of measurement thus far has focuses exclusively on a categorical (diagnostic 'caseness') approach to assessing depressive symptomology. However, depression symptoms that are likely due to a psychiatric cause (that is they are not explained by use of drugs or alcohol and were not due to a physical illness or injury) are common in the population. Figure 13.2 illustrates the prevalence of symptom groups stratified by *DSM-III* depression status (e.g., those that did or did not meet *DSM-III* diagnostic criteria for major depressive episode (MDE)). As shown by this figure, symptoms of depression are common *even among the group that did not meet diagnostic criteria* (i.e., approximately 24 per cent of the group that did not meet lifetime criteria for MDE still reported experiencing two weeks or more of dysphoria/anhedonia). This plot illustrates that all the signs and symptoms of depression are non-specific to the syndrome. Clearly these symptom groups occur much more frequently among those with a lifetime history of MDE, but they are certainly not absent in the group that did not meet diagnostic criteria. Incidentally, this highlights a common challenge in the measurement of psychopathology, in that the signs and symptoms that

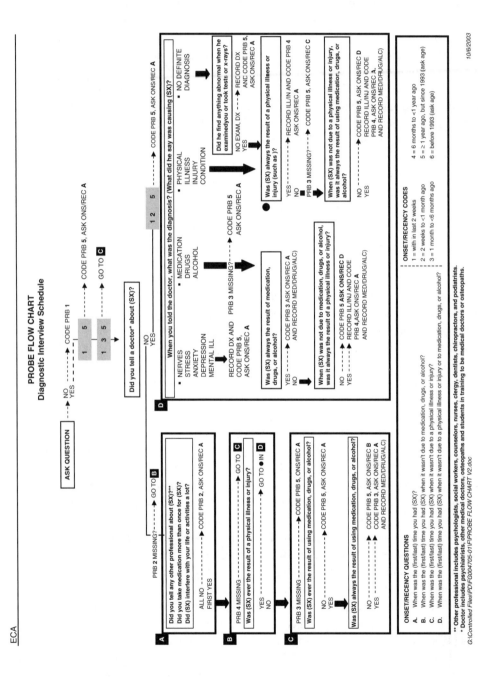

Figure 13.1 Interview algorithm of the Diagnostic Interview Survey (DIS) used to determine cases of major depressive episode in the Epidemiologic Catchment Area Project.

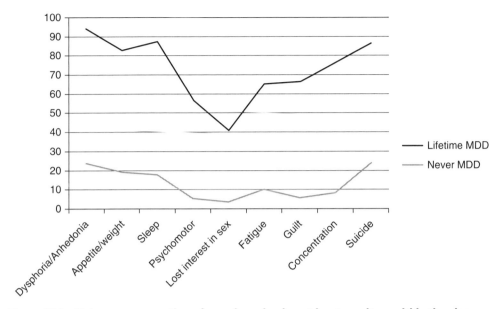

Figure 13.2   Values are proportion of sample endorsing at least one item within the nine symptom groups by lifetime MDE diagnosis. Values have been weighted to the U.S. population in 1980. Total *N* = 15,489 (four sites only: Baltimore MD; Durham NC; Los Angeles CA; St. Louis MO).

Note: Values have been weighted to the US population in 1980.

characterize a particular syndrome are often frequently common in the general population irrespective of case status and measurement instruments must be designed to provide appropriate diagnosis despite this trend.

Within the subset of respondents who met criteria for major depressive episode (*N* = 804), the patterning of symptom groups is similar across age groups (Figure 13.3). This indicates that, *conditional on meeting DSM diagnostic criteria*, the characteristics of depression syndrome do not vary substantially over the life course. However, the primary utility of measuring depression in the general population is not to characterize the symptoms of identified cases, but rather to *distinguish* cases from non-cases in order to estimate prevalence and incidence. If the accuracy of case identification varies over the lifespan, this has important implications

for both etiologic research and service planning and assessment.

Depression symptoms over the lifespan

The patterning and distribution of depression symptoms varies over the lifespan. Figure 13.4 displays the lifetime prevalence of the individual *DSM-III* DIS depression symptoms from the combined baseline Epidemiologic Catchment Area Project (see Table 13.1 for item wording). This plot illustrates that for almost all symptoms, the oldest cohort (aged 60 and older) has the lowest lifetime prevalence (a finding that has been replicated numerous times). This is a counterintuitive finding, as the oldest group should have the *highest* lifetime prevalence because they have had the longest time *ever* to experience a given symptom. This finding suggests that case

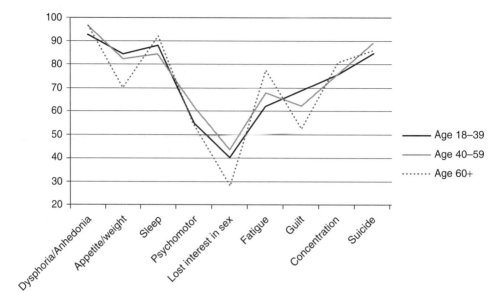

Figure 13.3   Values reflect the endorsement of the nine depressive symptom groups among the subset of the ECA sample that met criteria for DSM-III Major Depressive. Number that met DSM-III criteria, N = 804 (four sites only: Baltimore MD; Durham NC; Los Angeles CA; St. Louis MO).

identification of depression may not be consistent over the lifespan and that it may be necessary to employ different types of assessment strategies to ensure continuity of measurement over the lifespan.

The best setting in which to evaluate the utility of such strategies is in a longitudinal cohort study because it involves the repeated assessment of the same individuals over time as they age. While all five sites of the ECA Project completed interviews in 1981 and 1982, only the Baltimore site continued follow-up of the entire cohort beyond this in 1993 and 2004.

THE BALTIMORE EPIDEMIOLOGIC CATCHMENT AREA STUDY EXPERIENCE

The ECA interviews were framed after a revolution in psychiatric diagnosis, and

the 1981 cohort is thus the earliest in the nation to include a wide range of psychopathology, according to the newly revised *DSM-111* diagnostic criteria. The Baltimore ECA continued to utilize the DIS for the assessment of depression and other forms of psychopathology and whenever possible asked the identical items as the baseline survey (some items were added or changed as the instrument was updated to reflect the latest version of the *DSM*, as described in the footnote of Table 13.1). The additional person years of experience gave the opportunity for enhanced studies of natural history of psychopathology in the population, including studies of incidence and recurrence of common mental disorders, and consequences in terms of physical illness, disability, services use, and mortality.

What advantage was there to adding another wave of interviews, after the

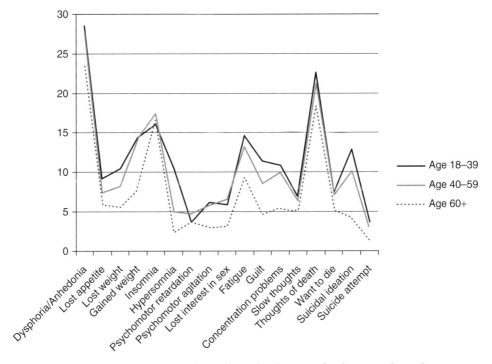

Figure 13.4   Values are proportion of sample endorsing *ever* having experienced symptom, regardless of MDE diagnosis. Total N = 15,489 (four sites only: Baltimore MD; Durham NC; Los Angeles CA; St. Louis MO).

Note: Mean percentage missing data across all symptioms by age group: 18–39 years = 1.75%; 40–59 years = 4.74%; and 60+ years = 12.85%. Values greater than zero indicate that the amount of missing data for that symptom was greater than the mean of all symptoms for the given age group, whereas values less than zero indicate that the amount of missing data for that symptom was less than the mean for all symptoms for the given age group.

passage of over a decade? Certain of the advantages are incremental in nature; certain advantages are unique to the situation of multiple waves of data; and certain advantages accrue because the investigators added new ideas and measures to the original design. The primary methodological and conceptual advantages to having multiple waves of data are the addition of person-years (i.e., the amount of time each respondent was observed) which is a critical determinant of identifying risk factors and consequences of psychopathology; better understanding of how environmental exposures accumulate over the life course (i.e., the notion of cumulative burden); and

the ability to explore the effects of age, period and cohort on the risk of mental health conditions. Longitudinal studies such as the Baltimore ECA also allow for a detailed description and more nuanced understanding of the influence of aging on health and mental health relative to cross-sectional studies that simply compare young and old age groups at a single point in time.

New survey research technologies have been integrated into each additional wave of follow-up. For example, for the 2004–2005 follow-up the DIS was translated into a Computer Assisted Personal Interview (CAPI) with the skip patterns of the Probe

Flow Chart (Figure 13.1) built directly into the instrument. This meant that interviews no longer had to memorize the series of questions that follow each symptom endorsement or the diagnostic algorithm for determining whether case status had been met. Also, information from earlier waves could be built into the CAPI instrument (i.e., whether the respondent had met diagnostic criteria for depression in the past).

The structure of the Diagnostic Interview Schedule as used in the ECA program facilitated several advances in epidemio-logic understanding of psychopathology. Inclusion of questions covering the entire diagnostic criteria allowed for descriptive data to be presented on rates of specific disorders and these epidemiologic data, for the first time, could be related to research in the laboratory or clinic, where the diagnos-tic level information was also used (Regier et al., 1984). The descriptive epidemiologic information included parameters which could not be studied earlier, such as incidence rates – the closest approximation of the population force of morbidity (Eaton et al., 1989a). The population structure of the diagnostic algorithm could be studied for the first time using new statistical procedures such as latent class analysis (Eaton et al., 1989b) and MIMC (Multiple Indicator Multiple Cause) modeling (Gallo et al., 1994). Further longitudinal stud-ies permitted better understanding of the natural history of the disorders, including the length of the prodrome, estimated separately for different symptom groups; (Eaton et al., 1997) the predictive value of aspects of the prodrome (Eaton et al., 1995); the predictive value of certain disorders for later physical conditions (Eaton et al., 1996; Gallo et al., 2000; Larson et al., 2001; Pratt et al., 1996), and the long-term outcome of the disorders, estimated without the bias of the clinic or the bias of a prevalence sample (Eaton et al., 2008).

NOTABLE ISSUES IN MEASUREMENT OF DEPRESSION OVER THE LIFESPAN

There are many general measurement issues that are relevant to the assessment of any psychological phenomena that are not specifically addressed here but have been the focus of much previous work (i.e., social desirability bias). In the case of social desirability bias, mental health conditions remain the target of social stigma (and arguably, outright discrimination) (Stuber et al., 2008; Phelan et al., 2008). Studies suggest that awareness of conditions such as depression in the United States has increased in recent decades (likely influ-enced by direct-to-consumer advertising of medications designed to treat mental health conditions) (An, 2008), but studies of social distance indicate that psychiatric conditions are still not interpreted by the lay public as 'health' conditions (Link et al., 1999). The impact of stigma on the assessment of depression is difficult to assess, but the reluctance to report symptoms may vary differentially across social groups and investigators have worked to address this issue by matching interviewers and respondents on age, sex, and race/ethnicity in order to reduce the social distance of this interaction with the express intent of increasing valid reporting (Jackson et al., 2004). Other constructs, such as criminal history, illicit drug use, and even body weight, are also subject to social desirability bias (Latner et al., 2008), and investigators have employed a variety of solutions to remedy this (i.e., preference for self-report rather than interviewer-administered questionnaires; including nonsensical items to identify participants who endorse (or fail to endorse) questions in a systematic way; and obtaining Certificates of Con-fidentiality from the Federal Government in order to protect respondent reports from subpoena). Other common factors that influence measurement accuracy more generally include cultural variation (i.e., language of interview) and selection bias, particularly as it relates to social desirability (e.g., persons who agree to participate in the survey may be more willing or less willing to endorse sensitive items relative to those who refuse).

These threats to measurement validity undoubtedly influence of measurement of depression, but they do not necessarily have unique implications for measurement over the life course. The key appeal of longitudinal research is the ability to compare characteristics within the same person across several points in time; clearly the validity of such a comparison is predicated on stability of measurement of the construct of interest. Four main measurement concerns pertaining to assessing depression over the lifespan are: (1) construct validity, (2) non-response bias, (3) attribution of symptoms, and (4) conceptual discontinuities.

Construct validity

Reliability and validity of the diagnosis of depression are intrinsically linked – the *DSM* criteria have been designed to promote reliability across raters and within raters across time. The advances of these criteria, which are operationalized by the DIS and similar instruments, have not resolved the lack of a 'gold standard' against which to assess diagnostic validity. In the absence of a gold standard, traditional measures of validity such as sensitivity and specificity lose some of their interpretive value (Eaton et al., 2007a). Other methods of assessing validity, including external construct validity (i.e., familial clustering, similar sets of environmental exposures, similar course, and common treatment response), have been suggested as alternatives (Kraemer, 2007). However, the measurement error implied by poor

reliability directly reduces the statistical power to detect such associations, and thus it is unclear how to interpret poor external validity. The issue is particularly important for life course research because such factors may vary over the lifespan. The lessening of family history and emergence of vascular disease as a risk factor for depression over the lifespan in later life is just one example of how the influence of risk and protective factors (e.g., those characteristics used to determine external validity) vary with age (Alexopoulos, 2006). These changing risk profiles influence the ability to reliably measure depression even with well-characterized instruments.

Non-response bias

Another important concern regarding measurement of constructs associated with social stigma like depression is non-response (Tourangeau and Yan, 2007). Respondents have the right to refuse to answer any item, and thus several categories of survey items – income and religious involvement in particular – often have a high percentage of missing data because of this. Patterns of missing data may vary not only by item but also by age, as ability or willingness to respond truthfully to particular items changes over the lifespan or may be influenced by period or cohort effects.

In the baseline ECA interview, the average percentage of missing data across the 17 items of major depression does vary significantly by age, with adults age 60 and older having the highest average percent missing (12.85 per cent), followed by middle-aged respondents (4.74 per cent) and younger adults (1.75 per cent) ($p < 0.001$). Cognitive impairment and the need to use proxy respondents in later life is one obvious explanation for changes in the amount of missing data in later life. Figure 13.5 displays the deviations

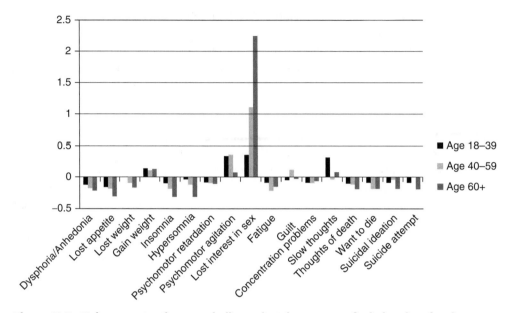

Figure 13.5 Values greater than zero indicate that the amount of missing data for that symptom was greater than the mean of all symptoms for the given age group, whereas values less than zero indicate that the amount of missing data for that symptom was less than the mean for all symptoms for the given age group. Total N = 15,489 (four sites only: Baltimore MD; Durham NC; Los Angeles CA; St. Louis MO).

from these age-group specific percentages for each symptom (Individual Item % Missing – Average % Missing Across All Items). It illustrates whether specific depression items were more or less likely to have missing data *relative* to the average responsiveness for each age group, thus accounting for the differences in degree of missing data across the age groups. The plot illustrates that the items show similar patterns of missing data within each age group (i.e., older adult are not substantially more likely to refuse to answer items on suicidal ideation relative to younger adults). This analysis also shows that the only item with a large amount of missing data relative to the average for each age group is the item concerning lost interest in sex, as is expected based on previous work on surveys of sexual behavior (Tourangeau and Yan, 2007). It is important to note, however, that this analysis of non-response does not

account for respondents who answer 'No' rather than 'I don't know' to these items (e.g., social desirability).

Recall bias, or systematic inaccurate reporting associated with the passage of time since an event, is another form of measurement error that is an important threat to the validity of measuring depression over the lifespan. Clearly the relative strength of recall bias is inversely proportional to the amount of time between interviews. In the case of the Baltimore ECA, that length is substantial – 12 years – and as a result, the consistency of symptom reporting is generally poor. For example, the kappa coefficient for lifetime experience of dysphoria/anhedonia from the 1981 interview to the 1993 Baltimore follow-up is only 0.32 (Thompson et al., 2004). However, this analysis demonstrated that age was not associated with incorrect recall, which suggests that while recall bias should be addressed with more frequent follow-ups, the influence of this phenomenon on measurement of depression over the lifespan may be minimal.

Differences in symptom attribution

Measurement error over the lifespan for specific symptoms of depression can come in two forms: (a) the symptom itself is endorsed differentially across age groups, and (b) the symptom, when endorsed, is differentially attributed to psychiatric versus non-psychiatric causes. Data from the Baltimore site indicate there is evidence to support this first scenario – older adults do report fewer depressive symptoms than their younger counterparts. In particular, they may be less likely to report feelings of sadness (dysphoria) relative to younger cohorts (Gallo et al., 1994; Gallo and Rabins, 1999).

As discussed above, behavioral and somatic symptoms of depression (e.g., concentration problems, fatigue, appetite disturbances, and sleep disturbances) can have causal attributions that are not related to mental health, and in order to differentiate 'psychiatric' symptoms from symptoms due to these alternate explanations, the DIS uses a Probe Flow Chart (Figure 13.1). Interviewers would memorize the pattern of questions appropriate for each symptom endorsement and follow the chart in order to arrive at a determination as to whether the reported symptom (i.e., insomnia) was (a) severe enough to be considered impairing, and (b) not always due to medication, drugs, or alcohol or a physical illness or injury. If a symptom was considered severe (e.g., the respondent either told a doctor or other professional about it, sought treatment for it, or reported that it interfered with their life or activities a lot – see the left side of the Probe Flow Chart) and was not always due to these alternate causes, it was considered a psychiatric symptom (indicated by a '5' on the Probe Flow Chart). Other fully-structured diagnostic instruments that have been developed since the DIS, such as the CIDI, (Robins et al., 1988) employ similar probe structures to differentiate psychiatric attributions from other causes of these non-specific symptoms.

One way to assess whether competing causes of symptomology contribute to the lower prevalence of depression syndrome among older adults is to examine whether the attribution of symptoms to non-psychiatric causes (e.g., illness/injury or medication/drugs/alcohol) differs by age. Figure 13.6 shows the distribution of causal attributions for items from three selected symptom groups – appetite/weight, sleep, and fatigue. These panels illustrate that for many – but not all – symptoms, when the oldest cohort reports experiencing a symptom it is more likely to attribute it to a non-psychiatric cause than the younger age groups. Attributions for insomnia in particular do not vary by age, whereas attributions of fatigue and appetite disturbances to non-psychiatric causes are reported more frequently with increasing age. Thus, for many symptoms, not only are older adults *less likely to endorse* the items, *even when they do endorse* them they are *less likely* to be designated by the DIS diagnostic algorithm as potentially psychiatric in nature relative to younger adults. This finding is consistent with previous evidence from other samples showing an increase in physical illness attributions for symptoms among older adults (Knäuper and Wittchen, 1994). Measurement of other expressions of psychopathology that are characterized by somatic and behavioral complaints, such as anxiety disorders (i.e., panic disorder), and cases of co-occurring psychiatric and substances use disorders ('dual-diagnosis') are also likely impacted by this issue of symptom attribution.

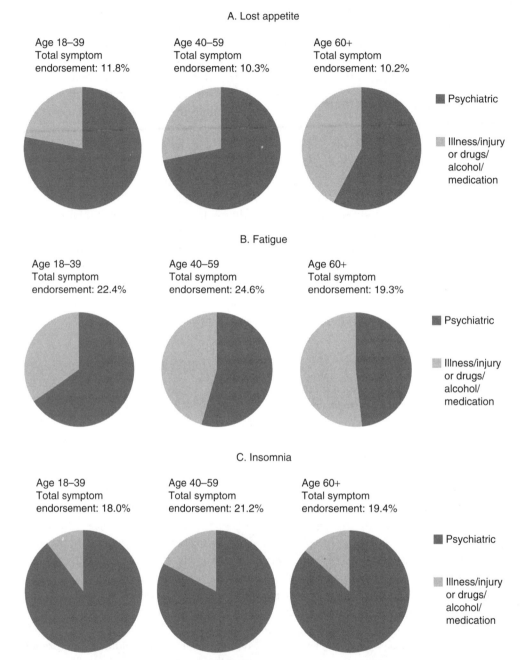

Figure 13.6   Some depression symptoms have potential causal attributions other than being psychiatric in nature, such as being due to illness and/or injury or the use of medication, drugs, or alcohol. These charts display the distribution of causal attributions for three depression symptoms among those who reported having experienced the symptom: (A) Lost appetite, (B) Fatigue, and (C) Insomnia. Total *N* = 15,489 (four sites only: Baltimore MD; Durham NC; Los Angeles CA; St. Louis MO).

Long prodromal period

The measurement of psychopathology should take into account the length of the prodromal period and thus account for symptom onset that pre-dates the fulfillment of the complete diagnostic criteria. The measurement of depression over the lifespan is also impacted by the natural history of this condition which is characterized by an episodic, but often enduring, course (Eaton et al., 2008) and an extended period of prodromal symptomology before onset (Eaton et al., 1997). The symptoms of depression often have onset several years before diagnostic criteria is met. For example, among cases of MDE in the Baltimore ECA, feelings of dysphoria typically onset five years prior to meeting diagnostic criteria. Other symptoms, such as appetite disturbances and suicidal ideation, have much shorter prodromal periods, typically two years (Eaton et al., 1995, 1997). It is unresolved whether the time from symptom onset to disorder onset varies over the lifespan, but these findings partly explain why symptoms of depression are prevalent even among those who do not meet diagnostic criteria – some of them are in the prodromal period and will go on to develop the disorder. Respondents who reported feelings of dysphoria, for example, are seven times more likely to progress to meeting diagnostic criteria for major depression relative to those who did not experience that symptom. Sleep disturbances are also highly predictive of disorder onset, whereas weight and appetite changes are less so (Eaton et al., 1995). However, a large portion of respondents who reported those symptoms will never go on to meet diagnostic criteria, which suggests that researchers interested in primary prevention of depression should focus on developing measures that focus on those signs and symptoms that are most

relevant to the precursors and prodomal aspects of this disorder.

Conceptual discontinuities

The factor most directly relevant to measurement of depression across ages concerns discontinuities in expression of distress and relevant risk factors over the lifespan. Three examples of the impact of these discontinuities are: depression during childhood, post-partum depression, and so-called vascular depression in later life.

Childhood

There is substantial debate as to the nature and expression of psychopathology in childhood, and whether disorders in childhood are etiologically distinct from their counterparts in adulthood (Achenbach, 1982). Many of the measures used to assess psychopathology in childhood, such as the Child Behavior Checklist (CBCL), are designed to assess general distress and not a specific condition and generally do not have equivalent adult measures. There are also issues regarding assessment modality (e.g., children often have limited insight into their own behavior and emotions and may be unreliable) (Fallon and Schwab-Stone, 1994), and thus many assessments utilize reports from parents, caregivers, and teachers in order to assess potential psychopathology. Fortunately, there is a version of the Diagnostic Interview Schedule designed for use in children (the DIS-C), which allows for a demonstration of the impact of this discontinuity on measurement. Both derive their symptom items and diagnostic algorithms from the *DSM* (Schaffer et al., 1996). The DIS-C differs from the adult-oriented DIS in terms of utilizing multiple assessment modalities (e.g., child and parent reports) and has diagnostic algorithms that can be used to synthesize reports from these multiple sources (i.e., symptoms are considered present if they are reported by either the child or the parent). The DIS-C has modules for the assessment of depression, but it also focuses on forms of pathology more relevant to childhood outcomes, such as attention deficit hyperactivity disorder (ADHD), conduct disorder (CD), and oppositional defiant disorder (OD). However, both the DISC and the DIS utilize lay interviewers rather than trained mental health professionals in order to be able efficiently and affordably to measure psychopathology in the community. The key question as to the concordance between DISC and DIS diagnostic categories remains unresolved – there are few, if any, longitudinal studies available that used both these measures and have followed individuals from childhood until mid-life. This disconnect between adult and childhood measurement instruments is perhaps even more acute in areas where distinct childhood measurement instruments have not been developed.

Childbirth

Another span of the life course that has implications for depression measurement and has received considerable attention from researchers is the periods surrounding childbirth (see Boyd et al., 2005 for an extensive review of measurement of post-partum depression). Briefly, three scales that have been specifically developed to assess post-partum depression (PPD): the Edinburgh Postnatal Depression Scale (EPDS) (Cox et al., 1987), the Post-partum Depression Screening Scale (PDSS) (Beck and Gable, 2000), and the Bromley Postnatal Depression Scale (Stein and van den Akker, 1992). The EPDS is the most widely used of these instruments and consists of 10 items related to the affective and cognitive aspects of depression and largely excludes symptoms focused on somatic symptoms (i.e., appetite changes) that are

normally experienced in the post-partum period. The PDSS is a longer instrument and includes additional items related to the shift in personal identity and social roles of new mothers. Finally, the Bromley includes both closed and open response items and assesses both current and lifetime (i.e., past pregnancies) PPD. The development of measures specific for this stage of the life course (and, presumably, only for women), is clearly motivated by a desire to better capture and understand the phenomenology of this state, an approach whose soundness and validity certainly merit consideration. In this instance, distinct measures for PPD beg the question as to whether depression subsequent to childbirth is really a 'unique' form of the syndrome. The DIS does not have any questions specific to depressive symptoms post-childbirth, and thus this question remains unresolved by this research.

Later adulthood

The measurement of depression potentially lends insight into a broader set of methodological considerations related to both construct stability and measurement of depression in later (aged $\geq$ 60) adulthood. Foremost, epidemiologic surveys consistently show that the lifetime prevalence of depression syndrome decreases with age after mid-life, (Eaton et al., 2007b) despite the fact that, logically, older persons should have higher lifetime prevalence since they have been at risk for a longer period of time. These studies also show, however, that point prevalence, and even first lifetime incidence, of depression syndrome decline with age. These epidemiologic findings contrast with many clinical studies and research with symptom scales which reveal an elevated prevalence of mood disturbances among older adults (Gallo et al., 1994). There is evidence that this discrepancy between diagnostic schedules and depressive symptom scales may be due to the tendency for older adults to be less likely to endorse feelings of dysphoria, which is one of the core characteristics (the other being anhedonia) of depressive disorder (Gallo et al., 1994). This has led some researchers to suggest that the nature of depression in later adulthood is fundamentally different than earlier in life (Newmann et al., 1991, 1996), and express a preference for the term 'depletion syndrome'.

During the later stages of the lifespan, concerns about confounding and measurement bias due to medical comorbidity are paramount, as illustrated above. There is also concern about the effect of neuropsychiatric conditions associated with aging, such as Alzheimer's and Parkinson's disease, on insight and ability to report on mood changes. One example of the importance of accounting for physical and cognitive decline when measuring older adults is embodied by the 'vascular depression hypothesis' put forth by Alexopoulos (Alexopoulos, 2006). This syndrome is characterized by depressive symptomology (psychomotor retardation and lack of interest, but not the essential features of depression syndrome, dysphoria or anhedonia), poor insight, functional disability, and executive dysfunction. It is thought to be due to underlying brain pathology – which distinguishes it from episodes of depression earlier in the life course – often but not always attributable to cerebrovascular disease. Whether this condition represents a distinct diagnostic entity is still strongly debated by nosologists, researchers, and clinicians. Still, the emerging body of empirical evidence aimed at parsing out the degree to which a respondent's ability to endorse a particular mood state or behavioral or somatic complaint at the very least speaks to a methodological issue related to psychiatric measurement

across the lifespan worthy of further consideration.

It is unlikely that the measurement of depression across lifespan would benefit from the development of discrete, life-phase specific, instruments. Two scales that have been developed specifically for the identification of depression in later life include the Geriatric Depression Scale (GDS) and the Cornell Scale for Depression in Dementia (CSDD). The GDS is a 30-item inventory that includes items on memory complaints and concentration difficulties, anhedonia and boredom, withdrawal from social life, and hopelessness (Yesavage et al., 1983). The CSDD is, as the name implies, specific to populations with significant cognitive impairment (Alexopoulos et al., 1988). The difficulty is that the scales assume a different nosologic entity without testing that assumption. Progress in understanding the evolution of depression through the lifespan, from childhood through adulthood, and including the post-partum period and old age, will be most rapid when a life course cohort is studied with a range of symptoms including those relevant to all putative nosologic entities, and including a range of etiologic theories. That will allow dissection of the concept of depression and its possible subdivision into more discrete diagnoses.

Summary

There are many potential explanations for the consistent yet counterintuitive finding of lower than expected lifetime prevalence of depression among older cohorts, including measurement error, recall bias, and age-related changes in the expression of depressive symptomology. Factors such as differential survivorship (e.g., depression influences morbidity and mortality such that those with a history of depression do not survive into older age) and cohort effects (e.g., the social environment is more 'depressogenic' now than it was when these elderly cohorts passed through the peak risk period for depression) may also be operating (Gallo, 1995). How these factors influence measurement of depression over the lifespan remains an area of active research, but investigators should be cognizant of these issues when designing studies and interpreting results of studies of psychopathology in the population.

IMPLICATIONS FOR THE MEASUREMENT OF DEPRESSION OVER THE LIFESPAN

Epidemiologic research suggests that the expression of depression changes both quantitatively (severity, magnitude) and qualitatively (characterization, correlates, precursors, consequences) over the life course. It has been argued that it would be invalid 'to argue that the disorder changes simply because it failed to match the threshold required for the formal diagnosis' (Andrews et al., 2007). That may be true under a static view of psychopathology, but under a developmental framework it is permissible and even expected that the nature, the presentation, and subsequently the measurement, of depression changes over the life course, a notion that is commonly accepted in the study of psychopathology in children and adolescents (Hudziak et al., 2007). The DSM criteria for major depression are applied uniformly to all periods of development, and thus one would expect that the measurement error inherent in applying those criteria to also change. Due to the influence of age on variability of presentation of psychopathology at early and later periods of the life course, dimensional conceptualizations of depression may be more appropriate and reliable compared to categorical ones during those

periods. For example, if heterogeneity of the category of depression 'caseness' increases with age (that is, the differentiation between case and non-case becomes less distinct), relying on dichotomous characterizations will reduce statistical power to identify true associations. Indeed, it has been argued that continuous measures of psychopathology are preferable to categorical ones simply because available statistical methods for evaluating associations *require* that the outcome be transformed into a continuum if it is not already (i.e., probability or log-odds) in order to evaluate the relative influence of multiple risk factors (i.e., multiple logistic regression) (Wheaton, 2007). However, it is not necessary to abandon the syndromic, categorical notion of depression in order to account for variability across age. A developmentally informed categorization of depression would take into account variation in typical signs and symptoms across the lifespan. The concept of 'depression without sadness' in later life, described by Gallo and Rabins (1999), is a prime example of using epidemiologic research and the developmental framework to inform the conceptualization of depression syndrome across various developmental periods (Gallo and Rabins, 1999).

Irony and measurement of depression

Irony is characterized by a contrast between what is expected and what is observed, and the simultaneous acceptance as both as legitimate (Gray, 1960). Irony may be a useful framework for understanding the discrepancy between various and changing etiologic factors for depression over time and the need to preserve continuity of measurement of over the life course.

What does it mean to be a 'case' of depression as assessed by the Diagnostic Interview Schedule or any other diagnostic measure in terms of the causal nature of this condition? To be a case of tuberculosis or myocardial infarction implies a set of known etiologies (e.g., *Mycobacterium tuberculosis* or blockage of a blood vessel, respectively) that are common to all cases and are relatively proximal to the condition. In contrast, depression 'caseness' does not imply any specific etiology, and in fact often suggests the interaction of multiple potentially distinct causal pathways. This quality of ironic deception – that depression cases that appear identical in symptomology can be unrelated etiologically – is a useful heuristic for conceptualizing measurement of depression over the life course and across demographic groups.

One response to the multifaceted etiology of depression over the lifespan has been the development of subgroup-specific measures. For example, the development of the Geriatric Depression Scale was an attempt to better identify depression among older adults (Yesavage et al., 1983), and, as discussed above, there are now screening scales available for use specifically during the post-natal period to assess post-partum depression (Boyd et al., 2005). However, the fact that depression has multiple causes implies that tailoring measurement strategies to different 'types' of depression over the life course (e.g., post-partum depression, vascular depression) is unwarranted. Depression cases at age 40 are just as etiologically diverse as those that occur during other periods of life, and it may be that the experience of depression later in life is influenced by previous episodes. Thus, having different measures of depression for different life events or stages disrupts continuity of measurement without providing any advantage in terms of being more specifically related to an etiologic model.

Another example of ironic deception in measurement of depression is the

tension between validity (e.g., concordance between diagnosis and 'true' case status) and reliability (e.g., repeatability) of this diagnosis over time (Faraone and Tsuang, 1994). As discussed earlier, there is no 'gold standard' in psychiatry with which to compare diagnostic assessments against in order to determine how the proximity of a diagnosis to the 'truth'. Relative to a clinical assessment (the 'lead standard' of psychiatric categorization), the DIS has relatively high specificity (ranging between 80 to 98 per cent) and only moderate sensitivity (ranging from 27 to 92 per cent) (Eaton et al., 2000, 2007a), indicating that this instrument is successful at identifying 'true' non-depressed individuals as such, but often misclassifies 'true' cases of depression as non-depressed. In general, reliability is argued to be a pre-requisite for validity, but in the absence of a gold standard it is unclear how that relationship operates or should be measured. In one of the few studies of its kind, Rice and colleagues (1992) demonstrated that the concordance for *lifetime* major depressive disorder over a six-year period was only 74 percent, although the reliability increased in a graded fashion according to severity of the condition as indicated by number of symptoms at baseline (Rice et al., 1992). Faraone and Tsuang (1994) argued that an unreliable diagnosis, such as depression, can still display characteristics of validity (e.g., familial aggregation), and suggest that alternate methods of assessing validity, such latent class analysis may be more appropriate for understanding the imperfect overlap between 'true' depression status and diagnosis (Faraone and Tsuang, 1994).

Current measures of depression are driven by atheoretical descriptive phenomenonology, as discussed above, and as a result have an ironic quality because they apply to a phenomenon that has multiple, distinct, and potentially unrelated etiologies that vary across individuals and within individuals over time, and these measures describe this phenomenon fairly consistently despite the differing ways in which it arises. In this sense, two mutually exclusive qualities of depression co-exist: it is a phenomenon that, in part, is understood by sociologists, clinicians, geneticists, philosophers, etc., as an experience that has certain qualities and causes, many of which do not overlap across these disciplinary groups; and yet it is also a phenomenon whose primary descriptive symptom characteristics – melancholy, disruptions in behavior and social life – have changed very little over the centuries, despite major theoretical shifts in the social sciences and medicine.

Diagnostic and dimensional measurement of depression revisited

As discussed above, Figure 13.3 demonstrates two factors critical to the dimensional approach to measuring depression: (a) symptoms of depression occur at a non-zero rate among the group that does not qualify for the diagnosis of depression, and (b) there is no point in the distribution of depressive symptoms or a so-called cardinal symptom that clearly differentiates depressed from non-depressed groups. The fact that depressive symptoms are relatively continuously distributed in the population has several important implications for taxonomy, research, and clinicians (Horwitz, 2007; Schwartz, 2007; Wheaton, 2007), and has been an important consideration in the development of the latest version (version V) of the APA's *Diagnostic and Statistical Manual of Mental Disorders* which is due to be published in 2012 (Regier, 2007).

Psychiatric taxonomy has been the topic of heated debate for decades, and an exhaustive review of this literature is beyond the scope of this chapter. However, we will draw attention to the potential importance of a distinction articulated by Haslam (2003) between conceptualizing depression as a 'discrete' kind as opposed to a 'practical' kind (Haslam, 2003). To view depression as a discrete kind is to say that depression is categorically different (e.g., a discrete state) from non-depression. The difficulty with this position is that there is nothing specific to depression that makes it 'essentially distinct' from non-depression (i.e., specific genetic marker/family history or life event). In contrast, to view this phenomenon as a practical kind is to say that depression is a complete continuum, with no inherently non-arbitrary place to distinguish between depressed and non-depressed. Under this approach, a cut-point to distinguish between the two is made legitimate because there is some portion of the 'elevated symptom' group that is at increased risk of unwanted consequences (e.g., suicide, unemployment, health problems) relative to the 'low symptom' group.

The distinction between discrete and practical kinds has important implications for etiologic and epidemiologic investigations. For example, in order to generate an estimate of prevalence of any condition, which is the proportion of the population that meets case criteria, an investigator must apply some sort of mutually exclusive classification system to the population to determine the numerator. However, if depression is actually a practical kind (e.g., a continuous latent construct) then these estimates of prevalence will always be biased (Eaton et al., 2007a). Prevalence is used to determine need for health services, and thus biased estimates can substantially affect both the availability and economic cost of services. This distinction affects research expectations for the types of causal factors (and subsequently preventive strategies) likely to be most important for this condition. If depression is actually a continuous latent construct, then researchers should focus on identifying risk factors that would produce that type of distribution (e.g., additive model, accumulation of risk factors over time). In contrast, if depression is actually a discrete latent construct, then we should be looking for risk factors that would produce a corresponding type of distribution (e.g., unique events, clustering of risk factors at a given point in time) (Horwitz, 2007). This particular set of concerns, ranging from biased estimates to appropriate assumptions regarding prevalence and distribution at the population level, speak to the wider range of implications that the distinction between discrete and practical types of constructs has for the conceptualization and measurement of a whole range of concepts across the social sciences).

Finally, the distinction between understanding depression as a continuum (practical kind) versus a category (discrete kind) directly affects clinical practice. A clinician is ultimately faced with a dichotomous decision as to whether or not to treat a person they determine is experiencing depression. Under the assumption that depression is a continuum, there is no clear rationale for a clinician to decide to treat someone with five symptoms rather than someone with four, or to treat two individuals with the same symptoms differently. This is of course confounded by the reality that individuals experiencing depression have their own thresholds for seeking treatment, and this threshold may change over time. In this instance, as is the case with other psychopathology, measurement decisions related to cut scores have genuine clinical implications with regard to the provision of appropriate care. Ultimately, a decision regarding whether to treat depression must be made by both the individual seeking treatment, and

the provider (whether that person is a mental health specialist or not). Population studies of depression and other mental health conditions must be both responsive to the needs of health practitioners (e.g., they must provide guidance for evidence-based medical practice) while also flexible enough to develop and utilize measures that have limited usefulness regarding treatment decisions but may be more appropriate for studies of etiology. For example, latent class modeling of psychiatric symptoms assessed by instruments like the DIS can be used to determine the overlap and distinguishing features of forms of psychopathology that are often treated as distinct in clinical practice (i.e., anxiety and depression). Such analyses have demonstrated that most 'distinct' psychiatric diagnoses are largely explained by a clustering of internalizing and externalizing factors. (Krueger, 1999) Such research is useful in studies of etiology because (1) comorbidity of psychiatric conditions is the rule rather than the exception, and (2) there are few – if any – exposures that have been definitively isolated to specific disorders.

CONCLUSION

Research involving measurement of depression in the population must balance clinical relevance with the need to assess and document appropriately the natural history and varying expressions of depressive symptomology over the life course. Studies such as the Epidemiologic Catchment Area Project demonstrate the utility of linking psychiatrists and epidemiologists to design instruments appropriate for measuring complex phenomena such as depression. Clinical studies can inform such community-based research by conducting thorough examinations of the life histories of persons who experience depression, and by critically examining the evidence base behind the definitions, and differentiations, of clinical syndromes. Population researchers who aim to improve measurement instruments can inform clinical practice by exploring the predictors of trajectories of depression symptomology and by identifying targets for intervention. Consistent measurement of depression over the lifespan is critical to these efforts, as well as to maintaining a consistent language across clinical and research settings.

REFERENCES

Achenbach, T. M. (1982) *Developmental psychopathology*. New York: Wiley Press.

Alexopoulos, G. S. (2006) 'The vascular depression hypothesis: 10 years later', *Biological Psychiatry*, 60: 1304–05.

Alexopoulos, G. S., Abrams, R. C., Young, R. C. and Shamoian, C. A. (1988) 'Cornell scale for depression in dementia', *Biological Psychiatry*, 23: 271–84.

An, S. (2008) 'Antidepressant direct-to-consumer advertising and social perception of the prevalence of depression: Application of the availability heuristic', *Health Communications*, 23: 499–505.

Andrews, G., Brugha, T., Thase, M. E., Duffy, F. F., Rucci, P. and Slade, T. (2007) 'Dimensionality and the category of major depressive episode', *International Journal of Methods in Psychiatric Research*, 16: S41–S51.

Aneshensel, C. S., Clark, V. A. and Frerichs, R. R. (1983) 'Race, ethnicity and depression: A confirmatory analysis', *Journal of Personality and Social Psychology*, 44: 385–98.

Beck, C. T. and Gable, R. K. (2000) 'Postpartum depression screening scale: Development and psychometric testing', *Nursing Research*, 49: 272–82.

Boyd, R. C., Le, H. N. and Somberg, R. (2005) 'Review of screening instruments for postpartum depression', *Archives of Womens Mental Health*, 8: 141–53.

Cox, J. L., Holden, J. M. and Sagovsky, R. (1987) 'Detection of post-natal depression: Development of the 10-item Edinburgh postnatal depression scale', *British Journal of Psychiatry*, 150: 782–6.

Dohrenwend, B. P. and Dohrenwend, B. S. (1982) 'Perspectives on the past and future of psychiatric epidemiology', *American Journal of Public Health*, 72: 1271–9.

Eaton, W. W., Anthony, J. C., Gallo, J. J., Cai, G., Tien, A., Romanoski, A., et al. (1997) 'Natural history of diagnostic interview Schedule/DSM-IV major depression', *Archives of General Psychiatry*, 54: 933–99.

Eaton, W. W., Armenian, H., Gallo, J. J., Pratt, L. and Ford, D. E. (1996) 'Depression and risk for onset of type II diabetes: A prospective population-based study', *Diabetes Care*, 19: 1097–1102.

Eaton, W. W., Badawi, M. and Melton, B. (1995) 'Prodromes and precursors: Epidemiologic data for primary prevention of disorders with slow onset', *American Journal of Psychiatry*, 152: 967–72.

Eaton, W. W., Dryman, A., Sorenson, A. and McCutcheon, A. (1989b) 'DSM–III major depressive disorder in the community: A latent class analysis from the NIMH epidemiologic catchment area programme', *British Journal of Psychiatry*, 155: 48–54.

Eaton, W. W., Hall, A. L. F., MacDonald, R. and McKibben, J. (2007a) 'Case identification in psychiatric epidemiology: A review', *International Review of Psychiatry*, 19: 497–507.

Eaton, W. W., Kalaydjian, A., Scharfstein, D. O., Mezuk, B. and Ding, Y. (2007b) 'Prevalence and incidence of depressive disorder: The Baltimore ECA follow-up, 1981–2004', *Acta Psychiatrica Scandinavica*, 116: 182–8.

Eaton, W. W., Kramer, M., Anthony, J. C., Dryman, A., Shapiro, S. and Locke, B. Z. (1989a) 'The incidence of specific DIS/DSM–III mental disorders: Data from the NIMH epidemiologic catchment area program', *Acta Psychiatrica Scandinavica*, 79: 163–78.

Eaton, W. W., Muntaner, C., Smith, C., Tien, A. and Ybarra, M. (2004) 'Center for epidemiologic studies depression scale: Review and revision (CESD and CESDR)', in M. E. Maruish (ed.), *The use of psychological testing for treatment planning and outcomes assessment* (3rd edition). London: Lawrence Erlbaum, 363–77.

Eaton, W. W., Neufeld, K., Chen, L. S. and Cai, G. (2000) 'A comparison of self-report and clinical diagnostic interviews for depression: Diagnostic interview schedule and schedules for clinical assessment in neuropsychiatry in the Baltimore epidemiologic catchment area follow-up', *Archives of General Psychiatry*, 57: 217–22.

Eaton, W. W., Shao, H., Nestadt, G., Lee, B. H., Bienvenue, O. J. and Zandi, P. (2008) 'Population-based study of first onset and chronicity in major depressive disorder', *Archives of General Psychiatry*, 65: 513–20.

Fallon, T. and Schwab-Stone, M. (1994) 'Determinants of reliability in psychiatric surveys of children ages

6 to 12', *Journal of Child Psychology and Psychiatry*, 35: 1391–1408.

Faraone, S. V. and Tsuang, M. T. (1994) 'Measuring diagnostic accuracy in the absence of a "gold standard"', *American Journal of Psychiatry*, 151: 650–7.

Gallo, J. J. (1995) 'Epidemiology of mental disorders in middle age and late life: Conceptual issues', *Epidemiologic Reviews*, 17: 83–94.

Gallo, J. J., Anthony, J. C. and Muthen, B. O. (1994) 'Age differences in the symptoms of depression: A latent trait analysis', *Journal of Gerontology*, 49: 251–64.

Gallo, J. J., Armenian, H. K., Ford, D. E., Eaton, W. W. and Khachaturian, A. S. (2000) 'Major depression and cancer: The 13-year follow-up of the Baltimore epidemiologic catchment area sample', *Cancer Causes and Control*, 11: 751–8.

Gallo, J. J. and Rabins, P. V. (1999) 'Depression without sadness: Alternative presentations of depression in late life', *American Family Physician*, 60: 820–6.

Gray, J. C. (1960) 'Irony: A practical definition', *College English*, 21: 220–2.

Haslam, N. (2003) 'Kinds of kinds: A conceptual taxonomy of psychiatric categories', *Philosophy, Psychiatry and Psychology*, 9: 203–17.

Helzer, J. E. and Robins, L. N. (1988) 'The diagnostic interview schedule: Its development, evolution, and use', *Social Psychiatry and Psychiatric Epidemiology*, 23: 6–16.

Horwitz, A. V. (2007) 'Distinguishing distress from disorder as psychological outcomes of stressful social arrangements', *Health*, 11: 273–89.

Hudziak, J. J., Achenbach, T. M., Althoff, R. R. and Pine, D. S. (2007) 'A dimensional approach to developmental psychopathology', *International Journal of Methods in Psychiatric Research*, 16: S16–S23.

Jackson, S. W. (1990) *Melancholia and depression: From Hippocratic times to modern times,* Yale: Yale University Press.

Jackson, J. S., Torres, M., Caldwell, C. H., Neighbors, H. W., Nesse, R. M., Taylor, R. J., et al. (2004) 'The National Survey of American Life: A study of racial, ethnic, and cultural influences on mental disorders and mental health', *International Journal of Methods in Psychiatric Research*, 13: 196–207.

Kessler, R. C., Berglund, P., Demler, O., Jin, R., Koretz, D., Merikangas, K. R., et al. (2003) 'The epidemiology of major depressive disorder: Results from the National Comorbidity Survey replication (NCS–R)', *JAMA*, 289: 3095–105.

Knäuper, B. and Wittchen, H. U. (1994) 'Diagnosing major depression in the elderly: Evidence for response bias in standardized diagnostic interviews?' *Journal of Psychiatric Research*, 28: 147–64.

Kraemer, H. C. (2007) 'DSM categories and dimensions in clinical and research contexts', *International Journal of Methods in Psychiatric Research*, 16: S8–S15.

Krueger, R. F. (1999) 'The structure of common mental disorders', *Archives of General Psychiatry*, 56: 921–6.

Larson, S. L., Owens, P. L., Ford, D. E. and Eaton, W. W. (2001) 'Depressive disorder, dysthymia, and risk of stroke: Thirteen-year follow-up from the Baltimore epidemiologic catchment area study', *Stroke*, 32: 1979–83.

Latner, J. D., O'Brien, K. S., Durso, L. E., Brinkman, L. A. and MacDonald, T. (2008) 'Weighing obesity stigma: The relative strength of different forms of bias', *International Journal of Obesity*, 32: 1145–52.

Lincoln, K., Chatters, L. M., Taylor, R. J. and Jackson, J. S. (2007) 'Profiles of depressive symptoms among African Americans and Caribbean blacks', *Social Science and Medicine*, 65: 200–13.

Link, B. G., Phelan, J. C., Bresnahan, M., Stueve, A. and Pescosolido, B. A. (1999) 'Public conceptions of mental illness: Labels, causes, dangerousness and social distance', *American Journal of Public Health*, 89: 1328–33.

McPherson, S. and Armstrong, D. (2006) 'Social determinants of diagnostic labels in depression', *Social Science and Medicine*, 62: 50–8.

Murphy, J. M. (2002) 'Symptom scales and diagnostic schedules in adult psychiatry' in M.T. Tsuang and M. Tohen, (eds) *Textbook in psychiatric epidemiology* (2nd edition). New York: Wiley-Liss.

Narrow, W. E., Rae, D. S., Robins, L. N. and Regier, D. A. (2002) 'Revised prevalence estimates of mental disorders in the united states: Using a clinical significance criterion to reconcile 2 surveys' estimates', *Archives of General Psychiatry*, 59: 115–23.

Newmann, J. P., Engel, R. J. and Jensen, J. E. (1991) 'Changes in depressive–symptom experiences among older women', *Psychology of Aging*, 6: 212–22.

Newmann, J. P., Klein, M. H., Jensen, J. E. and Essex, M. J. (1996) 'Depressive symptom experiences among older women: A comparison of alternative measurement approaches', *Psychology and Aging*, 11: 112–26.

Phelan, J. C., Link, B. G. and Dovidio, J. F. (2008) 'Stigma and prejudice: One animal or two?' *Social Science and Medicine*, 67: 358–67.

Pratt, L. A., Ford, D. E., Crum, R. M., Armenian, H. K., Gallo, J. J. and Eaton, W. W. (1996) 'Depression, psychotropic medication, and risk of myocardial infarction: Prospective data from the Baltimore ECA follow-up', *Circulation*, 94: 3123–9.

Robins, L. N. and Regier, D. A. (eds) (1990) *Psychiatric disorders in America: The epidemiologic catchment area study*. New York: Free Press.

Regier, D. A. (2007) 'Dimensional approaches to psychiatric classification: Refining the research agenda for DSM-V, an introduction', *International Journal of Methods in Psychiatric Research*, 16: S1–S5.

Regier, D. A., Myers, J. K., Kramer, M., Robins, L. N., Blazer, D. G., Hough, R. L., et al. (1984) 'The NIMH epidemiologic catchment area program: Historical context, major objectives, and study population characteristics', *Archives of General Psychiatry*, 41: 934–41.

Rice, J. P., Rochberg, N., Endicott, J., Lavori, P. W. and Miller, C. (1992) 'Stability of psychiatric diagnoses: An application to the affective disorders', *Archives of General Psychiatry*, 49: 824–30.

Robins, L. N. (1989) 'Diagnostic grammar and assessment: Translating criteria into questions', *Psychological Medicine*, 19: 57–68.

Robins, L. N., Wing, J., Wittchen, H. U., Helzer, J. E., Babor, T. F., Burke, J., et al. (1988) 'The composite international diagnostic interview: An epidemiologic instrument suitable for use in conjunction with different diagnostic systems and in different cultures', *Archives of General Psychiatry*, 45: 1069–77.

Schaffer, D., Fisher, P., Dulcan, M. K., Davies, M., Piacentini, J., Schwab-Stone, M. E., et al. (1996) 'The NIMH diagnostic interview schedule for children version 2.3 (DISC-2.3): Description, acceptability,

prevalence rates, and performance in the MECA study', *Journal of the American Academy of Child and Adolescent Psychiatry*, 35: 865–77.

Schwartz, S. (2007) 'Distinguishing distress from disorder as psychological outcomes of stressful social arrangements: Can we and should we?' *Health*, 11: 291–9.

Stein, G. and van den Akker, O. (1992) 'The retrospective diagnosis of postnatal depression by questionnaire', *Journal of Psychosomatic Research*, 36: 67–75.

Stuber, J., Meyer, I. and Link, B. (2008) 'Stigma, prejudice, discrimination and health', *Social Science and Medicine*, 67: 351–57.

Thompson, R., Bogner, H. R., Coyne, J. C., Gallo, J. J. and Eaton, W. W. (2004) 'Personal characteristics associated with consistency of recall of depressed or anhedonic mood in the 13-year follow-up of the baltimore epidemiologic catchment area survey', *Acta Psychiatrica Scandinavica*, 109: 345–54.

Tourangeau, R. and Yan, T. (2007) 'Sensitive questions in surveys', *Psychological Bulletin*, 133: 859–83.

Whaley, A. L. and Geller, P. A. (2003) 'Ethnic/racial differences in psychiatric disorders: A test of four hypotheses', *Ethnicity and Disease*, 13: 499–512.

Wheaton, B. (2007) 'The twain meet: Distress, disorder, and the continuing conundrum of categories', *Health*, 11: 303–19.

Yesavage, J. A., Brink, T. L., Rose, T. L., Lum, O., Huang, V., Adey, M., et al. (1983) 'Development and validation of a geriatric depression screening scale: A preliminary report', *Journal of Psychiatric Research*, 17: 37–49.

14

Description and Discovery in Socio-spatial Analysis: The Case of Space Syntax

Bill Hillier and Noah Raford

INTRODUCTION

It is commonly acknowledged that the human habitat is becoming an increasingly urban one. This is a process which has been at work in fits and starts for most of human history. In antiquity, for example, the largest city in the world was Athens, Greece, with a population of 235,000–300,000 citizens and slaves (Chandler, 1987). Rome later eclipsed Athens as the Western world's largest city. Although both ultimately declined in both size and importance, these urban centres possessed all the basic social and physical components that would characterise urban life for the next 2,500 years – components such as increased population density, monumental public buildings, craft specialisation, education in the arts and sciences, formalised and non-family based social interaction,

centralised food storage and distribution, and a complex infrastructure of roads, waterways and communication networks (Childe, 1952).

This process of centralisation and complexification of human society has intensified and accelerated over time. Nearly 60 per cent of the world's population will live in or around a city in 2030, a number estimated to be nearly five billion people (United Nations Population Division, 2008). Contemporary world cities such as London, New York, and Tokyo, for example, as well as a host of others such as Lagos, Mumbai, or Sao Paolo, have become 'megacities', places with over 10 million inhabitants, both locally diverse countless ways and globally connected through a complex web of cultural, material and financial exchange (Hall, 1984; Sassen, 2001). Commensurate with these physical shifts are a range of profound social and cultural changes which are related to urbanisation. These include changes to life variables such as family size, life space, and education rates, as well a host of less tangible outcomes such as language, political participation, and social complexity. The city, in both physical and social terms, has become the main locus of human life.

Amidst these changes, politicians, policy makers, planners, architects, and consumers are making a range of choices about the shape of our environment that will have profound and long-lasting effects on both the social and physical fabric of the city. By their very nature, changes to the physical structure must be long lasting; things like road building and property development are expensive, large, and durable. Social change, although perhaps moving at a faster rate, is no less complex and long lasting. Yet despite the profound changes we are already facing in today's urban environments, not to mention the complexities and uncertainties of tomorrow's cities, very little effort has been made to systematically study how these physical and social changes are intertwined, and how the choices of today will affect the individuals and societies of tomorrow who will forced to use them.

Why is this the case? In this chapter we argue that there is a gap between social theory and spatial design, and that the inability of contemporary theory to join them is not a function of their lack of relationship, but instead a function of our lack of ability to measure them properly and thus construct evidence-based theories and testable hypotheses. The gap between space and society, in other words, is a measurement challenge first and foremost. We describe this challenge by outlining how contemporary urban sociologists have conceptualised this link, then we introduce the development of space syntax theory as a means of first measuring space in and

of itself (that is, as an objective, empirical entity) and second, using measurement to generate new insights into social theory *vis-a-vis* a process known as *configurational analysis*. We then offer space syntax theory as a theory of socio-spatial measurement, linking objective spatial layouts with social processes through an objective platform of empirical measurement. We propose that such a platform enables a new examination of the problem of space in society, or society in space, through empirical study of real world phenomena, in a way that creates the possibility for surprising outcomes and new theoretical insights. We then compare this research process with traditional Popperian approaches, as well as contemporary approaches to generative social science, and then close by arguing that space syntax provides a platform for overcoming the problem of measurement, with important consequences for the future of urban environments.

THE PROBLEM OF MEASUREMENT (OR THE LACK THEREOF) IN SOCIETY AND SPACE

'Form poses a problem which appeals to the utmost resources of our intelligence, and it affords the means which charm our sensibility and even entice us to the verge of frenzy. Form is never trivial or indifferent; it is the magic of the world' (Chermayeff, 1982). Ratio, proportion and measure, embodied through the study of geometry, are at the heart of architecture and urban design. These principles were found to be so important in antiquity that they were often imbued with philosophical and cosmological significance. Vitrivius, for example, explicitly linked the proportions found in nature to ideal proportions in buildings, a concept later visualised by Da Vinci's in his famous

'Vitruvian Man'. This drawing, considered by many to be a representation of the highest Renaissance ideals of order, balance and proportion, is thought to propose an ideal relationship between humanity, God, and the universe at large, *vis-a-vis* the measures and proportions of the human body. Other examples include Blake's iconic painting of a bearded, bemuscled Creator kneeling over the sphere of the Earth and wielding a large golden compass ('The Ancient of Days'), or Le Corbusier's contemporary 'Modular', a more secular attempt to link human and natural proportion to an ideal sociology through architecture and urban form.

Measurement then, as expressed through the geometric aspects of architecture, has always been an important link between the physical world of human design and the metaphysical world of social, political, and cosmological significance. It would be natural to expect then, that given the importance and ubiquity of this connection, as well as the increasing sense of urgency stemming from ever accelerating urbanisation, there would be a clear understanding and commonly accepted understanding of the concepts of 'space' and 'society', and that the linkage between the two would have been well theorised, measured, and tested by now.

Surprisingly this is not the case. There are indeed enormous amounts of scholarship on both architectural and social theory individually, as well as a few significant attempts to link them. But beyond commonsense and accumulated practical experience about how they are connected and affect each other, there is little evidence of real substance upon which reliable theory could rest.

Take urban design, for example. In his review of urban design theory over the last 50 years, Cuthbert (2007) objects that 'urban design is self-referential and neither informed by, nor committed to, any external authority in intellectual terms'. He concludes that 'to be scientific, a discipline must have either a real or theoretical object of enquiry', and that contemporary urban design theory has neither. His review of definitions of urban design concludes that nearly all of its popular definitions have nearly no level of refutability, 'the mark of insignificant theory'.

Urban sociology offers little more hope, at least with regards to a coherent and testable theory of space and society. Many of sociologist's brightest thinkers dismiss the idea that studying space on its own is even possible or desirable, as would be necessary to identify the relationship between one independent variable and another the manner necessary for testing hypotheses. Anthony Giddens is exemplary in this regard when he writes, '… to suppose that space has its own intrinsic nature … is logically questionable and empirically unfruitful. Space is not an empty dimension along which social groupings become structured, but has to be considered in terms of its involvement in the constitution of systems of interaction. … in human geography spatial forms are always social forms.' (1984: 198)

It might be reasonably expected that an increasingly self-conscious society, driving headlong towards a more urban future and aware of the high-cost risk of errors that led, for example, to the early demolition of much social housing in the 1960s and 1970s, might have provided the stimulus for collaborations to try and find answers to these questions. This is not the case, and even the most simple questions posed by designers, such as, 'will this work for these people?' or 'is this solution better than that in this context?' actually conceal far reaching questions about the relations between spatial patterning and social outcomes to which answers have rarely been sought, let alone found.

In the absence of testable propositions linking spatial design with social outcomes, sociologists have abandoned the question of space, while spatial practitioners and theorists have practically abandoned the goals of science. What we find instead is that at any given time a number of popular, theory-like propositions may exist which link spatial forms to social outcomes, but that these ideas are almost totally untested, and thus go on virtually unchallenged, and we find that some of their proponents are even adverse to the very idea of testing them. Most such ideas emerge fully formed (or half-baked, depending on one's perspective) from the general background of ideas and beliefs fashionable at the time, gaining popularity based upon the influence of their main proponents, exerting influence over building and development for a period of time, only to be replaced by some other quasi-theory which rises in fashion due to whatever other reason it may become popular. Although seemingly unrelated to the world of Popperian theory, evidence, and hypothesis, such trends can nonetheless wield tremendous power and often carry with them a force associated with well tested paradigmatic ideas in science or dogmatic faith in religion or political ideologies.

Some examples; in the second half of the 20th century it was widely believed that breaking large residential developments up into small inward looking courtyards or piazzas would promote stronger local communities, that lower population densities would lessen crime and social malaise, that open plan schools would support child-centred learning, and even that public open spaces with 'good enclosure' would be successful and well used. These ideas, often presented as solutions to past problems, were later found to not only fail in their original goals, but even worse, to create new problems and perpetuate old challenges (Hillier, 1988). Residential developments shaped by the idea of enclosure, for example, turned out to be overly fragmented and cut off from the public realm and shared the fate of others in being pulled down or radically redesigned (Hillier et al., 1983). Ideas about density and crime are changing dramatically in response to new concepts in urban design, and it has been found that higher density, mixed used developments are often more safe than the suburban cul-de-sacs purported to be the solution to urban crime (Haughey, 2005; Harries, 2006; Hillier and Sahbaz, 2007). Open plan schools and the child-centred learning they were associated with are also under fierce attack, and open spaces, such as Trafalgar Square, have been radically improved by redesigning them to integrate into the urban area and its movement patterns, at the cost of a reduction in enclosure. All of these examples are particularly interesting as they seemed self evident at the time to their advocates and informed design practice over an extended period, even their evidence-base was always poor to non-existent. In the absence of hypothesis testing and experimental evidence we are often forced to learn the hard way, through direct experience paid for in years of bad decisions and lost opportunity.

The lack of understanding between space and society is not for lack of effort. On the contrary, the 20th century saw the emergence of many of the 'founding fathers' of urban social theory, most of who sought to theorise and test the relationship between urban spatial form (or architectural form) and social process such as family relations, community participation, migration patterns, crime and criminality, and other such topics (Tonnies, 1887; Simmel, 1908, 1950; Wirth, 1938; Durkheim, 1933). These thinkers indeed produced much of the theory that is taught to this day, laying down the foundations of not only urban sociology, but much of social science as we now know it. Efforts have only intensified in the last 25 years, marked by a series of seminal texts which are social theoretical and focus on such questions as the nature and future of cities, and the relation between human societies and their spatial form, for example Lefebvre (1974), Sennett (1970, 1977), Harvey (1973, 1996), Soja (1989, 1996, 2001), Castells (1996), to name only the most influential.

For many, these city-centred books have formed the cutting edge of reflection on a changing society. While these texts may offer important insights into and commentary on urban social life, many of which share a background in the Marxist critique of capitalism, in general they are mostly aimed at the macro level of the changing economic and social processes within which built environments are formed, and their implications for our experience of the city, and thus rarely engage the levels of resolution at which built environment professionals intervene in the real world. Their relevance to design-level theories tends then to be more contextual than substantive, and their reliance on testable hypothesis and empirical falsification is sparse, if extant at all.

As a result, urban sociology has been unable to provide the kind of guidance needed by design and planning professionals in their daily work, while design and planning theory has been of little value for urban social theory in its quest to understand the unfolding of the modern world. The two disciplines have drifted apart and we find contemporary architectural and urban theory concerning itself mostly with questions of form and aesthetics, while contemporary urban sociology has turned away from the early theoretical ambition of its founding fathers to understand the relations between social morphology and settlement form and towards a more exclusive focus on the study of the changing characteristics and spatial distributions of urban populations, and the range of experience and problems they engender, such as the inter-relation of ethnic or socio-economic groups.

The later shift to a more limited point of view in urban sociology is perhaps best summarised by Peter Saunders (2007) in his book *Social Theory and the Urban Question*, in which he writes:

> Despite their very different approaches and concerns, Weber, Durkheim and Marx and Engels all came to very similar conclusions as regards the analysis of urban questions. All agreed that the city played a historically specific role in the development of western capitalism, but they all agreed that once capitalism has become established, the city ceased to be a theoretically significant category of analysis. This was because it was no longer the expression and form of a new mode of production (Marx), or because it ceased to be the basis of human association and social identity (Weber), or because it no longer corresponded to the geographical boundaries of the division of labour (Durkheim). ... The city, in other words, was not seen as a significant object of study in its own right, and urban questions were addressed only insofar as they could contribute to an understanding of certain processes associated with the development of modern capitalism. (p. 249)

He adds in his preface that: '...each of these different approaches to urban sociology has foundered on the attempts to fuse a theory of specific social processes with an analysis of spatial forms. The conclusion ... is that these two questions are, with one minor exception [which Saunders calls the 'social significance of space' which he suggests is of very limited interest] distinct and mutually exclusive'. Others support this sentiment. Gidden's perspective has already been introduced, but Soja is equally clear:

> ... a key first step in recognizing a socio-spatial dialectic is to recognise that physical space has been a misleading epistemological foundation upon which to analyze the concrete and subjective meaning of human spatiality ... Space in itself may be primordially given, but

the organization, and meaning of space is a product of social translation, transformation, and experience. (Soja, 1989: 79–80)

So is Soja's mentor, Lefebvre:

instead of uncovering the social relationships (including class relationships) that are latent in spaces, instead of concentrating our attention on the production of space and the social relationships inherent in it ... we fall into the trap of treating space 'in itself', as space as such ... and so fetishize space in a way reminiscent of the old fetishism of commodities where ... the error was to consider 'things' in isolation, as 'things in themselves'. (Lefebvre, 1974: 90)

If these authors are right then the prospect of finding useful linkages between social theory and the spatial and physical form of the built environment seem bleak, since they are essentially arguing that no such relation exists.

In this chapter we argue the contrary position; that there is indeed an examinable connection between society and space, and that to engage in its investigation is fundamentally a problem of measurement and description, and how one deals with this problem of measurement is the key to understanding both modern urban design practice and modern social theory.

We therefore suggest that the missing ingredient linking physical form and social theory is measurement, and that if appropriate methods of measurement were found, they would enable us to create a more rigorous testing platform upon which the key questions of urban sociology could be addressed.

We suggest that through the development of space syntax theory, we have taken an important step in this direction, laying the groundwork for a unified, evidence-based theory of space and society which could improve our understanding of what society is and how it works, as well as simultaneously translating these insights

into an actionable, decision-relevant format for urban designers and policymakers.

The following section explores what the space syntax measurement platform looks like and what it suggests for urban social theory.

SPACE OR SOCIETY FIRST?

The question about society and its spatial form, in whatever mode or format it is posed, offers a fundamental choice. It can either be approached from society to space, or from space to society, that is by working from social theory towards the spatial environment, or from the spatial environment towards social theory. To most social scientists it has always seemed self-evident that we must take the former route, since it is surely society that determines space and not space that determines society. The approach to the city that this generates is one of trying to see the spatial environment as the spatial *output*, and so as the *by-product*, of social, economic and perhaps cognitive processes. The 'society-first' assumption might reasonably be called the *spatiality paradigm*, since it does not question the idea the link from society to space should be sought through an examination of the *spatiality* of social processes. This is clearly the underlying assumption of the cutting edge texts from Lefebvre, Harvey, Soja, Castells and others that we referred to earlier, which are in all cases attempts find the city and its space as the product of much wider processes of economic and social change.

In this context, attention to spatial patterns without reference to the social processes creating those patterns is to turn away from the reasons for studying space. By turning space itself into an object of thought in its own right there is, according to the protagonists of the *spatiality paradigm*, a danger of falling into precisely the western centred, overly abstracted, unselfconscious, asymmetric view of the social universe of which the principle strands of the spatiality paradigm offer a fundamental critique. Studying the forms of the material world other than in the light of their social causes seems to be to take a step back into the western darkness. For writers like Soja and Harvey (among others), this reason for the exclusion of real space from the agenda is quite explicit. Both started their academic careers as part of the 'quantitative revolution' of the 1960s, which saw the quantification of spatial patterns as part of a move towards a universal scientific geography set on a mathematical foundations. Both later rejected this view of space as denuding space of its essential interest: its social formation. For these authors, the idea that space in itself is a worthwhile object of study then risks a repetition of what these authors had come to see as the intellectual error of the 1960s (Soja, 2001).

The problem with paradigms, however, is that they prevent questions, even obvious questions, from being raised. In the case of the *spatiality paradigm* there are such obvious questions: are the spatial patterns through which social patterns are materialised then arbitrary? Does social life generate a endless proliferation of momentary patterns with no relation to each other, only to their social causes? Is space completely *amorphous*, and so *nothing*, until given shape by social agency? A moment's reflection suggests that this cannot be the case. If we say space reflects society, we mean that we can detect in space some describable pattern which has in some sense been generated by social forces. We cannot within the realm of human reason (which may of course be mistaken) both say this and expect these patterns to be arbitrary, since the very expectation of influence *implies* certain consistencies through which

similar social forces would produce similar patterns, and different social forces different patterns. Indeed, that this is the case is clearly a key, if unstated, assumption of most of the writers we have reviewed. If the patterns are arbitrary, it is not clear if it would be possible to argue in a coherent way that space was being shaped by society. As argued in *The Social Logic of Space* (Hillier and Hanson, 1984) for there to be a *social logic* of space, there must in the first instance be a some kind of *logic of space* on which this can be built.

To understand the space of social phenomena, then, we must also investigate the 'space of space'. Without this, the spatiality paradigm seems to have two consequences, one practical and the other theoretical. Practically speaking, the outcome is the paradigmatic exclusion of *real space* from the *theoretical* agenda, even when it is part of the *empirical* agenda, and this would in itself deter engagement between social theory and those who create our built environment. The theoretical consequence is that the fundamental pre-occupation of the founding fathers with the possible *agency* of spatial transformation in social morphology, and so an independent role in creating the society–space nexus, is more or less excluded from thought.

It was these reflections that led, in the early 1980s, to an attempt to turn the question round, and re-establish the theoretical links between the spatial and social worlds that had been so influential in setting the foundations of modern social theory (Hillier and Hanson, 1984). The idea was to look at the society–space relationship 'space first', by examining the patterns of *real space* found in the built environment and asking in what sense these could be seen to be the outcome of social and economic processes. This approach was called *space syntax*, to emphasise its initial focus on real space, and this has now grown into a research community of several hundred worldwide, supporting a biannual symposium attracting over 250 papers per conference (www.spacesyntax.org), as well as spin-out companies applying the method to real projects.

What follows will be a brief overview of the space syntax theory of space and its social embedding, with special attention given to the importance of measurement as a key to unlock their critical interrelationship. Readers seeking a more thorough recent introduction could refer to (Hillier and Vaughan, 2007) written for a social science audience, (Hillier, 2006) written for an architectural audience, or (Hillier, 2007) written for a cognitive science audience.

SPACE SYNTAX AS A THEORY OF SOCIO-SPATIAL DESCRIPTION

There was a major problem in the space syntax research programme right from the start: how to *describe* the difference between one spatial pattern and another. This first came to light through trying to characterise the differences in the space patterns of the social housing estates of the 1960s and 1970s, some of which were already beginning to show signs of precipitate decline – and so presented a challenge to socio-spatial thought – and ordinary urban space patterns based on networks of streets. In research terms, it was clear that if spatial and social patterns were to be compared, then the spatial variable had to be controlled. The problem of *spatial description* was fundamental.

In fact the lack of means to describe the familiar and common patterns of space that structure our built environment reflects a very much deeper difficulty, one to do with the nature of human minds and how we occupy the world and move about

in it: there is no language to describe the difference between one pattern of space and another. Language has terms that deal precisely with spatial relations involving at most three entities, for example, the English prepositions such as *between*, *inside*, *beyond*, and *through* are all terms which describe with some precision the relation of three things. Words like *among* describe more, but at a cost of less precision. In general, language lacks terms to describe complex patterns of spatial relations, and in fact complexes of relations of any kind.

The reason for this is that spatial relations, and relations in general, are so fundamental to how our 'embodied minds' exist in the world that they form part of the mental apparatus we think *with*, rather than *of*. In this sense space is analogous to language. When we speak or hear we think *of* the words, but *with* the syntactic and semantic rules that allow us to form words into meaningful sentences. It is this unconscious understanding of patterns that make speaking and hearing possible. Space is the same. We deal with complex spatial patterns *competently* but *intuitively*, and, again as with language, we don't really understand how we do this. This opens up an interesting possibility. We can, as with linguistic science, study the complex patterns of space that have been produced in different social, economic, and cultural conditions, and the ways in which people use space, and through this try to expose the *structure* and cultural variability of what seems, *prima facie*, to be a human *language of space*.

Progress was made on the description problem by using the basic ideas of spatial relation built into language to create more general tools for describing and comparing forms of spatial complexity. This was called the *configurational* approach. Configuration was defined as *relations which take into account other relations* (as the prepositions do), and methods developed to measure the relations between each space in a complex and all the others, and in this way to assign 'configurational' values to individual spaces describing the links of each to all others. Core to this approach was the construction of new objects of spatial measurement, which have been many and varied over the years. Instead of relying upon the 'primary' measures of geometry such as length, width, height, proportion and ratio, which were found to be poorly connected to behaviour throughout the 1970s on environment and behaviour, the key insight in space syntax was to articulate the connectedness of space as a *network of relations*, which could be objectively measured using the mathematical tools of graph theory, network analysis, and topology.

The consideration of space as an objective network of relations, which could be measured quantitatively and expressed as a graph, was the breakthrough insight of early space syntax work. This insight drew inspiration from the mathematics of graph theory, which found that any system of elements which interact with each other could be represented by a mathematical object called a graph (Bollobás, 1979). A graph was composed of a collection of nodes and links, technically termed 'edges'. Thus, as summarised the interacting components of the system could be reduced to a set of nodes, and the interactions among the components are represented by edges, allowing for quantitative measurement of their relationships and position. Although this insight had its roots in structural sociology from the early 1970s, building on ideas dating back to the early 1950s (Freeman, 1977, 1979; Bavelas, 1948, 1950; Leavitt, 1951; Shimbel, 1953; Shaw 1954, 1964), it had received little attention by urban planners and social theorists up until this point. Network analysis has

become quite popular and useful in a range of other fields in the last 10 years (for an excellent review see Newman et al., 2006), including in the field of urban spatial measurement (Crucitti et al., 2006), but this was the first attempt within urban spatial analysis to consider the role of space as an independent variable. This opened the door for a more rigorous testing platform that was used for empirical falsification of the role of space in a range of social and anthropological questions.

An early example of the results of this approach was the discovery that the relative position of rooms within the spatial network of a building interior appeared to be strongly correlated with the social function of those rooms. Working with samples of vernacular houses it was also possible to use these formal techniques to show more general consistencies across cultures in the way in which space was used to express different social ideas. For example, the more segregated a space was with respect to all others in a dwelling, then the more strongly it tended to be defined as a special social category, and the stronger the rules governing its access and use. For example a 'front parlour' in the UK tradition was the least spatially integrated ground floor room in the house, and was rarely used, but it was also the best furnished and decorated, and housed the most important memorial items. Its position by the front door meant that it could be used to support formalised encounters, such as those involving difficult class relations, for example, when the vicar or the insurance man called. This tendency to segregate certain kind of spaces whose conceptual importance coincided with the rarity of their use, in its extreme form becomes the idea of the sacred, which is often expressed by positioning the most sacred objects, such as a religious altar, in the 'deepest space' from the entrance. These transcultural commonalities were later shown to be related to certain simple mathematical principles governing the effect on the shaping and placing of objects on ambient space (Hillier, 1996, 2002, 2007).

The *function* in building could now, for the first time, be given a clear *spatial* meaning. The function of a space was not simply a reflection of what went on in the space and the furnishings and equipment that supported the activity, but also of *configuration values* describing the positioning of the space with respect to all other spaces in the layout. By learning to measure the different ways in which spaces could be embedded in layout, and applying the measures to, say, samples of vernacular houses, it could be shown that social and cultural patterning was actually present in the plan of a house and its functioning, as well as in the minds of the inhabitants. Society could be found in the form of the artefact, and this could be expressed in a simple mathematical way (Hillier et al., 1987; Hanson, 1999).

Similar patterns between spatial configuration and social use were found at the larger urban scale. By treating individual streets and open spaces as nodes, and the connections between them as links, it was possible to measure the relative centrality and importance of any street within the network. This quantitative exploration revealed surprising regularities in spatial structure, which we termed *configurational inequalities*. Some streets, it was found, were consistently better connected and more central within the network of urban relationships than others. In fact the entire network itself seemed to display a compelling spatial logic, whereby a pattern of most accessible routes could usually be identified, linking together clusters of less connected, more isolated of streets. These relationships, it was further discovered, tended to form a generic pattern is most cities, a pattern

we termed the *deformed wheel*: a 'hub' of streets at or near the centre, strong 'spokes' reaching out towards the edges in all directions, and often part of the 'rim' on the edge of the settlement. Figure 14.2 shows the case of Nicosia within the walls.

These underlying spatial patterns seemed to compel a social interpretation. It was found, for example, that although the deformed wheel was a purely topological description of network shape, without any consideration of land use, urban zoning law, or social history, there was a remarkable correlation between topological centrality and certain forms of land use and economic activity. The most active streets and spaces in a settlement were to be found on the most central and accessible links, while the areas of lower accessibility and centrality (those at the interstices of the wheel) tended to be quieter residential areas. Aside from their descriptive utility, strong statistical evidence was found which linked configurational variables with other outcomes such as pedestrian and vehicle volume (Penn et al., 1998), retail and commercial land use location and value (Enström and Netzell, 2007; Matthews and Turnbull, 2007), legibility and wayfinding (Peponis et al., 1990; Weisman, 1981; Penn, 2003; Penn and Kim, 2004; Raford, 2006), pedestrian traffic and safety (Raford and Ragland, 2004, 2006), crime and social exclusion (Hillier, 2004; Hillier and Shabaz, 2005; Baran et al., 2007; Nubani and Wineman, 2005) and obesity and public health (Baran et al., 2008).

It was clear that the pattern brought to light by spatial analysis was also a social pattern, in that its *raison d'être* was to concentrate certain uses and certain activities in certain places, while dispersing and discouraging them in others. The deformed wheel as a measurable, configurational entity, thus functioned as a probabilistic device to generate and modulate the interface between the inhabitants of the settlement and the visitors and strangers with whom they shared a micro-economic interdependence.

This ability to analyse streets networks in terms that related to their social functioning then led to a discovery that, in its turn, led to a new social theory of the city. The discovery was that the spatial configuration of a street network was *in and of itself* a major factor – probably the major factor – in shaping movement flows. (Hillier et al., 1993; Hillier and Iida, 2005) This suggested that spatial configuration was in good part responsible for the ways in which patterns of human *co-presence* emerge in the network. Once this was clear, it also became clear that through its influence on movement flows and co-presence, the structure of the street network also shaped land use patterns (Hillier, 1996), in that movement-dependent land uses like retail would naturally migrate to locations which the network had made co-presence rich, while others, often including residence, would prefer the contrary. Once a shop went to a location, it would act as an attractor for more movement, and this would set in train multiplier effects through which the settlement would evolve into the *dual* form of a *foreground* network of linked centres, each scaled according to its position in the network, set into a *background* network of residential space (Hillier, 1999). The more integrated foreground, or global, network tended to take a *universal* form because it was generated by micro-economic activity, and other things that people do together, while the background, more localised and more segregated, network was much more strongly shaped by cultural factors, which would be different from one cultural region to another, and even within the same city (Hillier and Vaughan 2007).

THE EFFECTS OF MEASUREMENT ON SOCIAL THEORY: FORMING TESTABLE PROPOSITIONS ABOUT REAL SPACE

The invention of new ways of measuring space, as an empirical subject of study in and of itself, allowed for the creation of testable propositions which linked spatial patterns to social life. They satisfy our demand for *testable* propositions, since they make clear predictions about the relations between space and its use. But they are also theoretical propositions which link directly to social theory, both to the preoccupations of the *spatiality paradigm* and to the founding fathers preoccupations with the relations between spatial factors and social *morphology*.

The methodologies of space syntax and their associated social theory are now increasingly also used both to reformulate and address research questions about cities and to create a more rigorous and evidence based prediction of social outcomes from spatial forms at the design stage. Examples of research questions that have been addressed recently through space syntax include the spatial and social pathology of failing housing estates (Hillier, 1996; Hillier and Vaughan, 2007), the economic and social development of self-generated settlements (Hillier and Netto, 2002), the spatialisation of migration groups (Vaughan and Penn, 2006; Vaughan, 2007), the spatial definition of urban areas (Hillier and Vaughan, 2007), the spatial dynamics of work environments (Penn et al., 1999) and the micro-analysis of spatial patterns of urban crime (Hillier, 2004; Hillier and Shabaz, 2007).

The space syntax package of method and theory is also used on an expanding portfolio of real projects, not least through the UCL spin-out company Space Syntax Limited (www.spacesyntax.com). The application procedure involves first making a model of the urban area in which development is proposed, and testing it by directly observing existing movement and land use patterns, and correlating these with spatial patterns. To the degree that the model is able to account for the existing functional patterns, a tested model exists with which to generate and test conjectural solutions to the design problem in hand. In this sense, evidence based design can include both *site-specific* evidence provided by the context of a development and the theoretical evidence provided by the accumulation of studies. Once the tested model exists, candidate designs produced by built environment professionals can themselves be treated as testable propositions by inserting the proposed spatial pattern into the model and re-running the analysis to see how the proposed pattern works in the context of, and affects, the pattern of the surrounding area. Typically, a series of improving designs are explored, gradually converging on the pattern that most fulfils the social objectives of the design. The aim of this procedure is to set design more and more into the context of understanding of the *self-organising processes* which are pervasive in all cities, so that design can work with these processes rather than, as so often in recent history, under the influence of social ideologies masquerading as theory, against them.

The space syntax research agenda has had important theoretical implications for urban social theory. It has been seen how the space-society issue has long been formulated as one of the key questions in social geography, yet also one of the most elusive. In their 1997 reader *Space and Social Theory*, Benko and Strohmeyer identify at least 56 different areas where space was a significant category of thought. Crang and Thrift (2000) subsequently observe that, 'Space is the everywhere of modern thought. It is the flesh that flatters the bones of theory. It is an all purpose nostrum to be applied whenever things look sticky'.

Space syntax points a way out of this quagmire by offering an analytic theory of space and society, as well as a host of measurement techniques that can be used to test theoretical propositions against empirical phenomena. It suggests that space is inherently social in its nature, in that spatial configuration bounds or encourages the social activities which are likely to occur within it, and that society itself is inherently spatial. So strongly are these two concepts related, we argue, that society can be accurately described as an embedded space-time network, bound by and embodied in space and therefore subject to something akin to measurable sociospatial laws.

This proposition has several implications for social theory. First, we are compelled to the conclusion that cities, seen spatially, are strongly relational systems (perhaps we should say 'strongly configurational systems'), that is systems in which the relations of each element to all other are more important for the structure and functioning of the system than intrinsic or virtual properties of the elements themselves. (Hillier, 1999) Early social network researchers found that an individual's position within their social network strongly affects their level of influence and access to information (see Freeman, 1977 for a review of early studies). The same is true for spatial networks, and because most interaction is embedded in spatial networks, there may be important structural isomorphisms between them, in that the shape of one strongly influences the shape of the other. Second, it also suggests that space and society are 'dual systems', in the important sense that each seems to be made up of material events which take place in space-time, such as interactions and encounters, and informational entities such as the codes and conventions which seems to govern these material events locally. We might say that society has both hardware (interactions) and software (rules governing interaction), as do cities (buildings and the rules which connect them). We also suggest that space and society seem to be for the most part (in spite of utopias and ideal cities) emergent systems arising from distributed processes, rather than designed systems. Crucially, both space and society appear to be partly or even largely *nondiscursive*, in that human beings operate at least their local patterns competently, without being able to say what it is that they are doing, so that while each is the outcome of human activity, and is utilised by human beings in everyday life, analytically speaking we have at best an unclear idea what it is that we understand. Finally, this marriage suggests that both types of system seem, in spite of their bottom-up construction, to exhibit some degree of top-down as well as bottom-up functionality, in that just as, say, movement and land use patterns are functions of the overall structure of the urban grid, so individual social behaviours seem to be - though to a varying degree – functions of the overall pattern we call society.

This interpretation adds a new level of analytical rigour to Giddens' previous arguments linking space and society. Giddens (1984) has argued that social structures are virtual, or immaterial, entities, but they appear in space-time as concrete 'situated practices', that is as social behaviours and interactions that occur, as they must, in real space-time locations. Giddens' key spatial argument is that these virtual social structures are *produced* and even more importantly *reproduced* by being realised in space time. In other words, society may be 'virtual', but it only really exists and projects itself through time by being realised in dispersed space-time practices. So the pattern of situated practices is not itself the structure of society, but it is *through* dispersed situated practices that the virtual structure of society is made real for us and, more importantly, *reproduced*. Giddens makes – and is probably arguing from – an analogy with language. Language, he argues, exists in the same way. It is only by being used – that is projected into space-time by being spoken and written – that the virtual structure of language is perpetuated through generations. This is a simple, but very subtle argument, since it allows space to play a critical role in society without any whiff of the spatial mechanism or determinism that seems to terrorise sociology in the form of environmental determinism.

Space syntax provides the analytical theory and measurement methodologies which go beyond Giddens' notional connection by demonstrating real socio-spatial linkages in empirical phenomena. The difference allows for more fruitful investigation into the nature of society, as it manifests itself space and time. The hope of the space syntax paradigm is to contribute its own speciality – the study of space itself – to a more synthetic and less philosophically constrained inter-disciplinary effort to find clear formulations for these problems and so some prospect of better resolutions. Space syntax is not the opposite of the spatiality paradigm presented above, but its 'other half'. As such, it is the means by which the social study of space can engage fully both with its own theoretical development and also with the real world issues which await its attention.

IMPLICATIONS FOR THE PHILOSOPHY OF SCIENCE

There are also philosophical implications for measurement raised by this research agenda. At the beginning of space syntax research effort we attempted to take a strictly Popperian approach towards scientific inquiry, that is, the creation of theoretical ideas first and then the test of these ideas through empirical falsification. We rapidly found that most of our initial theories were wrong, however, and that the experiment we set up to test them lead instead to the creation of unexpected phenomena which undermined our understanding and so in time forced it to grow. This process began to take a path closer to that described by Hacking (1983), whereby the discovery of unexpected new phenomena through observation, experimentation, or simulation, precipitates a crisis of theory and leads to new directions of understanding. By basing our inquiry on a platform of extrinsic measurement, we found that our observations and simulations revealed unexpected 'created phenomena' which, over time, actually became the basis of our theory of measurement.

This process is similar to that emerging in other simulation-based generative social sciences, particularly that of agent-based modelling (Epstein, 2006). Agent-based models, for example, provide computational demonstration that a given series of local rules are in fact sufficient to generate some macrophenomena of interest. Does this kind of 'created phenomena' constitute explanation, not to mention proper theory? Epstein argues 'that demonstration is taken as a necessary condition for explanation itself,' and that, if you can't simulate it, you can't really explain it. Generative social sciences are therefore primarily *deductive*, in that they deduce theoretical propositions based on the measurement (and simulation) of real world phenomena.

In that they are primarily deductive, such approaches are also by necessity explicitly descriptive. Epstein suggests that, 'generative sufficiency is a necessary, but not sufficient condition for explanation' (2006).

This suggests that they ultimately fall short of final causal falsification in a way which would satisfy Popper. This does not imply they lack value for social science, however. The ability to describe a system in enough detail to accurately simulate it, as is done in space syntax through configurational analysis, provides a platform for formulating more rigorous theoretical proposition, as well as for comparing them to how well they correspond to empirical phenomena in the real world.

Such an approach towards theory, measurement, and understanding is a significant step closer to real science than what has existed historically in urban social theory. Real science, in this light, is all about being careful enough in the observation of the world, and clear enough in the way ideas about it are formulated, for those ideas to be proved wrong by the world. Science is not the imposition of abstract schemes of thought on the physical world, but the constant demolition such schemes of thought and their replacement with tentative and temporary alternatives.

Space syntax does not claim to be science – that is something to be achieved – but it does *aspire to* the standards of science by seeking to be sufficiently clear and consistent in its descriptions of what space is like, and sufficiently careful in its observations of space at work for tentative theoretical formulations to be proved wrong. When ideas have been shown to be wrong, then often it is protracted attention to the world at work, and the confrontation of unexpected and unexplained phenomena, that lead to the formulation of a new ideas which can then be clarified and tested (Hacking, 1983).

This more pragmatic view of how science works has interesting affinities with the philosophy of Deleuze. A guiding notion in Deleuze's work is *transcendental empiricism* (Deleuze, 1963). Defined in contradistinction to Kant's *transcendental idealism*, through which the mind imposes its categories on the world, Deleuze's concept means that the world with all is complexities and contradiction is the most fertile source for our thought. It is the world that leads us to move beyond the accepted conceptualisations which structure thought, and guide us to new concepts and new modes of thought. Deleuze's philosophy is usually thought of as being somehow antithetical to science, but with one more step it surely *is* science. In science, the source of new theoretical ideas is rarely simply abstract thought. More often it is the bringing to light of new phenomena which are inconsistent with our existing theoretical models, and so demand novel theoretical thought inspired by the intractability of the world to the abstractions we impose on it.

This has been exactly the case in the development of the space syntax research programme. By taking a 'measurement descriptive' approach to the society-space problem, we have found that a spatial analysis of society is not an alternative to the social analysis of space, but actually the *means to it*. To understand the space of different fields of human activity, we must first investigate the 'space of space'. By clarifying how space is *manipulable*, we can see how it is *manipulated*, and why it works for a *particular* social purpose. This is to say no more than that to understand what space is saying we must learn its language. Space has an active and structured engagement with social life, and without understanding this we cannot fully realise the theoretical promise of the social study of space. With a theorisation of the 'space of space' in place, we can both set up testable propositions for space creation, and link back to the founding fathers of social theory in their acknowledgement that space was a factor in human existence.

REFERENCES

Baran, P., Rodríguez, D., Khattak, A. (2008) 'Space syntax and walking in a new urbanist and suburban neighbourhoods', *Journal of Urban Design*, 13: 1.

Baran, Smith, and Toker (2007) 'The space syntax and crime: Evidence from a suburban community', Proceedings of the Sixth Space Syntax Symposium, Istanbul, 2007.

Bavelas A. (1948) 'A mathematical model for group structures', *Human Organization*, 7: 16–30.

Bavelas A. (1950) 'Communication patterns in task oriented groups', *Journal of the Acoustical Society of America*, 22: 271–82.

Benko and Stromeyer (1997) *Space and Social Theory: Interpreting Modernity and Postmodernity*. Blackwell.

Bollobás, B. (1979) *Graph theory: An introductory course*. New York/Berlin: Springer-Verlag.

Castells, M. (1996) *The rise of the network society*. Blackwell.

Chandler, T. (1987) *Four Thousand Years of Urban Growth: An Historical Census*. Lewiston, New York: St. David's University Press.

Chermayeff, S. (1982) *Design and the public good: selected writings*, Cambridge, MA: MIT Press.

Childe, G. (1952) *New light on the most ancient near east*. London.

Crang and Thrift (2000) *Thinking space*. London and New York: Routledge.

Crucitti, P., Latora, V. and Porta, S. (2006) 'Centrality measures in spatial networks of urban streets', Phys. Rev. E 73, 036125. Doi:10.1103/PhysRevE.73.036125.

Cuthbert, A. (2007) 'Urban design: Requiem for an era – review and critique of the last 50 years', *Urban Design International*, 12: 177–223.

Deleuze, G. (1963) *Kant's critical philosophy*. Trans. Hugh Tomlinson and Barbara Habberjam 1983: London: Althone Press.

Durkheim, E. (1933) *On the Division of Labor in Society*. New York: Macmillan.

Enström, R. and Netzell, O. (2007) 'Can space syntax help us in understanding the intraurban office rent pattern? Accessibility and rents in downtown Stockholm'. *The Journal of Real Estate Finance and Economics*, 36: 289–305.

Epstein, J. (2006) *Generative social science: Studies in agent-based computational modeling*. Princeton, NJ: Princeton University Press.

Freeman, L. C. (1977) 'A set of measures of centrality based on betweenness', *Sociometry*, 40: 35–41.

Freeman, L. C. (1979) 'Centrality in social networks: Conceptual clarification', *Social Networks*, 1: 215–39.

Giddens, A. (1984) *The Constitution of Society*. London: Polity Press.

Hacking, I. (1983) *Representing and Intervening*. Cambridge University Press.

Hall, P. (1984) *The World Cities*, 3rd edition. New York: St. Martin's Press.

Hanson, J. (1999) *Decoding Homes and Houses*. Cambridge University Press.

Harries, K. (2006) 'Property crimes and violence in United States: An analysis of the influence of population density', *International Journal of Criminal Justice Sciences*, 1, 2.

Harris, C. and Ullman, E. (1945) 'The nature of cities', *Annals of the American Academy of Political and Social Science*, 242: 7–17.

Harvey, D. (1973) *Social Justice and the City*. Baltimore: Johns Hopkins University Press.

Harvey, D. (1996) *Justice, Nature and the Geography of Difference*. Blackwell.

Haughey, R. (2005) *Higher-Density Development: Myth and Fact*. Washington, DC: ULI–the Urban Land Institute.

Hillier, B. (1988) 'Against enclosure', in N. Teymur, T. Markus and T. Wooley (eds) *Rehumanising Housing*. London: Butterworths. pp. 63–85.

Hillier, B. (1996) *Space is the Machine*. Cambridge University Press E-edition 2007, online at www.spacesyntax.com

Hillier, B. (1999) 'Centrality as a process', *Urban Design International*, 4: 107–27.

Hillier, B. (2002) 'Society seen through the prism of space', *Urban Design International*, 7: 3–4 22 pp.

Hillier, B. (2004) 'Can streets be made safe?', *Urban Design International*, 9: 31–45.

Hillier, B. (2006) 'The golden age for cities ? How we design cities is how we understand them', *Urban Design*.

Hillier, B. (2007) 'Studying cities to learn about minds', in C. Holscher, R. Conroy-Dalton and A. Turner (eds) *Space Syntax and Spatial Cognition* SFB/TR8 Universitata Bremen.

Hillier, B. and Burdett, R., Peponis, J. and Penn, A. (1987) 'Creating life: Or, does architecture determine anything?', *Architecture & Comportement/Architecture & Behaviour*, 3 (3): 233–50.

Hillier, B. and Hanson, J. (1984) *The Social Logic of Space*. Cambridge University Press.

Hillier, B. and Iida, S. (2005) 'Network effects and psychological effects: A theory of urban movement COSIT conference 2005', in A. Cohn and D. Mark (eds) *Spatial Information Theory Lecture Notes in Computer Science 3603*. Springer Verlag. pp. 473–90.

Hillier, B. and Netto, V. (2002) 'Society seen through the prism of space: Outline of a theory of society and space', *Urban Design International*, 7 (3–4): 181–203.

Hillier, B. et al. (1983) 'Space syntax: A new urban perspective', *Architects Journal*.

Hillier, B., Penn, A., Hanson. J., Grajewski, T. and Xu, J. (1993) 'Natural movement: Or configuration and attraction in urban pedestrian movement', *Environment & Planning B: Planning & Design*, 19: 29–66.

Hillier, B. and Shabaz, O. (2005) 'High resolution analysis of crime patterns in urban street networks: An initial statistical sketch from an ongoing study of a London borough', Proceedings of the Fifth Space Syntax Symposium, Delft, 2005.

Hillier, B. and Shabaz, O. (2007) 'Beyond hot spots; using space syntax to understand dispersed patterns of crime risk in the built environment'. Invited paper to conference on crime analysis at the Institute of Pure and Applied Mathematics, University of California at Los Angeles, January 2007.

Hillier, B. and Vaughan, L. (2007) 'The city as one thing', *Progress in Planning*, 67: 205–30.

Leavitt, H. J. (1951) 'Some effects of certain communication patterns on group performance', *Journal of Abnormal and Social Psychology*, 46: 38–50.

Lefebvre, H. (1974, 1991) *The Social Production of Space*. Tr. Nicholson-Smith D. Blackwell. Translated from *La Production de l'Espace*.

Matthews, J. and Turnbull, G. (2007) 'Neighborhood street layout and property value: The interaction of accessibility and land use mix', *Journal of Real Estate Finance and Economics*, 35.

Newman, M., Barabási, A. L. and Watts, D. (2006) *The Structure and Dynamics of Networks*. Princeton, NJ: Princeton University Press.

Nubani, L. and Wineman, J. (2005) 'The Role of Space Syntax in Identifying the Relationship Between Space and Crime', Proceedings of the Fifth Space Syntax Symposium, Delft, 2005.

Penn, A. (2003) 'Space syntax and spatial cognition: or why the axial line?', *Environment and Planning B: Planning and Design*, 35: 30.

Penn, A., Hillier, B., Banister, D. and Xu, J. (1998) 'Configurational modelling of urban movement networks', *Environment and Planning B: Planning and Design*, 25: 59–84.

Penn, A. and Kim, Y. (2004) 'Linking the spatial syntax of cognitive maps to the spatial syntax of the environment', *Environment and Behavior*, 36: 483.

Peponis, J., Zimring, C. and Choi, Y. (1990) 'Finding the building in wayfinding', *Environment and Behavior B*, 22: 555–90.

Raford, N. (2005) 'Pedestrian movement and the urban experience in fractured spatial systems: the case of

Boston, Massachusetts', *World Architecture: Special Issue on Space Syntax*, Shanghai, China, November 2005.

Raford, N. and Ragland, D. (2004) 'Space syntax: Innovative pedestrian volume modeling tool for pedestrian safety', *Transportation Research Record: Journal of the Transportation Research Board*, 1878.

Raford, N. and Ragland, D. (2006) 'Pedestrian volume modeling for traffic safety and exposure analysis: The case of Boston, Massachusetts', UC Berkeley Traffic Safety Center. Paper UCB-ITS-TSC-RR-2006-4. http://repositories.cdlib.org/its/tsc/UCB-ITS-TSC-RR-2006-4

Sassen, S. (2001) *The global city : New York, London, Tokyo*. Princeton, NJ: Princeton University Press.

Saunders, P. (2007) *Social Theory and the Urban Question*, 1st edition. London: Routledge.

Sennett, R. (1970) *The Uses of Disorder: Personal Identity and City Life*. New York.

Sennett, R. (1977) *The Fall of Public Man*. New York: Knopf.

Shaw, M. E. (1954) 'Group structure and the behavior of individuals in small groups', *Journal of Psychology: Interdisciplinary and Applied*, 38: 139–49.

Shaw, M. E. (1964) 'Communication networks', in L. Berkovitz (ed), *Advances in Experimental Social Psychology*. vol. 6. New York: Academic Press.

Shimbel, A. (1953) 'Structural parameters of communication networks', *Bulletin of Mathematical Biophysics*, 15: 501–07.

Simmel, G. (1908) *Soziologie*. Leipzig: Duncker & Humblot.

Simmel, G. (1950) *The Sociology of Georg Simmel*. Compiled and translated by Kurt Wolff, Glencoe, IL: Free Press.

Soja, E. (1989) *Postmodern Geographies: The Reassertion of Space in Critical Social Theory*. London: Verso.

Soja, E. (1996) *Thirdspace: Journeys to Los Angeles and Other Real-and-Imagined Places*. Cambridge, MA: Blackwell.

Soja, E. (2001) 'In different spaces: Interpreting the spatial organization of societies', Proceedings of the Third Space Syntax Symposium, Atlanta.

Tonnies, F. (1887) *Gemeinschaft und Gesellschaft*, Leipzig: Fues's Verlag, translated in 1957 as '*Community and Society*', now available from Transaction Publishers (1988).

United Nations Population Division (2008) *World Population Prospects, 2008*, accessed online at http://esa.un.org/unpp/index.asp

Vaughan, L. (2007) 'The spatial form of poverty in Charles Booth's London', *Progress in Planning*, 67 (3): 231–50.

Vaughan, L. and Penn, A. (2006) 'Jewish Immigrant Settlement Patterns in Manchester and Leeds 1881', *Urban Studies*, 43: 653–71.

Weisman, G. (1981) 'Evaluating architectural legibility: Wayfinding in the built environment', *Environment and Behavior*, 13: 189–204.

Wirth, L. (1938) 'Urbanism as a way of life', *American Journal of Sociology*, 44: 1–24.

Fundamental Issues in Measurement

15

Understanding the Intangibles of Measurement in the Social Sciences[1]

Madhu Viswanathan

A central theme of this handbook is to provide understanding of some of the intangibles of measurement. Intangible issues in measurement relate to aspects that have not been sufficiently articulated or form the implicit knowledge that experienced researchers may possess that has not been explicated. Some such intangibles may appear to be 'common sense' issues that may not be so common or make sense when carefully explored. In this chapter, some of the intangibles of measurement in the social sciences are discussed with a view to explicating the issues involved and providing direction for the design and use of measures and methods. The material in this chapter is reprinted or adapted from *Measurement Error and Research Design* (Viswanathan, 2005).

We begin with an overview of measurement and the measure development process.

The vast literature on measurement has had a statistical emphasis without sufficient elucidation of the nature of measurement error. In the view of the author, this is the central intangible issue in measurement that needs to be clarified and demystified. Therefore, this chapter provides a very detailed discussion of measurement error. Understanding measurement error provides a basis to then address some intangible issues in how measures are used in research design. We then contrast the continuum from physical to psychological measurement, with a view to explicating intangible issues relating to different types of measures and measurement approaches. We end with a broader discussion of intangibles relating to the assumptions of measurement, and the need to enrich approaches to measurement in the social sciences beyond what is easily measurable.

OVERVIEW OF MEASUREMENT AND MEASURE DEVELOPMENT

Measurement 'consists of rules for assigning symbols to objects so as to (1) represent quantities of attributes numerically (scaling) or (2) define whether the objects fall in the same or different categories with respect to a given attribute (classification)' (Nunnally and Bernstein, 1994: 3). This element of the definition emphasizes understanding what these attributes really mean, that is, fully understanding the underlying concepts being measured. Rules refer to everything that needs to be done to measure something, whether measuring brain activity, attitude toward an object, organizational emphasis on research and development, or stock market performance. Therefore, these rules include a range of things that occur during the data collection process, such as how questions are worded and how a measure is administered. Numbers are central to the definition of measurement for several reasons: (a) Numbers are standardized and allow communication in science, (b) numbers can be subjected to statistical analyses, and (c) numbers are precise. But underneath the façade of precise, analyzable, standardized numbers is the issue of accuracy and measurement error.

A number of steps have been suggested in the measure development process (Churchill, 1979; Gerbing and Anderson, 1988) that are adapted here (Figure 15.1). As in many stepwise processes, these steps are often blurred and iterative. These steps emphasize that traversing the distance from the conceptual to the operational requires a systematic process. Rather than consider a concept and move directly to item generation, and use of a resulting measure, the distance between the conceptual and the operational has to be spanned carefully and iteratively.

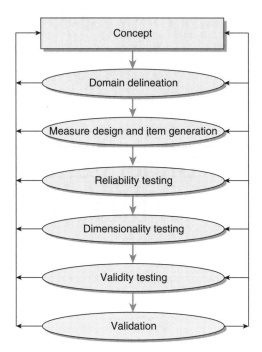

Figure 15.1   Steps in the measure development process.

The very idea of measurement suggests an important distinction between a concept and its measurement. Hence, the literature distinguishes between conceptual and operational definitions of *constructs* (i.e., concepts specifically designed for scientific study) (Kerlinger, 1986). Larger distances between the conceptual and the operational have at least two implications. As the distance increases, so, too, do measurement error and the number of different ways in which something can be measured. This is akin to there being several ways of getting to a more distant location, and several ways of getting lost as well!

Domain delineation involves explicating both what the construct is and is not. At its core, this step involves understanding what is being measured by elaborating on the concept, *before the measure is designed and items in the measure are generated.* Domain delineation is a step in the conceptual domain and not in the operational domain. Domain definition and delineation is an important step that enables understanding the conceptual as it relates to the operational. Measure design and item generation follows domain delineation. Before specific items can be generated, the design of the measure needs to be determined. Important here is the need to think beyond measures involving agreement–disagreement with statements, and also beyond self-report measures. Measures can range from observational data to behavioral inventories. Subsequent steps in measure development relate to empirical testing of the psychometric properties of the measure and purifying it, by assessing its reliability, freedom from random error, and validity, freedom from random and systematic error. Central to measure development and use is a clear and detailed understanding of the meaning of measurement error.

UNDERSTANDING MEASUREMENT ERROR

There is perhaps no bigger intangible in measurement than in the meaning of measurement error itself. In fact, the nature of measurement error should be understood in each stage of developing measures and in their use and errors in developing and using measures are closely interrelated. In this section, types of errors in measurement are discussed in great detail with a view to explicating this intangible aspect of measurement. Our aim here is to provide as careful a dissection of error as possible. Our discussion begins with random and systematic error and provides finer discrimination and a detailed taxonomy of errors.

Random error

Random error is any type of error that is inconsistent or does not repeat in the same magnitude or direction except by chance. Using the example of a weighing machine, random error occurs when repeated readings for a person whose weight has not changed are 'all over the place'. Gulliksen (1950) defines random error in a statistical sense in terms of the mean error, the correlation between the error and the true score, and correlation between errors being zero. Nunnally (1978) uses the example of a chemist who, because of blurred vision, reads a thermometer incorrectly and consequently records the temperature to be slightly higher or lower, over many readings, leading to a distribution of errors. Bagozzi (1984) describes random error as the result of several forces (such as variations in data collection) that tend to cancel out in the long run. Ghiselli (1964) describes unsystematic variation as occurring when no trend is discernible from differences in responses across occasions.

In essence, a way to visualize random error conceptually is to examine whether inconsistent responses are provided across time (or items) when the phenomenon in question has not changed (such as an enduring trait). The very notion of consistency implies consistency across some unit, such as time or items. Some causes of random error include complex wording or language, questions requiring estimation, vagueness in questions or response categories (Churchill, 1979; Nunnally, 1978), the nature of administration through distracting factors and inconsistent administration procedures (cf. Churchill, 1979), and personal factors such as mood. Random error may be due to some aspect of the item, such as ambiguous wording, that causes respondents to provide a response with some variation (e.g., 'Numbers are redundant for most situations' may be an item where what represents 'most situations' may vary considerably). Such random error may attenuate correlations between an item and other items or measures.

Considering consistency across time for illustrative purposes, the presence of such factors as ambiguity can lead to responses that are not consistent over time. Respondents may be unable to provide consistent responses for a variety of reasons, such as not knowing the answer because it requires estimation ('How much beer did you drink last year?'), unclear wording, ambiguity in wording ('Do you exercise regularly?') or double-barreled questions ('Do you like the price and quality of this product?'). Respondents may provide an answer that is inconsistent, such as taking a wild guess. The test of inconsistency across time is whether a different (i.e., inconsistent) response would have been obtained if the question had been posed again. The assumption in retesting is that respondents do not recall their previous answer (hence, a sufficient time interval is needed). This is akin to a weighing machine not having any memory of previous weights. Moreover, the phenomenon is assumed to be unchanged. Thus, the notion of inconsistency across time is premised on some sort of retesting, even if actual retesting does not occur. A thought experiment has to be conducted: Will the question lead to consistent responses across time when the phenomenon has not changed?

Systematic error

Systematic error is any error that has a consistent effect. Systematic error results from consistent but inaccurate responses. Gulliksen (1950) refers to systematic error as constant error, using the example of a tape measure that has stretched over time, leading to constant underestimation. Using the example of a weighing machine, readings that are consistently off in one direction reflect systematic error, although additional nuances are discussed subsequently. Causes of systematic error could be leading or biased questions, or aspects of the measurement process that typically cause respondents to be unwilling to provide an accurate response (e.g., 'Do you support the president's stance on …?'). Being unwilling to provide an accurate response, respondents may provide a response that is inaccurate, yet consistent. For example, with a leading question, respondents may consistently provide a response that is more acceptable.

The literature on questionnaire design has often distinguished between respondents being *unable* versus *unwilling* to provide a response. Unwillingness to provide an accurate answer typically arises with threatening questions, such as those on sensitive topics requiring private information. Inability to provide an accurate answer arises because of factors such as difficult or ambiguous questions. Factors such as leading questions may lead respondents to provide inaccurate but consistent responses, as will be discussed under systematic error. Random error is usually caused by a respondent's inability to answer questions accurately. However, it should be noted that random error might also be due to respondents being unwilling to provide a response and therefore filling in a random response. For example, if a question on income is viewed by respondents as being intrusive, they may deliberately provide a wildly inaccurate answer. Similarly, respondents may also provide consistent responses when they are unable to answer accurately, such as through using the middle alternative. Moreover, the distinction between inability and unwillingness is itself often blurred as a function of the underlying psychological mechanisms involved in response generation. Nevertheless, a useful rule of thumb is that inability may lead to random error, and unwillingness may lead to systematic error.

Types of random and systematic error

Although generic definitions of random and systematic error were provided above, finer distinctions need to be made within these types of errors for a complete understanding of measurement error.

Idiosyncratic versus generic random errors

A distinction can be made between idiosyncratic random error, which affects a small proportion of individuals in an administration – such as those that result from mood or language difficulties – and generic random error, which has a broad-based effect across a sizable proportion of respondents in an administration, such as those that result from item-wording effects. Using the example of a weighing machine, if reading errors in a study of weight are restricted to a small proportion of individuals – say, errors due to reading the weight from different angles – then large sample sizes will likely minimize such error. Such error may occur because of a number of factors, such as language difficulties, the individual in question being in an extreme mood, or an error in the mechanics of completing the response. The key here is that such error is restricted to a small proportion of the entire sample and hence is not likely to affect overall statistics. Such a distinction is useful in understanding the relationship between certain sources of random error commonly discussed in the literature, such as mood, and likely outcomes in terms of error. For instance, mood is often suggested as a source of random error, when it may well be a source that leads to idiosyncratic

random error that can be minimized through the use of sufficiently large sample sizes. If sources of random error, such as mood state, are assumed to conform to a normal distribution, then outliers that cause random error are likely to be idiosyncratic in nature.

Generic random error is reflected in the responses of a sizable proportion of respondents. Typically, such generic random error is likely to be caused by factors with pervasive effects, such as item wording (e.g., ambiguous wording) or the nature of the setting (e.g., a noisy setting). The distinction between idiosyncratic random error and generic error may be blurred as a function of the proportion of respondents who are affected by a factor or error source, such as mood. For example, differences in language ability may be idiosyncratic, whereas item wording problems may be more broad-based and may affect a sizable proportion of respondents, thereby leading to generic random error. Nevertheless, the distinction between idiosyncratic and generic random error is very useful in conceptual examination of the likely outcomes of specific sources of error and enables the researcher to identify and categorize the likely nature of error. Factors such as mood are often suggested as sources of random error along with other factors, such as ambiguous wording. Here, a useful distinction can be made between sources that are likely to lead to idiosyncratic random error versus those likely to lead to generic random error.

Random error in measures attenuates observed relationships (Nunnally, 1978), although it can inflate relationships in multivariate analysis (Bollen, 1989). When a measure with random error and unreliability is related to a measure of a different construct in substantive research, the observed relationship is likely to be smaller than the true relationship. Whereas the effect of idiosyncratic random error can be minimized through larger sample sizes, generic random error in the measurement of a construct attenuates relationships. The effects of errors on relationships hold on average and relate to expected values rather than individual outcomes. In a statistical sense, idiosyncratic random error is a form of sampling error that can be minimized with larger samples. In this regard, Nunnally (1978) has pointed out the importance of large samples in measurement because measurement indicators, such as coefficient alpha, themselves have a degree of precision or a confidence interval associated with them as a function of sample size.

Random error within versus across administrations

As the various descriptions of the concept of random error suggest, a fundamental characteristic of random error is that it is expected to average out over many readings to a mean of zero. Such averaging could be across different units, across time or administrations, or across items within a single administration. Hence, an important distinction is between random error within an administration – reflected in inconsistent responses within a single administration – and random error across administrations or occasions – reflected in inconsistent responses across administrations. For instance, random error in items in an administration may average out across multiple items, assuming a large set of items. Similarly, random error could average out across a large set of administrations. In practice, however, large sets of administrations are not feasible, which is another reason for minimizing random error during measure development.

A response to an item may be sensitive to factors across administrations, such as interactions with settings and mood.

As mentioned earlier, it is useful to distinguish between idiosyncratic random error, and generic random error that affects the entire administration. If responses to an item have idiosyncratic random error in both administrations, such error is addressed through large samples. Factors such as mood have been mentioned in the literature as potential sources of random error (Churchill, 1979). An item requiring aggregation across events or behaviors (e.g., 'Generally speaking, retail outlets do not cheat') may lead to different responses for people in a negative mood. If such a pattern of responses is restricted to a small proportion of individuals (i.e., is idiosyncratic), such a possibility can be minimized through large samples and the assumption of a normal distribution of mood in the first and second administrations. On the other hand, an interaction between an item and a variable, such as setting or interviewer effect, that varies across administrations and affects a sizable proportion of respondents will likely lead to random error across administrations. For example, if an item is prone to interviewer effects and there is inconsistency across administration in the degree to which interviewers lead the respondents, or in interviewer appearance and associated perceptions of socially desirable answers, this could cause generic random error across administrations. If other aspects of administrations are inconsistent, such as the use of distracting settings in one administration, all of the items or the items that are susceptible to distracting factors (e.g., more difficult items) may be affected. In this regard, Ghiselli (1964) distinguishes between varying unsystematic factors that vary across individuals on a single occasion (e.g., comfort of seating, lighting, hearing based on distance from instructor, and transient individual factors such as fatigue) and constant unsystematic factors that affect all individuals in a similar way but vary across occasions (e.g., poor lighting throughout an administration). Varying unsystematic factors can cause idiosyncratic and generic random error within an administration as well as across administrations, whereas constant unsystematic factors can cause generic random error across administrations.

Idiosyncratic random error does not affect stability assuming sufficient sample sizes. Generic random error within administrations can lead to generic random error across administrations, as indicated by the negative directionality of the relationship between such error and the stability of an item.

Additive versus correlational systematic error

As noted, one way of visualizing systematic error is in terms of a thermometer or a weighing machine that consistently deviates from the true value in a specific direction by a constant sum, say, as a result of an error in calibrating the zero point on the device (Figure 15.2). For example, the illustration in the top left of Figure 15.2 displays the measured score as being less than the true score by a constant. Such error is a type of systematic error called additive systematic error. Additive systematic error inflates or deflates responses by a constant magnitude and may result in reduced correlations with other items. It should be noted that additive systematic error can be constant across responses and therefore have no effect on relationships, or it can be partial in the sense that the additive effect deflates or inflates responses to one end of the scale and restricts variance (Figure 15.2). For example, the illustration

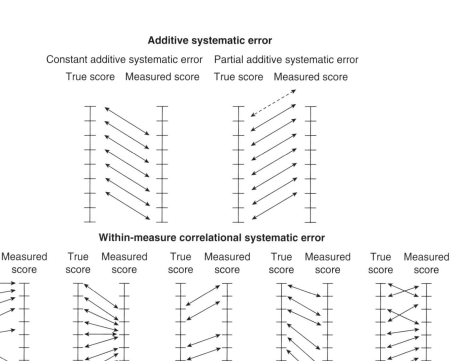

Figure 15.2   Types of systematic error.

on the top-right in Figure 15.2 displays a constant addition to the measured score over and above the true score which is deflated due to the upper end of the scale, with each arrow representing data for an individual. Such additive error could be caused by several factors, such as leading questions, interviewer bias, unbalanced response categories, consistently lenient or stringent ratings due to wording or other factors, or a tendency to agree or disagree. Factors that cause responses to be consistently off in one direction across respondents lead to additive systematic error.

However, such additive systematic error (i.e., consistent error that deviates by a constant magnitude from the true score) is not as problematic in academic research when compared to survey research. Academic research emphasizes accurate estimates of relationships between variables rather than accurate estimates of absolute values (Groves, 1991). Additive errors matter only to the extent that they reduce scale variance and consequently deflate correlations. In this regard, Nunnally (1978) highlights the importance of relative standing in typical statistical analyses used in the social sciences, which are correlational in nature. Correlations are largely influenced by relative standing of values on variables (Nunnally, 1978). To the extent that relative standing along variables is preserved, correlations are not significantly affected.

A more problematic form of systematic error is correlational systematic error, which consistently deflates or inflates the relationship between two or more variables (Figures 15.2 and 15.3). Correlational error occurs when individual responses vary consistently to different degrees over and above true differences in the construct being measured; that is, it is a result of different individuals responding in consistently different ways over and above

true differences in the construct. Using the weighing machine example, if readings are off in a certain direction and also in proportion to somebody's weight, then that is an example of correlational error (e.g., if the weighing machine shows an additional 5 lb for a 100 lb person and an additional 10 lb for a 200 lb person). In the bottom half of Figure 15.2, the measured score diverges or converges or varies in other consistent ways when compared to the true score. This is over and above an additive effect and represents consistent variations to different degrees.

Correlational systematic error occurs if different individuals interpret and use response categories in consistent but different ways. For example, an item with correlational systematic error due to a common method, such as extreme response anchors, could lead to the use of middle response categories, whereas an item with correlational systematic error due to a common method, such as moderate response anchors (e.g., like-dislike), could lead to the use of extreme response categories. Correlational systematic errors can be caused by the use of response scales of a similar format across items, including what are referred to in the literature as method factors. For example, say, a certain set of response categories is employed (say, *very good* to *very bad*) and respondents interpret the categories in certain ways (*very good* means more or less positive for different respondents). In this scenario, the covariance across items will be due, at least partially, to the method factor, or the use of identical response formats (see Andrews, 1984). Similarly, correlational systematic error may arise as a result of other aspects of the research method, such as variation in the interpretation of the instructions and the questions (Andrews, 1984). Such error may arise out of items tapping into different traits.

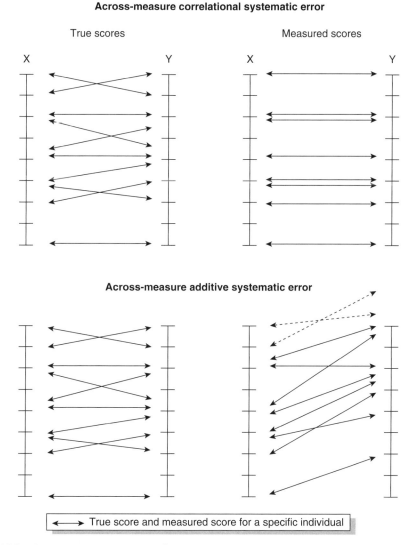

Figure 15.3   Across-measure systematic error.

Additive systematic error in an administration can have either no effect or a negative effect on stability and test–retest correlations. Additive systematic error is likely to have no effect or to attenuate relationships due to decreased variance. It should be noted that any constant additive error, by definition, cannot affect correlations. The point here, however, is that if there is an additive effect and finite end points to a scale, then responses are all biased upward (or downward) toward the end of the scale, thus reducing its variance and its ability to covary.

Correlational systematic error can strengthen or weaken observed relationships (Nunnally, 1978). Consistent differences across individuals over and above the construct being measured may be positively correlated, negatively correlated, or not correlated with the construct.

Within-measure correlational systematic error
Correlational systematic error can be distinguished within measures versus across measures. The latter refers to correlational systematic error that occurs between measures of different constructs. Within-measure correlational systematic error occurs between different items of a measure. It can be the result of responses to items being influenced by the use of a common method or by different trait or specific method factors that may or may not be related to the trait being measured (Figures 15.2 and 15.3). Within-measure correlational systematic error due to a common method factor is used to refer to aspects of the method that are common across all items, such as response categories (Figures 15.2 and 15.3). This is similar to the use of the term *common method factor* in a multitrait, multimethod context (Campbell and Fiske, 1959).

Within-measure correlational systematic error due to a common method factor may arise from the use of the same response format, similar stems, or the completion of items in close proximity, and it can typically lead to inflated relationships between items of a measure. Within-measure correlational systematic error can also occur as a result of items measuring different traits or method factors than intended. Within-measure correlational systematic error can have a positive influence on stability, such as the consistent measurement of a different but stable method factor or construct.

An example of within-measure correlational systematic error is halo error in the completion of items within a measure – a tendency to provide similar responses across items that are thought to be related. In this regard, researchers have demonstrated how responses to earlier items of a measure can affect responses to later items, with the latter becoming more polarized and more consistent with adjacent responses (Feldman and Lynch, 1988; Knowles, 1988; Simmons et al., 1993). Knowles and Byers (1996) demonstrate the increased reliability of later items through the clarifying role played by earlier items. Such error can be as a result of a within-measure halo effect in that a general impression based on earlier items influences responses to later items. Therefore, responses to later items are consistent with responses to earlier items.

Across-measure systematic error
Whereas within-measure correlational systematic error occurs between items of a measure, across-measure correlational systematic error occurs across measures of different constructs (Figure 15.3). In Figure 15.3, true versus measured scores for two variables are displayed. Essentially, across-measure correlational systematic error occurs if measures of different constructs are influenced by a trait or a method factor, or by different but related traits or method factors, thus inflating or deflating true correlations between them. A common method factor that affects both measures is a source of across-measure correlational systematic error. For example, the use of the same paper-and-pencil method (that taps, say, a response style of using certain parts of the scale) is likely to inflate correlations. Likewise, if subsequent measures are influenced by earlier ones, then the scales completed first introduce systematic error in later measures. For example, hypothesis guessing may result from responses to the first measure influencing responses to the second measure. Use of common instructions or even the same page for different measures can also cause correlational systematic error (Lennox and Dennis, 1994). Across-measure correlational systematic error also

occurs when a subset of items from measures, rather than entire measures, is influenced by a different trait or method factor. For instance, a subset of items may share a specific context.

It should be noted that across-measure systematic error could also lead to an additive effect that does not affect correlations. Completion of one measure may lead to inflated responses on a subsequent measure (i.e., across-measure constant additive systematic error). When finite endpoints play a role, such inflation could decrease correlations (i.e., across-measure partial additive systematic error). Whereas the correlational type can inflate or deflate correlations, the additive type can either deflate or not affect correlations. Therefore, the broader term, across-measure systematic error, is used here. Narrower terms that specify the correlational or additive nature of error are used to describe the specific types of across-measure systematic error.

In summary, a host of errors identified in the literature fall under the rubric of systematic errors of an additive or a correlational nature. Systematic errors can be distinguished within measures versus across measures. Within-measure correlational error can occur because of a common method and also because of different traits or specific method factors. Detailed understanding of measurement error provides the foundation to address intangible issues in the design of measures and methods.

USING MEASURES IN RESEARCH DESIGN

The in-depth discussion of the nature and types of measurement errors have a number of implications for psychometric testing, for understanding different types of measures, and for different research methods, such as survey and experimental

methods (Viswanathan, 2005, 2008). These implications represent some of the intangible aspects of measurement that have not been explicated sufficiently in the literature. Here, we focus on intangible issues relating to using measures in research design. This area is particularly germane as researchers make a variety of assumptions about how existing measures can be used and there is a lack of sufficient discussion on such issues.

Modification and use of validated measures

A common situation that researchers face is the need to use previously developed scales in research methods rather than developing measures for specific studies. Scales previously validated for reliability, dimensionality, and validity are often employed by researchers in methodological design. Design considerations, such as the separation or grouping of key variables, may require the modification of existing measures. Recommendations are discussed at the level of items, measures, administration, and construct.

When using existing measures, research design can be enhanced by beginning with a careful methodological review of the literature, as distinct from a substantive review. A methodological review should begin with clear conceptual definitions of constructs rooted in relevant literature. The construct as defined should be delineated from related constructs by explication of relevant domains. Current definitions may need to be modified if constructs are not sufficiently distinguished or clearly defined. Constructs may not be properly defined in past research for a variety of reasons, including their 'self-evident' nature. However, anything short of a clear definition warrants further attention. Available measures need to be examined carefully in a variety of ways. First, items need to be examined in light of the conceptual definition of a construct. This is not to second-guess prior work as much as it is to obtain correspondence between the conceptual and the operational. An existing measure may not capture all of the dimensions of a construct as defined. An important aspect of the domain may have been excluded. Measures are a work in process needing constant improvement. However, considerable conceptual and empirical support should be provided for modifying previously validated measures. A methodological review, which parallels a substantive review of the literature, should cover various measures of a construct in terms of psychometric properties. Such a review should take into consideration the sample and usage conditions of previous psychometric work. As discussed earlier, measures are not tested in isolation but in specific usage contexts.

Items may need to be added to measures to cover certain aspects of the domain or to add a new dimension. In such situations, items could be added at the end of the measures rather than modifying existing items. Thus, the original measure is preserved in terms of items and sequencing. The within-measure halo effect and other such effects present during prior validation are not disrupted. Items in a measure perform well for many reasons, not all of which are apparent or foreseeable. Measure assessment is both deductive and inductive; the latter suggesting that items may work empirically for a variety of known and unknown reasons, with the proof being in the empirical results. A specific sequencing of items could contribute to their performance. Therefore, changes in sequencing can be detrimental, while also adding new variations and making it more difficult to attribute differences in results to the appropriate sources.

When adding items, new items and the entire measure should be evaluated using all psychometric procedures in order to create a basis for deleting or modifying items. Researchers should exercise caution in modifying individual items of previously validated measures. Such modification requires extensive conceptual and empirical support. A sufficient rationale, as well as empirical evidence of psychometric properties, is required for modifying either the number or labeling of response categories. Vague wording of anchors, extreme or nonextreme wording of end anchors, and a reduction or increase in the number of response categories can lead to systematic as well as random error.

At the measure level, new items should be added at the end of measures and supported by the assessment of psychometric properties at the item and measure levels. It may be necessary to add items in order to allow for a sufficient number of items representing each dimension after measure purification and item deletion. This allows the researcher to purify a measure and have an adequate number of items in the final measure (generally, a minimum of approximately four items, with broader constructs requiring a higher minimum). As discussed, researchers should exercise utmost caution in deleting existing items of previously validated measures, providing extensive conceptual and empirical support as bases. Modified measures should be assessed empirically before their use in substantive studies. The use of short forms, different sequencing, and the use of fillers require appropriate psychometric support. At the administration level, researchers should articulate a rationale and/or provide empirical evidence for using measures in different populations.

Rethinking at the construct level and consequent changes to measures should avoid modifying existing items but should rather add items at the end of measures. Thus, the entire measure and individual items can be assessed. A sufficient number of items per dimension are needed, as discussed earlier. Such modifications also require empirical testing for all psychometric procedures. Because construct-level changes are fundamental, they require a careful review of the literature. Deleting or modifying existing items as a result of construct-level changes requires extensive conceptual and empirical support. Ideally, validation should be conducted before conducting substantive studies to avoid investing effort in research designs involving unreliable or invalid measures.

When previously validated scales are employed without modification, psychometric properties should be reported. Again, the key here is that measures have to be assessed in usage conditions, and that reliability and validity are properties of measures in specific usage conditions. Researchers should provide evidence of reliability and validity of the measures used in a study, whether or not these measures have been validated previously. Deviations from previous findings in terms of dimensional structure may require data analyses to be adjusted accordingly. For instance, if a scale has been validated previously as being unidimensional, and two dimensions are found during usage, then substantive results ideally should be reported for each of these possibilities. Similarly, if a previously validated scale has items that need to be deleted, results should be reported for the original version as well as the modified version of the scale. Essentially, the previously validated scale has to display appropriate psychometric properties under specific usage conditions; otherwise, substantive results based on the scale are open to question. When any validation as described above is conducted concurrent with, or prior to, hypothesis tests, sufficient sample sizes must be used in studies to enable psychometric testing

and to minimize idiosyncratic random error.

Using unvalidated measures

Measures that have not been validated previously are often used in methodological design. Such measures may have no prior evidence of psychometric properties or may, at most, provide evidence of reliability, usually coefficient alpha, based on their use in substantive studies. Relevant here is a methodological review as discussed earlier. Validation for such measures ideally should be conducted before the measures are used in research methods to test substantive hypotheses. This minimizes the likelihood of investing in unreliable or invalid measures. Such measures may need to be modified to maintain a sufficient number of items for each dimension. When validation is conducted concurrent with hypothesis tests, variables must be added to the design to incorporate validity tests. Such an approach, of course, runs the risk of placing all the eggs in one basket. Therefore, the measure itself could include additional items to allow for item deletion and measure purification. Whereas data are readily available for tests of reliability and dimensionality, the addition of a few variables can make validity tests possible. A methodological review of past use of measures also can be employed to infer evidence of validity. Sufficient sample sizes must be used to enable psychometric testing and to minimize idiosyncratic random error.

The emphasis on conceptual and empirical work is not to discourage re-evaluating existing measures. Rather, measures need to be evaluated and improved constantly, and measure development is an ongoing process. However, such re-evaluation has to be done carefully, with full consideration of previous work on a measure. Researchers may put together some measures for the purpose of a study without sufficient conceptual or empirical work. Hence, measures need to be examined carefully in many situations.

Designing collection of data on multiple measures

Researchers in the social sciences use surveys with organizational or individual foci and collect data on a variety of measures of constructs. Essentially, a research method consists of measurement and/or manipulation of several variables. How these variables are sequenced and administered bears on the nature of error that is likely to result. When reporting these methodological issues, the rationale that researchers provide for the sequencing of measures used in hypothesis tests is often insufficient or absent. Such a rationale should account for across-measure systematic error that is likely when data are collected on multiple measures. Discussion of such error would be appropriate both in developing the rationale for the research design before the fact, and in the interpretation of results. For example, a study of relationships between organizations may sequence a host of such measures as opportunism and power, without sufficient discussion of the rationale in terms of reducing across-measure systematic error. Or, a study may sequence a number of scales with similar response categories contiguously. Some plausible sources of error, such as hypothesis guessing, halo effects, and common method factors, require explanation in such situations. Rationale for specific design of methods and appropriate interpretation of results should be presented. Strong tests can be designed or strong evidence can be inferred from results by assessing the separation or grouping of central variables in light of hypothesized relationships between them as discussed.

Additionally, pilot tests can be used to assess likely sources of error in research methods. Pilot tests are sometimes used in an experimental context to assess demand artifacts and in a survey setting to assess the wording of individual items. However, they also can be used to assess plausible sources of systematic error in correlational designs. Similar tests conducted concurrently with hypothesis tests (e.g., immediately following collection of data on variables in hypothesis tests) in substantive studies rather than pilot tests can facilitate the interpretation of findings, although they are no substitute for sound methodological design. The 'causal mentality' often employed in experimental research to design independent variables is just as pertinent in sequencing variables in correlational designs or in sequencing dependent variables in experimental designs to counter across-measure systematic error. As discussed, research design can be enhanced through a careful methodological review of the literature.

If existing measures of a construct are not chosen for use, then the rationale for a new measure needs to be provided. Similarly, the use of specific existing measures needs to be supported as well. If existing measures that lack psychometric testing are to be used, then studies can build in additional testing, such as validation tests. However, such designs run the risk of putting all eggs in one basket. A more efficient design can be achieved by separately testing measures before investing resources in substantive studies. A common problem in using existing measures is the need to supplement items to cover subdomains. A key recommendation here is to employ sufficient numbers of items for each dimension to allow for item deletion and a resulting scale with four items. A four-item scale may be the minimum number to demonstrate psychometric properties in most situations, although a larger minimum would apply for constructs covering complex domains. The practice of having one or two items because of length of questionnaires is not recommended because reliability may not be achievable or demonstrable.

Although measure assessment prior to its use in substantive testing is strongly recommended, if such a step is not employed, the substantive study should be planned to accommodate psychometric assessment. The problem with such an approach is the confounding of methodological and substantive explanations. In addition to traditional methodological artifacts, lack of measurement reliability or validity undermines the validity of the research design.

Perhaps the most effective and efficient step in methodological design is preliminary work prior to a substantive study, be it pretesting, pilot testing, or measure development work. However, this key step is often short changed in light of pragmatic concerns such as time pressure or the lack of easy access to samples. Whereas the former requires adequate planning and the added realization of the high payoff involved, the latter is often a significant problem, particularly when respondents are not conveniently accessible for a variety of reasons (e.g., managers in organizations). Through preliminary work, in addition to a sound basis for a specific methodological study, a basis is also in place for a program of research. The payoff from a sound methodological basis can extend to several studies in a program of research. Ideally, the measures employed in a study should have demonstrated psychometric properties that enable confidence in them, and thus in the results of a study. When there is considerable uncertainty on multiple fronts, it is difficult, perhaps impossible, to draw meaningful conclusions. For example, if the relationship between two measures of different constructs is nonsignificant, is this because (a) the two constructs in question are not related, or (b) unreliable or invalid measures have been used for one or both of the constructs? In this regard, from a theoretical standpoint, measurement is often described as a large-sample theory (Nunnally, 1978), emphasizing the importance of large samples in measure development to minimize uncertainty due to sampling error.

Illustrative scenarios on using measures in research design

Some illustrative scenarios that commonly occur in using existing and/or unvalidated measures are described to bring out key issues. Say, a construct has been measured with a scale available in the literature. However, the construct itself has not been defined conceptually anywhere in the literature. This scenario occurs often and may warrant careful examination of the domain of the construct and definition. The available scale may capture only some aspects of the domain. Alternatively, the scale may capture a slightly different, perhaps somewhat narrower, construct. Definitions and dimensions are assumed, a sort of logic of 'everyone knows what it means'. There are also situations where the dimensionality of a scale has been assessed through factor analysis, yet no conceptual definition of the construct or proposed dimensions is available. One of the first steps in any research and in any presentation of research should be the definition of constructs. In other words, it is essential to understand what is being researched and what is the thing being measured. Such definition of previously undefined constructs or redefinition may lead to the addition of new items.

Another common scenario occurs where a scale measuring a specific construct is available in past research and coefficient alpha is reported, but no other psychometric properties have been assessed. Can the scale be used as is? In this scenario, the psychometric evaluation of the scale is limited to internal consistency. It is well worth the effort to examine the definition and individual scale items for representation of content. If additional items are required, they could be added to the end of the scale to maintain the sequencing of the original scale. However, items in the original scale may warrant modification because they capture a different construct or a method factor. Here, either additional items can be added or, in extreme cases, the original items can be modified. Addition of items instead of modification may lengthen measures. Essential in this scenario is the need to empirically reassess internal consistency and assess dimensionality and validity. Clearly, modifying a validated scale requires appropriate empirical support; however, mere reporting of coefficient alpha is not sufficient validation.

Another common scenario involves developing several new scales as a part of a research project to measure constructs being studied. Due to time constraints, however, data are collected for measure assessment concurrent with hypothesis testing. This scenario effectively puts all the methodological eggs in one substantive study basket. Pretesting, whether of measures or manipulations, may be relatively cost-effective for the effort involved. At the least, a small pilot study may identify wording problems. In the event that all eggs have to be put in one basket, it is important to carefully conceptualize constructs, delineate their domains, and edit items. A sufficient number of items to start with is essential to allow for an adequate number after purification (usually at least four at the end of the process). Broader constructs may require a larger minimum number of items.

Consider another scenario where a study uses samples that are difficult to access, say, employees of specific organizations. Several constructs are measured by single-item scales to reduce the length of the survey and increase the response rate. In this scenario, the problem lies in the inability to achieve or demonstrate psychometric properties of scales. An alternative here is to use short forms of measures. These short forms of measures could be validated in separate studies, in terms of both empirical evidence and conceptual examination to assess coverage of the domain with a representative set of items. Such an approach may lead to a trade-off between reliability and content validity (e.g., choosing items with the highest item-to-total correlations vs. items that cover the domain of the construct). Ideally, a similar sample should be used, but as a last resort, the short form could be validated in more easily available samples, provided such samples are logically reasonable alternatives (e.g., senior graduate students in business with appropriate work experience in place of managers in research on business administration). If single items need to be employed as a last resort, they should be validated in separate studies by demonstrating a high covariation with other items of the measure, through high covariation with another measure of the construct, and through high stability (reliability across time). Such evidence, when available in previous validation work, could be used to justify the research method.

Consider another scenario where a study employs measures that are based on objective numbers (e.g., return on investment, market share). Given the availability of such numbers, these measures are considered reliable and valid. In this scenario, it is important to understand what construct is being measured. Return on investment (ROI) is an objective number, yet the aim really is to assess performance. There are many dimensions to performance; it is not self-evident that ROI alone would capture these dimensions. A second issue here is the use of objective numbers. Such measures can be usefully supplemented by subjective measures, such as self-report ratings of ROI or of performance vis-à-vis major competitors or the industry. Objective numbers can themselves be standardized based on industry averages. A key issue here is that absolute numbers are interpretable when compared to some reference point. The design of subjective ratings may enable interpretation of objective measures as well, by highlighting the limitations of objective measures and the nature of reference points against which to compare them. Such multiple approaches likely enhance clarification of constructs and their domains and provide multiple measures and a test of convergent validity.

An opposite scenario is also common, using self-report measures exclusively. Consider a situation where organizational research is conducted and measures are assessed exclusively through self-reports by employees. Here, alternative measures from independent sources should be considered. A self-report measure of a construct can be supplemented with another measure of the construct based on secondary data. Convergence between very different approaches to measuring the same construct provides strong evidence of validity. Using independent sources of data for measuring different constructs is also a way of reducing across-measure systematic error.

FROM PHYSICAL TO PSYCHOLOGICAL MEASUREMENT

So what is measurement in the social sciences? How do the soft numbers in these soft sciences compare to the hard numbers from measurement in the physical sciences? How do the different types of measures used in the social sciences compare and contrast? This broader topic covers a host of intangible issues that require explication. A brief journey through physical measurement of inanimate objects to physiological measurement, often coupled with physical measurement in this discussion, to psychological measurement is instructive. Measurement in the social sciences has similarities to measurement in these diverse disciplines. The discussion that follows oversimplifies distinctions and sweeps entire disciplines into clear-cut categories. Nevertheless, it is intended to stimulate thinking from a broader perspective. In fact, differences in measurement within the social sciences are quite large, reflecting characteristics of physical and physiological measurement to different degrees.

Considering the concept of length, the distance between the conceptual and the operational is minimal. Even here, the measurement of length is far from obvious with larger distances and, of course, with astronomical distances. In other words, the underlying construct is physically discernible, directly paralleling the measurement of the construct. Measurement involves calibrating a ruler or tape with equally spaced distances based on conventional agreement. An external comparison standard is available. Reliability or consistency is likely to be affected by human error in reading. Through mechanization, such error can be reduced or even eliminated. Multiple readings are akin to multiple-item scales and enhance reliability. Test–retest reliability can be assessed by direct comparison of lengths. Thus, if a tape expands over time, it affects test-retest reliability. Because an absolute standard is available, reliability does not have to hinge on relative ordering. In fact, availability of an absolute standard is related to consistency in measurement of the phenomenon. The ratio scale property per se is not the key characteristic; it is the availability of an established external standard against which a measure can be assessed. The ratio scale property is not necessary, a temperature scale being an example. Time is similar to length in that the distance between the conceptual and the operational is small, at least in the past 300 years! Weight is perhaps more abstract than length – the construct is discernible through the sensory mode – but the correspondence between the construct and its measurement is not as apparent as for length. Again, an external standard is established and available that converts weight into calibrated intervals and presents symbols representing weights. Moreover, the measure follows from the conceptual definition, say, gravitational pull or how heavy an object is, but perhaps not as directly as length.

With physical properties, external measurement standards are available. Physical phenomena may appear more or less constant relative to psychological phenomena. However, many factors may impinge on physical measurement. For instance, the measurement of wind chill requires specifying measurement conditions, such as feet above the ground. The wind chill index represents a formative indicator of how cold air feels on human skin. Whereas effect indicators are those where constructs cause responses on indicators or items, causal or formative indicators cause or form the overall measure of a construct. For example, a measure of socioeconomic status is defined by a weighted combination of its components, such as income and education. The measure of a construct, by definition, is 'caused' or 'formed' by its indicators. It combines wind speed about 5 feet above the ground (human face level) with a calculation of heat transfer, skin tissue resistance, clear night sky conditions, and a calm wind threshold of 3 miles per hour. Although formed by precise observations and calculations, this measure requires certain assumptions, such as feet above the ground and wind at calm conditions. Administration conditions have to be specified for measurement. Extraneous factors may affect accurate measurement, say, wind conditions in measuring speed. Physical measurement is far from clear-cut, as discussed, because of variations in administration. Consider battery life measured through tests that simulate usage conditions in toys. Such specification necessarily incorporates some usage conditions while excluding others. Thus, some aspects of battery life are captured, and not others. Alternatively, the construct has to be redefined to be narrower. This is because 'battery life' is an abstraction imposed by researchers. This example illustrates how physical constructs can be placed on a continuum where some involve abstractions, only slices of which are captured in measurement. Physical measurement is also based on assumptions about conditions, and about factors that lead to a phenomenon, with measurement procedures excluding some factors and including others. It is conceivable to form a summary measure that sums up items (or measurements) across different conditions somewhat like sampling from a domain of items.

Physiological measurement falls somewhere between physical measurement and psychological measurement. Here, human beings, rather than inanimate physical objects, are the focus. Although conscious control over physiological responses may be difficult, a variety of factors can lead to changes in readings. For example, blood pressure can be affected by posture or other factors. Yet external validation is possible (i.e., absolute measurement that is not generated by respondents).

Considering constructs in the social sciences, responses are influenced by myriad psychological factors. Whereas physiological observations are not usually under conscious control, self-reports can be influenced by many factors, such as complex motivations for self-presentation. Also, external standards of measurement generally are not available. (A qualification is appropriate here because ability tests and other such measures are similar to physical measurement in many respects.) Rather, there are many metrics or units of measurement, usually relative rather than absolute. Thus, validation usually rests on relative ranking rather than absolute criteria. Differences from absolute values are usually not meaningful because the notion of some precise absolute value is not available. An absolute standard is available when a narrow concrete physical/sensory dimension is captured. Alternatively, when a numerical scale, such as stock market performance or IQ, is agreed upon by convention, absolute differences are relevant.

Psychological attributes, of course, relate to the mind and necessarily involve abstract attributes. Thus, the distance between the conceptual and the operational is relatively large. Moreover, responses are provided by humans rather than merely recorded in the case of physical attributes. Complexities in human cognition and motivation influence responses, thus necessitating multiple nuanced items. Observations of human behavior, while involving only recording similar to physical measurement, typically purport to capture abstract psychological constructs. Measurement of constructs is usually indirect.

With physical measurement, different types of error can creep in through administration. Random error can occur because of, say, deviations in administering a measure. Either test–retest or multiple readings (i.e., interval of almost no time) can be employed.

Errors can occur in reading. A parallel here is with research associates or interviewers administering methods including observations. Say the observational method is employed to assess 'information search' by recording the number of products examined in a store. Clear specification of the behavior to be recorded is needed, such as 'definition of an instance when products are removed from a shelf.' In observations in physical measurement, the human element is involved in administering a measure and recording a reading. However, for psychological constructs, the observed element is an indicator of a latent construct. Moreover, the element needs clear definition, and measurement is subject to administration errors. Research associates who deviate from instructions can cause a variety of errors. But additionally, the measurement technique has inherent error in that the element of observation is an imperfect indicator of the underlying construct, say, 'information search' (i.e., it is sampled from the domain of information search). This example captures the essence of the difference between physical and psychological measurement. Any item or measure is inherently imperfect in psychological measurement. Any item typically captures only a slice of an underlying construct. Moreover, there is error in the relationship between the item and the slice that it purports to capture. In a sense, the relationship between a construct and an item can be viewed as probabilistic in psychological measurement and deterministic in physical measurement.

Constructs in physical and physiological research are, of course, not necessarily concrete, narrow dimensions. Because abstract thinking is a part of the psychological makeup of human beings, psychological constructs that capture such thinking may be expected to be abstract, whereas physical and physiological constructs may be expected to be relatively concrete. However, when abstract thinking is applied to phenomena in the physical or physiological realm, abstract constructs are created. Consider medical research, where indications of narrow constructs, such as blood pressure, are then used to diagnose conditions. Levels of a variety of physiological indicators form or define conditions. Indicators of individual dimensions are combined to assess more abstract constructs. Such models (e.g., for disease diagnosis) could be considered as substantive relationships between constructs. However, they can also be viewed from a measurement perspective. Specific dimensions are combined to define a broader construct. Thus, certain symptoms in combination point to disease (i.e., formative indicators). For instance, cancer detection may involve looking for missing cells, reoriented cells, or sequencing of genetic codes. However, a judgment has to be made by viewing these characteristics in the larger context of the patient's history; otherwise, a computer program rather than a pathologist would be able to make judgments. Paralleling the mind-body distinction, measurement involves psychological or physical characteristics. Physical attributes can be narrowly defined and translated on an available standard. They are discernible through sensory mechanisms or through symbolic representation (e.g., calories). The psychological element is manifest in human error, including bias; in reading and administration; and in machine error. In physiological measurement, the psychological element is also manifest in the degree to which it influences the physiological, that is, in the degree to which the mind can be used to manipulate physiology. Abstracted constructs, such as diagnosis of diseases, involve the use of narrow indicators of physical characteristics to draw broader inferences. Note that the measurement of physical characteristics

has error, sometimes considerable error, as well.

So, does the notion of a latent construct as used in the social sciences occur in physical or physiological measurement? If measures are observable, and each individual observation is of a slightly different aspect, then conditions or categories, such as diseases, are inferred from a combination of observations. Clearly, what underlies the symptoms is the disease. But each symptom is not an indicator of the disease as each item is a measure of a psychological construct. The item-as-measure model applies to abstract constructs capturing psychological phenomena. Here, the latent construct is an abstraction, and items are created to capture it in different ways. In physiological observations such as blood pressure, the parallel to multiple items is multiple readings. A different method to measure blood pressure would represent just that, and convergent validity would be germane. However, the notion in psychological constructs of developing a set of items rather than a single item to capture a latent construct is not paralleled for a relatively concrete physical or physiological measurement, that is, for a narrow construct that can be captured by a single item, such as weight or temperature. Hence, the measure is relatively close to the construct it captures. However, even a physical dimension such as battery life is an abstraction in the sense of covering a domain of applications or usage situations. As the distance between the conceptual and the operational increases, the potential for developing multiple measures of a construct increases. Restated, as distance decreases, the potential for developing multiple items as measures decreases. As the abstractness of constructs increases, multiple items are needed to cover the domain and to capture these constructs in different ways through different nuanced items. Dimensions are latent, and it is not fruitful to assign each item to be a different dimension. This could lead to countless dimensions, one for each item nuanced by wording – actually, an idiosyncratic combination of content and method. Thus, sets of items typically are used to represent single dimensions and cover the domain. Given the need to cover an abstract domain, dimensions or factors are not sliced narrowly but rather cover a sizable subdomain. For concrete measurement, different ways of measuring a concrete construct represent different measures rather than different items. Multiple repeated readings are the closest parallel to multiple items.

Note that the inherent nature of measurement is quite different in physical measurement - observing a physical reading versus some form of self-report or observation in psychological measurement. Hence, wording issues and the need for multiple items that are similar become critical in psychological measurement. Important here are different ways of getting at something while accounting for human differences in understanding items and generating responses. Moreover, the need to cover a domain, which does not rise to the level of multiple dimensions, is important. Thus, latency and abstractness of the construct and complexity in human self-reporting necessitate multiple-item scales.

The aim in psychological measurement is to approximate an abstract domain through a sampling of items (i.e., domain sampling) (Nunnally, 1978). The key word here is 'approximate' – physical measurement that is relatively concrete could be captured by a single item. Psychological measurement and construct definition aim for some parsimony. Thus, constructs are approximated by a sampling of a domain. This is not purely deductive reasoning; it is both deductive and inductive. Conceptual or empirical analysis may suggest that a domain has to be split into dimensions.

Such dimensions are then the unit of analysis approximated by a set of items. Carefully selected multiple items serve to enhance representation of the domain, an issue germane to validity. To the extent that items belong together, they enhance internal consistency reliability. Covariance across items enhances coefficient alpha.

Human error is involved in physical measurement. But this is often perceptual and sometimes motivational (say, in biased reading). The researcher, rather than the respondent, is involved in the recording of responses. A latent feeling is not being translated into a response to an item by a respondent or observer. Thus, in psychological measurement, uncertainty about capturing a domain because of distance between the conceptual and the operational, and uncertainty about human perception and response generation because of self-reports or observations by human beings, are two reasons to generate multiple items assuming an item-as-measure model. Another reason overlaps with multiple readings in physical measurement – the notion of averaging across error-filled trials. The notion of the use of multiple items and reliability as a sort of averaging is somewhat incomplete. It applies to physical measurement more than to psychological measurement. In psychological measurement, each item is also somewhat different, trying to capture different aspects of an abstract domain. Moreover, nuances in wording are used to elicit accurate responses from respondents. The latter is a way of assessing consistency across similar items, whereas the former is essentially getting at slightly different aspects of the domain.

Thus, physical measurement can involve aspects of psychological measurement, imperfect measurement of slices of constructs due to researcher-imposed abstractions, and various types of errors due to administration. In psychological measurement, the first issue is accentuated and qualitatively different, and the second issue involves some unique elements due to conscious responses being produced by human beings. Note that physiological measurement of attributes under human control falls on the margin between physical and psychological measurement. Thus, unique in psychological measurement is the human element in responses and the need for nuanced items. As noted earlier, sweeping distinctions between physical and psychological measurement are employed here for purposes of the discussion. However, differences in measurement within physical or within psychological measurement are vast. For instance, there are relatively concrete constructs in psychological research.

Another issue here is a type of measurement that falls along the continuum from physical to psychological measurement: the use of objective data on natural occurrences. When disparate concrete measures are studied to gain insight into a construct such as pace of life, a germane issue is whether these measures necessarily should converge if they are tapping into the same construct. Although the need for such convergence is evident when using an item-as-measure model and developing multiple items to tap into a construct, objective data from available sources do not fall into these neat categories. Rather, items aiming to measure pace of life, such as time taken for a transaction at the post office or pace of walking at a downtown area, are each idiosyncratic and naturally occurring, rather than responses to a carefully designed set of items. Such specific items are influenced by many factors in addition to the construct in question. The same is true of organizational indicators, such as R&D expenses or percentage of new products. In fact, each such concrete measure may provide some insight into the phenomenon, yet not be considered

as measuring the same thing in terms of the degree of convergence among measures. Each different measure of, say, pace of life can in turn provide insight into different slices of a phenomenon, thus adding to understanding. In contrast, a self-report scale of pace of life summarizes it with all its implications into self-report items that are likely to covary. Measures formed from secondary data or natural observations do not fit into the category of a multiple-item scale and all the related criteria. The model of a latent construct measured by covarying items maps onto traditional self-reports on multiple items. But this model is not as easily transferable to items that are objective data on natural occurrences. Data based on natural occurrences have parallels with physical measurement of concrete things that are then accumulated into a broader construct, or physiological measurement, such as using physiological indicators to arrive at an overall diagnosis of a condition.

In a sense, the item-as-measure model of conceptualization corresponds to or maps onto a measurement process where respondents provide self-reports to items. The process of measurement corresponds to the nature of the relationship between items of a measure and the underlying construct. The measurement model suggests that levels of the underlying construct lead to responses on individual items. In actual measurement, the latent construct causes responses on items of a measure. Each item is capturing some aspect of the underlying construct. Each item is carefully constructed to capture primarily the construct, although it is subject to other influences. Although each item captures some different aspect of the domain of a construct, responses to items are expected to be correlated because they are caused by the same underlying construct. Objective data, on the other hand, are, in some sense, naturally occurring and subject to many influences, one of which is the construct in question. Rather than being carefully constructed items that primarily capture the construct in question, they are naturally occurring and also happen to (sometimes coincidentally or accidentally) provide data on a construct. Structured observations are somewhere in the middle, essentially the continuum being from self-reports on items to structured observations in response to carefully designed stimuli to naturally occurring events.

BROADER ISSUES IN MEASUREMENT IN THE SOCIAL SCIENCES

We close this chapter with a discussion of some broader issues on the role of measurement in science. Again our emphasis is on intangible issues that require further explication and relate to the fundamental assumptions of measurement and the tendency in research to measure the measurable.

Assumptions of measurement

Measure development procedures assume that a construct can be isolated and examined. By measuring or manipulating individual constructs, relationships between constructs are studied and substantive hypotheses about these relationships are tested. The very notion that numbers can be assigned to attributes of people, objects, or events is premised on being able to study attributes or constructs separate from other constructs. After all, measurement relates to rules for assigning numbers to attributes of people, objects, and events. As discussed below, this is not the case for many phenomena. A complex network of constructs may influence a phenomenon and may not be separable into individual constructs for purposes of measurement.

Quantitative research involves a basic assumption that constructs can be isolated and measured or manipulated. The basis for psychometric measurement is that a single construct is being measured. In fact, the very idea of quantitative measurement involves identification and definition of an isolated construct. Phenomena or sets of isolatable constructs are studied in an experimental or survey context. Note that these quantitative approaches ideally require such isolation. Controlled experiments and correlational studies aim for such isolation. Natural experiments are quasi-experiments in that constructs are not strictly isolated. Yet alternative explanations could be accounted for at a conceptual level. In correlational and experimental studies, conceptual arguments need to be made to isolate constructs and understand interrelationships. For instance, manipulations of constructs such as product status may involve potential confounds, requiring conceptual arguments in addition to empirical evidence against alternative explanations. In designing high, medium, or low levels of status of, say, a restaurant, several other variables, such as price or quality perceptions, may be manipulated. Are results then due to status levels, or price or quality differences? Some constructs may be difficult to isolate for manipulation. Others may be impossible to measure because of their level of abstraction. In such scenarios, conceptual arguments have to be made against possible alternative explanations for findings. For instance, in the example above, alternative explanations in terms of quality or price differences rather than status differences have to be countered. A series of studies may need to be designed to show that the results can be uniquely explained by a variable, such as status, and by ruling out alternative explanations. For instance, the effect of status on a number of variables could be studied, or the effect of a number of variables on status could be studied.

A construct is also sometimes assumed to be unchanged in quantitative research; therefore, consistency is assessed over time. However, such an assumption does not hold if the phenomenon is changing. Consider a longitudinal study of a construct with a specific underlying dimensional structure. At a certain point in time, a scale may be shown to have internal consistency, stability, dimensionality, and validity. If the phenomenon in question changes over time, however, then several possibilities arise. Consider a scenario where an individual difference variable is being measured and may change over time (e.g., current mood). For such constructs, internal consistency, dimensionality, and validity can be assessed. However, stability is not germane because mood is transitory rather than enduring. Alternatively, the internal structure of a scale may change over time. Consider, for example, an individual trait of a social psychological nature, such as social identity, that changes over time. The internal structure in terms of the underlying dimensions may vary over time. The parallel here is with internal structures of constructs that vary across cultures. Constructs may be specific to cultures. Alternatively, measures may be specific to cultures with underlying constructs being identical in internal structure across cultures.

A key requirement for longitudinal studies where a construct is changing is a validated measure as a starting point. A starting frame of reference and point of comparison is provided by such measures. Thus, over time, changes in internal structure can be assessed, such as stronger relationships between dimensions of a construct, without added uncertainty about measurement to begin with. A similar argument applies in cross-cultural measurement.

Well-developed measures of constructs in one culture provide a baseline or a comparison point for measure development in other cultures.

The assumption in quantitative research that a single construct can be isolated and measured or manipulated has important implications for conceptual and methodological issues. Can a single construct be isolated conceptually? Methodologically? Quantitative measurement may not be a viable research method in many situations. Qualitative research offers an alternative in such situations. When constructs cannot be isolated and studied, the researcher serves as the measurement instrument in understanding a complex pattern of interrelationships between constructs. The assumptions underlying quantitative measurement should be noted, that there are isolatable constructs that can be studied. In fact, as discussed, some constructs cannot be easily isolated and manipulated. In such situations, conceptual arguments have to be made for one explanation versus another. Rather than completely isolating constructs in either a manipulation or a measurement, alternative arguments could be ruled out conceptually. Pushing this line of reasoning further, qualitative research is a viable approach for studying a number of interrelated constructs that cannot be isolated but have to be studied as complex relationships. Conceptualizations in qualitative research can be more organic in nature rather than of a strict linear, causal form.

Measuring the 'measurable'

There is an understandable tendency in science to measure what is easy to measure. Over time, these measures take on a life of their own to the point where they become the only things worth measuring. A case in point is some ability testing. With such tests, the emphasis is on demonstrating measurement properties that are relatively easy to demonstrate (i.e., reliability or consistency). This stands to reason because a reasonable level of consistency is necessary for further inquiry. But validity is an entirely different story that requires fuller understanding of that thing being measured. Although predictive validity can be shown through the use of a criterion, such as grade point average in college, the criterion variable itself may suffer from the issue of measurability. Meaningful constructs of success or accomplishment are very difficult, often impossible to capture. The point to note is that empirically demonstrable psychometric properties such as reliability may often be the tail that wags the dog. So what is to be done? At a minimum, a clear understanding of that thing that is being measured is indispensable. If measurement drives the research, then the construct should be defined appropriately, resisting the temptation to use narrowly construed measures to represent broad constructs. At an extreme, each item can be construed as a measure of something – a very concrete construct. However, this is an inefficient way of conducting scientific research. Multiple items enhance reliability by averaging, but also by using items measuring slightly different things that covary with each other.

Rigorous scientific research is often associated with isolating constructs and studying them through specific methods. Such reductionism comes at a price – the inability to study the big picture. The rigor and precision that is possible by isolating and studying specific constructs leads to a problem of measuring the measurable and researching the researchable. It is manifest in finding different ways to study narrow issues. Paradoxically, more sophisticated methods may be applied to study narrower and narrower issues. A variation on this notion is the use of a tried and tested research method to look for problems it can solve (somewhat like finding a hammer on a weekend at home and then looking for nails to pound in). All of this is part of the marketplace of ideas where different types of research compete with each other. The purpose here is not to pass judgment on different types of research or individual research projects as much as to make broader observations at the level of disciplines and methods. Researchers choose programs of research for a variety of reasons, including interest, and different types of research serve to build a picture.

Several points are noteworthy with regard to measuring the measurable, and therefore putting the measurement 'cart' ahead of the construct 'horse'. Although a pragmatic consideration of what is measurable is, of course, relevant, it is sometimes the only consideration. Assumptions about what is measurable may need to be challenged. Innovative ways of measuring difficult constructs may need to be attempted. Innovation also extends to the conceptual level, where conceptually rich constructs and complex relationships between constructs are visualized. Although all such hypothesized relationships cannot be tested rigorously through quantitative measurement, they should nevertheless be conceptualized. Moreover, qualitative research provides a way of assessing a constellation of constructs wherein the researcher is the instrument. Such research requires a different kind of rigor. Rigor is often associated with certain quantitative, reductionist approaches. But a narrow view of rigor can result in narrow issues being studied. Different research questions require different types of research methods. Some complex phenomena require rigorous qualitative research; the alternative is to not research the phenomena at all. Perhaps rigor, which is sometimes used to refer exclusively to the use of a specific research method or a data analysis technique, should be extended to the nature of conceptual thinking as well as the fit between research methods and research objectives. The nature of evidence differs for different phenomena; establishing causality between smoking and cancer involves a different type of evidence than establishing causality between information processing goals and memory. Proof is different in the physical versus social sciences and so, too, within the social sciences. A narrow view of methodological rigor can lead to a narrow focus on narrow research questions.

Several metaphors could be used to characterize a narrow substantive or methodological approach: lenses or filters or mental compartments or more extreme paradigmatic straitjackets. A story about the elephant and the six men who could not see is one such metaphor. One version of the story relates how each man touched a different part of an elephant; one thought the tail was a piece of rope, another thought a leg was a tree trunk, and so on. If the elephant is the phenomenon under study, the aim is to see as much of the elephant as possible through substantive theories and methodologies, while realizing that many parts remain to be seen. A narrow substantive focus may narrow the methodological focus, which in turn may narrow substantive insights.

CONCLUSION

This chapter aimed to explicate some of the intangibles of measurement in the social sciences and provide direction for the design and use of measures and methods. Perhaps no single issue characterizes this need to explicate intangibles than that of the meaning of measurement error itself. A clear and detailed understanding of measurement error forms the foundation that permeates the development as well as the use of measures and the design of research methods. The chapter then covered some intangible issues; in using measures in research design, in understanding different types of measures ranging from the physical to the social sciences, and finally in broader issues in the role of measurement in social science. These are, of course, just some of the intangible issues in measurement, and other issues relate to different types of measures (e.g., stimulus-centered versus respondent-centered scales), measurement in experimental design, etc. (Viswanathan, 2005, 2008), as well as the numerous issues relating to measurement in different contexts covered in this handbook, such as cross-cultural measurement. Ultimately, by explicating intangible issues in measurement, research design can be improved and a wide range of phenomena in social science research can be studied more rigorously.

NOTE

1 The material in this chapter is reprinted or adapted from *Measurement Error and Research Design* (Viswanathan, 2005) and appears here with the kind permission of Sage.

REFERENCES

Andrews, F. M. (1984) 'Construct validity and error components of survey measures: A structural modeling approach', *Public Opinion Quarterly*, 48: 409–42.

Bagozzi, R. P. (1984) 'A prospectus for theory construction in marketing', *Journal of Marketing*, 48: 11–29.

Bollen, K. A. (1989) *Structural equations with latent variables.* New York: Wiley.

Campbell, D. T. and Fiske, D. W. (1959) 'Convergent and discriminant validation by the multitrait-multimethod matrix', *Psychological Bulletin*, 56(3): 100–22.

Churchill, G. A., Jr. (1979) 'A paradigm for developing better measures of marketing constructs', *Journal of Marketing Research*, 16(2): 64–73.

Feldman, J. M. and Lynch, J. G., Jr. (1988) 'Self-generated validity: Effects of measurement on belief, attitude, intention, and behavior', *Journal of Applied Psychology*, 73: 421–35.

Gerbing, D. W. and Anderson, J. C. (1988) 'An updated paradigm for scale development incorporating unidimensionality and its assessment', *Journal of Marketing Research*, 25(5): 186–92.

Ghiselli, E. E. (1964) *Theory of psychological measurement.* New York: McGraw-Hill.

Groves, R. M. (1991) 'Measurement error across disciplines', in P. P. Biemer, R. M. Groves, L. E. Lyberg, N. A. Mathiowetz and S. Sudman (eds), *Measurement error in surveys.* New York: Wiley. pp. 1–25.

Gulliksen, H. (1950) *Theory of mental tests.* New York: Wiley.

Kerlinger, F. N. (1986) 'Constructs, variables and definitions', in *Foundations of behavioral research.* 3rd edition.New York: Holt, Rinehart and Winston. pp. 26–44.

Knowles, E. S. (1988) 'Item context effects on personality scales: Measuring changes the measure', *Journal of Personality and Social Psychology*, 55: 312–20.

Knowles, E. S. and Byers, B. (1996) 'Reliability shifts in measurement reactivity: Driven by content engagement or self-engagement?', *Journal of Personality and Social Psychology*, 70(5): 1080–90.

Lennox, R. D. and Dennis, M. L. (1994) 'Measurement error issues in substance abuse services research: Lessons from structural equation modeling and psychometric theory', *Evaluation and Program Planning*, 17(4): 399–407.

Nunnally, J. C. (1978) *Psychometric theory.* 2nd edition. New York: McGraw-Hill.

Nunnally, J. C. and Bernstein, I. H. (1994) 'Introduction', in J. C. Nunnally and I. H Bernstein (eds), *Psychometric theory.* New York: McGraw-Hill.

Simmons, C. J., Bickart, B. A. and Lynch, C. J. (1993) 'Capturing and creating public opinion in survey research', *Journal of Consumer Research*, 20(2): 316–29.

Viswanathan, M. (2005) *Measurement error and research design*, London: Sage Publications.

Viswanathan, M. (2008) 'Measurement error in experimental designs in consumer psychology', in C. P. Haugtvedt, P. H. Herr and F. R. Kardes (eds) *Handbook of consumer psychology*, New York: Lawrence Erlbaum Associates. pp. 1133–59.

16

Towards a More Rigorous Scientific Approach to Social Measurement: Considering a Grounded Indicator Approach to Developing Measurement Tools

Eric Tucker

INTRODUCTION

Social measurement creates the possibility for a more rigorous scientific understanding of the social world. The movement towards rigorous measurement instrument design merits attention because the quality of such tools shapes the quality of social scientific understanding. This chapter proposes a 'grounded indicator approach' to social research that is both critical of current efforts to develop measurement tools and intended to enhance measure development.

Concepts are explanatory devices that social scientists create to understand the world. As such, concepts do not exist 'out there', but rather to make communication more efficient and effective. When made operational, concepts are translated into indicators; that is, into measures or proxies. In chemistry, an indicator is a substance that changes colour in the presence and quantity of a certain ion. For a social scientific indicator to have validity, it must measure accurately those aspects of the phenomenon it intends to measure (Hammersley, 1987, 1998). If the precision or accuracy is weak, so too is the validity of the indicator. Social measures should be both analytic and sensitising – they should provide useful descriptions, explanations, and applications.

This chapter calls for rigour and science in the development of instruments of social measurement. As researchers descend from the concept to the operational indicator, they go through a range of phases with varying degrees of rigour and deliberateness. Rigour minimises the gap between the indicator and the corresponding constellation of social practices and occurrences. Rigour, here, refers to the accuracy, precision, validity, and integrity of the measurement enterprise. A scientific approach to social measurement reflects systematic investigation, observation, description, and explanation of social phenomena.

The measurement-related methodological question this chapter asks is how to move away from the contemporary emphasis on verification as the primary mechanism to secure the validity and reliability of indicators. I posit that minimising measurement error might best be achieved by a greater emphasis on the generation and modification phases as complementary to verification efforts. I look at the potential for empirical social research that focuses upon the generation and modification, in addition to the verification, of indicators. I argue that statistical verification is an internally consistent, but incomplete, approach to maximising rigour. To complement and refine the strengths of statistical verification, flexible and emergent research methods might be used to generate more thorough understandings of a particular social phenomenon, which might

in turn be used to develop higher quality indicators.

This chapter proposes the development of a 'grounded indicator approach' for social scientific research. A 'grounded indicator approach' is defined herein as the purposeful systematic generation of indicators from social scientific data. A grounded indicator approach derives indicators from the empirical study of phenomena the concept represents. This chapter outlines a grounded indicator approach and methodology, and then explores its potential strengths and limitations. It concludes by addressing certain concerns of potential critics.

PART I: LOCATING THE GROUNDED INDICATOR APPROACH WITHIN THE FIELD OF MEASUREMENT

This section frames the Grounded Indicator Approach within the broader field of social measurement.

Measurement is at the centre of social science research. A concern to develop and improve measurement unites the social sciences and is the continual focus of debate. The literature regarding the production of quality measurement instruments is vast, and this section aims merely to identify certain streams within the field of measurement and situates the Grounded Indicator Approach within them.

First, the notion of a gap between established instruments and the social world permeates the social sciences, which regularly identify areas where the quality of established measures is lower than desired. Some examples may illustrate the nature of such gaps. For instance, Shriver (1995) discusses how the measurement of current cost data in financial accounting has a systematic overstatement bias when estimating the value of industrial machinery. Powers et al. (1994) study how typed replicas of handwritten essays receive lower average scores, demonstrating the challenge of using written essays to indicate writing skill. Frisbie and Cantor (1995) study the validity of alternative methods for spelling assessment finding differential outcomes for different instruments. Potenza and Stocking (1997) explore the challenge of flawed test questions that fail to capture particular skills. Galvez and McLarty (1996) work around the limitations of demographic indicators that omit temporary residents. Whether social scientists discuss current costs, handwriting, spelling, flawed questions, or temporary residents, the gap between social reality and what the indicator captures is a recurring measurement challenge.

Second, both current measurement literature and practice tend to over-emphasise verification and correspondingly de-emphasise the process of generating new, situation-specific indicators. However, researchers involved in fields from psychology and economics to environmental policy and city planning are engaged in developing and modifying domain-specific measurement approaches. Methodologically oriented measurement literature thus lags behind measurement practice, and researchers should highlight methodological considerations, theoretical insights, and challenges in all stages of measure design. Current literature on measurement is underdeveloped. This chapter proposes the broadening of the research stream focused on discovering, developing, and provisionally verifying the integrity of new measures through rigorous thought, systematic collection, and analysis of data related to the construct in question.

The development of measures for constructs is an ongoing priority for the social sciences. Examples abound: Putnam (1993, 2000), Putnam et al. (1994), Florida (2002, 2005), Laumann (1994), and

Sen (1973, 1987, 1999, 2002) represent first-tier researchers who take this challenge seriously. Indeed, across the social sciences operationalising concepts is a priority. For example, Currie et al. (2004) develop and validate a short-form of internalised homophobia reflecting contemporary attitudes. The design of the Human Development Index of well-being (inspired by Sen) has spurred a robust research community (e.g. Gormely, 1995, Acharya and Wall, 1994). Noble et al. (2004) describe the development of a scale assessing attitudes towards working single parents. Le et al. (2005) construct a student readiness inventory of the psychosocial and academic-related skills that predict university performance and retention. These studies represent the generation of new indicators across the social sciences.

Modification of existing and emerging indicators works in tandem, and iteratively, with generation. I will discuss various factors that call for indicator modification. First, indicators sometimes miss the mark, requiring adjustment, e.g. Farrall and Ditton (1999) suggest 'fear of crime' measures are inaccurate and then use social research to enhance theorisation and measurement. Second, as alternative methods to measure existing concepts emerge, options are weighed, and modification ensues. For instance, Sharpe and Abdel-Ghany (1997) test alternative measurement strategies for capturing the value of homemakers' time. Third, items (variables) that operationalise a given construct may require modification. For example, Walden et al. (1994) compare two different approaches to estimating out-of-pocket health expenditures. Fourth, when the definition of a concept changes the indicators also require modification. Stratton (1994) re-examines the empirical definition of involuntary part-time employment, saying that current indicators overstate its frequency. Similarly,

Carlson et al. (1994) describe how the evolving definition of the family unit driven by increases in divorce, re-marriage, and single-parenting provokes adaptation. Fifth, changing conditions necessitate indicator evolution. Teague (2000) discusses how modification transformed the instrument of the 2001 England and Wales Census, particularly with regard to sub-populations. Existing measures require rigorous adaptation to keep pace with societal change. Researchers modify when indicators are inaccurate, new approaches to measurement emerge, contextual conditions or the concept's definition change, and the variables require adaptation.

Third, the field of measurement places high priority on the statistical validation of emergent indicators. However, the indicators themselves are often based on logical deduction, assertion, and speculation, rather than rigorous scientific research. Empirical research that aims to improve indicator design and quality is a small fraction of published work. Journals of measurement print relatively few articles on research geared towards empirical generation and modification. Instead, scales appear as 'already always' existent and in need of statistical verification. This chapter addresses what social scientists spend relatively little time conducting research upon: how to operationalise constructs through concept definition, category development and domain delineation, item generation, the subsequent scale development, and modification. Researchers instead tend to focus on statistical tests to secure validity and reliability.

Examples of articles that focus on how constructs are conceptualised and developed represent one strand of current indicator design and improvement. Stevenson and Evans (1994) discuss conceptualisation and measurement of Cognitive Holding Power. Giancarlo et al. (2004) report on the development of a new instrument to measure mental motivation. Dowson and McInerney (2004) examine the development and validation of the Goal Oriented and Learning Strategies survey. Asher and Defina (1995) study the shortcomings of measures of income inequality that relate to age-income profiles and propose improvements in conceptualisation. Wolfe et al. (2004) compare the quality of scales of teacher perception of instructional environments, focusing on dimensionality, internal consistency, and category effectiveness. Articles describing the design and improvement of indicators are abundant.

Finally, measurement error should be at the centre of discussions of measure design. Viswanathan argues that 'measurement error should be understood in each stage of developing measures and their use', suggesting that 'errors in developing and using measures are closely interrelated' (2005: 386). Researchers and methodologists alike reflect on the specific threats to validity and reliability encountered, and offer nuts and bolts discussions of indicator development that minimise measurement error. Authors such as Viswanathan (2005) and Salkind (2004, 2005) provide basic analyses. Bollen elaborates upon more advanced psychometric procedures to detect and reduce measurement error (Bollen, 1998a, b, Bollen and Lennox, 1991). By reporting innovative approaches to indicator design that minimise error, researchers can share principles and practices to guide the next generation.

Rigorous concepts for social research

My call for rigorous enquiry is inspired by Husserl's insight that, 'only ideals have a rigorous identity' (1970d: 313). Ideals (in this usage) are pure; they are possible types that have exact specifications. For instance, a triangle has exactly three sides. Ideals can be 'practically applied to the world of sense-experience', but researchers must be careful to distinguish between the *type* 'triangle' and the construction paper-cut out *token* (Husserl, 1970b: 24). The bodies encountered in the social world, for instance, are never geometrically 'pure' shapes. A pure straight line or circle never occurs in the life-world. Encountered shapes (and, indeed, social phenomena) are marked by deformations and vagueness. According to Husserl, 'the things of the intuitively given surrounding world fluctuate, in general and in all their properties' (1970a: 25).

The notion of Ideal Types here refers to a descriptive category honed to facilitate communication amongst social scientists. Ideal Types make reading social practices meaningful, describing the essential without seeking to understand the contingent. For instance, to understand the meaning of 'going to the store' one does not need to understand the contingencies (e.g. which route to take). The meaning of a particular Ideal Type is distinct and precisely defined. The social phenomena themselves are not so clear and would remain unintelligible if applicable, exact concepts were not created. Ideal Types are more or less exact and functional. Returning to the example of geometry, an isosceles triangle has at least two (of three) sides that are exactly the same length. The properties of an isosceles triangle give it a functionality that is helpful for answering certain questions.

The social world has several characteristics that make Ideal Types more conceptually complicated than geometric shapes: its infinite complexity and diversity; its fluidity; the inability of social researchers to control and experiment with much human phenomena; the subjective meaning of human action; reactivity to the researcher's humanity; and the significance of occurrences to individuals. While logic may be sufficient to distinguish the features

of a plain or the curvature of an arc, creating new specific Ideal Types to represent social phenomena, I suggest, requires the rigour of the social scientific method. Further, a given social interaction can never be exhausted by a single concept because that concept only delineates one aspect of the interaction. Ideal Types are human constructs and as such offer a partial and limited perspective of understanding social reality.

PART II: DEFINING A GROUNDED INDICATOR APPROACH

This chapter sets out to offer some methodological insights based on an empirical research project (Tucker, 2007a, b), which suggested the potential for a new approach to measurement development in social science. I suggest naming such an approach a 'Grounded Indicator Approach' (GIA), and define it as one that entails the generation, modification, and verification of measures through empirical social research.

The chapter's goal is to outline this proposal for a GIA, explain its basic tenets, outline some potential benefits, defend its relevance, and respond to potential criticisms. I propose signposts to help researchers know when they stray too far from the grounded generation route. When the road to conducting grounded indicator research becomes more familiar, researchers will be able to discover alternative routes, and invest in new methodological vehicles.

A full description of the features, aims, advantages, and procedures of the GIA would require more breadth and depth than possible in this chapter alone. This chapter does not, therefore, provide a foundational, generalised description of GIA, nor a detailed manual. Nor does it seek to explain the core concepts and procedures that GIA might eventually entail. Given the formative stage of GIA's development as a notion, I offer a preliminary proposal rather than an extensive, detailed conjecture of how this approach might eventually work. In this sense, the goal is 'to stimulate rather than freeze thinking about the topic' (Glaser and Strauss, 1967: 9).

Features of a grounded indicator approach

The Grounded Indicator Approach (GIA) uses empirical data derived from the observation of real phenomena to generate, modify, and validate its indicators. In this way it is distinguished from other approaches to generation and modification based on logical deduction, assertion, and speculation. The term 'grounded' refers to an emphasis on indicators that emerge from and in relationship to data regarding empirical phenomena. Social evidence serves as the foundation of grounded indicators, which are built up from the ground of empirical research, and thus are firmly rooted in the context of production. The GIA is both an emerging set of methodological propositions and an ongoing methodological discussion that employs the conceptual distinctions that this chapter introduces.

The GIA entails conducting empirical research at each of the three major phases of indicator development: generation, modification, and validation. I argue that the current measure development practice overemphasises rigorous, statistical verification (validation) of indicators for concepts whose nature and dimensions have been clarified through logic, speculation, and deduction. Notions of excellence in measure development adhere too much to verification, and thus de-emphasise indicator generation and modification.

Social research into aspects of the three phases of measure development, with a GIA, occurs in an iterative, systematic manner: (i) *Generation*: Generation is the first stage of development and production where the potential indicator comes into being. It includes exploratory research, literature review, concept definition, measure conceptualisation, domain delineation, item generation, and scale generation. The GIA proposes that each component of generation be subject to the rigours of social science research. (ii) *Modification*: Modification is the process of altering scales and items in order to improve their function. Efforts to hone measurement instrument design might include expert review, piloting, systematic adjustments, evidence-based revision, identification of gaps between the instrument and measured phenomenon, multiple locations and multiple condition testing, and systematic assessment of the advantages of various measurement options. (iii) *Verification*: It encompasses most existing statistical techniques to secure validity and reliability. It includes reliability testing, dimensionality testing, validity testing, and validation. Procedures included in this category include: item-to-total correlations, item means, test-retest correlations, factor loadings, residuals, and cross-construct correlations.

The features of the GIA that I propose would include:

- A process of grounding indicators in social research (i.e. purposeful systematic generation of indicators from data). It would seek to derive indicators from the study of phenomena relevant to the concept being operationalised. Grounded indicators are developed and provisionally verified through systematic collection and analysis of social scientific data.
- Minimisation of measurement error through the rigorous application of appropriate social scientific research methods at each stage of measure development.
- The differentiation of generation, modification, and verification as distinct phases in measure development. The GIA differs from

approaches where verification is statistically rigorous but the generation and modification stages are based upon logical deduction, assertion, and speculation. It recommends the reassessment of the relative priority that each of the three phases receive given the current relative over-emphasis of verification and relative de-emphasis of generation and modification.

- A research process that moves step-wise between the conceptual and the operational domains in an iterative, systematic manner, involving the purposive use of evidence, argumentation, and professional judgement as researchers descend the ladder of abstraction from the concept to the operational indicator.
- Standards of scientific research including the definition of assumptions, stipulations of procedures, defence of presuppositions, adherence to transparency, and openness to professional peer consideration and scrutiny.
- Methodologies best suited to respond to particular questions and development stages. The GIA embraces a methodological pluralism that includes qualitative and quantitative data, a focus on both meaning and behaviour, competing notions of the role of natural science as a model, experimental and natural settings, and the use of induction and deduction.

The GIA can create indicators suited to their supposed purpose. It is contrasted with indicators developed through 'logical deduction from a priori assumptions' (Glaser and Strauss, 1967: 3). Viswanathan contends that these steps are often blurred and iterative.

> The steps in the process emphasize that traversing the distance from the conceptual to the operational requires a systematic process. Rather than consider a concept and move directly to item generation, and use of a resulting measure, the distance between the conceptual and the operational has to be spanned carefully and iteratively (Viswanathan, 2005: 5).

The GIA means that grounded indicators 'not only come from the data, but are systematically worked out in relation to the data during the course of the research' (Glaser and Strauss, 1967: 6). As the

paragraph above suggests, the generation of grounded indicators involves empirical research at each phase and entails purposeful systematic empirical research and thinking whether the task at hand is delineating the dimensions of a concept or developing items.

Aspirations and aims for the grounded indicator approach

Aspirations that I hold for the eventual grounded indicator research conducted by social researchers include that it has the potential to do the following.

- Promote the gradual accumulation of understanding within a research community about the operationalisation of a particular concept through the progressive conduct of empirical social research aimed at producing data sets that inform the generation, modification, and verification of indicators.
- Benefit from an increased appreciation for conducting research to design and improve indicators as well as for the relative value of investing empirical social research resources into the generation and modification of high-quality measurement instruments.
- Accept the importance of high-quality indicators and promote the notion of measure development as a unique contribution that social scientific researchers can make to knowledge.
- Acknowledge the unique contributions that the labour of professional, policy, critical, and public social scientists can contribute to measure development.
- Hold relevance to the development of a range of measurement tools, including surveys, tests, and observations.
- Minimise the gap between the measurement instruments developed and the social world.
- Provide approaches and techniques for the development of instruments that measure the difficult to measure, including unobtrusive measures, measurement for evaluation, and measuring the elusive.

Further, the Grounded Indicator Approach (GIA) aspires to engage in the following broad conversations, in that it fulfils the following.

- Promotes multidisciplinary, interdisciplinary, and international research discourses on social measurement.
- Advocates the exploration of how social scientists in general design measures, what problems they encounter, and how they overcome these challenges.
- Encourages the publication of autobiographical reflections of researchers through real-world cases that illustrate trends, issues, and significant principles in measurement design concretely.
- Examines the relationship between the theory and practice of measurement and addresses measurement at methodological, procedural, and conceptual levels through the publication of accounts of the process of generating indicators and scales.
- Seeks to broaden understanding about the diverse and emergent ways researchers might develop measurement instruments.
- Engages in a sustained conversation with a comprehensive set of dialogues on the methods, contexts, fundamental issues and practices of measurement as a feature of research design in the social sciences.

Thus, the GIA will potentially encompass conversations with a range of researchers including psychologists, educationalists, political scientists, and sociologists. Although practitioners in particular sub-fields (e.g. RASCH or Item Response models) may not see the immediate connection, I envision a dialogue that engages all of these sub-fields.

In making the case for this enterprise, I hope to encourage interest in rigorous measurement as central to social scientific research while broadening the meaning of measure development. Governments, corporate initiatives, research institutes, and non-governmental agencies use measurement instruments. Indicator generation, however, is a unique contribution of social scientists.

I have the following aims for grounded indicators when they are developed.

- Provide thorough, accurate, valid, and reliable descriptions, interpretations, and explanations.
- Meet extant standards for indicator quality, including coherence, consistency, clarity, integration, parsimony, and scope.
- Be workable and usable in practical applications.
- Be both analytic (i.e. they will designate characteristics of concepts) and sensitising (i.e. they will illuminate phenomena and yielding a 'meaningful' picture).
- Possess 'wide applicability' in a range of contexts and users.
- Be based on acknowledgment of the threat of 'decadent measurement', pointing the way toward critical, reflective social scientific measurement.
- Provide novel perspectives on the social world and facilitate theoretical advances.
- Facilitate a critical, reflective relationship between the evidence produced through social measurement and the resultant explanations.

The GIA advances the position that indicator adequacy cannot be divorced from the manner of its generation. Grounded indicators fit the data available about the social phenomena that they seek to operationalise, because they are derived from and then illustrated by data.

GIA research aims to produce workable indicators meaningfully relevant to the phenomena and capable of describing it: they are operable, functional, and capable of measuring the phenomena they intend to measure. The feasibility of the GIA undergirds this proposal. I would not suggest the approach if I did not believe that it could generate indicators more successful than those logically deduced and then verified.

The grounded indicator approach and social evidence

Social science sometimes suffers from an uncritical relationship between evidence produced through research and the resultant explanation. Evidence is peculiarly social in that its use and validity are a matter of public articulation, assessment, and deliberation. The GIA seeks to correct circumstances when the generation, interpretation, analysis, and communication of indicators and their meaning take pathological forms. At times social scientists 'make the case' with indicators pathologically – that is, with explanative forms that exhibit habitually maladaptive and compulsive characteristics, and manifest functions of oppression and social disease. By disease I mean an abnormal, harmful tendency. Pathological explanation uses grossly atypical and spectacularly ill-conditioned data to dismiss typicality. Non-pathological explanation, in contrast, tends to remove exceptional cases from the centre of discussion.

Although the notion of pathological explanation will be developed more fully elsewhere, it is sufficient to note that indicators may make phenomena intelligible through deviation from healthy description. I reference the work of Lewis Gordon (1995a, b, 1997a–c, 2000, 2006), Franz Fanon (1967a, b), Edmund Husserl (1910, 1931, 1960, 1970a–d), Nelson Maldonado-Torres (2006), Maurice Merleau-Ponty (1962), Jean-Paul Sartre (1948, 1956), and Alfred Schutz (1962, 1970) and Schutz and Luckmann (1973) to argue that indicators too often rest on 'taken for granted' assumptions, and instead need to begin with a description of the foundational structures of the everyday life-world. By bracketing extant disciplinary assumptions about measurement methodology, the GIA might help to acknowledge and grapple with the threat of pathological explanation.

Alfred Schutz introduces a notion of the 'taken for granted' in the everyday life-world (1962). Social scientists who would explain human action and thought in non-pathological ways, I suggest, must begin by describing the foundational structures of this everyday life-world (the 'natural attitude'), the reality in which one continuously participates as one eats breakfast, drinks tea, or walks in the park. Elsewhere, I've described how I integrate such an effort into my own research (Tucker, 2007a).The life-world is the fundamental, paramount reality that conscious, normal adults take for granted in the attitude of common sense. By 'taken for granted', Schutz means the unquestionable, everyday state of affairs that is unproblematic until further notice. For humans in the natural attitude the world is never a mere aggregation of coloured spots, incoherent noises, or centres of cold and warmth. Humans see trees, listen to music, and experience hugs, finding themselves in a world taken for granted and self-evidently 'real'. It is the unexamined ground, the taken-for-granted frame holding all problems that the researchers must overcome. Researchers assume the validity of this personal stock of knowledge until further notice.

Social scientists must, I argue, attend to a precise analysis of the inducements through which they are motivated to regard an experience as in need of explication. Said another way, social scientists need to consider their experience as in need of re-explication, a step that interrupts the course of the chain of self-evidency. The Grounded Indicator Approach starts with that premise.

The grounded indicator approach: An example from researching social capital

An extended example of Grounded Indicator Research (GIA) focused on a particular stage of operationalisation (conceptualisation) may help illustrate the broader methodological argument. Defining social capital as the relationships and networks that facilitate collective action and access to resources, this researcher undertook two case studies that were designed to generate categories which describe some of the possible practices that potentially contribute to its formation or deformation. The first examines Urban Debate Leagues (UDLs) in American cities. The second explores Get Out The Vote (GOTV) infrastructures that focused on young voters in 'swing states' in the 2004 American Presidential campaign. The categories this grounded research produced illuminate potentially operable dimensions of social capital formation, hopefully advantageously positioning future measurement instrument design.

I conducted empirical research to investigate whether minimising measurement error might best be achieved by a greater emphasis on the generation and modification phases of development. It further suggests that statistical verification is an internally consistent, but incomplete, approach. The research focused on identifying some major categories, generated from the analysis case study data, which describe the social practices that potentially contribute to the formation or deformation of social capital. Such categories, it was hoped, would illuminate potentially operable dimensions of the concept and suggest features that merit further consideration.

Ethnographic research methods, among flexible and emergent approaches, were thus be used to generate more thorough understandings of a particular social phenomenon, which might in turn be used to develop higher quality indicators.

This research began as a pilot enquiry into how to best describe the education-enhancing and education-enabling relationships and networks I observed led me to explore indicators for social capital. The lack of agreement on a focused, rigorously articulated conceptualisation and set of indicators frustrates those eager to make social capital usable as a tool for evidence-based public policy and school improvement.

Each case had two parallel *data collection* phases. Phase One involved conducting a process evaluation of the programming initiatives. Phase Two involved conducting repeated, in-depth interviews to get a sense of how participants perceived and gave meaning to the programme. This approach generated data that speaks to both the structural and the textural features of the life-world. Structural features happen in spatial and physical reality. Textural features result from meaning making and human interpretation. The subsequent *data analysis* process was also multi-tiered. First, comprehensive, synthetic descriptions of the essential features of the program (UDLs or GOTV Infrastructures) and of the textural descriptions were generated through empirical phenomenological analysis. Second, these evaluative descriptions were shared with practitioners and expert reviewers who offered feedback that was incorporated into final descriptive reports. Third, these final descriptions were used as the raw material for category generation and development. I explain how the methods and the criteria employed lend themselves to 'category' development.

I conducted two compressed ethnographic investigations (Walford, 2001) selected for their relation to the research questions. I collected in-depth, unstructured data from existing social settings in order to describe some of the unique, sensitising aspects of each case that highlighted potentially essential features of the relevant social phenomena. I suggest that the features and strengths of ethnography, specifically, and qualitative research, more generally, make it uniquely suited to contribute to the development of new indicators and the improvement of existing indicators. Each case was selected in order to:

- extend to and shed insight into core dimensions of social capital, including structural and cognitive features; micro-, meso-, and macro-features; bonding, bridging and linking; strong and weak ties; intense and limited ties; formal and informal ties; homogenous and heterogeneous groups; network density and structural holes; network orientation; and considerations of quality and quantity;
- represent an exemplary instance of practices that attempt to contribute to the formation of social capital, expose those relationships and networks that are open to intervention, and distinguish those strands of social capital that facilitate access to resources and enable collective action;
- help operationalise the notions of the social embeddedness of individual choices and actions (Coleman, 1988); of the structuration of human action (Giddens, 1984); and of the constrained project (Schutz and Luckmann, 1973);
- contribute to the generation of categories that are both analytic and sensitising;
- allow focus on potentially education-enhancing aspects of relationships and networks; and
- facilitate access to sites and to a range of data sources.

Through the research, I developed categories of social capital formation that indicated that particular social practices might contribute substantially to social capital formation or deformation. I then developed a three-fold framework component: *actions*, *contexts*, and *discourses*. Each component reflected a qualitative data analysis process similar to that undertaken for category development.

I developed a three-component framework to classify categories: *actions*, *contexts*, and *discourses*. *Actions* entail purposive procedures moving towards an envisioned goal. Categories considered as actions include establishing hubs for communication and activity, reaching out through personal networks, communication with target communities, recruiting participants, focusing on participant retention, providing resources to learn how to participate, engaging in advocacy efforts, creating an expense list, making an effort to secure financial support, maximising quality of contact, and embracing role- and task-differentiation. *Contexts* are meaning-structures that serve as settings for social actions. Categories defined as contexts include making space for supporters to contribute, navigating the spatial context of networks, and assumption of membership expectations. These structures also include a context of common action, inspiration, being defined by the opposition, urgency, and relevance. *Discourses* are extended, interactive communication practices dealing with a particular topic, including acknowledging participant contribution, articulating the rationale for a given tool, articulating incentives to participate, and translating private concerns into group concerns. *Discourses* also include discourses of interiority, realisability, and efficacy.

The purpose of introducing this work is to demonstrate the nature of systematic, empirical research at all phases of research. Category development, like all stages of operationalisation, benefits from the rigors of social research.

PART III: EXPLORING THE RELEVANCE OF GROUNDED INDICATORS

Having made the case for the grounded indicator approach as potentially improving measure quality and the resulting evidence and explanation, I turn to the relevance of grounded indicators. Do measures of poverty and well-being developed in Western Europe mean the same thing in Lagos, Nigeria, or in rural Burkina Faso? Should the definitions of rape developed in 1970s New York City be transposed without adaptation to contemporary South Africa or Pakistan? What does it mean to translate performance input measures from a drug rehabilitation non-governmental organisation (NGO) in Delhi to an urban education reform NGO in Chicago? Do the self-report indicators of condom use for commercial sex workers developed in Baltimore have the same validity in the agricultural fields of Ethiopia? Fundamentally, these questions are about the *relevance* of indicators. The question is, *why do indicators generated in one context matter in another?* Why are the months spent generating, modifying, and validating indicators something other than profoundly idiosyncratic? Why should other researchers and practitioners treat grounded indicators as important and, indeed, why use them? A critical discussion of the concept of relevance and the applicability of grounded indicators to situations beyond the context of creation follows.

On one side, a strong universalising tendency might urge researchers to embrace the general application of grounded indicators to other settings and contexts. On the other, a strong particularising tendency might argue indicators generated in one context cannot be legitimately applied to other situations – the general relevance of the findings is low. Each position has strengths and weaknesses, and researchers surely desire some happy middle ground. These tendencies ultimately have components that nest within each other. In a Venn diagram of the two, tendencies components overlap. The by-product of both tendencies, the synergy and the synthesis of universalising and particularising urges, will prove most fruitful. But where is the overlap?

As Walford observed, 'one of the difficulties that pervades social science and educational research is the lack of agreement about the meaning of words' (2001). Indeed, researchers seem to mean

a range of things when they say the word 'generalisability' or relevance. In order to understand the strength and some of the limitations of the universalising and particularising tendencies, I will look at a range of definitions and perspectives on each side.

Universalising indicators entails seeing them as universally applicable. In the strong formulation of this position, indicators become applicable to all purposes, conditions, or situations – they have worldwide scope, limitless applicability, and encompass all members of the social world. No one advocates this strong (overstated) position, but some writers on generalisability come close. Kaplan argues that for a finding to be generalisable, it must be truly universal and unrestricted with regard to time and space (1964). From this perspective, indicators must thus be applicable 'always and everywhere,' provided that the appropriate conditions are satisfied. They would have enduring value that is context-free. Some authors compliment this perspective, adding that the goal of science, and thus of scientific measurement, is to speak authoritatively and generally about diverse populations and times. Campbell and Stanley might comment that indicators should hold validity to a range of populations, settings, and treatments (1963). Robson's more subtle formulation might suggest that the generalisability of indicators refers to the extent to which they are generally applicable to contexts, situations, times, or persons other than those in which the indicators were developed (2002).

The particularising tendency, in its opposition to the general or universal application of grounded indicators, is wary of the possibility that particulars will be ambushed behind generalisations. First, the unique and specific aspects of the people, things, places, categories, and times studied leave their residue on the indicators generated.

Second, the contexts where grounded indicators will be applied must be treated individually; the details are worthy of note and may need to be specified. Walford captures some of this dilemma when he wrote that qualitative research 'requires a focus on a very small number of sites, yet there is often a desire to draw conclusions which have a wider applicability than just those single cases' (2001: 15). The strong form of the particularlising tendency is overly concerned with details about the circumstances of application. It demands exacting attention to the particulars of the context of application.

Some reject notions of generalisability entirely. Denzin suggests that interpretivists believe that when any given instance of social interaction is thickly described, it will disclose some of the structure and essential meaning of the life-world (1997). Lincoln and Guba attack generalisability in its classical sense of freedom from time and context, as represented by Kaplan or Smith, arguing that there are always many conditions, contingencies, and disjunctions (1979). Human action always has an embodied perspective and a time and place. Cronbach et al. point out that valid conclusions corrode with time (1972). Lincoln and Guba (1997) also write that generalisations do not exist 'out there' in nature, but rather are actively generated by researchers. As a product of imagination, generalisations are thus temporally and contextually relative. They are mere inductive, logical statements rather than universal truths.

Given the strong cases of both sides, what should researchers want indicators to be able to do? The GIA aims to limit the application of indicators to contexts where they have dubious fit and working capacity. Grounded indicators have a sociological meaning that is hopefully both analytic and sensitising while helping to account for and interpret what emerges

in new situations. It is always possible for an indicator to be tenuously connected and not clearly applicable. One goal of a GIA is the generation of indicators with more clearly delimited boundaries of applicability. Humility about the broad applicability of grounded indicators is necessary, but the goal is the development of indicators that are generally applicable and possess descriptive, explanatory, and predictive power.

Indicators operationalise concepts, which are themselves 'used to define, describe and suggest possible explanations for some phenomenon or activities, they do often also try to make links both to grand theory and to micro-level theory' (Walford, 2001: 148). Concepts offer models that are simplifications of complex realities. Particular indicators bring conceptual models into the everyday world by focusing on a particular feature at the expense of others. Others might concentrate on completely different aspects. The indicators that researchers choose to operationalise a concept, thus influences the story their models tell. Indeed, different indicators can produce distinct, even contradictory models. These contradictions, however, can be fruitful.

In order to tease out which portions of universalising and particularising tendencies overlap, researchers need to discuss specific proposals. Where these tendencies overlap and co-mingle, researchers may find that they inspire a productive synthesis – for ultimately, researchers hope to understand better when indicators generated in one context are applicable in another.

Relevance refers to the degree to which an indicator can be legitimately compared across groups. Gomm et al. might say that the generalisability of an indicator references its general relevance and applicability (2000). Goetz and LeCompte might argue that the potential for applicability of an indicator relates to 'comparability' and 'translatability' (1984). How well does the context of creation compare to that application? Does the indicator translate, in that it solicits information in the context of application fluently? Indicators, as efforts to capture concepts, may have features in common with telling metaphors, illustrative jokes, and illuminating comments. Indicators hope to capture the essential dimensions of Ideal Types, and highlight and enhance understanding of particular aspects of the concept.

Lincoln and Guba ask when and whether a working hypothesis (in this case, an indicator) developed in Context A is applicable in Context B (1985). Their answer embodies a subtle particularlising perspective. The degree to which an indicator is transferable from one context to another, they might say, is a direct function of the empirical similarity of the two contexts. They call this 'fittingness', or the extent of congruence between the contexts of creation and of application. This implies that researchers involved in generating grounded indicators by collecting data in a particular situation should describe and appraise the case's locale rigorously. This means the researcher must ask himself, *what information might a reader interested in applying this indicator need to decide about transferability?* The person seeking to apply a grounded indicator to a new context presumably requires information about both contexts (Stake, 1995).

The analytical relevance of concepts

Grounded indicators are generated through case study research. Yin argues that while survey research relies on statistical generalisation secured through sampling strategies, case studies rely on analytical generalisation, where the researcher strives to generalise particular results to a broader

theory (1994). The relevance of the findings to theory is not assumed automatically, but instead must be tested through the replication of findings in additional contexts. By extension, indicators become relevant on the basis of a theory about how the concept and the indicators relate. No set number of cases will allow the generation of grounded indicators to be representative of some population. The generation of indicators that are valid measures for concepts entails generalising these indicators to theory.

An example illustrates this point. Yin discusses Jane Jacobs, who lived in and wrote about New York and was an early voice warning that 'urban renewal' (i.e. housing projects, highways, business districts) destroyed neighbourhoods (Jacobs, 1961). She advocated 'mixed-use' urban space, suggesting that streets and neighbourhoods should be understood as dynamic organisms, and that sidewalks, parks, neighbourhoods, and the economy function synergistically. She further suggested that high densities of people are vital for vibrant city life, economic growth, and prosperity. Jacobs proposed a theoretical vision for urban planning based on a case study of New York City. This theory might be operationalised with indicators examining phenomena such as neighbourhood parks and small blocks. The core question regarding the relevance of these indicators to new contexts of application is primarily whether her theory of urban planning is fitting for the context. It may be relevant in Paris, Portland, and Pittsburgh but not in Delhi, Dar es Salaam, or Djibouti. It may need to be adjusted for Harbin, Hiroshima, and Hong Kong. Trying to figure out whether the indicator is fitting or translatable only makes sense in a context where the theory and accompanying concepts are appropriate to the context of application.

Recognising the provinciality of measurement in the social sciences without resorting to particularism

In contemplating Michael Burawoy's notion of provincialising the social sciences, I argue for the provincialisation of social indicators. The social sciences have, Burawoy argues, worked to transcend historicity by hiding their 'origins behind universalistic knowledge claims' and securing 'their scientific truth by defining their methodology (positivism) as context free' (Burawoy, 2005a: 1). Tackling the insularity of measure design and research in the North Atlantic social sciences entails recognising efforts to universalise the problems of very particular societies (Burawoy, 2005b: 418). Grounded indicators must be grounded in their methodology, their specific context of production, and the creator's participation in the world he or she seeks to comprehend – in other words, in their particularity.

Christine Inglis calls upon researchers to recognise the provinciality of American sociology, meaning that we must 'open and expand it to other forms of sociological knowledge' (2005: 385). She suggests that it sets international research agendas, influences global careers, and globalises 'conceptual frames, theoretical paradigms and methodological practices' (Burawoy, 2005b: 427). National sciences are benchmarked to standards that revolve around publications in Western (predominantly American) journals. It is not just South Africa and Kenya, but Taiwan and Norway that feel the strain. Fourcade-Gourinchas demonstrates how the remote problematics of US economics inhibit other economists to investigate issues of pressing local, national, and regional concern (2003). Thus, the US commands 'an impressive concentration of resources and research facilities' and benchmarking pulls national social sciences away from measurement challenges of national urgency (Burawoy, 2005b: 16).

Positivist measurement fails to recognise its own implication in the world it measures. Post-positivistic efforts acknowledge the conditions of the production of knowledge. Positivism focuses on an indicator's correspondence to reality. Grounded indicators focus on developing and operationalising concepts that make communication about social phenomena more efficient and effective. GIA focuses on the accumulation of conceptual clarity and the growth of knowledge. The conditions for positivistic assumptions about measurement are eroding. Riveting grounded indicators to those assumptions does not serve the interest of reflexive, scientific enquiry into measurement.

GIA does not seek to develop measures that are applicable to all contexts. Scholars working within gender studies, ethnic studies, Africana studies, and postcolonial studies have damaged the notion of context-free knowledge. The assumptions and conditions that gird universal indicators have been unmasked and criticised, (Gordon, 1995b; Dussel and Mendieta, 1996, 2003; Fanon, 1967; Said, 1978, 1994; hooks, 1981, 1996, 2000; Spivak, 1999). As critical social scientists revealed the assumptions of universalising measurement to be arbitrary and unscientific, public social scientists have entered 'a dialogue with local knowledges demonstrating the limits of all-purpose recipes' (Burawoy, 2005d: 15). GIA does not call for a '*reactive devolution* into scattered and defensive nativist particularisms, but the *reconfiguration*' of the social scientific labour involved in developing indicators (Burawoy, 2005d: 16). This will mean acknowledging that American indicators seem universal largely because American social sciences are prominent. As national social sciences engage with national problems and local issues, grounded indicators will become indiginised both through local generation and purposeful adaptation and translation. Grounded indicators seek wide applicability but recognise their own specificity.

PART IV: RESPONDING TO CRITICS OF THE GROUNDED INDICATOR APPROACH

To expand upon my proposal for a GIA, this section responds to seven potential concerns.

The cost efficiency of the grounded indicator approach

Some critics might charge that the GIA is too time intensive, or suggest that it is not feasible to spend a considerable amount of time on indicator generation and modification. I respond in several ways. First, the GIA *is* time intensive – it recommends that research time and resources be allocated to the systematic, empirical generation and modification (as well as verification) of indicators. I suggest that this relative emphasis on these early phases of indicator development will prove fruitful – the return on investment will be favourable.

Second, indicator development currently consumes considerable time and resources; the GIA merely aims for greater scientific rigour. Generation and modification are currently largely based on assertion and argumentation by researchers. This modified 'truth by authority' approach is not necessarily efficient or effective. The relative efficiency of the current approach to generation and modification, when compared to empirical research that

conducts tests and makes systematic observations about the empirical world, is not a given. The missteps and misadventures that accompany non-systematic approaches may not be productive. GIA defends social scientific methodologies as reliable and efficient when compared with speculation or assertion.

Third, development of quality indicators is a priority. Indicators facilitate learning and information exchange, raise the profile and comprehensibility of social phenomena, suggest social trends, help identify gaps in understanding about social issues, improve policy decision making by facilitating planning and enhancing evidence-based consensus, and facilitate the development of models. Quality indicators enhance intervention design, evaluation, and performance. Given the important role that high-quality indicators play in facilitating all other aspects of research, the social sciences must bring a more scientific approach to these challenges.

Several quick points are also worth mentioning. Fourth, GIA proposes that researchers continually review the research and thoughts that comprise a particular measurement tool. GIA, inspired by Mills (1959), urges researchers to avoid the bureaucratisation of reason and discourse and instead to focus upon the relationship of social practices to social structures, and historical contexts. GIA is one way to fulfil the promise of social sciences because it rests upon the sociological imagination and quality of mind. Fifth, GIA aims to minimise measurement error, which should be at the centre of research design discussions. Measure development entails taking the necessary steps to develop reliable and valid measures. Minimising measurement error should be the priority at each stage in instrument development and should guide social research. Sixth, GIA promotes Cooper's notion that a healthy community (in this case, a healthy research community) is efficient, in that it achieves much when given little (1988). I suggest that GIA will produce significant results with relatively modest investments. Although systematic, purposeful research into matters such as item generation, scale creation, scale modification, and piloting is certainly time intensive – the relative cost for improvements with regard to measurement error and reliability are low.

The feasibility of the grounded indicator approach

Some critics might argue that GIA is a fruitless undertaking because the production of grounded indicators is impossible. Several responses merit mention. First, there is no evidence one way or another, as an empirical matter, as to whether a relative emphasis on generation and modification will prove to be efficient. Whether GIA is a fruitful undertaking is a question that must be worked out through methodological argumentation and then practice. Second, the GIA retains all the advantages of current verification techniques. It merely suggests that a rigorous scientific approach to generation and modification is missing from the process of social measure development and that adding this rigour would make a difference. Third, the GIA is not universally appropriate. With the development of any given indicator, the question is whether the benefits of a GIA (validity, workability, fittingness, etc.) are worth the investment. Fourth, the accumulation of scientific knowledge *is* worth investment. This chapter defends a social scientific approach to measure development. This entails making a large number of empirical observations about a particular social phenomenon that aim to be minimally biased and prejudiced. The researcher then identifies and describes

patterns that explain what is happening in a manner that facilitates communication and aids understanding. Certainly, observations may fail for various reasons, including inappropriate expectations, inaccurate observation statements, and selective concentration. Even if systematic social research designed to inform the generation of indicators is riddled with limitations, it will still be productive.

The demands placed on indicators

Some social scientists argue the position that indicators will never be perfect and that imperfect proxies are adequate for most studies. The GIA, in suggesting that existing measures are often imperfect, dubious, or misspecified, and in advancing a more rigorous scientific approach to measure development, seems directly opposed to this position. This is a complex question, and several issues are worth consideration.

First, modelling of higher-level complexity from lower-level simplicity certainly reflects one significant orientation of social science. Clear and parsimonious indicators that model complex phenomena are the ideal. I do not advocate wildly complicated, incoherent measurement tools, but aspire towards simple models that are sufficiently complex to answer the questions at hand and explain the phenomena studied. The more complicated and multi-dimensional a model becomes, the greater the number of possible interpretations about what relationships mean.

Second, the desire to develop grounded indicators does not necessarily imply a call for more complicated models. GIA developed indicators are not intended to capture the full variety and complexity of the social world, but instead to measure what they intend to measure and measure it accurately. Quality and workability of indicators are the goal, but simple models are not by definition of higher quality or more workable. If a simple, clear proxy delivers a picture that is neither valid nor reliable, the utility of simplicity is minimal in that instance. Further, a poorly understood concept can cause a measurement instrument to become more, not less, complicated.

Third, there is a threshold of measurement error and quality below which indicators are inappropriate for use. Researchers at times differ with regard to the location of that threshold. The question is what quality of observation is needed to draw rigorous, scientific conclusions. The current standards and procedures to secure validity (such as criterion, content, and construct validity) fail to produce sufficient levels of rigour. GIA is committed to the development of quality indicators as foundations of good models.

Fourth, rather than aiming for simplicity in and of itself, the GIA aims to produce of measurement instruments that offer explanations and descriptions that facilitate social scientific understanding of the world. Grounded indicators do not aim to reflect the way things are in the world, but rather to have internally consistent proxies that paint a coherent, accurate, and useful picture. For instance, modelling light as either a wave or as a particle reflects aspects of reality. Grounded indicators aim towards proxies that understand the agreement and disagreement models produce. Simple models do not always provide workable explanations.

The time frame and scope of the grounded indicator approach

The legitimate concern exists that producing 'grounded indicators' takes time and that a single research project will never achieve an appropriate end result. However, GIA is intended as a process

of enquiry that is collective rather than individual. GIA research entails a research community that checks results of particular studies, sceptically assesses conclusions, and divides labour. This section proposes aspects of a GIA research community.

Professional activities focused on measurement currently emphasise statistical verification. This emphasis takes the development of indicators for granted and unintentionally undermines the mandate for this foundational work. For established procedures, a researcher's principle task in ensuring quality is to verify its validity and reliability. But emphasis on verification curbs the generation of new measures. The GIA assumes and subsumes rigorous validation of indicators once they are at the appropriate stage – but only to the extent that these approaches serve the broader call for the development of grounded indicators. Even researchers made prominent through their role in the development of new indicators and scales often do not publish accounts that focus primarily on how their indicators were developed. By focusing on the validation phase of development, such researchers shift attention away from the process of systematic, scientific generation and modification.

GIA seeks to strengthen the mandate for the generation of indicators through social research. By proposing the codification of GIA, I argue for its legitimacy as a task for social scientists throughout the trajectory of their academic careers. Codification of grounded indicator methodologies may encourage the social sciences to use research to generate more and better indicators. Codified grounded methodologies, by increasing the standing of research for indicator development, will also help grounded indicator researchers to, in the words of Glaser and Strauss, 'defend themselves against verifiers who would teach them to deny the validity of their own scientific intelligence' (1967: 6). Professional tendencies to favour certain research practices are, I hope, susceptible to influence and argumentation.

I propose the development of venues for discussion and publication of how indicators ought to be developed. Interestingly, researchers who have successfully created new concepts and indicators generally do not publish accounts of the process of generation and modification, but focus instead on describing verification and application. Although an audience would exist, few venues for the publication of how indicators and scales are developed and how challenges were overcome currently exist. Little is known about the practice of measure design in social sciences until psychometric and validation procedures are completed. Accounts of the social research conducted to distinguish concepts, delineate categories, and operationalise those dimensions deserve attention. GIA aims to set in motion a new professional discourse.

I propose that research communities fully investigate indicators in early phases of development. Contemporary measurement practice tacitly pre-supposes that indicators emerge in full-grown form, ready to be validated. In practice, most existing indicators are seriously underdeveloped. Researchers submit indicators to premature empirical testing and, in failing to understand the concept or its domains, misunderstand the results. Unless conceptual clarification is paired with empirical validation, Viswanathan argues, statistical tests are difficult to interpret (2005). Some researchers run complex statistical tests (such as psychometric diagnostics, and variations of confirmatory and exploratory factor analysis and validity tests) before they genuinely understand the construct.

Finally, the GIA proposes the gradual development of indicators through the scientific accumulation of knowledge and understanding during social research. Grounded indicator research aims for the cumulative development of knowledge regarding constructs, categories, and indicators. The approach entails the progressive building up from data generated through the study of phenomena. The vision is for those directly involved in gathering and analysing data in relation to the discovery of categories and the design of indicators to participate in a ever-developing discussion, allowing thinking on constructs, categories, and indicators to become 'quite rich, complex, and dense, and makes its fit and relevance easy to comprehend' (Glaser and Strauss, 1967: 32). Findings from grounded indicator research do not 'freeze' understanding, or treat a category as fixed and firmly established. Instead, findings open the door for continued research oriented towards generation, modification, and validation.

CONCLUSION

This chapter make the case for the viability of what I have called the grounded indicator approach (GIA) to measure development. The GIA entails the generation, modification, and verification of measures through empirical social research. The goal of this chapter was to propose a GIA, explain its basic tenets, discuss its relevance, and respond to potential criticisms.

GIA opens several areas for further methodological enquiry. First, the notion of a GIA needs to be further related to social science measurement literature. GIA will benefit from a sustained engagement with measurement development, design, and testing within the social sciences. Researchers, such as the contributors to this handbook, have overcome challenges to develop measures, and can offer insights about the process. By identifying and engaging the most vital and significant new thinking on measurement, the GIA could spark multidisciplinary, interdisciplinary, and international discussions that engage trends, issues, and significant principles in measurement design concretely. The GIA needs to work between the theory and practice of measurement and consider the contribution it can make to measurement at methodological, procedural, and conceptual levels. A GIA should encompass the diverse and emergent ways researchers measure the social.

Second, conducting grounded indicator approach research in all phases of measure design will provide insight into this methodological proposal. In order for grounded indicator methodology and procedure to influence measure design, studies refining GIA-methodologies are required. Researchers interested in the application of grounded indicator research will benefit from both continued theoretical advances and descriptions of novel approaches to instrument design. For GIA to become typified by creativity and innovation, it will have to attract researchers with a range of disciplines, commitments, and priorities.

This chapter offers a tentative and preliminary sketch of the nature of a GIA,. The presumption that social measurement constitutes rigorous, rationally ordered enquiry stems from a confidence that overlooks the criteria social science holds for other phases of research design. The GIA calls for the social sciences to sustain their professed commitment to the rational, systematic approach to measure design.

REFERENCES

Acharya, A. and Wall, H. J. (1994) 'An evaluation of the United Nations' Human Development Index', *Journal of Economic and Social Measurement*, 20(1): 51–66.

Asher, M. A. and Defina, R. H. (1995) 'Age-adjustment of income inequality trends: A methodology critique', *Journal of Economic and Social Measurement*, 21(1): 33–44.

Bollen, K. A. (1998a) 'LISREL Models', in P. Armitage and T. Colton (eds) *Encyclopedia of biostatistics*. Sussex: John Wiley. pp. 2305.

Bollen, K. A. (1998b) 'Structural equation models', in P. Armitage and T. Colton (eds) *Encyclopedia of biostatistics*. Sussex: John Wiley. pp. 4363–72.

Bollen, K. A. and Lennox, R. (1991) 'Conventional wisdom on measurement: A structural equation perspective', *Psychological Bulletin*, 110(3): 305–14.

Burawoy, M. (2005a) 'Provincializing the social sciences', in G. Steinmetz (ed.) *The politics of method in the human sciences: Positivism and its epistemological others*. Durham: Duke University Press. pp. 508–26.

Burawoy, M. (2005b) 'Response: Public sociology: populist fad or path to renewal?' *British Journal of Sociology*, 56(3): 417–32.

Campbell, D. T. and Stanley, J. C. (1963) *Experimental and quasi–experimental designs for research*. Boston: Houghton Mifflin.

Carlson, B. L., Cohen, S. B. and Johnson, A. E. (1994) 'Family unit constructs, dynamics, and analysis in the household component of the NMES', *Journal of Economic and Social Measurement*, 20(3): 215–36.

Coleman, J. S. (1988) 'Social capital in the creation of human capital', *American Journal of Sociology*, 94 Supplement: S95–120.

Cooper, A. J. (1988) *A voice from the south*. New York: Oxford University Press.

Cronbach, L. J., Gleser, G. C., Nanda, H. and Rararatnam, N. (1972) *The dependability of behavioral measurements: Theory of generalizability for scores and profiles*. New York: Wiley.

Currie, M. R., Cunningham, E. G. and Findlay, B. M. (2004) 'The short internationalized homonegativity scale examination of the factorial structure of a new measure of internalized homophobia', *Educational and Psychological Measurement*, 64(6): 1053–67.

Denzin, N. K. (1997) *Interpretive ethnography: Ethnographic practices for the 21st century*. London: Sage.

Dowson, M. and McInerney, D. M. (2004) 'The development and validation of the goal orientation and learning strategies survey (GOALS-S)', *Educational and Psychological Measurement*, 64(2): 290–310.

Dussel, E. and Mendieta, E. (1996) *The underside of modernity : Apel, Ricoeur, Rorty, Taylor, and the philosophy of liberation*. Atlantic Highlands, N.J.: Humanity Books.

Dussel, E. and Mendieta, E. (2003) *Beyond philosophy: ethics, history, marxism, and liberation theology.* Lanham: Rowman and Littlefield Publishers.

Fanon, F. (1967a) *Black skin, white masks.* New York: Grove Press.

Fanon, F. (1967b) *A dying colonialism* (1st edition). New York: Grove Press.

Farrall, S. and Ditton, J. (1999) 'Improving the measurement of attitudinal responses: An example from a crime survey', *International Journal of Social Research Methodology*, 2(1): 55–68.

Florida, R. (2002) *The rise of the creative class: And how it's transforming work, leisure, community and everyday life.* New York: Basic Books.

Florida, R. (2005) *The flight of the creative class: The new global competition for talent* (1st edition). New York: HarperBusiness.

Fourcade-Gourinchas, M. (2003) *The construction of a global profession: The case of economics.* Department of Sociology, University of California, Berkeley. Unpublished.

Frisbie, D. A. and Cantor, N. K. (1995) 'The validity of scores from alternative methods of assessing spelling achievement', *Journal of Educational Measurement*, 32(1): 55–78.

Galvez, J. and McLarty, C. (1996) 'Measurement of Florida temporary residents using a telephone survey', *Journal of Economic and Social Measurement*, 22(1): 25–46.

Giancarlo, C. A., Blohm, S. W. and Urdan, T. (2004) 'Assessing secondary students' disposition toward critical thinking: Development of the California measure of mental motivation', *Educational and Psychological Measurement*, 64(2): 347–64.

Giddens, A. (1984) *The constitution of society: Outline of the theory of structuration.* Berkeley: University of California Press.

Glaser, B. G. and Strauss, A. L. (1967) *The discovery of grounded theory: Strategies for qualitative research.* Chicago: Aldine Publication Co.

Goetz, J. P. and LeCompte, M. D. (1984) *Ethnography and qualitative design in educational research.* Orlando: Academic Press.

Gomm, R., Hammersley, M. and Foster, P. (2000) *Case study method: Key issues, key texts.* Thousand Oaks: Sage Publications.

Gordon, L. R. (1995a) *Bad faith and antiblack racism.* Atlantic Highlands, N. J.: Humanities Press.

Gordon, L. R. (1995b) *Fanon and the crisis of European man: An essay on philosophy and the human sciences.* New York: Routledge.

Gordon, L. R. (1997a) *Existence in black: An anthology of Black existential philosophy.* New York: Routledge.

Gordon, L. R. (1997b) *Her Majesty's other children: Sketches of racism from a neocolonial age.* Lanham, MD: Rowman and Littlefield.

Gordon, L. R. (2000) *Existentia Africana: Understanding Africana existential thought.* New York: Routledge.

Gordon, L. R. (2006) *Disciplinary decadence: Living thought in trying times.* Boulder: Paradigm Publishers.

Gormely, P. J. (1995) 'The Human Development Index in 1994: Impact of income on country rank', *Journal of Economic and Social Measurement*, 21(4): 253–67.

Hammersley, M. (1987) 'Some notes on the terms "validity" and "reliability"', *British Educational Research Journal*, 13(1): 73–81.

Hammersley, M. (1998) *Reading ethnographic research: A critical guide* (2nd edition). London: Longman.

hooks, b. (1981) *Ain't I a woman: Black women and feminism.* Boston: South End Press.

hooks, b. (1996) *Killing rage: Ending racism.* New York: H. Holt and Co.

hooks, b. (2000) *Feminist theory: From margin to center.* Cambridge: South End Press.

Husserl, E. (1910) *Phenomenology and the crisis of philosophy: Philosophy as a rigorous science, and Philosophy and the crisis of European man.* New York: Harper and Row.

Husserl, E. (1931) *Ideas: General introduction to pure phenomenology.* London: G. Allen and Unwin, New York: Macmillan.

Husserl, E. (1960) *Cartesian meditations: An introduction to phenomenology.* The Hague: Martinus Nijhoff.

Husserl, E. (1970a) 'The attitude of natural science and the attitude of humanistic science: Naturalism, dualism, and psychophysical psychology', in E. Husserl (ed.) *The crisis of European sciences and transcendental phenomenology: An introduction to phenomenology.* Evanston, IL: Northwestern University Press. pp. 315–34.

Husserl, E. (1970b) *The crisis of European sciences and transcendental phenomenology: An introduction to phenomenology.* Evanston, IL: Northwestern University Press.

Husserl, E. (1970c) 'Idealization and the science of reality – The mathematization', in E. Husserl (ed.) *The crisis of European sciences and transcendental phenomenology: An introduction to phenomenology.* Evanston, IL: Northwestern University Press. pp. 301–14.

Husserl, E. (1970d) 'The Vienna lecture', in E. Husserl (ed.) *The crisis of European sciences and transcendental phenomenology: An introduction to phenomenology.* Evanston, IL: Northwestern University Press. pp. 269–99.

Inglis, C. (2005) 'Four sociologies, multiple roles', *British Journal of Sociology*, 56(3): 395–400.

Jacobs, J. (1961) *The life and death of great American cities*. New York: Random House.

Kaplan, A. (1964) *The conduct of inquiry: Methodology for behavioral science*. San Francisco: Chandler.

Laumann, E. (1994) *The social organization of sexuality: Sexual practices in the United States*. Chicago, IL: University of Chicago Press.

Le, H., Casillas, A., Robbins, S. B. and Langley, R. (2005) 'Motivational and skills, social, and self–management predictors of college outcomes: Constructing the student readiness inventory', *Educational and Psychological Measurement*, 65(3): 482–508.

Lincoln, Y. S. and Guba, E. G. (1985) *Naturalistic inquiry*. London: Sage.

Maldonado-Torres, N. (2006) 'Toward a critique of continental reason: Africana studies and the decolonization of Imperial cartographies in the Americas', in L. R. Gordon and J. A. Gordon (eds) *Not only the master's tools: African-American studies in theory and practice*. Boulder, CO: Paradigm. pp. 51–84.

Merleau-Ponty, M. (1962) *The phenomenology of perception*. London: Routledge.

Mills, C. W. (1959) *The sociological imagination*. Oxford: Oxford University Press.

Noble, C. L., Eby, L. T., Lockwood, A. and Allen, T. D. (2004) 'Attitudes toward working single parents: Initial development of a measure', *Educational and Psychological Measurement*, 64(6): 1030–52.

Potenza, M. T. and Stocking, M. L. (1997) 'Flawed items in computerized adaptive testing', *Journal of Educational Measurement*, 34(1): 79–96.

Powers, D. E., Fowles, M. E., Farnum, M. and Ramsey, P. (1994) 'Will they think less of my handwritten essay if others word process theirs?' *Journal of Educational Measurement*, 31(3): 220–33.

Putnam, R. D. (1993) 'The prosperous community: Social capital and public life', *The American Prospect*, 4(13): 35–42.

Putnam, R. D. (2000) *Bowling alone: The collapse and revival of American community*. New York: Simon and Schuster.

Putnam, R. D., Leonardi, R. and Nanetti, R. Y. (1994) *Making democracy work: Civic traditions in modern Italy*. Princeton: Princeton University Press.

Robson, C. (2002) *Real world research: A resource for social scientists and practitioner-researchers* (2nd edition). Oxford: Blackwells.

Said, E. (1978) *Orientalism*. New York: Pantheon Books.

Said, E. (1994) *Representations of the intellectual: The 1993 Reith Lectures*. New York: Pantheon Books.

Salkind, N. J. (2004) *Statistics for people who (think they) hate statistics*. Thousand Oaks, CA: Sage Publications.

Salkind, N. J. (2005) *Tests and measurement for people who (think they) hate tests and measurements*. Thousand Oaks, CA: Sage Publications.

Sartre, J. P. (1948) *Anti-Semite and Jew*. New York: Schoken Books.

Sartre, J. P. (1956) *Being and nothingness: An essay on phenomenological ontology*. New York: Philosophical Library.

Schutz, A. (1962) *The problem of social reality* (Vol. 1). The Hague: Martinus Nijhoff.

Schutz, A. (1970) *The phenomenology of the social world*. Evanston, IL: Northwestern University Press.

Schutz, A. and Luckmann, T. (1973) *The structures of the life–world* (Vol. 2). Evanston: Northwestern University Press.

Sen, A. K. (1973) *On economic inequality*. Oxford: Clarendon Press.

Sen, A. K. (1987) *On ethics and economics*. Oxford and New York: Blackwell.

Sen, A. K. (1999) *Development as freedom* (1 ed.). New York: Alfred Knopf.

Sen, A. K. (2002) *Rationality and freedom*. Cambridge: Belknap Press.

Sharpe, D. L. and Abdel-Ghany, M. (1996) 'Discrimination due to race and gender in the youth labor market: Is it a double jeopardy?' *Journal of Economic and Social Measurement*, 22(1): 43–64.

Shriver, K. A. (1995) 'The measurement of current cost data: Implications of economic analyses', *Journal of Economic and Social Measurement*, 21(1): 17–31.

Spivak, G. (1999) A *critique of postcolonial reason: Towards history of the vanishing present*. Cambridge: Harvard University Press.

Stake, R. E. (1995) *The art of case study research*. London: Sage.

Stevenson, J. C. and Evans, G. T. (1994) 'Conceptualization and measurement of cognitive holding power', *Journal of Educational Measurement*, 31(2): 161–81.

Stratton, L. S. (1994) 'Reexamining involuntary part-time employment', *Journal of Economic and Social Measurement*, 20(2): 95–116.

Teague, A. (2000) 'New methodologies for the 2001 census in England and Wales', *International Journal of Social Research Methodology*, 3(3): 245–255.

Tucker, E. (2007a) 'Measurement as a rigorous science: How ethnographic research methods can contribute to the generation and modification of indicators', in Geoffrey Walford (ed.) *Methodological Developments in Ethnography* (Studies in Educational Ethnography, Volume 12) Amsterdam, New York, Oxford, Elsevier. pp. 109–36.

Tucker E. (2007b) *Towards a More Rigorous Scientific Approach to Social Measurement: An Empirical and Methodological Enquiry into the Development of Grounded Indicators of Social Capital Formation.* Doctoral Thesis. Oxford University.

Viswanathan, M. (2005) *Measurement error and research design.* Thousand Oaks: Sage.

Walden, D. C., Miller, R. and Cohen, S. B. (1994) 'Comparison of out-of-pocket health expenditure estimates from the 1987 National Medical Expenditure Survey and the Consumer Expenditure Survey', *Journal of Economic and Social Measurement,* 20(2): 117–36.

Walford, G. (2001) *Doing qualitative educational research: A personal guide to the research process.* London: Continuum.

Wolfe, E. W., Ray, L. M. and Harris, D. C. (2004) 'A RASCH analysis of three measures of teacher perception generated from the school and staffing survey', *Educational and Psychological Measurement,* 64(5): 842–60.

Yin, R. K. (1994) *Case study research: Design and methods* (2nd edition). Thousand Oaks: Sage.

17

Measuring Conceptualisations of Morality: Or How to Invent a Construct and Measure it too

Remo Ostini

When social scientists set out to measure a construct they usually (hopefully) have a good idea of what it is that they are trying to measure. Some ideas in social science, however, are difficult to define and morality is one of those. With many such ideas, and this is certainly true of morality, a typical approach is to assert a definition or carve off an obviously relevant subsection of the construct – and measure that instead. With respect to morality, examples of this approach include altruism (e.g., Hoffman, 1981); prejudice (e.g., Reynolds et al., 2001); group norms (e.g., Terry and Hogg, 1996); moral norms (Gorsuch and Ortberg, 1983); justice reasoning development (e.g., Kohlberg, 1969,

1976; Colby and Kohlberg, 1987); justice as a social psychological variable (e.g., Skitka and Crosby, 2003); traits and habits (e.g., Volz, 2000); care and responsibility (e.g., Gilligan, 1982); and character (e.g., Hogan, 1973). Cooperation is a popular proxy for morality in contemporary evolutionary psychology research (e.g., Stone et al., 2002).

Each of these variables represents an important and relevant element of the commonly understood notion of morality. This very fact, however, indicates that none of these variables alone provides a comprehensive description of morality.

An alternative approach is to define the construct in the process of measuring it.

This is a somewhat old-fashioned approach that was effectively used in much foundational personality research. Taking this approach presumes a dispositional notion of morality. This bootstrapping type of process was used in the project described in this chapter.

In moral psychology research, both Loevinger's (1976) Ego Development measurement tool and Kohlberg's Moral Judgement Interview (Colby and Kohlberg, 1987) are examples of the measurement tool development process strongly affecting the form of the construct that ends up being measured. However, both Kohlberg and Loevinger's highly intensive, content analysis-based approaches were strongly theoretically driven. The project described in this chapter attempts to move away from a developmental focus and is driven by the notion that there is no compelling theory – and certainly no settled theory – of moral psychology to use as the basis for designing a measure of morality.

CONSTRUCT DEFINITION

Usually, on the surface at least, knowing what is to be measured is not a major difficulty for a social scientist. Typically, people want to measure something because they have something to measure – and they know what it is. Often in the social sciences, however, the situation is more complicated – primarily because we intend the numbers that we collect to represent something beyond what they tell us directly. That is, we are often trying to measure unobservable phenomena or attributes. For example, when we count the spelling errors that a person makes on a test we don't usually particularly want to know just how many errors the person made. Rather, we would like to think we have gathered valuable information on that person's spelling prowess more generally, including on words not included in the test, including in situations far different from the test-taking setting, and including times other than the specific time that the test was taken. Whether or not the test actually does these things requires evidence.

When measuring typical performance (e.g., personality) rather than maximal performance (e.g., ability) the process is further complicated by two factors. First people are often more motivated to do their best on a test of their ability, perhaps partly because it is easier to do your best on a task that demonstrates an ability (e.g., correctly solving a mathematics problem) than it is on a task that demonstrates accurate self-awareness (e.g., reporting how true it is that you are usually a happy person). Second, related to the preceding issue is the fact that it is far easier to answer untruthfully (deliberately or not) on measures of what people are normally like. It is difficult to succeed in deliberately convincing a tester that you are a better speller than you 'really' are – though it is easy to convince them that you aren't as good as you could be. It is often much easier to respond to measures of typical performance in ways that make you look better, or more the way you would like to be, than you 'truly' typically are.

Measuring morality is difficult for two reasons. First, it is, in fact, difficult to know what morality is – not only is the notion of morality unobservable but it is difficult to know what it is we aren't observing. Everyone knows what morality is when they see it but describing it in a sufficiently concrete manner to allow it to be measured is very difficult. This is because there is a preciseness required of descriptions of attributes to be measured that is very difficult to achieve with morality without the testing materials becoming superficial or without ending up with check-list of more or less badness. Indeed, one of the complications with measuring morality is that it can conceivably be measured as an ability, in the manner of Hartshorne and May (1928), for example, or in the context of how people usually think about morality. This project aims to measure people's understanding of morality, not their ability to be moral.

The second difficulty with measuring morality is that, even if it were possible to identify a conceptualisation of morality with which the researcher was satisfied and which could be clearly specified, it is still difficult to put in place a process by which behavioural responses or observations can be obtained and turned into numbers that accurately embody and signify varying amounts of this conceptualisation of morality. This two-part difficulty is a technical problem involving test construction and the application of an appropriate measurement model. It is addressed in the following sections on item generation and item analysis.

ITEM GENERATION

Once a construct has been clearly defined the measurement task is then determining the best way to represent the construct so that observations about its presence or absence in people can be made. If a construct has been precisely and explicitly defined, this can be a relatively simple matter of identifying an appropriate task for people to undertake. Often it comes down to a process of item writing that flows in a logical and transparent manner from the definition.

Sampling moral concepts

When measuring morality 'from scratch' the problem of item generation in the absence of a precise construct definition

is formidable. The technical challenge is how best to sample the item universe. This is a particularly acute challenge when you are trying to avoid *a priori* definitions of the construct – which effectively means that the universe from which you sample items does not have firmly constituted boundaries. The approach taken in this project was to define the universe in the same process as generating measurement items. This is a labour-intensive process and ultimately it is difficult to know precisely how comprehensive you have been. If done carefully, however, this process has the advantage of producing a definition of morality that is meaningful to the people being measured. It also allows the possibility of identifying aspects of morality that the researcher may not have considered for inclusion in a measure of morality.

Different ways to implement this approach include sampling ideas about morality from moral philosophy; from nursery rhymes; from moral theology; from literature generally; or from all of these sources, as well as any other relevant texts on the nature of morality.

The approach taken in this project was more direct. I asked people. In my initial interview sample I used a structured interview (Appendix 17.1) to ask 20 honours/postgraduate university students what morality meant to them. Students with four or more years of tertiary study experience were initially chosen because they were expected to be more able to express, in words, complex abstract ideas – such as what morality might be. Some support for this expectation came from subsequent interviews with urban and rural members of the general public that resulted in interviews that were one-third and one-quarter as long as the original interviews, respectively, for responses to the same set of 10 questions. The 20 questions are an attempt at a slightly more sophisticated way of asking people to describe morality – rather than walking up to them and saying 'So. What's morality?' They are simple questions, not complex dilemmas to solve but they are hard to answer. People who were interviewed often commented that they hadn't really thought about these questions – though they thought they should have.

Students across a range of physical and social sciences, arts, and humanities were interviewed in an attempt to get a breadth of experiences and worldviews in the sample. This was essentially a process of trying to get a good representation of corporate, naïve morality; at least within an (over?)educated, Western sample.

Interviews were transcribed verbatim and each transcript was separated into statements containing a single idea about morality. Ultimately, the 20 interviews produced 1,219 separate statements about morality. These statements became the raw material for this project's attempts to measure morality. They were the potential items.

Examples of the types of statements generated by the interviews included the following.

Caring about others is the dominant feature of a good person.
Everyone is born good.
Well intentioned people can disagree on what is the right thing to do.
Evil does exist and people can do it.
The boundaries between right and wrong are defined by social custom.
There is a part of you that will decide what is morally right and morally wrong regardless of how you have been influenced by society.

This type of interview data practically begs for qualitative analysis – and such analysis has begun. That analysis is not, however, the focus of this chapter. It is not in the first instance at least, an integral part of the attempt to measure morality.

Ultimately the results of the qualitative analysis will be juxtaposed with the results of the quantitative structural analysis which underlies this project's attempts to measure morality. To the extent that they parallel the quantitative results, they provide support for the picture of the morality construct painted by the quantitative analysis. To the extent that they diverge from the quantitative structure, the qualitative results can highlight weaknesses, shortcomings, and outright holes in the construct being measured.

Item selection 1.0

Initially, statements (items) that duplicated an idea were excluded. About half of the statements contained duplicate ideas. For the remaining 600 statements, rather than putting them all into one questionnaire, every fourth item was allocated, sequentially, to a separate questionnaire. This produced four, 150-item questionnaires. Even 150 statements about morality, especially such raw statements as those from verbatim transcripts, are hard work for respondents. Respondents were given a 5-point Likert scale ranging from 1 – 'Nothing like what I think' to 5 – 'Exactly what I think' to evaluate statements. The questionnaires were called the Moral Concepts Scale (MCS).

Completing the questionnaire typically took people 30–40 minutes. One respondent became agitated and tore up the questionnaire after a few dozen questions because the process was too stressful. Another respondent took the questionnaire home and spent the better part of two days carefully responding, in detail, to each question – often ignoring the 5-point Likert scale.

Once collected into reasonably manageable (for most people) questionnaires, the strategy was to give the questionnaires to as many people as possible and to use the item analysis process to weed out the bad items.

There are two main features to this approach. First, moral concepts were sampled through a structured interview process which generated over a 1,000 statements about morality. These concepts were then organised by getting people to respond to questionnaires containing the statements.

There are at least three problems with this approach. It is expensive, both in time and resources. It demands a lot of respondents – both in the sense of sample size, and in terms of what respondents are being asked to do. It is unfundable.

ITEM ANALYSIS

The goal of item analysis is to ensure that the items in the measuring instrument are operating effectively. This means that items are discriminating, operate in the same manner for different groups in the population to be measured (e.g., items are not more difficult for men to answer than women), and usually that, as a group, the items measure across a range of ability or trait levels. This is to ensure that the test can differentiate people who have more or less of the attribute being measured.

Structural analysis

When test construction begins with a well-defined construct, structural analysis might be considered part of the test validation process. That is, the construct definition specifies the expected structure of the attribute being measured and the structural analysis tests whether this is found in the data. The general question is whether people are responding to the measuring instrument in a way that shows that the elements of the test (usually items) are holding together in the manner that is expected. Most commonly, tests are designed to measure a single, undifferentiated construct, in which

case, the goal is to obtain a unidimensional structure with all items in the test hanging together, that is, all being strongly related to each other.

Since the process of developing the MCS did not begin with a precise definition of morality the structural analysis process becomes complicated. To begin with, the structure of the construct cannot be tested – only described. As a result, the structural analysis becomes part of the process of defining the construct.

Prior to compiling all of the interview responses into four questionnaires, it was important to show that the process of (almost) blindly constructing a measure and using test construction procedures to make sense of the data – and ultimately define the construct – would actually work. This process is not one that is generally recommended for test construction and it was eminently possible that there would simply be too much noise for any true response variation to be detected. It was also possible that there would be no 'true' variation in the data – if, for example, the item generation process produced nothing but a random set of unconnected statements about morality. It was expected that the process would produce a set of items that captured the effects of the underlying construct, morality – but this was an expectation that needed to be tested before committing large amounts of resources to the project. To this end, a single 150-item pilot questionnaire was constructed and administered to 1,050 people.

Data screening

An extensive data screening process was used to try and reduce the amount of noise in the data. Responses with large numbers of missing data (10 per cent of an entire questionnaire; $N = 7$) were excluded. Univariate and multivariate normality were assessed and items with large departures from normality were flagged as potentially problematic. Two influential case analyses were conducted on questionnaire items: one based on regression diagnostics (standardised residuals and Mahalanobis distance) and one using the influence function described by Thissen et al. (1980). Finally, a multivariate outlier analysis along the lines suggested by Gnanadesikan (1977) was used to identify outlying items and respondents. Items that failed checks on multiple indicators were excluded. The screening process was quite severe on items, reflecting the assumption that there was likely to be considerable noise in these untested items.

Data structures

For the next stage of the analysis 999 people and 93 items survived data screening and were retained. This involved seeing which, if any, items went together. It was anticipated that different sets of items would cohere and that the coherent sets of items would represent different aspects of morality. It was also expected that items would share a relationship with each other through their association with an underlying morality construct.

These data were investigated through two types of analyses. The first set of analyses involved four linear, multivariate statistical techniques that are commonly used to investigate the structural properties of response data. In this set of analyses the data were analysed by means of two metric (Principal Components Analysis: PCA, and Factor Analysis: FA) and two non-metric (Cluster Analysis: CA, and Multidimensional Scaling: MDS) statistical techniques. The relationships among the four techniques have been elaborated in a number of places (see, e.g., Davison, 1985; Kruskal, 1977; MacCallum, 1974;

Shephard, 1980) and although it is rare for the techniques to be used in tandem, they are all techniques that can legitimately be used with Likert-type scale data.

The second type of analysis used with these data was a non-linear scaling procedure based on non-parametric item response theory. Known as Mokken scaling (see, e.g., Molenaar and Sijtsma, 2000), this procedure provides a method for assessing the dimensionality of a set of data (van Abswoude et al., 2004). It has the potential to avoid the types of problems that can occur when categorical data is analysed using linear statistical techniques (see, e.g. McDonald, 1982; Wainer, 1982).

Multiple analyses for identifying data structure were used primarily because the item selection process was not being driven by substantive theory regarding the construct. The goal was to attempt to avoid capitalising on chance relationships identified through the variance minimising procedures, estimation routines, and convergence criteria driving each of the methods. The rationale here is, fundamentally, to spread the risk of producing spurious results.

This is not a true cross-validation process because the same data were used with each statistical technique. It was more of an overlapping validation process where the item structures identified by each technique were compared and those groups of items that were consistently identified as belonging together by multiple methods were treated as enduring, and therefore likely to be meaningful.

Results: linear analyses

The four linear analyses selected to assess the structure of the MCS data are among the most commonly used statistical analyses for analysing data structure. However, within these analyses, there is little in the way of definitive tests to identify the 'correct' structure for a set of data. This is especially true when the analyses are exploratory in nature. Instead, within each technique, a set of semi-formal rules of thumb have developed over time to become accepted methods for choosing the 'best' solution for a given technique, that is, the solution that can be adopted as providing an optimal outcome in terms of the likely structural properties of a given set of data. This solution can be described as an exemplar solution.

This process allows, and indeed often requires, that multiple analyses be performed and that the exemplar solution is chosen from among this set of possible, plausible, exploratory solutions. An alternative approach is to compare the solutions obtained from each of the multiple analyses and identify structures common across the different solutions within an analytical technique. These structures are typically sets of items that are identified by the statistical technique as belonging together. That is, they are repeatedly identified, for example, as loading on the same factor or being part of the same cluster across repeated, tentative, factor or cluster analyses, respectively. Comparing structures across solutions within specific statistical techniques can produce what might be called consensus structures – in contrast to the exemplar solutions produced through the application of each technique's rules of thumb.

In this project, only one un-rotated PCA was conducted on the MCS data set to emphasise the variance maximisation rationale of this analytical technique and to clearly differentiate it from factor analysis. The PCA result was therefore, both the exemplar and the consensus solution for this technique. With each of the other three analytical techniques, however, multiple tentative, exploratory analyses were conducted. The selection rules that have developed for

each technique over time were then applied to arrive at an exemplar solution for the FA, CA, and MDS, respectively. The multiple analyses that were conducted within each of these techniques were also compared to each other to identify consensus structures in the data.

The exemplar solutions and the consensus structures identified for each analytical technique essentially form the data for the results of the structural analysis. The results are the common structures that are found when the PCA, FA, CA, and MDS exemplar solutions across the four techniques are compared. A parallel set of comparisons across consensus structures form a second set of results.

This process is unusual enough to warrant reiteration. To summarise, multiple solutions (factor analyses, cluster analyses, and multidimensional scalings, respectively) were obtained. Usual procedures were employed to find the 'best' analysis for each statistical technique – these are called the respective technique's exemplars. The multiple solutions for each technique were also compared to each other (within a given technique), rather than picking the 'best' solution. Factors, clusters, and dimensions that were repeatedly found across the multiple tentative solutions were identified – these are the consensus structures. Finally, exemplar structures were compared across statistical techniques. Consensus structures were similarly compared across statistical techniques.

Exemplar comparisons

Common item structures across exemplar solutions were obtained by comparing dimensional structures on an item-by-item basis. For example, items identified as belonging to the first principal component were compared for overlap with the items in each factor, dimension, and cluster of the other techniques' exemplar analyses.

The same comparisons were conducted for each exemplar principal component, factor, cluster, and dimension. Notable overlap was defined as greater than 50 per cent identical items in any pair of comparison structures for structures described by four items or more. Three-item structures required 100 per cent overlap to be considered notable.

Summarising item structure overlap over all of the exemplar comparisons resulted in a set of 10 item structures, of four items or more, that recurred repeatedly. These item structures are listed in Table 17.1, together with internal consistency estimates. Examination of item content suggested common themes were being measured by these structures. Titles indicating what these themes appear to be are also listed in the table.

Consensus comparisons

Multiple PCA, FA, MDS, and CA analyses were conducted in the process of selecting the exemplar analyses. Consensus structures were obtained by comparing item structures across these analyses within each statistical technique. As expected, there was considerable overlap among principal components, factors, clusters, and

dimensions, respectively. The consensus structures that were found were then themselves compared across the four statistical techniques to produce higher order structures. The rationale was that rather than comparing item structures across individual (exemplar) analyses for the four statistical techniques, a set of structures that were found to be common to multiple analyses conducted within each technique would first be identified and these consensus structures would then be compared across techniques. Comparing item structure overlap across these consensus structures identified a set of nine common structures. These structures, together with proposed labels and internal consistency estimates, are presented in Table 17.2.

Overall, these results demonstrate considerable overlap in item structures among the four different statistical techniques. This occurred even though the comparisons were made across analyses that had different numbers of components, factors, clusters, and dimensions. This suggests that item structures identified in multiple analyses are durable and likely to be important. It should be noted that simple structure, in a factor analytic sense, has not been preserved in these analysis although there are only five

Table 17.1 Common item structures identified among exemplar analysis comparisons

Title	Items	α
Goodness	2, 5, 21, 38, 39	.48
Tolerance and moral self-confidence	7, 12, 18, 27, 52	.55
Descriptive morality	21, 26, 63, 78, 101	.30
Moral realism	30, 56, 57, 83, 110, 114	.54
Responsibility	35, 36, 40, 43	.46
Compunction/integrity	35, 88, 103, 122, 138, 139	.57
Social context	63, 66, 74, 94, 96	.56
Conscience	67, 73, 86, 99	.44
Objectivity – relativity	69, 82, 84, 87, 91, 101, 104, 147, 148	.66
Moral identity	86, 103, 113, 115, 119, 122, 123, 130, 141, 144, 146	.75

Table 17.2 Common item structures identified among consensus analysis comparisons

Title	Items	α
Goodness	2, 4, 5, 21	.44
Tolerance and moral self-confidence	7, 12, 18, 27	.45
Acceptability of hurt	20, 22, 29, 51, 55	.47
Moral evasion	35, 88, 122, 139	.44
Responsibility and failure	36, 40, 41, 43, 49	.57
Moral malleability	69, 82, 87, 91, 104, 147, 148	.64
Moral certitude	77, 80, 88, 92, 139	.44
External, prescriptive morality	94, 95, 96, 97	.59
Life definition	103, 113, 115, 119, 122, 130, 141, 144, 146	.71

items that are part of more than one structure in the exemplar structures and only two such items in the consensus structures.

Results: non-linear analysis

The Mokken Scale analysis of the MCS data reinforced the results obtained from the four linear analyses. Limiting interpretable dimensions to those with four items or more resulted in the identifications of seven interpretable dimensions. This is slightly fewer than the 10 exemplar structures identified and the nine consensus structures found. However, the majority of the non-linear structures replicated structures found in the linear analyses. Only two structures appear to be unique to the non-linear analysis. These are structures representing a notion of concreteness of moral reality (*a moral issue will impinge on other people rather than just on the abstract*) and a notion of moral force (*sometimes there are moral issues where you have to cross the barrier and impose your moral choices on other people*).

The remaining five non-linear structures are very similar to equivalent consensus and exemplar structures, though not identical. For example, while the primary dimension is again associated with the concept of identity and defining life and morality it incorporates items that attempt to define morality explicitly as well as focussing on the importance of morality to defining one's life and moulding one's identity.

Non-linear analysis succeeded in improving the reliability of the moral concept structures that were identified, supporting the theoretical rationale for using this data analytical approach with this particular Likert-type data. Improved reliability is reflected in the higher total scale reliability from the non-linear analysis ($\alpha = 0.84$) compared to the exemplar ($\alpha = 0.82$) and consensus analyses ($\alpha = 0.79$).

Summary so far

These analyses suggest that morality, at least in the form that is used in everyday speech, consists of something in the vicinity of seven to ten dimensions. This represents a proof of concept to the extent that it strongly suggests that there is something about morality in the questionnaire items, we can find it, and it seems to be meaningful.

At this point, the meaningfulness of the moral dimensions is largely based on interpretations of the content of the items that form the enduring data structures. There are two tentative conclusions that we can make about morality, as measured in the MCS, from the results in Tables 17.1 and 17.2. First, the primary concept that has been found is the importance of morality to people in defining their lives. For some people their sense of morality is what gives their lives meaning. Other people aren't the least bit interested in morality. At best it's a nuisance that they have to deal with to be able to get on with what is really important in their lives. This is perhaps best considered to be a valence dimension. Second, most of the other dimensions are more like content dimensions that describe what morality means to people. People vary in the importance which they attribute to each of these dimensions as things that they perceive to be important aspects of morality. Content dimensions include relativism, which shows up in a couple of different forms. In some cases it has split into an 'it depends' dimension (malleability) and a dimension that is almost the opposite (certitude/objectivity). Other content dimensions reflect external prescriptions of morality (e.g., socially defined standards) as well as an internal dimension (conscience). Responsibility and tolerance are two further dimensions of morality that this questionnaire appears to measure.

Four questionnaires

Being confident that the item generation and test construction process could produce questionnaires that contained information about morality that was worth measuring, the project focus moved on to the item analysis of the full complement of ideas from the interviews – as represented in the four questionnaires. Fundamentally, the focus of this stage of the MCS development process was to broaden the sampling of items being used to measure morality. Specifically, the goal was identifying items that measured well. A secondary goal, while people were kindly filling out questionnaires for us, was to obtain some early data on what kind of moral construct was being measured. To this end, several rounds of data collection included variables that might be considered relevant to morality. This allowed some preliminary concurrent validity analyses to be conducted with MCS constructs. In the structural analysis, moral dimensions appeared meaningful because they persistently emerged through multiple analyses and because they contained items with consistent, interpretable meaning. The concurrent validity analyses of this stage of the process were designed to clarify the meaning of the dimensions by identifying their relationships to other, relevant variables.

Rather than brutally culling items through the exacting data screening process used in the proof-of-concept structural analysis, the focus on the four-questionnaire (4Q) analyses was to find items that measure morality – rather than predominantly trying to exclude items that seem to contribute to noise.

Item response theory

In addition to considering whether individual items were highly skewed and whether they were related to the overall construct being measured (foci of the earlier item analysis) item analysis at this stage of the process included the use of item response theory (IRT) analysis. IRT contains a number of useful features for test construction and use. For example, the detection of poor items can be formalised through the use of item-model fit statistics. While there are limitations to the specific fit indices, they allow the possibility of an explicit test of item functioning. IRT also provides tests of model-data fit at the entire test/questionnaire level. So, for example, while a questionnaire made up of Likert-type items may not fit an intuitively appropriate rating scale model, it may fit a more general model (Ostini, 2001) – and this can be tested explicitly.

With IRT, items can also be selected based on the range of the trait continuum that they measure and how well they discriminate – using sample invariant item parameters, when model assumptions are met. IRT also provides conditional measures of precision. IRT measures of precision take the form of functions that vary across the trait continuum. Furthermore, these measures of precision are available at both the item level (Item Information Function) and at the test level (Test Information Function: TIF). So, while IRT test information provides a measure of how precisely a set of items in a test are measuring the trait in question, in a role that is analogous to classical test theory reliability (Baker, 1992) the TIF has the advantage of providing measures of precision at each trait or ability level rather than a single global measure.

By fitting an IRT model to the MCS data, the 4Q analysis implicitly took advantage of the sample invariance of the model parameters. Item fit statistics were explicitly used to help select items. Finally, an idiosyncratic feature of Rasch and Rasch-type polytomous models that shows category boundary ordering was used to investigate how the ordered response scales were working. The modelling of reversed boundaries can be used as a diagnostic tool to help provide understanding of the cognitive processes at work in responding to an item and probably indicating that something is wrong with the item (Andrich, 1988).

There are many IRT models than can be applied to Likert-type items (Ostini and Nering, 2006) and there is some evidence that, despite fundamental theoretical differences that can produce much heated argument, the different models produce remarkably similar outcomes in terms of person measurement (Ostini, 2001). Given this state of affairs and the desire to identify reversed boundaries, the extended logistic model (Andrich, 1988) was used in these analyses.

The 4Q stage of the MCS development process used skewed items analysis, item-total correlations, IRT item-fit, and reversed boundaries as indicators of poorly functioning items. These analyses were conducted to identify items to exclude from further analysis. Items that were flagged as problematic on two or more of these indicators were excluded from further analyses. Between 19 (MCS version D) and 25 (MCS version A) items were excluded on the basis of these analyses.

Items with very heavily skewed response distributions were retained for an Imp scale. The Imp scale is a simple scale for identifying implausible responding that takes advantage of the fact that some moral statements are utterly, fundamentally implausible while others are almost impossible to disagree with. These items are used in a diagnostic scale to check whether respondents are attending to the statements in the questionnaire or simply responding at random. Repeatedly responding to Imp items in the tails of their distributions is

considered evidence of a likely response bias – specifically, inattention or faux contrariness. The location of the cut-off for the Imp scale that best indicates inattentive or contrary responding is an empirical question that is yet to be conclusively answered.

CONSTRUCT VALIDATION

There are two broad approaches that can be followed when validating tests. One approach involves developing and evaluating test norms. For example, are people who have more of the attribute being measured ranked higher on the test? An alternative approach is to lay out a set of theoretically justified, expected relationships with other variables and test to see whether they eventuate. While failure to find the expected connections may indicate a poorly hypothesised (or tested) set of relationships, it may also be necessary to consider whether the measure is not working as intended.

Generally, construct validation involves asking whether the test is measuring what it was built to measure. This is difficult with the MCS in part because finding what morality was one goal of building this test. This means that the construct definition and construct validation processes are intertwined.

Validating the MCS

Factor analyses were periodically conducted on data from each questionnaire as the slow process of data collection unfolded. No definitive factor structures were sought, or found, meaning simply that no factor solution was identified as the 'best' solution obtainable for a questionnaire in terms of simple structure; variance accounted for (high item communalities); strength of factors (multiple high factor loadings); and reproducibility.

There were factors that tended to come up repeatedly in multiple analyses, both within individual questionnaires as well as across questionnaires (e.g., life definition, relativism) while other factors came and went depending on when and with which questionnaire analysis was conducted (e.g., religion and conscience). Many of the moral concepts that were identified in these analyses corresponded to the kinds of concepts identified in the 'proof-of-concept' structural analyses. The removal of fewer items through the 4Q item analysis process tended to contribute to there being more factors (10–14) often containing larger numbers of items than in the item structures identified in the structural analysis. Within this fluid construct status environment, relationships with other cogent/relevant constructs were tentatively investigated.

Table 17.3 Four-questionnaire data collection design including validation variables showing numbers of respondents

Validation variables	MCS version			
	MCS 3a	MCS 3b	MCS 3c	MCS 3d
	570	635	576	583
Internal State Awareness (ISA)	73	81	51	97
Eysenck Personality Inventory (EPI)	82	125	154	167
Social Values (VS)	73	—	—	—
Political Orientation (LC)	82	—	—	—
Big 5 Personality (IPIP)	—	81	—	—
Guilt (PFQ)	—	125	—	—
Emotional Intelligence (EI)	—	—	154	—
Multidimensional Personality Questionnaire (MPQ)	—	—	51	—
Religion (SRDS)	—	—	—	89
Empathy (IRI)	—	—	—	167

Table 17.3 lists the 10 validation variables investigated in the course of MCS 4Q data collection. These investigations are far from conclusive, but they add to the tapestry of information about morality as portrayed by the MCS. To the extent that they demonstrate intelligible relationships with relevant variables; these sorts of results encourage further development of the MCS and indicate the types of moral concepts that the MCS is measuring.

For example, investigations using the Eysenck Personality Inventory (EPI) suggested that personality, as represented by the EPI dimensions of neuroticism and extroversion, is more closely related to MCS dimensions than are emotional intelligence or guilt. Conversely, empathy and measures of liberalism and conservatism are more strongly related to more MCS dimensions than is EPI personality.

Investigations using the Big 5 personality factors produced positive conscientiousness-relativism and agreeableness-relativism relationships. At the same time, more dimensions measured by the MCS were found to have significant and sometimes stronger relationships with a measure of Internal State Awareness than with Big 5 personality dimensions. Similarly, a measure of social values was found to have many, often strong, relationships with MCS dimensions, on a scale that dwarfed the relationships between the same social values and a measure of Kohlbergian moral judgement (Ostini and Ellerman, 1997).

Over the entire range of constructs whose relationships with the MCS were investigated results were sometimes unexpected, but taken together indicate that the construct being measured by the MCS is a complex representation of morality.

The purpose of the 4Q stage of the project was essentially to identify items that didn't work – without necessarily knowing why they didn't work. The concurrent validity step of simultaneously administering scales measuring constructs expected to be related to people's moral concepts was essentially a way to maximise the information that respondents were providing for the effort that they were making – and perhaps to make the experience more interesting for them. It seems unnecessarily mean and harsh to put people through the process of responding to 150 raw statements about morality simply to weed out a few hundred items. In the end these results give us more confidence that the MCS is measuring dispositional aspects of morality in a form that most people would recognise.

At its most basic level, the item analysis process itself contributes to evidence of the construct validity of the MCS. In particular, to the extent that items in the measure relate to each other and to an aggregate score on the measure they indicate that the MCS is measuring a coherent construct.

Content analyses of the original interview transcripts together with interviews conducted in two other, demographically distinct samples are also being undertaken. To the extent that these analyses identify similar concepts in the interview text as the statistical procedures have identified in the MCS response data, they too will provide evidence of construct validity. Of course, to the extent that they find the interviews to be incoherent or replete with a range of ideas that may be tenuously related to morality, the content analyses would undermine the construct validity of the MCS.

Another way to clarify the type of construct being measured by the MCS is to administer the test to people in groups that differ in relevant ways. Unlike Kohlbergian measures, one would not expect moral philosophy students or seminarians to score higher on the MCS – at least in part because a *higher* MCS score does not equate to a *better* score. It is however, conceivable that there will be cultural differences in which MCS dimensions are prioritised among different groups (e.g. East-West; Rural-Urban; Affluent-Poor). To the extent that groups that might be expected to espouse quite different social norms are differentiated on MCS dimensions, this supports the capacity of the MSC to measure something important.

Next steps

Following the 4Q stage of the MCS development process, 140 items were flagged as functioning poorly. The remaining 360 items have been combined into two questionnaires. The next stage of data collection and analysis will determine whether these are parallel measures or whether they measure different aspects of morality. While these questionnaires contain the best functioning items from the original set of 600, it is likely that further item refinement or removal will occur. Future analyses are expected to be more definitive with the development process arriving at the point where there is less noise in the data with items that measure morality better and items that are more strongly interrelated. Relationships with other constructs should also become clearer.

Ultimately, however, morality is difficult to measure. For that reason, final scaling of items and respondent measures will use IRT. Even if IRT only provides a modest improvement in measurement precision over simple summation methods it will be valuable for scoring respondents – as it becomes clearer what they are being scored on – in addition to its contributions in analysing items for test construction purposes.

The measures that result from this program should give us a clearer idea of the multifaceted nature of morality – and a way to measure them well. This in turn, should allow relationships with other cogent variables to become clearer and help us to know how morality operates in people's lives. Once we know what we're measuring and once we know that we're doing it well, we will have a comprehensive measure of moral conceptualisation that can also be used in theoretical and applied behavioural and social science research.

CONCLUSION

This chapter describes a moderately convoluted process that has been pursued with the aim of measuring morality, as it really is. This endeavour has been complicated by the fact that no one really knows what morality really is – or if they do, they cannot convince many other people that they are right. Breaking the fundamental rule of being clear at the outset about what is being measured has resulted in an unusual and somewhat arcane structural analysis and a blurring of the construct definition and validation aspects of the test construction process.

In contrast, it is more common in academic research for people to know exactly what they want to measure and to simply assume that they are doing so when they build an instrument. Measurement need not be difficult but this is not an excuse for ignoring the need to do it well. It seems that research in some academic disciplines is awash in measures that are assumed to be measuring the intended attribute and are assumed to be measuring it well enough – often purely on the basis of a plausible looking set of test questions and a Cronbach's alpha of greater than 0.70. It is worth recalling that it does not matter how large a sought-after effect is if the tool that is being used to measure it is measuring an irrelevant attribute or is measuring a relevant attribute so imprecisely that the effect is impossible to detect.

Thorndike (1997) suggests that complex measurement tools in the physical sciences are accepted because the results that they produce are 'consistent, verifiable, and useful' (p. 12). In that spirit, it can be argued that the final test or any measurement instrument in the social sciences lies in the question, 'Is it working?' That is, will the numbers obtained from the test being constructed allow the user to efficiently and properly perform the tasks for which the test is intended – whether that involves applied decision-making or theory building. Answering this question involves three pivotal elements: (i) that the measurement instrument is used in a way that allows it to work as intended (this is the test administration question); (ii) that it measures what was intended (this is the validation question); and (iii) that it measures well (this is the item analysis question). If these questions can be answered positively then the effort that has gone into building the measurement tool will have been worthwhile.

REFERENCES

Andrich, D. (1988) 'A general form of Rasch's extended logistic model for partial credit scoring', *Applied Measurement in Education*, 1: 363–78.

Baker, F. B. (1992) *Item response theory: Parameter estimation techniques*. New York: Marcel Dekker.

Colby, A., and Kohlberg, L. (1987) *The measurement of moral judgment*. (Vol. 1). Cambridge: Cambridge University Press.

Davison, M. L. (1985) 'Multidimensional scaling versus components analysis of test intercorrelations', *Psychological Bulletin*, 97: 94–105.

Gilligan, C. B. (1982) *In a different voice*. Cambridge, Mass: Harvard University Press.

Gnanadesikan, R. (1977) *Methods for statistical data analysis of multivariate observations*. New York: John Wiley and Sons.

Gorsuch, R. L., and Ortberg, J. (1983) 'Moral obligation and attitudes: Their relation to behavioral intentions',

Journal of Personality and Social Psychology, 44: 1025–8.

Hartshorne, H. and May, M. A. (1928) *Studies in the nature of character*. New York: Macmillan.

Hoffman, M. L. (1981) 'Is altruism part of human nature?', *Journal of Personality and Social Psychology*, 40: 121–37.

Hogan, R. (1973) 'Moral conduct and moral character', *Psychological Bulletin*, 79: 217–32.

Kohlberg, L. (1969) 'Stage and sequence: The cognitive developmental approach to socialization', in D. A. Goslin (ed.) *Handbook of socialization theory and research*. Chicago: Rand McNally. pp. 347–480.

Kohlberg, L. (1976) 'Moral stages and moralization: The cognitive-developmental approach', in T. Likona (ed.) *Moral development and behavior: Theory, research and social issues*. New York: Holt, Rinehart and Winston.

Kruskal, J. (1977) 'The relationship between multidimensional scaling and clustering', in J. Van Ryzin (ed.) *Classification and clustering*. New York: Academic Press. pp. 17–44.

Loevinger, J. (1976) *Ego development: Conceptions and theories*. San Francisco: Jossey Bass.

MacCallum, R. C. (1974) 'Relations between factor analysis and multidimensional scaling', *Psychological Bulletin*, 81: 505–16.

McDonald, R. P. (1982) 'Linear versus nonlinear models in item response theory', *Applied Psychological Measurement*, 6 (4): 379–96.

Molenaar, I. W. and Sijtsma, K. (2000) *MSP5 for Windows: A program for Mokken scale analysis for polytomous items*. Groningen: iec Progamma.

Ostini, R. (2001) *Identifying Substantive Measurement Differences Among a Variety of Polytomous IRT Models*. Unpublished doctoral thesis, University of Minnesota, Minneapolis, MN.

Ostini, R. and Ellerman D. A. (1997) 'Clarifying the relationship between values and moral judgement', *Psychological Reports*, 81: 691–702.

Ostini, R. and Nering, M. L. (2006) *Polytomous Item Response Theory Models*. Thousand Oaks, CA: Sage.

Reynolds, K. J., Turner, J. C., Haslam, A. and Ryan, M. K. (2001) 'The role of personality and group factors in explaining prejudice', *Journal of Personality and Social Psychology*, 37: 427–34.

Shephard, R. N. (1980) 'Multidimensional scaling, tree-fitting, and clustering', *Science*, 210: 390–8.

Skitka, L. J. and Crosby, F. J. (2003) 'Tends in the social psychological study of justice', *Personality and Social Psychology Review*, 7: 282–5.

Stone, V. E., Cosmides, L., Tooby, J., Kroll, N. and Knight, R. T. (2002) 'Selective impairment of reasoning about social exchange in a patient with bilateral limbic system damage', *Proceedings of the National Academy of Sciences of the United States of America*, 99 (17): 11531–6.

Terry, D. J. and Hogg, M. A. (1996) 'Group norms and the attitude-behavior relationship: A role for group identification', *Personality and Social Psychology Bulletin*, 22: 776–93.

Thissen, D., Baker, L. and Wainer, H. (1981) 'Influence-enhanced scatterplots', *Psychological Bulletin*, 90: 179–84.

Thorndike, R. M. (1997) *Measurement and evaluation in psychology and education* (6th edition). Upper Saddle River, N.J.: Prentice-Hall.

van Abswoude, A. A. H., van der Ark, L. A. and Sijtsma, K. (2004) 'A comparative study of test data dimensionality assessment procedures under nonparametric IRT models', *Applied Psychological Measurement*, 28: 3–24.

Wainer, H. (1982) 'Robust statistics: A survey and some prescriptions', in G. Keren (ed.) *Statistical and methodological issues in psychology and social sciences research*. Hillsdale, N.J.: Erlbaum. pp. 187–214.

Volz, J. (2000) 'In search of the good life', *Monitor on Psychology*, 31: 68–9.

APPENDIX 17.1

OPEN-ENDED INTERVIEW QUESTIONS

1. How would you describe a good person?
2. How would you describe a bad person?
3. What does the word morality mean to you?
4. What does it mean to say something is morally right or wrong? What makes an issue moral?
5. What does responsibility mean to you?
6. What does fairness mean to you?
7. When there are conflicting views on moral issues is there a correct way to solve the moral problem, or is everybody's opinion equally right?
8. Why should people be moral?
9. If you had to say what morality meant to you, how would you sum it up?
10. Those are all the questions that I have, is there anything that you would like to add?

18

The Problem with Poverty: Definition, Measurement and Interpretation

Robert Walker, Mark Tomlinson, and
Glenn Williams

Although almost everybody believes that they know what poverty is, it is surprisingly difficult to define and measure.

The Oxford English Dictionary definition of poverty seems straightforward: 'the condition of having little or no wealth or material possessions'. However, for this definition to acquire practical value, it is necessary to interpret the weasel word 'little', little in relation to what? Furthermore, the focus on wealth, 'the abundance of possessions', sits uneasily alongside official definitions of poverty that mostly rely on measures of income.

For the British public, if focus groups are to be believed, poverty is a phenomenon of the developing world, understood: 'as part of the vocabulary of aid-oriented charities

and international NGOs. It seems to suggest an abject end-state, which applies clearly to images of malnourished "third world" children, or if pressed to consider the British context, a bygone age of Dickensian squalor' (Castell and Thompson, 2007: 10). Yet, over half of Britons responding to opinion polls regularly agree that there is 'quite a lot' of poverty in Britain today', with only about 40 per cent thinking that there is 'very little' (Park et al., 2007). This discrepancy seems to reflect differences in deep-seated values. Some people hold the view that poverty is the product of unfairness and social injustice, low benefits and insufficient government action, while others believe that poverty results from indolence exacerbated by high benefits and profligate public expenditure. While the latter group tends overwhelmingly to adhere to a strict definition of poverty ('someone cannot eat and live without getting into debt'), the former are more prepared to countenance one that refers to a person's inability to buy 'things that others take for granted'.

There are also national cultural differences in the understanding of poverty (Table 18.1). Swedes are more likely to attribute poverty to modern progress and injustice than either Britons or Americans.[1] Americans and Britons are more prone to blame poverty on laziness or lack of willpower; 39 per cent of Americans hold to this view, four times the number in Sweden and twice that in Spain. At a political level, UK Prime Minister Margaret Thatcher and German Chancellor Helmut Kohl in the 1980s both denied that poverty existed in either of their countries; discussion was kept alive within Europe by the French, Irish and Italian governments that promoted use of the term 'social exclusion' as a euphemism.

There is more of a shared understanding of poverty among the poor in economically advanced countries. The common experience is of personal failure in societies that rate success in terms of conspicuous consumption (Edin et al., 2000; Beresford et al., 1999; Schwarz, 1997; Clasen et al., 1998). Feelings of worthlessness are reinforced by the sense, real or imaginary, that other people view people who are poor as feckless, dishonest, or as scroungers. Only close relatives and true friends offer succour, support that may be made difficult to accept by the stigma of personal failure (Edin and Lein, 1997; Middleton et al., 1994). The word poverty itself is shunned, being shameful; people, instead, describe their everyday experiences: 'lives which are mundane, limited, constrained, full of drudgery or struggle' (Castell and Thompson, 2007: 11).

Having demonstrated the rapidity with which a common sense understanding of poverty evaporates, let us make clear the ontological stance from which we engage with the topic in the ensuing discussion. We begin by defining the distribution of resources (material, social and personal) measured relative to need; affluence lies at the top end of the distribution and hardship towards the bottom. Poverty is taken to be the unacceptable lowest quantile of this distribution. We believe that hardship exists as an empirical reality that is variously but directly experienced by individuals (and indirectly by the communities in which it occurs). However, we consider poverty to be a political construct with no one-to-one correspondence to a reality experienced by a particular set of individuals. Because the very word poverty predicates the demand

Table 18.1   Views on the causes of poverty

Percentages

Causes	Great Britain (1999)	Germany (1999)	Spain (1999)	Sweden (1999)	US (1997)	Causes
Injustice in society	32	45	48	49		
Part modern progress	23	17	10	33	44	Circumstances beyond control
Unlucky	16	11	20	11		
Laziness/lack of willpower	25	24	20	8	39	Insufficient effort
None of these	4	3	2	0	17	Both
Total	100	100	100	100	100	

Source: World Values Survey (2008) and Weaver (2000).

for action to eradicate it, poverty becomes a rallying cry for social change. It is a rhetorical device used as a weapon in political competition and an administrative tool that services the political debate with statistics and provides a baseline against which to measure the effectiveness of anti-poverty policies.

In theory, hardship can be directly measured although that is not to deny the difficulty of deciding what kind of resources are to be set against what measure of need. Poverty, on the other hand, is fixed by positioning of the poverty threshold. The underlying distribution of resources to needs is continuous with a maximum value asymptotically approaching infinite affluence and a minimum value that results in death. Poverty is politically constructed by bifurcating this distribution, fixing the quantile below which individuals will be counted as poor.[2] The severity of poverty is then defined as the amount by which a poor individual's hardship score falls short of the poverty threshold.

Given this ontological position, we could devote the remainder of this chapter to explaining the different levels at which governments fix 'official' poverty thresholds. However, we leave others to map this terrain (e.g., Veit-Wilson, 1998) and write *as if* poverty were synonymous with hardship, ignoring our concern that academics and researchers often amalgamate and/or confuse the two. We briefly review the various and sometimes competing conceptions of poverty and conclude that they can be reconciled in a multi-dimensional representation of poverty. We subsequently report, and, in part, evaluate, our recent attempts to measure poverty[3] conceptualised in this way. Then, in 'reverse' semi-autobiographical fashion, we draw on analysis to argue that time and space[4] are not merely the ether in which poverty occurs but serve to shape the phenomenon and, thereby, to create

not one kind of poverty but many. Finally, we return full circle briefly to consider methods that social scientists have proposed to assist politicians in establishing poverty thresholds and report tentative results from the implementation of an approach first suggested 20 years ago (Walker, 1987).

CONCEPTIONS OF POVERTY

Student textbooks are prone to present scientific measurement as a linear process in which a concept is first clearly defined, an indicator then devised and a scale created, the aspiration being that the indicator adequately captures the essence of the concept in any relevant context. However, the history of poverty research demonstrates a recursive process in which an apparently self-evident but poorly articulated concept is itself defined with reference to available indicators. The early pioneers of poverty research, for example, Henry Mayhew (1851), Charles Booth (1892) and Seebohm Rowntree (1901) in Britain and W.E.B Du Bois (1899) and Robert Hunter (1904) in the US, witnessed large numbers of their fellow citizens existing in squalor, without sufficient food, decent clothing or adequate heating or sanitation. Their interest in measurement was moral and instrumental rather than scientific; they wanted to mobilise political support to change policies so as to ameliorate the conditions of the poor. Moreover, this heavy mix of morality and politics demanded that they show that the paupers' impoverishment was not of their own making and due to lack of resources rather than profligate spending. Hence, these pioneers paid considerable attention to establishing how much income their poor respondents had, as well as how much it cost to provide for the basic necessities of life.

Much later, notably in the 1960s when policies stimulated by the pioneers had been implemented, matured and developed and economic growth had lifted almost everyone above subsistence levels, a new generation of academic activists, including Brian Abel-Smith and Peter Townsend (1965) in Britain and Harrington (1962) in the US, pointed out that the basic necessities of life had also changed and that lack of income was preventing people from engaging in the activities and expenditure expected of them, causing them to be excluded and stigmatised. While Townsend (1979) compiled a list of items and activities that people went without, his main aim was to demonstrate an income level below which the probability of going without – deprivation – increased significantly.

Townsend's attempt to develop indicators of consumption attracted much criticism because of their normative basis and failure to take account of personal preferences (Piachaud, 1981). Nevertheless, his argument that poverty was inherently relative was gradually accepted and incorporated into official (and de facto official) measures of poverty, first in Britain and then in Europe (although the US still persists in an official definition of poverty that is neither automatically nor systematically altered with rising living standards [Blank, 2008]). Furthermore, until very recently official measures relied entirely on income as the metric of poverty, usually crudely adjusted (equivalised) by household size and composition to take account of presumed economies of scale arising from shared living accommodation and lower consumption by children (Banks and Johnson, 1994). The poverty threshold was (and continues to be) defined as equivalised household income below an arbitrary proportion (usually, 40, 50 or 60 per cent) of the national median.[5] In 2004/5, Britain followed the European example, replacing the historic but domestically derived McClements equivalence scale with the inelegantly named 'modified OECD' one.

This reliance on low income as an index of poverty no doubt reflects the comparative ease with which income can be measured since direct measures of deprivation are difficult to devise.[6] However, as Ringen (1988) argues, low income and deprivation are intrinsically different and predicate contrasting policy responses. Income poverty can be resolved by ensuring that the poor have higher incomes whereas additional income does not guarantee reduced deprivation. For Ringen, poverty equates to consumption that is so low as to exclude poor people from a 'normal way of life'. Income, he asserts, is an indirect and inadequate measure of poverty. The generic warning is that while, other things being equal, simple measures are preferable to complex ones, simplicity can be seductive, introduce bias and, Ringen would argue in this case, lead researchers inadvertently to measure the wrong concept.

A plethora of studies have constructed indicators of deprivation (Berthoud et al., 2004; Calandrino, 2003; Gordon et al., 2000; Nolan and Whelan, 1996). Some, following Townsend, determine *a priori* lists of possessions and activities and record the numbers of people who lack them. Increasingly, though, possessions and activities are selected as indicators because they are believed by the majority of respondents to be 'social necessities' that 'nobody should have to do without' (Gordon and Pantazis, 1997; Gordon et al., 2000). This 'democratic', 'majoritarian' or 'consensual' approach makes the measure inherently relative. Typically, to avoid the problem of 'deprivation through choice', respondents are asked whether they lack possessions or fail to engage in activities because they are short of income. Normally a deprivation threshold is set in terms of a prescribed but arbitrary number of possessions or activities that cannot be afforded. However, sometimes the individual possessions and activities are treated as measurable indicators of a latent concept, deprivation, not considered to be amenable to direct measurement (Whelan and Maitre, 2005).

Studies that compare material deprivation and income poverty show them to be only moderated correlated. Calandrino (2003), for example, finds 32 per cent of British lone parents to be both poor and multiply deprived and another 36 per cent to be either poor or deprived. These findings appear to lend support to Ringen's contention that the two concepts should be differentiated and, in turn, to demonstrate the universal importance of defining concepts and selecting indicators with care. It should be noted, however, that the lack of association between income poverty and material deprivation could simply be an artefact of cumulative measurement errors or result from differential time lags since material deprivation arising from a fall in income may only become apparent when possessions depreciate and are abandoned (Berthoud et al., 2004).

As already noted, much of the policy community in the US continues to reject the reframing of poverty as a relative concept. This is partly a product of practical politics, pragmatically premised on achieving small improvements in the official poverty index, the political ownership of which, distinct among key statistical measures, resides within the White House (Blank, 2008). Absolute poverty has other political advantages. It can, for example, be ameliorated by the effects of passive policies, such as economic growth, that lift the incomes of the poor above the poverty threshold. Relative poverty, in contrast, can only be eradicated by active redistribution of income (and/or other resources, economic

or social)[7] and has the counterintuitive characteristic of often rising during periods of economic. This latter phenomenon occurs when the poverty threshold is set relative to median income and economic growth is accompanied by rising income inequality.[8] Perhaps not surprisingly, therefore, absolute measures of poverty, or, at least, quasi-absolute measures that hold a relative threshold constant in money terms, are enjoying somewhat of a renaissance. They have recently been reintroduced alongside relative measures in Britain (DWP, 2007a) and are included among the Laeken indicators used to monitor the impact of the European social inclusion agenda (Atkinson et al., 2002). In addition, both Irish and British governments have adopted composite measures that count people as poor only if they fail to meet both a relative income and a material deprivation threshold (DWP, 2003; Nolan and Whelan, 1996).[9]

While it is still common place to present absolute and relative poverty as competing concepts, Amartya Sen (1999) has convincingly sought to reconcile them. He argues that poverty is not (just) a lack of income but rather the failure of a person to achieve minimum capabilities that are context specific and hence relative. People fulfil such capabilities through the functioning of commodities that they need to acquire – a bicycle or car, for example, to get to work – and a person's failure to do so is a source of shame. While capabilities and functioning vary by context and are inherently relative, shame is universal and absolute and constitutes the core meaning of poverty. Sen's effort to reconceptualise how researchers understand poverty thus has profound implications for measurement. Although the universality of this construction has yet to be tested across diverse cultures and different levels of economic development,[10] the idea is given considerable credence by the testimonies of worthlessness felt by poor people that have been cited above. Alongside shame, poor people talk of the difficulty of making ends meet, the immediate and more long-term difficulties and hassle of budgeting, the challenge of rationing claims of children and partners on limited resources and the risk of borrowing becoming unmanagcable indebtedness.

A considerable number of studies have also reported psychological strain associated with poverty although they differ in the direction of causality that is assumed (Payne, 2006). Either way, whether mental ill-health is a product or a cause of poverty, the evidence is that stress-related illnesses are a common part of the experience of being poor. Similarly, there is evidence that social isolation occurs as either a manifestation or a consequence of poverty but that, once a person is marginalised, the twin phenomena become self-reinforcing; the person lacks the support, information and contacts that might help them to find work or, in other ways, to engage more fully in society (Gallie et al., 2003; Cattell, 2001). A further manifestation of poverty that is widely reported is exclusion from civic participation. This occurs for a complex range of reasons including alienation and perceived powerlessness. However, it may also be the result of more prosaic factors including reliance on public transport, limited access to childcare and the time constraints imposed by the need to make do with limited resources (Pantazis et al., 2006).

An additional consideration is the complex interplay between poor people and the places in which they live. Among other reasons, including the legacy of history, constraints imposed by access to housing mean that people with low incomes are geographically concentrated, often in areas with poor amenities and higher rates of crime and antisocial behaviour. There is considerable controversy about the extent to which the experience of personal poverty is compounded by locality, but it is certain that poverty is mediated by place and place by people's poverty (Dorling et al., 2007).

One response to the growing appreciation of these different facets of poverty has been to complement an income-based measure with sets of other indices, illustrated by the 18 Laeken indicators used by the European Commission (NPI, 2007) and the 41 measures employed by the UK government (DWP, 2007a). Another response has been increasingly to reference the multi-dimensional nature of poverty although most attempts at measurement have not progressed beyond the use of multiple measures and indexes, frequently assembled from different data sources and often pertaining to different samples of individuals. Even when measures do relate to the same individuals, the multi-dimensionality is sometimes lost by combining the individual scores into a single scale (Gordon et al., 2000).

The most common way of handling the multi-dimensionality of poverty is to employ factor analytic techniques in which a battery of variables collected through a survey of individuals is reduced analytically to a smaller set of composite indicators termed factors. The factors are, in essence, weighted summations of the individual variables (Calandrino, 2003). Unfortunately the factors accumulate the measurement error associated with the original variables which becomes especially problematic when one is interested in measuring change by comparing factors derived from variables collected at different times since an unknown proportion of the change observed in the factors will be due to differences in measurement error. Often the factors also have to be 'rotated', that is adjusted through a process of matrix multiplication, in order to facilitate interpretation and the optimum rotation will vary between one set of data and another. So, while factor analysis allows the multiple dimensions of poverty to be simultaneously measured, the compounding of measurement error and the use of different rotations makes the technique unsuited to monitoring change in poverty rates over time (Haase and Pratschke, 2005; Loehlin, 1992).

To summarise, poverty is now usually conceptualised to be relative, although with absolute components, and to be multi-faceted or multi-dimensional. However, systematic measurement of multi-dimensional poverty has hitherto proved troublesome.

MEASURING MULTI-DIMENSIONAL POVERTY

Rationale and strategy

Before reporting on some of our recent attempts to overcome the traditional difficulty of measuring poverty multi-dimensionally, it is necessary to explain how we interpret the concept of multi-dimensional poverty. We take a person-centric view, asking 'what do low income people experience as poverty?' The answer drawn largely from qualitative literature is that they recognise all the facets of poverty cited above: low income; material deprivation; depressing, sometimes frightening, neighbourhoods; stress in budgeting; psycho-social stress; shame, isolation and exclusion (Walker and Collins, 2004). To convert this experience into a measurement, we define each aspect of poverty as a dimension and create a composite poverty score for individuals based on their score on each of the dimensions measured simultaneously. The presumption, then, is that a person's experience of poverty is, at any instance, simultaneously shaped by their score on each of the constituent dimensions. No assumption needs to be made about the direction of possible causality between the various dimensions of poverty: while psychological distress may be caused by income poverty in a previous period, its presence is an integral part of the experience of poverty in the present, however, or whenever, it was caused.

The technique employed to accomplish the measurement task is structural equation modelling (SEM). Like standard factor analysis (subsequently called exploratory factor analysis), SEM reduces a large number of variables to create scores on a smaller number of factors. The variables are conceptualised as observed manifestations of underlying or latent concepts. Each observed variable in a structural equation model (SEM) has an error term associated with it, allowing measurement error to be isolated and controlled for in a way that is impossible with factor analysis. Unlike exploratory factor analysis, a SEM requires a strong theoretical justification before the model is specified. Thus, the researcher decides which observed variables are to be associated with which latent unobserved factors in advance. This aims to avoid the problems of instability and rotated solutions associated with exploratory factor analysis.

The basic measurement model fitted to data from the British Household Panel Study (BHPS) is shown in Figure 18.1 (see Tomlinson et al. [2008] for the full model). The BHPS commenced in 1991 with an initial sample of around 10,000 individuals resident in some 5,000 households and interviews are repeated annually. The analysis covers alternate years during the period 1991–2003 reflecting biannual inclusion of key variables. Even so, data limitations mean that the dimensions of shame and neighbourhood deprivation are not included in the composite measure, although the latter dimension has successfully been

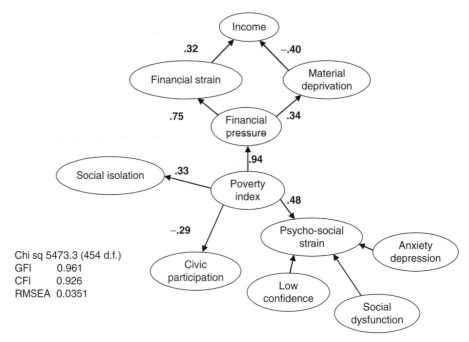

Figure 18.1   Measurement model for poverty index.
Source: Tomlinson et al. (2008).

modelled in analysis covering a shorter period (Tomlinson et al., 2008)

The ellipses in Figure 18.1 are latent unobserved variables, the dimensions of poverty. In most cases, these dimensions are measured with respect to observed variables taken from the BHPS but omitted from the diagram. Each of the observed variables has an associated error term while coefficients or loadings indicate how closely the observed and latent variables are related. Some of the latent variables in the model are measured by other latent variables and each has a residual term associated with it (not shown) because none of the latent variables is fully accounted for by the variables associated with it. The poverty index itself is defined and measured by four latent variables: 'financial pressure'; social isolation'; 'civic partic- ipation' and 'psychological strain'. Like- wise, 'psychological strain' is measured

with respect to three latent variables ('anxiety/depression', 'low confidence' and 'social dysfunction') that are, in turn, mea- sured with respect to the 12-item General Health Questionnaire (GHQ) included in the BHPS. 'Financial pressure' reflects both the 'financial stain' incurred in making ends meet in the short term and 'material deprivation', the real effects of long- term financial hardship on the household. 'Material deprivation' and 'financial strain' are themselves partly defined by household income.

By making assumptions about the dis- tributions of the variables and error terms in the model, the coefficients are estimated using maximum likelihood statistical tech- niques and a variety of fit statistics is available to assess the validity of the models constructed (see Klein, 2005; Byrne, 2001). The coefficients are shown in standardised form in Figure 18.1 and indicate that the poverty index is shaped, or weighted, most by 'financial pressure', itself more closely associated with 'financial strain' than with 'material deprivation'.[11] 'Psychological strain' is more important in the index than 'social isolation', while the coefficient attached to 'civic participation' is of similar size to that for 'social isolation' but has the opposite sign (because increased poverty is associated with less civic participation).

Process

It should be recognised that the model in Figure 18.1 is the product of an iterative process. We began with expectations about the dimensions of the poverty index and the variables needed to measure them based on a careful reading of the literature (Tomlinson et al., 2008). Many of what we considered the most appropriate variables were not available, none relating to shame or, early in the period, to neighbourhood environment. Many were not as we would have specified them. The measures of civic participation, for instance, related only to largely unspecified membership organisations, while the measures of material deprivation related solely to the possession of consumer durables with no indication of whether this reflected preference or constraint. The General Health Questionnaire scale provides a generic measure of psychological well-being and is not necessarily an ideal index of psychological strain (Goldberg and Williams, 1988). Moreover, it was only administered to persons aged over 16 which meant that we could not include children in our measure of poverty. (We considered ways of creating a measure of 'household stress' so as to include children, for instance, by setting a household value equal to the stress reported by the household head or to the mean or highest of the stress levels reported by adults, but none proved satisfactory.)

Importantly, the model relationships were modified to improve the statistical fit of the model. We did not begin, for example, with the concept of 'financial pressure', but anticipated that 'financial strain' and 'material deprivation' would each contribute directly to the poverty index. However, in the modelling it became evident that the difficulty of making ends meet, though conceptually different from a lack of possessions, was nevertheless closely related to it with the two components possibly being cumulative. Including income in the model was driven by theoretical concerns that echo the positions of Townsend and Sen; poverty is the inability to participate due to lack of resources. However, adding income added little to the statistical properties of the model while reducing its parsimony; income loaded onto both 'financial strain' and 'material deprivation' rather than directly onto the poverty index. In terms of the recorded distribution of poverty or trends over time, there was very little difference between an index that included income and one that did not.

The preferred model, then, is obviously a compromise between theoretical aspirations, data availability and data quality. We were able to check the robustness of the technique, although not the precise model, using a second study, the Family and Children Survey (FaCS), a panel of families with children initiated in 1999 with a sample of low-income families but expanded in 2001 to include all families. For comparison, we estimated two models based upon a subset of variables contained in both surveys in 2001. This necessitated estimation of only three latent constructs (financial strain, material deprivation and housing) and one second-order poverty index as before. The coefficients between the observed variables and the latent variables proved to be very similar as did the size of the coefficients between the three latent first-order variables and the overall index. There were some differences (the FaCS model, for example, assigned greater weight to financial strain than to material deprivation) but these differences are not large and comparison of the average scores for the indexes by different social groups gave similar results. We concluded, therefore, that despite different sampling frames and different respondents (the 'head of household' in the BHPS but the 'recipient of Child Benefit' for FACs), policy questions or hypotheses tested using these models would give similar results whichever survey was used (Tomlinson et al., 2007).

Interpretation

Figure 18.2 shows the mean and median scores for the poverty index fitted to BHPS data for odd numbered years between 1991 and 2003. This is analogous to plotting the inverse of the trend in average equivalised household income used in traditional measures since, unlike income, the poverty index is a direct measure of poverty and high scores indicate extreme poverty. The mean score declines steadily throughout the period from around 0.43 to 0.16. The steadiness of the trend is in notable contrast to the jagged pattern produced by exploratory factor analytic techniques, one illustration of the advantages that SEM has in its treatment of measurement error. The decline in the score is consistent with a fall in poverty, as recorded over this period using traditional income based measures, and suggests a general rise in social well-being. Unfortunately, it is not possible straightforwardly to assess the strength of the fall in the index because the scores are not standardised in any way. Moreover, since a negative score is possible, meaning that a score of zero does not indicate the absence of poverty, it cannot be presumed that that the average poverty index more than halved. The growing difference between the mean and median scores over the period points to widening inequalities (especially during the last years of the Major government, 1993–1997).

In order to provide headcounts of poverty it was necessary, as with income-based measures, to transform the continuous poverty index into a dichotomous variable by selecting a threshold poverty score. The threshold was fixed to yield a 25 per cent poverty rate in 1991 which approximated to poverty rates recorded by traditional income-based measures at the time. On this basis, the proportion of adults defined as

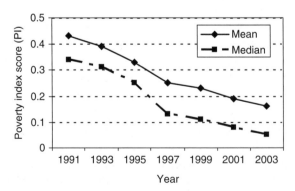

Figure 18.2   Mean and median scores for the poverty index, UK, 1991–2003.
Source: Tomlinson et al. (2008).

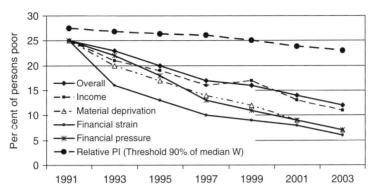

Figure 18.3   Headcount poverty rates, UK, 1991–2003.
Note: Poverty rates set as 25% for 1991 (except relative measure).
Adapted from: Tomlinson et al. (2008).

poor fell gradually over the whole period from the initial 25 to 12.9 per cent in 2003 (Figure 18.3). Moreover, it is possible to disaggregate the contribution made to this trend by the individual components. By using subsets of the coefficients employed to calculate the overall poverty score from the model, it is uniquely possible to calculate poverty rates for each component of the index (selected ones being shown in Figure 18.3). The 'material deprivation' and 'financial stain' components were calculated without income included (which was calculated separately), while 'financial pressure' combined the coefficients for income, material deprivation and financial strain.

Poverty rates based on the 'financial strain' and 'material deprivation' components of the index both fell much faster than income, declining by three-quarters as opposed to one half; that is, from 25 per cent in 1991 to around seven per cent in 2003. Rates of poverty defined in terms of 'financial strain' decreased more quickly in the early part of the period (as, to a lesser degree, did those associated with 'material deprivation') at a time when unemployment, inflation and interest rates were all falling. Poverty experienced as

financial pressure, a product of the effects of income, financial strain and material deprivation, occurred slightly later during the last years of the Major era when inequality was more evident. The other components, 'psychological strain', 'civic participation' and 'social isolation', all remained fairly constant indicating that the major falls in the overall index were largely due to improvements in people's material well being and the easing of 'financial strain'.

Reflecting Sen's analysis of capabilities and shame, the poverty measure used in the foregoing analysis reflects both absolute and relative conceptualisations of poverty. The income measure was deflated, removing the tendency with the absolute measures for people to be floated out of poverty simply as a result of economic growth. The measure of material deprivation, while socially salient in 1991, was not weighted to take account of market penetration. A number of the constituent items would have become cheaper and more widely diffused during the subsequent 13 years leading one to expect that material deprivation would fall naturally. The indices of strain were measured in absolute terms.

It is possible to construct a relative measure by fixing the poverty threshold relative to entire distribution of the poverty scores. However, the traditional method of simply setting the threshold as a fraction of median (or mean) proved to be inappropriate. This was because the possibility of negative values for the poverty index made it impossible to calculate a fixed baseline. The strategy adopted was to 'normalise' the poverty index before calculating headcounts of *relative* poverty. This was achieved by first computing from the model the maximum value (PI_{max}) that the poverty index (PI) could take (i.e., when someone had no income, no possessions, maximum stress, no social contact, no civic participation, maximum financial strain, etc.). PI was then transformed into a normalised index W

$$W = (-PI) + PI_{max} \qquad (18.1)$$

Equation 18.1 reverses the distribution and sets a minimum at zero. It therefore effectively creates an index, not of poverty per se, but of its opposite, labelled W for 'well-being'. A person who is as badly off as one can be will have score of zero ($W = 0$).[12] Everyone else is measured relative to that hypothetical person and no-one can have a negative score.

Relative poverty rates were then calculated as fractions of the median of index W. Since the mean and median of W gradually increased between 1991 and 2003, it is not surprising to discover that falls in poverty rates on this relative measure were noticeably less than with the original measure: a fall of between a sixth and a third rather than a half (Figure 18.3). However, it was apparent that the more severe the measure of poverty employed, the larger the proportionate fall in the headcount rate, suggesting that changes were progressive with the poorest of the poor gaining most.

Briefly to summarise: SEM facilitates the development of multi-dimensional measures of poverty that permit poverty rates to be meaningfully compared and tracked over time, while allowing simultaneous tracking of the constitute dimensions. Thus, we are able to conclude that poverty, measured as a multi-dimensional concept, fell in Britain both in absolute and relative terms between 1991 and 2003, driven more by reductions in material deprivation and financial strain than by increases in income per se.

POVERTY DYNAMICS

Thirty years ago poverty tended to be conceptualised as static with an immutable distinction between the poor and the non-poor and an implicit assumption that, class-like, the two groups rarely exchanged places (Walker, 2005a). Now poverty is understood to be dynamic and the focus has switched to poverty spells, most of which turn out to be short-lived. That said, some people are poor for very long periods while recurrent spells of poverty, contrary to predictions based on the concept of a stable poverty class, appear to be the norm rather than the exception (Jenkins and Rigg, 2001). Cross-sectional poverty rates are now routinely accompanied by counts of the number of people poor for a number of years within a given period (DWP, 2007b).

The shift of emphasis from poor people to spells of poverty was driven by technical considerations. First, with the launch of the US Panel Study of Income Dynamics (PSID) in 1968, it became possible to observe respondents' circumstances change over time (Duncan, 1984). Secondly, it came to be realised that early estimates of the duration of poverty, which summed the number of years observed during which a person was poor, were understatements, biased by failing to take account of poverty occurring before or after the observation period (Walker with Ashworth, 1994). This, the problem of 'spell censorship', Bane and Ellwood (1986) showed could partially be overcome by focussing on spells rather than individuals, borrowing survival analysis techniques from medical research.

Taking duration into account

Dissociating spells of poverty from people is nevertheless problematic. It makes invisible the experience of repeated spells and diverts attention from poverty rates (for which there is no analogue). It is, therefore, worth reflecting on work published 15 years ago that asked basic questions about how poverty should be measured if explicit account was taken of time (Ashworth et al., 1994). Nicholson (1979) and Atkinson (1984) initiated the debate by suggesting that a truly satisfactory measure of poverty would need to combine lack of resources with duration. Leaving aside the choice of accounting period, the time over which resources are matched against needs, and the observation period (preferably as long as possible) discussed elsewhere (Ashworth and Walker, 1994), Atkinson argued that there is 'some level of income deficiency which is serious enough even for short periods and a lesser extent of deprivation which becomes serious if it lasts long enough' (Atkinson, 1984: 15).

Nicholson's generic formulation of poverty measured over time was:

$$P = CT \qquad (18.2)$$

where C is the income deficit, the amount by which income falls short of the poverty standard and T is the duration. Statistics that count the number of years poor assign C the value of one. At this date, little thought was given to the multi-dimensional nature of poverty but C could be substituted by the distance between the aforementioned poverty index score (PI) and the poverty threshold.

It is worth discussing how this generic concept has been operationalised not least because of the growing importance of temporal measurements in many social science disciplines but also because of what it can reveal about the nature of poverty itself. Adopting different terminology and notation than that used by Atkinson and Nicolson, Ashworth et al. (1992) provide a more specific definition of what they call absolute cumulative poverty, Y_i^*, the income deficit for individual i summed over each accounting period covered by a study:

$$Y_i^* = \sum_{t=1}^{T} [(e_{it} - y_{it}) \, |x = 1] \qquad (18.3)$$

where Y_i^* is absolute cumulative poverty; y_{it} is income in year t; e_{it} is needs in year t; T is observation period (ideally a life stage or other intrinsically meaningful period); and $x = 1$ if in poverty and 0 if not in poverty.

This formulation, following Nicholson, makes no allowance for the fact that the same absolute shortfall in income will impose different financial constraints depending on the needs and size of the household unit. One response to this deficiency is to adjust the absolute measure by the equivalence scale implicit in the original measure of needs. Equivalised cumulative poverty, Y_i^{**}, is defined:

$$Y_i^{**} = \sum_{t=1}^{T} [(e_{it}/c) - y_{it} \, |x = 1] \quad (18.4)$$

where c is an equivalising constant.

A more readily interpretable approach, which achieves the same effect, involves summing [1 – (income to needs ratio)] for years in poverty to yield, Y_i^{***}, the cumulative income deficiency ratio:

$$Y_i^{***} = \sum_{t=1}^{T} [1 - (y_{it}/e_{it}) | x = 1] \quad (18.5)$$

A value of unity indicates that a shortfall in income equivalent to the needs for one year has been experienced over the period observed. It can be shown that Y_i^{**} and Y_i^{***} have identical distributions.

None of the above measures takes account of spells of relative prosperity experienced during the observation period. This can be achieved by removing the conditioning from the above equations so that each entity is cumulated over the entire observation period rather than over spells of poverty:

$$D_i^{*} = \sum_{t=1}^{T} [(e_{it} - y_{it})] \quad (18.6)$$

where D_i^{*} is the absolute life-stage income deficit.

$$D_i^{**} = \sum_{t=1}^{T} [(e_{it}/c) - y_{it}] \quad (18.7)$$

where D_i^{**} is the equivalised life-stage income deficit and

$$D_i^{***} = \sum_{t=1}^{T} [1 - (y_{it}/e_{it})] \quad (18.8)$$

where D_i^{***} is the life-stage income deficiency ratio.

A final measure, P, life-stage poverty, records instances where equivalised income during the observation period falls short of needs, that is:

$$P_i = D_i^{***} \quad \text{if and only if } D_i^{**} > 0 \quad (18.9)$$

These measures each highlight different features of poverty when viewed through a temporal lens and taken cumulatively add greatly to understanding of the nature of the poverty experience as demonstrated by Ashworth et al. (1994). They compare the results of applying these various measures to a cohort of American children born between 1968 and 1973 and followed for 16 years of childhood (Table 18.2). Care should be taken in interpreting the maximum and minimum values which sometimes appear as outriders to the distributions. The first five measures relate only

Table 18.2   Temporal measures of poverty for US children, 1960s–1980s

US dollars						
Quintiles	Absolute cumulative poverty	Equivalised cumulative poverty	Cumulative income deficiency ratio	Equivalised childhood income deficit	Childhood income deficiency ratio	Childhood poverty
Maximum	13	9	0.00	−1,262,014	−136.10	49
4th	3,499	2,904	0.33	−166,996	−18.01	15,112
3rd	9,501	6,484	0.70	−87,397	−9.43	34,029
2nd	21,468	13,880	1.50	−34,864	−3.76	44,319
1st	51,336	33,671	3.36	14,186	1.53	58,205
Minimum	285,917	112,205	12.10	112,206	12.10	112,206
Mean	32,732	18,472	1.99	−89,761	−9.68	39,931
Medium	15,692	9,272	1.00	−62,148	−6.70	40,661
Prevalence	38	38	38		38	9

Source: Ashworth et al. (1993).

to children who experienced some poverty, 38 per cent of the cohort. (The equivalising constant (c in Equation 18.4) represents the needs of a male and female couple aged 21–35 years, i.e., $9,272.51 in 1987 US dollars.)

Comparing the first two columns shows that taking account of family size substantially reduces the apparent level of cumulative poverty. Because childhood poverty was more frequent in large families than small ones, the equivalisation process also has the effect of slightly reducing the apparent inequality in the distribution of cumulative poverty (the Gini coefficient [not shown] falls from 0.62 to 0.56). Even so, it is clear that poverty, measured as the cumulative shortfall in income, is far from equitably distributed even among the children who experienced poverty.

The cumulative income deficiency ratio highlights the pattern of inequality. The mean value of the ratio is 1.99, indicating a shortfall in income during periods of poverty which is very nearly equivalent to the income required to meet the needs of a family for two years. The distribution is much skewed with the mean being almost twice the median.

The final three columns in Table 18.2 take account of the income received during periods of relative prosperity which, for all but 25 per cent of children who suffered poverty, more than compensated for the shortfall in income experienced whilst in poverty. It can be calculated from Table 18.2 that, for the average child experiencing poverty, family income during childhood exceeded needs by about 64 per cent. For children in the fifth decile, this value is in excess of 120 per cent.

In the final column of Table 18.2 the accounting period is set equal to childhood and the prevalence poverty rate drops from 38 per cent to 9.4 per cent. The distribution is less skewed than for the other measures.

The deficit for those in the fifth quintile roughly equates with the annual needs allowance for a two parent, two child household, while that for the first quintile is four times as great.

There are unresolved difficulties with the composite measures of poverty presented above, that hold more general relevance for measurement. For example, it is self-evident that the consequences of a shortfall equivalent to annual needs that is concentrated in one year are likely to be more severe than the same shortfall spread over several years. However, all the measures treat a given shortfall in the income to needs ratio as equivalent irrespective of the length of time over which it occurs. A more fundamental criticism is that all the measures derived from the Nicholson and Atkinson formulations ignore the timing and sequencing of poverty spells and the possibility that these, together with severity, might actually define different kinds of poverty (Walker with Ashworth, 1994).

Temporal patterning and living standards

In the period since the arrival of panel data first made it possible to take explicit account of time in the study of poverty, attention has shifted from a focus on duration to an emphasis on sequence and periodicity resulting in a reappraisal of the very concept of poverty itself. By way of illustration, Table 18.3 links temporal patterning and severity by defining six poverty sequences based on the frequency, duration and spacing of spells experienced during childhood:

1 *Transient poverty*, a single spell of poverty lasting a single year;
2 *Occasional poverty*, more than one spell of poverty but none lasting more than one year; in practice, the duration of relative prosperity

Table 18.3   Severity and temporal patterning of childhood poverty, US, 1960s–1980s

Pattern/type of poverty*	% of all children	% of children experiencing poverty	% of all childhood poverty	Income to needs ratio during poverty spells Mean (SD)	Income to needs ratio during childhood Mean (SD)
No poverty	62				3.31(1.60)
Transient	10	27	5	0.71(0.26)	2.63(1.30)
Occasional	3	8	4	0.69(0.21)	1.82(0.49)
Recurrent	16	41	53	0.67(0.15)	1.21(0.45)
Persistent	5	14	12	0.70(0.14)	1.66(0.63)
Chronic	2	5	13	0.59(0.09)	0.66(0.08)
Permanent	2	5	13	0.46(0.13)	0.46(0.13)
All	100	100	100	0.67(0.20)	2.68(1.63)

* See text for definitions.
Source: Adapted from Ashworth et al. (1993).

always exceeds the duration of poverty in this cohort;

3   *Recurrent poverty*, repeated spells of poverty, some separated by more than a year arid some exceeding a year in length

4   *Persistent poverty*, a single spell of poverty lasting between two and 13 years;

5   *Chronic poverty*, repeated spells of poverty never separated by more than a year of relative prosperity; and

6   *Permanent poverty*, poverty lasting continuously for 15 years.

The robustness of this typology was subject to sensitivity analyses. The rise or fall in the income to needs ratio required to cross the poverty threshold was varied in order to test for 'false transitions' and different poverty thresholds were used and all permutations yielded similar substantive results (Ashworth et al., 1994).

It should be noted that the focus on childhood has both substantive and technical significance in the measurement of poverty. Childhood poverty has been shown to scar individuals for life, having a marked detrimental effect on child outcomes (Ermisch et al., 2001; Hobcraft, 1998). At the technical level, by defining poverty relative to a complete life-stage, problems of censorship bias are avoided. The first column in

Table 18.3 reports the mean cumulative income deficiency ratio for each poverty type (medians reveal a similar pattern). It shows that there is very little difference in the severity of poverty encountered by children experiencing transient, occasional, recurrent or persistent poverty (although, as comparison of the standard deviations indicates, experience is more varied among the first two types of poverty). However, it is evident that poverty among children who were permanently poor, or who suffered very brief spells of respite, was very severe even when account is taken of differences in household composition. For the former group, annual income amounted to only 46 per cent of need and for the latter group, it averaged 59 per cent during spells of poverty.

The second column in Table 18.3 takes account of the income received in years when income exceeded needs to give a measure of childhood living standards. As the duration of poverty increases, so the number of years in which to acquire income in excess of minimum needs falls. Not surprisingly, therefore, the income to needs ratio falls steadily with duration with the turnaround point occurring at between eight and nine years: children who were in poverty for any longer were entrenched in a childhood of penury.

The figures suggest that transient poverty was typically a one off aberration from an accustomed way of life. Certainly, children who experienced a single year of poverty generally did not spend the remainder of their childhood living on the margins of poverty. The ratio of income to needs for these children, when averaged over the 15 years of childhood, was 2.63 compared with 3.31 for children who were never poor. Indeed, one in six of transiently poor children had an income-to-needs ratio that exceeded the average for children who were never poor. This finding underlines the methodological dangers of taking individual data points and cross-sectional measures as indicative of a static reality.

In terms of childhood living standards, the position of children who encountered occasional short spells of poverty was comparable with those who experienced a single spell of persistent poverty. In both cases the income deficits incurred during years of poverty were generally more than offset by income received in more prosperous years. Nevertheless, taking childhood as a whole, income levels were not high. At first sight, the apparent similarity between these groups may be a little surprising since 65 per cent of the first group were in poverty only twice and none for more than four years, whereas 32 per cent of the second group had spells lasting five or more years. However, the repeated spells of occasional poverty often represented small downward fluctuations in the financial circumstances of families living for long periods on very constrained budgets. Persistent poverty, on the other hand, frequently constituted a major departure from accustomed living standards of the kind associated with relationship breakdown, redundancy and substantial loss

of earning power occasioned by illness and disability. In this instance, the temporal sequence and frequency of observations shapes the difference between a one off aberration and a persistent state.

Recurrent poverty appears qualitatively different again, defining childhoods characterised by severe and lasting hardship. Thirty one per cent of the children in this group lived in families where, over the period of their childhood, income fell short of need, while for another 30 per cent income exceeded needs by only 30 per cent. If recurrent poverty, afflicting 16 per cent of all US children growing up in the 1970s and 1980s, was the most common experience of poverty, the very worst experience was reserved for the two per cent of children in permanent poverty. Family income fell short of needs by an average of 54 per cent and, for 24 per cent of these children, by more than 66 per cent – poverty of a third-world order. Chronic poverty was also severe, with lifetime resources never rising above the needs threshold, but such children were at least one rung above the destitution faced by children who were permanently poor.

To summarise, time and dynamics are important. Time is not just the medium in which life and poverty takes place, it arguably shapes the experience of poverty. Measurement tools and efforts more broadly would often be remiss not to take the influence of time into account. Transient poverty may be no more than an unwelcome deviation in an otherwise prosperous life, whereas permanent offers no hope[13] and occasional and recurrent poverty sees people's hopes and aspirations repeated dashed by circumstance, luck or inadequacy. Figure 18.4 suggests that these distinctions identify different social phenomena with unique spatial manifestations. In the 1970s and 1980s permanent poverty among American children was largely

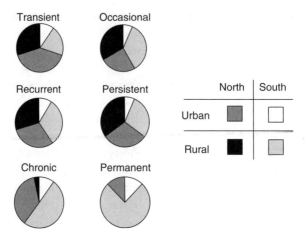

Figure 18.4   Spatial characteristics of childhood poverty in the US, 1960s–1980s.
Source: Walker with Ashworth (1994).

confined to the South, notably in rural areas, whereas transient poverty was exclusively a feature of the urban North. Permanent and chronic poverty were also largely restricted to non-white American children (not shown [Walker with Ashworth, 1994]). How such different types of poverty find expression in the multiple dimensions discussed earlier in this chapter is, as yet, unknown.

FIXING THE POVERTY LINE

While Townsend (1979), Gordon and Pantazis (1997) and Desai (1981) have argued that the binary threshold between the poor and the non-poor has empirical reality, that a real distinction exists in behavioural and experiential terms between the poor and the non-poor, we take the view (as already explained) that the choice of threshold is arbitrary. Nevertheless, to the extent that the poverty threshold takes on a political reality, as a stimulus for change or as a measure of policy effectiveness, the method by which it is fixed is profoundly important. In exploring this issue, we hope to provide insight more generally into methods available to researchers who need

to impose a binary threshold on a continuous variable of political or social signficance.

There are three broad methods for fixing the poverty threshold: arbitrary determination; normative judgement and attitudinal assessment (Walker, 2005b). The first method is well illustrated by the aforementioned thresholds used by the European Commission and set at 40, 50 or 60 per cent of median household income. While of considerable and growing political significance, any substantive meaning is tenuous and historic. In their seminal work introducing the concept of relative poverty to Britain, Abel Smith and Townsend (1965) set poverty thresholds as multiples of the prevailing level of social assistance, itself long disconnected from its subsistence origins (Mansfield, 1986). The 100 per cent social assistance threshold provided a direct measure of policy effectiveness while the more generous 140 per cent threshold became target promoted by welfare rights activists. The latter was found to equate with approximately 50 per cent of mean earnings and this formulation was subsequently taken up internationally, but later altered with the median substituted for the mean so that the poverty threshold would be less affected to increases in inequality.

Normative thresholds, such as the official US poverty line, typically involve appointed experts determining an appropriate level of adequacy. Two variants warrant mention. The first requires experts to define and cost a comprehensive budget that they judge is necessary for families of varying sizes to get by financially; this is the approach used by the German and Swedish governments and the Family Budget Unit in the UK. The second, employed in the US, involves costing a core budget and applying a multiplier to generate a poverty threshold.

The third common method for determining poverty thresholds, attitudinal assessment, has already been discussed in relation to the consensual measures employed by Gordon et al. (2000). It entails asking representative population samples how much income is needed for people to make ends meet, or the kinds of possessions or activities that all people in their community ought to be able to afford.

Walker (1987) criticised normative and consensual measures for failing to capture either the interactive process through which consensus is achieved or the commitment of respondents to support political action needed to tackle poverty at the level defined. Instead he proposed a methodology that replaced 'the single panel of experts with a judicious mix of group and depth interviews with members of the public [that] could provide the basis for directly determining a socially approved budget' (p. 222). First used to estimate the cost of children (Middleton et al., 1994), the method has subsequently been employed by lobbyists in Canada and New Zealand and, in Jersey, by the government to inform decisions about the choice of social assistance rates (Fisher, 2007; Middleton, 2000). Its most recent application is that undertaken in Britain for the Joseph Rowntree Foundation. This

sought to establish 'a minimum acceptable standard [for Britain] below which it is unacceptable (scientifically, morally and socially) in today's society for any individual or family to fall' (Middleton and Bradshaw, 2006: 6).

In this latest formulation, members of the public were asked to draw up lists of basic necessities and were serviced by researchers and experts who costed, critiqued and challenged the lists in order to test their substantive and political robustness (Figure 18.5). The results (Bradshaw et al., 2008) suggest that poverty thresholds based on 60 per cent of median disposable income fall short of what the British public consider to be an acceptable minimum; depending on household type, they would set the minimum income standard or poverty line at between 69 and 78 per cent of median disposable income (Table 18.4). Likewise, benefit levels appear to be out of line with what respondents believe to be necessary. While the agreed minimum income standard was less than the means-tested benefits threshold for pensioner couples, it was 2.3 times that for single persons and, respectively, 73 per cent and 59 per cent more than benefit threshold for couples with two children and lone parents with one child.

An important by-product of the Rowntree methodology is that it provides a way of empirically estimating the equivalence scales used to adjust income to take account of differences in household composition (Table 18.5). While respondents are initially asked to specify the requirements of individuals they also engage in discussion and assessment of the economies in scale arising from shared living: for example, common housing costs and the possibility that clothes might be handed on to younger siblings of the same sex. The results suggest that, in terms of public experience, abandonment of the McClements' equivalence scale in favour of the modified OECD one was

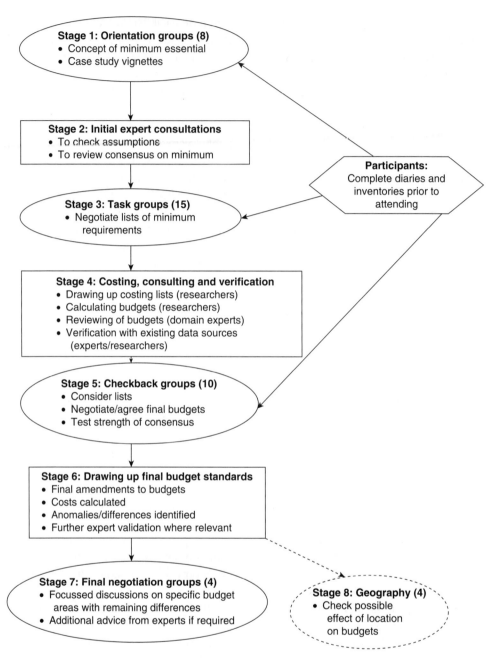

Figure 18.5 Establishing a minimum income standard.

a retrograde step. Compared to the consensual Rowntree index, the latter understates the additional burden that additional children impose on families and slightly overstates the cost of living alone.

This latest method of setting thresholds is not without its problems. It is costly, difficult to update easily and impossible to apply to all the myriad living arrangements that characterise modern society

Table 18.4   Rowntree minimum income standard: Comparison with 2007/8 benefit rates, actual expenditure of benefit recipients and 60 per cent of median disposable income

Before housing costs

Family type	Rowntree minimum income standard £,p (2007)	Per cent of actual expenditure by people receiving out of work benefits	Per cent of out of work benefit income	Per cent of equivalised median earnings
Single person	148.37	125	230	78
Couple pensioner	205.55	92	95	69
Couple plus two children	372.49	135	173	74
One parent, one child	210.35	135	159	70

Calculated from Bradshaw et al. (2008).

Table 18.5   Rowntree minimum income standard: Comparison of equivalence scales

Equivalence scales, Couple = 1.0 (before housing costs)

Family type	Rowntree minimum income standard	McClements	Modified OECD
Single person	0.63	0.61	0.67
Single pensioner	0.58	0.61	0.67
Childless couple	1.00	1.00	1.00
Couple pensioner	0.87	1.00	1.00
Lone parent, toddler	0.89	0.90	0.90
Couple, two children (pre and primary school)	1.58	1.58	1.40
Couple, three children (pre, primary and secondary school)	1.95	1.87	1.60

Source: Bradshaw et al. (2008).

and, hence, to provide secure estimates of the numbers living below the threshold set.[14] The method implicitly prioritises consumption and material deprivation over other dimensions of poverty. No attempt is made, for instance, to cost psychosocial strain although exchanges in the group discussions make clear that respondents were trying to establish thresholds that, while not unduly generous, sought to minimise hardship that acts as a stressor. A proclaimed strength is that the method is explicitly political. It takes the negotiated beliefs of the public and presents them as evidence that existing standards and policies are socially unacceptable. Whether the British government will follow the example of the States of Jersey and use consensual measures of adequacy to establish benefit levels is to be seen.

CONCLUSION

We began and now end with the assertion that poverty is a political rather than a scientific construct. We do not deny that hardship is a social reality and, indeed, have argued that the unequal distribution of society's resources that leaves a proportion of the population unable to engage in the activities associated with full citizenship is pernicious, with multiple consequences and dimensions. As social scientists, we can provide measures of hardship and explore its causes and consequences. Much has been achieved, but much remains to be done. We know too little about the multiple manifestations of hardship, its immediate and longer term consequences; about the factors that protect individuals and the processes and measures than can bring spells of hardship to an early end; and about the reasons why repeated episodes of hardship are so common. The statistical and substantive properties of many of the basic measures of hardship are still not yet well understood.

Social science can also provide the conceptual and technical tools to devise poverty thresholds that turn social realities into political ones. We believe that social scientists have an obligation so to do. Social science may also be able to help in the specification of polices most likely to be effective in reducing poverty. However, what social science can never do is to end the debate about what poverty is and what should be done about it.

NOTES

1 Note, though, that a different question was asked of Americans.

2 The difference between hardship and well-being is discussed below. Suffice to say that the dimensions on which hardship is measured give greater weight to the concerns of those who define themselves to be in hardship. Empirically hardship and wellbeing are likely to be negatively correlated with each other.

3 Strictly 'hardship'.

4 Limitations of space cause us to prioritise the role of time rather than space in shaping the nature of poverty.

5 Relative poverty lines used to be fixed in relation to mean income which proved to be very susceptible to high outliers. The mean is sometimes still used by the OECD since it imposes less stringent data requirements.

6 Atkinson (1995), though, prefers income to expenditure because he is concerned to promote the human right to adequate minimum resources rather than living standards per se.

7 This could be achieved by changing the distribution of primarily labour market income, (perhaps by a minimum wage or a cap on high salaries), secondary incomes by means of progressive direct and indirect taxation) or tertiary incomes via targeting services differentially towards people with low incomes.

8 Recession can have the opposite effect as happened in Russia after the collapse of the Soviet Union.

9 These composite measures are less sensitive to increasing inequality often associated with economic growth.

10 A proposal to do this is currently being developed by the authors.

11 The models were run in AMOS 6.0 in conjunction with SPSS 14 on wave 1 of the BHPS. Cross-sectional weighting was applied and listwise missing data deletion applied. The fit statistics are all quite respectable (GFI and CFI greater than 0.9 and RMSEA less than 0.05). Scores for the PI were saved and these form the basis of the analysis that follows. The procedure in AMOS 6.0 produces a set of linear equations that can be used to compute scores for all the latent concepts in the model based on a weighted summation of the observed variables. The outcome is an equation the coefficients of which, termed 'factor weights', were saved and used to compute scores for all successive waves. Therefore, factor weights from Model 1 in wave 1 were used to compute PI scores for all waves for the first set of analyses.

12 There is the potential here for a treatise length discussion about the relationship between poverty and well-being. The strategy was to provide a technical fix to a technical problem but the resultant conceptual difficulties are recognised although left to another day.

13 Since the future is unknown hope is always possible and the duration of poverty is unknowable to those who live it. Nevertheless, people accommodate to reasonable expectations (Walker and Collins, 2003).

14 The family living arrangements costed by Bradshaw et al. (2008) cover 95 per cent of single unit households and 79 per cent of all households.

REFERENCES

Abel Smith, B. and Townsend, P. (1965) *The Poor and the Poorest*. London: Bell.

Ashworth, K., Hill, M. and Walker, R. (1992) *Economic Disadvantage during Childhood*. Loughborough, UK Loughborough University of Technology, Centre for Research in Social Policy. Working Paper 170.

Ashworth, K. and Walker, R. (1994) 'Measuring claimant populations: Time, fractals and social security', in N. Buck, J. Gershuny, D. Rose and J. Scott (eds), *Changing Households*. Colchester: ESRC Research Centre on Micro-social Change. pp. 114–29.

Ashworth, K., Hill, M. and Walker, R. (1993) 'A new approach to poverty dynamics', *Bulletin de Methodologie Sociologique*, 38: 14–37.

Ashworth, K., Hill, M. and Walker, R. (1994) 'Patterns of childhood poverty: New challenges for policy', *Journal of Policy Analysis and Management*, 13(4): 658–80.

Atkinson, A. (1984) *The Economics of Inequality*. Oxford: Oxford University Press.

Atkinson, A. (1995) *Incomes and the Welfare State: Essays on Britain and Europe*. Cambridge: Cambridge University Press.

Atkinson, A., Cantillon, B., Marlier, E. and Nolan, B. (2002) *Social Indicators: The EU and Social Exclusion*. Oxford: Oxford University Press.

Bane, M-J. and Ellwood, D. (1986) Slipping in and out of poverty: the dynamics of spells', *Journal of Human Resources*, 21(1): 1–23.

Banks, J. and Johnson, P. (1994) 'Equivalence scales and public policy,' *Fiscal Studies*, 15(1): 1–23.

Beresford, P., Green, D., Lister, R. and Woodward, K. (1999) *Poverty First Hand: Poor People Speak for Themselves*. London: CPAG.

Berthoud, R., Bryan, M. and Bardasi, E. (2004) *The Relationship between Income and Material Deprivation over Time*, Leeds: Department for Work and Pensions Research Report 219, Corporate Document Services.

Blank, R. (2008) 'How to improve poverty measurement in the United States', *Journal of Policy Analysis and Management*, 27(2): 233–54.

Booth, C. (1892) *Life and Labour of the People in London* (1889–1903). London: Macmillan.

Bradshaw, J., Middleton, Davis, S. A., Oldfield, N., Smith, N., Cusworth, L. and Williams, J. (2008) *Minimum Income Standards in Britain*. York: Joseph Rowntree Foundation.

Byrne, B. (2001) *Structural Equation Modelling with AMOS*. Mahwah: Lawrence Erlbaum Associates.

Calandrino, M. (2003) *Low-Income and Deprivation in British Families*. London Department for Work and Pensions: Working Paper 10.

Castell, S. and Thompson, J. (2007) *Understanding Attitudes to Poverty in the UK:Getting the Public's Attention*. York: Joseph Rowntree Foundation.

Cattell, V. (2001) 'Poor people, poor places, and poor health: the mediating role of social networks and social capital', *Social Science and Medicine*, 52: 1501–16.

Clasen, J., Gould, A. and Vincent, J. (1998) *Voices Within and Without: Responses to Long-term Unemployment in Germany, Sweden and Britain*. Bristol: The Policy Press.

Desai, M. (1981) '*Is poverty a matter of taste? An econometric comment on the Piachaud-Townsend debate*', London: London School of Economics (unpublished).

Dorling, D., Rigby, J., Wheeler, B., Ballas, D., Thomas, B., Fahmy, E., Gordon, D., and Lupton, R. (2007) *Poverty, Wealth and Place in Britain, 1968 to 2005*. Bristol: Policy Press.

Du Bois, W. (1899) *The Philadelphia Negro, A Social Study*. Philadelphia: The University of Pennsylvania Press (Republished, 1996)

Duncan, G. (ed.) (1994) *Years of Poverty, Years of Plenty*. Ann Arbor: Institute for Social Research.

Department for Work and Pensions (DWP) (2003) *Measuring Child Poverty*. London: Department for Work and Pensions.

Department for Work and Pensions (DWP) (2007a) *Opportunity for All: Indicators Update 2007*. London: Department for Work and Pensions. http://www.dwp. gov.uk/ofa/reports/2007/OpportunityforAll2007.pdf

Department for Work and Pensions (DWP) (2007b) *Households below Average Income (HBAI) 1994/95–2005/06*. London: Department for Work and Pensions. http://www.dwp.gov.uk/asd/ hbai/hbai2006/contents.asp

Edin, K. and Lein, L. (1997) *Making Ends Meet: How Single Mothers Survive Welfare and Low-Wage Work*. New York: Russell Sage Foundation.

Edin, K., Lein, L., Nelson, T., and Clampet-Lundquest, S. (2000) *Talking to Low-income Fathers*. Joint Center for Poverty Research, University of Chicago, Newsletter, 4, 2.

Ermisch, J., Francesconi, M. and Pevalin, D.J. (2001) *Outcomes for Children in Poverty*, DWP Research Report No. 158. Leeds: Corporate Document Services.

Fisher, G. (2007) *An Overview of Recent Work on Standard Budgets in the United States and Other Anglophone Countries*. Washington, DC: Department of Health and Human Services. http://aspe.hhs.gov/ poverty/papers/std-budgets/report.pdf

Gallie, D., Paugam, S. and Jacobs, S. (2003) 'Unemployment, poverty and social isolation: Is there a vicious circle of social exclusion?,' *European Societies*, 5(1): 1–32.

Goldberg, D. and Williams, P. (1988) *A Users Guide to the GHQ*. London: Institute of Psychiatry.

Gordon, D. and Pantazis, C. (1997) *Breadline Britain in the 1990s*. Aldershot: Ashgate.

Gordon, D., Adelman, L., Ashworth, K., Bradshaw, J., Levitas, R., Middleton, S. et al. (2000) *Poverty and Social Exclusion in Britain*. York: Joseph Rowntree Foundation.

Haase, T. and Pratschke, J. (2005) *Deprivation and Its Spatial Articulation in the Republic of Ireland*. Dublin: NDP.

Harrington, M. (1962) *The Other America: Poverty in the United States.* New York: Macmillan.

Hobcraft, J. (1998) *Intergenerational and Life-Course Transmission of Social Exclusion: Influences and Childhood Poverty, Family Disruption and Contact with the Police.* London: London School of Economics, CASE paper 15.

Hunter, R. (1904) *Poverty.* New York: Macmillan.

Jenkins, S. and Rigg, J. (2001) *The Dynamics of Poverty in Britain.* London: Department for Work and Pensions, Working Paper 157.

Klein, R. (2005), *Principles and Practice of Structural Equation Modelling*, Second Edition. New York: Guilford Press.

Loehlin, J. (1992) *Latent Variable Models: An introduction to Factor, Path and Structural Analysis.* Hillsdale: Erlbaum.

Mansfield, M. (1986) 'The political arithmetic of poverty', *Social Policy and Administration*, 20(2): 47–57.

Mayhew, H. (1851) *London Labour and London Poor.* London: Griffin, Bohn, and Company.

Middleton, S. (2000) 'Agreeing Poverty Lines: The Development of Consensual Budget Standards Methodology', in J. Bradshaw and R. Sainsbury (eds), *Researching Poverty.* Aldershot: Ashgate. pp. 59–76.

Middleton, S. and Bradshaw, P. (2006) *A Minimum Income Standard For Britain.* Loughborough: Centre for Research in Social Policy.

Middleton, S., Ashworth, K. and Walker, R. (eds) (1994) *Family Fortunes: Pressures on Parents and Children in the 1990s.* London: CPAG.

Nicholson, J. (1979) 'The assessment of poverty and the information we need', in *Social Security Research: The Definition and Measurement of Poverty.* London: HMSO. pp. 9–58.

Nolan, B. and Whelan, C. (1996) *Resources, deprivation and poverty.* Oxford: Clarendon Press.

NPI (2007) *The Poverty Site.* London: New Poverty Institute http://www.poverty.org.uk/summary/eu.htm

Pantazis, C., Gordon, D. and Levitas, R. (eds.) (2006) *Poverty and Social Exclusion in Britain: The Millennium Survey.* Bristol: The Policy Press.

Park, A., Phillips, M. and Robinson, C. (2007) *Attitudes to poverty: Findings from the British Social Attitudes survey.* York: Joseph Rowntree Foundation.

Payne, S. (2006) 'Mental Health, Poverty and Social Exclusion', in C. Pantazis, D. Gordon and R. Levitas (eds), *Poverty and Social Exclusion in Britain: The Millennium Survey.* Bristol: The Policy Press.

Piachaud, D. (1981) 'Peter Townsend and the Holy Grail', *New Society* (10th Sept.) 419–421.

Ringen, S. (1988) 'Direct and indirect measures of poverty', *Journal of Social Policy*, 17(3): 351–65.

Rowntree, B. S. (1901) *Poverty, A Study of Town Life.* London: Macmillan and Co.

Schwarz, J. (1997) *Illusions of Opportunity: The American Dream in Question.* New York: W. W. Norton & Company.

Sen, A. (1999) *Commodities and Capabilities.* Delhi: Oxford University Press.

Tomlinson, M., Walker, R. and Williams, G. (2007) '*Using structural equation models to measure poverty: comparing the BHPS and FACS*', Families, youth, community and justice: New survey datasets for social research, Economic and Social Data Service workshop, Royal Statistical Society, London, 8th May.

Tomlinson, M., Walker, R. and Williams, G. (2008) 'Measuring poverty in Britain as a multi-dimensional concept, 1991 to 2003', *Journal of Social Policy*, 37(4): 597–620.

Townsend, P. (1979) *Poverty in the United Kingdom, a Survey of Household Resources and Standards of Living*, London: Penguin Books and Allen Lane.

Veit-Wilson, J. (1998) *Setting Adequacy Standards: How Governments Define Minimum Incomes.* Bristol: Policy Press.

Walker, R. (1987) 'Consensual approaches to the definition of poverty: Towards an alternative methodology', *Journal of Social Policy*, 16(2): 213–25.

Walker, R. (2005a) 'Opportunity and Life Chances: The Dynamics of Poverty, Inequality and Exclusion', in P. Diamond and A. Giddens (eds.) *The New Egalitarianism.* London: Polity Press. pp. 69–85.

Walker, R. (2005b) *Social Security and Welfare: Concepts and Comparisons.* Milton Keynes: Open University Press/McGraw-Hill.

Walker, R. with Ashworth, K. (1994) *Poverty Dynamics: Issues and Examples.* Aldershot: Avebury.

Walker, R. and Collins, C. (2004) 'Families of the Poor', in J. Scott , J. Treas and M. Richards (eds.) *Blackwell Companion on the Sociology of the Family*, Malden: Blackwell Publishers. pp. 193–217.

Weaver, K. (2000) *Ending Welfare as We Know It.* Washington DC: Brookings Institution Press.

Whelan, C. and Maitre, B. (2005) 'Vulnerability and multiple deprivation perspectives on economic exclusion in Europe: A latent class analysis', *European Societies*, 7(3): 423–50.

World Values Survey (2008) http://www.world valuessurvey.org/

19

Ethical Issues in Social Measurement

Martin Bulmer and Josephine Ocloo

"Oh, the monster!' exclaimed the Reverend Dr Folliott, 'he has made a subject for science the only friend he had in the world'.'

Thomas Love Peacock, Crotchet Castle

ETHICAL RESPONSIBILITY IN SOCIAL SCIENCE

Ethics is a matter of principled sensitivity to the rights of others. Being ethical limits the choices we can make in the pursuit of truth. Ethics say that while truth is good, respect for human dignity is better, even if, in the extreme case, the respect of human dignity leaves one ignorant of human nature. Such ethical considerations impinge upon all scientific research, but they impinge particularly sharply upon research in the human sciences, where people are studying other people. Social scientists engaged in measurement necessarily need to consider ethical issues that arise in the course of their research and this chapter considers

some of the issues which arise. The opening quotation hints at the dilemma which is involved in trying to treat other human beings as the subject of scientific investigation, and the dilemmas to which this may give rise.

The social science research community has responsibilities not only to the ideals of the pursuit of objective truth and the search for knowledge, but also to the subjects of their research. Just as in other sciences, with human subjects in the physiological laboratory, patients in the medical school, or students in the psychological laboratory, so members of the public whom the social researcher encounters while out in the field need to be considered from an ethical standpoint. Researchers always have to take account of the effects of their actions upon those subjects and act in such a way as to preserve their rights and integrity as human beings. Such behaviour is ethical behaviour. When social inquiry attempts to create measurement tools, these have or may have an ethical dimension which needs to be considered.

Consider two examples. A social policy researcher is investigating the adequacy of social security provision for persons who have recently been bereaved. How does the government grant payable to the estate of the deceased person compare to the actual cost of a simple funeral? The social researcher plans to interview the spouses of recently deceased elderly people in order to assess this issue. A second example concerns the study of teenage pregnancy and the availability of contraception (see Holland et al., 1998; Lee, 1993). Researchers interview adolescents in order to throw light on these issues and test theories. In both these cases, what are the researchers' responsibilities in conducting the research? The elderly widow or widower may be upset or distressed to be asked questions about the loss of their spouse, and so the issue needs to be handled sensitively. If the researcher is seeking to evaluate the degree of distress, or the degree of financial hardship which the respondent experienced, as a result of the loss of their spouse, how is this to be measured, and is the measurement of such distress a legitimate activity? Does the value of the knowledge which will be gained from the research outweigh the costs to the individual in providing the information for the researcher? Is the measurement attempted and the intrusion which it involved justified in the pursuit of greater knowledge?

In the second example, the young person being asked about their sexual knowledge, experience and behaviour needs to be approached with care, possibly with the permission of parents. If the person is under the age of 16, particular problems arise because of the issue of consent to take part in research on the part of children. Parents or proxies such as teachers may be required to give consent for those

under the age of 16. Lee (1993) has a good discussion of some of the approaches that can be taken to broach sensitive topics in surveys. What may appear to be technical problems of research can have ethical implications. For example, in asking young people who are teenagers about their sexual knowledge and experience, great care must be taken not to assume too great a degree of knowledge or experience on the part of the respondent, inviting them to assume a level of knowledge beyond what they possess. Research in this area, though perfectly possible, frequently arouses objections from persons such as parents, teachers and school governors who object to the young person being exposed to questions about matters which they consider to be beyond their knowledge or unsuitable for the age of the child. Though frequently underestimating the degree of knowledge and understanding which children may possess about sexual matters, there is an undoubted ethical dimension to the measurement of a young person's knowledge or experience of sexual behaviour which the social researcher cannot ignore.

GLOBAL ISSUES SUCH AS THE CONTROVERSY ABOUT INTELLIGENCE

Social scientists can tackle questions of very broad scope, which raise issues about the ethical justification for the activity which is being undertaken in the name of research. Is it justifiable for the social scientist, for example, to draw attention to differences in aptitude or ability not just between individuals in society, but between social groups? This has been a live issue in educational research for most of the twentieth century, and much research into educational inequalities has had to grapple with this issue.

Part of the debate has been about the relative weight of environmental and hereditary factors in determining educational performance and life chances, which does have an ethical dimension but it is first and foremost a scientific issue of how explanations are constructed and framed, and how proof is adduced. Some features of the controversies over group differences in ability and attainment do, however, have a directly ethical dimension, and highlight the question of what it is justifiable to assume in seeking to measure social differences.

There is not space to review the entire course of the controversy, but one work will suffice by way of example to show the nature of the arguments which can be engendered. In the mid 1990s, US psychologist Richard Herrnstein and political scientist Charles Murray published *The Bell Curve* (1994), a best-selling book which argued that intelligence could predict many kinds of social difference better than socio-economic status or education level. A particularly controversial part of the book suggested that racial differences in intelligence existed and that these differences might be genetic. These conclusions in particular were very fiercely contested, provoking the American Psychological Association to set up a special task force to investigate the research reported in the book. This concluded that many of the statements in the book were supported by evidence, but that there was no direct evidence that the inter-racial differences were genetic. The basic findings of black–white difference in the bell curve of intelligence as measured by tests were not seriously disputed, but its interpretation was. The observed differences in average test score achievement between ethnic groups varies according to the populations studied and the type of tests used. Black–white average IQ differences appear to increase with

age. Many social scientists challenged the suggestion that such differences were biologically grounded.

Measurement of group difference in intelligence thus posed ethical questions, which it proved very difficult to resolve on the basis of scientific consensus. The policy implications of these theories were considerable, and the wider political implications far-reaching. Solving such ethical issues of measurement is far away and it indicates the depths into which such ventures can lead.

WHAT IS MEASURED – THE CASE OF HAPPINESS

The measurement of intelligence is a mainstream part of social science and educational testing and selection. Measurement issues can arise where social science pushes out its boundaries into other areas not hitherto deemed part of social measurement. The lines of the American poet E. E. Cummings come to mind:

who cares if some one-eye son of a bitch
invents an instrument to measure spring with.

Do social scientists venture where less confident souls would hesitate to go?

A case in point is provided by the growing vogue for the study of 'happiness', which has indeed spawned a branch of economics known as 'happiness economics'. Consideration of this issue perhaps recalls Peacock's adage from *Crotchet Castle*. Is *everything* to be made the 'subject of science'? As with many phenomena with which the social sciences are concerned, the study of 'happiness' involves both careful conceptual analysis, and the devising of measuring tools with which the term can be measured in empirical research. There is perhaps a disjunction between the two aims, for while the conceptual analysis can be quite sophisticated, the measurement of happiness relies extensively on subjective self-reports by respondents as to how happy they are feeling. The classic social survey question, asked in the US General Social Survey starting in 1972, has had the following wording: 'Taken all together, how would you say things are these days, would you say that you are very happy, pretty happy, or not too happy?' Consistent results have been obtained from such a question, but some criticise it as being too subjective, involving, if response to the question is scaled, no standard metric in terms of which the individual can place himself or herself on a scale with certainty.

Others working on the subject (e.g., Oswald, 1999) point to some of the correlates of unhappiness, which they find is particularly associated with unemployment, divorce and severe ill-health. Richard Layard (2005) has particularly emphasised the association between unhappiness and mental ill-health, and has had some success in persuading government to change policies for the making available of cognitive behavioural therapy. The study of happiness by economists has been part of a focus upon economic growth, but seeking to suggest that growth measured purely in terms of money or wealth is not adequate and that the consumer's satisfaction must be measured in other ways. The study of 'happiness economics' displays considerable ingenuity, including devising indicators which can be taken as proxies for 'happiness', but worries about the construct validity of the measures which are proposed remain. Do they adequately tap the concept which is invoked, and can indeed 'happiness' be distilled into an unambiguous measure to be operationalised in empirical research?

Questions such as the General Social Survey question on feeling very happy/pretty happy/not too happy quoted earlier do not adequately tap a person's quality of life, which is what is being measured in this field. Are there ethical issues raised by social scientists engaged in what might be termed 'bogus measurement'? There is no doubt that most of the indicators used by happiness economists are justifiable, such as unemployment or extent of mental ill-health in the community, but is it misleading to make a direct connection between these and the presence or absence of happiness? My own position is an agnostic one, the research field seems an interesting one, but I worry that it may be seen to be offering more than it can deliver.

THE SOCIAL SCIENTIST POSES UNWELCOME QUESTIONS TO RESPONDENTS

'Happiness' might be said to be a 'hazy' concept. Whether it is measurable is debatable. Much of the data which social science researchers collect, however, is much more specific and concrete, for instance, the information about financial circumstances and benefits following bereavement referred to in the opening paragraphs of this chapter. To what extent can the collection of such data give rise to ethical questions? How does the sociological researcher weigh the sensitivity of topics in designing a questionnaire and determine what is permissible?

It is clear from the history of social research that there are sensitive questions involved here. The Population Census is a special type of research inquiry, because it is undertaken by government, usually at decennial intervals, and with legal powers behind it requiring completion. This means that the coverage of censuses has to be approved by Parliament. There are several types of question which have proved controversial at one time or another (cf. Bulmer, 1979). Early in the twentieth century, one UK census included a question asking of adult women the number of children ever born to them. This question did not refer to marital status or present relationship, and was included for purposes of fertility projection based on census data. It led to objections, however, that the head of the household filling in the form would have to ask embarrassing questions to female domestic servants in their employment, and that the question was unsuitable. In the mid-twentieth century, consideration was given at successive censuses to including a single question on gross income in the schedule, but was not proceeded with because of objections to having to provide this information on a compulsory basis. In the 1971 Census, a post-census income survey was conducted, which achieved a response rate around 50 per cent. This response level was so low that the results of the income survey were not published, and indirectly this provided support for the decision not to include the question in the main census.

From the 1991 Census, a question on ethnic origin was included in the census, replacing previous inferences about the presence of ethnic minorities based on data on country of birth and parent's country of birth (Bulmer, 1996). This change generally commanded agreement, but there have been minority voices among social scientists questioning whether the inclusion of such a question was an unalloyed good thing. Some of the objections were based upon recall of record keeping practices in some European countries before WW2, where religion was recorded, and such data were used during the wartime Nazi occupation to deport members of the Jewish populations of those countries to concentration camps.

Research in other areas may give rise to ethical questions about measurement. Sociologist Sylvia Walby has undertaken research into domestic violence and sexual assault using the British Crime Survey (Walby and Allen, 2004; Walby and Myhill, 2001). Conducting survey research into these issues is a sensitive matter, and raises a number of methodological problems in terms of respondents' willingness to respond, use of screening questions to identify those to be questioned more intensively, gender matching of interviewer and respondent, presence or absence of other household members at the interview, and how to elicit information about violence or assault in a non-threatening manner (see also Lee and Stanko, 2005). Is the social scientist justified in intruding into very private areas of behaviour, involving experiences which are likely to have been disturbing for the respondent, in order to increase the supply of research knowledge about subjects which are undoubtedly of importance in the public policy arena?

CONFIDENTIALITY: CAN DATA BE PROTECTED?

Measurement in social research is particularly associated with large-scale inquiries such as censuses and surveys. Social researchers need to consider their ethical responsibilities in relation to the handling of data resulting from such large-scale enquiries as the results of a population census or a survey. Researchers give respondents assurances about the confidentiality of the information that they provide, and that individuals will not be able to be identified from the resulting research, and it is the researcher's responsibility to ensure that this is respected. In the case of the census, government carries this out and usually makes completion compulsory, with legal sanctions available against those who do not cooperate. The questions asked in a census require legislative approval, and usually only basic factual information which is easily measurable is included in the census questionnaire. Census offices go to great lengths to ensure that the data which they hold is entirely confidential. This is part of the 'legislative bargain' which is part of the approval which the census obtains when it is planned.

With census data (which covers the entire population), special precautions are taken: the individual data are not released outside the census office; in UK small area tabulations, random error is injected into the tables; and in the individual and household samples available from the UK Census (the sample of anonymised records), certain mainly geographical variables are suppressed or altered to prevent people deducing facts about individual respondents. In longitudinal research, where individuals and households may be followed over a period of time, special precautions need to be taken to keep secret the identities and locations of participants, and these precautions need to be re-doubled if data matching or linking is involved.

With survey data, in addition to omitting respondents' names and addresses, their geographical location is frequently not accurately identified, thus maintaining confidentiality. Proper arrangements for the custody of the paper questionnaires or the electronic files resulting from the survey need to be made. The implications of the survey need to be considered. (In the UK, this may involve consultation with the Office of the Information Commissioner, see the web site: http://www.ico.gov.uk).

Various methods have been used to ensure the confidentiality of large datasets. A variety of different models are available (see Boruch and Cecil, 1979: 93–126) to ensure insulation of different files from each other, and to keep the identifying links separate from the data to which they relate. Statistical methods, such as random error injection and randomised response (Lee, 1993: 82–6),

have often been attempted. The most effective recent innovation is computer-assisted self-interviewing (CASI), in which respondents answer questions themselves on the interviewer's lap-top computer without the interviewer being involved, thus ensuring privacy in the interview and a degree of confidentiality of the resulting data. There is further discussion of practical methods to be used to protect data in Boruch and Cecil (1983).

THE REGULATORY FRAMEWORK OF RESEARCH ETHICS: A CASE STUDY

In recent years, some have argued that the system of ethical regulation erected in the biomedical sciences has become a threat to freedom of inquiry in the social sciences. British sociologist Robert Dingwall (2008) has put forward a trenchant argument of this kind, suggesting that once ethical review bodies are created, they tend to take on a life of their own, and even in the health services, efforts to roll back the role of ethics committees in hospitals and health trusts are resisted by such bodies who see their self-interests threatened. Measurement is an important part of all health research, so measurement issues are involved in this area.

There is considerable substance to the rumblings of dissatisfaction with NHS Research Ethics Committees, which was acknowledged in a Department of Health Ad Hoc Committee report in 2005 (Department of Health, 2005). This found that such committees interpreted their responsibilities too widely, and that many surveys and studies of NHS staff did not require ethical review. The report noted the charge of inconsistency in decisions reached between individual cases. NHS Research Ethics Committees (RECs) were criticised for having attempted to reach judgements about the scientific merit of proposals, which, it was pointed out, was beyond the terms of reference of RECs. Those involved in national surveys of UK health, in which much pioneering health measurement is involved, carried out by research nurses, such as height and weight, heart condition, blood pressure and lung function report that the demands of research ethics committees are a serious hindrance to their work.

It is right that health research, including medical research, should be subject to ethical review, and in the United Kingdom, the National Health Service has an elaborate system of ethics committees which review biomedical research involving human subjects. In recent years, however, they have extended their remit to cover social science research and social research, so that some members of such committees claim that any inquiry into a patient's experience of medicine, including their description of the conditions and symptoms which they suffer, must be subject to ethical review. For instance, it has been argued that if you are asked in a survey whether you suffer from a condition such as asthma, such a question must first be approved by the NHS research ethics system.

Dingwall's critique ranges wider than simply the UK system. Dingwall considers that institutional review boards infringe the First Amendment to the US Constitution, which protects freedom of speech and freedom of the press. In the UK, he argues that there is a danger that informed consent becomes fetishised, and regarded as the 'be-all and end-all' of ethical review. The extent of social measurement is being curtailed. One recent extreme manifestation of this is the requirement by some ethics committees that consent forms, signed, for example, by young persons under the age of 18, and separately by their parents, require a witness to sign the consent form, as if the human subject or their parents were

signing a will! Dingwall's argument is an extreme one, and may be consulted as part of an examination of the case for and against ethical review.

There is no doubt, however, that in relation to social science research, some ethics committees are capable of behaving in an officious manner (e.g., Elwyn et al., 2005), and place obstacles in the way of conducting social research. This raises another issue in relation to the ethics of measurement, are there external hindrances to measurement of social aspects of health, as a result of the UK system of ethical review which is in place. There is also a set of questions about the transparency of ethical review, both by universities and in the NHS COREC system. Neither system provide usually for appeal against decisions reached, which are sometimes disguised as 'opinions offered'.

Medical sociologist Eliot Freidson (1970) long ago pointed to the dangers in medical sociology of social science research being compromised by the failure of sociologists to adopt the perspective of a critical outside observer of medicine in the public good. The danger is that insufficient independence can lead to sociologists adopting the distorted view that medicine has of itself, in terms of its scientific knowledge and mission. Some of the problems arise from an over-close relationship between UK universities and the National Health Service as a funder of training (e.g., of nurses) within those institutions. There is more likelihood of disagreement.

Other factors that have led to the growth in this area of sociology are, increased governmental involvement in medical care, creating research opportunities and funding for sociologists to study the organisation and delivery of medical care. Sociologists have also become increasingly involved in teaching medical students in medical schools, and since the 1960s, the social and political struggles over health and medical care have become major social issues drawing researchers into the field. Medical sociology is now one of the largest sub-specialisms in British sociology, with its own annual conference run in competition with the main BSA conference. Some sociologists have come to see the organisation of medicine and the way medical services are delivered as social problems in themselves. Sociologists of medicine, such as Freidson, point out that this approach to sociological research can best be achieved by persons operating from independent positions outside the formal medical setting (Freidson, 1970: 42).

How health-related social science research is regulated is important because it throws light upon how the ethics of measurement operates in practice. There are significant questions in the relationship between the academic researcher and the wider society which are caught in this nexus, particularly the salience of both physical and social measurement in the health field.

Some of these issues can be illuminated by a discussion of a particular case. This involved the author and a PhD student working under his supervision, who is co-author of this chapter, and concerns our dealings with the University Research Ethics Committee in a university in the south of England. The case study relates to a full-time PhD student carrying out research on patient safety and patient empowerment. The research was being conducted as part of an ESRC CASE Studentship in partnership with a leading voluntary organisation in the patient safety field. A major part of the PhD project involved the student working with this organisation to develop a network of user groups whose members had been affected by medical harm. The student chose to study these as part of her research drawing upon

an action research methodology. Members of action groups were contacted via the voluntary organisation and no contact was involved with medical professionals or NHS premises in order to gain access to research subjects. (There is a fuller account in Bulmer and Ocloo (2009).)

The process of ethical review started with an application being made to the University's Ethics Committee after consulting with guidance on their website. The advice on the Ethics Committee website appeared to suggest that health-related research should always be referred first to the appropriate NHS Research Ethics Committee (REC), and the site quoted the Research Governance Framework for Health and Social Care document of 2001.

This document, *Governance Arrangements for NHS Research Ethics Committees*, stated in section 3.1 that

> Ethical advice from the appropriate NHS REC is required for any research proposal involving (a) patients and users of the NHS. This includes all potential research participants recruited by virtue of the patient or user's past or present treatment by, or use of, the NHS. It includes NHS patients treated under contracts with private sector institutions. (b) individuals identified as potential research participants because of their status as relatives or carers of patients and users of the NHS, as defined above.
>
> (Research on patients whose care is wholly private are outwith the system of ethical review.)

The guidance, however, created considerable confusion as it appeared to suggest that any research being carried out with patients who had ever used the NHS, was subject to ethical approval by an NHS Research Ethics Committee (REC). Therefore in order to clarify this position advice was sought from a senior member of COREC, the Central Office for Research Ethics Committees of the Department of Health at national level. He responded by confirming that recruitment via voluntary organisations – even for health-related research – did not require review by NHS REC's, as long as there was no intention to obtain information from NHS records. Obtaining ethical review from the University Committee was seen as the appropriate good practice in the circumstances advice was being sought on.

Given this advice an application was made to the University's Ethics Committee for research approval. This marked the beginning of a round of correspondence between the committee, the student and the student's supervisor that lasted for 11 months.

First round

The first round of this correspondence related to the original submission with the advice given from COREC that ethical review by the NHS REC system was not required if recruitment to the study was via voluntary associations. A multi-page protocol was submitted, with numerous attached documents. The opinion of the University Ethics Committee was that ethical approval was denied on the basis of the committee's view that NHS REC approval was required unless 'an explicit exclusion clause was be placed on participants currently receiving NHS treatment for a related condition'. The committee also raised a number of legitimate questions about the research proposal which were clarified in the second round.

Second round

The student then made a second submission to the Ethics Committee responding to a number of points raised and confirming that an exclusion clause would then be placed on the inclusion of participants in the research who were currently receiving treatment for a related condition. The aim of this

response was to expedite matters in order that ethical approval could be achieved without further delay. This prompted a further response from the Ethics Committee which stated that while they accepted the points clarified by the applicant in response to their legitimate questions, before they were able to give a favourable ethical opinion, they wished to have a further response from the student to the suggestion that the committee would like the research proposal to be submitted to the local COREC. This it was stated was to see whether advice from them conflicted with advice taken previously by the student's supervisor stating ethical approval from an NHS Committee was not needed. It was further pointed out that advice had already been sought by the UEC from the local NHS REC Committee. This had confirmed that as the research did involve participants who had been treated for a certain condition by the NHS, and that the research was related to their experiences, then submission to an NHS REC was appropriate.

Third round

This led to a third submission to the University Committee. This pointed out the belief that given the understanding the committee appeared satisfied with responses to earlier questions on various issues related to the design of the study, the only outstanding issue was whether the proposal required an opinion from the NHS REC. To address this point, the revised application again stressed access to hospital or GP patients via the NHS was not being sought, conditions which automatically trigger NHS ethical review. Instead it was pointed out the research application had again been revised and that the primary focus was not on medical negligence but on a study of user empowerment in relation to patient safety. This was to be conducted through the work of the voluntary organisation in the CASE partnership and a network being set up with user groups and would also include a secondary analysis of data collected from support workshops for a range of people affected by medical harm.

The response to this third application from the Ethics Committee was to restate the position that as this protocol still involved potential NHS patients, the committee's position had still not changed, and therefore the protocol should be submitted to the appropriate NHS REC for review.

This situation was not resolved until after many further conversations with various parties, which included the Vice Chair, Secretary and the Chair of the NHS inter-area Ethics Committee, the MREC. Each of these individuals took the view that a study of persons recruited via a voluntary association did not fall within the remit of an NHS REC. The University's Ethics Committee eventually accepted this view. The total process from start to finish took 11 months.

Several issues arose from the case bearing on the ethics of measurement in this field.

a) The question of the extent of jurisdiction of ethics committees and the danger of their overstepping a line between carrying out appropriate ethical review and stepping into the territory of censoring research. Measuring medical harm is a sensitive issue, and one which impinges upon the professional standing of members of the health professions. This problem can be further exacerbated if NHS REC committees are in effect censoring social science research through the backdoor aided and abetted by university ethic committees dominated by health interests or who are misinformed by local NHS committees because of a lack of guidance from bodies such as the ESRC. This is compounded by the tendency of university ethics committees to play safe and to have virtually all of the university's research checked out by the NHS, just to play safe. This seems to have happened in this case.

b) Questions arise from the case study about how on the one hand the University Ethics Committee could have such a wide-ranging and draconian stipulation that in effect any research carried out with NHS patients required ethical approval, whilst on the other hand to apply this rule selectively with different cases. There was certainly evidence of local inconsistency in response to individual cases, though this was justified by the UEC that they proceeded on a case by case basis. They persisted to assert this to the end. The logic of their position was that ANY research into people's health, no matter how it was conducted, required reference to an NHS REC. Thus any sample survey which asked people questions about their health conditions, illness or treatment in principle required NHS ethical approval. Thus health measurement was subject to external review.

c) The case study raises issues about whether the University Ethics Committee was taking a harder line about NHS review because of the contentious nature of the issue being looked at, in this case, medical harm. How is the university to ensure freedom of inquiry when investigating topics of a sensitive nature in which professional interests may be involved?

d) Issues are also raised by this case about the way in which Ethics Committee can ask for changes in the research design either by default or intent, because of the feedback provided to the applicant. This criticism also extends to NHS committees, and was explicitly dealt with in the DoH Review (Department of Health, 2005), shaping the nature of a research project either explicitly or because a student begins to tailor their work to a design that they think will best allow them to gain approval as illustrated to some extent in the case study. Again, this is an instance of measurement being possibly constrained.

The ESRC Guidelines (ESRC, 2005), which were prepared after consultation with the Department of Health, strongly urged the avoidance of duplication in ethical submission, though in this case the UEC avoided such economy of effort. One of the concerning issues in detailed discussion was the willingness of the University Ethics Committee to behave like the handmaiden of the NHS REC. in the course of an argument with the Chair about the appropriateness of referring the matter to the REC. It was suggested that the secretary of the local NHS REC could be invited to a meeting of the UEC to lay down the law about the matter. Although this did not happen, it is disturbing that such a suggestion, with the severe infringement of academic freedom implied, should have been made at all. To what extent was university ethics policy dictated by fear of crossing the NHS as an organisation and jeopardising university funding for NHS training? The university in question had a nursing school funded wholly by the NHS, and aspired to be the site of a new medical school. The impression was gained that these interests of the university in NHS activity in some way coloured the reaction of the university to this proposal, and the reluctance to take the advice of the senior official in COREC that ethical review of this particular project was not required.

The case has been discussed in some detail because it shows the constraints which can operate, via the research ethics review system, upon empirical research outcomes involving measurement of patient experience within the National Health Service. Measurement is an integral part of such inquiries, and the system of research ethics review represents a possible constraint up on freedom of scientific investigation.

CONCLUSION

This chapter has reviewed a variety of ethical issues which arise in the course of the process of measurement in social science research. The initial quote from *Crotchet Castle* is intended to underline the dilemma which faces the human scientist, treating a human subject matter such as happiness

from the point of view of science, and in the process perhaps losing something of humanity in the process. But by the same token, social science may be a way of gaining more understanding of difficult issues, such as domestic violence, which are subject of moral condemnation but also quite widespread phenomena. The tension between measurement and scientific aspirations remains, and defies easy resolution.

REFERENCES

Boruch, R. F. and Cecil, J. S. (1979) *Assuring the Confidentiality of Social Research Data*. Philadelphia, PA: University of Pennsylvania Press.

Boruch, R. F. and Cecil, J. S. (1983) (eds) *Solutions to Ethical and Legal Issues in Social Research*. New York: Academic Press.

Bulmer, M. (1979) (ed.) *Censuses, Surveys and Privacy*. London: The Macmillan Press.

Bulmer, M. (1996) 'The ethnic group question in the 1991 Census of Population', in D. Coleman and J. Salt (eds) *Ethnicity in the 1991 Census: Volume One, General Demographic Characteristics of the Ethnic Minority Populations*. London: HMSO. pp. 33–62.

Bulmer, M. and Ocloo, J. (2009) 'Looking forward: the researcher's perspective', in J. Strain, R. Barnett, P. Jarvis (eds) *Universities, Ethics and Professions: Debate and Scrutiny*. London: Routledge. pp. 127–38.

Department of Health (2005) *Report of the Ad Hoc Advisory Group on the Operation of NHS Research Ethics Committees*. London: Department of Health. (URL:http://www.dh.gov.uk/dr_consum_dh/groups/dh_digitalassets/@dh/@en/documents/digitalasset/dh_4112466.pdf

Dingwall, R. (2008) "The ethical case against ethical regulation in humanities and social science research", *Twenty-First Century Society*, Vol 3 (1), February, pp. 1–12.

Elwyn, G., Seagrove, A., Thornes, K. and Cheung, W. Y. (2005) 'Ethics and research governance in a multicentre study: Add 150 days to your study protocol', *British Medical Journal*, 330: 847.

ESRC (2005) *Research Ethics Framework*. Swindon: Economic and Social Research Council. (URL: http://www.esrcsocietytoday.ac.uk/ESRCInfoCentre/opportunities/research_ethics_framework/)

Friedson, E. (1970) *Professional Dominance: The Social Structure of Medical Care*. Chicago: Aldine Publishing Company.

Herrnstein, R. and Murray, C. (1994) *The Bell Curve: Intelligence and Class Structure in American Life.* New York: Free Press.

Holland, J., Ramazanoglu, C., Sharpe, S. and Thomson, R. (1988) *The Male in the Head: Young People, Heterosexuality and Power.* London: Tufnell.

Layard, R. (2005) *Happiness: Lessons from a New Science.* London: Allen Lane.

Lee, R. M. (1993) *Doing Research on Sensitive Topics.* London: Sage.

Lee, R. and Stanko, B. (2003) (eds) *Researching Violence: Essays on Methodology and Measurement.* London: Routledge.

Oswald, A. (1999) *A Non-Technical Introduction to the Economics of Happiness.* Warwick: Department of Economics.

Peacock, T. L. (1831) *Crotchet Castle.* London: T. Hookham.

Walby, S. and Allen, J. (2004) *Domestic violence, sexual assault and stalking: findings from the British Crime Survey.* London: Home Office Research, Development and Statistics Directorate, Home Office Research Study 276.

Walby, S. and Myhill, A. (2001) 'New survey methodologies in researching violence against women', *British Journal of Criminology*, 41: 502–22.

20

Measuring is More Than Assigning Numbers

Stephen Gorard

MEASUREMENT AS AN UNCONSIDERED CONCEPT

Measurement is fundamental to research-related activities in social science (hence this handbook). In my own field of education research, perhaps the most discussed element of education lies in test scores. Examination results are measurements; the number of students attaining a particular standard in a test is a measurement; indeed the standard of a test is a measurement. The allocation of places at school, college, or university, student–teacher ratios, funding plans, school timetables, staff workloads, adult participation rates, and the stratification of educational outcomes by sex, social class, ethnicity, or geography for example, are all based on measurements. Good and careful work has been done in all of these areas (Nuttall, 1987). However, the concept of measurement itself remains under-examined, and is often treated in an uncritical way. In saying this I mean more than the usual lament about qualitative–quantitative schism or the supposed reluctance of social scientists to engage with numeric analysis (Gorard et al., 2004a). I mean that even where numeric analysis is being conducted, the emphasis is on collecting, collating, analysing, and reporting the kinds of data generated by measurement, with the process of measurement and the rigor of the measurement instrument being somewhat taken for granted by many commentators. Issues that are traditionally considered by social scientists include levels of measurement, reliability, validity, and the creation of complex indices (as illustrated in some of the chapters contained in this volume). But these matters are too often dealt with primarily as technical matters – such as how to assess reliability or which statistical test to use with which combination of levels of measurement. The process of quantification itself is just assumed.

Although this chapter considers all of the issues above, what I want to do here is rather different. The first section discusses the general basis on which we allocate numbers to things and call the former 'measurements'. The next section reconsiders the usual classification of levels of measures, leading to a third section suggesting a flaw in the logic of creating complex indices (such as attitude 'measurements'). The next section looks at the kinds of errors that occur in measuring, leading to discussion of an even more serious logical flaw in the way in which we routinely handle errors in our measurements. The chapter ends by suggesting a fundamental change to the ways in which measurements are handled in social science. Thus, the chapter illustrates the limitations of a range of fundamental notions that are generally taken for granted in social science measurement. In doing so, it is intended to strengthen social science measurement by encouraging scepticism and parsimony, and by discouraging the obfuscation of unsustainable positions through increasing complexity of purportedly technical solutions to measurement problems.

WHAT IS MEASUREMENT?

When we say that we are measuring something, we generally imply a series of related preliminary steps that we have come to take for granted, and so to ignore. The danger in this lies in researchers remaining unaware of these pre-technical steps, and so mistaking the allocation of numbers to things as though it were measurement, leading to pseudo-quantification. For example, when we create a measure from scratch, the thing we seek to measure

must exist in the sense that we can observe it, whether directly or indirectly, otherwise our measurement of it is pointless.[1] It must be identifiable by some means and identified by us. And we must know something about its properties and behaviour, so that we can relate these to our measures of it. Put another way, even where the thing we seek to measure is a concept, like length, this concept must have manifest qualities that we can measure, like the way in which sticks of different length might protrude to different extents (Gorard et al., 2002). We must also have a measuring scale, based on numbers or their equivalents, and this scale must have a standard so that other users can comprehend and compare our measurements. The scale must have divisions or units that are related as directly as possible to changes in the properties and behaviour of the thing being measured, so that we can associate these changes with gradations in the measurement scale. We should also have a clear estimate of the accuracy of our measure, in the sense of how well changes in the scale can track changes in the properties and behaviour of the thing being measured. In other words, we need to have a good idea of the size of the error component in our measure.

Without any one of these components, measurement is largely an illusory exercise deceiving either the producer or the user. If the thing we are measuring does not exist, the idea of measurement makes no sense. If we know that it exists somehow and somewhere, but it is not readily identifiable by the qualities it makes manifest then we cannot hope to measure it at present. If we can identify it but have no idea in fact of how it varies over time, place, or other context then we cannot set up a measurement, because we cannot associate the measurement scale with these variations. We may later use an established measurement technique to measure new examples of the phenomenon, but at the outset we have to be able to associate existing variations in the phenomenon with gradations of our measure. Once we have met these preliminary requirements (among others perhaps) we have identified what seems to be a palpable quantity that is, in theory, capable of numeric summary. Next we need a suitable scale. If we do not have a scale capable of variation then we cannot associate scale variation with variation in our tentative quantity. If the scale does not have agreed and comprehensible steps within it, then we cannot convey variation in the quantity by variations in the scale. If we cannot directly associate variation in the quantity with variation in the scale – 'calibrate' our measure – then we are in danger of being misled or being misleading in our measurements. So, I emphasise this for what follows, we need two separate things – the object of measurement or its manifestation in the real world, and the measurement of it from the measuring scale.

These assumptions are largely unexamined when we first learn about and use simple measurements, such as the number of people in a room, and they remain so as we begin to create and use more complex scales such as how tall the people in the room are, and even the much more complex scale of how much time they have been in the room for. However, all such everyday measures meet the requirements above. We can learn to identify people and separate them from each other, from their surroundings, and from the remaining contents of the room. We can sense when a room is more or less crowded with people, and begin to associate that sense with the numeric scale of 'digits' (for small numbers we might literally draw an analogy between how many people and how many fingers). This scale is shared, comprehensible, and reliable. The scale goes up or down by one

for every new person entering or leaving the room. Barring computational mistakes, the scale is quite error-free, requiring no instruments, estimation, or fractions. It is a real number measuring scale.

Similarly, we can observe that the tops of some peoples' heads are further from the floor when standing upright, and that this characteristic remains relatively constant while they are in the room. We could even get people to stand in a line representing more or less of this characteristic of having their head further from the floor when standing upright. From such activity we could create an ordinal scale from shortest (less of this characteristic) to tallest (most). We could then select an item with a fixed amount of this characteristic (the shortest person, or a piece of furniture perhaps) and create a truer scale by using this item as a standard. The quantity of the characteristic can then be counted as a multiple of this standard. If the item used as a standard is commonly agreed or widespread, then this becomes the basis for a real number measuring scale, such as a ruler. It is more complex and so more prone to error than a scale of the number of people in a room – not least because tallness varies with posture, diurnally, and with age. But as long as we know these complications (or learn them once we have established the scale), we can take them into account when measuring tallness and when using the results for practical purposes. Time, or how long someone had been in the room, is more complex again and so even more prone to error, but it is similarly possible to convert to a quantity, and so arrive at a consensual, reliable, and useful scale to measure this characteristic.

A key point in all three examples is the analogous behaviour of the scale used to measure and of the thing being measured. We can see when people come or go and how this relates to changes in the number of people counted in the room. We can see how much one person's height protrudes beyond another, and how this relates to variation in a scale (perhaps by standing both people and the scale standard against a wall). It is the isomorphism between the numbers and the observations that gives us a measurement, and this depends on our correct identification of a quantity to be measured in the first place (Berka, 1983). I repeat, if people do not exist, or are not separated from their surroundings, or cannot be seen to protrude in relation to each other, then our quantities do not exist.

The examples so far are deliberately simple and everyday in scale, in order to illustrate the derivation of measurements from observations of the thing being measured (whether direct or indirect). Even these simple examples are imperfect, and require a certain number of assumptions that could be debated. The isomorphism between physical characteristics and measuring scales relies on imperfect judgement, for example. In social science, however, many researchers seek to go beyond relatively simple examples of creating measurements, such as the number of pupils in a school. As soon as they do so, their measurement problems and concerns will multiply. This means that they should be much more careful, explicit and humble in their approach.[2] It is not the mere assignment of number to things that leads to a quantity. No amount of 'quantification' will, by itself, establish a good and useful measurement. Obviously, anyone can simply assign a number to an object or to the imagined gradations within a concept. In this case we are using numbers as convenient labels – such as the serial numbers allotted to examination candidates for anonymity. What we must not do is mistake this process for real measurement.

Unfortunately, in ignoring the underlying premises of measurement, social science research has become saddled with quite a range of quantified items that are *not* clearly good and useful measures. In many examples in popular use, such as attitude scales and the like, we cannot calibrate the purported scale to the real thing as we are not sure what the real thing is. The object of measurement may not exist, may not be identifiable, or may not behave in an analogous manner to the numbers used as measures. For example, the problem with the well-known claim that 'intelligence is what IQ tests measure' is not so much whether IQ tests measure intelligence, but whether they measure anything (Prandy, 2002). We need to have a quantity identifiable by its qualities against which we can compare our measuring scale. If IQ is *really* only what IQ tests measure then IQ cannot be a real quantity, and so any attempt to measure it is liable to considerable confusion. The same might apply to 'attitude' measures.[3]

Explicitness is key to forming and using a good measure – and one that is reliable in the sense that it can reach the same result when used properly in the same situation by more than one researcher. If there is a dispute about the number of people in a room, it is possible to settle the matter by reference to the identifiable and separate things being measured. We have the measure (such as seven people) and we have bodies in a room that we can line up, and count repeatedly, until a consensus view is arrived at or a judgement becomes more general. Of course, there can still be errors of measurement but in principle they can be resolved by direct comparison of the figures and manifestation of the quality being measured. Resolving a dispute about the heights of people is more complex than about how many people there are, but still possible. We can get others to compare the ruler (standard of height) with the lengths of the people. In each example, we have explicit, stable, and easily re-counted evidence of a phenomenon and we have a separate system of measures. We can compare the two. The problem with extant efforts to operationalise IQ or attitudes is that we may have only the measurements. How then do we check for reliability or calibration or measurement error?

The rest of the chapter looks in more detail at this question, at the kinds of measurements used in social science, and assesses their suitability in terms of the ideas outlined so far.

ARE THERE LEVELS OF MEASUREMENT?

One of the aspects of measurement that is routinely proposed by social science researchers (instead of the importance of isomorphism perhaps) is that there are four levels of measurement (Stevens, 1992). These are termed ratio, interval, ordinal, and nominal. The claim is usually made that we need to be aware of these four because their characteristics affect how we should use and analyse them. Is this true, or is it better to go back to the ideas of measurement outlined so far, such as the need for isomorphism between measurement and measured, and so avoid the terrible fate that apparently awaits anyone who confuses their levels of measurement?

A ratio measure is one which meets all of the criteria described in the last section. One cannot have a ratio measure of a non-identifiable quantity, for example. There is a direct analogy between numbers on the scale and properties or behaviour of the thing being measured. Most significantly, when there are four people in a room this is more than two people in a room; it is exactly twice as many. When someone is six standard units tall, they are three times

as tall as someone two units tall, and so on. Conceptually, a further key point here is that the room can be empty, and the absence of a person will yield a measure of no units tall. Some scales can also have negative units, and these work in the mirror-opposite way to the positive units. Most people encounter such numbering systems in their everyday life, and most deal with them perfectly well without knowledge of measurement levels (or put another way any problems they have with such numbers are not usually about levels of measurement). Many of the figures used in social science, such as the examples at the start of the chapter, are similarly uncomplicated in this regard. These include the number of students and teachers in an establishment, the amount of government funding per pupil at school, the proportion of female pupils, the rate of participation of adults in part-time study, or the percentage of students deemed to have passed a test. All of these figures can be understood without reference to levels of measurement. Of course, many of them are much more complex and thus error-prone than a simple head-count. But it is not their ratio nature that makes them so. The complexity comes from real-life complications such as how to treat part-time or temporary staff, student mobility, missing data, or the definition of participation (see Gorard, 2008).

An interval measure is usually described as being like a ratio measure in all respects but without a genuine zero point (such as no people in the room, or no passes in a test). Thus, an interval measurement must also be of an identifiable quantity, and the scale and quantity must be able to vary proportionately and in tandem. However, it is difficult to think of a real-life example of such a measure. A temperature scale, such as Centigrade, is the most commonly cited example but this is not a scale often used in social research. Economic indices like the FTSE100 may be another, or they may have a zero even if it is unlikely to be used. And the distinction makes little difference to how we use ratio and interval scales in practice, apart from recalling that 20 degrees is not twice as hot (whatever that means) as 10 degrees. We may add or subtract interval numbers (to find that one room is 10 degrees hotter than another, for example), and I have never seen a statistical methods resource that suggests different models or tests for ratio and interval values, despite claiming that we need to know about the distinction so that we do not use the wrong kind of analysis.

So-called nominal measures are, in fact, not measures at all but categories of things that can be counted.[4] The sex of an individual would, in traditional texts, be a nominal measure. But sex is clearly not a quantity – although each sex could be allocated a number for shorthand. Even where the categories are expressed as numbers for some reason, these numbers cannot be used for arithmetic, and are not measures since there is no isomorphism between the quantity and its measure. There is no quantity, other than the frequency of individuals in each category of the variable 'sex' – i.e. how many females and how many males. Frequencies can be added, subtracted, multiplied, and divided just like ratio measures. Again, drawing a distinction here is pointlessly confusing. A frequency is a ratio measure. A category is not a measure at all. A category is a quality. Again, in everyday life there is little confusion over this.

The remaining level of measurement is termed ordinal, meaning that the scale has an order but no standard unit of measurement. An ordinal scale can be isomorphic with something observed, as long as the thing observed has an order to it but does not really increase or decrease along a continuum or in regular jumps.

An ordinal scale should *not* be used, and would not then be isomorphic, simply because of ignorance about the way in which the thing of interest varies. It should not be simply a sloppy interval measure. Ordinal 'measures' are quite common in current education research, and they have so many associated problems and issues – the so-called parametric strategy, and the latent nature of what they purport to measure, amongst others – that I leave further discussion of these for the next section. Suffice to say here that a true ordinal scale like a nominal scale is not really a measure at all (as defined above), but the most widespread (and so commercially successful) scales based on these premises are treated and analysed in the same way as ratio and interval scales anyway.

PROBLEMS WITH ORDINAL 'MEASURES'

Ordinal numbers are the same as nominal numbers in referring simply to categories of things that can be counted, and that can be treated accordingly. Again, the identification of a different level of measurement seems unnecessarily complex. The distinction is based on the claim that some sets of categories have an intrinsic order to them, and these are termed ordinal, whereas some categories do not, and these are termed nominal. The given example of an ordinal value might be the grades achieved in a school examination or test. But for most analyses, this order makes no difference beyond the obvious. In calculating the number of students achieving a certain combination of grades, such as A–C, a teacher is not going to add in the frequencies of students in grade D, for example. In the same way with a nominal scale representing full- and part-time employment and no employment, an analyst can calculate the number of all employed by adding the first two categories. They are not going to add in the unemployed category, except by mistake. Knowing the level of measurement here makes no practical difference. Whether a grade C is genuinely different to a grade D, and where the cut off point should be if so, is a difficult issue. But it is not one that is related to the level of measurement.

It is also important to realise that an intrinsic order is available for just about any set of categories. The serial numbers for TV channels on an old-fashioned analogue TV set could be treated as a nominal value having only arbitrary meanings, or could be placed or programmed in their order of appearance when flicking through with the channel 'advance' button, or the historical order in which they started broadcasting, or their transmission frequencies, and so on. All of these make sense, and appear to be at least as well ordered as many social or occupational class categories that commentators try to order in terms of skill or prestige (Rose, 1996; Erikson and Goldthorpe, 2002; Lambert, 2002). Many categorical variables in research are not intrinsically either ordinal or nominal. Instead, it depends how one looks at them.

When a set of categories are clearly intended to be ordinal, such as the order in which competitors finish a sprint race, any ensuing analysis will usually have available the much better and more genuine measures that underlie the order, such as the times taken. It is difficult to imagine a situation in which it would be better to analyse by using the ordinal data than the evidence used to create that order in the first place. Of course, if there is no good evidence to create the order in the first place (no sprint times) then there is no good order anyway.

The main reason why ordinal categories are treated separately to other categorical data by some researchers is because they want to claim that these are actually more like real numbers than they are like nominal categories. That is, analysts want to treat a numerical order of categories as though they were real numbers that can be added, subtracted, multiplied, or divided in a normal way. They want to be able to claim that a grade 'A' in an examination is worth 10 points and so five times as good as a grade 'E' scoring two points, for example. Therefore, if a grade B is worth 8 points, then a grade A minus a grade E is a grade B, and so on. This approach is common in statistical work, but it is of dubious value and rigour.[5] Categories such as examination grades are thresholds superimposed onto theoretically continuous levels of variation. They are not equal intervals, either in distance on a scale or in the proportion of cases within any grade. The difference in terms of underlying marks or performance between two students with different grades in an exam could be much less than the difference between two students with the same grades. The orders involved are not real numbers, and should not be treated as if they were. In everyday life, there is little confusion on this point. Only in traditional statistics is this confusion created, so that analysts can convert exam grades to points, and so on, so that they can then use a more convenient or more sophisticated analytic process. However, these analytic processes should only be available when researchers are in fact using real numbers (and often not even then, see below). What these analysts are doing is sacrificing clarity and even intellectual honesty in the name of technical sophistication.

In education and psychology research, a fairly common approach is to use questionnaires to measure latent variables like peoples' attitudes or their social 'capital'. A standard method to operationalise such constructs is to use scales of agreement and disagreement linked to items expressed as statements – such as Likert scales. The scale might vary from strongly agree, and slightly agree, to strongly disagree. These scale categories are then routinely converted to numbers (perhaps 1 for strongly agree, 2 for slightly agree, and so on), despite the lack of equal interval between the points on the scale. Each item is then intended to be a component of the measurement of a construct (or composite index). The set of items involved in the construct are completed by respondents, and then tested for reliability by looking at the correlations between the responses to each item, treating the scaled ordinal responses as real numbers. There are so many things to query with such an approach that it is hard to know where to start, particularly given that it is so widespread in use.

How is it possible to measure something, in the sense of establishing an analogous relationship between the object measured and the numbering scale, when the object measured is latent? This is very different from a concept of length emerging from differential protrusions (see above). With length we can test the concept directly. With latent constructs we only have the constructs. Converting agreement scales to equal interval numbers means that the numbers and the scale would not be isomorphic anyway. Yet, ironically the approach relies much more heavily on the real quality of the measurements involved because we do not have a direct explicit comparator on which to model our measurement.

Also we are no longer dealing with a single measure, but a composite formed from many. Does this make the overall composite measure better (or worse)? The notion that several questions or indicators can be combined to produce a better answer than just one is premised on sampling theory. It assumes that the variability of each indicator is equal to every other and that this variance is due solely to random error. This seems very unlikely (Anderson and Zelditch, 1968). How do we know that each item should have a specific weighting in creating the construct? Usually all items are given equal weight for no good reason (Nunnally, 1975: 8). The reliability of constructs is assessed in terms of correlation between items in the construct. If this is low, then non-matching items are rejected. But a high correlation is not, in itself, justification for a construct or latent measure. It could just mean that the researcher is asking the same question over and over again, and that one item would do instead. Nunnally (1975) suggests that in practical terms 'even a reliability of 0.90 is not high enough'. If the individual measures taken to create the overall construct are intended to be measuring the same thing to such an extent (0.9) then they will be repetitious (see below). If they are not intended to measure the same thing then how can we be justified in averaging them, or otherwise generating the composite? This is very different to contrasting two distinct measures, such as the number of pupils per teacher. It is more like those invalid UK league tables of Higher Education used in the press where the number of students with a first class degree is added to the number of computers and the library spend per annum etc.

One claim in response to this is that asking similar questions repeatedly leads to greater accuracy since random errors in responses are eliminated. Is this actually true? When we conduct a survey to create constructs, we must assume that a majority of respondents are able to answer any question correctly. If, on the other hand, a majority of respondents are not able to answer a question correctly then the survey is doomed from the start, and the use or non-use of constructs is irrelevant. 'Correctly' here means that respondents give the most appropriate response, that they would wish to retain on reflection, and which is supported by any available independent evidence. For example, someone born in the UK might correctly respond that they were born in the UK, retain this answer if allowed time to reflect on it, and could support it by reference to their birth certificate. A 'mistaken' answer, on the other hand, would be one that was inconsistent with other evidence, including the respondent's answers to other items within the construct.

When we conduct a survey to operationalise constructs, we assume that where respondents do not answer questions correctly then their errors are random in nature. We assume that errors are random for the sake of this argument because that is the assumption underlying the statistical treatment of constructs and their reliability. Of course, some incorrect responses will be systematic error (that is subject to non-random bias), but I will argue in the next section that these cannot be treated by statistical means, and that these techniques make the use or non-use of constructs irrelevant. For example, adult respondents might rarely overestimate their age, and more commonly understate their age, meaning that any measurement of age could have a slight bias. Techniques based on sampling theory cannot estimate or adjust for this bias.

In creating a construct we can only gain accuracy by asking different versions of the same question when two or more responses from the same individual differ. If we ask the same or very similar questions several times we gain nothing if the answer to each version of the question is consistent with every other. For example, if an individual responds correctly with their age to one question and their valid date of birth to another question then the response to one of the questions alone is sufficient. We only learn something from repetition of the question when the second response differs substantially from the first.

Therefore, it follows that most people who change their answer between the first usually correct answer and the second answer will be making a mistake on the second answer. Some respondents will give the same answer both times, whether correct or incorrect, but these are unaffected by the repetition. If the errors are truly random then a certain proportion of those who gave the correct answer to the first question will give an incorrect answer to the second version of the same question. A similar proportion of those who gave an incorrect answer to the first question will give a correct answer to the second version of the same question. But there will be more people giving a correct answer than an incorrect answer first time (see the first assumption). Therefore, for those answers that differ, the answers to the second question will be more likely to be in error than the first answer.

Therefore, asking a question more than once reduces rather than increases the accuracy of the evidence we collect from the survey. This conclusion has been confirmed by simulation.[6] Why do many researchers not notice this problem? I suspect because, unlike a simple measure like length, they are dealing with something that they cannot otherwise calibrate. In such situations, we can have no idea of the 'correctness' of responses, other than their consistency. We are stuck with a circular definition like IQ – the construct is what the construct measures. Or perhaps researchers are confused about the issue of reliability, within items of the construct (rather than across test–retest situations). Where items in a construct have high internal consistency or high reliability they are merely asking the same thing repeatedly (in the same way that if we know someone's date of birth we also know their age). Where they do not have this high internal consistency, they are not asking the same question in effect, and so are not the subject of this discussion.

The suggestion that in building constructs we create a more accurate measure of the underlying variable fails in almost every way. Overall, surveys are better at collecting 'factual' information like date of birth than 'imaginary' data such as attitudes to car ownership.[7] However, because constructs are usually based on imaginary things that we cannot confirm apart from with the use of similar survey instruments with exactly the same limitations, and since we have no way of knowing the real answer, we can never test empirically what we gain in accuracy by asking questions several times in different ways. We do know that there are clear opportunity costs. Asking what is effectively the same question again and again leaves less room in a questionnaire of fixed length for questions on other things. The repetition also leads to boredom among respondents, which may affect response rates and the integrity of responses. Using only the best single item (perhaps the one with the highest loading in a factor analysis generated when developing the questionnaire) allows us to reduce the length of the questionnaire in order to increase completion and response rates (once the measure has been developed for use). This, it seems to me, is a far surer path to quality than using constructs in areas other than assessment. Constructs such as multiple item tests *can* work better in assessment for a number of reasons, most notably because they are more properly measurements given that the composer can have a good idea beforehand of what the correct response should be to each item. In examinations there is, in essence, a correct answer (or answers) for which marks are awarded, and these can be moderated for consistency between examiners. This is not to defend assessment *sui generis* but to point out that, in its own terms, it seeks to find out whether the candidate can correctly describe an answer that is already known. Attitude scales, on the other hand, generally seek to find out something

so far unknown. The ultimate arbiter of the attitude is the respondent not the examiner.

I repeat, the problem with constructs such as attitudes and preferences is that there is no explicit thing – e.g. the correct answer, or the number of people in the room – with which the purported measure can be compared. Therefore, it is hard to see attitude scales and the like as real measures of anything very much. Even in those situations where they correlate highly with something explicit (a human behaviour for example) there is a danger of tautology. For example, people who choose to go swimming might be more likely to report wanting to go swimming, and so on. In this case, where we have the behaviour itself it is a better measure than the report of preference or intention – which is a weak proxy. It is also often, when tested in non-tautological conditions, an inaccurate proxy. For example, students' reported attitudes to science at school are weakly but inversely related to their subsequent choice of studying science subjects or not (Gorard and See, 2009).

THE BEHAVIOUR OF ERRORS IN MEASUREMENT

Knowing whether we have the correct figure is a key component of measuring. Whatever kind of measurement we use, and however good the scale we devise, there are likely to be some errors in the figures that emerge. It is a condition of good and safe measurement that we have some idea of the scale and possible impact of such errors, and I focus on this issue here because it is usually ignored in traditional resources in favour of concerns over sampling variation (see next section). A measure is intended to react isomorphically with the quantity of which it is a measure. Measurement error is an indication of the failure of that isomorphism. As such, it has nothing to do with sampling variation. Measurement error can come from mis-specification of the scale, mis-calibration, mis-reading, mis-recording, and errors in transcription or recall. One common source of simple mistakes comes from copying, such as when transferring a long list of numbers from paper to computer or calculator. Intriguingly, errors are also introduced merely by entering numbers into a computer or calculator even when the numbers are entered entirely correctly. A computer stores all of its numbers in binary, and only allocates a specific number of binary digits to each number. The process of converting base ten numbers into binary numbers, therefore, automatically introduces small errors to some numbers, even where they start out as perfect representations of the reality we are measuring.[8] We have no reason to assume that all such sources of error are random in nature; in fact we have a considerable body of evidence to show that they are non-random (Gorard, 2006a). Researchers are more likely to mis-read or mis-type data in such a way as to support their favoured ideas, for example. A ruler that was calibrated to be too short would consistently over-estimate lengths, rather than provide any kind of random variation around the 'true' length. Thus, the techniques of statistical analysis based on random error and sampling theory are of no general use in assessing the general quality of a measurement. Standard errors, confidence intervals, and significance levels, for example, do not, and cannot begin to, help us estimate the importance of such errors in our measurements.

In research situations there are many sources of genuine error that are unaddressed by traditional statistical analyses concerned only with sampling variation. Many purported measures in common use in

social science probably contain a very high proportion of measurement error.[9] These include attitude scales, the categorisation of ethnic groups or occupational classes, the allocation of national examination grades, or definitions of poverty. What they all have in common is a high level of imprecision – some, like attitude scales, more because of the vagueness of what is being measured, and some, like the allocation of national examination grades, more because the size of the operation leads to mistakes and imperfect moderation between assessors. While we can take steps to minimise the chances of the second kind of error, we cannot guarantee their absence.

Why do errors matter so much? Surely, we can just use the best available figures, analyse them accurately, and be aware that our results will not be perfectly accurate. Well – consider the following example. We calculate the mean score in a school test for a group of boys, and find the answer 60 per cent. We also calculate the mean for a group of girls, and find the answer 70 per cent. Let us imagine that both means are around 90 per cent accurate. An error component of one part in ten may seem reasonable when considering either figure in isolation. But this means that the real boys' score actually lies between 54 and 66 per cent (i.e. 60 plus or minus 6). The real girls' score lies between 63 and 77 (i.e. 70 plus or minus 7). If we subtract the girls' mean from the boys', the manifest answer is 10. But the true answer could be anywhere between 23 (77–54) and −3 (63–66). Remember, these are not probability calculations. Confidence intervals are no help here. The difference −3 is as likely as any other answer. Therefore, despite both figures initially being 90% accurate, when we subtract the two figures we genuinely have no idea whether the result is positive or negative. The actual range for the answer, from −3 to +23 (or 26), is nearly three times the size of the surface answer (which is 10). The range of measurement error involved is far greater than the range of the answer itself. The relative measurement error in the original measures has been propagated by the ensuing simple calculation.

This propagation of initial measurement errors is usually ignored in training texts, because it remains largely unaddressed by traditional statistical analysis. Even where we have relatively accurate initial figures to work with, the process of conducting arithmetic with numbers changes the size of the error component relative to the numbers. Even such a simple technique as above, when subtracting two numbers, manages to convert an error of just 10 per cent to an error of 260 per cent of the figures involved. What has happened is that the initial numbers were so close that the subtraction makes them almost negligible in the result, leaving the answer to be made up almost entirely of error. This happens in real-life calculations all of the time. You may be able to imagine what happens to the error components in more complex analyses. Value-added analyses of school performance, for example, routinely involve finding the difference between two sets of similar-sized numbers each with high levels of initial error. Knowing about the propagation of errors, how much faith would you want to put in the results?

Two important points emerge from this consideration. First, there is no standard acceptable amount of error in any measurement. The relevance of the error component is a function of scale, and of the use to which the measurement is put. Second, the relative size of the error in any result is not determined by the accuracy of the original measurements. It depends on the precise steps in the ensuing computation. Of course, it helps if the initial readings are as accurate as possible, but whether

they are accurate enough depends on what is done with the readings, and how the error component propagates as it is used in calculations. It is important to recall that every statistical, arithmetic, or mathematical operation conducted with measurements is also conducted with their error components. If we square a variable, then we also square its error component and so on. The more complex the calculations we conduct the harder it is to track the propagation of errors (even if we are aware of them at source), and so make an informed judgement of the ratio of error to final result. In extreme cases, the manipulation of variables leads to results almost entirely determined by the initial errors and very little influenced by the initial measurements. When answering a typical analytic question, such as 'is there a real difference between two figures', we need to take into account, in a way that traditional analysis simply ignores, the likely scale of any errors. Why is this not done as standard?

MISPLACED EMPHASIS ON RANDOM ERRORS

One of the main reasons why consideration of real measurement error issues, such as bias and propagation, are routinely ignored is the false belief that measurement error is handled by statistical testing and estimation. The basis of statistical testing derived from sampling theory is the calculation of a conditional probability. This probability becomes the p value used for significance testing, and also for standard errors, confidence intervals and often in deciding which variables to retain in complex statistical modelling. The calculation of the probability is grounded in various assumptions, such as a random or randomised sample and complete measurement of all cases in the selected sample (de Vaus, 2002). The probability is intended to help decide whether two sets of measurements (perhaps two sub-samples) could have come from the same overall group (see Gorard, 2010 for more discussion of this).

> Application of NHST [null hypothesis significance testing] to the difference between two means yields a value of p, the theoretical probability that if two samples of the size of those used had been drawn at random from the same population, the statistical test would have yielded a statistic (e.g., t) as large or larger than the one obtained. (Nickerson, 2000: 242)

If the p value calculated in this way is less than a certain level, traditionally 5 per cent, then the null hypothesis (often the 'nil' null hypothesis of no difference) is rejected. Standard reputable texts on methods for statistical analysis are in agreement over the conditional nature of null hypothesis testing, even though they may all express this condition in different ways (Carver, 1978). 'The final step in the testing process is to see whether the proportion from the random sample is sufficiently far from the proportion assumed by the null hypothesis to warrant the rejection of the null hypothesis' (Fielding and Gilbert, 2000: 248). 'The null hypothesis is presumed true until statistical evidence, in the form of a hypothesis test, indicates otherwise – that is, when the researcher has a certain degree of confidence, usually 95% to 99%, that the data does not support the null hypothesis' (Wikipedia, 2008).

The probability of the data/sample encountered in any new research is conditional upon the null hypothesis (rather than the other way around), and is routinely used to accept or reject the null hypothesis, where the null hypothesis is usually one of no difference. Why does this matter?

The logic is a modified form of the argument of *modus tollendo tollens,* or denying the consequent. If the null hypothesis is assumed true we can calculate the probability of observing data as (or more) extreme than the data we did observe. If this probability is very small it suggests that the null hypothesis is not likely to be true. Of course, the formal *modus tollens* is not based on probability but certainty. The argument goes:

> If A then B
> Not B
> Therefore, not A

This argument is indisputable, and its soundness can be proved by logic trees or truth tables. However, when converted to a likelihood argument, the argument says:

> If the null hypothesis (H) is true then we can calculate the probability of observing data (D) this extreme
> The probability of D (given H) is very small
> Therefore, the probability of H is very small

This second argument is more complex than the simple *modus tollens.* Unlike the formal logic version, it allows for a false positive result (or Type I error) when H is rejected incorrectly because the small probability of observing D has occurred despite H (as it will on a small percentage of occasions). By definition a Type I error (incorrect rejection of the null hypothesis) is only possible if the null hypothesis is true. The truth of the null hypothesis itself is not derivable from p since p only exists assuming the null hypothesis to be true. Many specific events, when closely described, can be deemed low probability, and the occurrence of a low probability event is not, in itself, any evidence of it not being due to chance (as this term is usually interpreted, Gorard, 2002). Sitting down to a game, the gamer would not declare a die biased just because it rolled two threes in succession. Nor would they do so if they were dealt three cards in the same suit from a standard pack. Yet both of these gaming events are less likely than the 5 per cent threshold used in traditional statistical analysis.

This likelihood version of *modus tollens* also allows for a false negative result (or Type II error) where the probability of D is found to be not very small, and so H is not rejected even where it is not true. In general, users of statistics tend to understand these limitations of the method, either formally or intuitively. They may reason that as long as the conditional probabilities of D and H are clearly linked, so that a low value for $p(D|H)$ means a low value for $p(H|D)$ and *vice versa*, the approach is useful and valuable. As Nickerson (2000: 251) says: '... to many specialists, I suspect, it seems natural when one obtains a small value of p from a statistical significance test to conclude that the probability that the null hypothesis is true must also be very small'. But this is not so at all. Reversing D and H leads to two statements that are clearly not equivalent in real life (or indeed in science, logic, maths, or statistics). The probability of carrying an umbrella if it is raining is not the same as the probability of it raining if one carries an umbrella. *Modus tollens* does not work with likelihoods.

The p value for a statistical test is the probability of getting the data we did given that the null hypothesis of no difference between sample and population (or two sub-samples) is true. For the p value to be calculated the null hypothesis must be assumed as true. By definition, therefore, the p value by itself cannot be used to judge or even help judge the likelihood of the truth of the null hypothesis. Yet what analysts seem to want from statistical testing is precisely that ability to judge the probability of the null hypothesis. And this is what they usually report the p value as

being, and how they use it in practice. The widespread practice of significance testing rests on a crucial confusion between these two conditional probabilities.

The assumptions of significance testing only really work when the prior probability of the null (and alternate) hypothesis is 50 per cent. In this unlikely circumstance the probability of the data observed given the null hypothesis – $p(D|H)$ – is the same as $p(H|D)$ and so the null hypothesis could be plausibly retained or rejected with likelihood $p(D|H)$. Even then, of course, it is still not clear that one study leading, however convolutedly, to $p(H|D)<0.05$ should be able to over-ride completely a prior $p(H)$ of 0.50 in this manner. In other circumstances, indeed in most conceivable circumstances, even this is not possible, which means that statisticians not only have to claim a series of rather unrealistic assumptions such as a perfect random sample with full response, no dropout and no measurement error, they also have to claim that all of their null hypotheses have a 50 per cent likelihood before any data is collected or analysed. In other words, statistical analysis must assume no prior knowledge of any kind.

Nickerson (2000: 247) provides numerous examples of specialists in statistics routinely ignoring this distinction between pD|H and pH|D, and shows that false beliefs about these conditional probabilities are 'abundant' in the literature. These examples include social scientists and statisticians 'of some eminence', such as Fisher himself. This 'belief that p is the probability that the null hypothesis is true' (Nickerson, 2000: 247) is an even more fundamental error than the less common but still prevalent mistaken belief that $1 - p$ is the probability of any specific alternate hypothesis being true.

As analysts, we can convert the probability of getting the data we did given the null hypothesis into the more useful probability of the null hypothesis given the data we obtained, by using Bayes' theorem. But to do this requires us to know $p(H)$ – the unconditional probability of the null hypothesis being true in the first place. So, apparently tautologically, in order to find the empirical probability of the null hypothesis we must know how likely it is beforehand. Analysts might reasonably use their *a priori* subjective judgement of the null hypothesis being true to substitute for $p(H)$. In which case the new p value is an estimate of how far that subjective view of the null hypothesis might be affected by the new empirical evidence (see Gorard et al., 2004b). But almost none of the material published in mainstream social science research journals, follows such a procedure. Most analysts simply appear to misinterpret the conditional probability of the new data as though it were the probability of the null hypothesis conditional upon the new data. Falk and Greenbaum (1995) claim that the lack of a clear relationship between $pD|H$ and $pH|D$ discredits the whole logic of significance testing, which answers a question we would never knowingly ask, but leads us to conclude we have some kind of answer to the questions we might actually want answered – such as how probable is the hypothesis, how reliable are the results, and what is the size of the effect found?

There have been many criticisms of statistical testing over decades (Gorard, 2006a), and many examples of misuse of the method such as widespread acceptance of p values based on non-probability samples, or dredging datasets via multiple use of a technique whose probability calculations are predicated on one-off use (Wright, 2003). What is demonstrated in this chapter is far more fundamental. It is that the easy assumption that a low value for $p(D|H)$ means a low value for $p(H|D)$

is false. *Modus tollens* does not work with probabilities – or, expressed differently, it requires a further probability in order to make it work at all. Since at least the writing of Jeffreys (1937) it has been well established that a small value of $p(D|H)$ (such as less than 0.05) can be associated with a probability of H that is actually near 1. A null hypothesis significance test is therefore: '… based upon a fundamental misunderstanding of the nature of rational inference, and is seldom if ever appropriate to the aims of scientific research' (Rozeboom, 1960: 417).

Unfortunately, reflective consideration of errors in measurement and analysis has been almost completely overshadowed by a mechanical procedure designed for dealing only with random variation. This procedure is almost impossible to use correctly as intended in social research (as opposed to agricultural trials, for example), and even when used correctly has a logical flaw. It deals only with random variation, which our consideration of genuine measurement errors shows to be only a small part of the problem. And as now revealed, it is a fatally flawed way even of dealing with random variation. Nothing like this based on sampling theory and analysis of random variation can save ill-designed number scales applied to obscure concepts from the charge of pseudo-quantification. On the other hand, rejecting significance tests makes the use of numbers less problematic and so encourages their use in research (Gorard, 2006b). We should continue where possible to randomise our cases to treatment groups in trial designs, and to select samples at random in passive designs where population figures are not possible. We do this because it helps minimise systematic bias, not because it means we can then use significance tests and everything that stems from techniques predicated on random errors.

RETHINKING THE USE OF MEASUREMENT

If accepted, the argument here suggests that confusion between the measurement of observable events and the habit of assigning numbers to imagined events (including perceptions, attitudes, and intentions) has possible dangers. These dangers include the opportunity costs of conducting research with flawed techniques when the time, money, effort, and access to research sites could have been used to better effect. They include the vanishing breakthroughs that occur when insecure research knowledge is rolled out into policy or practice (Harlow et al., 1997). Perhaps almost as importantly, the possible dangers include the ethical and methodological distortion of new researchers by their mentors. Let the pendulum swing back a little towards scepticism about the easy allocation of numbers to things, and about the replacement of the basic pre-technical steps in creating a measurement by increasingly complex models and techniques. Let us think a little more (but a little less defensively) about the real process of measurement. Perhaps we can then help build the capacity to find and use appropriate measures in social science, that will be of genuine help to the societies we are ostensibly doing the research to benefit.

NOTES

1 A genuine measurement is not the same as the thing being measured. A person's height exists independently of any measuring scale. If the height did not exist then the measuring scale would be useless (or perhaps worse than useless). This is a key point for this chapter.

2 A measuring scale for a latent variable is inherently more problematic than for a simple measure like the number of people in a room. Both scales might be useful, and both might have problems, but the latter is the more likely to have serious problems, and the more likely in extreme to be so inaccurate as to be pseudo-quantification. I realise that there are a large number of latent measurement scales in popular use in social science. There is not the space here to discuss the validity of all of these scales individually. Nunnally (1975: 9) says

> ... the best general approach ... is to develop an instrument that correlates as highly as possible with a particular factor or intellect or personality. This requires that the items be homogeneous with respect to content ... Thus, a good item for a vocabulary test is one that correlates well with the total score ... methods of item analysis and test construction became clear: namely one should select those items that correlate well with the test as a whole and throw out those items that do not ...

This clear explanation from an expert in psychometrics lays bare the tautology involved in such purported measurements. The point about the spurious nature of this internal reliability is dealt with later in the chapter. Here, the key point for readers to note is that this passage only addresses the measure itself, and does not consider at all the correlation (isomorphism) between the measure and the thing it is supposedly measuring.

3 To clarify, it is the isomorphism (correlation) between the behaviour of the measuring scale and the thing being measured that allows proper quantification. If IQ scales work well for the purposes intended, perhaps by accurately predicting performance in school or occupation, then they are a true, but probably still problematic, measure. IQ here is intended to illustrate the broader principle being proposed, that a true measuring scale must measure something other than itself.

4 Ratio and interval measures do not have to be continuous in their scaling, as should be clear from the examples used thus far. It is not the theoretically continuous nature of underlying temperature that makes Centigrade an interval scale. In everyday terms, the number of people in a room is based on a measuring scale involving only whole units. The saltatory nature of the scale used does not mean that it is not a ratio scale. So-called nominal measures are quite different, as the example of sex should make clear. The ideas of ratio and interval make no sense with this example, largely because the points on the scale (such as male or female) are not really measures at all, as defined so far in the chapter. They are merely categories. It makes no sense to ask whether male is some ratio of female. The measures involved are the frequencies of cases in each category, not the categories themselves. And frequencies are clearly on a ratio scale, despite what most textbooks might claim.

5 This is not to suggest that an examination grade could not be given a numeric name. The point is that whether they are letters or numbers, such grades are neither ratio nor interval in nature. A grade 2 at GCE O level in the UK was in no real way twice as much of anything as a grade 1, and the difference both in frequency and exchange-value between a grade 1 and a 2 was not the same as between a 3 and a 4. The grades are categories rather than measures. The only measures they are based on are the underlying scores used to allocate the grades. To convert the scores into letter grades and then convert the grades into numbers and then use those numbers as though they were scores is a good illustration of the mess researchers get into, and widely accept, once the desire for quantification over-takes the principles of establishing a measure. Better by far to use the underlying scores (and what kind of measure these are is debatable, but not dealt with here). In the absence of these scores researchers must be careful when working with grades. They are not like the number of people in a room, since the underlying score for an individual with an A grade may be nearer to an individual with a B grade than two individuals with A grades are to each other. We can, however, use the frequencies of individuals in each grade category, or the probability of reaching a threshold grade, for example, as real numbers.

6 For a simple example, using an Excel spreadsheet, creates a large set of random numbers (perhaps 1 or 0) in one column. Treat this as the underlying theoretically 'true' answer sought by an instrument (of course, this is the essential knowledge we lack in practice and which makes latent measurement so much more dangerous than everyday measurement). Choose an overall 'accuracy' of response level such as 90 per cent, and create a second column identical to the first except that each number has a 10 per cent chance of randomly flipping from 0 to 1 or vice versa. Treat this as the response to the first item in the instrument. Create a third column from the first in the same way. Treat this as the response to the second item in the instrument. Both sets of 'responses' will be around 90 per cent accurate in isolation. What do we gain or lose by aggregating the two item responses? Try it. You will find, however, you resolve differences between items (does 0 followed by 1 count as half, for example?), that the combined result is less than 90 per cent accurate. The more items you add, the less accurate the aggregate result becomes.

7 An individual's views on cars might be more properly sought via in-depth conversation or, better yet, observation.

8 It is well-known that some numbers in denary (decimals) are irrational, like pi, and that others would take an infinite number of decimal places, like the ratio 1/3. Use of figures such as these in analysis (other than mathematics) involves putting up with a minor representational error in practice. The size and

therefore the impact of that error is best considered in relative terms, as a fraction of the number in which it is an error. We do not always know this relative error precisely, but we can estimate its upper bound (for example, in representing the number 1/3 as a 6 figure decimal fraction: 0.33333, the maiximum error would be bounded by 0.00001). It should also be well-known to all readers that both the absolute and relative representational errors in figures alter when the number base is altered. The unwieldy decimal of the ratio 1/3 is handled easily and with no error term in number base three (as 0.1), for example. The apparently simple decimal fraction 1/10 (or 0.1), on the other hand, cannot be represented accurately in one byte (8 binary digits). The closest we could achieve in binary would be 0.0001100 which is equivalent to 0.09375 in decimal, or 1/16 plus 1/32. We introduce an error of more than 6% simply by storing the decimal 0.1 on the computer! Extending the number of bits used to represent the decimal ratio 1/10 reduces the relative error but will never eliminate it (the absolute error in 8 bits is .00625 or 1/10 of 1/16 and so the sequence simply repeats *ad infinitum*). There are, by definition, an infinite number of such potential problems when using a computer or calculator, but they are systematic to the number bases involved. They are certainly not random, and cannot be dealt with by any technique predicated on them being random. Three further points should be stressed for readers who have not considered these elementary concerns for measurement before. First, the example of a never-ending binary number is used as an illustration. These kinds of representational errors can occur though with any value held in a limited number of bits (as all must be). Second, these representational errors are, of course, additional to errors of any kind in the measuring process itself. Third, the initial relative error in any measurement changes during analysis so that, on average, the relative error will increase half of the time on every single arithmetic step of a calculation. Yet analysts almost never check the behaviour of these systematic errors and their propagation, relying on the false assurance of rituals based on random sampling theory. The relative error can quite easily grow to such proportions that we say the analysis is 'ill-conditioned', meaning that the manifest result is terribly sensitive, and owes more to the error than to the substantive measurements involved (Gorard, 2001). It is very possible that whole areas of social science are based on such ill-conditioned models. The field of school effectiveness is one such candidate, in which assessment scores at two points in time are subtracted from each other to leave most of the 'gain' score susceptible to high relative error propagating from the inevitable errors in both sets of assessment scores. One 'analyst' – a top professor of school effectiveness no less – once remonstrated with me that school effectiveness cannot be so flawed since they had found one school in an area, which had had four successive years of positive value-added. If I tell readers that there were at least 16 schools in the area, that the 'effective' school had been identified *post hoc*, and that no other school in the area had the same four-year record, then I hope all of you can see why this claim is so ridiculous. If not, I point out that there was also one school with four successive years of negative scores, one with three negative followed by one positive, one with two negative followed by a positive and a negative, etc.

9 In quite simple everyday kinds of measurement that we might use in social science, even where completion of a questionnaire, for example, is compulsory by law, and where we have access to some way of judging, it is clear that we have high levels of missing data. According to official statistics in the UK the most prevalent cell in any analysis of the social class of students in higher education is 'unknown' (Gorard et al., 2007). In subsequently assessing the proportion of students in any social class, the measurement error introduced by this missing data (of the order of 30 per cent) must be added to any concerns we have about the class categories themselves (such as their timeliness or their equal appropriateness for all ages and sexes, and their threshold effect), and to any errors made by those 70 per cent of respondents who did answer, plus errors in entering or coding the responses, plus any representational errors (see above). I think it is fair to say that this relatively simple measure contains a very high proportion of measurement error. Of course, with psychometric data and similar it is not so easy to estimate the measurement error (one of the main points made in this chapter), but let us not allow this inevitable ignorance to fool us into working on the basis that the relative error will be any less than in the social class example.

REFERENCES

Anderson, T. and Zelditch, M. (1968) *A basic course in statistics, with sociological applications.* London: Holt, Rinehart and Winston.

Berka, K. (1983) *Measurement: Its concepts, theories and problems.* London: Reidel.

Carver, R. (1978) 'The case against statistical significance testing', *Harvard Educational Review*, 48: 378–99.

de Vaus, D. (2002) *Analyzing social science data: 50 key problems in data analysis.* London: Sage.

Erikson, R. and Goldthorpe, J. (2002) 'Intergenerational inequality: A sociological perspective', *Journal of Economic Perspectives*, 16(3): 31–44.

Falk, R. and Greenbaum. C. (1995) 'Significance tests die hard: The amazing persistence of a probabilistic misconception', *Theory and Psychology*, 5: 75–98.

Fielding, J. and Gilbert, N. (2000) *Understanding social statistics.* London: Sage.

Gorard, S. (2001) *Quantitative methods in educational research: The role of numbers made easy.* London: Continuum.

Gorard, S. (2002) 'The role of causal models in education as a social science', *Evaluation and Research in Education*, 16(1): 51–65.

Gorard, S. (2006a) 'Towards a judgement-based statistical analysis', *British Journal of Sociology of Education*, 27(1): 67–80.

Gorard, S. (2006b) *Using everyday numbers effectively in research*: Not *a book about statistics.* London: Continuum.

Gorard, S. (2008) 'Who is missing from higher education?', *Cambridge Journal of Education*, 38(3): 421–37.

Gorard, S. (2010) 'All evidence is equal: The flaw in statistical reasoning', *Oxford Review of Education*, (forthcoming).

Gorard, S. and See, BH. (2009) 'The impact of SES on participation and attainment in science', *Studies in Science Education*, (forthcoming).

Gorard, S., Prandy, K. and Roberts, K. (2002) *Introduction to the simple role of numbers*, Occasional Paper 53. Cardiff University School of Social Sciences.

Gorard, S., Rushforth, K. and Taylor, C. (2004a) 'Is there a shortage of quantitative work in education research?', *Oxford Review of Education*, 30(3): 371–95.

Gorard, S., Roberts, K. and Taylor, C. (2004b) 'What kind of creature is a design experiment?', *British Educational Research Journal*, 30(4): 575–90.

Gorard, S., with Adnett, N., May, H., Slack, K., Smith, E. and Thomas, L. (2007) *Overcoming barriers to HE.* Stoke-on-Trent: Trentham Books.

Harlow, L., Mulaik, S. and Steiger, J. (1997) *What if there were no significance tests?* Marwah, NJ: Lawrence Erlbaum.

Jeffreys, H. (1937) *Theory of probability.* Oxford: Oxford University Press.

Lambert, P. (2002) 'Handling occupational information', *Building Research Capacity*, 4: 9–12.

Nickerson, R. (2000) 'Null hypothesis significance testing: A review of an old and continuing controversy', *Psychological Methods*, 5(2): 241–301.

Nunnally. J. (1975) 'Psychometric theory 25 years ago and now', *Educational Researcher*, 4(7): 7–21.

Nuttall, D. (1987) 'The validity of assessments', *European Journal of Psychology of Education*, 11(2): 109–18.

Prandy, K. (2002) 'Measuring quantities: The qualitative foundation of quantity', *Building Research Capacity*, 2: 2–3.

Rose, D. (1996) 'Official social classifications in the UK', *Social Research Update*, 9: 1–6.

Rozeboom, W. (1960) 'The fallacy of the null hypothesis significance test', *Psychological Bulletin*, 57: 416–28.

Stevens, J. (1992) *Applied multivariate statistics for the social sciences.* London: Lawrence Erlbaum.

Wright, D. (2003) 'Making friends with your data: Improving how statistics are conducted and reported', *British Journal of Educational Psychology*, 73: 123–36.

21

Is Social Measurement Possible, and Is It Necessary?

Martyn Hammersley

To Lord Kelvin's famous remark that 'when you cannot measure it, when you cannot express it in numbers, your knowledge is of a meagre and unsatisfactory kind', the Princeton economist Jacob Viner is said to have quipped: 'When you *can* measure it, when you *can* express it in numbers, your knowledge is still of a meagre and unsatisfactory kind'

(Prewitt, cited in Merton et al., 1984: 330; emphasis added)[1]

There is a particularly pernicious form of Pythagoreanism, according to which the ostensively qualitative features of human life are squeezed insensitively, and without second thought, into a quantitative mould. ... There are many things in human life that may not be quantitative. They are no worse for that. If nonquantitative, they can be investigated in terms of their own 'categories' and such investigation is no less scientific than measurement. Quantitative structure is but one (important) kind amongst many and it holds no franchise over scientific method in its entirety.

(Michell, 1999: xiv)

The principle 'Let's get it down to something we can count!' does not always formulate the best research strategy; 'Let's see now, what have we here?' may point to a more promising program. Measurement, in short, is not an end in itself. Its scientific worth can be appreciated only ... [if] we ask what ends measurement is intended to serve, what role it is called upon to play in the scientific situation, what functions it performs in inquiry.

(Kaplan, 1964: 171)

Measurement of 'nature's capacities' is possible, and in many respects has been successfully accomplished (Cartwright, 1989; see also Duncan, 1984: Chapter 5). Furthermore, measurement has often been taken to be an essential feature of science, with the result that many social scientists have pursued rigorous measurement because they see it as required in order to produce scientific knowledge.[2] Symptomatic of this perspective is the influence of what Merton et al. (1984) refer to as 'the Kelvin dictum', which (at the instigation of William F. Ogburn) was inscribed on the new Social Science Research Building at the University of Chicago in 1929 (see Wirth, 1940).

The original, full quotation from Kelvin is as follows:

> In physical science a first essential step in the direction of learning any subject is to find principles of numerical reckoning and methods for practicably measuring some quality connected with it. I often say that when you can measure what you are speaking about, and express it in numbers, you know something about it; but when you cannot measure it, when you cannot express it in numbers, your knowledge is of a meagre and unsatisfactory kind: it may be the beginning of knowledge, but you have scarcely, in your thoughts, advanced to the stage of *science*, whatever that may be. (Sir William Thomson [later Lord Kelvin] 1889:73–4; cited in Merton et al., 1984)[3]

Despite the influence of this dictum, the argument that it is possible and necessary to measure social phenomena has been subject to considerable challenge, as the quotations at the head of this chapter indicate. Qualitative researchers, especially, usually deny the feasibility of, and the need for, measurement. Indeed, the defects of many forms of psychological and social measurement have long been one of the grounds used in challenging the claims and the value of quantitative work.[4]

While the problems surrounding measurement have often been acknowledged by quantitative researchers, they have usually been treated as technical in character; in other words as susceptible to remedy through further refinements in measurement technique (see, for example, Bulmer, 2001). By contrast, critics have often taken these problems to indicate the folly of the whole enterprise. And they have supported this conclusion by philosophical and methodological arguments of various kinds. They have insisted, for example, that human actions, unlike the behaviour of physical objects or even of animals, are constituted by meanings or reasons, and that by their very nature these are not susceptible to measurement. Quantitative researchers' attempts to measure them have been criticised, for instance, for assuming that people employ standard meanings (ones that are common across a population and stable over time) that can be understood independently of the local social contexts in which they arose. Qualitative researchers have also argued that measurement falsely assumes the operation of fixed patterns of causal relation; instead, they claim, social phenomena are by their very nature processual and contingent in character, and therefore not measurable. In more recent formulations, the argument has been that social phenomena are discursively constructed, and that the only feasible analytic task is to describe the discourse practices involved, or perhaps even to expose and challenge them. Indeed, attempts at social measurement have themselves sometimes been subjected to discourse analysis, this being designed to reveal how they construct the phenomena they purport to represent (see, for instance, Mulkay et al., 1987; Ashmore et al., 1989; Desrosières, 2001). So, the assumptions about the nature of social inquiry built into much qualitative research and much current social theory are at odds with any conception of social science that puts rigorous measurement at its core.[5]

At the same time, however, some commentators on qualitative research have argued that it cannot escape the need to measure the phenomena with which it deals (see Naroll, 1962, 1973; Moles, 1977; Denzin, 1978; Hammersley, 1986). In this spirit, it is often pointed out that, despite their frequent rejection of causal analysis in favour of interpretivism or constructionism, qualitative researchers nevertheless often aim at explaining outcomes of one kind or another in terms of the operation of various factors; so that, in practice, they are engaged in much the same task as any other kind of social scientist. Furthermore, while the sensitising concepts that qualitative inquiry usually employ are important in the development of new theoretical ideas, it may be impossible to subject competing knowledge claims to effective assessment without clarifying and developing key concepts into more definitive forms; and without relating these to instances in a rigorous fashion (see Hammersley, 1989). Moreover, many of the knowledge claims that qualitative researchers put forward are intrinsically quantitative in character: they refer (albeit usually in verbal terms) to frequency, duration, degree, or extent. In short, it has been concluded by some commentators that it is impossible to do qualitative research, or at least to do it well, without employing measurement processes of *some* kind.

In this chapter I want to examine several key issues involved in these arguments. To do so I will employ a broad interpretation of the nature of social measurement, considering some major obstacles it faces, as these relate to both qualitative and quantitative work. It seems to me that these obstacles are too often glossed over on both sides of the divide.[6] Furthermore, we need to remove the debate over measurement from the context of paradigm battles between competing social science approaches, in order to recognise and address problems that virtually all social scientists face.

In offering any answer to the questions posed in my title, much depends of course upon what we mean by the term 'measurement'; and, beyond this, on what we take the functions of measurement to be. These will be my first topics.

THE MEANING OF 'MEASUREMENT'

There are at least two quite different, but influential, definitions of 'measurement' within the methodological literature. First,

there is what is probably the most common approach, exemplified by specifying so-called *levels* of measurement (Stevens, 1946).[7] This is founded on Stevens' definition of 'measurement' as 'the assignment of numerals to objects or events according to rules' (p. 677). On his influential account, the assignment of instances to labelled categories constitutes the 'nominal level of measurement'. This is distinguished from ranking, and from two forms of metric measurement (interval and ratio scales).[8] The second, more restrictive, definition of the term 'measurement' denies this title to categorisation counts and even to rankings, insisting that measurement is always concerned with the *degree* to which phenomena possess some characteristic. From this point of view, at least an interval scale and preferably a ratio scale is required for scientific measurement to take place: 'if the sums do not add up, the science is wrong. If there are no sums to be added up, no one can tell whether the science is right or wrong. If there are no ratio-scale measurements, there can be no sums to add up' (Laming, 2002: 691; see also Johnson, 1936; Michell, 1999: 14).

There is another issue about what counts as measurement that is relevant here. This concerns the degree to which measurement must involve the use of explicit, standardised techniques – rather than reliance upon human judgement, whether that of researchers or informants. A central aspect of the development of at least some natural sciences has been the attempt to replace human judgement with mechanical or electronic forms of measurement, alongside efforts to extend the sources of evidence beyond human perceptual capabilities. On this model, many commentators would insist that measurement in the social sciences requires the use of explicit, standardised procedures that at least *minimise* the role of human judgement in producing evidence; in order to maximise the chances of valid measurement (Wilks, 1961: 5). As Wilks indicates, the model here is not just that of natural science but also that of modern, mass production methods. What is involved is a notion of procedural objectivity (Eisner, 1992), and sometimes this is taken to *ensure* validity. For example, Bovaird and Embretson (2008: 283) claim that:

> A measure is standardized if there are uniform procedures to ensure that the measure is administered and scored the same way each time it is used. If so, two individuals who receive the same score can be interpreted to possess the same amount of the attribute.

A more fundamental issue than how 'measurement' is to be defined concerns what the function is of the activities that are included under this heading, interpreted in the broadest sense to include categorisation. This is the next issue I will explore.[9]

THE FUNCTIONS OF CATEGORISATION AND MEASUREMENT

It is important to recognise that typologies and quantitative dimensions are implicit in much ordinary everyday talk. Categories are used to formulate events or persons, and the latter may also be described verbally in ways that place them on one or more dimensions, such as 'bigger/smaller', 'more/less well-known', 'more/less important', 'more/less intelligent', 'more/less frequent', and so on. So, it is not the case that category schemes and conceptual dimensions are alien notions imposed upon social life by quantitative researchers; they are already built into it. What such researchers seek to do, often, is to render everyday schemes and dimensions, and their application, more systematic and rigorous, *in particular ways*; in the belief

that this is essential for scientific work. So what is necessary is to assess how they do this, and whether what they attempt is possible and necessary.

One of the tasks that the work of classification and measurement addresses, and the one I will focus on here, is what we might call the evidential grounding of concepts; in other words, the task of linking them to evidence that will serve as grounds for allocating objects to categories, or to particular points on a scale, in terms of the relevant conceptual property. The implication of the term 'grounding' is not that concepts are generated out of pure thought, and therefore need to be linked to 'the empirical realm' on the ground. Generally speaking, the concepts that we employ in any research project will have come out of ordinary experience of the world and/or from the literature produced by previous research. We may also generate concepts, or identify which ones are relevant to the phenomena being investigated, through the process of abduction. The key point is, though, that in carrying out any investigation we will need to link the concepts we have selected and developed to evidence that will allow us to check the likely validity of the knowledge claims in which those concepts are embedded. In the case of classification, we will need to be able to identify relevant objects and place them in categories that map the property which the concept implies. With measurement, it is a matter of identifying relevant objects and then assigning them to an appropriate position on a scale that accurately represents the character of the property. So, 'grounding' is a functional category, it does not refer to an empirical as against a theoretical realm, but rather to providing grounds for knowledge claims.

Occasionally, concepts will relate directly to what can be used as evidence for classification or measurement. For example, two classic case studies in the sociology of education focused on the effects of streaming (tracking) in secondary schools, and the researchers had little problem in determining which students were in which stream, since class lists were available and these determined membership (Hargreaves, 1967; Lacey, 1970). However, such directly groundable concepts are rare. Usually, evidence has to be indirect. So, for example, the studies just mentioned investigated whether streaming generates a polarisation in secondary school students' orientations, in particular whether anti-school attitudes increase among those placed in lower streams. Given this task, they had to find some means of identifying positive and negative attitudes towards school. For this purpose they used a range of indications: what students said to one another about the school, about teachers, about school work etc; how they behaved in lessons; what they said in response to questions in interviews and written questionnaires about their attitudes towards school; their friendship choices; and their participation in after-school activities.[10]

In the discussion above I have avoided the usual phrasing – to the effect that concepts must be 'operationalised' – because this term is potentially misleading. It could be taken to imply that concepts can (and should) be *defined* in terms of standard measurement operations. While few quantitative researchers today would accept operationism in its full form, for example, treating intelligence as no more than 'what intelligence tests measure', there is a very strong tendency for them to assume that, alongside any conceptual definition, there must be an 'operational definition' in terms of a standard set of indicators, usually a measurement instrument of some kind.[11] However, we need to distinguish clearly between the property being measured and

any dimension this implies, a scale that would represent it, and any particular instrument that could be employed to locate objects at points on this scale in terms of amounts of the property. One problem with the notion of operationalisation is that it tends to obscure these distinctions. Indeed, it is perhaps a legacy of operationism that it is very common, in the social and psychological sciences, for scales and measurement instruments to be conflated with one another, and also for them to be treated as effectively defining the property they are intended to measure.[12] By contrast, in physical measurement the distinctions are usually retained. For instance, mercury thermometers can be used to measure both degrees Fahrenheit and degrees Celsius, and there are other kinds of thermometer that can be used to measure on each of these scales. Moreover, heat as a dimensional property is conceptualised independently of both scales and measurement instruments. The key point is that how we think about any property we are investigating, how we devise a categorical scheme or scale to represent it, and how we assign objects to their appropriate category or place on the scale are three quite different undertakings, even though the judgments we make in relation to each will affect the others.

The conflation of these three aspects of the process of grounding concepts in evidence is closely associated with, and reinforces, the tendency to assume that classification or measurement must, in the name of rigour, be carried out through the use of standard operations – explicit procedures that everyone can apply in the same way. Thus, in much quantitative research, measurement procedures have taken the form of closely specified, standard routines that a researcher must adhere to, on the grounds that this will increase measurement reliability (in the sense of consistency across observers and occasions).[13] However, while using standardised techniques may sometimes be possible and desirable in social science, there are good reasons to believe that it may not always be either. More importantly, to assume that it is essential is to mistake a means for the function it performs. There is no intrinsic requirement that the grounding of concepts in any particular study be achieved via standardised operations. While each object must be classified or measured in terms of the same concept definition, the indications we use to assign objects are not part of the concept and can legitimately differ when dealing with different objects. Furthermore, there is no reason to assume that such variation in measurement practice would increase the likelihood of error, though it might well increase the risk of inconsistency between observers.

So, the use of a standard set of indicators, or of a measurement instrument, is simply one strategy that can be employed to classify or measure; furthermore, standardisation is not necessarily very effective in improving the validity of any attempt to ground concepts. There are at least three reasons why quantitative researchers often believe that standard operations or measuring instruments are required, and these need to be distinguished. First, there is the idea that by adopting a standard procedure the grounding process will be made more objective, in the sense that it will eliminate the effects of subjective or idiosyncratic factors on the part of the researcher and others. A second argument is that standard operations are necessary where more than one person is going to collect the data, so as to try to ensure that the same data will be collected irrespective of which researcher is involved. For example, it is argued that this is important in survey interviews as a prerequisite for assuming that any differences in responses

to questions are not a product of variation in the behaviour of interviewers. The third argument is that a specification of standard operations or procedures is essential if it is to be possible for the research to be replicated, so as to check that the results were not a product of extraneous factors, including those emanating from the subjective characteristics of the researcher.

These arguments are not as compelling as they are often taken to be. The first, and most fundamental, one focuses on how the subjectivity of both researchers and respondents/informants can threaten validity. However, this overlooks the fact that the influence of subjective factors can never be entirely eliminated, and that distinctive capabilities on the part of researchers (and informants) may be essential for producing the knowledge required. In most of its forms, in the physical as well as the social sciences, measurement involves some observational judgement; even if it is only looking at a dial to read off the figures, or making a decision about into which category a respondent's answer falls.[14] Indeed, even where data are produced entirely electronically, researchers must draw inferences from them; and this is never just a matter of deductive logic or of mathematical inference. While some older models of the research process drew a very sharp boundary between theory and data, most recent philosophical views recognise that this is at most a functional distinction; which implies that judgement and interpretation are always likely to infuse what are treated as data. So, avoiding human judgement is impossible; the key issue is how to improve the validity of the particular sorts of judgement employed.[15]

There is a fundamental fallacy that lies beneath the idea that grounding concepts must involve the use of standard operations. This is the false contrast that is sometimes drawn between procedures and judgements, with the former being treated as objective (or, at least, as potentially objective) the latter while/is viewed as inevitably subjective, in other words as necessarily leading to error. Part of the problem here is that the term 'subjective' can have different meanings, and that these carry discrepant implications for the task of grounding concepts. 'Subjective' is often taken to refer to what goes on inside people's heads, rather than what occurs 'on the outside' in their behaviour. So, judgements are often treated as, by their very nature, private rather than public, and therefore as not open to checking by others. And, from this, the leap is frequently made to the conclusion that judgements are idiosyncratic, in the sense of reflecting the characteristics of the person rather than accurately representing what is being judged.[16] But this line of thought is defective. Much twentieth-century, analytic philosophy was concerned with disabusing us of the misconception that statements about subjective matters are simply expressions of inner experience. It has been pointed out that when we talk about such things, even to our-selves, we are using publicly available language and cultural conventions to do so. From this point of view, judgements, like other subjective phenomena, are not inscrutable, private experiences that cannot be evaluated, and which therefore must be simply accepted or rejected. Nor are they necessarily idiosyncratic, and neither does idiosyncrasy, necessarily imply inaccuracy. Of course, it is true that they *can* be inaccurate, and that we may need to employ means to improve or check them. But this is no reason always to avoid or minimise them; nor is there any alternative that can *ensure* accuracy.[17]

Not only is relying entirely upon pro-cedure impossible, since some element of judgement will almost always remain, but attempting to do this will often be counterproductive. This is because reliance on procedures prevents us from using our observational and interpretative skills, and our relevant background knowledge, in drawing inferences about the nature of the phenomena with which we are dealing. While guidelines may be useful, these frequently operate best as an aid to judgement, for example, in reminding us what may need to be taken into account, what could indicate what, and so on. However, to try to turn such guidelines into standardised decision rules that substitute for judgement will often increase rather than reduce error. For example, in observing and recording what actions are taking place in some situation we must have the capacity to 'read' the behaviour involved, and the environment to which it is attuned. Very often, in part, this is a matter of understanding the language that people are using to communicate with one another. But this is not just a matter of knowing the vocabulary and grammar of that language, we also need to have pragmatic competence in it, in order to grasp what it is being used to do on any particular occasion. And this is closely involved with understanding people's intentions, their likely reasons for doing what they are doing, the motives that might lead them to react in the way that they do to others' actions, and so on. Where we are observing a scene that is already familiar to us, we probably already have these capabilities; it is usually only when we are a stranger that the need for them becomes obvious. Here, in order to be able even to describe what is going on, at least in terms that will allow us to develop and assess social science explanations, we need to 'learn the culture' of the people involved.[18]

Attempts to avoid bias coming from the subjectivity of the people being studied face similar problems. It is claimed that standardisation increases the chances that responses from experimental subjects or survey respondents are comparable because each has been presented with more or less the same stimulus. However, this argument is based on some highly questionable (in effect, behaviourist) assumptions concerning human communication. We must ask: Can it be assumed that standardisation of physical stimuli, for example, in the form of printed items on a questionnaire, ensures that people's responses are equivalent? The answer to this is almost certainly 'no'. The idea implicit in this assumption is that people respond to stimuli on the basis of at least an approximation to an algorithmic and universal model: in terms of which the verbal elements of the stimulus are translated via rules, plus use of a semantic dictionary and perhaps also a factual encyclopaedia, into a standard meaning. However, there is a great deal of work in linguistics, philosophy, and the social sciences which makes clear that human communication does not operate in this fashion, that it is a more complex and indeterminate process: it involves mutual adaptation and negotiation of meaning in order to coordinate actions.[19] Thus, in interpreting questions in an interview, or items on a questionnaire, respondents will attribute intentions and motives to the researcher, these attributions will shape their answers, and people may differ in how they do this in ways that are unrelated to the variable being measured.[20] There is also the problem that, in practice, it is never possible entirely to standardise the circumstances in which people respond to tests, answer questions in interviews, and so on. For instance, they may complete postal or online questionnaires in a variety of contexts (in their lunch break at work, lying in bed on a Sunday morning, alone or with other people, etc), and these could affect their responses. Nor is it clear that there is a positive, linear relationship between

degrees of standardisation and degrees of validity; and, in the absence of this, approximations to standardisation cannot be treated as facilitating increased validity even 'other things being equal'.

For all these reasons, it is doubtful that standardisation of data collection processes can be relied upon to minimise the effects of extraneous factors. More than this, such standardisation, as well as efforts to render consistent how observers or interviewers code responses, may lead to systematic error. In other words, consistency may be attained at the cost of accuracy. For instance, in using standardised interviews to elicit responses that are taken to indicate pro- or anti-school attitudes among students it would not be unreasonable, in principle, for the coding rules to treat any response which is negative towards teachers as signifying an anti-school attitude. However, background information could tell us that students who are highly committed to educational achievement may have negative attitudes towards at least some teachers, and that what students say and do varies considerably across contexts (see Fuller, 1980; Hammersley and Turner, 1980). In the construction of attitude-measuring instruments problems of this kind are sometimes recognised, and attempts made to control for the error involved by comparing response patterns across several items intended to measure the same property.[21] But there are two potential problems here. The first is how to separate out consistency across responses produced by systematic error from that generated by the property being measured. The second arises from the fact that relying upon a questionnaire represents a very narrow range of indicators for the property. As indicated earlier, there is a diversity of indications that could be used for assessing students' attitudes towards school. However, what is frequently found when very different kinds of indicator are used to measure the same property is that there is limited correspondence among the results.[22] What this usually tells us is that much work remains to be done in clarifying the property concept that is being grounded, and in developing effective means for grounding it. And the key point is that achieving improved grounding depends upon conceptual and empirical work: we must *discover* how best to ground our concepts.

The other two arguments often used to support the idea that reliance upon standardised measurement procedures is essential can be dealt with much more briefly. The second, about the need for consistency in survey research, draws on the same assumptions as the first argument. Furthermore, it relates to only one, albeit important, kind of research: that where multiple interviewers or observers are employed. In this sense it is a pragmatic matter, rather than relating to the essential character of measurement. As regards the third argument, it should be noted that replication is simply one means by which to assess the likely validity of the findings of a study, and it can only be used where the research process can be repeated in more or less the same way. There is no reason to argue that because replication is a useful strategy all research should be designed so as to facilitate it. This would be to allow the tail to wag the dog.

So, it must not be assumed that, in seeking to ground concepts in evidence, it is essential to employ some standardised procedure or instrument, or that doing this will necessarily increase the accuracy of the results produced. Indeed, for the reasons I have suggested, it may introduce systematic error. In the next section I want to examine a rather different issue, but one that also raises serious questions about the usual approach taken to the task of measurement, as well as about some treatments of categorisation.

CLASSICAL AND FUZZY CATEGORIES

Categorisation or classification is a key analytic strategy in its own right (see Becker, 1940; McKinney, 1954, 1966, 1970; Tiryakian, 1968; Lofland, 1971: 13–58; Bailey, 1994). It is also fundamental to all measurement, in that we are always measuring a property that belongs to the members of some *type* of phenomenon. The key point I want to make here is that it is often assumed, explicitly or implicitly, that a fundamental requirement of scientific categorisation is that it takes a classical or Aristotelian form. This requires that the categories belong to an explicit system, with each being defined in terms of a set of essential features, preferably ones that can serve as criteria for identifying members of the category.

However, there are some good reasons to believe that the categories used in social science not only often do not correspond to the classical model, but perhaps also cannot do so. First, it is important to note that considerable empirical work is often required in order to develop a categorical scheme that can represent variation in the phenomena being studied. Initially, in abducting categories – for example, in the manner recommended by Glaser and Strauss (1967; see also Strauss and Corbin, 1998) as part of grounded theorising – the aim cannot and should not be to produce a set of categories that are mutually exclusive and exhaustive. This would obstruct the creative process involved. Any form of more systematic, classical categorisation must represent a further step beyond the initial more flexible, overlapping categories generated in the process of abduction. This is because we often need to *discover* what are fruitful categories. Our concepts should not always be taken over automatically from commonsense classifications or from existing theories. What this indicates is that an important part of the research process can be to find good questions to ask about the topic of interest, and perhaps even the best way to characterise the topic itself. There is a tendency in much discussion of categorisation and measurement to overlook the need for this process of development: to treat clearly formulated research questions and their associated categories as the *starting point*, rather than as an important product of the inquiry process. What is overlooked here is that reformulation of the initial research question, and development and refinement of the categories being used, may sometimes need to continue throughout data collection and well into data analysis within particular studies.

Beyond this, though, there are also a couple of reasons why achieving category systems that have the classical form may actually be impossible in social science. The first relates closely to the discussion in the previous section. It stems from the fact that the categories involved in scientific work include not simply those that are key concepts in the arguments developed by researchers but also those that are embedded in any evidence used to generate, and to assess the likely validity of, those arguments. There is a common view which portrays science as founded upon transparent procedures 'all the way down'. But it has been pointed out that scientists rely upon 'knowledge how' not just on 'knowledge that'; in other words, they place tacit reliance on capabilities that necessarily operate outside the immediate focus of attention, and in some cases beyond the realm of consciousness altogether.[23] Moreover, these capabilities or skills cannot be fully explicated in propositional terms. They are matters of practical competence that humans have developed in their ordinary engagement with the world, and there may also be specialised capabilities that

researchers have developed. It is certainly true that, as I noted earlier, there has been much effort on the part of natural scientists to make explicit the procedures they use, and even to develop various kinds of electronic apparatus that replace some of the human practices previously involved. However, these can never be replaced completely, and in the context of social science there is even less scope for reducing the role of human judgement.

But the key point here is that the categories involved in these practical capabilities on which researchers rely do not seem to take the classic Aristotelian form. In other words, they do not usually operate via a set of necessary and sufficient conditions that govern their usage. Instead, cultural categories generally seem to operate on the basis of family resemblances, with people using prototypes or exemplars as a basis for determining what counts and does not count as an instance (Rosch, 1999; see also Taylor, 2001, 2003).[24] Furthermore, the meaning of any cultural category is usually context-sensitive: what it includes, and does not include, depends upon the context in which it is being used, including the purposes it is serving. Not only will people interpret the same category in somewhat different ways according to circumstances, but also what level of clarity is required may vary in the same way.

So, a first problem facing attempts to produce classically rigorous classifications stems from the fact that, at some level, social research will always depend upon social scientists' ordinary cultural capabilities; that it may not be possible to explicate these fully in propositional terms; and that these practices depend upon flexible, context-sensitive categorisation.

The character of people's everyday categorisations has consequences for social science in a second way too. This arises to the extent that, in order to describe and explain their behaviour, we need to include in our accounts some representation of the categories that underlie people's discriminations among situations, differentiation across types of other people, identification of strategies available for use, and so on. And this is surely unavoidable in social science.[25] The crucial point is that, if everyday categories have a flexible, fuzzy, context-sensitive character, then we should not pretend that they can be incorporated into analytic categories that have an Aristotelian form: to do so would be to introduce distortion. This suggests that, for this reason too, we may have to work with analytic categories that are themselves based more on family resemblances, and perhaps also rely on the use of prototypes or exemplars (rather than criteria specifying necessary and sufficient conditions) to identify instances. In addition, we will need to find a way of taking into account the contextual sensitivity of the categories that the people we are studying use.

These two problems are of significance not only for quantitative researchers' attempts to measure social phenomena, but also for any attempt by qualitative researchers to engage in the kind of rigorous classification recommended by writers like McKinney, Tiryakian, and Bailey (McKinney, 1954, 1966, 1970; Tiryakian, 1968; Bailey, 1994). And they represent major obstacles. However, a caveat is in order here. While it is unlikely that we can avoid reliance upon everyday competences – replacing these with formal, fully explicit, classical categorisation procedures – there may well be a need for researchers to exercise these practical competences in ways that are more careful, reflective, and explicit than is frequently the case in everyday life; specifically in order to try to achieve research goals. We should note that reflective deliberation about how categories should be defined and interpreted, and

collective discussion designed to bring interpretations into closer agreement, occur in several other areas of human activity; notably those where much hinges on the decisions that result. Examples include legal definition of offences and medical diagnosis of illness. So, the fact that we must rely upon practical cultural capabilities that involve fuzzy categories does not mean that we should simply accept the practical categorisations built into everyday usage as they stand: these can be refined for particular purposes, even if we will never be able fully to explicate them, or to turn them into classically defined, 'transparent' forms. Indeed, not only is such refinement possible it will often be essential. For example, many years ago Lofland rightly criticised what he labelled as a tendency towards 'analytic interruptus' among qualitative researchers: the use of categories that had not been properly specified through the systematic development of typologies (Lofland, 1970, 1971: Chapter 2; see also Bendix, 1963, Hammersley and Atkinson, 2007: Chapter 8 especially pp. 172–5). And his criticism continues to apply to much qualitative work today.

So, we need not treat the fuzzy nature of our categories as an insurmountable barrier to social science, nor perhaps even to social measurement. At the same time, we must recognise the serious problems that this causes for current classification and measurement strategies. Furthermore, considerable work may be necessary in order to clarify categories and develop ways of identifying instances of them in effective ways.

MEASUREMENT BY FIAT?

The problems surrounding categorisation I have just discussed parallel some that relate more specifically to the task of measurement, defined in the narrow sense as involving interval and ratio scales. A key problem here concerns whether the object-properties to be measured have the character that is demanded by metric measurement; in other words, whether they have a quantitative structure. This is a point that is obscured by Stevens' definition of 'measurement', in which reference to capturing the nature of some property is omitted. Michell has argued that in the field of psychology, where attempts at measurement of human behaviour have been most highly developed, there has been a failure to investigate this fundamental issue (Michell, 1997, 1999, 2000, 2002). He claims that it has been simply *assumed* that the properties to be measured are at least ordinal in character, and that the methods used to gauge them effectively generate an interval scale. He describes this as a scandal (Michell, 2002: 103). In effect, what he is identifying here is what, many years ago in the field of sociology, Cicourel labelled 'measurement-by-fiat' (Cicourel, 1964: 12); in other words, measurement that fails to ensure that the assumptions built into the measurement procedure correspond to the structure of the phenomena being measured.[26] As these writers have pointed out, an instrumentalist attitude, according to which all that matters is whether the use of a measurement procedure generates 'significant' findings, is inadequate (see Michell, 1999: 21). In social science any differences discovered are generally probabilistic and small, and there are many sources of error, within measurement procedures and elsewhere, which could generate spurious findings, including stable ones across several studies.

Any adequate classification or measurement depends upon a sound understanding of the phenomenon being classified or measured, and of the processes involved in any indirect indicators that are being relied upon. Duncan sums up the point with an example from physical measurement:

> I hope it is clear that most of the story of temperature measurement has to do with experimental determination of the quantitative laws of expansion of substances and with the deepening of the theoretical understanding of heat and thermodynamics, as well as learning how to construct reliable and sturdy instruments. There is not really much to be learned from the concomitant contentions about how to assign numbers to objects ..., except that the strictly numerical part is quite secondary. The Kelvin scale is a scientific achievement of the first order, not merely because it provides a scale with mathematically powerful properties, but because it incorporates a profound understanding of how a certain class of phenomena works. (Duncan, 1984: 149)

So, the argument is that we need to develop our understanding of the concepts we are employing, and that this is part and parcel of improving our knowledge of the phenomena to which they refer. Similarly we must develop our understanding of the social processes underlying the indicators we use.[27] It is hardly a secret that there are fundamental uncertainties about many of the concepts that are central to social science (see Sartori et al., 1975; Sartori, 1984; Walker, 1995; Williams, 2001). Furthermore, there is no reason to suppose that all these analytic categories will be open to metric measurement – and even some of the categories that are amenable to this, in principle, will not be open to it in practice at any particular time, given the limited capabilities and resources available to us. This may, of course, indicate that the research problem being addressed is simply not tractable, at least at present. However, alternatively, it may mean that we must rely upon ranking or categorisation instead of measurement in the narrow sense. I am not suggesting that whatever strategy is available to us should be treated as sufficient; very often it will not be. Rather, I am arguing that no research strategy ought to be ruled out simply on the grounds that it does not conform to some preconceived model of science, or because it does not allow mathematical inference of kinds thought desirable.[28] The key issue is whether it can help us provide an adequate answer to the research question(s) we are addressing.

Furthermore, there will often be a great deal of conceptual work, and basic exploration of the phenomena being studied, that must be done before any process of analytic classification or measurement can be developed very far. Nor will the need for this necessarily stop once attempts at classification or measurement begin. In short, we require a much more thoughtful approach to the grounding of concepts than is currently common in much quantitative and qualitative research.

CONCLUSION

In this chapter I have tried to clarify the nature of the task that classification and measurement are designed to address. My aim has been to make clear that we must assess any attempts to categorise or measure phenomena in the context of how far these enable us to answer worthwhile research questions, rather than in terms of prior views about the form that categorisation and measurement *ought to* take. I have also identified some serious problems that these tasks involve; problems which arise, in large part, from what seems to be the nature of social phenomena, and in particular from the character of human social action.

Are we to conclude that these problems make social measurement impossible? I think it would be foolish to draw this conclusion. Whether or not some body of evidence provides adequate support for the answer offered to a particular research question will depend upon the nature of the question, the sorts of evidence that are available, what is taken to be the appropriate level of adequacy, and so on. It is as dangerous to generalise about what is impossible as it is automatically to assume that something *is* possible. Furthermore, it is necessary to adopt a pragmatic attitude towards social research, to recognise that what is possible cannot be determined on the basis of philosophical or statistical argument alone. To a large degree, we must *find out* what is and is not possible. And this, in turn, depends upon our current capabilities and resources, which may develop over time.

Equally, though, we must make robust evaluations of our attempts at classification and measurement. It is essential to recognise that adopting a pragmatic approach does not mean treating whatever we find we *can* do as *good enough*, as if what is possible determines what is necessary. Furthermore, in my view most current social science is weak in this respect. The problems discussed in this chapter represent major challenges; and – as Cicourel, Michell, Duncan, and others have pointed out – there has been a longstanding and common tendency to turn a blind eye to them, in the hope that they will go away. What is required instead is, first of all, sober recognition of the limits on what it is possible for social science currently to achieve, and an avoidance of excessive claims about the validity of the findings produced. In my view such excess is not uncommon in both quantitative and qualitative studies. A second requirement is to pay more careful attention to the methodological problems we face. We need to understand their nature more clearly, to recognise their implications for what we can and cannot do, and to find ways of dealing with them that enable us to produce better quality knowledge about the social world. Ignoring these problems is not a rational option on either side of the methodological divide.

NOTES

1 Viner's comment occurred in a Round Table discussion on quantification, see Wirth, 1940: 177.

2 On the history of measurement see, for example, Woolf (1961) and Robinson (2007). For the history of *social* measurement see Duncan (1984), who rightly points out that there is a sense in which 'all measurement is social' (p. 35). See Michell (2007) for a critical history of social measurement theory. For an account of the 'theory and practice' of measurement across both the natural and the social sciences, see Hand (2004); while Viswanathan (2005) provides a recent discussion of measurement in the context of social science. For an earlier discussion focusing on non-random error, see Zeller and Carmines (1980). Kempf-Leonard (2004) has edited an encyclopaedia that includes entries on many aspects of social measurement.

3 The paper by Merton et al. recounts their efforts to discover the original form of 'Kelvin's dictum'. Interestingly, this had already been identified by Kaplan (1964: 172).

4 For an early example see Phillips (1971: chapter 2 and *passim*).

5 A glance at the *Handbook of Qualitative Research* (Denzin and Lincoln, 2005) will provide confirmation of this statement. Earlier in his career Denzin treated measurement as an essential part of social research (see Denzin, 1970).

6 For a recent discussion of measurement theory that, like many others, effectively takes most of the issues discussed in this chapter for granted see Bovaird and Embretson, 2008.

7 Kaplan (1964: Chapter 5) and others have put forward more elaborate outlines of measurement levels.

8 Producing a scale for temperature with an absolute zero, in other words a ratio scale, was of course one of Lord Kelvin's great scientific achievements. For discussions of Stevens' work on scales see Newman (1974) and Matheson (2006). While his approach has been extremely influential, within psychology and beyond, it has been subjected to considerable criticism (see, for example, Duncan, 1984: Chapter 4; Velleman and Wilkinson, 1993; Michell, 1997, 1999, 2000, 2002).

9 For a discussion of the functions of measurement in the physical sciences (see Kuhn, 1961; see also Duncan, 1984: Chapter 5).

10 While principally qualitative in character, these studies also used some quantitative measures, and in this respect can be categorised as early examples of mixed methods research. On the whole programme of research to which they belong see Hammersley, 1985.

11 The term 'definition' can, of course, mean different things (see Robinson, 1954). There is also some dispute about what the term 'operational definition' meant for early operationists (see Hardcastle, 1995; Feest, 2005).

12 See, for instance, the discussion in Mueller (2004).

13 While now entrenched in usage, it seems to me that this definition of 'reliability' as 'consistency' is ideological, in the sense that it trades on the commonsense connotation of 'can be relied upon', while meaning something quite different. Furthermore, as Zeller and Carmines (1980: Chapter 1) note, consistency is only desirable in the absence of systematic error.

14 Though it is often more than this. It is important to remember that the use of any physical measurement device is located within some form of social practice, without which measurement could not take place. For example, in taking a person's temperature a thermometer must be applied to the right part of the body (in the mouth, under the arm, etc) and in a context where the person's temperature is not likely to be 'artificially' raised or lowered, not to mention the fact that the thermometer must be read correctly. In short, measuring instruments are tools, and all tool use is dependent upon social practices that involve common understandings and the negotiation of contingent situations. Furthermore, as the case of medicine indicates, evidence from standardised instruments often needs to be combined with that from non-standardised sources.

15 See Campbell's arguments that 'qualitative knowing' always underpins 'quantitative knowing' (Campbell ,1988a, b). He writes: 'Qualitative, commonsense knowing of wholes and patterns provides the enveloping context necessary for the interpretation of particulate quantitative data' (1988a: 365). Also relevant in this context is Daston and Garrison's (2007) discussion of different notions of objectivity in physical science, and of the 'somersault' history of the meaning of the term (pp. 29–35).

16 One source of this tendency is the arguments of Bacon and others to the effect that science should rely upon the abilities of ordinary human beings, not on specialised knowledge and skills, in the way that was true of humanistic scholarship in the Renaissance (see Gaukroger, 2001: 127 and *passim*). Gaukroger notes the parallel between Bacon's conception of the collective work of scientists and the demand made on Jesuits that they carry out instructions 'as if they were but corpses' (p. 128). It is perhaps from this context that the notion of scientific 'rigour' gets its sense!

17 Newell (1986) covers this, and much other relevant, philosophical ground.

18 This is, of course, the longstanding argument about the need for Verstehen in social research

(Becker, 1950: Chapter 4; Truzzi, 1974; O'Hear, 1996).

19 See, for example, Grice (1991) and Sperber and Wilson (1986). There has been increasing recognition of this problem, if not usually of its depth, in the literature on survey research (see, for example, Johnson et al., 1997), though much actual social research practice ignores it.

20 All human answering relies upon such attributions, as Schegloff (1971) illustrated many years ago in a study of the apparently simple matter of giving strangers directions.

21 Though Heath and Martin (1997) suggest that, in fact, this is rarely done in social measurement.

22 The classic example is LaPiere's study of prejudice and discrimination against minority ethnic groups (LaPiere, 1934; see also Deutscher, 1973).

23 For a classic argument along these lines, see Polanyi (1959, 1966).

24 An alternative terminology here, drawn from biology, is the distinction between monothetic/monotypic (corresponding to what I have called classic or Aristotelian) and polythetic/polytypic categories (see Bailey, 1994: 7–8, Beckner, 1959: Chapter 2). This idea was applied in anthropology by Needham (1975). Also bearing on this issue, there has been considerable discussion within the philosophical literature about the nature of vagueness; on which see, for example, Williamson (1994). Equally relevant is Kuhn's (1970, 1977) discussion of the role of exemplars in science and Elgin's (1996: Chapter 6) discussion of 'exemplification' in cognition more generally.

25 One interpretation of the implications of this for measurement, somewhat at odds with my argument in this chapter, is Cicourel (1964).

26 Cicourel borrowed this term from Torgerson (1958: 21–2). Duncan (1984: 144 and *passim*) takes a rather similar view to Michel in his evaluation of much social measurement. His doubts about the idea of a 'correlational science of inexact constructs', and his denunciations of 'statisticism' (pp. 226–33), remain as pertinent today as they were 25 years ago.

27 Closely associated with this is a need to ensure that the meanings of those terms which are integral to the evaluation of classifications and measurements, such as validity and reliability, are soundly based and clear. I do not believe this currently to be the case (see Hammersley, 1987, 1991).

28 The range of available statistical techniques has, of course, increased considerably since Stevens first identified differences in the kind of statistical analysis each level of measurement allows. In particular, there has been considerable development in the analysis of categorical data. However, this generally requires categorisation on what I have called the 'classical' model. For attempts to address this through notions of fuzzy sets and family resemblance relations see Ragin (2000) and Goertz (2006).

REFERENCES

Ashmore, M., Mulkay, M. and Pinch, T. (1989) *Health and Efficiency: A Sociology of Health Economics*. Milton Keynes: Open University Press.

Bailey, K. D. (1994) *Typologies and Taxonomies: An Introduction to Classification Techniques*. Thousand Oaks CA: Sage.

Becker, H. P. (1940) 'Constructive typology in the social sciences', in H. E.Barnes, H. Becker and F. B. Becker (eds) *Contemporary Social Theory*. New York: Russell and Russell.

Becker, H. P. (1950) *Through Values to Social Interpretation*. Durham NC: Duke University Press.

Beckner, M. (1959) *The Biological Way of Thought*. New York: Columbia University Press.

Bendix, R. (1963) 'Concepts and generalizations in comparative sociological studies', *American Sociological Review*, 28(4): 532–9.

Bovaird, J. A. and Embretson, S. E. (2008) 'Modern measurement in the social sciences', in P. Alasuutari, L. Bickman and J. Brannen (eds) *The Sage Handbook of Social Research Methods*. London: Sage.

Bulmer, M. (2001) 'Social measurement: what stands in its way?', *Social Research*, 68(2): 455–80.

Campbell, D. T. (1988a) 'Qualitative knowing in action research', in E. S. Overman (ed.) *Methodology and Epistemology for Social Science: Selected Papers by Donald T. Campbell*. Chicago: University of Chicago Press.

Campbell, D. T. (1988b) ' "Degrees of freedom" and the case study', in E. S. Overman (ed.) *Methodology and Epistemology for Social Science: Selected papers by Donald T. Campbell*. Chicago: University of Chicago Press.

Cartwright, N. (1989) *Nature's Capacities and Their Measurement*. Oxford: Oxford University Press.

Cicourel, A. V. (1964) *Method and Measurement in Sociology*. New York: Free Press.

Daston, L. and Garrison, P. (2007) *Objectivity*. New York: Zone Books.

Denzin, N. K. (1970) *The Research Act*. Chicago: Aldine.

Denzin, N. K. (1978) *The Research Act, Second edition*. New York: McGraw-Hill.

Denzin, N. K. and Lincoln, Y. S. (eds) (2005) *Handbook of Qualitative Research, Third edition*. Thousand Oaks CA: Sage.

Desrosières, A. (2001) 'How real are statistics? Four possible attitudes', *Social Research*, 68(2): 339–55.

Deutscher, I. (1973) *What We Say/What We Do: Sentiments & Acts*. Glenview, Ill.: Scott, Foresman.

Duncan, O. D. (1984) *Notes on Social Measurement: Historical and Critical*. New York: Russell Sage Foundation.

Eisner, E. (1992) 'Objectivity in educational research', *Curriculum Inquiry*, 22(1): 157–71.

Elgin, C. (1996) *Considered Judgment*. Princeton NJ: Princeton University Press.

Feest, U. (2005) 'Operationism in psychology: What the debate is about, what the debate should be about', *Journal of the History of the Behavioral Sciences*, 41(2): 131–49.

Fuller, M. (1980) 'Black Girls in a London Comprehensive School', in R. Deem (ed.) *Schooling for Women's Work*. London: Routledge and Kegan Paul.

Gaukroger, S. (2001) *Francis Bacon and the Trans- formation of Early-Modern Philosophy*. Cambridge: Cambridge University Press.

Glaser, B. G. and Strauss, A. L. (1967) *The Discovery of Grounded Theory*. Chicago: Aldine.

Goertz, G. (2006) *Social Science Concepts: A User's Guide*. Princeton NJ: Princeton University Press.

Grice, P. (1991) *Studies in the Way of Words*. Cambridge MS: Harvard University Press.

Hammersley, M. (1985) 'From ethnography to theory: A programme and paradigm for case study research in the sociology of education', *Sociology*, 19(2): 244–59.

Hammersley, M. (1986) 'Measurement in ethnogra- phy: The case of Pollard on teaching style', in M. Hammersley (ed.) *Controversies in Classroom Research*. Milton Keynes: Open University Press.

Hammersley, M. (1987) 'Some notes on the terms "validity" and "reliability"', *British Educational Research Journal*, 13(1): 73–81.

Hammersley, M. (1989) 'The problem of the concept: Herbert Blumer on the relationship between concepts and data', *Journal of Contemporary Ethnography*, 18(2): 133–59.

Hammersley, M. (1991) 'A note on Campbell's distinction between internal and external validity', *Quantity and Quality*, 25(4): 381–7.

Hammersley, M. and Atkinson, P. (2007) *Ethnogra- phy: Principles in Practice, Third edition*. London: Routledge.

Hammersley, M. and Turner, G. (1980) 'Conformist pupils?' in P. Woods (ed.) *Pupil Strategies*. London: Croom Helm.

Hand, D. J. (2004) *Measurement Theory and Practice: The World through Quantification*. London: Arnold.

Hardcastle, G. L. (1995) 'S. S. Stevens and the origins of operationism', *Philosophy of Science*, 62(3): 404–24.

Hargreaves, D. (1967) *Social Relations in a Secondary School*. London: Routledge and Kegan Paul.

Heath, A. and Martin, J. (1997) 'Why are there so few formal measuring instruments in social and political research?', in L. Lyberg, P. Biemer, M. Collins,

E. de Leeuw, C. Dippo, N. Schwarz and D. Trewin (eds) *Survey Measurement and Process Quality*. New York: Wiley.

Johnson, H. M. (1936) 'Pseudo-mathematics in the mental and social sciences', *American Journal of Psychology*, 48(2): 342–51.

Johnson, T., O'Rourke, D., Chavez, N., Sudman, S., Warnecke, R., Lacey, L. and Horm. J. (1997) 'Social cognition and responses to survey questions among culturally diverse populations', in L. Lyberg, P. Biemer, M. Collins, E. de Leeuw, C. Dippo, N. Schwarz and D. Trewin (eds) *Survey Measurement and Process Quality*. New York: Wiley.

Kaplan, A. (1964) *The Conduct of Inquiry: Methodology for Behavioural Science*. New York: Chandler.

Kempf-Leonard, K. (ed.) (2004) *Encyclopedia of Social Measurement*, 3 volumes. Amsterdam: Elsevier.

Kuhn, T. S. (1961) 'The function of measurement in modern physical science', *Isis*, 52: 161–90. (Reprinted in Kuhn 1977).

Kuhn, T. S. (1970) *The Structure of Scientific Revolutions*, 2nd edition. Chicago: University of Chicago Press.

Kuhn, T. S. (1977) *The Essential Tension*. Chicago: University of Chicago Press.

Lacey, C. (1970) *Hightown Grammar*. Manchester: Manchester University Press.

Laming, D. (2002) 'A review of *measurement in psychol- ogy: A critical history of a methodological concept*', *Quarterly Journal of Experimental Psychology A*, 55: 689–92.

LaPiere, R. T (1934) 'Attitudes versus actions', *Social Forces*, 13(2): 230–7.

Lofland, J. (1970) 'Analytic interruptus and interactionist imagery', in T. Shibutani, (ed.) *Human Nature and Collective Behavior: Papers in Honor of Herbert Blumer*. Englewood Cliffs NJ: Prentice-Hall.

Lofland, J. (1971) *Analyzing Social Settings*. Belmont CA: Wadsworth.

Matheson, G. (2006) 'Intervals and ratios: The invari- antive transformations of Stanley Smith Stevens', *History of the Human Sciences*, 19(3): 65–81.

McKinney, J. C. (1954) 'Constructive typology in social research', in J. T. Doby, E. A. Suchman, J. C. McKinney, R. G. Francis and J. P. Dean (eds) *An Introduction to Social Research*. Harrisburg PA: Stackpole.

McKinney, J. C. (1966) *Constructive Typology and Social Theory*. New York: Appleton-Century-Crofts.

McKinney, J. C. (1970) 'Sociological theory and the process of typification', in J. C. McKinney and E. A. Tiryakian (eds) *Theoretical Sociology: Perspectives and Developments*. New York: Appleton- Century-Crofts.

Merton, R. K., Sills, D., L. and Stigler, S. M. (1984) 'The Kelvin dictum and social science; an excursion into the history of an idea', *Journal of the History of the Behavioral Sciences*, 20: 319–31.

Michell, J. (1997) 'Quantitative science and the definition of measurement in psychology', *British Journal of Psychology*, 88: 355–83.

Michell, J. (1999) *Measurement in Psychology: Critical History of a Methodological Concept*. Cambridge: Cambridge University Press.

Michell, J. (2000) 'Normal science, pathological science and psychometrics', *Theory and Psychology*, 10(5): 639–67.

Michell, J. (2002) 'Stevens's theory of scales of measurement and its place in modern psychology', *Australian Journal of Psychology*, 54(2): 99–104.

Michell, J. (2007) 'Measurement', in S. P. Turner and M. W. Risjord (eds) *Philosophy of Anthropology and Sociology*. Amsterdam: Elsevier.

Moles, J. A. (1977) 'Standardization and measurement in cultural anthropology: A neglected area', *Current Anthropology*, 18(2): 235–58.

Mueller, C. W. (2004) 'Conceptualization, operationalization, and measurement', in M. S. Lewis-Beck, A. Bryman and T. F. Lia (eds) *The Sage Encyclopedia of Social Science Research Methods*. Thousand Oaks CA: Sage.

Mulkay, M., Ashmore, M. and Pinch, T. (1987) 'Measuring the quality of life: A sociological invention concerning the application of economics to health', *Sociology*, 21(4): 541–64.

Naroll, R. (1962) *Data Quality Control – A New Research Technique: Prolegomena to a Cross-Cultural Study of Culture Stress*. New York: Free Press.

Naroll, R. (ed.) (1973) *A Handbook of Method in Cultural Anthropology*. New York: Columbia University Press.

Needham, R. (1975) 'Polythetic classification: Convergence and consequences', *Man* 10(3): 349–69.

Newell, R. W. (1986) *Objectivity, Empiricism, and Truth*. London: Routledge and Kegan Paul.

Newman, E. B. (1974) 'On the origin of "scales of measurement"', in H. R. Moskowitz, B. Scharf, and J. C. Stevens (eds) *Sensation and Measurement: Papers in Honor of S. S. Stevens*. Dordrecht: Reidel.

O'Hear, A. (ed.) (1996) *Verstehen and Humane Understanding*. Cambridge: Cambridge University Press.

Phillips, D. L. (1971) *Knowledge from What? Theories and Methods in Social Research*. Chicago: Rand McNally.

Polanyi, M. (1959) *Personal Knowledge*. Chicago: University of Chicago Press.

Polanyi, M. (1966) *The Tacit Dimension*. Garden City, NY: Doubleday.

Ragin, C. (2000) *Fuzzy-Set Social Science*. Chicago: University of Chicago Press.

Robinson, A. (2007) *The Story of Measurement*. New York: Thames and Hudson.

Robinson, R. (1954) *Definition*. Oxford: Oxford University Press.

Rosch, E. (1999) 'Reclaiming concepts', in R. Nunez and W. J. Freeman (eds) *Reclaiming Cognition: The Primacy of Action, Intention and Emotion*. Exeter UK: Imprint Academic. Published simultaneously in *The Journal of Consciousness* Studies, 6(11–12): 61–77. Also available at (accessed 19.02.08): http://psychology.berkeley.edu/faculty/profiles/erosch1999.pdf

Sartori, G. (ed.) (1984) *Social Science Concepts: A Systematic Analysis*. Beverly Hills CA: Sage.

Sartori, G., Riggs, F. W. and Teune, H., (1975) *Tower of Babel: On the Definition and Analysis of Concepts in the Social Sciences*. Occasional Paper No. 6. Pittsburgh PN: International Studies Association

Schegloff, E. A. (1971) 'Notes on a conversational practice: formulating place', in D. Sudnow (ed.) *Studies in Social Interaction*. New York: Free Press.

Sperber, D. and Wilson, D. (1986) *Relevance, Communication and Cognition*. Oxford: Blackwell.

Stevens, S. S. (1946) 'On the theory of scales of measurement', *Science*, 103: 677–80.

Strauss, A. L. and Corbin, J. M. (1998) *Basics of Qualitative Research*, 2nd edition. Thousand Oaks CA: Sage.

Taylor, J. R. (2001) 'Linguistics: prototype theory', in N. J. Smelser and P. B. Baltes (eds) *International Encyclopedia of the Social and Behavioral Sciences*. Amsterdam: Elsevier.

Taylor, J. R. (2003) *Linguistic Categorization*. Oxford: Oxford University Press.

Thomson, Sir William (Lord Kelvin) (1889) *Popular Lectures and Addresses, volume 1*. London: Macmillan.

Tiryakian, E. A. (1968) 'Typologies', in D. L. Sills (ed.) *International Encyclopedia of the Social Sciences*. New York: Free Press.

Torgerson, W. (1958) *Theory and Method of Scaling*. New York: Wiley.

Truzzi, M. (ed.) (1974) *Verstehen: Subjective Understanding in the Social Sciences*. Reading, MA: Addison-Wesley.

Vellemann, P. F. and Wilkinson, L. (1993) 'Nominal, ordinal, interval, and ratio scale typologies are misleading', *American Statistician*, 47: 65–72.

Viswanathan, M. (2005) *Measurement Error and Research Design*, Thousand Oaks, CA: Sage.

Walker, R. (1995) 'The dynamics of poverty and social exclusion', in G. Room (ed.) *Beyond the Threshold: The Measurement and Analysis of Social Exclusion*. Bristol: Policy Press.

Wilks, S. S. (1961) 'Some aspects of quantification in science', in H. Woolf (ed.) *Quantification: A History of the Meaning of Measurement in the Natural and Social Sciences*. Indianapolis: Bobbs-Merrill.

Williams, M. (2001) 'Complexity, probability and Causation: implications for homelessness research'. This can be found at (accessed 11.03.08): http://www.whb.co.uk/socialissues/mw.htm

Williamson, T. (1994) *Vagueness*. London: Routledge.

Wirth, L. (ed.) (1940) *Eleven Twenty-Six: A Decade of Social Science Research*. Chicago: University of Chicago Press.

Woolf, H. (ed.) (1961) *Quantification: A History of the Meaning of Measurement in the Natural and Social Sciences*. Indianapolis: Bobbs-Merrill.

Zeller, R. A. and Carmines, E. G. (1980) *Measurement in the Social Sciences*. Cambridge: Cambridge University Press.

The Real World Practice of Measurement

22

Sensitive Issues and the Difficulty to Measure: The Case of Measuring Child Sexual Abuse

Will Tucker and Ross Cheit

INTRODUCTION

Child Sexual Abuse (CSA) is not new. Records of, and laws against, sexual maltreatment of children date back to at least ancient Babylon (Sommerville, 1982). More recently, the past 30 years have seen a marked increase in awareness of, and societal and policy responses to CSA. Among numerous books, conferences, and studies, are the *Journal of Child Sexual Abuse* and *Child Abuse and Neglect*. A 'selection' of US federal child welfare laws lists 47 statutes passed since the 1974 Child Abuse Prevention and Treatment Act which established the National Center on Child Abuse and Neglect (Child Welfare Information Gateway, 2008). In spite of this increase in social policy and social science

attention, those who study child maltreatment still face significant difficulties as they attempt to answer the first question about CSA: How much does it happen?

CSA may seem clear-cut: it either happened or it did not. But measuring its frequency is not simple: there is disagreement over what constitutes an instance of CSA, not every incident is reported, not every report can be substantiated, and not every substantiated case is referred for child protective service action or criminal prosecution – so the actual incidence of it is impossible to quantify without estimation and inference.

Measuring CSA is subject to the many methodological difficulties facing social scientists more generally: divergent definitions, protected populations, and reliance on the reports of others – which, whether from victims or bureaucrats, are often controversial or contested. Often unnoticed in these discussions is the volatile political atmosphere that accompanies most allegations or studies. It is both in these large and small controversies and in the administrative complications of counting CSA that this particular measurement challenge can provide lessons for social scientists, from the furious responses that follow even one allegation of abuse, to the over-arching debates between policymakers, advocates, and researchers, such as the 'wars' over whose estimates of abuse disclosure rates are most accurate (Pipe et al., 2007b).

Definitions and responses to CSA have long been controversial. Indeed, political movements often have driven response to CSA. In the late 1800s, Societies for the Prevention of Cruelty to Children arose from the already influential Society for the Prevention of Cruelty to Animals, and child advocacy became a cause of an early feminist movement (Myers, 1994b). The past 30 years' growth in interest can also partially be traced to the feminist movement of the 1970s and 1980s. Barbara Nelson's *Making an Issue of Child Abuse* (1984) described the successful growth of movements against child abuse in the 1970s, arguing that CSA had become an 'agenda-setting,' and 'noncontroversial' issue (pp. 126–7). This may seem true today, as on the surface, CSA appears to be apolitical. Yet within a year of the publication of Nelson's book, several controversial cases received extensive media coverage, the advocacy group Victims Of Child Abuse Laws (VOCAL) had formed, and what many have called a 'backlash' had begun (Hechler, 1988; Whittier, 2009). Today, for all the supposed agreement about CSA (a 1995 poll showed 97 per cent of respondents were aware of 'Child Sexual Abuse' and a vast majority (74 per cent)

believed it a major problem or somewhat of a problem in their state (Tabachnick et al., 1997), CSA is highly controversial and politically charged, and measurement occurs within this context.

On this point, Christopher Jencks' defense of and warning for social scientists in *The Homeless* (1994) is relevant. He noted that as soon as a social problem 'became a political issue, legislators and journalists began asking for numbers' (p. 1). These numbers, whether roughly estimated by advocates or gathered by bureaucrats or social scientists with some methodological rigor, are at the center of political debates. Jencks, therefore, reminds his readers of the importance of differentiating between 'political' and 'scientific numbers.'

We, however, argue that for CSA (and perhaps for more areas than researchers would care to admit), there are not 'scientific' or 'political' numbers. Instead, whether we acknowledge it or not, there are almost no numbers that are not informed by some sort of micro- or macro-level agenda. So, how to address questions of measurement when 'no number is innocent,' (Stone, 2002: 167) and each individual record or incident is open to, and often subject to, charged debate, and when efforts to standardize and aggregate measurements are influenced by the same pressures? And if all is so difficult and political, then why even try to count? These are the questions that this chapter aims to address. In taking up these particular questions, which focus on CSA, this chapter seeks to raise measurement-related methodological questions of broader relevance to researchers across the social sciences.

WHY IS IT IMPORTANT TO COUNT?

As with other problems, society has a stake in the measurement of CSA because there are broader consequences related to the frequency, severity, and response to its occurrence. At the simplest level, CSA is important because it harms individuals and families, both initially and over time. Studies show that in the initial aftermath of abuse, children suffer from psychological, physical, emotional, and social trauma and instability (Lanktree et al., 1991; Lewin, 2007; Noll et al., 2006; Browne and Finkelhor, 1986). Prospective and retrospective studies have shown that these negative outcomes can persist and grow as victims age (Briere and Elliot, 1994; Putnam, 2003), even resulting in later substance abuse (Bailey and McCloskey, 2005), court involvement (Goodkind et al., 2006), eating disorders (Hund and Espelage, 2005), and attempted suicide (Roy and Janal, 2006). Working with CSA victims may even have a 'vicarious' adverse impact on clinicians (Way et al., 2004).

Second, by any measure, CSA is a significant problem that affects too many people. The United States' National Child Abuse and Neglect Data System, which gathers reports from state agencies nationwide, shows CSA incidence rates from 2000 to 2006 ranging from 78,120 to 88,656 substantiated cases per year. Community samples show significant variance, which will be discussed later, but generally from 12 to 35 per cent of women and 4 to 9 per cent of men report unwanted sexual experiences before age 18 (Putnam, 2003). The magnitude of CSA makes it a pressing concern for policy and research.

Third, CSA is defined by statute as criminal and subject to criminal justice system enforcement. Furthermore, there may be ways to prevent CSA (through community media campaigns or offender treatment programs) or alleviate negative outcomes (Rispens et al., 1997; Rheingold et al., 2007). But to gauge the success or impact of these programs, we need an accurate measure of what the programs aim to prevent – the incidence of CSA – to see trends and changes.

Additionally, many of the difficulties researchers, clinicians, and others face in measuring CSA grow from, or are directly related to, difficulties in responding to allegations and reports of it. Working toward more accurate methods of measuring, CSA may also lead to innovative and effective institutional responses. This potential can be seen in innovations now underway or advocated in many jurisdictions, including vertical integration of prosecution, Children's Advocacy Centers (CACs) and interdisciplinary investigation and response teams (Williams, 2006; Faller and Palusci, 2007).

Finally, accurately counting even the most difficult to measure of social problems is important and necessary. As our policy and political discourse is increasingly guided by evaluation and 'what works,' demand for numbers also increases. Absent rigorously collected scientific numbers, political numbers fill the vacuum. Although we attempt to show that the line between the two is less clear than one might assume, the dangers of letting purely political numbers guide our discussion of and response to CSA are clear. CSA is all too common, and it can be devastating for children, family, and communities. It requires a broad-based response that is serious, thoughtful, and measured.

DIFFICULTIES DEFINING CSA

To measure CSA, we must ask – how do we define an instance of it? Even if we began at the highly unlikely baseline that a) we were able to collect all relevant facts surrounding an alleged incident, and that b) none of the facts were disputed, it would still be difficult to define what makes up a 'true' incident of CSA. In fact, there is no consensus about any of the words that make up the term.

Defining the occurrence of CSA – like research focused on several other social constructs – entails specifying the population vulnerable to it. In the case of CSA, this means defining who counts as a 'child.' Social science researchers have used different definitions. In retrospective prevalence studies, many studies define victims of CSA as under 18 years of age (Abma et al., 1997; Gallup organization, 1995; Saunders et al., 1992). Others define CSA as occurring to victims as under 17 (Bagley, 1991), 16 (Nance, 1991; Siegel et al., 1987), 15 (Briere and Runtz, 1988), or even under 13 years of age (Mullen et al., 1988). Another set of retrospective studies does not ask for specific ages, but instead whether participants were abused 'while growing up' or 'as a child' (MacMillan et al., 1997; Kercher and McShane, 1984). Finkelhor (1979), with standards he and other researchers used in later studies, defined the age of a 'child' victim in relation to the age of the perpetrator – if the victim was under 12 years old and the perpetrator was at least five years older, then it was abuse. Similarly, if the victim was aged between 13 and 16 and the perpetrator was at least 10 years older, it also was CSA. Unsurprisingly, these studies vary in their estimates of CSA prevalence.

If social scientists are not agreed on which age defines childhood, or during which ages a young person may be a victim of CSA, laws and policy are not much clearer. In the United States, for instance, each state has its own 'age of consent,' at which persons are judged to have the legal capacity to consent to sexual activity. In most of the states, this ranges from 16 to 18 years of age, although many states have specific, and varying, definitions for statutory rape and sexual abuse, requiring minimum age differences or positions of authority (Hines

and Finkelhor, 2007). Worldwide, ages of consent are generally between 12 and 18, although again laws do not necessarily provide clarity (Waites, 2005).

'Sexual' is also difficult to define. Some actions are accepted by nearly all researchers, advocates, and policymakers as sexual and inappropriate – forced intercourse, for example. But other actions, such as touching of various types and degrees, are more ambiguous.

Context is an important factor in whether an action is considered sexual. If a basketball coach pats a player's behind during a game, few would remark on it. If the same action occurred in other situations, it would likely be subject to mandatory reporting laws.

It might be tempting to consider the intent of the adult or perpetrator, or the understanding of the child. But these are, for practical purposes, nearly impossible to measure (and easy to deny), and the distinction between sexual and not sexual is not easily drawn.

'Abuse' is similarly difficult to define. One starting point might be whether the action or behavior is wanted or unwanted. But even this is not unambiguous. If a young child does not want to be given a bath, few would consider it abusive for a parent to ignore their protests. But what if an uncle, cousin, or babysitter did so?

Administrative definitions provide guidance on the scope and meaning of CSA definitions. The US Department of Health and Human Services' National Incidence Studies offer two ways to define abuse: the 'Harm' standard, which requires that an act or omission result in 'demonstrable harm' in order to be classified as abuse; and the 'Endangerment' standard, which includes children in counts if considered in danger of harm from abuse (Sedlak and Broadhurst, 1996: 4–5). But even administrative definitions do not fully resolve the definitional ambiguity. For instance, a social worker, mandatory reporter, or social scientist might disagree in good faith about what constitutes harm or endangerment of harm? As discussed earlier, CSA is associated with many negative outcomes for victims. But if a child is resilient enough to avoid those negative outcomes, does that mitigate the abuse?

Unsurprisingly, researchers answer these questions in different ways. In a meta-analysis of CSA research methodologies, Goldman and Padayachi (2000) noted that researchers used different definitions of 'sexual abuse.' Some create a scale of 'severity' of abuse. Some include only physical contact, others also include non-contact abuses, some only include 'unwanted' sexual behaviors, or behaviors that were 'wanted' by the victims. Still others left it to participants to decide if they had been sexually abused. Although the nature of CSA might make differences in definitions seem understandable, constructs across the social sciences have analogous situations. Researchers have divergent perspectives on which actions constitute constructs, under what circumstances, and for what populations.

The intention of discussing these ambiguities is not to parse words, but rather to emphasize the difficulties of defining even a single case of CSA, and suggest that for practical purposes, it is impossible to achieve consensus amongst researchers and practitioners on an objective, standard definition. For instance, at what age does it become inappropriate for parents to continue to hand-bathe their child? Who should make that decision, and how? Why then, and not a year later or earlier? These questions highlight the range of issues that complicate definitions. Researchers and administrators have tried different tactics: draw a bright line at some point, or attempt to develop a reasonable standard, and rely on the judgment of professionals to deal with individual reports.

Furthermore, there are a wide variety of actors who respond to instances of CSA, and these actors tend to have different operating assumptions and definitions, professional training, and motivations. For instance, Child Protective Services workers may operate under more inclusive and flexible definitions of CSA than do police officers, who work with specific criminal definitions. Generally speaking, clinicians may be more interested in perception of incidents, focusing more on cases where a child feels abused or displays adverse effects. Prosecutors may only want to move forward with prosecution on cases that they have the strongest chance to win, so they may focus on cases with as little ambiguity as possible.

Responding to social and political shifts, these pressures have changed over time, along with definitions of CSA. Gordon (1988), part of the movement to focus 'unprecedented' attention to incest and sexual abuse in the 1970s, was surprised to find that social workers in the 1890s had discovered similar evidence of CSA and responded similarly in their investigations. By the 1920s, though, a decline in feminist political movements coincided with a transformation of the perceived problem of sexual abuse, from intra-family 'carnal abuse,' to stranger-rape on the streets, often brought on by the victims' own behavior. This brought different responses:

A battered woman, terrified of her husband, is told by their daughter, who has become a 'sex delinquent', behaving 'vulgarly', that her father has criminally assaulted her. The mother says 'she would speak to him.' At court the police chief says he is doubtful about taking up the case as the girl's word is the only evidence the Government could produce; he would not question the father 'as it would be asking [him] to incriminate himself.' The daughter was committed to an institution. (Gordon, 1988: 59)

Gordon argued that, in the presence or absence of feminist and political movements 'the very same evidence of sexual abuse will be differently defined' (p. 61).

Although this chapter focuses on CSA measurement in the US, much of the argumentation is applicable globally. Just as definitions of and responses to CSA have changed over time in the US, what is considered and counted as CSA has been socially constructed differently in other places. Whether or not an incident is considered abuse is partially determined by cultural context, a related and well-known example being clitorectomies, called, depending on one's cultural perspective, either female circumcision or female genital mutilation. Different societies may define or construct CSA differently, but 'in every country where researchers have asked about it, they have found that an important percentage of the adult population ... acknowledges a history of sexual abuse' (Finkelhor, 1994). Finkelhor's epidemiology of 20 countries has been joined by reviews of CSA prevalence studies in Europe, sub-Saharan Africa, and Central America, all showing prevalence rates similar to the wide range of results in North American studies (Lampe, 2002; Lalor, 2004; Speizer et al., 2008). Prevalence surveys have yielded results within or near North American ranges in Turkey (13.4 per cent), China (16.7 per cent F, 10.4 per cent M), Malaysia (6.8 per cent), Nicaragua (20 per cent M, 26 per cent F), Palestinian Authority (45.6 per cent), Tanzania (27.7 per cent), Sweden (3.1 per cent M, 7.1 per cent F), Spain (17.9 per cent), and New Zealand (23.5 per cent), and other places (Alikasifoglu et al., 2006; Chen et al., 2004; Singh et al., 1996; Olsson et al., 2000; Haj-Yahia and Tamish, 2001; McCrann et al., 2006; Edgard and Ormstad, 2000; Pereda and Forns, 2007; Fanslow et al., 2007). Available evidence indicates

CSA is universal, although defined, approached, and counted differently by various cultures and societies.

There are also social and political pressures within societies. For instance, reporting CSA may be influenced by a prestige bias. As Stone (2002) notes, 'Measurement, like a mirror, triggers a natural desire to look good' (p. 178). At the risk of speaking too generally, almost all of us hope, or like to think that CSA is less likely to occur in our own families, neighborhoods, cities, states, or countries. There are advocates for children who are more inclined to believe allegations of CSA, who remember that many cases are never reported. There are also civil libertarians who view allegations more skeptically, and emphasize high-profile cases where allegations were ultimately deemed false.

There is no easy-to-use definition or response to CSA that can anticipate the details of every potential case. And how a researcher defines CSA influences drastically the numbers you get when you start counting. A study by Roosa et al. (1998), provides a convincing example. Asking 2003 young women to complete a sexual history questionnaire, they analyzed the results using different definitions of sexual abuse. Depending on whether the definition included non-contact abuse, a broader definition of contact abuse, or abuse committed by peers, friends, or boyfriends, they detected prevalence rates ranging from 18 to 59 per cent – a difference of over 300 per cent. In sum, the manner in which CSA is defined and socially constructed shapes what is counted, and the results of counting.

CURRENT MEASUREMENTS OF CSA

In addition to the definitional issues that influence measurement, actual efforts to count CSA encounter real-world challenges. In general, there are currently two ways CSA is quantified: incidence reports and studies, which attempt to document the number of reported cases of child maltreatment over a certain time horizon; and retrospective or prevalence studies, which ask adults if they were maltreated as children. Each has benefits and drawbacks: incidence studies, while difficult and time-consuming, can show how many reports of maltreatment reach those institutions charged with responding to CSA, but cannot and do not count the numerous cases where a child does not quickly disclose or an adult does not quickly recognize signs of potential abuse and hence almost certainly significantly underestimate the problem. Retrospective studies, on the other hand, may offer a more complete picture of the scale of abuse and neglect, but are also subject to concerns about memory and methodology. The methodological strengths and limitations of incident report- and retrospective survey-based measurement, respectively, have implications both for social scientists interested in CSA, and those focusing on other social constructs.

Incidence studies usually combine data from existing bureaucratic sources, such as Child Protective Services (CPS) records, criminal justice, or law enforcement reports. The National Child Abuse and Neglect Data System (NCANDS) analyzes case-level data of CPS agencies from almost all states (and DC and Puerto Rico), and issues an annual aggregation of CPS reports (Child Welfare Information Gateway, 2008). The National Incidence Study of Child Abuse and Neglect (NIS) attempted a more ambitious, rigorous estimate of incidence. Only three have been published so far, the most recent (NIS-3) in 1996 from 1993–4 data. The NIS-4, scheduled for release in 2009, combines a representative sample of CPS

data from jurisdictions with estimates from 'sentinels,' or professionals who come into frequent contact with children, to estimate unreported cases. These national studies of incidence measure how many cases are reported, rather than how many actually occur in a given time period. A handful of additional studies have attempted to quantify incidence outside bureaucratic data, by surveying youth directly either in random phone surveys or in specific situations, such as psychiatric hospitals (Finkelhor et al., 2005; Lanktree et al., 1991).

Retrospective or prevalence studies, on the other hand, usually survey a (sometimes random) group of adults and ask them, retrospectively, if they had experienced CSA. Substantial retrospective analysis of the prevalence of CSA began in 1979, when Diane Russell surveyed 930 women from a probability sample of the San Francisco phone book, reporting that 38 per cent of women had experienced contact abuse. Many methodological variations and pseudo-replications followed – changing who, how, where, and when similar questions were asked. These prevalence studies, while replicable, differ so greatly from each other that they are not easily comparable. Prevalence studies give researchers greater methodological control: they decide the sample and questions, and can administer surveys directly. They are also easier and cheaper to administer – a survey of a college student body is a less daunting project than canvassing state or county CPS offices for records and then deriving the relevant statistics.

These methodological flexibilities have resulted in significant variance amongst prevalence studies. One meta-analysis found a range in the results of retrospective prevalence studies between 2 and 62 per cent. The Roosa et al. study (discussed above) found that how CSA was defined resulted in a 300 per cent difference in abuse rates, while Finkelhor (1994) found that the number of questions the surveys asked was the best predictor of prevalence rates. Of six studies asking women a single question to ascertain abuse history, five had rates under 13 per cent. Of eight studies asking two or more questions, seven had rates over 19 per cent. Similarly, Gorey and Leslie (1997) found that surveys' response rate was associated with prevalence, suggesting that non-abused targets are less likely to respond to surveys, potentially inflating prevalence rates in studies with poor response rates.

CSA seems to have differential frequency across various segments of the population. Almost all studies – incidence or prevalence – have found that female children are more likely to be reported victims of CSA than males. The NIS-3 found that reports of sexual abuse for female victims were three times as likely (Sedlak and Broadhurst, 1996). Similarly, prevalence rates are uniformly higher – one meta-analysis of 22 studies argued for a 'reasonable' estimate of 30 to 40 per cent prevalence for women, and a rate for men of 'at least' 13 per cent (Bolen and Scannapieco, 1999). Victim characteristics such as disabilities or an absent parent seem to be associated with higher risk of reported abuse (Westcott and Jones, 1999). And although a disproportionate number of lower socioeconomic status (SES) families are involved with CPS, SES does not seem to be associated with higher risk of CSA reports (Finkelhor, 1993). Children are also at risk of CSA from infancy, and while CSA is less frequent at ages 0 to 2, 'children's risk of sexual abuse ... is relatively constant from age 3 on' (Sedlak and Broadhurst, 1996).

Aside from these risk factors, many studies have attempted to measure and compare prevalence rates in population sub-groups –

recent examples include Latino men who have sex with men, HIV-positive patients in the American Deep South, and married observant Jewish women (Arreola et al., 2005; Whetten et al., 2006; Yehuda et al., 2007). Because of differences in methodology and doubts of the authors themselves about their samples' representativeness (Yehuda et al., mention it was 'not feasible to obtain a representative sample' (p. 1704)), it is difficult to compare such rates conclusively.

As we have discussed, researchers cannot be sure that there are no significant differences across ages or ethnicity in victimization rates – but in the absence of strong data indicating otherwise, it makes sense to take it as the null hypothesis. While it may be equally likely to occur, after the abuse occurs, victims, families, and institutions respond in vastly different ways.

DISCLOSURE (OR NON-DISCLOSURE) AND IMPLICATIONS FOR COUNTING

The rate at which sexual abuse is reported or disclosed is the subject of a considerable amount of debate – Pipe and colleagues (2007b) refer to it as 'the disclosure wars.' In addition to legitimate methodological concerns, discussions of disclosure rates are particularly heated because of implications for the numbers of and responses to CSA. It is one methodological area where politics are clearly visible. Debates over numbers are 'one of the most prominent forms of discourse in public policy,' as one side 'wants measures to make these perennial problems look low and declining, while the other wants to make them look high and growing' (Stone, 2002: 167, 183). Social scientists are either conscious participants in this discussion, or subject to the pressures of both sides, but they should not ignore it, as 'every number is a political claim about "where to draw the line'" (Stone, 2002: 167). Rates of CSA disclosure have significant implications for where to draw the line.

Although many crimes leave evidence or have witnesses, CSA often leaves no physical evidence, and victim and offender as the only witnesses. In cases where there is evidence, medical or otherwise, it is still often private, and must be uncovered. As a result, discovery of CSA often depends on a report or disclosure of abuse. Unfortunately, this process cannot be standardized. Young children may not be able to find the words to describe their abuse. When and if children disclose CSA, it is rarely to a social worker or police officer, but often to a caretaker or trusted adult (Arata, 1998). This inserts an extra level between law enforcement, child protection, and the report of the incident, and decreases the likelihood that a child will disclose in a manner that translates into a report if the offender is familiar to them (Hanson et al., 1999).

Studies that have attempted to quantify the proportion of reports to actual incidence have shown varied results. An early randomized survey found that, of adults who reported sexual abuse as a child, only 3 per cent had reported to authorities (Timnick, 1985). London et al. (2008) recently reviewed 13 retrospective surveys of adults, finding relatively consistently that many, if not most, victims of CSA did not disclose the abuse. Of adults who reported abuse in surveys, only 31 to 45 per cent disclosed the abuse as a child (meaning 55–69 per cent did not). Even more strikingly, in the studies that specifically asked about reporting the abuse to authorities, only 5 to 13 per cent said they had done so. Two large-scale retrospective studies that used national probability samples, Finkelhor et al. (1990) and Smith et al. (2000), found 38 and 28 per cent, respectively, of those reporting

abuse indicated that they were disclosing it for the first time during the survey. Those victims who do disclose – to authorities or otherwise – often do not do so immediately. One survey of 300 patients found that CSA victims who disclosed abuse waited a mean of 2.3 years to disclose, reporting fear or embarrassment as the reasons for delay (Kellogg and Huston, 1995). A study of 90 sexually abused children found a similar average delay of two years between abuse and disclosure (Henry, 1997). Many victims of CSA never disclose their abuse during childhood.

Memory may play a role in delay or lack of disclosure. Psychiatrists have argued that memories of traumatic events may be repressed, a phenomena known as 'Dissociative Amnesia' (APA, 2000). There is some empirical evidence indicating that CSA may trigger dissociative amnesia – one study that interviewed victims 17 years after their documented cases of abuse found that 38 per cent did not disclose any sexual abuse (Williams, 1994). A similar study that interviewed 96 adults 20 years after documented cases of CSA found that 37 per cent did not recall or disclose the abuse (Widom and Morris, 1997). However, a more recent study found that 81 per cent of adults with abuse history previously documented by the researchers disclosed abuse during interviews approximately 13 years later (Goodman et al., 2003).

Exactly what these numbers mean is controversial. Compared to the two previous prospective studies, some have argued that Goodman and colleagues' (2003) study design might skew toward those more likely to remember and disclose abuse later. Thirteen years earlier in a study with the same researchers, all participants had reported abuse to authorities, and were interviewed by researchers as many as seven times (Freyd, 2003; Cheit, 2003). Others have argued that there are many reasons why victims may not mention their abuse when asked years later (Laney and Loftus, 2005). Though we do not know to what degree, it is likely that memory and disclosure issues result in substantial under-reporting of CSA.

Many incidents of CSA are not reported to authorities immediately or ever, and indeed never reach institutions as potential cases. Researchers understand that incidence data from reports to CPS agency measure only a portion of abuse – 'the tip of the iceberg,' but what portion is unclear and debatable. Unfortunately, what appears on survey responses or institutional radar may not be any easier to measure, or any further removed from political debates.

FALSE POSITIVES AND NEGATIVES

Even when researchers and institutions are able to investigate reports of abuse, they may not accurately determine if it has occurred. When children are questioned about suspected abuse, four outcomes are possible. They could give a true positive or a true negative, and accurately disclose that they were or were not abused. These are ideal outcomes for clinicians and researchers, and are not particularly controversial. However, there are two other documented possibilities. There are false negatives – when a child denies or does not disclose abuse that did occur. There is also the potential for false positives – when a child reports abuse that did not occur. These two categories are not only particularly relevant to efforts to measure and quantify the frequency of CSA, but also for societal and institutional responses. If false positives or false negatives are considered common, our societal and institutional responses could shift significantly. This perhaps can be seen in a study that surveyed attitudes of professionals who dealt with

CSA. Judges and law enforcement officers were significantly more skeptical about childrens' reports of abuse than were CPS or mental health workers (Everson et al., 1996).

Understanding factors that contribute to false positives or negatives in the case of CSA might well have broader methodological significance. False positives are particularly difficult to measure. It may at first seem unclear why or how a child would accuse falsely. Some have argued that 'false accusations' are frequent in divorce and custody cases (Schreier, 1996). Gardner (1992) claimed that the 'vast majority' of CSA allegations in divorce cases were false. A recent Canadian study found that the rate of intentionally false allegations of maltreatment was three times higher in cases involving custody disputes (12 versus 4 per cent) – but also noted that none of the 'intentionally false' reports of CSA originated with the alleged child victim (Trocmé and Bala, 2005). Accusations in custody disputes, however, are likely already treated with skepticism, and are among the first to be screened out (Jones, 1993).

Some researchers stress the potential for unintentional false positives, pointing to suggestive questioning in high-profile cases in the US in the late 1980s and early 1990s (Loftus and Ketchum, 1994; Ceci and Bruck, 1995). Children may disclose in a way that may be misunderstood as abuse, or disclose abuse that they believe happened or are led to believe happened. Most research on childhood development indicates that autobiographical memory can be extensive and accurate, and is probably not significantly worse than in adults (Baker-Ward et al., 1993; Fivush, 1993). Much of the research on suggestibility of memories has found that by age 10 or 11, children appear to be suggestible, but not more so than anyone else (Saywitz and

Snyder, 1993). However, some research has found that young children, especially pre-schoolers, can be more suggestible than adults and older children (Ceci and Bruck, 1995; Goodman and Clarke-Stewart, 1991). Ceci and Bruck and colleagues have emphasized child suggestibility in their research, and have found that it is possible to suggest a memory to a young child (Ceci and Bruck, 1993; Bruck et al., 1995). No researchers have attempted to 'suggest' a memory of CSA (such a study could not meet institutional ethical standards), so it is unclear how much of this distinct body of suggestibility research is actually transferable to CSA. It may seem counter-intuitive that a memory of a potentially traumatic event such as sexual abuse could be falsely suggested to a child, but there is some experimental evidence that indicates it is possible (Bruck et al., 1995).

There is also the question of disclosures of abuse that are later recanted. London et al. (2008) reviewed ten studies and found ranges of recantation between 4 and 27 per cent, with most at the lower range of that scale. They concluded that 'the frequency of recantation is relatively low and only occurs in a minority of children who previously made claims of CSA' (p. 35). It is not entirely clear in these studies if abuse actually occurred, or if the original disclosure or the later recantation is false. Put differently, these reports might represent either true negatives or false negatives.

The question of false negatives heightens certain methodological debates in the measurement of CSA. London et al. (2007) looked at results from 24 studies of disclosure patterns of children believed to be abused, finding rates ranging from 24 to 96 per cent of abused children disclosing the abuse. They argued that the variation in the disclosure rates was less related to victim characteristics and was more closely associated with methodological considerations. For instance, studies that only used a sample of victims who had previously disclosed abuse or had strong indications of abuse had high rates of disclosure. Similarly, studies of cases previously substantiated by CPS investigators had high rates of disclosure. One could conclude, as did the authors, that in cases where there is a higher likelihood of actual CSA, that disclosure rates are higher.

The representativeness and external validity of these studies using samples of substantiated or previously disclosed cases is not universally accepted, however. Considering that instances of CSA usually have few witnesses, and little to no physical or corroborating evidence, 'suspicion,' 'substantiation,' and the report or disclosure of a child could almost be considered synonymous. If we accept the premise that substantiated cases (incidence rates) of CSA are the 'tip of the iceberg,' then it is likely that samples with high rates of previous disclosure, or high rates of suspicion and substantiation, are not representative of the universe of CSA victims. Lyon (2007), attempted to minimize 'suspicion bias' and 'substantiation bias' by reviewing 26 studies which examined children who had contracted gonorrhea, 'among the most convincing corroborative evidence,' of CSA. In 21 studies from 1965 to 1993, there was an average disclosure rate of 43 per cent – that is, only 43 per cent of children who presented to doctors with gonorrhea (which could only be acquired through sexual contact) admitted to sexual contact, even after (sometimes) repeated interviews.

Critics point out that children with STIs in general, and gonorrhea in particular, make up a small and perhaps unrepresentative sample of all abused children. Moreover, samples that expressly did not previously disclose any abuse may be a subset of abused children more likely to remain silent, deflating the disclosure rates (London et al., 2008). Nevertheless, it is hard to discount the conclusion that over half of children with gonorrhea respond in the negative to direct questions about CSA; and that, consistently across 21 studies, false negatives were as likely as, if not more likely than, true positives.

The aim of this chapter is not to settle the methodological disputes between these debating camps, which would require more than our allotted pages and more data than now exist. Rather, it is to point out that the current state of research is open to, and subject to, both interpretation and manipulation. Reasonable people may disagree – some may consider it more important to minimize the number of false positives to protect innocent people accused of crime. Others may suggest that it is a higher priority to ensure that innocent children are protected and try to cast potential nets as broadly as possible to minimize false negatives.

But there are also less reasonable disagreements, positions, and agendas. These methodological debates can allow political agendas to don the mantle of compromise, moderation, and reasonableness, and introduce ambiguity and uncertainty into cases (such as young children infected with gonorrhea) where there probably should not be any. The understandable gray areas at the margins of what is considered CSA (non-contact abuse, for instance), can be used to insinuate ambiguity into all accusations. Those accurately accused of abuse can manipulate methodologies to argue that false positives might be more likely than they actually are, and to use social science debates to obfuscate and impeach the credibility of a child accuser. Experts hired by the defense in criminal and civil trials may be more likely to

cherry-pick the studies they cite and to point to methodological shortcomings of those less useful to their clients' cases. And it may be that research agendas that either minimize or focus on the role and frequency of false negatives or false positives respond to and are informed, and perhaps inspired, by political actors, advocates, and agendas. Moreover, they can significantly impact how society perceives the entirety of CSA, and on how our institutions – and the street-level bureaucrats who exercise discretion within them – respond to it. As Goodman and Goodman-Brown (2007) noted, 'Concerns over false reports affect how children are questioned – or are not questioned – about sexual abuse, which in turn affects the likelihood and process of disclosure.'

These debates are of interest for social scientists, as they underscore difficulties in counting social phenomena. There is significant methodological and political controversy about false positives and negatives – the scope and nature of CSA and how it is reported – before CPS, law enforcement, or researchers even begin to count, investigate, or respond. This, in turn, influences our institutional counting of and response to CSA, for as Stone (2002) noted, 'the reason we try to predict rain, after all, is to decide whether to carry an umbrella' (p. 167).

INSTITUTIONAL RESPONSES TO CSA AND COUNTING DIFFICULTIES

There is significant ambiguity and little consensus about what constitutes CSA, and what indicates it has occurred or not. An additional challenge with using institutional data as a proxy measure for frequency of CSA is that institutional responses to CSA remain far from standardized. Reports of CSA navigate a complex network of agencies. CSA is both a criminal offense and an issue of child endangerment involving law enforcement agencies, Child Protective Services, criminal justice, and family courts – and each report could take more than one potential path, depending on which agency hears it. Incidents of CSA are reported (or not); screened for investigation; investigated; substantiated; referred for further action (whether prosecution, removal from home, or therapy); and then that action may be taken by CPS or criminal justice institutions. At each of those steps, some alleged incidents move forward, and some are screened out. Each of these steps and decisions could be influenced by a variety of factors, making it difficult to get accurate counts.

Gathering and using data and estimates from institutional records – whether at the local, state, or national level – is difficult and risks inaccuracies. In the case of measuring CSA, there are almost guaranteed to be confounding factors, because at each level a) we are probably unlikely to get all of the facts, and b) there probably will be conflicting versions of events left to someone to reconcile. Neither gathering relevant facts nor reconciling them will likely be done by social scientists, and so researchers are left to both rely upon the discretion of a variety of street-level bureaucrats and to try to generalize across individuals, groups, locations, and even time. Thus, CSA measurement is dependent on methods that are less than scientific. Since using institutional data means aggregating thousands of incident-level decisions and responses to CSA, it is useful to look at some of the factors that influence those decisions and responses.

Reporting (mandatory and otherwise)

Reporting rates influence the accuracy of measurement efforts. As discussed above, available evidence indicates that child victims often do not disclose incidents of actual abuse; and even if they do tell their families, that information may not make it to institutions. Reported incidents of abuse represent only a portion of all incidents; and it is unclear what proportion it is and if it changes between jurisdictions or over time – making it difficult to draw conclusions.

An additional influence on reported numbers of CSA may be the mandatory reporting laws that many jurisdictions (including all of the US and Australia) have enacted for professionals who work with youth and children. Reasonable suspicions of abuse must be reported, albeit with differences in the required timeframe and method of reporting. These reports currently make up some 56.3 per cent of reported cases of child abuse in the US (Child Welfare Information Gateway, 2008). Evaluations of the effectiveness of mandatory reporting vary – some argue that it is better to cast a wide net, and uncover as many cases of CSA as possible (Ainsworth, 2002). Others argue that it may spread limited CPS resources too thinly, or inflate numbers and lead to an increase in frivolous or false accusations (Van Voorhis and Gilbert, 1998; Robin, 1991). However, studies have also found that professionals, even under mandatory reporting laws, often fail to file paperwork or report suspected child abuse to authorities (Gunn et al., 2005).

Screening, categorization, and miscounting

Many reports or allegations of abuse are screened out and never investigated, or are misclassified – which can affect overall CSA measurement. When CSA is reported, whether by a victim or mandatory reporter, it is usually to an abuse, child protection, or law enforcement hotline. These 'gatekeepers' can forward a report to another agency, refer it for investigation, or screen it out and not follow up. Whitcomb (1992) reminds us that many reports 'are screened out at each gate' (p. 5). In 2006, 38.3 per cent of all referrals were screened out prior to investigation by CPS agencies (Child Welfare Information Gateway, 2008). Studies have found that CPS workers tend to screen out those that involve custody disputes, and have reporters with a history of unfounded allegations, with incomplete information, with no indication or risk of harm, without a specific incident mentioned, or when the maltreatment was by a non-caretaker (Haskett et al., 1995; Jones, 1993).

The impact of categorization perhaps can be seen sharply in infant homicide, discussed in Chapter 28 of this volume by Marc Reidel (p. 561), citing Overpeck et al. (1999) who argued that difficulty and hesitancy in classifying suspicious incidents as 'intentional' means that actual rates of infant homicide could be 'almost 20 per cent greater than reported rates.'

Many reports are also screened out after investigation, when a perpetrator or suspect cannot be identified, when there is insufficient information to prove or disprove allegations, or when the allegation seems false (Whitcomb, 1995). Levels of training of investigators and quality of investigation vary, and some studies indicate that aspects of the forensic evaluation can lead to false positives or negatives (Herman, 2005). Most states classify cases into two categories depending on if there is or is not evidence indicating abuse (either substantiated and unsubstantiated, or founded and unfounded). In 2006, five states also classified cases as 'indicated' when abuse could not be verified by legal standards but there was reason to believe it occurred. To prepare the annual report, states 'crosswalk' their data into NCANDS' classifications. Although the state-level results do not

mirror the national proportions, state data are pooled into the following results: 25.2 per cent of investigations resulted in substantiations, 3.0 per cent 'indicated' abuse, and 60.4 per cent were unsubstantiated cases (Child Welfare Information Gateway, 2008).

Our measures of incidence rates are counts of 'substantiated' cases – but it is worth noting that classifying a case as 'unsubstantiated' does not mean that abuse did not occur (Drake, 1996). As Smith et al. (2006) note, 'many concerned observers of the CPS believe that 'true' instances of child abuse often go unsubstantiated because of problematic investigatory techniques or idiosyncratic decision-making by protective service personnel' (p. 358). It is likely that some reports are screened out when there is enough evidence to warrant investigation, or are classified as unsubstantiated when CSA did occur; and that these 'errors' in counting happen at different rates for different caseworkers, jurisdictions, and time periods. This likely affects our counts of CSA incidence, but we do not know how much.

Resources and caseloads

Organizational features and constraints also seem to affect how CPS agencies respond to and count allegations of CSA. Urban jurisdictions may be more likely to have specialized staff and plans for dealing with allegations of abuse than rural offices with smaller staffs. Jones' (1993) review of CPS decision-making literature found evidence that workers are more likely to investigate when they do not feel overburdened, and that the number of reports received in a day is associated with whether the report is investigated.

CPS case workers currently average 62 investigations per worker per year, a number that has been relatively stable since 2000

(Child Welfare Information Gateway). The National Incidence Study (NIS-3) indicated that between 1986 and 1993 the number of investigations conducted by Child Protective Services remained constant, but the number of reported cases increased significantly, and the percentage of substantiated cases was cut almost in half – suggesting there may be limits to investigative capacities (Sedlak and Broadhurst, 1996). Given state budget crises and economic downturn, resources dedicated to CPS agencies may not increase soon. While a recent study of 1997–2002 NCANDS data did not find a negative relationship between increasing caseloads and numbers of substantiated cases (Almeida et al., 2008), the quantifiable impact of organizational factors on counting CSA remains unknown.

Children's advocacy centers

In many jurisdictions, various agencies that respond to CSA may not fully cooperate. Martell (2002), analyzing factors which influenced prosecution and child removal, found that the agency that started an investigation (CPS versus criminal justice) was likely to act on it – and called agency response 'finder's keepers' (p. 167). In addition to a lack of a strategic or coordinated response to CSA, this could also indicate that in some jurisdictions where a report is made influences whether or not it is included in incidence data.

The first Child Advocacy Center (CAC) was formed in 1985 in Alabama to coordinate community and agency response to child abuse. In January 2009, there were 722 CACs listed on the National Children's Alliance website. CACs use Multidisciplinary Teams (MDT) of prosecutors, investigators, law enforcement officers, and/or mental health and medical professionals to simultaneously and comprehensively investigate and reduce stress on children and families. CACs, in general, respond to cases of CSA differently than do CPS agencies alone, and this seems to create different results and counts. Smith et al. (2006) compared reports sent to CPS agencies versus those sent to a CAC, and found higher rates of case substantiation for the CAC (along with higher rates of law enforcement involvement and medical exams). Efforts to promote MDTs have not all been positive, as Sedlak et al. (2006) found that in one county, structures set up to support inter-agency collaboration actually impeded case sharing. While there has not been extensive empirical study, it seems likely that CACs and other innovative institutional responses would have different rates of investigation and substantiation, and therefore different counts of CSA incidence (Cross et al., 2007; Jones et al., 2007).

Discretion

Partially because of the structure of our agencies, and partially because of the nature of CSA, one cannot simply follow a checklist to diagnose it – institutional response relies on the discretion of street-level actors such as teachers, social workers, police officers, lawyers, judges, and child advocates. Power of discretion is perhaps most famously recognized in prosecutors, about whom Supreme Court Justice Robert Jackson (1940) argued: 'The prosecutor has more control over life, liberty, and reputation than any other person in America' (p. 18). A recent example from Texas' 143rd Judicial District illustrates this: A District Attorney gained notoriety for declining to prosecute 80 per cent of the cases brought to him by law enforcement (compared to the average Texas prosecutor, who declined to prosecute 18 per cent). He took forward only one case of sexual assault or indecency with a child out of 58 forwarded to him in six years – and ignored a case involving two officials at a juvenile prison sexually assaulting young men, which allegedly included DNA evidence and a partial confession (Blakeslee, 2008).

Although decisions earlier in the process – whether in reporting, investigating, substantiating, removing a child, or referring for prosecution – may be less dramatic, these actors still exercise significant discretion. These decisions are influenced by many expected factors, such as the decision-makers' background and training, or the available evidence. But there may be other, harder to quantify influences. Social scientists have found that narratives and anecdotes may bias and influence decision-making (Winterbottom et al., 2008). CPS and criminal justice staff have reported in interviews that media coverage 'can and does forcefully impact agency protocols,' (Martell, 2002: 217), and observers have pointed out the importance of media coverage and media assessments of institutional responses to CSA (Goddard and Saunders, 2001). Political factors may also influence individuals' decision-making. Defenders of the Texas DA, for instance, asserted that he provided the type of justice his district wanted (he won re-election in 2008). Clearly, political agendas and narratives, and the political use of social science research can influence those decisions.

Researcher access and methodological issues

Social scientists who attempt to measure or study CSA must navigate the challenges of designing professional, principled research methodologies on ethically fraught terrain. Both children and perpetrators (particularly if incarcerated) are considered protected populations, and submitting a research proposal on CSA almost certainly will result in an intensive review and possible constraints from an Institutional Review Board. Direct work with victims, or even the records and facts of their cases, is difficult to arrange and rare – and when it is possible, researchers themselves are often subject to mandatory reporting laws (Walsh et al., 2004). This means that researchers become reliant on institutional data and the interpretations, judgments, and discretion of others. And even this is not always possible – as even public institutions often hesitate to grant researchers' access to records.

Trends in institutional data

Difficulties in accurately counting social phenomena like CSA mount when comparing numbers over time. Indeed, the role of politics and social attitudes is particularly magnified when comparing data over time. As Murray Straus argued in 1979 as research on child abuse was beginning in earnest (cited in Bogden and Ksander, 1980):

> Such statistics do not indicate that there is any more child abuse now than there was 5, 10 or 100 years ago ... What the ever increasing statistics on child abuse indicate is a changing standard of family relationships. We are no longer willing to tolerate the level of violence to which children have been subjected for centuries.

In contrast, David Finkelhor and Lisa Jones have taken notice of and spurred discussion on what would be an encouraging trend – the decline in reported incidence of CSA. They argue that

> We believe the evidence for the existence of a decline in youth victimization is extremely strong ... Something positive is going on in the social environment. Not only is there encouragement to be drawn from this development, but also, there are important lessons

to be learned. If something is working, it is incumbent on us to find out what, and to try to do more of it or expand its impact in some way (Finkelhor and Jones, 2006).

Finkelhor and Jones provide corroborating evidence – for instance, parallel decreases in cases involving confessions or children with STIs, and declines in other child welfare indicators such as runaways. They discuss various potential reasons why the numbers may have decreased, from the availability of abortions and a decline in unwanted children to shifting social values and awareness and the availability of pharmacological treatments for mental illness. But for all the potential reasons they give, they overlook the role that the political struggles (or 'wars,') of the same time period may have played in influencing the baseline numbers or the trends that they discuss. In an earlier study, including telephone interviews of CPS officials in 43 states, Jones et al. (2001) posited that a 'backlash' may have some impact on reporting rates, but found that the 'majority' of respondents did not feel that 'fears of legal repercussions' were an important factor. Characterizing the political battles over CSA as dealing with 'fears of legal repercussions,' however, ignores that two sides of a political struggle have been consciously and publicly arguing about where to 'draw the lines' defining what should and should not be considered CSA. This apparent reluctance to discuss or analyze the role that politics plays in CSA measurement is not unique to Finkelhor and Jones. It is evident in most of the studies we have discussed. But ignoring the political aspects of measurement ignores a confounding variable that may have a significant impact on the validity and reliability of estimates – certainly the political actors and advocates hope to do so.

Examining the same incidence measures – the annual compilation of CPS data by the NCANDS – it is clear we should be particularly cautious when drawing inferences. In 2000, there were 87,480 reported cases of CSA in the US. In 2006, there were 78,120. At first glance, this seems to indicate a decrease in reported cases of 9,360, or 10.7 per cent (the decrease since 1992 is even more striking, at 53 per cent). On closer examination, the conclusion is less clear. For instance, take the cases of Utah and Nevada, two neighboring states of nearly identical populations (~2.6 million), both growing (Utah experienced 14.2 per cent population growth between 2000 and 2006, Nevada 24.9 per cent), and no obvious differences that would produce significantly different incidences of child abuse. In Nevada, there were 5,775 substantiated cases of child maltreatment in 2000, of which 261 were cases of sexual abuse. In 2000 in Utah, there were 8,729 cases of child maltreatment, with 1,713 being cases of sexual abuse. Researchers might rightly ask if the 6.56:1 ratio of CSA incidence raises concerns about the validity of indicators, or suggests actual differences in incidence?

The 2006 numbers are perhaps even more confusing. While nationwide numbers of cases decreased, in Utah there were 13,043 cases of maltreatment, and 2,322 were CSA – both increases over 2000. In neighboring Nevada, though, there were 5,345 cases of abuse or neglect, and 193 were sexual abuse – both decreases from 2000. The two neighboring states have almost identical population sizes. Yet one has twelve times as many substantiated cases of CSA and its counts have increased since 2000, while the other has much smaller numbers which have decreased since 2000. We would want to know much more about how decisions are made in these and all states before interpreting the national numbers. It is probably better to be cautious before we infer that children in Las Vegas are twelve times less likely to be subject to sexual exploitation than those in Salt Lake City. What does the national decline in substantiated cases really mean? As Leventhal (2001) cautioned, it is unclear if it represents 'good news or false hope.' We would caution against interpreting these trends to mean anything more than that substantiated cases have declined.

POLITICAL EFFECTS ON COUNTING

For those who work in the field of CSA, forces and incentives push in various directions. Unfortunately, there are probably more incentives to hide than to reveal facts. A perpetrator probably does not want notoriety as a sexual abuser of children. Victims and their families also are unlikely to want the label 'sexually abused.' Extended families may not want to know about an incident, or to tell others. Neighbors, communities, nations – nearly all would rather that the abuse had not occurred, and that might mean ignoring signs of it or inducing a community-wide amnesia.

Measurement is adversely affected by factors that tend to suppress disclosure and honest discussion. Child victims who are already self-conscious would not want everyone to know, and may have been threatened or told to keep it secret. There is evidence of Post-Traumatic Stress Disorder-like symptoms in CSA victims. The stigma and social pressures on them – particularly when an abuser is a known adult who violated their trust – may make it difficult for them to trust others enough to disclose. They may even repress those unfortunate memories and have Dissociative Amnesia. Offenders may also

feel some of these internal pressures and motivations – such as guilt and regret – in addition to perhaps having more practical reasons they would not want their actions to become public knowledge.

But there are also many external pressures that influence the validity of efforts to quantify CSA, some of which we have discussed. Books about CSA have titles such as *The Battle and the Backlash* and social scientists refer to certain methodological debates as 'memory wars' and 'disclosure wars.' Perhaps researchers attempting to measure CSA should not be surprised by such contentiousness – after all, the beginning of the child protection movement grew partially from feminist movements which still remain contentious, and early strategists saw the issue as political (Whittier, 2009; Nelson, 1984). Some argue that the early child protection movement moved too quickly and to excess; and that advocates made claims that were exaggerations at best, such as 'children don't lie about sexual abuse.' A series of highly visible cases in the 1980s gained notoriety when 'the charges turned bizarre,' with allegations of 'strange rituals, possibly satanic,' and publicly fell apart (Hechler, 1988: 131, 17). Some have imputed these cases to have methodological implications about what should be considered CSA.

What has followed has probably accurately been described as a 'backlash.' One social scientist characterized this backlash as an argument that the 'child protective system is out of control; that child protection is on a witch-hunt; that child abuse hysteria is rampant; that child protection professionals are comparable to Nazis, McCarthyites, KGB agents, and so on; and that professionals are the problem' (Myers, 1994: 17). In return, many of those who are skeptical about the extent of CSA worry about being called accomplices or sympathizers themselves.

It is worth reviewing the extent of this backlash, to get a sense of implications it may have for broader efforts to quantify CSA. Organizations such as Victims Of Child Abuse Laws (VOCAL) were founded to support those who deemed 'wrongfully accused,' and exert political influence to redefine abuses. Costin and colleagues (1996) in *The Politics of Child Abuse*, asserted that professionals, social workers, and attorneys were part of a 'sexual abuse industry.' Others expressed the viewpoint of Philip Jenkins (1998), describing the response to CSA as a 'moral panic,' reminiscent of witch-hunts. Discussion began to focus on 'the real victims of the war against child abuse': those who had been 'falsely' accused (Wexler, 1988).

Conflict about how to define, respond to, and thus count CSA was probably inevitable. There are active civil liberties organizations and advocates, and constitutional protections for the accused – and it is important and appropriate to weigh and provide safeguards for concerns of both the accused and the victim. But we may too quickly ignore that not every argument is in good faith. If, at the lowest estimates, there are 78,250 cases of CSA a year, and, if by conservative estimates, one in four women and one in eight men have been victims of sexual abuse, it is quite likely that there is a non-trivial number of abusers involved in these rather public, methodological discussions of what should be considered CSA, and what should be considered a false accusation. It should also be noted that some of those who study or work in CSA may have been abused as children, which could influence their views.

The conflict we see in societal response to CSA, Conte points out, is likely a manifestation of a conflict within individuals – and in efforts to operationalize this construct, it is important to realize that 'complex psychological, cultural, and political processes are involved in recognizing and responding to childhood sexual abuse' (Conte, 1994: 227). Efforts to measure CSA must be grounded with an understanding of these emotionally, politically, and culturally-charged complexities.

If, as we have seen, the counting of CSA depends at every stage on a great deal of discretion, we must also acknowledge that that discretion and decision-making are likely to be influenced by the politics of CSA. And if this is true even in cases of 'noncontroversial' sexual abuse, it is also true of social science and policy research in general.

CONCLUSION: INNOVATING AND IMPROVING MEASUREMENT

Methodological difficulties related to the measurement of CSA are not new. Disagreements on definitions and discussions have continued for decades, as has the realization that a single measure or definition will not serve the needs of all researchers and practitioners who do work on CSA. As Haugaard and Emery (1989) stated, the danger in using different definitions and methodologies is that 'the concept of child sexual abuse will become muddled, research results will be more difficult to compare, and those reading the results will be misled.' Roosa et al. (1998), who found differences in prevalence rates of 300 per cent depending on the definition used, use even starker language: 'The current diversity in measurement serves as a barrier … to accumulating and communicating useful information about this phenomenon.'

So what can researchers do? What can be measured accurately and reliably? Social scientists and commentators have long advocated changes and improvements in CSA measurement, a review of which is beyond the scope of this chapter. The recommendations of Finkelhor and Wells' (2003) for improving national data systems and the discussions of Walsh et al. (2004) of methodological issues in research design provide useful specific improvements for researchers and policymakers.

The following four conclusions are drawn from these sources and others, both for their importance to CSA research and for their potential usefulness for other areas of study.

First, social scientists should design research and analyze data with an understanding of the political pressures weighing on discussions of controversial issues like CSA. It may not be necessary or even advisable to be a partisan in these debates, but it may be harmful to ignore them and assume that numbers generated by institutions and research are not both subject to pressures from and use or manipulation by political movements. If researchers continue to design studies and analyze data without considering the political pressures that influence measurement at every stage, they will continue to find confusing and perhaps even contradictory counts. Those who wish to accurately represent social problems must approach them without illusions, looking at societal trends and pressures from the past, present, and future. (For instance, increased availability of cameras and camera phones has led to various scandals in child protection. In the coming years, it is likely that these developments will not only lead to a change in policy and institutional response, but also affect measurement.) Researchers might design studies to look closely at the political pressures weighing on decision-makers, and see how their decisions are affected by them. A fuller understanding of why certain incidents move through the system and others do not, why some cases are counted and others not, combined with institutional

numbers, would provide a clearer picture of the scope of CSA.

Second, every effort should be made to standardize collection procedures and open national, aggregated data sets to researchers. For instance, as we have discussed, our chief incidence measure, substantiated cases reported voluntarily to the National Child Abuse and Neglect Data System (NCANDS) provides imperfect measures. Aggregating data from states with different record-keeping systems, NCANDS ends up weighting equally reports from Arizona, which files all of one child's allegations into a single, most 'severe' category, and reports from Connecticut, which reports up to eight allegations per child (Finkelhor and Wells, 2003). NCANDS is a federally established and funded arm of the Department of Health and Human Services. Changes in federal regulations and legislation could streamline and implement new data systems for state CPS agencies that could allow for some state autonomy while creating core categories and definitions for national analysis, and make (privacy protected) data sets more full and available for researchers.

Third, researchers beginning new, independent measures of CSA should carefully plan and rigorously test instruments and design before being put into the field. As previously discussed studies showed, methodological differences such as the definition of abuse (Roosa et al. 1999), the number of questions the instrument asked (Finkelhor, 1994), or response rate (Gorey and Leslie, 1997) can result in significant differences. Walsh et al. (2004) argues for psychometric evaluation of questionnaires for 'acceptable' psychometric properties before using any surveys or questionnaires in the field. In light of the impact methodological variations can have on results, it is even more important that researchers in

CSA share instruments, design studies with best practices from both previous studies and instrument design theory in mind, and carefully design methodologies to avoid the documented biases we have seen.

Fourth, social scientists should develop instruments and studies to fill in the gaps in institutional data sets, particularly in understanding how decisions are made, discretion is exercised, and incidents find their way into reports and databases. Recent studies have taken innovative steps to illuminate these missing pieces in the epidemiology of CSA: such as vignette-based measurements of decision-making in reports of abuse by CPS workers (Benbenishty et al., 2002; Lazar, 2006) or mandatory reporters (Hinkelman and Bruno, 2008; Webster et al., 2005); or evaluation of CACs and other non-standard institutional responses and programs with experimental and other strong methodological designs (Smith et al., 2006; Walsh et al., 2007). These and other studies represent a promising start, but these efforts should be expanded, as too much of current understanding of CSA and institutional responses is based on anecdote, conjecture, and politics instead of solid qualitative and quantitative research.

If social scientists attempt to quantify and analyze the pressures and politics that influence decisions in cases of CSA, we will be left with a clearer understanding of what these measurements mean. We have hope that by counting CSA in careful, rigorous, accurate way, we can craft responses that will lead to lower counts in the future.

REFERENCES

Abma, J. C., Chandra, A., Mosher, W. D., Peterson, L. S. and Piccinino, L. J. (1997) 'Fertility, family planning, and women's health: New data from the 1995 national survey of family growth', *Vital and Health Statistics. Series 23, Data from the National Survey of Family Growth*, (19): 1–114.

Ainsworth, F. (2002) 'Mandatory reporting of child abuse and neglect: Does it really make a difference?' *Child & Family Social Work*, 7(1): 57–63.

Alikasifoglu, M., Erginoz, E., Ercan, O., Albayrak-Kaymak, D., Uysal, O. and Ilter, O. (2006) 'Sexual abuse among female high school students in Istanbul, Turkey', *Child Abuse & Neglect*, 30(3): 247–55.

Almeida, J., Cohen, A. P., Subramanian, S. V. and Molnar, E. E. (2008) 'Are increased worker caseloads in state child protective service agencies a potential explanation for the decline in child sexual abuse?: A multilevel analysis', *Child Abuse & Neglect*, 32(3): 367–75.

American Psychiatric Association (2000) Task Force on DSM-IV. Diagnostic and statistical manual of mental disorders DSM-IV-TR. in American Psychiatric Association [database online]. Washington, D.C.

Arata, C. M. (1998) 'To tell or not to tell: Current functioning of child sexual abuse survivors who disclosed their victimization', *Child Maltreatment*, 3(1): 63–71.

Arreola, S. G., Neilands, T. B., Pollack, L. M., Paul, J. P. and Catania, J. A. (2005) 'Higher prevalence of childhood sexual abuse among latino men who have sex with men than non-latino men who have sex with men: Data from the urban men's health study', *Child Abuse & Neglect*, 29(3): 285–90.

Bagley, C. (1991) 'The prevalence and mental health sequels of child sexual abuse in a community sample of women aged 18 to 27', *Canadian Journal of Community Mental Health*, 10(1): 103–16.

Bailey, J. A. and McCloskey, L. A. (2005) 'Pathways to adolescent substance use among sexually abused girls', *Journal of Abnormal Child Psychology*, 33(1): 39–53.

Baker-Ward, L., Gordon, E. N., Ornstein, P. A., Larus, D. M. and Clubb, P. A. (1993) 'Young children's long-term retention of a pediatric examination', *Child Development*, 64(5): 1519–33.

Benbenishty, R., Segev, D., Surkis, T. and Elias, T. (2002) 'Information-search and decision-making by professionals and nonprofessionals in cases of alleged child-abuse and maltreatment', *Journal of Social Service Research*, 28(3): 1–18.

Blakeslee, N. (2008) 'The reluctant prosecutor', *Texas Monthly*, October 2008.

Bogden, R. and Ksander, M. (1980) 'Policy data as a social process: A qualitative approach to quantitative data', *Human Organization*, 39(4): 302–9.

Bolen, R. M. and Scannapieco, M. (1999) 'Prevalence of child sexual abuse: A corrective metanalysis', *Social Service Review*, 73(3): 281–313.

Briere, J. N. and Elliott, D. M. (1994) 'Immediate and long-term impacts of child sexual abuse', *The Future of Children*, 4(2): 54–69.

Briere, J. and Runtz, M. (1988) 'Symptomatology associated with childhood sexual victimization in a nonclinical adult sample', *Child Abuse & Neglect*, 12(1): 51–9.

Browne, A. and Finkelhor, D. (1986) 'Impact of child sexual abuse: A review of the research', *Psychological Bulletin*, 99(1): 66–77.

Bruck, M., Ceci, S. J., Francoeur, E. and Barr, R. (1995) ' "I hardly cried when I got my shot": Influencing children's reports about a visit to their pediatrician', *Child Development*, 66(1): 193–208.

Ceci, S. J. and Bruck, M. (1993a) *Child witnesses: Translating research into policy*. Vol. 7SRCD. Ann Arbor: University of Michigan.

Ceci, S. J. and Bruck, M. (1993b) 'Suggestibility of the child witness: A historical review and synthesis', *Psychological Bulletin*, 113(3): 403–39.

Ceci, S. J. and Bruck, M. (1995) *Jeopardy in the Courtroom: A Scientific Analysis of Children's Testimony*. Washington, D.C.: American Psychological Association.

Cheit, Ross E. (2003) 'The limitations of a prospective study of memories for child sexual abuse', *The Journal of Child Sexual Abuse*, 12(2): 105–111.

Chen, J. Q., Dunne, M.P. and Han, P. (2004) 'Child sexual abuse in China: A study of adolescents in four provinces', *Child Abuse & Neglect*, 28(11): 1171–86.

Child Welfare Information Gateway (2008) 'Major federal legislation concerned with child protection, child welfare, and adoption', in U.S. Department of Health and Human Services, Administration on Children, Youth and Families; Children's Bureau [database online]. [cited 1/15/2009]. Available from http://www.childwelfare.gov/pubs/otherpubs/majorfedlegis.cfm.

Child Welfare Information Gateway (2006) and United States Children's Bureau. 'Child abuse and neglect', in Child Welfare Information Gateway [database online]. Washington, D.C.

Conte, J. R. (1994) 'Child sexual abuse: Awareness and backlash', *The Future of Children*, 4(2): 224–32.

Costin, L. B., Karger, H. J. and Stoeszm D. (1996) *The politics of child abuse in America*. New York: Oxford University Press.

Cross, T. P., Jones, L. M., Walsh, W. A., Simone, M. and Kolko, D. (2007) 'Child forensic interviewing in children's advocacy centers: Empirical data on a practice model', *Child Abuse & Neglect*, 31(10): 1031–52.

Drake, Brett (1996) 'Unraveling "Unsubstantiated"' *Child Maltreatment*, 1(3): 261–71.

Edgardh, K. and Ormstad, K. (2000) 'Prevalence and characteristics of sexual abuse in a national sample of Swedish seventeen-year-old boys and girls', *Acta Paediatrica*, 89(3): 310–19.

Everson, M. D., Boat, B. W., Bourg, S. and Robertson, K. R. (1996) 'Beliefs among professionals about rates of false allegations of child sexual abuse', *Journal of Interpersonal Violence*, 11(4): 541–53.

Faller, K. C. and Palusci, V. J. (2007) 'Children's advocacy centers: Do they lead to positive case outcomes?' *Child Abuse & Neglect*, 31(10): 1021–9.

Fanslow, J. L., Robinson, E. M., Crengle, S. and Perese, L. (2007) 'Prevalence of child sexual abuse reported by a cross-sectional sample of New Zealand women', *Child Abuse & Neglect*, 31(9): 935–45.

Finkelhor, D. (1994a) 'Current information on the scope and nature of child sexual abuse', *The Future of Children*, 4(2): 31–53.

Finkelhor, D. (1994b) 'An international epidemiology of child sexual abuse', *Child Abuse & Neglect*, 18(5): 409–17.

Finkelhor, D. (1993) 'Epidemiological factors in the clinical identification of child sexual abuse', *Child Abuse & Neglect*, 17(1): 67–70.

Finkelhor, D. (1984) *Child sexual abuse: New theory and research*. New York: Free Press.

Finkelhor, D. (1979) *Sexually victimized children*. New York: Free Press.

Finkelhor, D., Hotaling, G., Lewis, I.A. and Smith, C. (1990) 'Sexual abuse in a national survey of adult men and women: Prevalence, characteristics, and risk factors', *Child Abuse & Neglect*, 14(1): 19–28.

Finkelhor, D., Ormrod, R., Turner, H. and Hamby, S. L. (2005) 'The victimization of children and youth: A comprehensive, national survey', *Child Maltreatment*, 10(1): 5–25.

Finkelhor, D. and Wells, M. (2003) 'Improving data systems about juvenile victimization in the united states', *Child Abuse & Neglect*, 27(1): 77–102.

Finklehor, D. and Jones, L. (2006) 'Why have child maltreatment and child victimization declined?' *Journal of Social Issues*, 62(4): 685–716.

Fivush, R. (1993) 'Developmental perspectives on autobiographical recall', in Gail S. Goodman and Bette L. Bottoms (eds) *Child victims, child witnesses: Understanding and improving testimony*. New York: Guilford Press. pp. 1–24.

Freyd, J. J. (2003) 'Memory for abuse: What can we learn from a prosecution sample?' *Journal of Child Sexual Abuse*, 12(3): 97–103.

Gallup Organization (1995) *Disciplining children in America: A Gallup poll report*. Princeton, N.J.: Gallup Organization.

Gardner, R. A. (1992) *True and false accusations of child sex abuse*. Cresskill, N.J.: Creative Therapeutics.

Goddard, C. and Saunders, B. (2001) 'Child abuse and the media', *Child Abuse Prevention Issues: 14*. National Child Protection Clearinghouse, Australia. Available online: http://www.aifs.gov.au/nch/pubs/issues/issues14/issues14.html

Goldman, J. D. G. and Padayachi, U. K. (2000) 'Some methodological problems in estimating incidence and prevalence in child sexual abuse research', *Journal of Sex Research*, 37(4): 305–14.

Goodkind, S., Ng, I. and Sarri, R. C. (2006) 'The impact of sexual abuse in the lives of young women involved or at risk of involvement with the juvenile justice system', *Violence against Women*, 12(5): 456–77.

Goodman, G. S. and Clarke-Stewart, A. (1991) 'Suggestibility in children's testimony: Implications for sexual abuse investigations', in John Doris (ed.) *The suggestibility of children's recollections*. Washington DC: American Psychological Association. pp. 92–105.

Goodman, G. S., Ghetti, S., Quas, J. A., Edelstein, R. S., Weede, K., Redlich, A. D., Cordon, I. M. and Jones, D. P. H. (2003) 'A prospective study of memory for child sexual abuse: New findings relevant to the repressed-memory controversy', *Psychological Science*, 14(2): 113–18.

Goodman, G. S. and Goodman-Brown, T. (2007) 'Foreword', in M.-E. Pipe, M. E. Lamb, Y. Orbach and A.-C. Cederborg (eds) *Child sexual abuse: Disclosure, delay, and denial*. Mahwah: Lawrence Erlbaum Associates. pp. vvi–ix.

Gordon, L. (1988) 'The politics of child sexual abuse: notes from American history', *Feminist Review*, 28: 56–64.

Gorey, K. M. and Leslie, D. R. (1997) 'The prevalence of child sexual abuse: Integrative review adjustment for potential response and measurement biases', *Child Abuse & Neglect*, 21(4): 391–8.

Gunn, V. L., Hickson, G. B. and Cooper, W. O. (2005) 'Factors affecting pediatricians' reporting of suspected child maltreatment', *Ambulatory Pediatrics*, 5(2): 96–101.

Haj-Yahia, M. M. and Tamish, S. (2001) 'The rates of child sexual abuse and its psychological consequences as revealed by a study among Palestinian university students', *Child Abuse & Neglect*, 25(10): 1303–27.

Hanson, R. F., Resnick, H. S., Saunders, B. E., Kilpatrick, D. G. and Best, C. (1999) 'Factors related to the reporting of childhood rape', *Child Abuse & Neglect*, 23(6): 559–69.

Haskett, M., Wayland, K., Hutcheson, J. and Tavana, T. (1995) 'Substantiation of sexual abuse allegations: Factors in the decision-making process', *Journal of Child Sexual Abuse*, 4(2): 19–47.

Haugaard, J. J. and Emery, R. E. (1989) 'Methodological issues in child sexual abuse research', *Child Abuse & Neglect*, 13(1): 89–100.

Hechler, D. (1988) *The battle and the backlash: The child sexual abuse war*. Lexington, Mass.: Lexington Books.

Henry, J. (1997) 'System intervention trauma to child sexual abuse victims following disclosure', *Journal of Interpersonal Violence*, 12(4): 499–512.

Herman, S. (2005) 'Improving decision making in forensic child sexual abuse evaluations', *Law and Human Behavior*, 29(1): 87–120.

Hines, D. A. and Finkelhor, D. (2007) 'Statutory sex crime relationships between juveniles and adults: A review of social scientific research', *Aggression and Violent Behavior*, 12(3): 300–14.

Hinkelman, L. and Bruno, M. (2008) 'Identification and reporting of child sexual abuse: The role of elementary school professionals', *The Elementary School Journal*, 108(5): 376–91.

Hund, A. and Espelage, D. (2005) 'Childhood sexual abuse, disordered eating, alexithymia, and general distress: A mediation model', *Journal of Counseling Psychology*, 52(4): 559–73.

Jackson, R. (1940) 'The federal prosecutor', *Journal of the American Judicate Society*, 24(June): 18.

Jencks, C. (1994) *The homeless*. Cambridge, MA: Harvard University Press.

Jenkins, P. (1998) *Moral panic : Changing concepts of the child molester in modern America*. New Haven, CT: Yale University Press.

Jones, L. M., Cross, T. P., Walsh, W. A. and Simone, M. (2007) 'Do children's advocacy centers improve families' experiences of child sexual abuse investigations?' *Child Abuse & Neglect*, 31(10): 1069–85.

Jones, L. M., Finkelhor, D. and Kopiec, K. (2001) 'Why is sexual abuse declining? A survey of state child protection administrators', *Child Abuse & Neglect*, 25(9): 1139–58.

Jones, L. (1993) 'Decision making in child welfare: A critical review of the literature', *Child & Adolescent Social Work Journal*, 10(3): 241–62.

Kellogg, N. D. and Huston, R. L. (1995) 'Unwanted sexual experiences in adolescents: Patterns of disclosure', *Clinical Pediatrics*, 34(6): 306–12.

Kercher, G. A. and McShane, M. (1984) 'The prevalence of child sexual abuse victimization in an adult sample of Texas residents', *Child Abuse & Neglect*, 8(4): 495–501.

Lalor, K. (2004) 'Child sexual abuse in sub-Saharan Africa: A literature review', *Child Abuse & Neglect*, 28(4): 439–60.

Lampe, A. (2002) 'The prevalence of childhood sexual abuse, physical abuse, and emotional neglect in Europe', *Zeitschrift fur Psychosomatische Medizin und Psychotherapie*, 48(4): 370–80.

Laney, C. and Loftus, E. (2005) 'Traumatic memories are not necessarily accurate memories', *Canadian Journal of Psychiatry*, 50(13): 823–8.

Lanktree, C., Briere, J. and Zaidi, L. (1991) 'Incidence and impact of sexual abuse in a child outpatient sample: The role of direct inquiry', *Child Abuse & Neglect*, 15(4): 447–53.

Lazar, A. (2006) 'Determinants of child protection officers' decisions in emergency situations: An experimental study', *Child & Youth Care Forum*, 35(3): 263–76.

Leventhal, J. (2001) 'A decline in substantiated cases of child sexual abuse in the United States: Good news or false hope?' *Child Abuse & Neglect*, 25: 1137–8.

Lewin, L. C. (2007) 'Sexually transmitted infections in preadolescent children', *Journal of Pediatric Health Care*, 21(3): 153–61.

Loftus, E. F. and Ketcham, K. (1994) *The myth of repressed memory: False memories and allegations of sexual abuse.* New York: St. Martin's Press.

London, K., Bruck, M., Ceci, S. J. and Shuman, D. W. (2007) 'Disclosure of child sexual abuse: A review of the contemporary empirical literature', in M.-E. Pipe, M. E. Lamb, Y. Orbach and A.-C. Cederborg (eds) *Child sexual abuse: Disclosure, delay, and denial.* Mahwah: Lawrence Erlbaum Associates. pp. 11–39.

London, K., Bruck, M., Wright, D. B. and Ceci, S. J. (2008) 'Review of the contemporary literature on how children report sexual abuse to others: Findings, methodological issues, and implications for forensic interviewers', *Memory*, 16(1): 29–47.

Lyon, T. D. (2007) 'False denials: Overcoming methodological biases in abuse disclosure research', in M.-E. Pipe, M. E. Lamb, Y. Orbach and A.-C. Cederborg (eds) *Child sexual abuse: Disclosure, delay, and denial.* Mahwah: Lawrence Erlbaum Associates. pp. 41–62.

MacMillan, H. L., Fleming, J. E., Troome, N., Boyle, M.H., Wong, M., Racine, Y.A., Beardslee, W.R. and Offord, D.R. (1997) 'Prevalence of child physical and sexual abuse in the community – results from the Ontario health supplement', *Jama-Journal of the American Medical Association*, 278(2): 131–5.

Martell, D. R. (2002) *Child placement and criminal prosecution: A study of the relationship between criminal justice and protective service interventions in cases of child abuse.* PhD Dissertation for Brandeis University.

McCrann, D., Lalor, K. and Katabaro, J. K. (2006) 'Childhood sexual abuse among university students in Tanzania', *Child Abuse & Neglect*, 30(12) (DEC): 1343–51.

Mullen, P. E., Romansclarkson, S.E., Walton, V.A. and Herbison, G.P. (1988) 'Impact of sexual and physical abuse on womens mental-health', *Lancet*, 1(8590): 841–5.

Myers, J. E. B. (1994a) *The backlash: Child protection under fire.* Thousand Oaks, CA: Sage Publications.

Myers, J. E. B. (1994b) 'Child abuse: The response of the legal system', in Mark Costanzo and Stuart Oskamp (eds) *Violence and the law.* Thousand Oaks, CA: Sage Publications.

Nance, K. (1991) 'Statewide poll dispels myths of child sexual abuse', *Lexington Herald-Leader (KY)*, 12/1/1991, sec A.

Nelson, B. J. (1984) *Making an issue of child abuse : Political agenda setting for social problems.* Chicago: University of Chicago Press.

Noll, J. G., Trickett, P. K., Susman, E. J. and Putnam, F. W. (2006) 'Sleep disturbances and childhood sexual abuse', *Journal of Pediatric Psychology*, 31(5): 469–80.

Olsson, A., Ellsberg, M., Berglund, S., Herrera, A., Zelaya, E., Pena, R., Zelaya, F. and Persson, L.A. (2000) 'Sexual abuse during childhood and adolescence among Nicaraguan men and women: A population-based anonymous survey', *Child Abuse & Neglect*, 24(12): 1579–89.

Pereda, N. and Forns, M. (2007) 'Prevalencia y características del abuso sexual infantil en estudiantes universitarios españoles', (Prevalence and Characteristics of Child Sexual Abuse in Spanish University Students), *Child Abuse & Neglect*, 31(4): 417–26.

Pipe, M.-E., Lamb, M. E., Orbach, Y. and Cederborg, A.-C. (2007a) (eds) *Child sexual abuse: Disclosure, delay, and denial.* Mahwah: Lawrence Erlbaum Associates.

Pipe, M.-E., Orbach, Y., Lamb, M. E. and Cederborg, A.-C. (2007b) 'Seeking resolution in the disclosure wars: An overview', in M.-E. Pipe, M. E. Lamb, Y. Orbach and A.-C. Cederborg (eds) *Child sexual abuse: Disclosure, delay, and denial.* Mahwah: Lawrence Erlbaum Associates.

Putnam, F. W. (2003) 'Ten-year research update review: Child sexual abuse', *Journal of the American Academy of Child & Adolescent Psychiatry*, 42(3): 269–78.

Rheingold, A. A., Campbell, C., Self-Brown, S., de Arellano, M., Resnick, H. and Kilpatrick, D. (2007) 'Prevention of child sexual abuse: Evaluation of a community media campaign', *Child Maltreatment*, 12(4): 352–63.

Rispens, J., Aleman, A. and Goudena, P. P. (1997) 'Prevention of child sexual abuse victimization: A meta-analysis of school programs', *Child Abuse & Neglect*, 21(10): 975–87.

Robin, M. (1991a) 'The social construction of child abuse and "false allegations"', *Child & Youth Services*, 15(2): 1–34.

Robin, M. (1991b) *Assessing child maltreatment reports: The problem of false allegations*. New York: Haworth Press.

Roosa, M. W., Reyes, L., Reinholtz, C. and Angelini, P. J. (1998) 'Measurement of women's child sexual abuse experiences: An empirical demonstration of the impact of choice of measure on estimates of incidence rates and of relationships with pathology', *Journal of Sex Research*, 35(3): 225–33.

Roy, A. and Janal, M. (2006) 'Gender in suicide attempt rates and childhood sexual abuse rates: Is there an interaction?' *Suicide and Life-Threatening Behavior*, 36(3): 329–35.

Rush, F. (1980) *The best kept secret: Sexual abuse of children*. Englewood Cliffs, N.J.: Prentice-Hall.

Saunders, B. E., Villeponteaux, L. A., Lipovsky, J. A., Kilpatrick, D. G. and Veronen, L. J. (1992) 'Child sexual assault as a risk factor for mental disorders among women: A community survey', *Journal of Interpersonal Violence*, 7(2): 189–204.

Saywitz, K. J. and Snyder, L. (1993) 'Improving children's testimony with preparation', in G. S. Goodman and B. L. Bottoms (eds) *Child victims, child witnesses: Understanding and improving testimony*. New York: Guilford Press. pp. 117–146.

Schreier, H. A. (1996) 'Repeated false allegations of sexual abuse presenting to sheriffs: When is it munchausen by proxy?' *Child Abuse & Neglect*, 20(10): 985–91.

Sedlak, A. J., Schultz, D., Wells, S. J., Lyons, P., Doueck, H. J. and Gragg, F. (2006) 'Child protection and justice systems processing of serious child abuse and neglect cases', *Child Abuse & Neglect*, 30(6): 657–77.

Sedlak, A., Broadhurst, D. D., National Center on Child Abuse and Neglect and Westat, and James Bell Associates (1996) *Third national incidence study of child abuse and neglect : Final report*. [Washington, D.C.]: U.S. Dept. of Health and Human Services, Administration for Children and Families, Administration on Children, Youth and Families, National Center on Child Abuse and Neglect.

Siegel, J. M., Sorenson, S. B., Golding, J. M., Burnam, M. A. and Stein, J. A. (1987) 'The prevalence of childhood sexual assault – the Los-Angeles epidemiologic catchment-area project', *American Journal of Epidemiology*, 126(6): 1141–53.

Singh, H. S. S. A., Yiing, W. W. and Nurani, H. N. K. (1996) 'Prevalence of childhood sexual abuse among Malaysian paramedical students', *Child Abuse & Neglect*, 20(6): 487–92.

Smith, D. W., Letourneau, E. J., Saunders, B. E., Kilpatrick, D. G., Resnick, H. S. and Best, C. L. (2000) 'Delay in disclosure of childhood rape: Results from a national survey', *Child Abuse & Neglect*, 24(2): 273–87.

Smith, D. W., Witte, T. H. and Fricker-Elhai, A. E. (2006) 'Service outcomes in physical and sexual abuse cases: A comparison of child advocacy center-based and standard services', *Child Maltreatment*, 11(4): 354–60.

Sommerville, C. J. (1982) *The rise and fall of childhood*. Beverly Hills, CA: Sage Publications.

Speizer, I. S., Goodwin, M., Whittle, L., Clyde, M. and Rogers. J. (2008) 'Dimensions of child sexual abuse before age 15 in three Central American countries: Honduras, El Salvador, and Guatemala', *Child Abuse & Neglect*, 32(4): 455–62.

Stone, D. A. (2002) *Policy paradox: The art of political decision making*. New York: Norton.

Tabachnick, J., Henry, F. and Denny, L. (1997) 'Perceptions of child sexual abuse as a public health problem – Vermont, September 1995', *Morbidity and Mortality Weekly Report*, 46, (34) (8/29/1997): 801–3, http://www.cdc.gov/mmwr/preview/mmwrhtml/00049151.htm

Timnick, L. (1985) '22% in survey were child abuse victims', *Los Angeles Times*, 8/25/1985.

Trocmé, N. and Bala, N. (2005) 'False allegations of abuse and neglect when parents separate', *Child Abuse & Neglect*, 29(12): 1333–45.

United States Bureau of the Census (2003) State & county quickfacts, in The Bureau [database online] Washington, D.C.

Van Voorhis, R. A. and Gilbert, N. (1998) 'The structure and performance of child abuse reporting systems', *Children and Youth Services Review*, 20(3): 207–21.

Waites, M. (2005) *The age of consen : Young people, sexuality, and citizenship*. Houndmills, Basingstoke, Hampshire; New York: Palgrave Macmillan.

Wakefield, H. and. Underwager, R. C. (1988) *Accusations of child sexual abuse*. Springfield, Ill: C.C. Thomas.

Walsh, C., Jamieson, E., MacMillan, H. and Trocmé, N. (2004) 'Measuring child sexual abuse in children and youth', *Journal of Child Sexual Abuse*, 13(1): 39–68.

Walsh, W. A., Cross, T. P., Jones, L. M., Simone, M. and Kolko, D. J. (2007) 'Which sexual abuse victims receive a forensic medical examination? the impact of children's advocacy centers', *Child Abuse & Neglect*, 31(10): 1053–68.

Way, I., van Deusen, K. M., Martin, G., Applegate, B. and Jandle, D. (2004) 'Vicarious trauma: A comparison of clinicians who treat survivors of sexual abuse and sexual offenders', *Journal of Interpersonal Violence*, 19(1): 49–71.

Webster, S. W., O'Toole, R., O'Toole, A. W. and Lucal, B. (2005) 'Overreporting and underreporting of child abuse: Teachers' use of professional discretion', *Child Abuse & Neglect*, 29(11): 1281–96.

Wells, S. J., Lyons, P., Doueck, H. J., Brown, C. H. and Thomas, J. (2004) 'Ecological factors and screening in child protective services', *Children and Youth Services Review*, 26(10): 981–97.

Westcott, H. L. and Jones, D. P. H. (1999) 'Annotation: The abuse of disabled children', *Journal of Child Psychology and Psychiatry*, 40(4): 497–506.

Wexler, R. (1990) *Wounded innocents: The real victims of the war against child abuse*. Buffalo, NY: Prometheus Books.

Whetten, K., Leserman, J., Lowe, K., Stangl, D., Thielman, N., Swartz, M., Hanisch, L., Van Scoyoc, L. and Moore, M. (2006) 'Prevalence of childhood sexual abuse and physical trauma in an HIV-positive sample from the deep south', *American Journal of Public Health*, 96(6): 1028–30.

Whitcomb, D. (1992) *When the victim is a child.* 2nd editiom. Washington, D.C.: US Department of Justice.

Whittier, N. (2009) *From self-help to the state: The politics of child sexual abuse.* New York: Oxford University Press.

Widom, C. S. and Morris, S. (1997) 'Accuracy of adult recollections of childhood victimization, part 2: Childhood sexual abuse', *Psychological Assessment*, 9(1): 34–46.

Williams, D. M. (2006) 'Children first: National model for the vertical prosecution of cases involving murdered and physically abused children', *Journal of Aggression, Maltreatment & Trauma*, 12(3–4): 131–48.

Williams, L. M. (1994) 'Recall of childhood trauma: A prospective study of women's memories of child sexual abuse', *Journal of Consulting and Clinical Psychology*, 62(6): 1167–76.

Winterbottom, A., Bekker, H. L., Conner, M. and Mooney, A. (2008) 'Does narrative information bias individual's decision making? A systematic review', *Social Science & Medicine*, 67(12): 2079–88.

Yehuda, R., Friedman, M., Rosenbaurn, T. Y., Labinsky, E. and Schmeidler J. (2007) 'History of past sexual abuse in married observant Jewish women', *American Journal of Psychiatry*, 164(11): 1700–6.

23

Indirect Measurement

David J. Bartholomew

BACKGROUND

Measurement is part of everyday life. Robinson's *The Story of Measurement* (Robinson, 2007) illustrates how the measurement of things, mundane and esoteric, is something we are all familiar with. We look at the thermometer to tell us whether to put on an extra coat. The financial pages of the newspaper will give us indexes of share prices to tell us how the financial markets are performing. As we drive to work, the speedometer will enable us to keep within the speed limit and the fuel gauge will indicate when we should stop to fill up. Our computer will tell us how many e-mail messages are awaiting our attention and the clock on the wall will mark the passage of time. In such a manner we are endlessly fed with numbers which both inform us and guide our decisions. In this welter of numerical information, which is thrust upon us, there lurks a host of questions which we scarcely pause to think about. We are easily lulled into a state of mind in which

it is easy to accept, without question, that these numbers contain meaning which we will instantly recognise.

My own entry into the field of measurement was neither direct nor planned and it had two different origins which were quite unconnected. The first arose out of my interest in stochastic models for social processes – the attempt to understand the aggregate dynamics of social systems in terms of the seemingly random behaviour of the individuals of which they were composed. This work appeared in many publications culminating in Bartholomew (1973). This book included some discussion of the measurement of such things as labour turnover and social mobility but only in a subsidiary role. The second approach was through my interest in establishing factor analysis, and related latent variable models, as a respectable branch of statistical theory. The general approach was set out in Bartholomew and Knott (1999). It quickly became apparent to me that this field included an important and highly controversial topic known as the problem of factor scores. This problem is concerned with how one should assign individuals to points on a latent scale on the basis of their scores in a set of tests.

In both cases, the starting point was a statistical (probability) model and this led inexorably, but painfully slowly, first to the realisation that many, if not most measurement problems, could be expressed as problems either of estimation or prediction using a fitted model. The second realisation was that estimation problems arose when we were thinking of measuring something which was a characteristic of a population, or aggregate, whereas prediction referred to a single individual. In technical language, the former involved the estimation of a parameter and the latter the prediction of the value of a random variable. The working out of these insights is the substance of *The Statistical Approach to Social Measurement*, Bartholomew (1996) and it forms the backbone of this chapter. This approach stands in seeming contrast to much of the preceding work in sociology, psychology, economics and elsewhere which had been predominantly intuitive and *ad hoc*. However, this distinction is more apparent, than real because model construction is often a formalisation of what had already been implicit. Like all attempts at systematisation, it provides a justification for much current practice but also the base for new extensions. Throughout this chapter we shall seek to integrate the formal and the informal approaches to measurement.

There are many definitions of measurement but one which will serve us here is that it is *the assigning of numbers to objects in a way which, in some sense, reflects their magnitudes*. A moment's reflection, however, will show that not all such numbers are the same – some are 'more equal than others'. Some are simply

obtained by counting. The number of emails waiting or the number of people ahead of us in the Post Office queue is a perfectly straightforward numerical statement about the world around us. Other numbers may only give a rank order, while others may be arrived at by using a measuring instrument like a weighing machine. There might be debate about how these numbers should guide our actions, but little argument about what is actually measured. Anyone else, looking at the same situation, will arrive at the same answer.

The same is not true of the temperature of a room. Physics defines temperature in terms of the degree of activity of the molecules which make up the air. We cannot see these molecules or directly measure what they are doing so we have to rely, instead, on some indirect indication. For example, the length of a narrow column of a liquid, such as mercury, depends on the ambient temperature and so changes of this length will indicate changes of temperature. But how do we convert this length into a number? And how do we cope with the fact that the size of changes of length will depend on what liquid we use? Even if we all use the same liquid, that still leaves the question of how temperature and length are related.

Things become even worse when we move into the social field and eavesdrop on the debates which take place there. We find terms like intelligence, inequality, mobility and depression being used just as if they were measurable quantities like the things we count. People are said to have more or less of these things in much the same way as they have larger incomes or bigger houses. Some politicians would have us believe that reducing tax rates will increase our happiness. Such statements are quantitative and they imply an ability to measure the things which are spoken of in a way which is generally recognised and understood. Although there certainly are things in the social field which can be measured in a straightforward fashion, such as the number of centenarians in the country, many more are ill-defined and can only be measured indirectly. We clearly need to think of measurement in general enough terms to cover this variety of circumstances.

WHY MEASUREMENT IS IMPORTANT

Measurement in the social sciences is just as important as in other, more easily quantifiable fields. This is, partly at least, because measures enter so often into political and social debate. They are intended to bring clarity and precision to debates but, so often, they cloud rather than clarify the issues under discussion.

We motivate our thinking by starting with the related concepts of equality and diversity. Both are generally considered 'a good thing' but, so often, they appear to be in opposition to one another. Equality is good and politicians count it to their credit if they can demonstrate that inequalities in wealth have decreased. At the same time diversity is also a good thing and diversity means difference, but difference spells inequality! It is clear, therefore, that we cannot sensibly speak of either in unqualified terms. To emphasise the point we turn to other, familiar examples. In the academic world, it is the business of examiners to detect and quantify differences (diversity of ability) and they would be regarded as in dereliction of duty if, for example, all degree candidates were awarded the same class of degree. On the other hand, employers are expected to ensure that all ethnic groups are proportionately represented in their workforces. They must not discriminate on any criterion which is held to be irrelevant to the duties to be performed. All individuals

must have equal opportunities. It will be immediately clear that there are distinctions to be made here if we are to avoid confusion.

Disputes often bring to light a lack of clarity about what it is one is trying to measure. Indeed, an important function of measurement theory is to help us clarify what it is we are talking about. This is especially true in the case of the example which we have already mentioned, namely intelligence. Thus measurement is not simply the assigning of numbers to objects in a way which reflects their magnitude. It is also a way of getting our ideas as clear as possible on what it is we are talking about. One way of putting it is to say that there has to be a 'dialogue' between the measure and the concept. As we bring the two into greater harmony we increase our understanding of the subject matter. Intelligence is one of those concepts which is widely used – as though everyone knows exactly what is meant by the term. We all speak of someone as being very intelligent or that A is more intelligent than B as though it is self-evident that such assertions are meaningful. But they are not. Such statements presuppose that intelligence is a well-defined entity for which a measuring instrument is available. There is, of course, such a measure in the shape of the *Intelligence Quotient* (IQ) which is often treated as though it is synonymous with intelligence. IQ does have many practical uses but it does not adequately capture all that we habitually mean by intelligence. Indeed, it is often pointed out that measured values of IQ are sometimes at variance with subjective judgements about relative intelligence. This simply reflects the fact that IQ does not adequately cover all that we mean when we speak of intelligence. Judging these matters requires a subtle interplay between possible measures and the concept which we are trying to capture.

SOCIAL MEASUREMENT: THREE WAYS OF CLASSIFYING MEASURES

We already have the rudiments of a classification of measures; we now make it explicit. First, and most fundamental, there is *direct* and *indirect* measurement. Some things can be directly observed, for example the number of car drivers in a population or the ratio of male to female births in a country. These may be easy or difficult to measure in practice but there is no problem, in principle, about doing it. On the other hand, there are indirect methods, with which this chapter is primarily concerned. We have already mentioned intelligence and quality of life but there are many others. Secondly, we classify measures according to whether they refer to some aspect of a population, or aggregate, as opposed to whether they refer to individuals.

Finally, each of these categories may be sub-divided according to whether or not they are derived from probability models. Intuitive methods are difficult to define precisely but easy to illustrate as we shall shortly see.

All of these distinctions will become clearer as the discussion develops. For the present, they serve to provide a structure for our presentation.

ARE INDIRECTLY MEASURED QUANTITIES *REAL*?

Discussions of measurement can easily become bogged down in philosophical debates about whether the thing being measured is *real*. For most purposes this issue is irrelevant; the important question concerns usefulness. Nevertheless, it is desirable to dispel some misunderstandings at the outset. A quantity can be real enough yet beyond the reach of direct measurement. For example, we might wish to measure

something like personal wealth, which certainly exists but which, for one reason or another, we are not able to measure directly. An alternative is to approach it indirectly by measuring other correlates of wealth such as occupation, possession of a second home and suchlike. However, most of the cases we meet are not like this but are what are better referred to as *constructs*; that is, entities which we invent to facilitate our thinking about the social world. Intelligence is a prime example, but there are many others such as social mobility and conservatism. Essentially, these scales are constructed mentally to facilitate our thinking about the quantity and to economise in the effort required to do so. They are not necessarily well-defined and one purpose of measurement is to make them more precise, as we have noted.

Both versions of these concepts, whether real or constructed, are *unobservable* in practice, if not in principle, but they are treated in essentially the same way. In technical language they are *latent* or *hidden*. The theoretical problem we then confront is how to learn something about things which are latent from things that we can directly observe.

AGGREGATE-LEVEL MEASUREMENT

In both individual- and aggregate- level measurement, we shall adopt a two-pronged attack. First, we shall follow the intuitive route where we proceed by a mixture of intuition and analogy. Second, we shall try to see the problem in a more general way, in terms of a probability model, which tries to capture the essence of the problem mathematically.

Aggregate- and individual-level measures are easily confused. For example, intelligence provides a salutary lesson of the misunderstanding which can result from treating an individual measure as though it applied to a population. James Watson, the co-discoverer of the double helix structure of DNA, was alleged to have claimed that Blacks were less intelligent than Whites. Essentially, this is a statement about populations, but the IQ measurements, on which it was based, are at the individual level and tell us nothing, directly, about group differences. To measure the 'intelligence' of any population, and hence to justify statements at that level, would require us to think first in aggregate terms about how best to describe the distribution of individual measurements.

Some of the most important measurement problems at the population level are also the most difficult. They relate to dynamic systems where the interest is often in measuring change. The oldest and most thoroughly discussed problem of this kind is that of index numbers for measuring price levels, or what is often referred to as the cost of living. Such measures aim to capture the essence of the changing levels of the prices of a multitude of items over a period of time and the changing quantities of them which are used. Social, or occupational, mobility, with which my own interest began, is another example. Here again the complexity of the changing patterns of movement between classes somehow has to be captured by a single index.

At the aggregate level we may well need a different model for each situation, but in the case of individual level measurement, as we shall see, we are often able deal with a whole class of measurement problems together. However, we begin at the aggregate level.

MEASURING INEQUALITY

Here we look at the measurement of population characteristics taking as an example the measurement of inequality.

This has most commonly been discussed in relation to inequalities in wealth or income but has also been used for measuring health provision inequalities and discriminating power in risk management. In fact, any variable, which can be thought of as the 'size' of something, will be grist to the mill. Inequality is a characteristic of a population, not of any individual member of it. It can be approached in a purely intuitive, or empirical, way or as a model-based method on the lines described above. We take each approach in turn.

We begin with the empirical approach, guided by analogy and intuition. In doing this we follow the path taken by Corrado Gini in relation to income or wealth. Gini is best remembered, perhaps, as the inventor of a coefficient which bears his name. In a population of individuals each will have an income. Those incomes will differ and our aim is to find a measure of those differences. In the case of two individuals there is no problem because the difference between their incomes is the natural and obvious measure of inequality. However, the answer we get will obviously depend on the currency in which income is measured. Converting from pounds to dollars, for example, will give a different answer. It makes sense, therefore, to make our measure independent of the currency used. This may easily be done by expressing incomes in relation to some average value which thus plays the part of a common currency. From now on, therefore, we suppose that all incomes are expressed in units of the average. When we move on to several individuals there are many such differences we ask, for example, how should they be combined into a single measure? One obvious possibility is to take their average. In essence this gives us the Gini coefficient. It has the great advantage of being interpretable – it is exactly what it says it is – the average income difference. Interestingly, the Gini coefficient can also be derived by following a seemingly different route using what is known as the Lorenz curve. A common way of reporting inequality is to say, for example, that 5 per cent of the people have 80 per cent of the income. This suggests a considerable degree of inequality but why pick on this particular comparison? There are other such comparisons. We might add, for example, that 10 per cent have 90 per cent and so on. Percentages such as those we have given could be plotted one against the other and they would then form what is known as the Lorenz curve. In a strictly equal society any x per cent of the people would have x per cent of the income and the Lorenz curve would then be a diagonal line rising from the point (0,0) to the point (100,0). The further the actual curve is below this diagonal, the greater the inequality. The area between the two curves measures inequality and is equivalent to the Gini coefficient. If we multiply the area by two we shall have a measure varying between 0 and 1 – the upper end of the range corresponding to the greatest degree of inequality. This measure has been widely used at a descriptive level: for typical human populations the value might come out to be around 0.3 or 0.4.

A MODEL-BASED APPROACH

Gini's approach is perfectly adequate as an empirical means of measuring inequality but it is helpful to see the problem in a more general context, because it gives us a framework for tackling other, similar problems. In this way we identify a class of problems for which we can provide a general solution.

The first step is to recognise that we are dealing with values of a random variable whose pattern of variation is described by a probability distribution. The problem is then essentially one of finding the appropriate summary measure for the distribution. Elementary statistical courses take the student through a series of such measures beginning with measures of location, then moving on to measures of dispersion, kurtosis and so on. A measure of location is concerned with size and a measure of dispersion with the degree of spread. It is clear that the idea of inequality comes close to the idea of dispersion but, as noted above, it suffers from the disadvantage of being scale-dependent. We have seen that this can be dealt with quite easily by expressing the variable in units of the mean. This is the same as computing the coefficient of variation, usually denoted by σ/μ, where σ is the standard deviation and μ is the mean. A second empirical way is, at first sight, more subtle, but it provides a link with what follows. It is to look not at the individual values but at their logarithms. The reason is at once apparent by noting that $\log ax = \log x + \log a$. This says that if we multiply any number x by a positive constant a and then take its logarithm, we get the sum of the logarithms of a and x. If, therefore, we were to go back and pose our original problem in terms of the logarithm, rather than the original variable, we could again look to the variance (or standard deviation) without the trouble of finding that the measure was scale dependent. Adding a constant, $\log a$ in this case, makes no difference to the variance. This suggests that there might be other cases where we might take logarithms, namely those where we have a non-negative variable and where we require a scale-independent measure. It is easy to show that, in some cases, the standard deviation of the logarithm is quite close to the coefficient of variation.

So far we have not really moved very far beyond the empiricism of Gini's method.

What we have done is to gain access to a more general problem of finding a scale-free measure of dispersion of a frequency distribution. It certainly represents progress to have reduced the problem to one where there is a known solution, but we can go further. There is no obvious empirical way of relating Gini's coefficient to either the coefficient of variation or the standard deviation of the logarithms. If they were all to depend, at a deeper level, on some more fundamental property of the distribution, then we would have reason to feel that we had captured the essence of inequality. There is, in fact, a little-known, but simple, connection between the average difference and the variance of a set of numbers which serves to draw attention to the similarity between a variance and the mean average difference as used in Gini's coefficient. It may be shown that

$$\sigma^2 = \tfrac{1}{2} \sum (x_i - x_j)^2 / n(n-1) \quad (23.1)$$

where the summation is over both i and j. The variance is, therefore, half the average of the squared differences between the xs whereas the Gini coefficient is the average of the absolute differences.

If there were some reason for expecting $\log x$ to be normally distributed there would be a rationale for basing a measure of inequality on its standard deviation since this is the parameter which summarises the variation. It is an empirical fact that many distributions of size are in fact lognormal, meaning that their logarithms have a normal distribution. We know that normal distributions tend to arise when a variable can be regarded as the sum of independent parts. If the logarithm is to be a sum then the variable itself must be a product and there are plausible reasons for expecting this to be the case with many size distributions. For example, let us imagine that value of wealth is arrived

at by a series of steps. Suppose present wealth increases in one step by an amount which is proportional to current wealth. This is plausible because, for example, money earned as interest is usually determined on a percentage basis, as are pay rises. If those increments are independent, then, under the foregoing assumptions, the distribution of total wealth after several steps will be approximately lognormal.

None of this shows that size distributions will be precisely lognormal of course, merely that there will be a tendency in that direction. Insofar as that turns out to be the case, the standard deviation of the distribution will be a reasonable measure of inequality and that is all we need. It is therefore this parameter, σ say, which captures the essence of what we mean by inequality. Unsurprisingly, both of the other measures we have mentioned are functions of σ only and, furthermore, they turn out to be almost proportional to one another. We have

$$\text{coefficient of variation} = (\exp \sigma^2 - 1)^{\tfrac{1}{2}} \quad (23.2)$$

and

$$\text{Gini coefficient} = 2\Phi(\sigma \sqrt{2} - 1) \quad (23.3)$$

where $\Phi(.)$ is the normal distribution function. The important thing is that both measures, which were first thought of on purely empirical grounds, now appear to be linked to something more fundamental, namely a probability distribution.

It should be clear from this example what the general strategy is. First, we specify a probability model for the process which underlies the quantity to be measured. Then we identify what aspect, i.e. parameter, of the model, corresponds most closely to what it is we wish to measure. In this example, which was particularly simple, the model was a probability distribution of the logarithm of the size variable. In the case of social mobility we would have to have a model describing the dynamics of the problem as family lines move from one generation to the next. Such a model might require several parameters and we would then have to see what combination of them best matched our notion of mobility.

INDIVIDUAL-LEVEL MEASUREMENT

We begin with the intuitive approach. If we cannot measure something directly, the next best thing is to measure something else which is closely related to it. In the case of temperature, the length of a column of mercury is related to the degree of agitation of the molecules surrounding the bulb of the thermometer. In this case the relationship is a precise one; a given increase in activity will always produce the same increase in length. In the social sciences relationships are seldom so exact. For example, the size of a person's bank balance might be extremely difficult to observe so, instead, we might find it less intrusive to observe the value of the house in which they lived. We might reasonably expect the latter to be an indicator of the former, but the relationship would be far from exact. The same would be true of any other indicators available to us like age or the number of clubs to which the person belonged. The position is even worse with such things as intelligence or attitude to abortion, neither of which could be directly measured, even in principle. But, even in such cases, we might feel that indicators, such as answers to questions in a test or social survey, were telling us something relevant. Where the relationship between indicators and the underlying quantity of interest is imprecise we might expect to do better if we used several indicators rather than one. But if this is the case, how should

we combine them into a single measure. Or, put another way, how can we extract from the indicators, the information which each conveys about the latent variables and then combine the result into a single entity? This is the problem with which this section is concerned.

In my school days, form masters were required to arrive at a 'form order' at the end of each term. For this purpose, subject teachers were required to submit to the form master a percentage mark in their subject for each boy. The form master then added up the marks for each boy and ranked the members of the class according to the total mark achieved. This rank order then appeared on the end-of-term report. It was accepted, without question, that the resulting order reflected the current standing of each boy. In other words, a measure of attainment had been arrived at by adding up the component marks. Any suggestion that the marks might have been combined by multiplying them, or adding up their squares would have been regarded as bizarre. But what is the rationale for the simple addition rule which underlies so much assessment in education and elsewhere?

There is a closely parallel situation which, at first sight, might seem to provide a justification for the addition rule. It comes from the simple average. Suppose we wish to measure the time it takes for someone to run 400 metres using the seconds hand on a wrist watch. We know that any particular measurement is uncertain because of the difficulty of matching the precise start and finish points with the position of the second hand. Different judges will get slightly different answers because of these uncertainties. The watches, if several are used, might also run at different speeds giving rise to further errors. Most of us would feel that we would get a better estimate by forming the average of the readings obtained. It is easy to provide a rationale for this feeling. It is because we feel that there is a 'true' time which would be given by the sophisticated instruments used in modern high-level athletics. Each of our amateur measurements might be thought of as an approximation to this true time. If there is no obvious reason for expecting them to be biased in one direction or the other, then those times which are too long would be roughly balanced by those which are too short. In the long run, then, we would expect the resulting average would be much nearer to the true value than any measurement taken singly. The only difference between adding and averaging is that in the latter case we divide by the number of cases and this makes no essential change; it only alters the scale, but nothing else. What we have just argued can be expressed in more precise mathematical language but this verbal argument conveys the essence of the matter.

Again, imagine that these are not marks accumulated over a term but marks acquired in a series of examinations taken over a short period. It might now be argued that everyone has an 'off day' and therefore that one should ignore the one or two lowest marks and use instead the average of the best subjects. This argument presumes that it is the best that people can do which comes closer to what we actually wish to measure. Other, even more subtle considerations, might be brought into play. For example, there is often a greater spread of marks in mathematics than in, say, history so that the 'cancelling out' argument we used in justifying the averaging process might be less effective here, in that deviations in mathematics might have a greater influence on the final outcome than we would wish. It is becoming clear that the idea of simple averaging is not really adequate to cope with the variety of situations we face. This becomes even more obvious when we move on to other examples.

It might seem that the example of school subject marks with which we started would be covered by this argument. If each subject mark were to be regarded as an unbiased but uncertain measure of ability, then the average of such marks would seem to be a better estimate of ability than any mark taken by itself. Up to a point this might be true, but one can easily imagine the kinds of argument which would take place when such issues are considered. It might be claimed that some subjects were better or more important indicators and therefore should have more weight. Mathematics, Science and English are often regarded as more important than some other subjects. Different people might have different ideas on what the weights should be. A simple way of assigning extra weight would be to double the marks on some subjects. Once arguments of this kind are admitted, it is clear that the case for simple averaging is beginning to break down.

Measuring an individual's quality of life is an important field which illustrates why the idea of simple averaging is not enough. The term *quality of life* covers two distinct concepts, though each, in different ways, exemplifies the problem. Quality of life can refer to individuals who are undergoing medical treatment which affects their ability to cope with everyday matters. A measure might then be based on such indicators as: mobility, ability to dress themselves, quality of sleep, eating problems and suchlike. In another sense quality of life refers to the ordinary life of healthy people for which relevant indicators might be air and water quality, ambient noise levels, pollutants in the atmosphere and unemployment levels. This latter interpretation might, equally well, be treated at either the individual or aggregate level.

A moment's reflection reveals the problems of trying to construct an overall measure as a sum of such quantities.

The indicators are totally different kinds of variable and will be measured in different units. Water and air quality might be expressed in parts per ten million of some impurity say, sound in decibels, ability to dress or feed oneself might be binary variables of the yes/no variety, unemployment a percentage, and so on. The value of any sum derived from such quantities would depend crucially on the units adopted and would thus be virtually meaningless. One possible way out of the difficulty is to express all variables in comparable units such as multiples of their standard deviations. It would then make more sense to add them, although this does not exclude the possibility of going on to weight them differentially according to their perceived importance.

Another possibility is to convert all the indicators to binary variables. If they were continuous variables we could simply record whether or not they exceeded some arbitrarily chosen threshold. In the case of income, for example, we could record whether or not it exceeded, say, £40,000 per year. The choice of threshold is not critical but it might most conveniently be chosen somewhere in the middle of the range. If the indicators were categorical, we could divide the categories into two groups and record into which group the indicator fell. If the categories were ordered, we would normally amalgamate adjacent categories. This strategy has many advantages. Adding up the number of variables which exceeded their thresholds amounts to simply counting the number in that category.

Second, the calculation is very straightforward and easily interpretable. The disadvantage, of course, is that in dichotomising the variables we are throwing away information. This is relatively more serious if there are few indicators that have been treated in this manner. However, this loss may be partly offset if many of the indicators themselves are rather imprecise; in such cases it may be easier to agree on a binary value than on an exact measure. For example, when assessing psychiatric symptoms it might be easier to agree on whether they are present or absent, than on the precise value to give to their magnitude. In any case, a measure based on binary indicators might be a useful first step to a more adequate one. In an educational context, this might simply involve the counting of the number of correct answers. It is reassuring to know that such widely used procedures can claim to be optimal.

We shall now aim to justify this claim by setting it in the context of a measurement model. Virtually the whole of modern statistics depends on the idea of a model. Our theoretical approach to individual-level measurement will be based on a model describing the link between the indicators and the entity to be measured. We shall then appeal to elementary probability laws in order to extract all the information which the indicators give us about the quantity to be measured. First, it will be necessary to say something about what a probability model is. We shall do this in a way which is closely linked to our objectives.

A model is an abstract representation of the measurement situation. Once we have a model, the path to the solution is largely a matter of routine. It will facilitate the argument if we employ a modicum of algebra but in little more than a notational role.

A measure is constructed from a set of indicators. In practice, they will have names, like 'unemployment' or 'mark in arithmetic'. In the theory, we shall denote them all by the symbol x and we shall distinguish one from the other by subscripts, thus: $x_1, x_2 \ldots x_p$ are the scores and there are p altogether. The single latent variable which we aim to measure will be denoted by y. The model specifies how the xs are related among themselves and, in particular, to y. As this relationship is assumed to be probabilistic, the calculus of probability will show us how to bridge the gap from one to the other.

The first thing is to decide what constitutes a possible set of indicators. If any x is an indicator of some quantity, y, it must be correlated with y. That is, if x increases there must be a corresponding change in y, otherwise x is not an indicator! Any x which does not have that property is of no use to us. First of all then, we are looking for indicators which are correlated with y – the more highly correlated the better. It then follows that, if we have two such indicators, they must be correlated with one another. This arises from their common dependence on y. Changes in y thus necessarily induce changes in both indicators. Conversely, if y does not change from one set of xs to another there will be no correlation between them. Holding y constant thus causes all the inter-correlations to vanish.

This idea is so fundamental that we remark that it is already likely to be familiar to the reader in another guise in connection with *spurious correlation*. For example, if two things like spelling ability and height in children are positively correlated, we know that we cannot infer a causal link between the two because their correlation may be due to their common dependence on a third variable, such as age in this case. To see whether there really is a causal relationship we would have to hold age constant, that is, look at children of the same age and see whether the correlation persisted. If it vanished, we could infer that age explained the correlation; in other words, the correlation was *spurious*. Variation in age would thus have induced a spurious correlation between the two otherwise unrelated variables.

In a sense, the situation is reversed when we consider the measurement problem. There we are deliberately looking for indicators whose correlation would vanish if we were able to hold the third, latent variable, fixed. If we are able to find a set of indicators which are all positively correlated among themselves, then it is at least possible that these correlations could all be induced by a single unobserved quantity, which we might identify with the quantity we wish to measure. The problem is then to find a way of getting back to the y from the xs.

This route back is provided by the calculus of probability and we shall now indicate, in general terms, how this comes about. The xs and y all vary and so their variation must be described by a joint probability distribution. If we can specify this, we can find the distribution of y conditional on the xs. This distribution tells us everything there is to know about y given the xs. In other words, it extracts all the information the xs have to tell us about y. If it turned out that this distribution depended on the xs in a particularly simple way, then it might give us a clue about how to measure y. The remarkable thing is that in a wide class of circumstances the dependence is exceptionally simple, in that the conditional distribution of y depends on a single function and, furthermore, that function is a linear combination of the xs. This is, essentially, the same idea as that which arises when we speak of a *sufficient statistic* in statistical estimation. Thus, we would have provided a justification for using linear combinations, and also a way of calculating what the weighting should be. We no longer have to rely on intuition. Our intuition has been used instead to specify a reasonable model from which we are led inexorably to a suitable measure. As far as I am aware, this discovery was first set out in Bartholomew (1984) and has subsequently appeared in many guises. The core idea is embodied in the *sufficiency principle* which we shall now explain.

The justification of our claim that linear combinations of indicators may be optimal is now set out in a simplified form suitable for our purposes in this chapter. It is necessarily technical, but this section may be omitted by those unfamiliar with probability as long as its main conclusion is understood.

As before, we denote the set indicators by $x = (x_1, x_2, \ldots x_p)$ and the latent variable for which we wish to construct a measure by y. The essential starting point is to define the conditional distribution of any x given y. To do this we note that a great many important distributions belong to the so-called exponential family whose density function may be written

$$f(x_i|y) = \phi(x_i)\xi_i(y)\exp x_i\theta_i (i = 1, 2, \ldots p) \tag{23.4}$$

where θ_i is some function of y. It follows that, if the xs are conditionally independent (as they must be if y is to be fully explained by the association among the xs) the joint distribution of the xs, conditional on y is obtained as the product of the individual distributions

$$f(x \mid y) = \prod_i \phi(x_i)\xi_i(y) \exp \sum_i x_i\theta_i. \tag{23.5}$$

Since we are interested in the distribution of y *given* x, we require the conditional distribution

$$f(y|x) = f(y)f(x \mid y)/f(x) \tag{23.6}$$

where

$$f(x) = \int_y f(y)f(x \mid y)dy \tag{23.7}$$

If we substitute the expression for $f(x \mid y)$, given above, into $f(y|x)$, it will be found

that the terms involving x cancel, apart from the one involving $\sum \theta_i x_i$. In general, this sum depends on y through θ_i and since we have made no assumption about the scale of y, there is nothing to prevent us from choosing this to make θ a linear function of y. Thus if $\theta_i = \alpha_{i0} + \alpha_{i1}y$, it will be seen that, apart from the constant term, the conditional distribution of y given x depends on x only through the linear combination $\Sigma_i\alpha_{i1}x_i$.

The conditional density $f(y|x)$ thus depends on x only through this function of the xs (which is thus *sufficient* for y). Thus, all the information in the indicators is contained in this simple function. The practical question which arises is whether or not this covers a large enough number of cases to be practically useful. The exponential family does, in fact, include many of the commonly used distributions, notably the normal distribution and the Bernoulli distribution. The latter arises in the important practical case of binary data – where responses are of the yes/no variety. In that case

$$f(x \mid y) = \prod_i \{\pi_i(y)\}_i^x \{1 - \pi_i(y)\}_i^{1-x}$$
$$= \exp \Sigma_i x_i \text{ logit } \pi_i(y)$$
$$\times \exp \log \sum_i \{1 - \pi_i(y)\} \tag{23.8}$$

where x_i is 1 or 0, according to whether the response is positive or negative (e.g. 'yes' or 'no') and $\pi_i(y)$ is the probability of a positive response on the ith item for an individual at the point y on the latent scale. This is of the required form if

$$\text{logit } \pi_i(y) = \alpha_{i0} + \alpha_{i1}y \tag{23.9}$$

and this implies that $\pi_i(y)$ has the form of a logistic growth curve increasing from 0 to 1 as y increases, which is reasonable.

The family also includes the Poisson and Gamma distributions, and in a slightly generalised form, the multinomial distribution.

Thus, we have established that a linear combination of the xs provides an effective summary of all the information the data contains about the latent variable in a wide variety of practically important cases.

VALIDITY AND RELIABILITY

It is possible to start at the other end by trying to set out criteria by which good measures might be judged. We might argue that, although it is difficult to lay down principles for constructing a good measure, it is much easier to recognise a good one when we see it. If we could lay down some criteria which any measure should possess, we could easily check whether any proposed measure had them. This is a course of action which has often been used in social measurement. Two such widely used criteria are *validity* and *reliability*. Validity is concerned with whether something measures what it is supposed to measure, and reliability with how precisely it does so.

Validity is an important criterion and various adjectives are used to qualify it. 'Construct', 'predictive' and 'convergent' are just three of the forms of validity which will be encountered in the literature. But whatever qualifications we introduce, the concept is essentially circular in character. For the only way we can judge validity is by comparing the proposed measure with something which is already known to share something with the variable in question. But if we had some such measure why, it may be asked, should we need another? There are, of course, good answers to this somewhat cynical question but the mere posing of it serves to highlight the dilemma we face. Why should we be trying to construct a new measure of something if we already know enough about it to make the judgement required in assessing its validity?

The point may be illustrated by thinking of a measure formed by taking the sum of a set of indicators. Imagine that we had enquired whether such a method is valid. We might have sensibly argued that any valid measure should increase in value if any one component of the sum were to be increased. After all, the 'more' we have of whatever that indicator 'indicates', the higher should be the resulting measure. A sum clearly meets this requirement. But if, at an earlier stage, we had considered whether this item should be included in the first place, we would have to say that we had done it because we believed it to be positively correlated with the latent quantity and therefore should be included! Hence the circularity.

Reliability has to do with reproducibility. If we have occasion to independently measure the same thing two, or more, times we would hope to get much the same answer on each occasion. It is clear that this is very much akin to measuring variability – the less variable the results yielded by a measuring instrument, the better it is. One common way of measuring the variability of a measure is to look at the reduction in variance which we could achieve if the true value were known to us. In the aggregate case, where the measure is a parameter of a model, we would aim to minimise its sampling variance. In the individual case, we would look at the variance of the measure itself. In the latter case we need some standard with which to compare it and this is provided by what the variance would have been had we not conditioned on the latent variable.

BIBLIOGRAPHICAL BACKGROUND

The literature on measurement is enormous. Some is focussed on measuring physical quantities, but social science concerns are also prominent. A good general introduction to the whole field is provided by Hand (2004). Psychology has been the centre of activity for much measurement work and the sub-field of psychometrics has spawned its own journals and books, sometimes in isolation from what was going on in adjacent fields. Michel (1990) is a book length introduction and Anastasi (1985) and Narens and Luce (1986) give useful accounts of the position reached by the mid-1980s. Two important examples which often escape the net of reviews such as this are the measurement of uncertainty, treated in Lindley (1971) and of utility discussed in Moore (1983). All of these articles are reproduced in my four-volume edited work *Measurement* (Bartholomew, 2006) which includes over 60 original articles spanning the whole history of the subject from Sir Francis Galton to the present day. Although still not exhaustive, this does provide a representative picture of the many-faceted character of the history, and in itself provides a comprehensive introduction to the literature.

REFERENCES

Anastasi, A. (1985) 'Some emerging trends in psychological measurement: A fifty year perspective', *Applied Psychological Measurement*, 9: 121–38.

Bartholomew, D. J. (1973) *Stochastic Models for Social Processes*, 3rd edition. Chichester: Wiley.

Bartholomew, D. J. (1984) 'The foundations of factor analysis', *Biometrika*, 71: 221–32.

Bartholomew, D. J. (1996) *The Statistical Approach to Social Measurement*. San Diego: Academic Press.

Bartholomew, D. J. (2006) *Measurement, (4 vols)*. London: Sage Publications.

Bartholomew, D. J. and Knott, M. (1999) *Latent Variable Models and Factor Analysis*. London: Arnold.

Hand, D. J. (2004) *Measurement*. London:Arnold.

Lindley, D. V. (1971) A 'numerical measure of uncertainty', in D. V. Lindley (ed.), *Making Decisions*. London: Wiley Interscience. pp. 13–28.

Michel, J (1990) *An Introduction to the Logic of Psychological Measurement*. Hillsdale, N.J.: Lawrence Erlbaum Associates.

Moore, P. G. (1983) 'The concept of utility', in P. G. Moore (ed.), *The Business of Risk*. Cambridge University Press. pp. 63–79.

Narens, L. and Luce, R. D. (1986) 'Measurement: The theory of numerical assignments', *Psychological Bulletin*, 99: 166–80.

Robinson, A. (2007) *The Story of Measurement*. London: Thames and Hudson.

24

Increasing the Measurement Accuracy of Consumption Intentions

Brian Wansink

Behind the goal of many interventions – from public health education to advertising campaigns – is that of altering the incidence, frequency, or volume of a behavior. This could involve reducing the incidence or frequency of smoking, reducing the volume of calorie intake, increasing one's minutes of physical activity, or increasing the purchase or intake of healthy produce or packaged goods. Unfortunately, there are not helpful measures for estimating and screening the effectiveness of these interventions. Since measuring actual consumption can be prohibitive in terms of time and money, we present quantitative and qualitative measures which can be examined prior to the launch of an intervention. Last, we examine promising psychographic differences that if correctly measured may explain the differing effectiveness of different interventions. We then discuss implications for general issues in social science measurement.

There is often an assumed relationship between attitudes and behaviors. That is, people are asked about products because it is thought that it is reflective of what they might buy; they are asked about political candidates because it reflects on how they would vote; they are asked about dieting because it reflects on how much food they would eat (Wansink, 1994a). In other words, when behavior is impossible to measure, such as with an unreleased new product, or an upcoming presidential campaign, we often use attitude measures as a surrogate for behavior (Wansink et al., 2009a).

There is a basic, but frequently useful conceptualization of the attitude-behavior connection, and it involves an intermediate step of behavioral intentions (cf. Fishbein and Azjen, 1975). This basically contends that attitudes are related (to some extent) to behavioral intentions, and these intentions are, in turn, related to actual behavior. Certainly there are a lot of other factors in the equation. In the final analysis, however, a good predictor of behavior may be if both behavioral intentions are extreme and if attitudes toward it are extreme.

For instance, measuring a person's relative attitude toward a soft drink might be related to her intentions toward consuming that soft drink within the next week, and these intentions might be related to actual purchase. Similarly, one's attitude toward exercising and eating less might be related toward the intention to 'lose 10 pounds before my high school reunion,' and this is likely to be somewhat related to actual weight loss. While a number of other factors make these relationships imperfect, it is often believed there is a general mapping from one to the other. Indeed the insights in this chapter are based on two decades of work on identifying the subtle environmental cues that nudge unknowing consumers in directions that influence their behavior below their level of awareness (cf. Wansink, 2004a, 2006).

In many cases, it is more practical and less expensive to examine consumption intentions than it is to conduct a study where actual consumption is examined. Indeed, when food safety is a concern (Wansink, 2004b) when hypotheticals are being examined (Pennings et al., 2002), or when a vulnerable population is being examined (Wansink and Payne, 2008), consumption intentions are the best way to proceed.

In other cases, it would be useful to know if different interventions had a likelihood of success before launching them. This would be true of an anti-smoking campaign, weight loss counseling, a new family-planning website, a new curriculum to tackle adult illiteracy, or a new soy-based product being developed (Wansink and Park, 2002; Wansink and Cheong, 2002). Figure 24.1 shows how these interventions might eventually influence consumption. The consumption intentions we believe will mediate consumption can be measured both quantitatively and qualitatively. A description of new techniques to answer these questions will be outlined and tested. When dealing with behaviors and

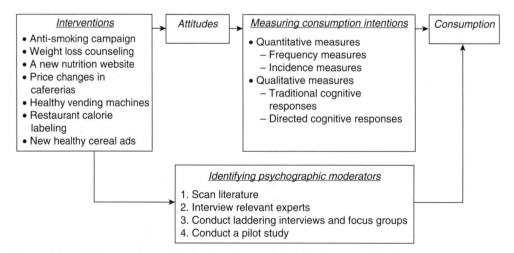

Figure 24.1   How to estimate the impact of a consumption intervention.

intended behaviors of consequence, the direct predictive ability of a measure is critical. With quantitative measures of behavioral intent, an important distinction will be made between frequency and incidence, showing when one measure is more relevant than the other. With qualitative measures of behavioral intent, new methods of directing cognitive responses toward consumption will be discussed and explored.

The second critical part of Figure 24.1 is its emphasis on identifying and measuring psychographic variables that could moderate the impact of the intervention on consumption. For instance, a person who has a very high degree of self-discipline may show less responsiveness to an intervention than one who has a low degree of self-discipline. Being able to account for self-discipline would increase the precision of any measures of consumption. This could be done either by using it as a covariate or by separately analyzing different groups of people based on them being low, moderate, or high in their self-discipline.

While direct measures of consumption can be made in some cases (cf. Wansink, 2009), there are many more occasions when it would be less costly, more convenient, and more practical to know – even in a preliminary manner – how one's intentions might be drifting. In some cases, it can allow intervention before it is too late.

This chapter has three purposes: 1) To show how different *quantitative* measures of intentions will alter the accuracy of estimating the impact of an intervention; 2) to show how different *qualitative* ways of asking for open-ended feedback will alter the accuracy of the possible impact of an intervention, and 3) to suggest key individual differences – psychographic – measures that could moderate the accuracy of these measures of consumption intention.

QUANTITATIVE MEASURES THAT PREDICT CONSUMPTION

Measures of one's consumption intentions (for a particular time period, such as 'within the next two weeks') can be obtained either through likelihood measures (incidence), or through estimates of one's consumption volume. Incidence can be directly obtained by asking an individual how likely ('Highly Unlikely' = 1 to 'Highly Likely' = 7) it will be that he/she exhibits a consumption behavior an upcoming time period. This could be how likely they think it will be that they smoke, eat a dessert, buy something from a vending machine, or eat an apple. Consumption intentions can also be measured by asking one to estimate the volume a product he or she might possibly consume within a similar time period. This could be how many packs of cigarettes one plans to smoke, how many desserts they will eat, how many vending machine trips they will make, how many apples they will eat, or when they will stop eating dinner (Wansink et al., 2007)

These two different measures of consumption intent – incidence and volume – have different relative strengths. With infrequent consumers, volume estimates will be skewed toward 0 units (especially over a relatively short period of time). This is partially a drawback of numerical estimates that provide no gradation between 0 and 1 unit. In such cases, volume estimates would provide less variance and less information than an estimate of incidence or consumption likelihood. As a result, incidence estimates would allow a greater gradation in response and would be more sensitive in detecting any potentially different effects these interventions might have on consumption.

In contrast, with frequent or heavy consumers, a volume estimate is likely to be more accurate than a likelihood estimate.

This is because the distribution of these volume estimates is more likely to be normally distributed (Pearl, 1981). As a result, a volume estimate of one's consumption intent is likely to provide more variance and more information about the intended consumption of heavy users than is a likelihood measure, which would undoubtedly be at or near 1.0 (100 per cent probable). Under these circumstances, estimates of volume (versus frequency) would be a more accurate estimate of a heavy user's actual consumption.

Empirical findings

The effectiveness of these different measures was examined by Wansink and Ray (1992) when they exposed 239 subjects from Parent-Teacher Associations to a series of interventions for one of three different brands (Campbell's Soup, Jell-O Brand Gelatin, and Ocean Spray Cranberry Sauce). The correspondence between intentions and consumption was most impressive when the subjects were divided (i.e., segmented) into heavy users and light users based on their prior year's consumption of the brand. Consumers who consumed more than the median amount for each brand were classified as relatively 'heavy users' and the rest as 'light users' (Jacoby and Chestnut, 1978).

In general, both measures of consumption intention (likelihood and volume estimates) were effective in predicting subsequent consumption, depending upon how frequently one has tended to consume the brand in the past. Heavy users were more accurate in estimating their *consumption volume* than in estimating their 'likelihood' of using these three products ($r = .62, .46,$ and $.23$). In contrast, light users were not as accurate in estimating their consumption volume but were instead much more accurate in estimating the consumption

likelihood ($r = .42, .78,$ and $.49$). When contrasted with research that indicates that consumption volume predictions are often very low (Pilgrim, 1957; Cassidy, 1981), the results from Table 24.1 show that volume predictions can be very accurate when frequent users are examined. The results of this study are described in more detail elsewhere (Wansink and Ray, 2002).

Implications for increasing predictive validity

These results make two important illustrations. First, attitude measures will not always be sensitive enough to measure consumption-related intentions. Second, consumption intentions can be measured through incidence or through volume estimates, and each measure is effective under different circumstances. Heavy users are most accurate when predicting their future consumption volume. Light users are most accurate when predicting their likelihood of consumption.

These results can be extended to entire product categories. That is, if a researcher is trying to estimate the impact that an

Table 24.1 Some examples of individual difference variables that might moderate an intervention and consumption

Need for cognition
Motivation
Involvement
Prevention-focused
Health-conscious
Introverted
Innovator
Emotional
Rational
Self-Monitoring
Self-centered
Detail-oriented
Obsessive
Suggestibility
Need for approval
Education
Curiosity

intervention will have on the consumption of a product category that, relative to other categories, is infrequently consumed, likelihood measures may be more generally accurate than volume measures. However, if the product category is one that, relative to other categories, is frequently consumed, volume measures may be more accurate. In this study, for example, the typical household ate 29.1 cans of soup per year, but only 2.7 cans of cranberry sauce. It may be that soup is a product category where consumption intentions are best estimated through volume measures, while consumption intentions for cranberry sauce would be best estimated through likelihood measures. This relationship should be even stronger when examining the heavy users of a frequently consumed category, or when examining the light users of an infrequently consumed category. Indeed, volume estimates provided relatively accurate estimates of consumption for heavy users ($r = .62$) of soup and likelihood estimates provided relatively accurate estimates of consumption for light users ($r = .49$) of cranberry sauce.

The findings described here underscore the importance of consumption-related measures over the simple measures of attitude that are typically collected when screening an intervention. Specifically, it is important to understand that volume estimates best approximate the actual consumption of heavy users (or of frequently consumed brands) and that likelihood estimates are best used with light users (or with infrequently consumed brands).

The general notion here is that when we want to better understand how an intervention – such as an advert, website, curriculum, treatment, and so on – influences behavior, we need to ask in a way that generates valid and relevant, not irrelevant, responses. The more specific we can narrow the universe of responses, the

more we will be able to explore the most meaningful insights.

In this case, these findings underscore the importance of taking consumption-related measures in intervention pre-studies, instead of simply using attitude measures. Specifically, it is important to understand that volume estimates best approximate the actual consumption of heavy users, or frequently engaged behaviors and that likelihood estimates are more accurate with light users, or with infrequently engaged behaviors. Additional information about these interventions can be obtained by examining the thoughts or cognitive responses that are generated by the intervention. These cognitive responses can best be examined using *either* pre-exposure elicitation exercises or directed post-exposure instructions.

QUALITATIVE MEASURES THAT PREDICT CONSUMPTION

While quantitative measures are perhaps the most obvious measure of consumption intentions, qualitative measures can provide some powerful insights as to *why* people will react to an intervention in the way they will. That is, they can tell us *why* one version of an ad is more effective at discouraging drug use, or why one in-store sign is more effective at encouraging milk consumption at meal time than another.

The most potentially valuable part of any intervention pre-study can be the open-ended questions – that is, the questions to which the respondents can make any reply they want (rather than just ticking one of the limited list of alternatives provided by the surveyor). Too often, though, the value of the responses to open-ended questions is wasted. They are either asked too broadly, or they direct a person to put down expedient answers to simply move on.

So while, in theory, a person could simply be presented an intervention and asked what thoughts went through their mind as they viewed it, this is likely to be ineffective because it is not focused specifically enough on consumption behavior. There is a solution to this.

Eliciting open-ended responses

Understanding the effectiveness of an intervention is greatly aided by knowing a consumer's thoughts as he or she views it. These thoughts help us better estimate the impact these interventions will have on attitudes and consumption, and they also suggest ways in which the interventions can be changed to be more effective. Unfortunately, the traditional procedure by which these thoughts are elicited may not yield valid or reliable findings (Russo et al., 1989).

The initial research with cognitive responses (or verbal protocols) was pioneered by Greenwald (1968) and then introduced into advertising by Wright (1973). Their work indicated that cognitive responses can mirror the actual thoughts that occur to people as they evaluate a persuasive message. In these studies, cognitive responses are typically elicited with instructions such as, 'Write down any thoughts that went through your mind while reading this.' These written thoughts are typically coded as either counter arguments, support arguments, or source derogations (Smead et al., 1981; Wright, 1980).

One problem with this coding scheme is that it does not specifically address thoughts that are consumption-related, nor does it necessarily encourage ones that could be of diagnostic value. Although a multitude of thoughts may be generated as one views an advertisement, only a small percentage of them will actually be communicated (Wright and Rip, 1980; Kidder, 1980).

After subjects see an intervention, they are typically asked to record their thoughts when viewing it. These instructions are general, and a portion of the random thoughts that results could be minimized if subjects had a better idea of what is expected of them (Ericsson and Simon, 1984). In short, when a researcher is focusing on consumption-related thoughts, the conventional procedure of simply asking for general reactions may not be as useful as procedures or questions that are less ambiguous.

Problems with current elicitation procedures

Although a multitude of thoughts may be generated when a person hears about an intervention or sees it, sometimes only a small percentage of them will actually be communicated (Wright and Rip, 1980). This becomes particularly evident when we compare the number of responses obtained when a subject speaks into a tape recorder to the reduced number that are instead obtained when the subject has to expend more effort and write them down (Kidder, 1980). Even verbalizing thoughts into a tape recorder eventually results in a subject recording fewer and fewer thoughts as they fatigue (Stemple and Westley, 1981).

Clearly, the more general the elicitation instructions, the greater the opportunity for irrelevant responses (Ericsson and Simon, 1978). It is important that any cognitive response elicitation procedure uncover the thoughts that are most related to the issue under examination, while minimizing the 'irrelevant' responses a subject verbalizes. Batra and Ray (1986), for instance, were interested in examining people's affective responses to viewing interventions. To accomplish this, they specifically asked subjects not to 'replay what happened in the ad.' By minimizing 'ad playback,' the researchers claim to have obtained more of the rich, affective responses that occurred during processing but that might not have been noted if the subject had spent time simply restating intervention content.

Before subjects see an advert, it is common to tell them that they will be asked questions about the intervention after viewing it. At the appropriate time, they are then typically asked to write down the thoughts they had when hearing about the intervention. These instructions are general, and a portion of the 'noise' that results could be minimized if subjects had a better idea of what is expected of them (Ericsson and Simon, 1984). In short, when a researcher is focusing on special types of thoughts – such as when they might consume a particular product – the conventional procedure of simply asking for general reactions to an ad would not be as useful as asking in a more directed and less ambiguous manner.

Two options for eliciting consumption-related responses

A person viewing an intervention may generate many thoughts about cognitive responses, but not all of them will be communicated because of time constraints or cognitive capacity constraints (Ericsson and Simon, 1984). To uncover these thoughts about a particular target issue, researchers have used either pre-exposure elicitation exercises, or directed post-exposure instructions.

If a subject is given no instructions prior to their exposure to an ad, he or she is free to think of any issues that come to mind. Pre-exposure elicitation exercises (such as practice tests or examples) frame a subject's processing by suggesting a range of issues which one might consider. One way this can be accomplished is by providing subjects with a hypothetical example or illustration of what another subject might have written when he or she viewed a related intervention (Keller, 1987). A second way this is accomplished is by providing subjects with a practice trial that is followed with standardized feedback. The feedback, for instance, can be presented in the form of a pre-written checklist which instructs them to reread their responses to ensure they are not simply writing down a replay of the intervention (Batra, 1984).

Providing subjects with pre-exposure elicitation exercises intensifies their processing of these target issues during exposure. In contrast, giving *directed post-exposure instructions* to subjects after they view an intervention encourages them to cognitively edit their less relevant thoughts before writing them down. One way this can be accomplished is by instructing subjects to address specific issues of interest (Wright, 1980). For instance, a researcher can ask subjects how they feel about using the product, if they agree or disagree with the ad, or if it reminds them of any past experiences with the product (Wright and Rip, 1980).

Pre-exposure elicitation exercises and directed post-exposure instructions both share risks of potential reactivity. The primary concern is that these procedures may 'force' a subject to generate thoughts about a particular target issue that would have otherwise never occurred to them (Turner, 1988; Nisbett and Wilson, 1977). As a result, such thoughts would be invalid, and would bias outcome measures such as beliefs, attitudes, or intentions. A direct way of testing for reactivity is by measuring the impact these different procedures have on critical outcome variables (Russo et al., 1989). Nonreactive procedures should have no influence the ratings of outcome variables when compared to that of a control group. In other words, if these different procedures are nonreactive, there should be no difference in the ratings of attitude and consumption intentions between subjects who are given pre-exposure elicitation exercises, directed post-exposure instructions, or neither.

Empirical findings

When people are viewing or experiencing different interventions we think will influence consumption, what is the best questioning procedure to use? The effectiveness of these two different elicitation methods was examined in a study that involved 74 adults who were recruited from Parent-Teacher Associations and who were given $6.00 for their effort (see Wansink et al., 1994 for details). This study found that using either pre-exposure elicitation exercises or directed post-exposure instructions increased the number of consumption-related thoughts generated by subjects, but was not reactive. That is, there were no corresponding differences in the attitude ratings or consumption intentions between subjects who were given pre-exposure elicitation exercises, directed post-exposure instructions, or neither.

In a general sense, these results are consistent with what Batra (1984) found when examining different types of elicitation exercises for different dependent variables. Batra's results showed that general instructions can be as effective as directed instructions, but only when accompanied by some form of vivid pre-elicitation exercise or illustration, such as an example or as a practice trial.

When should pre-exposure exercises be used in favor of directed post-exposure instructions? It is important to realize that both options are not always available. Involving subjects in pre-exposure exercises is not always feasible, and it can be constrained by the experimental design or time limitations. Under such circumstances, directed post-exposure instructions are the best alternative. When pre-exposure exercises can be used, they might elicit more thoughts about a target issue. It is important to note that the combination of the two procedures, however, provides no greater sensitivity than does either by itself.

A general method for increasing cognitive response sensitivity

Research dealing with cognitive responses is important because of the generalizations it makes regarding the cognitive response sensitivity (see also Wansink et al., 1994). In doing so, it suggests a general pre-testing method that can help researchers determine what procedure will be most appropriate for eliciting consumption-related cognitive responses. The general four-step method follows.

1 Select a number of pre-exposure elicitation exercises and directed post-exposure instructions believed to provide the greatest level of sensitivity toward consumption-related responses. Be certain to include a control condition.
2 Design the study by having the various procedures under examination represented between subjects factors. Statistical power can be increased by having subjects respond to multiple ads. Care should be taken to ensure that subjects are from a comparable pool as those who will be involved in the future studies.
3 Include outcome variables of interest to ensure that the different procedures do not generate reactivity (such as attitude ratings or consumption intentions).
4 Select the elicitation procedure that best achieves the objectives of the study without affecting outcome variables relative to the control condition. For instance, an objective may involve selecting the procedure which maximizes consumption-related thoughts, while minimizing unrelated thoughts such as intervention playback.

This section emphasizes the importance of increasing the consumption-related sensitivity of cognitive response elicitation procedures. Furthermore, it illustrates the steps researchers must go through if they seek to develop a stylized elicitation procedure for their own program of research. The study described here is taken from an ongoing program of research which suggests that either pre-exposure elicitation exercises (such as practice trials or prior exposure), or directed post-exposure instructions can increase this sensitivity without appearing to be reactive. The combination of the two procedures, however, provides no greater sensitivity than does either by itself.

PSYCHOGRAPHIC MEASURES THAT MAY MODERATE CONSUMPTION INTENTION ACCURACY

Qualitative and quantitative measures of consumption-related intentions can be powerfully efficient and generate invaluable insights when devising interventions. They can also be very noisy. Yet what may be written off as measurement error, could very easily be attributed to differences in response across different segments of consumers (Wansink et al., 2009; Wansink 1994b).

As an example, my Cornell Food and Brand Lab has a large-scale environmentally based weight-loss intervention called the National Mindless Eating Challenge. It is based on helping people implement the different strategies from *Mindless Eating: Why We Eat More Than We Want* (Wansink, 2006). Based on a person's psychographic characteristics we would recommend three small changes for them to make, and they would then track the number of days in the next month they successfully implemented that change and their weight at the beginning of the month and at the end.

After a few months of analyzing data, we found a parsimonious way to accomplish this with just two variables. We determined that for a particular eating problem (such as meal stuffing, snack grazing, restaurant indulging, etc.), all we needed to know what the extent to which they believed they controlled their immediate environment (e.g., do they do the purchasing and preparing of food, etc.) and the extent to which they have been successful making and keeping any habit change in the past (e.g, dieting exercise, not biting fingernails, etc.). By splitting people into these four different groups (high/high, high/low, low/high, low/low), we found their behavioral intentions came into line with their actual behavior.

When it comes to consumption, the segments that perhaps most important – and easiest to overlook – are psychographic segments. Psychographic and 'life style' research is sometimes referred to as AIO (Attitude, Interests, and Opinion research because the questions often focus on these types of variables). Psychographic variables may help us increase the precisions of our measures. If a certain personality trait – such as need for cognition, for instance – dramatically alters how a person responds to a manipulation or treatment, not accounting for it would lead our measures to be much noiser than necessary. Psychographic research resembles motivation research in that a major aim is to draw recognizably human portraits of consumers. But it also resembles more conventional research in that these portraits can be analyzed using standard statistical tools.

In this context of estimating an intervention's impact on consumption, the most obvious use of psychographic (or AIO) research is to draw portraits of target groups that would be more or less predisposed to being influenced. For almost any identifiable type of behavior there is at least the possibility of new insight when the behavior is viewed in the context of psychographics.

What are some examples of psychographic segments?

Linking an the effectiveness of an intervention to a behavior will be difficult if unaccounted groups of different people respond dramatically differently to the intervention. Such unaccounted noise would make us question the validity, accuracy, and reliability of our measures of that behavior.

By accounting for these differentially responding types of people, we can increase the strength of an effect and our confidence in the accuracy of our measures. This raises the question as to what are some psychographic measures that should be considered and measured?

One of the more widely known psychographic segmentation studies is one conducted by SRI International and called the VALS-2 Study (Values and Lifestyles). While many psychographic studies try to focus on measures and characteristics that might be uniquely related to a topic of interest (reducing binge drinking, determining taste profiles, understanding who is most likely to give donations to a college), the VALS study was conducted across categories and attempts to show more general psychographic segments that are relevant and can be used across a wide number of people and topics. Their psychographic approach sorts people into one of eight different groups. A general description along with the percentage of people in each category are noted below:

Fulfilleds – mature, responsible, well-educated professionals; well informed about world events; open to new ideas and social change; have high incomes; and are value-oriented.

Believers – conservative, predictable consumers favoring American products and established brands; have modest incomes; lives centered on family, church; and community.

Achievers – successful, work-oriented people deriving satisfaction from their jobs and their families; politically conservative and respect authority; favor established products that showcase their success.

Strivers – values similar to achievers but have fewer resources available; style and appearance are important to them as they strive to emulate the people they wish they were.

Experiencers – youngest segment with lots of energy to pour into physical and social activities; avid consumers who spend heavily.

Makers – practical people who value self-sufficiency; focused on family, work, and recreation with little interest in the outside world; unimpressed by material possessions.

Strugglers – lowest income and minimal resources; within their limited means, they are brand-loyal consumers; struggle to make ends meet.

Actualizers – highest incomes and maximum resources; high self-esteem; image is important as an expression of their taste, independence, and character; tastes lean toward the finer things in life.

These breakdowns are determined by cluster analyzing each person's answers to the questions noted below. Each of the scaled questions is answered using one of four categories: (1) mostly disagree; (2) somewhat disagree; (3) somewhat agree; (4) mostly agree. In addition to basic demographic measures, the psychographic questions are as follows:

1   I am often interested in theories.
2   I like outrageous people and things.
3   I like a lot of variety in my life.
4   I love to make things I can use every day.
5   I follow the latest trends and fashions.
6   Just as the Bible says, the world literally was created in six days.
7   I like being in charge of a group.
8   I like to learn about art, culture, and history.
9   I often crave excitement.
10   I am really interested only in a few things.
11   I would rather make something than buy it.
12   I dress more fashionably than most people.
13   The federal government should encourage prayers in public schools.
14   I have more ability than most people.
15   I consider myself an intellectual.
16   I must admit that I like to show off.
17   I like trying new things.

18   I am very interested in how mechanical things, such as engines, work.

19   I like to dress in the latest fashions.

20   There is too much sex on television today.

21   I like to lead others.

22   I would like to spend a year or more in a foreign country.

23   I like a lot of excitement in my life.

24   I must admit that my interests are somewhat narrow and limited.

25   I like making things of wood, metal, or other such material.

26   I want to be considered fashionable.

27   A woman's life is fulfilled only if she can provide a happy home for her family.

28   I like the challenge of doing something I have never done before.

29   I like to learn about things even if they may never be of any use to me.

30   I like to make things with my hands.

31   I am always looking for a thrill.

32   I like doing things that are new and different.

33   I like to look through hardware or automotive stores.

34   I would like to understand more about how the universe works.

35   I like my life to be pretty much the same from week to week.

What psychographic questions should I ask?

There are two basic approaches to deciding what psychographic measures to use. One involves using previously validated items, and the second involves developing *ad hoc* items that may be more specific or meaningful to the questions being investigated.

The most appropriate way to approach psychographic or individual difference measures is to use measures that have been validated in the literature and have been shown to be related to whatever is being studied. The purpose of this is to provide better predictive validity – to enhance the accuracy of the prediction. Table 24.1 gives an example of some of the individual difference measures that have been shown

to successfully differentiate different types of behavior in various fields. All of these characteristics are ones that have scales associated with them and which can be easily adapted to different uses. They are typically split into high-low groups based on median splits or on top-third/bottom-third splits.

A second approach to developing psychographic or individual difference questions is to do so on an intervention hoc basis that is relevant only to the questions being investigated. This is what we did to improve the effectiveness of the National Mindless Eating Challenge. But a warning is deserved. While this approach can provide some tempting and interesting criteria, it must ultimately be considered that the more idiosyncratic these measures are, the more difficult it will be to justify any interesting findings being related to them.

With this caveat in mind, how would you go about generating and isolating psychographic or individual difference variables that could enhance the predictive ability of what you are examining? Four approaches have proven useful with the work we have done in the Food and Brand Lab:

First, Scan the literature. Look for constructs that might be mentioned (even parenthetical) as being characteristics that influence attitudes or behaviors. While this literature can be academic, it can also be from the popular press. For instance, a journalist noted in a magazine article that eating some foods made her feel more feminine than other foods. Following this lead, we developed a gender-related scale that we found explained previously puzzling differences in the food between men and women. It indicated that men and women had some food preferences that could be traced to them perceiving the foods to be masculine or feminine to a similar extent as they perceived themselves (Wansink, 2006: 169).

Second, talk to relevant experts in this area. These may be researchers, or they may be what we call 'inside sources.' That is, they are inside sources of expertise based on their frequent interaction with the people of interest. For instance, in a study we conducted to better understand (and deter) binge drinking; my colleagues and I interviewed bartenders to begin developing personality profiles of those most predisposed to binge drinking and the overpouring of alcohol (Wansink and van Ittersum, 2005).

Third, conduct in-depth interviews or focus groups. When possible, conduct in-depth interviews or focus groups with the individuals in these areas that you most want to profile. The more extreme of a 'fanatic' they represent, the more useful will be their insights (Wansink, 2000). This can begin by having them describe themselves and then describe others that have similar preferences. The goal here is to begin gaining more confidence that some of the criteria that have been gathered will relate to some sub-segments of the population being considered.

Fourth, conduct a pilot study. When it is somewhat clear what some of the potentially distinguishing criteria are that are of interest, conduct a pilot study. The results from this study can be analyzed (through factor analysis and mean comparisons), and used to reduce unneeded questionnaire items before conducting your main study.

Example: a psychographic soup consumption story

One example of using psychographic questions involves a study done for a soup company. Over many years, this soup company had promoted all of its soups in a generic manner. There had recently been evidence, however, that different types of people preferred different types of soups. They reasoned that if they could make some rough generalizations as to what types of people preferred what types of soups, they could use this information to better promote their soups in a more tailored manner. That is, if health-oriented, outdoorsy people tended to prefer vegetable soup, the company could develop a more tailored 'vegetable soup ad' that was placed in magazines these people might read, and which touted health benefits, and perhaps even showed robust, outdoorsy people in the ad. To this end, they wanted to have psychographic and lifestyle profiles of their five most popular soups.

In conducting this research, the academic literature was first searched and a series of individual difference and personality variables related to different tastes were collected (along with the scales used to measure these items). Following this, a similar search was made of the popular press, and potentially defining characteristics were collected which might be worth further examining.

The second step was to consult with inside sources who might have insider knowledge in this area. Because of their frequent contact with soup eaters, it was thought that one inside source worth consulting would be to experience waitresses at diners. Thirty-two of these waitresses (with over 10 years experience each) were contacted and asked questions such as, 'If the soup of the day is chicken noodle, what kind of person orders that soup?' The majority of the waitresses had a number of observations about each type of soup lover, dealing with everything from the way they walked and talked, to what they wore and whether they had cat fur on them (Wansink and Park, 2000a). After these interviews, a number of converging insights had emerged. These insights were noted and examined in in-depth interviews of soup lovers.

The third step involved in-depth interviews with people who were self-proclaimed fanatics of one flavor of soup. These people were interviewed and asked to describe themselves and to try and differentiate themselves from the people who preferred other types of soup.

In all, the background literature, the waitress interviews, and the in-depth interviews suggested a number of personality criteria or constructs that might differentiate each of the five types of soup lovers (see Table 24.2 for a partial list). For each of these criteria, measures were found in the literature (or formed intervention hoc when necessary). The completed questionnaire was pretested and the final (reduced) version was next used on a sample of 1002 North American adults (Wansink and Park, 2000b). Table 24.2 gives an idea of what types of variables related to which type of soup users.

Structuring psychographic questions and analyzing answers

One means by which to ask psychographic questions is to have respondents indicate the extent to which they agree with various statements about their personality (such as those noted in Table 24.2). One common way this is done in academics (especially in paper surveys) is through an odd-interval, nine-point scale ranging from 1 = strongly disagree to 9 = strongly agree. Often the midpoints are not identified, but it is left up to respondents to interpolate these values. This appears reasonable to do.

A second way to ask questions is through a more abbreviated scale (such as done in the VALS2 example). Here an even-interval, four-point (or a six-point) scale is presented with the points identified as being mostly disagree, somewhat disagree, somewhat agree, and mostly agree. While it does not provide the range (or the midpoint) of the nine-point scale, this has been typically used in a number of formats, including paper, phone, or electronic.

There are additional ways to ask psychographic questions. Some researchers prefer to present two personality or AIO statements to respondents and ask them to indicate which he or she agrees with more. Other researchers prefer to ask the respondent to rank a set of statements from most to least agreement. These alternatives can help suppress the undesirable effects of 'essaying,' social desirability, and the like. They also can force discrimination among items that might otherwise be marked at the same scale position. But they are often difficult to administer and difficult for the respondent to handle.

Table 24.2 Lifestyle and personality variables used to differentiate soup preferences

Lifestyle	Personality
Active lifestyle: I am	Mentally alert: I am
outdoorsy physically fit a workaholic socially active	intellectual sophisticated creative detail oriented witty nutrition conscious
Family spirited: I am	Social: I am
family oriented a church goer	fun at parties outgoing not shy spontaneous trend setter
Homebody: I am	Athletic: I am
someone who enjoys being alone a homebody a good cook	athletic competitive adventurous
Intellectually stimulated past times: I am	Carefree: I am
a technology whizz a world traveler a book lover	down to earth affectionate a fun lover

Once the significant relationships have been found, the problem is to organize and understand them. Here factor analysis is useful at this point. As an illustration, one research study attempted to see if different psychographic profiles could be used to predict a person's consumption of their favorite soup (Wansink and Park, 2000a). Factor analysis was important in helping decrease the number of variables that needed to be examined. That is, those which were not highly loading on dominant factors in the pilot study were eliminated.

Are psychographic measures worth taking? Do they work?

It has been said that the relationships between psychographics and preferences for certain behaviors (or for products) are only superficial manifestations of more basic demographics. Yet two products with very similar demographic profiles can sometimes turn out to have usefully different psychographic profiles, and a demographic bracket in itself means little unless one has a clear picture of its lifestyle implications. Although correlations between psychographic variables and preferences seldom get higher than .3 or .4, the same is true of the relationships between demographics and product preference.

A classic area of consumer research is trying to predict choice and behavior based on personality of lifestyle traits. Efforts at successfully doing this, however, have been weak because the trait measures had questionable validity and reliability.

In the context of studying consumption, a justifiable concern was that the traits that were often investigated had little or no prior literature-based relevance to consumption. This probably should not be surprising in a developing area of investigation, such as consumption. Many of the most insightful

or informative insights may very well come from bottom-up 'brute' empirics. Still, much can be learned from the personality studies done throughout the 1970s and 1980s in consumer behavior. While most of these used only single-item scales, it has more recently been shown, however, that when even the same measures are taken at multiple times, the effectiveness and reliability of a scale's relation to actual behavior also increases.

One example of psychographic research worth noting deals with a psychographic study conducted by Market Fact's mail panel in which 1,000 questionnaires were mailed to homemaker members of this panel. In addition to the usual demographics and product consumption questions, the questionnaires contained about 300 'activity, interest and opinion' (AIO) statements to which the respondent indicated degree of agreement on a six-point scale.

Two of the products on the questionnaire were eye makeup and shortening. The demographic and product-consumption profiles of the consumers of these two products were vividly contrasting. In the AIO questions, the contrast deepened. Almost none of the items that correlated with use of eye makeup also correlated with use of shortening. AIO portraits did not always differ as much as the portraits of the eye makeup user and the shortening user. But even similar portraits sometimes show useful differences.

Perhaps the most obvious use of AIO research is to draw portraits of target groups. A less obvious use is to depict users of media vehicles. Psychographics can help in media selection by improving the analyst's understanding of the product-medium linkages found through direct cross tabulation. It also can shed light on topics other than products and media. For almost any identifiable type of behavior there is at least the possibility of new insight when the behavior is viewed in the context of AIO.

The typical approach of relating batteries of personality tests to different degrees of consumption (be it food, tobacco, alcohol, or television viewing) has been described as *ad hoc*, data mining, 'shot-in-the-dark,' or as random. Part of the problem is that the variables are seldom selected on the basis of some theoretical rationale.

One interesting attempt to reconcile this has been to examine the novelty value of different products and to try and relate them to the different consumer types that may be attracted to products that are either high or low in novelty value. As Goldberg pointed out, this personality trait has been termed 'venturesome ness' and is defined as the major value of innovative people.

Another notable study examined a number of women on the extent to which they were venturesome and on an estheticism-practicality scale. Subsequently analysis showed that these two traits could help them choose between two different types of toothpaste (Ultra Brita versus Colgate).

Yet another study found seven lifestyle clusters and labeled them (1) traditionalists; (2) frustrated; (3) life-expansionists; (4) mobiles; (5) sophisticates; (6) actives; and (7) immediate gratifiers. It was found that these lifestyle clusters related to certain behaviors with the traditionalists being more interested in shelf-stocking and cooking and baking, and the mobiles were higher in the self-indulgent and personal appearance product assortments.

The user of AIO data may use a large, highly diversified collection of statements or a more limited number of multi-item scales. Wells reports that the use of multi-item scales reduces the range of the topics that can be covered, and can obscure some novel, potentially interesting or useful relationships. Others prefer to ask questions that force people to rank a set of statements from most to least agreement in order to suppress 'yea-saying.' This ranking approach can also force discrimination among items that might otherwise have been marked on the same scale position. Rank-ordering can be useful in exploratory studies involving consumption intentions. Journal reviewers, however, often have problems with rank-ordering and its analysis. For this reason, rank-ordering can be done to generate insights, but rating scales are often best used for the more confirmatory research paper that might be sent to a journal.

This discussion has focused on issues related to accurately measuring consumption intentions – a more common analogue than measuring actual consumption, which can be more physically straightforward. It is critical to keep in mind that many of the issues discussed in this chapter will be equally relevant to measuring actual consumption and in reducing the noise between interventions and actual measures of behavior.

When the sample is large and the results are well-scattered, the simple way to analyze AIO data is by ordinary cross-tabulation. This has also been shown in a foundational study on cravings in which the food cravings of people were analyzed to show the different psychographic taste segments that existed with respect to snack food. The study found three groups – Classics, the Elaborates, and the Imaginers – each which have cravings triggered by different kinds of product or experience attributes. The Classics tend to prefer the basic version of a given product (such as the classic char-grilled hamburger and basic vanilla ice cream). The Elaborates tend to prefer a decorated version of the basic product (such as a bacon cheeseburger with the works, or an elaborate ice cream sundae). Whereas the elaborates have a high level of interest in the category, marketing messages were found to have little effect on them and their cravings. In contrast to elaborates, Imaginers may like either a basic or decorated version of the product, but they are also highly suggestible to marketing messages they are presented because they basically have a low level of interest in the category.

SUMMARY

An intervention in public health or in the marketing world can be very costly in dollars, time, expectations, and hope. Determining the effectiveness of such an intervention after-the-fact by using evaluation research would be more of an autopsy.

What is needed for interventions is to determine whether they will be effective before they are implemented. Research should be used to conduct a prescreening of possible options, not an autopsy after the fact.

Examining both quantitative and qualitative measures in prestudies can help narrow down which options are most likely to be effective. In addition, such measures will help indicate what changes can be made to increase the likelihood of success.

Further refinement of such investigations should take the psychographics of target groups into account. Doing so can sharpen the precision of measures and effectively show which segments are most promising – and least promising – to target with the intervention.

Since the mid-1960s, researchers have been identifying and measuring many important factors correlated with consumption. The next evolutionary step needs to be in the direction of understanding the 'whys' behind consumption. The focus needs to explain why – for instance – we eat how much we eat, not simply show it. This entails more of a focus on developing and testing process-models and theories of consumption.

Because much of this foundational research will be hit-and-miss, using situations where consumption intentions are measured can minimize the prohibitive risks of expensive, large-scale efforts such as clinical trials. Using consumption intention measures may more quickly and inexpensively allow more productive integration across studies and may help identify the more fundamental low-involvement drivers of consumption. Keeping a focus on the mechanisms or processes behind consumption – the whys behind it – will help the interdisciplinary area of food consumption progress in ways that can raise its profile and its impact on academia, on health practitioners, and ultimately on consumer welfare.

REFERENCES

Batra, R. (1984) 'Low involvement' message reception – processes and intervention implications. Unpublished dissertation, Graduate School of Business, Stanford University, Stanford, CA 94305.

Batra, R. and Ray, M. L. (1986) 'Situational effects of intervention repetition: The moderating influence of motivation, ability, and opportunity to respond', *Journal of Consumer Research*, 12: 432–45.

Cassidy, C. M. (1981) 'Collecting data on American food consumption patterns: An anthropological perspective', in Food and Nutrition Board National Research Council, *Assessing Changing Food Consumption Patterns*, Washington, D.C.: National Academy Press. pp. 135–54.

Ericsson, K. A. and Simon, H. A. (1978) 'Thinking aloud protocols as data', CIP working paper, Department of Psychology, Carnegie-Mellon University.

Ericsson, K. A. and Simon, H. A. (1984) *Protocol Analysis: Verbal Reports as Data*. Cambridge, MA: The MIT Press.

Fishbein, M. and Icek, A. (1975) *Beliefs, Attitude, Intention, and Behavior: An Introduction to Theory and Research*. Reading, MA.: Addison-Wesley Publishing.

Greenwald, A. G. (1968) 'Cognitive learning, cognitive response to persuasion, and attitude change', in A. G. Greenwald, T. C. Brock and T. C. Ostrom (eds.) *Psychological Foundations of Attitudes.* New York: Academic Press. pp. 63–102.

Jacoby, J. and Chestnut, R. W. (1978) *Brand Loyalty: Measurement and Management.* New York: John Wiley and Sons.

Keller, K. L. (1987) 'Memory factors in intervention: The effect of intervention retrieval cues on brand evaluations', *Journal of Consumer Research*, 14: 316–24.

Kidder, I. H. (1980) *Research Methods in Social Relations.* New York: Holt, Rinehart and Winston.

Nisbett, R. E. and Wilson, T. D. (1977) 'Telling more than we can know: Verbal reports on mental processes', *Psychological Review*, 84: 231–59.

Pearl, R. B. (1981) 'Possible alternative methods for data collection on food consumption and expenditures', in Food and Nutrition Board National Research Council, *Assessing Changing Food Consumption Patterns*, Washington, D.C.: National Academy Press. pp. 198–203.

Pennings, J. M. E., Wansink, B. and Meulenberg, M. M. E. (2002) 'A note on modeling consumer reactions to a crisis: The case of the madcow disease', *International Journal of Research in Marketing*, 19(2): 91–100.

Pilgrim, F. J. (1957) 'The components of food acceptance and their measurement', in J. Brozek (ed.) *Symposium on Nutrition and Behavior.* New York, National Academy Press. pp. 69–73.

Russo, J. E., Johnson, E. J. and Stephens, D. L. (1989) 'The validity of verbal protocols', *Memory and Cognition,* 17 (6): 759–69.

Smead, R. J., Wilcox, J. B. and Wilkes, R. E. (1981) 'How valid are product descriptions and protocols in choice experiments?' *Journal of Consumer Research*, 8: 37–42.

Stemple, G. H. and Westley, B. H. (1981) *Research Methods in Mass Communication.* Englewood Cliffs, NJ: Prentice-Hall.

Turner, C. K. (1986) 'Don't blame memory for people's faulty reports on what influences their judgments', *Personality and Social Psychology Bulletin*, 14: 622–9.

Wansink, B. (2009) 'Measuring food intake in realistic laboratory analog settings', in D. B. Allison (ed.) *Handbook of Assessment Methods for Obesity and Eating Behaviors.* forthcoming.

Wansink, B. (2006) *Mindless Eating: Why We Eat More Than We Think.* New York: Bantam-Dell.

Wansink, B. (2005) 'Consumer profiling and the new product development toolbox', *Food Quality and Preference*, 16(3): 217–21.

Wansink, B. (2004a) 'Consumer reactions to food safety crises', *Advances in Food and Nutrition Research*, 48: 103–50.

Wansink, B. (2004b) 'Environmental factors that increase the food intake and consumption volume of unknowing consumers', *Annual Review of Nutrition*, 24: 455–79.

Wansink, B. (2000) 'New techniques to generate key marketing insights', *Marketing Research*, (Summer): 28–36.

Wansink, B. (1994a) 'Antecedents and mediators of eating bouts', *Family and Consumer Sciences Research Journal*, 23(2): 166–82.

Wansink, B. (1994b) 'Developing and validating useful consumer prototypes', *Journal of Targeting, Measurement and Analysis for Marketing*, 3(1): 18–30.

Wansink, B. and Cheong, J.H. (2002) 'Taste profiles that correlate with soy consumption in developing countries', *Pakistan Journal of Nutrition*, 1(6): 276–8.

Wansink, B., Just, D. R. and Payne, C. R. (2009a) 'Mindless eating and environmental cues', *American Economic Review*, forthcoming.

Wansink, B. and Park, S.-B. (2002) 'Sensory suggestiveness and labeling: Do soy labels bias taste?' *Journal of Sensory Studies*, 17(5): 483–91.

Wansink, B. and Park, S.-B. (2000a) 'Accounting for taste: Prototypes that predict preference', *Journal of Database Marketing*, 7(4): 308–20.

Wansink, B. and Park, S.-B. (2000b) 'Methods and measures that profile heavy users', *Journal of Advertising Research*, 40(4): 61–72.

Wansink, B. and Payne, C. R. (2008) 'Consequences of belonging to the "clean plate club"', *Archives of Adolescent and Pediatric Medicine*, 162(10): 994–5.

Wansink, B., Payne, C. R. and Chandon P. (2007) 'Internal and external cues of meal cessation: The French paradox redux?' *Obesity*, 15: 2920–4.

Wansink, B., Payne, C. R. and van Ittersum, K. (2008) 'Profiling the heroic leader: empirical lessons from combat-decorated veterans of World War II', *Leadership Quarterly*, 19: 547–55.

Wansink, B. and Ray, M. L. (2000) 'Estimating an advertisement's impact on one's consumption of a brand', *Journal of Advertising Research*, 40(6): 106–13.

Wansink, B., Ray, M. L. and Batra, R. (1994) 'Increasing cognitive response sensitivity', *Journal of Advertising*, 23(2): 65–75.

Wansink, B. and Sobal, J. (2007) 'Mindless eating: The 200 daily food decisions we overlook', *Environment and Behavior*, 39(1): 106–23.

Wansink, B. and van Ittersum, K. (2005) 'Shape of glass and amount of alcohol poured:

Comparative study of effect of practice and concentration', *British Medical Journal*, 331(7531): 1512–14.

Wansink, B., van Ittersum, K. and Painter, J. E. (2005) 'How descriptive food names bias sensory perceptions in restaurants', *Food Quality and Preference*, 16(5): 393–400.

Wansink, B., van Ittersum, K. and Werle, C. (2009b) 'How negative experiences shape long-term food preferences: Fifty years from the World War II combat front', *Appetite*, forthcoming.

Wright, P. L. (1973) 'The cognitive processes mediating acceptance of intervention', *Journal of Marketing Research*, 10 (February): 53–62.

Wright, P. L. (1980) 'Message-evoked thoughts: Persuasion research using thought verbalizations', *Journal of Consumer Research*, 7 (September): 151–75.

Wright, P. L. and Rip, P. (1980) 'Retrospective reports on consumer decision processes', in J. C. Olson (ed.) *Advances in Consumer Research, 7.* Ann Arbor, MI: Association for Consumer Research. pp. 146–7.

Making Applied Measurement Effective and Efficient

Ujwal Kayandé

Consider the following applied measurement context: The senior management of a large retail chain believes that the quality of service offered in its stores is an important determinant of customer loyalty, eventually leading to better overall firm performance. Consequently, one of the most important operational objectives for the firm is to improve its quality of service. In order to align organizational goals with employee incentives, senior management decides to reward its store managers on the basis of each store's monthly 'service quality score'. The firm decides to measure service quality using a 10-item measurement scale, each item measured using a five-point Likert scale. A sample size of 100 customers from each store is deemed sufficient by management. A year into this program, the management are seriously concerned about their incentive program because the scores for most stores tend to be clustered around 4.2/5, suggesting that their

service quality scale has *little power to discriminate between stores*, even though the stores differ vastly on customer loyalty and performance. Their market research manager is baffled because the said scale was shown by several academic articles to have excellent measurement properties, including, for example, a Cronbach's alpha close to 0.95. Why is the scale then not able to discriminate between stores? In other words, *is the firm's measurement of service quality ineffective?* Consider the same context again. The market research manager digs deeper into the data to understand if some items are better than others at discriminating between stores. Instead, he finds that the score on any one item is a good predictor of the score on any other item, implying that each additional item beyond the first item is adding no new information. He wonders then as to why there should be 10 items in the scale – why not just one item? In other words, *is the firm's measurement of service quality inefficient?*

The purpose of this chapter is to present an applied measurement framework that will provide answers to two important questions: (1) What makes measurement effective? and (2) What makes measurement efficient? I argue that the nature of measurement in applied social sciences is such that its effectiveness and efficiency depend fundamentally on the purpose of measurement. The same data can provide 'good' information for one purpose and 'poor' information for another purpose. While my arguments might appear intuitive, most academics, in particular in applied disciplines such as marketing and information systems, ignore these arguments when they develop and/or recommend measurement instruments. Extant assessment of what is good or bad information is typically treated by academics as 'purpose-free', that is, independent of the purpose of measurement. A good example of such 'purpose-free' assessment of scale effectiveness is the rampant use of Cronbach's alpha as a measure of reliability, irrespective of whether the scale is stimulus-centered (e.g., quality of service offered by retail stores) or respondent-centered (an individual's need for cognition). Indeed, as Viswanathan (2005) points out, stimulus-centered scales 'place stimuli on a continuum' (p. 213), requiring consistency across respondents. The reliability of such scales is more appropriately assessed by inter-rater reliability measures, not Cronbach's alpha, which measures inter-item consistency. The framework in this chapter goes beyond such distinctions to present a comprehensive 'purpose-laden' approach, in which the purpose of measurement determines the *object* of measurement or the unit of analysis (e.g., stimulus or respondent), and consequently the effectiveness of measurement.

At the outset, I note that many, if not most, of the examples and measurement contexts discussed in this chapter will come from my discipline – that is, marketing. However, the problem I address is one that is equally applicable to any applied social science discipline. For example, in education, researchers might be interested in problems that require measures to discriminate between students, teachers, schools, districts, states, and/or countries. A measurement scale might be capable of discriminating between students, but might not perform as well when used to compare schools (or vice versa). Another example is that of comparing cultures on individualism or collectivism, an important measurement problem in the study of cultures. Once again, the researcher's interest might be in comparing cultures, not so much individual respondents, requiring measurement scales to be capable of discriminating between cultures, while generalizing over respondents within cultures. Whether a scale is capable of doing so requires an approach that (1) identifies conditions that affect an observed measure, and (2) determines measurement effectiveness taking into account those conditions and the purpose of measurement. My goal in this chapter is to offer such an approach.

This chapter is organized as follows. I first introduce my perspective on measurement, which is primarily influenced by the work of Cronbach and his colleagues. Subsequent to the conceptual discussion, I present a mathematical model of measurement effectiveness and efficiency, and an empirical illustration of the approach. Both are drawn largely from my joint work with Adam Finn published in 1997 in the *Journal of Marketing Research* (Finn and Kayandé, 1997). I then present two contrasting cases, both in the retail banking sector, to provide an illustration of how this approach can help make measurement effective and/or efficient in applied contexts. Finally, I draw upon the measurement literature to identify some guidelines to make applied measurement effective and efficient.

MEASUREMENT PURPOSE AND EFFECTIVENESS

Acquiring and interpreting information about the characteristics of objects has been a major focus of scientific inquiry in many disciplines. Such information is rarely acquired in its perfect form. Either the information acquisition process of a research study is limited to some extent, or the true state of an object's characteristic can never be known even if the information acquisition process is perfect. The information acquisition process can be limited because of several important reasons, one of which is the inability to measure the characteristic of interest under all possible conditions that affect the measurement procedure. For a simple example in the physical sciences, consider the measurement of the length of a table. A person with a ruler can take a measurement of the length. The measured length might depend on the person who measures the length and the particular ruler used by that person to measure the length. Thus, the measurement of the length of the table by one person with only one ruler can only be an approximation to the *true* length, if there is variation in the measure attributable to persons or rulers. On the other hand, the true state of the characteristic might be 'unknowable' because we can only represent the true state isomorphically (perhaps because the characteristic is socially constructed), or because of the inherently stochastic nature of the true state. In the social sciences, we often find such a limit in the information acquisition process *and* an inability to know the true state of the object's characteristic.

This combination results in a less than perfect 'measurement' of the characteristic of an object.

Social scientists have pursued the development of methods to improve the measurement of an object's characteristic, so that the true state of the characteristic is better represented, isomorphically or otherwise, by the measurement. A large number of these methods originated in education and psychology, although some were adaptations from statistics literature. Almost all methods are statistical in nature and this chapter is limited to methods that improve the quantitative measurement and representation of the true state of an object's characteristic, *assuming that the imperfections in measurement arise from the limits in the number of conditions under which a measurement of the characteristic can be made*. Whether a true state exists is controversial, and there are many philosophical perspectives on the issue. Although an interesting question, I abstract from it by *not assuming* the true state to be divinely determined. Instead, the true state is considered to be the 'limiting value of extensive observations' (Cronbach et al., 1972) of a stable characteristic of an object, consistent with the focus of this chapter on the number of diverse conditions under which the characteristic is observed.

Measurement of the characteristics of objects serves as the foundation for knowledge in several academic business disciplines (e.g., organizational behaviour, marketing, information systems, operations management, etc). Organizations, products, consumers, markets, employers, employees, and distribution channels are among the objects that are of critical interest to inquiry in our disciplines. Thus, almost every academic research study measures the characteristics of one or more of these objects, albeit in different ways. For example, the attitudes of consumers toward a behavior, the service quality provided by service firms, the satisfaction of a firm's employees, the image or reputation of a firm, the size of a market, market share of a brand, the demographics of a consumer population, and the choices made by consumers are commonly measured by academic researchers and practitioners. It is possible to directly observe some characteristics of some objects, e.g., choices made by consumers can be observed by grocery stores equipped to collect such data. On the other hand, characteristics of many types of objects are unobservable – they cannot be observed as a fact and are therefore isomorphically represented to facilitate their measurement. For example, the satisfaction experienced by an organization's employees or the service quality provided by firms are characteristics that are unobservable in an objective sense. In the marketing literature, for example, numerous scales have been developed ostensibly for the measurement of such characteristics, and as an indication of this activity, there are now at least two handbooks with details of multi-item scales (Bruner and Hensel, 1993; Bearden et al., 1993). Other disciplines use scales such as supplier management orientation (Shin et al., 2000) and user satisfaction with data (Karimi et al., 2005).

The effort to evaluate the effectiveness of measurement has largely focused on two aspects – the reliability and validity of the measurement instrument. These psychometric assessment tools are drawn from what is called classical test theory (see Allen and Yen, 2002), which originated in education and psychology. Classical test theory helps educational psychologists in evaluating the ability of a measurement procedure to reliably scale a student's ability or some other characteristic relative to other students in the population. As such then, classical test theory focuses largely on individual differences, or in other

words, on the scaling of some characteristic of individuals. When measurement instruments are evaluated on the basis of classical methods of reliability and validity, the researcher implicitly assumes that the measurement instrument will be used to discriminate between individuals. So, for example, if the researcher is interested in scaling consumers on their attitude toward an advertisement, then using classical methods is not wrong (although even this application of classical methods is somewhat limited, as explained later in this chapter). However, when the same classical methods are applied to evaluate a measurement instrument's ability to scale firms on some characteristic, say reputation, not only is the evaluation method wrong, but the results might be grossly misleading. Going back to the example at the beginning of this chapter, the 'reliability' of the service quality instrument was pretty high (Cronbach's alpha greater than 0.95), yet the scale was incapable of discriminating between stores. In other words, the measurement instrument was not effective in fulfilling the purpose to which it was put: discriminating between stores. The critical question that is asked in this chapter is whether measurement effectiveness when scaling a characteristic of individuals is the appropriate criterion to evaluate the information used to make various managerial decisions. Different managerial decisions require scaling of characteristics of *different* objects and therefore the appropriate scale evaluation criterion depends on the purpose of measurement.

Two specific issues deserve mention at this stage. First, classical test theory methods treat measurement error as a sample from a single undifferentiated distribution (Cronbach et al., 1972; Brennan, 1983). Any study of the evolution of statistical thought will certainly accord great importance to the revolutionary thinking of Fisher (1925), who suggested that variation in a measure can arise from several controllable sources, some of which are sources of error. The idea that variation can arise from several sources is the primary basis of the generalizability theory approach presented by Cronbach and his colleagues (Cronbach et al., 1972) in educational psychology. I note here that Cronbach was himself critical of classical test theory based methods, yet business disciplines continue to be enamoured by the same methods (to quote: 'I no longer regard the alpha formula as the most appropriate way to examine most data', Cronbach and Shavelson, 2004: 403).

Second, the chapter also suggests methods to improve the efficiency of the information acquisition process. Simply put, the data collection process for decision making can be made more efficient by taking into account the purpose of measurement. This is achieved by estimating the variation in measures attributable to different sources, deciding which sources constitute noise in measurement, and so are controllable, and which source(s) constitute a signal, and then constructing a measurement instrument that more effectively measures the characteristic of interest at lowest monetary cost.

MATHEMATICAL MODEL OF MEASUREMENT EFFECTIVENESS AND EFFICIENCY

In classical test theory, reliability is *assessed* as the degree to which a multi-item measurement instrument consistently scales a sample of individuals. Reliability can be expressed in mathematical form as

$$r = \frac{\sigma^2_{\text{true score}}}{\sigma^2_{\text{observed score}}} \qquad (25.1)$$

where, $\sigma^2_{\text{true score}}$ is the variation among respondents' mean scores and $\sigma^2_{\text{observed score}}$

is the sum of true score variance and error variance. Thus, a scale is seen as producing highly reliable information if it provides a consistent scaling of respondents. Many business measurement applications in marketing require the scaling of objects such as firms (comparing the service quality provided by firms, the supplier management orientation of firms, reputation of firms), advertisements (comparing the effectiveness of advertisements), or brands (comparing brand equity), rather than a scaling of individuals. Such scaling may require *generalization over individuals* in the population, it does not require scaling of the individuals. Thus, a reliability assessment method that considers only the scaling of individuals is limited in its scope.

As opposed to the limited view of classical reliability theory, generalizability theory (Cronbach et al., 1972; hereafter called G-theory) provides a multi-faceted view of measurement, where variation in measurement arises from multiple potentially *controllable* sources. For example, in measuring perceived quality of products in a category, variation could arise from multiple sources such as respondents, items, and products. Following the Fisherian logic of experimental design, G-theory assumes random sampling of one or more of these sources of measurement, allowing the researcher to estimate the variance attributable to each source. The random sampling assumption permits the researcher to use a random effects or variance components model to estimate the variation. Cronbach et al. (1972) defined a formula for the coefficient of generalizability, analogous to the reliability coefficient in classical reliability theory

$$E\hat{\rho}^2 = \frac{\sigma^2_{\text{universe score}}}{\sigma^2_{\text{universe score}} + \sigma^2_{\text{relative error}}} \qquad (25.2)$$

where $\sigma^2_{\text{universe score}}$ is the variance component associated with any object of measurement (analogue of the true score variance in classical reliability theory) and $\sigma^2_{\text{relative error}}$ is the sum of only those variance components that affect the scaling of the levels of the object of measurement. The notation[1] is meant to show that a generalizability coefficient is 'approximately equal to the expected value ... of the squared correlation between observed scores and universe scores' (Brennan, 1983: 17). For a study with items as the only facet of generalization, the coefficient of generalizability is equivalent to the classical reliability coefficient.

Because some of the terminology in this chapter is unique to G-theory, I note some basic definitions of terms. An 'object of measurement' is a factor, such as firms, advertisements, or brands, the levels of which need to be scaled by the measurement instrument. A 'facet of generalization' is a factor over which the researcher requires the findings to generalize. For example, a scaling of the service quality provided by firms should generalize over respondents in the population, thus making firms the object of measurement and respondents a facet of generalization. The levels of an object or a facet are the different elements constituting the factor. Six firms would constitute 6 levels of the object of measurement 'firms' and 200 respondents would correspond to 200 levels of the facet called 'respondents'. G-theory assumes that each random effect 'i' is normally[2] distributed with mean 0 and variance σ^2_i. A generalizability study (hereafter called a G-study) is the first stage of the two-stage procedure used in G-theory in which the variance components σ^2_i associated with each effect 'i' are estimated from empirical data. The second stage, called a decision study, is an applied study, the results of which are used to make decisions. Details of G-theory are

provided by Cronbach et al. (1972) and Brennan (1983). Rentz (1987) provides the most complete account in marketing; Shavelson and Webb (1991) provide a good introduction.

Scaling of the levels of an object of measurement is affected by every interaction of the object of measurement with a facet of generalization. A significant interaction between the object of measurement and a facet of generalization implies that the scaling of the levels of the object of measurement depends partially on the specific level of that particular facet of generalization. For example, if all respondents provided the same scaling of a sample of stores (i.e., perfect consistency between respondents), then the variance component associated with the interaction between respondents and stores would be equal to zero. The implication then would be that the scaling of stores does not depend on the respondent (indeed, if this were the case, the required sample size of respondents for decision studies comparing stores would likely be 1). Similarly, if all items generated the same scaling of stores, then the variance component associated with the interaction of stores and items would be equal to zero, providing support for a single-item scale to scale stores.

Relative error variance is the sum of the variance components associated with the interactions of the object of measurement with every facet of generalization and the random error variance. In a fully crossed study, if A is the object of measurement and B and C are facets of generalization, relative error variance can be expressed as

$$\hat{\sigma}^2_{\text{relative error}} = \frac{\hat{\sigma}^2_{\text{A X B}}}{N_{\text{B}}} + \frac{\hat{\sigma}^2_{\text{A X C}}}{N_{\text{C}}}$$
$$+ \frac{\hat{\sigma}^2_{\text{A X B X C, random error}}}{N_{\text{B}}N_{\text{C}}}$$

(25.3)

where N_B and N_C are the number of levels of facets B and C, respectively, to be used in a future decision study.

Equation 25.3 shows that the function for relative error variance is convex in the number of levels of the facets of generalization that will be used in a future study. Thus, the number of levels of the facets of generalization designed into a decision study determines the relative error variance, and therefore the expected G-coefficient.

The purpose of the measurement clearly defines the object of measurement and the associated sources of measurement error. Optimizing measurement implies identifying the most efficient allocation of resources along each of the sources that constitute error in a decision study. To structure the optimization problem, we let the decision maker choose the level of generalizability 'g' acceptable in the scaling of the object of measurement (which determines the acceptable noise in the information). The required level of generalizability will depend on the consequences that could flow from the decision study. Nunnally (1978) suggested rules of thumb such as 0.90 as the absolute minimum reliability for any applied study, with 0.95 being the desired level of reliability. The same guidelines could apply in the current context.

Given a desired generalizability, relative error variance can be reduced by sampling along the facets that contribute to error, much the same way the Spearman-Brown prophecy formula in classical reliability theory suggests that an increase in items results in higher reliability. Given three or four facets along which samples can be drawn, the question then is whether sampling should be equally distributed across facets. The answer is no, because facets contribute different amounts of error variance. Sampling should be in proportion to the size of the associated variance components. A desired level of generalizability may be achieved with several designs, each a different sampling along the facets (I call such designs iso-generalizability designs). The best choice from among these iso-generalizability designs will depend on their costs. The lowest cost design which satisfies the generalizability criterion will be the most efficient.

The optimization can be formally set up as follows. Assume the cost of measurement C is a function of the number of levels of each facet and object included in the measurement design, and the cost of each level of each facet and object. For a specific decision study, where the object of measurement is known from the managerial problem, cost C can be represented as

$$C = f(c_0, \tilde{C}, \tilde{N}, n_{object}) \qquad (25.4)$$

where c_0 is the fixed cost of the survey instrument, $\tilde{C}$ is a vector with elements representing the cost of an observation on each facet, $\tilde{N}$ is a vector with elements $n_1, n_2, \ldots, n_F$ representing the number of levels of F facets of generalization, and n_{object} is the number of levels of the object of measurement.

The cost C can be represented by different functions (such as additive or multiplicative) depending on the data collection method. The purpose here is to minimize the cost of the design subject to achieving a desired value g of the G-coefficient $E\hat{\rho}^2$. The relative error variance $\left[\hat{\sigma}^2_{relative\ error}(\tilde{N})\right]$ is a decreasing function in all F elements of $\tilde{N}$. Thus, the optimization problem can be formally stated as follows

$$\underset{\tilde{N}=(n_1, n_2 \ldots n_F)}{\text{Minimize}} \quad C = f(c_0, \tilde{C}, \tilde{N}, n_{object})$$

$$(25.5)$$

subject to

1 $\left[E\hat{\rho}^2(\tilde{N}) \right] = \dfrac{\hat{\sigma}^2_{object}}{\hat{\sigma}^2_{object} + \left[\hat{\sigma}^2_{relative\ error}(\tilde{N}) \right]} \geq g$, the

desired G-coefficient, and where $\hat{\sigma}^2_{object}$ and all

variance components that constitute $\hat{\sigma}^2_{relative\ error}$ are known *a priori* from a G-study.
2 Each element of $\tilde{N} \geq 1$.
3 Each element of $\tilde{N}$ is an integer.

This integer programming problem has no analytical solution. However, it can be solved by the branch-and-bound algorithm (Salkin, 1975), which is available in popular spreadsheet packages. The branch-and-bound integer programming algorithm has been used by Sanders and colleagues (1989) to minimize the total number of observations (product of the number of levels of all facets of generalization) needed to achieve a desired G-coefficient. In a second paper, Sanders et al. (1991) propose a method to maximize the G-coefficient by choosing the number of observations that can be accommodated within a budget constraint. Thus, the G-coefficient is specified as a result of the optimization, not as a constraint.

Marcoulides (1995) presented an optimization method that minimizes the error variance taking into account budget constraints. Thus, his method provides for an efficient allocation of resources along each facet. He derived an analytical solution for the optimum number of levels for each facet in a multi-facet design. The number of levels of each facet in such solutions is almost always a fraction, not an integer. He then rounds these numbers to the nearest integers around the solution. Mathematically, such an approach is flawed because it does not necessarily lead to the lowest cost of all possible *integer* solutions and/or the minimum error variance. Our formulation makes it clear that the chosen design will lead to at least the desired level

of generalizability and will simultaneously have minimum cost of all designs that do so. Moreover, these prior optimization papers use hypothetical, not empirical variance component data.

EMPIRICAL ILLUSTRATION WITH SERVICE QUALITY MEASUREMENT

The psychometric and economic advantages of the aforementioned G-theory approach are illustrated with an application to the measurement of service quality. Service quality measurement is an appropriate context for three reasons. First, service quality is an important managerial issue, so proprietary assessment studies abound (see the cases reported in Spechler, 1991). Improving service quality has been identified as a key strategy for firms to profitably differentiate themselves in the marketplace (Babakus and Boller, 1992; Boulding et al., 1993; Cronin and Taylor, 1992; Devlin and Dong, 1994; Parasuraman et al., 1988; Rust et al., 1995; Zahorik and Rust, 1992).

Secondly, service quality measurement is an area where there is a considerable discrepancy between the common practitioner reliance on a single-item scale for each aspect of service to be evaluated and the multi-item measurement scales advocated by academics. Practitioner studies commonly address managerial problems using single-item scales, of unknown reliability, which seem to fit the purpose at hand (Bolton and Drew, 1991a, b; Devlin et al., 1993; Schmalensee, 1994). By following the scale development paradigm put forth by Churchill (1979), Parasuraman et al. (1985, 1988) made a significant contribution to the service quality literature in developing SERVQUAL, a multi-item measure of perceived service quality. However, SERVQUAL consists of a large number of items (at least 21), even in the shorter one-column format which directly measures perceived performance relative to expectations (Parasuraman et al., 1994b).

Thirdly, the service quality literature is an example of an area in marketing where researchers have not recognized that the respondent is rarely the object of measurement. From a classical reliability theory perspective, SERVQUAL provides a highly reliable scaling of respondents' perceptions of five service quality dimensions (reliability, responsiveness, assurance, empathy, and tangibles), as indicated by coefficient alphas averaging 0.88 (Parasuraman et al., 1991). As is typical of almost all marketing measurement research, such high levels of reliability led the original developers of the scale to suggest that SERVQUAL will provide reliable information for such diverse purposes as tracking the service quality provided by a firm, assessing a given firm on each of the dimensions of service quality, categorizing a firm's customers into several perceived quality segments, evaluating the

level of service provided by each store in a multi-unit retail chain, and assessing a firm's service performance relative to its principal competitors (Parasuraman et al., 1988).

However, such a generalization incorrectly assumes that the reliability of a measurement instrument[3] can be assessed independently of the purpose for which it is to be used. As evidence to the contrary, research has shown inconsistency in the SERVQUAL factor structure when it is used in different service industries (Babakus and Boller, 1992; Carman, 1990). Criticisms and the defense of the SERVQUAL scale development procedure (Brown et al., 1993; Cronin and Taylor 1994; Parasuraman et al., 1993, 1994a; Teas, 1994) have also implicitly assumed that the object of measurement in all service quality applications is respondents.

Table 25.1 lists some of the management problems that would make a retailer need to measure service quality, and shows how different problems change both the object of

Table 25.1   Object of measurement as a function of the purpose of measurement

Purpose of measurement/ underlying management problem	Measurement need	(Object of measurement) scaling of	(Facets of generalization) generalize over
1. Determine the relationship between store characteristics and service quality of stores	The service quality being provided by each of the stores in the chain	Stores in the chain	Customers, aspects, items
2. Are customers being lost because our competitors are providing better service quality?	Identify how our chain's service quality compares with the service quality of our competitors	Competitors within an industry	Stores, customers, aspects, items
3. What areas of our business activity are most in need of management attention?	Identify what aspects of our service are most in need of improvement	Aspects of business activity	Stores, customers, items
4. How well are we doing on different aspects of our business activity relative to our competitors?	Identify the performance of our chain on different aspects relative to the performance of competitors on the same aspects	Aspects of the business activity of competitors within an industry	Customers, items
5. Determine whether those customers who pay full price are getting better service	Determine the service quality perceptions of different categories of customers	Customers	Stores, aspects, items

Source: Finn and Kayandé (1997).

measurement and what constitutes the error to be generalized over.

For example, the first problem is to determine what store-level factors influence the service quality provided by stores in a chain. Here the service quality provided by each store in the chain must be measured accurately, so that it can be related to the other store-level factors. Success requires reliable measures of the service quality *for each store*. There is no need to identify which customers thought they received the best or the worst service. The measurement needs to discriminate well between stores, whilst generalizing over the perceptions of different customers. Sources of variability that affect the consistency of mean scores obtained for the stores constitute error in scaling the stores. These sources include all interactions between stores and other facets, as well as the random error component. As shown in Table 25.1, other problems have different objects and consequent sources of error. Of course, one managerial study may address more than one of these problems.

To demonstrate this approach, Finn and Kayandé (1997) conducted a generalizability study of retailer service quality, and then used the estimated variance components to identify optimal measurement designs for five different service quality measurement applications, called decision studies. The five sources of variability, or facets, included in the G-study were retail sectors (or type of retailer), retail chains, aspects of service quality, the items used to measure service quality, and consumers. The G-study had consumers evaluate the service quality provided by a total of nine retailers, three chosen at random from amongst the well-known chains in three retail sectors – three each from department stores, fast food stores, and grocery stores. Each chain was evaluated on nine items, three items each for three aspects of service quality (tangibles, responsiveness, and empathy). The specific items used for these aspects were randomly chosen from the perception items used in the SERVQUAL scale (Parasuraman et al., 1991). Because of the work undertaken to refine SERVQUAL, these items are known to be suitable measures for the respective aspects. The specific items and the response format used are shown in Appendix 1.

From an experimental design perspective, retail chains in this study were nested within retail sectors, and items were nested within aspects. Respondents were asked to rate all nine chains on all nine items, so they were crossed with chains, sectors, items, and aspects. The more fully crossed the design of a G-study, the more sources of variability of measurement can be estimated (Cronbach et al., 1972). It is possible to optimize a nested measurement design for an applied study on the basis of a fully crossed G-study, but not vice-versa.

The data were collected by mail survey, obtaining 133 responses with usable data. The response rate was 35 per cent. Because Cronbach's alpha averaged 0.88 (range 0.67–0.96) across the scales, the data are comparable with those collected in previous service quality studies. Table 25.2 provides the estimated variance components for all the factors included in the study, along with the interactions. Variance components were estimated by the minimum variance quadratic unbiased (MIVQUE) estimation method (Hartley et al., 1978), available in SAS. Respondents, aspects, and items were assumed to be randomly chosen from their respective universes of consumers who shop at the retail chains, aspects of service quality, and items to measure aspects of service quality.

The estimated variance components due to retail chains, respondents, chains by respondents, and chains by respondents by aspects, and random error were relatively high.[4] Together they accounted for about 80 per cent of the total variance in service

Table 25.2   Analysis of variance and variance component estimates

Source of variation	Variance component	Total variance: %
Chains	0.694	14.17
Retail sectors	0.000	0.00
Respondents	0.850	17.23
Aspects	0.193	3.91
Scale items	0.074	1.45
Retail sectors by respondents	0.016	0.32
Retail sectors by aspects	0.000	0.00
Retail sectors by items	0.018	0.36
Chains by respondents	1.053	21.34
Chains by aspects	0.093	1.89
Chains by items	0.033	0.68
Respondents by aspects	0.260	5.27
Respondents by items	0.158	3.20
Retail sectors by respondents by aspects	0.000	0.00
Retail sectors by respondents by items	0.107	2.16
Chains by respondents by aspects	0.633	12.82
Error	0.751	15.23
Total	4.934	100.00

Source: Finn and Kayandé (1997).

quality scores. The estimates of the variance components for retail sectors and for the interactions of sectors by aspects and of sectors by respondents by aspects were negative. As shown in Table 25.2, such estimates are typically treated as if they were zero, because all negative estimates were very close to zero (Cronbach et al., 1972). The variance component associated with a nested facet (chains or items) is confounded with the variance component due to the interaction between the nested facet and the facet in which it is nested. For example, the variance component for items is confounded with the variance component for the interaction of items and aspects, because items are nested within aspects. Such confounding is explicitly recognized in this type of analysis.

I note here that the estimated variance components reveal something useful about the measurement context. First, only four

components (retail chains, respondents, chains by respondents, and chains by respondents by aspects) account for about 80 per cent of the variance, implying that there is much measurement invariance in these data. Specifically, the small variance components associated with the interaction of items and other facets (respondents, sectors, chains) suggests that the items essentially generate similar scaling of retail chains, retail sectors, and respondents. So if the purpose was to scale retail chains, the optimal number of items would most likely be one per aspect. However, the optimal number of respondents to scale retail chains is likely to be somewhat higher considering the relatively larger chains by respondents variance component. We now identify optimal designs (effective and efficient) for two managerial purposes.

REDUCTION OF ERROR VARIANCE IN APPLIED DECISION STUDIES

The variance components from the G-study can be used to calculate the expected G-coefficients for planned decision study designs or to identify the lowest cost design for a required G-coefficient. A major advantage of G-theory is that relative error variance is partially controllable through sampling along each facet included in a decision study because it is convex in the number of levels of the facets of generalization. For example, suppose a G-study shows the variance component associated with the interaction of retail chains with items is very small, close to zero. This means the scaling of retail chains is not dependent on items. Therefore, it would be inefficient to include more than one or two items in any future decision study in which chains are the object of measurement. However, we might expect the scaling of retail chains to vary across respondents. In such a case, increasing the number of respondents will improve the generalizability coefficient of a study in which chains are the object of measurement.

Table 25.3 quantifies the effect of increasing the number of items, aspects, and respondents on the generalizability coefficient for the service quality provided by retail chains within a retail sector. When retail chains are the object of measurement, the expected G-coefficient with just one item for one aspect and 25 respondents is about 0.75. Further, with one item per aspect, four aspects, and 35 respondents, the expected G-coefficient is about 0.90. This example illustrates how a generalizability coefficient can be forecast using the G-study data.

The differential reduction in error variance achieved by sampling along multiple facets also enables an optimal design to be chosen for a decision study. In the following section, the general optimization procedure of Equation 25.5 is used to design the optimal measurement for two illustrative managerial problems. Finn and Kayandé (1997) present three additional scenarios that illustrate how the purpose

Table 25.3 Reduction of error variance by sampling from multiple facets[a]

	G-study	Alternative decision studies			
$n_{sectors} =$	1	1	1	1	1
$n_{respondents} =$	1	25	35	50	100
$n_{aspects} =$	1	1	4	4	4
$n_{items} =$	1	1	1	1	1
Source of variation	*Estimate*	*Expected variance component[b]*			
Retail chain	0.69	0.69	0.69	0.69	0.69
Retail sector	0.00	0.00	0.00	0.00	0.00
Respondents	0.85	0.03	0.02	0.02	0.01
Aspects	0.19	0.19	0.05	0.05	0.05
Items[c]	0.07	0.07	0.02	0.02	0.02
Sector by respondents	0.02	0.00	0.00	0.00	0.00
Sector by aspects	0.00	0.00	0.00	0.00	0.00
Sector by items	0.02	0.02	0.00	0.00	0.00
Chain by respondents[d]	*1.05*	*0.04*	*0.03*	*0.02*	*0.01*
Chain by aspects	*0.09*	*0.09*	*0.02*	*0.02*	*0.02*
Chain by items	*0.03*	*0.03*	*0.01*	*0.01*	*0.01*
Respondents by aspects	0.26	0.01	0.00	0.00	0.00
Respondents by item	0.16	0.01	0.00	0.00	0.00
Sector by respondents by aspects	0.00	0.00	0.00	0.00	0.00
Sector by respondents by items	0.11	0.00	0.00	0.00	0.00
Chain by respondents by aspects	*0.63*	*0.03*	*0.00*	*0.00*	*0.00*
Error	*0.75*	*0.03*	*0.01*	*0.00*	*0.00*
Relative error variance	2.56	0.22	0.07	0.06	0.05
G-coefficient for chains	0.21	0.76	0.91	0.92	0.94

[a] All numbers truncated to two decimal places. Thus, a variance component of 0.00 does not necessarily imply that it is zero.
[b] Represents the estimated variance component for the random effect divided by the number of levels of the factors (other than the object of measurement) in the random effect.
[c] Because items are nested within aspects, all variance components that include items are divided by the number of items *and* the number of aspects.
[d] The variance components for the interactions of the object of measurement (chains) with the *facets of generalization* are in italics.
Source: Finn and Kayandé (1997).

affects effectiveness and efficiency of measurement.

Problem 1: benchmarking chains within one retail sector

Consider the benchmarking problem of comparing the service quality provided by five retail chains drawn from any one retail sector. Retail chains constitute the object of measurement for the study. Respondents are the raters of the service quality delivered by the chains, but it is expected that respondents could differ in their scaling of retail chains. Thus, the variance component due to the interaction between chains and respondents constitutes one source of measurement error variance. The items are all designed to measure service quality provided by each chain, but again it is expected that the scaling of chains could depend on the item used to measure service quality. Thus, the variance component due to the interaction of items and chains is the second source of measurement error variance. Similarly, the variance components due to the interaction between aspects and chains, and the three-way interaction between chains, respondents, and aspects are the other sources of error variance. Finally, random error variance, which is also confounded with several higher-order interaction variance components, constitutes another source of measurement error variance. Thus, relative error variance can be expressed mathematically as

$$\hat{\sigma}^2_{\text{relative error}} = \frac{\hat{\sigma}^2_{c \times r}}{n_r} + \frac{\hat{\sigma}^2_{c \times i}}{n_i n_a} + \frac{\hat{\sigma}^2_{c \times a}}{n_a}$$
$$+ \frac{\hat{\sigma}^2_{c \times r \times a}}{n_r n_a} + \frac{\hat{\sigma}^2_{\text{random error}}}{n_r n_i n_a}$$
$$(25.6)$$

Consistent with Equation 25.4, the cost function for the mail survey data collection method used in this study can be expressed as

$$C = f(c_0, \tilde{C}, \tilde{N}, n_{\text{chains}})$$
$$= c_0 + c_1 N_r + c_2(n_i n_a) n_c n_s$$
$$+ c_3(n_i n_a n_c n_s) n_r \qquad (25.7)$$

where c_0 is the fixed cost of the study; c_1 is the unit cost of selecting and communicating with a respondent; and c_2 is the unit cost of an additional item i when designing and formatting the data collection instrument. The multiplicative term $(n_i n_a)$ is necessary because a number of items taken together constitute an aspect. Also c_3 is the incremental cost of a lengthening of the study with an additional item on the data collection cost for each respondent; $c_0 = \$0$, $c_1 = \$5$, $c_2 = \$10$, $c_3 = \$0.20$ for all problems examined in this paper; n_r is the number of respondents, n_i is the number of items, and n_a is the number of aspects; n_c is the number of retail chains under investigation, in this case equal to 5; n_s is the number of retail sectors under investigation, in this case equal to 1; and N_r is the total number of respondents, equal to n_r for the crossed design and $(n_r n_c n_s)$ for the nested design.

Given this structure of the cost function, it is possible to minimize C over n_i, n_r, and n_a, subject to constraints suggested in Equation 25.5. Part I of Table 25.4 provides the optimal designs with the associated costs for a range of generalizability levels. Designs are described by the number of levels along each facet, assuming the same experimental design (crossing and nesting) as in the G-study. Note the sharp increase in costs to achieve generalizability levels of greater than 0.95. An interesting feature of these designs is that they require only one item per aspect. Technically, this result is due to the relative independence of the rating of chains and items, as reflected in the low variance component associated with the interaction of chains and items

Table 25.4 Optimal designs for retail chains as object of measurement, and crossed versus nested designs

$E\hat{\rho}^2$	σ^2_{rel}	I. Customers crossed with chains						II. Customers nested within chains					
		Facet sampling						Facet sampling					
		n_i	n_a	n_r	N_r[a]	N_t[b]	Cost ($)	n_i	n_a	n_r	N_r	N_t	Cost ($)
0.80	0.174	1	2	16	16	160	212	1	4	17	85	340	693
0.81	0.163	1	2	18	18	180	226	1	4	19	95	380	751
0.82	0.152	1	2	20	20	200	240	1	4	20	100	400	780
0.83	0.142	1	2	23	23	230	261	1	4	22	110	440	838
0.84	0.132	1	2	26	26	260	282	1	4	24	120	480	896
0.85	0.123	1	3	19	19	285	302	1	5	24	120	600	970
0.86	0.113	1	3	22	22	330	326	1	5	27	135	675	1060
0.87	0.104	1	3	25	25	375	350	1	5	30	150	750	1150
0.88	0.095	1	3	29	29	435	382	1	6	31	155	930	1261
0.89	0.086	1	3	35	35	525	430	1	6	35	175	1050	1385
0.90	0.077	1	4	31	31	620	479	1	6	40	200	1200	1540
0.91	0.069	1	4	38	38	760	542	1	8	41	205	1640	1753
0.92	0.060	1	5	38	38	950	630	1	7	52	260	1820	2014
0.93	0.052	1	5	50	50	1250	750	1	9	56	280	2520	2354
0.94	0.044	1	6	56	56	1680	916	1	10	67	335	3350	2845
0.95	0.037	1	7	68	68	2380	1166	1	12	80	400	4800	3560
0.96	0.029	1	9	82	82	3690	1598	1	15	100	500	7500	4750
0.97	0.021	1	13	99	99	6435	2432	1	17	145	725	12325	6940
0.98	0.014	1	18	159	159	14310	4557	1	24	225	1125	27000	12225
0.99	0.007	1	37	304	304	56240	14618	1	44	475	2375	104500	34975

[a] Total number of respondents.
[b] Total number of observations $= n_{items} \times n_{aspects} \times n_{respondents} \times n_{chains}$, where n_{chains} for this problem is 5.
Source: Finn and Kayandé (1997).

(only 0.7 per cent of total variance). Substantively, this result illustrates that the managerial preference for using a single item per aspect can in fact be optimal for certain types of problems.

Academic research on service quality (e.g., Parasuraman et al., 1994b) suggests benchmarking studies collect data separately from customers of each chain, nesting respondents within chains. We can calculate the variance components expected from such a nested design using the variance components from our fully crossed G-study. Thus, it is also possible to minimize C to solve for an optimal design while nesting respondents within the chains being benchmarked. Part II of Table 25.4 provides the optimal sampling and the costs associated with nested designs. Note that the number of

levels required for each facet (specially, the total number of respondents N_r) are much larger for the nested designs, and so are the associated costs.

Appendix 2 compares mathematical expressions for relative error variance for designs when (1) respondents are crossed with chains, and (2) respondents are nested within chains. It is obvious that a nested design will always require at least as many, and in most cases, larger samples of most facets than are required for a crossed design. Therefore, the reduction in cost with a crossed design is independent of the form of the cost function. This comparison illustrates the gain in efficiency from approaching survey measurement research from a generalizability and optimization perspective.

Problem 2: identifying priorities for quality improvement

Now consider a second problem that is associated with a different object of measurement. Suppose management is interested in determining which of five aspects of their retail chain's service quality are most in need of improvement. Because this problem requires a reliable scaling of the five aspects of service quality, aspects become the object of measurement. The number of chains in this design is fixed at one, but we require optimal designs for comparing any five aspects for any chain within any sector. Therefore, the object of measurement becomes aspects nested within chains, which are in turn nested within sectors. The generalizability coefficient for this design can be expressed as:

$$E\hat{\rho}^2 = \frac{\hat{\sigma}_a^2 + \hat{\sigma}_{sXa}^2 + \hat{\sigma}_{cXa}^2}{\left(\hat{\sigma}_a^2 + \hat{\sigma}_{sXa}^2 + \hat{\sigma}_{cXa}^2\right) + \hat{\sigma}_{\text{relative error}}^2} \tag{25.8}$$

where

$$\hat{\sigma}_{\text{relative error}}^2 = \frac{\hat{\sigma}_i^2 + \hat{\sigma}_{sXi}^2 + \hat{\sigma}_{cXi}^2}{n_i}$$

$$+ \frac{\hat{\sigma}_{rXa}^2 + \hat{\sigma}_{sXrXa}^2 + \hat{\sigma}_{cXrXa}^2}{n_r}$$

$$+ \frac{\hat{\sigma}_{rXi}^2 + \hat{\sigma}_{sXrXi}^2 + \hat{\sigma}_e^2}{n_r n_i}$$

As shown in Equation 25.8, relative error variance can be reduced by sampling more respondents and/or increasing the number of items. Table 25.5 provides optimal designs and the associated costs for generalizability levels ranging from 0.80 to 0.95. The cost function is identical to that in Equation 25.7, with number of aspects fixed at 5 and number of chains and sectors fixed at 1. Note that the number of items required for this problem is much higher than for Problem 1. This clearly illustrates

Table 25.5 Optimal designs for identifying priorities for quality improvement

$E\hat{\rho}^2$	σ_{rel}^2	n_i per n_a	n_r	Cost ($)
0.80	0.072	4	29	461
0.85	0.051	5	43	680
0.90	0.032	8	64	1232
0.95	0.015	16	132	3572

Source: Finn and Kayandé (1997).

the influence of the purpose of measurement on the optimality of a measurement design.

The stringent requirements for number of respondents (64) and number of items (8) per aspect to achieve generalizability of 0.90 probably results from the fact that SERVQUAL was not developed to distinguish between aspects, rather it was developed to distinguish between perceptions of respondents. Although Parasuraman et al. (1988) specifically claim SERVQUAL can provide reliable information for this issue, SERVQUAL items were originally selected and have since been refined for their ability to scale respondents. Thus, this problem illustrates an inadequacy of classical reliability theory methods.

ILLUSTRATIVE APPLICATION CASES

The main thesis in this chapter is that the effectiveness and efficiency of measurement depends fundamentally on the purpose of measurement. The previous section of the chapter provided a stylized illustration of the framework. The design of the empirical study was stylized because it was intended to demonstrate the full power of the framework to answer many applied measurement questions. In this section, I use data already collected by two organizations[5] to show how measurement programs in those organizations can be made effective and/or efficient.

The first case involved a customer satisfaction measurement program used by a large bank with 780 retail branches. Each month, the bank measured customer satisfaction using a three-item scale, collecting data from about 100 customers of each branch. Retail managers were rewarded on the basis of their branch's overall satisfaction score (incentives were determined on the basis of current performance relative to other branches). The total monthly cost of the program (including incentives) was about $500,000 (all estimates are from 2005–06). An analysis of the data suggested that the G-coefficient associated with the scaling of the branches was 0.98, assuming the firm continued to use the current design (monthly measurement of 100 customers per branch and a three-item scale). Reducing the benchmark G-coefficient to 0.95 (somewhat lower than 0.98, but acceptable nevertheless in an applied decision context), the bank would have to survey only 25 customers a month, reducing the overall cost of the program to only $121,000 a month. This analysis revealed the steep increase in number of customers and consequent survey costs for a small increase in effectiveness. Further analysis of this case included treating 'occasions of measurement' as an additional facet of measurement. We assumed that the measurements were undertaken on 12 randomly selected occasions in the year, allowing us to estimate whether the scaling of branches depended on the occasion of measurement. Interestingly, the variance component associated with the interaction of occasions and branches was very small, indicating that the scaling of branches was pretty much the same across the occasions of measurement. This information implies that the bank could safely reduce its measurement frequency from 12 times a year to perhaps a quarterly basis, further reducing the costs of the program.

The second case involved a service quality program used by a medium-sized retail bank with 100 branches. Each quarter, the bank (via its market research company) interviewed 15 customers from each branch, also obtaining a service quality score on a 22-item scale. Employees of the branches that scored among the top 20 branches in the country were rewarded with incentives each quarter. The total cost of the program was about $210,000 per quarter. An analysis of the data revealed that the measurement procedure, as currently implemented, was not effective because the G-coefficient associated with the scaling of retail branches was only 0.78. An analysis of the data revealed that to achieve a G-coefficient of 0.90, the bank should be sampling a minimum of 22 customers, implying additional survey costs of about $42,000 per quarter. Of note was the close to zero variance component associated with the interactions of branches and items, indicating that the scaling of branches did not depend on the items. The bank could possibly consider reducing the number of items in its survey, presumably also obtaining a better response rate to its surveys (therefore reducing the program cost).

These two cases provide illustrative contrasts in how the framework presented in this chapter can be used to improve the effectiveness and/or efficiency of applied measurement programs, even without collecting stylized data. In the first case, the bank was oversampling customers and occasions, therefore not efficient. In the second case, the bank was not effective and needed to increase its sample of customers.

DISCUSSION

There are three main arguments made in this chapter. First, that the purpose of applied measurement is not always scaling of respondents; indeed, the purpose might require the scaling of objects other than respondents. Second, each observed measure is a function of the conditions under which the observation was obtained; therefore, the effect of those conditions is important to understand. Third, researchers should think through the conditions that might affect observed measures and the purpose(s) to which the measures might be put; by doing so, the researcher can design effective and efficient applied measurement.

Business disciplines have largely followed classical test theory-based approaches to evaluate measurement effectiveness (see for example, Churchill's (1979) seminal scale development paradigm) and devoted a considerable amount of research to assessing and trying to improve the reliability and validity of multi-item measurement scales. But these methods implicitly assume that there is only one potential object of measurement to be scaled, that is respondents, perhaps tracing back through the psychological testing paradigm to a definition of a construct as 'some postulated attribute of *people*' (Cronbach and Meehl, 1955, italics added). As a consequence, the literature has largely ignored the fact that there are many different underlying reasons for conducting a measurement study. If these differences had no bearing on the measurement procedure, ignoring them would be acceptable. However, as argued in this chapter, the underlying purpose of measurement determines the object(s) of measurement and therefore cannot be ignored in the assessment and design of the measurement procedure.

Intriguingly, neither the practitioner nor the academic research community has wholeheartedly adopted the view of measurement advocated in this chapter (proposed first by Cronbach and his colleagues in 1963). The main reason for this resistance is that applied researchers are 'users' of methodology, and as such are interested in 'easy to use' and 'easy to justify' methods. Classical test theory methods are easy to use. Estimating Cronbach's alpha requires researchers to press a button in Statistical Package for Social Science (SPSS) without much, if any, consideration for the meaning of the formula. In stark contrast is the approach proposed herein where the researcher has to construct the G-coefficient *formula* before even being able to use it. Classical test theory methods are also easy to justify in applied disciplines because most measures are obtained on individuals, making it natural to think that constructs must be attributes of people, not other objects. Yet, the object of measurement could be other than respondents, in which case constructs are attributes of those objects, requiring the much harder methods of assessing measurement effectiveness. There is, unfortunately, no easy way to incorporate the approach proposed in this chapter. Yet, the costs of poor and wrong measurement are large, as are the benefits of effective and efficient measurement.

The concern about identifying the object of measurement is broader than what I have discussed here. In other research that I have published with my collaborator Adam Finn, we show that scale modification, scale adaptation, and construct validity assessment procedures are also subject to the same issues of incorrect objects of measurement (see Finn and Kayandé, 1999, 2004, 2005). Covariance matrices used in validity assessment are typically estimated across individuals, when it might be more appropriate to estimate covariance matrices over objects other than individuals and use those in construct validity assessment. I hope that I have argued forcefully enough in this chapter for academics to change their view of measurement so that there is a trickle down effect over time on academic research and practice.

I started this chapter with an applied measurement context that asked the questions: 'What makes measurement effective?' and 'What makes measurement efficient?' My primary argument in this chapter is that whether measurement is effective depends critically on what the measurement is being used for. If the measures are being used for scaling respondents, then using classical, traditional approaches to assess effectiveness is correct, even if limited. If the measures are being used to scale an object other than respondents, then classical, traditional approaches are not correct and could potentially be severely misleading.

Understanding the multiple sources of error, even if the purpose is to scale respondents, is important because doing so allows for a careful determination of how efficient the measurement procedure is, and additionally, how efficient the measurement procedure could be. The measurement of a characteristic of an object is influenced by the conditions under which the characteristic is measured. Assessing the extent to which these conditions contribute to the variance in the measure is important because it allows the applied researcher to 'optimize' future measurement by sampling from each condition in proportion to its variance contribution. But what is error variance and what is substantive variance is a decision only the researcher can make – a decision that rests solely on an articulation of the purpose of measurement. Generalizability theory '… enables you to *ask* your questions better; what is most significant for you cannot be supplied from the outside' (Cronbach et al., 1972: 199, italics added).

Identifying the multiple sources of variance in measurement requires the researcher to consider, *a priori*, what conditions might affect the measures and to what use might the measures be put. The empirical study described in this chapter was designed with a view to demonstrating the full range of questions that might be answered by the data. For example, more than acceptable levels of generalizability (.95) could be obtained with a single item per aspect, 7 aspects and as few as 68 respondents when benchmarking the service quality of retail chains within the same retail sector. This efficiency was achieved by recognizing the advantage of using a design crossing retail chains and respondents. Of course, using crossed designs is not possible in most empirical contexts. For example, in the two empirical application cases, customers could not have rated bank branches at which they were not customers. Therefore, a nested design was an inherent part of the data. However, nested designs do not preclude the researcher from delineating the sources of variation in the data, the purpose(s) to which the measures might be put, and working out how to make future measurement effective and efficient. The two cases with retail banks represented one example each of inefficient and ineffective measurement. Although collecting 'designed' data is most useful, researchers can also analyze already collected data and examine how to improve future measurement.

I conclude with a set of recommendations for researchers interested in improving applied measurement.

1 Identify the potential objects of measurement for a construct. Also identify other potential sources of variation.
2 Collect data by randomly sampling across each object of measurement and source of variation. If possible, collect crossed data.

3 Analyze data using variance component models, estimating variance component estimates for each source of variance.
4 Define an applied decision study, which requires the researcher to define the object of measurement.
5 Use the variance component estimates to calculate the generaliability coefficient for the specific decision study, usinq study sample sizes in the relative error variance term.
6 Optimize the applied decision study by choosing the numbers of levels for each of the facets of variation (i.e., efficiency), taking into account the cost of sampling on those levels and the desired generalizability coefficient (i.e., effectiveness).

Using this set of recommendations will hopefully improve the effectiveness and efficiency of applied measurement.

APPENDIX 1

Directions: The following statements ask how you feel about the service provided by some local area department store chains, grocery store chains, and fast-food chains. Please indicate the extent of your agreement with each statement about each chain. Circle a '10' if you very strongly agree, and circle a '0' if you very strongly disagree. If your feelings lie between these two extremes, circle a number in between '10' and '0' that best shows your level of agreement. There are no right or wrong answers – we are interested in your views of the service provided by the chains.

The following statements are about XYZ's department store chain:

1 XYZ's stores are visually attractive.
2 XYZ's employees appear neat and tidy.
3 XYZ's promotional materials are visually appealing.
4 XYZ's employees give you prompt service.
5 XYZ's employees are always willing to help you.
6 XYZ's employees are never too busy to respond to your requests.

7 XYZ's employees give you personal attention.
8 XYZ's employees have your best interests at heart.
9 XYZ's employees understand your specific needs.

Note: Each statement was accompanied by an 11-point scale anchored at the end-points by the labels 'Very Strongly Disagree' (= 0) and 'Very Strongly Agree' (= 10). The intermediate scale points were not labeled. Also, the statements were not numbered.

APPENDIX 2

Comparison of relative error variance in crossed versus nested designs

For a design with respondents crossed with chains,

$$\hat{\sigma}^2_{\text{relative error}} = \frac{\hat{\sigma}^2_{c \, X \, r}}{n_r} + \frac{\hat{\sigma}^2_{c \, X \, i}}{n_i n_a} + \frac{\hat{\sigma}^2_{c \, X \, a}}{n_a}$$
$$+ \frac{\hat{\sigma}^2_{c \, X \, r \, X \, a}}{n_r n_a} + \frac{\hat{\sigma}^2_{\text{random error}}}{n_r n_i n_a} \quad \text{(A2.1)}$$

For a design with respondents nested within chains,

$$\hat{\sigma}^2_{\text{relative error}} = \frac{\hat{\sigma}^2_r + \hat{\sigma}^2_{c \, X \, r} + \hat{\sigma}^2_{s \, X \, r}}{n_r}$$
$$+ \frac{\hat{\sigma}^2_{c \, X \, i}}{n_i n_a} + \frac{\hat{\sigma}^2_{c \, X \, a}}{n_a}$$
$$+ \frac{\hat{\sigma}^2_{r \, X \, a} + \hat{\sigma}^2_{r \, X \, a \, X \, s} + \hat{\sigma}^2_{c \, X \, r \, X \, a}}{n_r n_a}$$
$$+ \frac{\hat{\sigma}^2_{r \, X \, i} + \hat{\sigma}^2_{r \, X \, i \, X \, s}}{n_r n_i n_a}$$
$$+ \frac{\hat{\sigma}^2_{\text{random error}}}{n_r n_i n_a} \quad \text{(A2.2)}$$

where, r stands for respondents, c for chains, s for retail sectors, i for items, and a for aspects.

Note that the expression for the crossed design (A1) is a restricted version of the expression for the nested design (A2). Therefore, a nested design will always have at least as much relative error variance as a crossed design. Moreover, terms with variance due to respondents enter the nested design expression for relative error variance, and such terms will almost always be positive and among the highest in a service quality study. In such cases, relative error variance in a nested design will be much higher than that in a crossed design, implying therefore that greater sampling is required to attain the same level of generalizability.

NOTES

1 The generalizability coefficient is denoted by $E\hat{\rho}^2$. This notation is simple, yet imprecise because the generalizability coefficient is an estimate of the expected value of ρ^2. Thus, $E\hat{\rho}^2$ is not the expectation of the estimate of ρ^2, but the estimate of the expected value of ρ^2. It is used for simplicity, and should not be misunderstood to imply the expectation of an estimate.

2 The assumption of normality is not a strict requirement of G-theory. However, estimation and statistical inferences are simplified with an assumption of normality.

3 In the strictest sense, reliability is not a characteristic of a scale or instrument, it is a characteristic of the data or information gathered by using the scale. The same scale can produce data that are reliable and other data that are unreliable. However, because the term 'reliability of a scale or measurement instrument' is commonly used in marketing research, we use it loosely in this paper to make arguments. When we use the term reliability of a scale, it should be interpreted as the reliability of information gathered by using the scale.

4 The unbalanced nature of the data in our study does not allow for straightforward statistical tests on the variance components. Therefore, for the purpose of statistical inference only, we used a subset of 65 respondents who provided responses to every item in the questionnaire, to derive the variance components and the associated F-statistics. This subset, consisting of balanced data, accounted for 76% of the full unbalanced data; estimates of all variance components were similar in relative size

to the estimates from the full unbalanced data. All estimates greater than zero are significantly different from zero (ProbF < 0.05), except the estimate of the variance component associated with the interaction of sectors and respondents. All negative estimates are not significantly different from zero. Some F-tests are approximate and derived using Satterthwaite's (1946) method.

5 Because of confidentiality agreements with the supplier of the data, names of the organizations cannot be revealed.

REFERENCES

Allen, M. J. and Yen, W. M. (2002) *Introduction to Measurement Theory*. Long Grove, IL: Waveland Press.

Babakus, E. and Boller, G. W. (1992) 'An empirical assessment of the SERVQUAL scale,' *Journal of Business Research*, 24: 253–268.

Bearden, W. O., Netemeyer, R. G. and Mobley, M. F. (1993) *Handbook of Marketing Scales: Multi-Item Measures for Marketing and Consumer Behavior Research*. Newbury Park, CA: Sage.

Bolton, R. N. and Drew, J. H. (1991a) 'A longitudinal analysis of the impact of service changes on customer attitudes,' *Journal of Marketing*, 55 (January): 1–9.

Bolton, R. N. and Drew, J. H. (1991b) 'A multistage model of customers assessments of service quality and value,' *Journal of Consumer Research*, 17 (March): 375–84.

Boulding, W., Kalra, A., Staelin, R. and Zeithaml, V. A. (1993) 'A dynamic process model of service quality: From expectations to behavioral intentions,' *Journal of Marketing Research*, 30 (February): 7–27.

Brennan, R. (1983) *Elements of Generalizability Theory*. Iowa City, Iowa: ACT Publications.

Brown, T. J., Churchill, Jr., G. A. and Peter, J. P. (1993) 'Research Note: Improving the measurement of service quality,' *Journal of Retailing*, 69: 127–39.

Bruner II, G. C. and Hensel, P. J. (1993) *Marketing Scales Handbook: A Compilation of Multi-Item Measures*. Chicago. American Marketing Association.

Carman, J. M. (1990) 'Consumer perceptions of service quality: An assessment of the SERVQUAL dimensions,' *Journal of Retailing*, 66: 33–55.

Churchill, G. A., Jr., (1979) 'A paradigm for developing better measures of marketing constructs,' *Journal of Marketing Research*, 16, (February): 64–73.

Cronbach, L. J., Gleser, G. C., Nanda, H. and Rajaratnam, N. (1972) *The Dependability of Behavioral Measurements: Theory of Generalizability for Scores and Profiles*. New York: John Wiley and Sons.

Cronbach, L. J. and Meehl, P. E. (1955) 'Construct validity in psychological tests,' *Psychological Bulletin*, 52: 281–302.

Cronbach, L. J. and Shavelson, R. (2004) 'My current thoughts on coefficient alpha and successor procedures,' *Educational and Psychological Measurement*, 64 (3): 391–418.

Cronin, J. J. and Taylor, S. A. (1992) 'Measuring service quality: A reexamination and extension,' *Journal of Marketing*, 56 (July): 55–68.

Cronin, J. J. and Taylor, S. A. (1994) 'SERVPERF versus SERVQUAL: Reconciling performance-based and perceptions-minus-expectations measurement of service quality,' *Journal of Marketing*, 58 (January): 125–31.

Devlin, S. J. and Dong, H. K. (1994) 'Service quality from the customers perspective,' *Marketing Research*, 6 (1): 5–13.

Devlin, S. J., Dong, H. K. and Brown, M. (1993) 'Selecting a scale for measuring quality,' *Marketing Research*, 5 (Summer): 12–17.

Finn, A. and Kayandé, U. (1997) 'Reliability assessment and optimization of marketing measurement,' *Journal of Marketing Research*, 34 (May): 262–75.

Finn, A. and Kayandé, U. (1999) 'Unmasking the phantom: A psychometric assessment of mystery shopping,' *Journal of Retailing*, 75(2): 195–17.

Finn, A. and Kayandé, U. (2004) 'Scale modification in marketing: Alternative approaches and its consequences,' *Journal of Retailing*, 80(1): 37–52.

Finn, A. and Kayandé, U. (2005) 'How fine is C-OAR-SE? A generalizability theory perspective on Rossiter's procedure,' *International Journal of Research in Marketing*, 22 (1): 11–21.

Fisher, R. A. (1925) *Statistical Methods for Research Workers*. Edinburgh: Oliver and Boyd.

Hartley, H. O., Rao, J. N. K. and Lamotte, L. (1978) 'A Simple synthesis-based method of variance component estimation,' *Biometrics*, 34: 233–44.

Karimi, J., Somers, T. M. and Gupta, Y. P. (2005) 'Impact of environmental uncertainty and task characteristics on user satisfaction with data,' *Information Systems Research*, 15(2): 175–93.

Marcoulides, G. A. (1995) 'Designing measurement studies under budget constraints: Controlling error of measurement and power,' *Educational and Psychological Measurement*, 55 (3): 423–8.

Nunnally, J. C. (1978) *Psychometric Theory. Second Edition*. New York: McGraw-Hill.

Parasuraman, A., Berry, L. L. and Zeithaml, V. A. (1991) 'Refinement and reassessment of the SERVQUAL scale,' *Journal of Retailing*, 67 (Winter): 420–50.

Parasuraman, A., Berry, L. L. and Zeithaml, V. A. (1993) 'Research Note: More on improving service quality measurement,' *Journal of Retailing*, 69 (Spring): 140–7.

Parasuraman, A., Berry, L. L. and Zeithaml, V. A. (1985) 'A conceptual model of service quality and its implications for future research,' *Journal of Marketing*, 49 (Fall): 41–50.

Parasuraman, A., Berry, L. L. and Zeithaml, V. A. (1988) 'SERVQUAL: A multiple-item scale for measuring consumer perceptions of service quality,' *Journal of Retailing*, 64 (Spring): 12–40.

Parasuraman, A., Berry, L. L. and Zeithaml, V. A. (1994a) 'Reassessment of expectations as a comparison standard in measuring service quality: Implications for further research,' *Journal of Marketing*, 58 (January): 111–24.

Parasuraman, A., Berry, L. L. and Zeithaml, V. A. (1994b) 'Alternative scales for measuring service quality: A comparative assessment based on psychometric and diagnostic criteria,' *Journal of Retailing*, 70 (January): 201–30.

Rentz, J. O. (1987) 'Generalizability theory: A comprehensive method for assessing and improving the dependability of marketing measures,' *Journal of Marketing Research*, 24 (February): 19–28.

Rust, R. T., Zahorik, A. J. and Keiningham, T. L. (1995) 'Return on quality (ROQ): Making service quality financially accountable,' *Journal of Marketing*, 59 (April): 58–70.

Salkin, H. M. (1975) *Integer Programming*. Reading, MA: Addison-Wesley.

Sanders, P. F., Theunissen, T. J. J. M. and Baas, S. M. (1989) 'Minimizing the number of observations: A generalization of the Spearman-Brown formula,' *Psychometrika*, 54: 587–98.

Sanders, P. F., Theunissen, T. J. J. M. and Baas, S. M. (1991) 'Maximizing the coefficient of generalizability under the constraint of limited resources', *Psychometrika*, 56: 87–96.

Satterthwaite, F. E. (1946) 'An approximate distribution of estimates of variance components,' *Biometrics Bulletin*, 2: 110–14.

Schmalensee, D. H. (1994) 'Finding the perfect scale,' *Marketing Research*, 6 (Fall): 24–7.

Shavelson, R. J. and Webb, N. M. (1991) *Generalizability Theory: A Primer*. Newbury Park, CA: Sage.

Shin, H., Collier, D. A. and Wilson, D. D. (2000) 'Supply management orientation and supplier/buyer performance,' *Journal of Operations Management*, 18: 317–33.

Spechler, J. W. (1991) *When America Does It Right: Case Studies in Service Quality*. Norcross, GA: Institute of Industrial Engineers.

Teas, K. R. (1994) 'Expectations as a comparison standard in measuring service quality: An assessment of a reassessment,' *Journal of Marketing*, 58 (January): 132–9.

Viswanathan, M. (2005) *Measurement Error and Research Design*. Newbury Park, CA: Sage.

Zahorik, A. J. and Rust, R. T. (1992) 'Modeling the impact of service quality on profitability: A review,' *Advances in Services Marketing and Management*, 1: 247–76.

26

Contemporary Challenges of Longitudinal Measurement Using HRS Data

John J. McArdle

INTRODUCTION

Longitudinal data are collected for a lot of reasons – but what most researchers now agree upon is that we do this kind of data collection because we want to 'measure changes.' If we are studying individuals, these are labeled 'within person changes.' If we are studying larger units of aggregations, such as colleges or countries, these are often labeled 'within-unit changes.' Nonetheless, the key feature is that we examine change within the units we are studying. Many important issues in the measurement of change have been raised in classic treatments of the analysis of change (e.g., Harris, 1961; Cattell, 1966; Wohwill, 1973), and many of these have not fully been resolved (e.g., Burr and Nesselroade, 1991; Collins and Sayer, 2001). The purpose of this review is to highlight some classic challenges in the measurement of changes and to show how contemporary solutions can be used to deal with these issues.

Five classic challenges will be raised here: (1) separating individual changes from group differences; (2) options for incomplete longitudinal data over time; (3) options for nonlinear changes over time; (4) measurement invariance in studies of changes over time; and (5) opportunities for modeling dynamic changes. For each challenge we will describe the problem, and then review some contemporary solutions to these problems. This is not intended as an overly technical treatment, so only a few basic equations are presented, examples will be displayed graphically, and more complete references to the contemporary solutions will be given throughout.

Although each challenge could be focused on a completely different dataset, we use a common dataset to illustrate communalities of these challenges. Publicly available data from the *Health and Retirement Study* (HRS) and the *Asset and Health Dynamics of the Oldest Old Study* (AHEAD; see Juster and Suzman, 1995; Rodgers et al., 2003; McArdle, Fisher and Kadlec, 2007) are combined. The HRS-AHEAD studies have been heralded for their inclusion of cognitive measures in a national telephone-based survey of health and economics (see Herzog and Wallace, 1997). At the same time, the HRS-AHEAD studies have been criticized for lacking key many other issues, and we address these issues here. Prior research using cognitive data from the HRS-AHEAD has examined cohort-level changes in cognition, using longitudinal data from the HRS-AHEAD (1993–2000; e.g., Freedman, Aykan, and Martin, 2001; Rodgers, Ofstedal, and Herzog, 2003). Other studies have examined intra-individual differences in cognition by age (McArdle, Fisher and Kadlec, 2007).

Selected data from the Rodgers et al. (2003) paper are presented in Table 26.1. In the first part of this table, we list summary statistics for adults over the age of 50 on the overall cognitive scores collected among self-respondents across four waves (1993, 1995, 1998, and 2000) in a nationally representative sample of persons (using sampling weights) over the age of 50. These statistics are based on almost $n \sim 3{,}000$ who have participated in all four occasions of measurement, each about 2 years apart. In the second part of this Table (26.1b), we list the same statistics for all the people measures, most whom were not measured at all occasions. These include data collected on $N = 10{,}498$ individuals between the ages of 50 and 85 (median $= 71$) and $D = 25{,}029$ interviews. In this matrix we introduce a new binary variable termed *Dropout* (0,1), which indicates whether or

not the person has dropped out of the study. Of course, the increased sample size emphasizes the fact that we need to consider sampling and attrition. This paper uses the same cognitive data as Rodgers et al. (2003) but describes a series of analyses which capitalize on using new structural measurement techniques and all available HRS data (e.g., McArdle, Ferrer-Caja, Hamagami, and Woodcock, 2002; McArdle, 2007).

CHALLENGE 1: SEPARATING INDIVIDUAL CHANGES FROM GROUP DIFFERENCES

An initial concern here is the separation of inferences about (a) differences between people and (b) changes within people (McArdle, 2008). The current challenge can be stated as, 'what separation of groups and persons is best for my problem?'

A common solution to this problem is that simple subtraction of any two scores for any person is termed a 'difference score' and these are changes within a person over occasions which are formally written for each person as

$$D\{2, 1\}_n = Y[2]_n - Y[1]_n \qquad (26.1)$$

Although this equation is quite clear, one possible source of confusion is that we often use the formula for 'difference' to define a 'change.' This equation highlights the key purpose of most longitudinal measurement data – to detect differences in the patterns of individual changes. In addition, now that we have an explicit definition of changes (Equation 26.1), we can consider some key problems in their measurement (see Burr and Nesselroade, 1990).

Figure 26.2 gives a plot of the longitudinal data we use here. These data are raw scores for each person who come from

Table 26.1   Descriptive information on longitudinal data for primary participants in the Health and Retirement Survey (using HRS sampling weights; Rodgers et al., 2003)

[1a]: Descriptive statistics for the constant HRS sample ($n = 2,766$)

Variable	Mean	Std. Dev.	Minimum	Maximum	Notes
CA[1]	62.06	1416	2.9	100.0	0–35 rescaled as 0–100
CA[2]	62.46	1408	8.6	100.0	at Testing 2
CA[3]	60.93	1462	5.7	100.0	at Testing 3
CA[4]	58.33	1528	2.9	100.0	at Testing 4
Age[1]	81.92	485	65.2	100.9	AHEAD/HRS

Pearson correlations	CA[1]	CA[2]	CA[3]	CA[4]	Age[1]
CA[1]	1.00				
CA[3]	.613	.660	1.00		
CA[4]	.561	.607	.655	1.00	
Age[1]	−239	−.263	−.296	−.326	1.00

[1b]: Descriptive statistics for the entire HRS sample ($N = 10,498$)

Variable	Size	Mean	Std. Dev.	Minimum	Maximum	Notes
CA[1]	5,423	57.37	1611	0	100.0	0–35 rescaled
CA[2]	4,411	58.42	1619	0	100.0	at Testing 2
CA[3]	8,392	63.13	1578	0	100.0	at Testing 3
CA[4]	6,819	62.23	1547	2.9	100.0	at Testing 4
Age[1]	10.504	75.84	822	62	107.7	AHEAD/HRS
Dropout (0,1)	10,504	0.737	45.1	0	1	0=complete

Pearson correlations	CA[1]	CA[2]	CA[3]	CA[4]	Age[1]
CA[1]	1.00				
	(5,423)				
CA[2]	.695	1.00			
	(4,317)	(4,411)			
CA[3]	.637	.692	1.00		
	(3,508)	(3,449)	(8,392)		
CA[4]	.565	.610	.677	1.00	
	(2,933)	(2,879)	(6,566)	(6,819)	
Age[1]	−.258	−.280	−.357	−.350	1.00
	(5,423)	(4,411)	(8,392)	(6,819)	(10,504)
Dropout	−.305	−.327	.100	.211	−.453
	(5,423)	(4,411)	(8,392)	(6,819)	(10,504)

four occasions ($t = 4$) of measuring the cognitive abilities of Table 26.1 (CA[t]). The lines drawn here connect the data from one person over each occasion, so these lines are referred to as 'individual trajectories.' In order to be clear – the lines of Figure 26.1 are only drawn for a random set of 5 per cent of the overall HRS sample (i.e., $n \sim 500$). However, the summary statistics for the full set of CA[t] data are listed in Table 26.1. Among many possible group differences, we study different levels of Age-at-testing. Although not presented here, if we would display separate plots, it would appear that higher scores are found for persons who are younger (and have higher levels of education).

Let us now consider ways to analyze these kinds of longitudinal data. Following the logic of Equation 26.1, we can calculate the change scores for each pair of time points, and then write a regression equation in which this change is the dependent variable regressed on the group differences (i.e., age, dropout) between the people. This change-regression is an elementary description of what is widely known in statistics as a 'mixed model,' and this attempts to identify the 'between-person differences in within-person changes' (Nesselroade and Baltes, 1979). One popular collection of ideas about organizing group and individual differences in changes can be represented as a latent variable path diagram, and one of these is presented in Figure 26.2. Due to its flexibility, this classic idea about a model for changes has been revived in recent work (see Bayley, 1956; Rogosa, 1985; cf., Bryk and Raudenbush, 2000).

A comprehensive version of this mixed-model concept is termed a 'latent curve' or 'multi-level model' for the analysis of longitudinal data, and this can be written for multiple time points (t) as

$$Y[t]_n = g0_n + g1_n B[t] + u[t]_n \quad (26.2)$$

where the individual score (Y) at any time point (t) is considered a function of three underlying components: (1) the intercept score $g0$, which does not change over time – this is the constant part of the scores; (2) the slope score, $g1$, which does not itself change over time, but whose influence is multiplied through a group basis coefficient, $B[t]$ which can change over time for the whole group – this is the systematic change; (3) a unique or residual score $u[t]$ for the individual, which changes over time but is presumably uncorrelated with any other score – this is the random change. This organization of observations of multiple time points of data into only three underlying components is used to organize the individual differences in changes over time, and it is termed the 'level 1 model.'

Assuming we have some measure of group differences, measured and coded as X, it is also typical to propose an additional set of restrictions where we write regression equations

$$g0_n = v0 + \gamma0 X_n + d0_n, \quad (26.3)$$
$$g1_n = v1 + \gamma1 X_n + d1_n,$$

where two latent components from the previous equations ($g0, g1$) are now thought to be outcomes of the group differences in X with intercepts ($v0, v1$), slopes ($\gamma0, \gamma1$), and residuals ($d0, d1$). These equations are used to describe the group differences in the components of changes, so this is termed the 'level 2 model.'

Latent growth curve analyses can be calculated, using many available mixed-effects computer packages (e.g., SAS MIXED and NLMIXED; Littell et al., 1996; Verbeke and Molenberghs, 2000) and *structural equation modeling* programs (SEM; see Ferrer, Hamagami and McArdle, 2003). Because this can be examined as an SEM, the path diagram of Figure 26.2 may be a useful representation of this kind latent

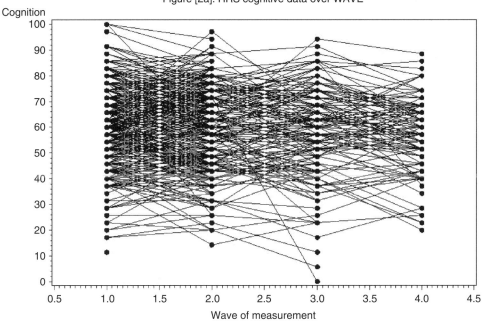

Figure 26.1   Plots of individual longitudinal trajectories (5% sample of the HRS primary participants).

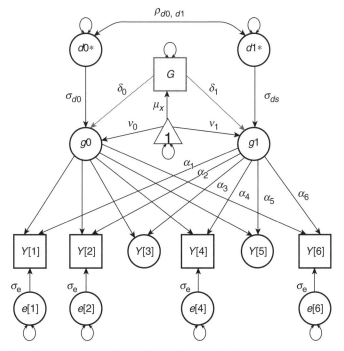

Figure 26.2   LCM with an external _X_ variable effecting both the common levels and slopes.

growth model. The observed variables are drawn as squares, the unobserved variables are drawn as circles, and the required constant is included as a triangle. Model parameters representing 'fixed' or 'group' coefficients are drawn as one-headed arrows while 'random' or 'individual' features are drawn as two headed arrows. In this case, the initial level and slopes are often assumed to have to be latent random variables with 'fixed' means (μ_0, μ_1) but 'random' variances (σ_0^2, σ_1^2) and latent variable correlations (ρ_{0s}). (The standard deviations (σ_j) are drawn in the picture to permit the direct representation of the covariances as scaled correlations.) The unique terms are assumed to be normally distributed with mean zero and variance (σ_u^2) and are presumably uncorrelated with all other components. In order to deal with incomplete cases we write the first level of variables as 'circles within squares' (as in McArdle, 1994; McArdle and Hamagami, 2001; McArdle and Nesselroade, 2003).

Using the available computer programs we can obtain the following numerical results. The first model fitted (2a) is a *no-change model* and was fitted to the raw data used to form Table 26.1b with only three parameters. The results include the three parameters which are expected to be constant over age: (a) a constant mean ($\mu_0 = 60.2$); (b) a constant covariance ($\sigma_0^2 = 178$), and (c) a constant unique variance ($\sigma_u^2 = 79$). The ratio of the two variance components leads to a high estimate of the intra-class correlation ($\eta^2 = 0.69$), and this indicated the individual scores are widely separated and positively correlated from one occasion to another. This model has a likelihood ($f_{MLE} = -10748$) that represents a notable statistical improvement (with $\chi^2 = 11337$ on $df = 1$) over the entirely random (i.e., zero correlation) case. A second model, labeled '+Drop' here, adds a single parameter to

assess the mean difference due to dropout on the previous results. These results imply the persons who later dropped out (for any reason) scored about 4 per cent points lower at the initial testing ($\beta_0 = -3.6$, with $\chi^2 = 86$ on $df = 1$), and this could be an important consideration.

The second model fitted (2b) is a linear mixed-effects model, using *wave-of-testing* as the basis for change – as in Figure 26.1. The results include three time-constant parameters ($\mu_0 = 60.5$, $\sigma_0^2 = 199$, and $\sigma_u^2 = 73$) plus three time-dependent slope parameters, indicating a very small decrease in means ($\mu_1 = -.09$) over every wave of testing, and increases in variances and covariances over every wave ($\sigma_1^2 = 1.4$, $\rho_{01} = -.30$). The linear wave model ($f_{MLE} = -10404$) is a statistical improvement over the entirely random model (with $\chi^2 = 10494$, on $df = 3$) and, more critically, a statistical improvement over the previous no-change level model ($\chi^2 = 843$ on $df = 3$). This improvement in fit appears substantial, but, as can be seen in Figure 26.1, these systematic changes over time represent only a very small average impact compared with the large overall variation in the individual growth curves. The group differences only show the dropouts were lower at the starting point ($\beta_0 = -5.0$), but it was not possible to estimate any differences in slope ($\beta_1 < .01$).

CHALLENGE 2: OPTIONS FOR INCOMPLETE LONGITUDINAL DATA OVER TIME

All longitudinal analyses require the choice of the *basis* or timing for analysis and, to the surprise of many researchers, this is not a fully restricted aspect of the analysis. Thus, the current challenge can be stated as is, 'what basis of timing is best for my problem?'

Part of this challenge comes from the new opportunities for dealing with incomplete data. Obviously there is a great deal of incomplete data in the HRS longitudinal study (see Table 26.1), but this is not an atypical problem in longitudinal research. The Rodgers et al. (2003) analysis described the use of a multiple imputation procedure for handling incomplete data. This method accounted for stable and time-varying covariates as well as covariation in the cognitive measures between and across waves (using IVEware). This approach seems reasonable for data missing over time, and it can be used when the incomplete due to attrition and other factors and not *missing at random* (MAR). The same sets of assumptions form the basis of any SEM analyses which includes 'all the data' – not simply the complete cases (e.g., McArdle, 1988, 1990; McArdle and Anderson, 1990). While we do observe non-random attrition, our goal is to include all the longitudinal and cross-sectional data to provide the best estimate of the parameters of change *as if everyone had continued to participate* (McArdle and Hamagami, 1991; Little, 1995; Diggle, Liang, and Zeger, 1994; McArdle et al., 1998; McArdle and Bell, 2000).

This mixed-model approach to growth curve analysis offers advanced techniques for dealing with the problem of *unbalanced* and *non-randomly incomplete data*. In computational terms, the available information for any subject on any data point (i.e., any variable measured at any occasion) is used to build up *maximum likelihood estimates* (MLE), using a numerical routine that optimizes the model parameters with respect to any available data. These MLE are based on fitting structural models to the raw score information for each person on each variable at each time (e.g., McArdle

et al. 2002). The goodness-of-fit of each model presented here will be assessed using classical statistical principles about the model likelihood (f_{MLE}). In most models to follow, we use the MAR assumption to deal with incomplete longitudinal records, but we test these assumptions whenever possible (e.g., Heyting et al., 1992; Little, 1995; Cnaan et al., 1997). This MAR assumption has become an incomplete data design problem (McArdle, 1994) which includes assumptions about age changes in different cohorts (e.g., Meredith and Tisak, 1990; McArdle and Anderson, 1990; Miyayzaki and Raudenbush, 2000).

This realization that we can deal with incomplete data has a fundamentally important impact on the possibilities for data analysis. In the latent growth model of Equation 26.2, the $B[t]$ represents a set of *basis coefficients* describing the function of the timing of the observations. Many alternative considerations for the description of these data can be conveniently considered as the specific variations of latent growth model [2] because we write

$$Y[t]_n = g_{0,n} + 0 \cdot g_{1,n} + u[t]_n \text{ or } \quad (26.4)$$
$$Y[t]_n = g_{0,n} + Wave[t] \cdot g_{1,n} + u[t]_n \text{ or}$$
$$Y[t]_n = g_{0,n} + Date[t] \cdot g_{1,n} + u[t]_n \text{ or}$$
$$Y[t]_n = g_{0,n} + Age[t] \cdot g_{1,n} + u[t]_n$$

In this equation the first model has no basis, and thus represents the no-change model stated earlier. The other three models have a basis ($B[t]$), but it is defined in a different way for each. These are comparable to fitting models with different x-axes (recentered, rescaled, etc.) to different forms of the Figure 26.1. Figure 26.3a shows the same raw data plotted over date-of-testing (with a 3-year timelag between times 2 and 3). As another alternative, Figure 26.3b shows the very same data plotted over the age-at-testing of the individuals. While this looks dramatically different form of the data,

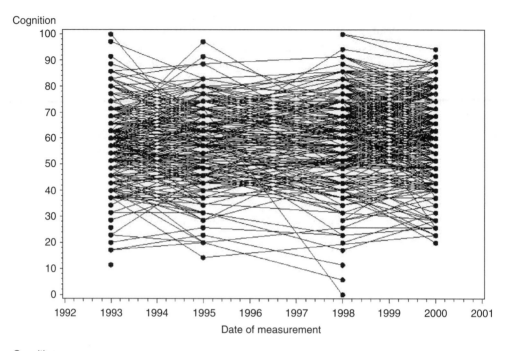

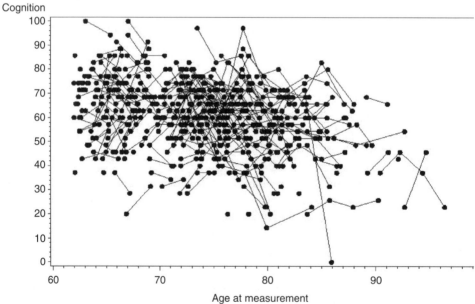

Figure 26.3 (a) HRS cognitive data over DATE-OF-TESTING. (b) HRS cognition scores over AGE-AT-TESTING.

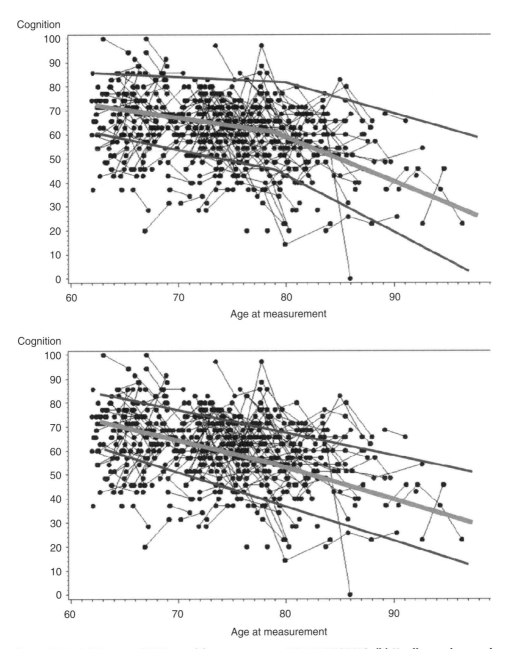

Figure 26.4   (a) Expected HRS cognition scores over AGE-AT-TESTING. (b) Nonlinear changes in HRS cognition scores over AGE of measurement.

especially the extreme scores, the points plotted on the y-axis are identical but the x-axis has changed. Since the results of any model depend on the scaling of the predictors, it follows that this choice of a basis for timing is one the most important sources of variance in longitudinal data, and is both an empirical and substantive issue.

These alternative models are nested under the random baseline model, but the three alternative models are not completely nested under one another, so no direct chi-square comparison can be strictly considered. In previous research where we have been interested in chronological age changes using date where there was no common starting point of specific interest ($t = 0$), it seemed most natural to use a timing of observation based on the observed or chronological age at the occasion of measurement (i.e., $t = $ Age). Of course, for this age-basis model to be viable, we need to presume the untestable MAR assumptions apply to this age dimension. This implies the score measured on a person at each age gives us some indication of their likely scores at the ages not measured, and persons measured at specific ages represent the age-based scores for anyone.

The third model fitted (Figure 26.3a) is a linear mixed-effects model using *date-of-testing* as the basis for change, now considering both the incomplete and complete trajectories of data points. The results include three time-constant parameters ($\mu_0 = 61.2$, $\sigma_0^2 = 186.0$, and $\sigma_u^2 = 71.2$) plus three time-dependent slope parameters indicating decreases in means ($\mu_1 = -1.4$) over every year of testing, along with increases in variances and covariances over each year ($\sigma_1^2 = 7.5$, $\rho_{01} = -.13$). Once again, as can be seen in Figure 26.3a, this is a relatively small average impact compared with the apparent variation in the individual growth curves. The linear date model likelihood

($f_{\text{MLE}} = -9995$) is a statistical improvement over the entirely random model (with $\chi^2 = 10903$, on $df = 3$) and a statistical improvement over the previous no-change level model (with $\chi^2 = 434$, on $df = 3$). The introduction of a contrast describing dropout differences (Drop) adds to these basic results, and suggest dropout impacted both the starting point (i.e., $\beta_0 = 13.5$, higher scores in 1993) and the year-to-year slope ($\beta_1 = -3.5$ additional difference per year). This accurately reflects the fact that dropout occurred at later dates, and that the persons who dropped out were on lower trajectories.

The fourth model fitted (Figure 26.3a) is a linear mixed-effects model using *age-of-testing* as the basis for change. This model was fitted with the chronological age recentered so $B[t] = Age[t] - 75$, so the results include the three time-constant parameters 'at age 75' ($\mu_0 = 59.8$, $\sigma_0^2 = 131.3$, and $\sigma_u^2 = 78.7$) plus three time-dependent slope parameters indicating decreases in means ($\mu_1 = -.83$) over 'every year of age,' and increases in variances and covariances ($\sigma_1^2 = .23$, $\rho_{01} = +.27$) over each year. Now, looking back to Figure 26.3b, this is a relatively large average impact compared with the apparent variation in the individual growth curves (i.e., -8.3 points lost per decade). The linear age model likelihood ($f_{\text{MLE}} = -9995$) is an improvement over the entirely random model (with $\chi^2 = 10903$, on $df = 3$) and a statistical improvement over the previous no-change level model (with $\chi^2 = 434$, on $df = 3$). The dropout differences do not alter these basic results, and suggest dropout differences at age 75 (i.e., $\beta_0 = -6.3$ lower scores for dropouts) and an additional year-to-year slope ($\beta_1 = -.25$ more decline per year). This suggests that the previous dropout results were age related, and once age is used as the basis, we see that the persons

Table 26.2 Alternative mixed-effects linear latent growth models for the longitudinal HRS Cognition Scores (individual $N = 10{,}498$ with data points $N_d = 25{,}029$)

Parameters and fits	Estimates from alternative latent growth models							
	2a: No change baseline (NCS)		2b: Linear change based on wave (LCW)		2c: Linear change based on date (LCD)		2d: Linear change based on age (LCA)	
	Base	+Drop	Base	+Drop	Base	+Drop	Base	+Drop
Fixed (Group) parameters								
Age 75 Mean μ_0	60.2	60.8	60.5	62.1	61.2	61.8	59.8	60.7
1-year Slope Mean μ_s	–	–	–.09	–1.6	–1.4	–1.5	–.83	–.81
Dropout on Intercept β_o	–	+3.6	–	–5.0	–	–13.4	–	–6.3
Dropout on Slope β_s	–	–	–	ne	–	+3.5	–	–.25
Random parameters								
Age 75 Variance σ_0^2	177.7	176.4	199.3	182.0	186.0	182.6	131.3	127.2
1-year Slope Variance σ_s^2	–	–	1.4	7.5	7.5	1.2	0.23	0.24
Level-Slope Correlation ρ_{0s}	–	–	–.30	–.11	–.13	–.22	.27	.25
Error Variance σ_e^2	79.3	79.2	72.5	67.3	71.2	67.9	78.7	74.2
Goodness-of-fit								
Overall Likelihood/parms	10748/3	10662/5	10404/6	9844/8	9995/6	9804/8	7879/6	7707/8
Random as Baseline χ^2/df	11337/1		10494/4		10903/2		12919/5	
No Change as Baseline χ^2/df	0/0		–843/3		–434/1		1582/4	

Notes: (1) The number of participants $N = 10{,}498$ and the number of data points $N_d = 25{,}029$; (2) The parameters for Wave are centered at $Wave[t] = 1$, those for Date are centered at $Date[t] = 1993$, and for Age are centered at $Age[t] = 75$; (3) Parameters are maximum likelihood estimates from minimizing the likelihood function $f = -2ll$ of the raw data using the SAS PROC MIXED program with HRS survey weights for the individuals; (4) The random baseline likelihood for the HRS PerCog variable is $f = 210898$ with $\mu_0 = 60.8$ and $\sigma_e^2 = 257.4$, so likelihoods are listed as $-2ll - 190000$; (5) All parameters are significant at the $\alpha = .001$ level unless there is an '*ns*' indicator, the '$=$' indicates a fixed parameter, the '*ne*' indicates a parameter that could not be estimated.

who dropped out were on much lower trajectories.

In the form of Equation 26.4 it becomes clear that the use of *Wave*[*t*] represents the fitting of a linear growth model through the four waves of data presented in Figure 26.1 (this seems closest to the regression approach by Rodgers et al. (2003) for cohort changes). The alternative use of *Date*[*t*] represents the fitting of a linear growth model through the longitudinal trajectory data presented in Figure 26.3a. The alternative use of *Age*[*t*] represents the fitting of a linear growth model through

Table 26.3 Alternative LINEAR and NON-LINEAR mixed-effects/latent growth models for the longitudinal HRS Cognition Scores (individual $N = 10{,}498$ with data points $N_d = 25{,}029$)

Parameters and fits	Estimates from alternative latent curve models			
	3a: Linear change based on Age per decade (LCA)	3b: Quadratic change based on age (QCA)	3c: Cubic change based on age (CCA)	3d: Two-part spline change based on age (SCA)
Fixed parameters				
Age 75 Mean μ_0	59.8	60.4	60.3	60.6
Slope 1 Mean μ_1	−8.3	−8.1	−7.5	−6.9
Slope 2 Mean μ_2	–	−1.2	−0.91	−9.5
Slope 3 Mean μ_3	–	–	−0.49	–
Random parameters				
Age 75 Var. σ_0^2	131.3	130.9	130.9	170.5
Slope 1 Var. σ_1^2	23.4	24.3	25.1	71.4
Slope 2 Var. σ_2^2	–	ne	ne	94.7
Slope 3 Var. σ_3^2	–	–	ne	–
Correlation $\rho_{0,s1}$	.27	.26	.26	.58
Correlation $\rho_{0,s2}$	–	ne	ne	−.26
Correlation $\rho_{s1,s2}$	–	ne	ne	1.00[b]
Error Variance σ_e^2	78.7	78.4	78.2	74.6
Goodness-of-fit				
Overall Likelihood/parms	7879/7	7926/10	7915/12	7826/10
Random as Baseline χ^2/df	13019/2	12972/8	12983/10	13072/6
No Change as Baseline χ^2/df	1682/3	1635/7	1646/9	1735/7
Sequential as Baseline χ^2/df	–	vs. linear 47/4	vs. Quadratic 11/2	vs. Linear 53/3

Notes: (1) The number of subjects $N = 10{,}498$ and the number of data points $N_d = 25{,}029$; (2) The parameters for Age are centered at $Age[t] = 75$ and scaled by $\Delta t = 10$ years – i.e., *per decade change* – and the two-part spline is centered at $Age[t] = 75$ as well; (3) Parameters are maximum likelihood estimates from minimizing the likelihood function $f = -2ll$ of the raw data using the SAS PROC MIXED program with HRS survey weights for the individuals; (4) The random baseline likelihood for the HRS cognitive ability ($CA[t]$) variable is $f = 210898$ with $\mu_0 = 60.8$ and $\sigma_e^2 = 257.4$; (5) All parameters are significant at the $\alpha = .001$ level unless there is an '*ns*' indicator, the '=' indicates a fixed parameter, the '*ne*' indicates a parameter that could not be estimated; (6) Boundary indicated by '*b*'.

the longitudinal trajectory data presented in Figure 26.3b, once again considering both the incomplete and complete trajectories of data points. Even with the large blocks of incomplete data, this picture of decline trajectories appears to be much clearer than in the previous two pictures because in Figure 26.3b we have substantially stretched out the *x*-axis to reflect more disparate ages. The changes are both over the wide *x*-axis (age differences between people) and in the narrow bands represented by the line segments (age changes within people). Given these results, and the MAR assumptions described above, there is evidence of a comparative advantage in using age-at-testing instead of wave or date-of-testing as the major dimension of group and individual change, so we pursue this approach in the rest of the analyses here.

CHALLENGE 3: DEALING WITH NONLINEAR CHANGES OVER TIME

It is possible to deal with nonlinearity of the changes over age in several ways, but the challenge is 'What form of nonlinearity is best for my problem?'

The simplest nonlinear models are based on altering the values of the basis $B[t]$ (as in McArdle and Nesselroade, 2003). The curve basis can be made to reflect specific nonlinear hypothesis, such as an exponential basis (i.e., $B[t] = [exp\{(-t - 1)\pi\}]$, with growth rate parameter π), and including individual coefficients in rates (π_n; McArdle and Hamagami, 1996; McArdle et al., 2002; see Heathcote et al., 2002). In another alternative basis we can allow the curve basis to take on a shape based on the empirical data (e.g., Rao, 1958; Tucker, 1958; Meredith and Tisak, 1990; McArdle, 1986). In this alternative the factor loadings ($B[t]$) are now estimated from the data as any factor loadings and we obtain what should be an *optimal shape* for the group curve.

But a far more common way to allow for nonlinear relationships is that this is to expand the basic specification equation to include multiple linear bases. We can write

$$Y[t]_n = g_{0,n} + B_1[t] \cdot g_{1,n} \qquad (26.5)$$
$$+ B_2[t] \cdot g_{2,n} + u[t]_n,$$

where the $B_1[t]$ and $B_2[t]$ represent different basis coefficients (i.e., $B_1[t]$ ne $B_2[t]$) which are added up to describing the function of the observations at different ages. One less simplistic feature of this model is that there is also an additional set of latent scores (g_2).

A wide variety of other options can be explored using Equation 26.5. For example, the linear model just used can be considered as the subset of Equation 26.5 where $B_2[t] = 0$. This can then be compared to the well known use of this model,

that is the *quadratic change* model where, for example, we use to include fixed coefficients $B_1[t] = Age[t]$ and $B_2[t] = \frac{1}{2} Age[t]^2$. This polynomial model can be extended to a *cubic change* model by introducing yet another set of coefficients ($B_3[t] = 1/3 Age[t]^3$) and scores (y_3). In all cases the means and variances and correlations among the parameters can be independently estimated using longitudinal growth data.

Another simple and popular variation is a *two-part spline* model fitted by first defining an age of turning or knot-point (e.g., $\tau = 75$) and then by writing fixed coefficients of $B_1[t] = \{Age[t]$ if $Age[t] < \tau\}$ and $B_2[t] = \{Age[t]$ if $Age[t] > \tau\}$. This simple coding creates the possibilities of two segments of age where the components of change can differ (e.g., before and after the age of 75). One common statistical problem arising in mixed models of this variety is that the correlation of the two age slopes hits a boundary condition ($\rho_{s1,s2} = 1$), so it is not really estimated and can be forced to zero without loss of fit. This lack of empirical identification is often due to few people with longitudinal measurements crossing both age segments, but this does not seriously bias the other estimates (as in Hamagami and McArdle, 2000). If no turning point age is defined substantively, τ can be estimated from the data (e.g., using NLMIXED; see Cudeck and Klebe, 2002; McArdle and Wang, 2007; Wang and McArdle, 2008).

The results of Table 26.4 include four alternative models of age changes. The first model (26.4a) is simply a reparameterization of the previous linear age model where we have rescaled $B[t] = (Age[t] - 75)/10$, so the intercepts are centered at the age of 75 and the slopes represent change per decade of age. The results exhibit the same fit as before, but the parameters of the slopes show

Table 26.4 Numerical results for a consecutive sequence of exactly identified common factor models to the eight cognitive sub-scales (see Table 26.5)

Statistic	$F = 0$	$F = 1$	$F = 2$	$F = 3$	$F = 4$
χ^2	25868.	5688.	474.	60.	2.
df	28	20	13	7	2
$D\chi^2$	–	20180.	5214.	414.	58.
Ddf	–	8	7	6	5
ε_a	.245	.136	.048	.022	.003
$-95\%(e_a)$	.242	.133	.044	.017	.000
$+95\%(e_a)$	.247	.139	.052	.027	.017
$rmsr$	.287	.156	.046	.009	.002

the average change is $\mu_1 = -8.3$ over 'every decade of age,' and substantial increases in variances and covariances ($\sigma_1^2 = 23.4$, $\rho_{01} = +0.27$) over each decade.

In model (26.4b) the same rescaled age basis was used in a quadratic change model, and there is a slight improvement in fit from the introduction of the new score (y_2) and four new parameters ($\chi^2 = 47$ on $df = 4$). The mean growth curve can be written using the stating slope ($\mu_0 = 60.4$), and two negative parameters, $\mu_1 = -8.1$ (per decade) and $\mu_1 = -1.2$ (per half decade squared). Unfortunately, a big problem here is that the additional variance and covariance terms associated with the second slope were 'not estimable' within this basis. To explore this problem, a *cubic change* model (26.4c) was fitted and, while improving the fit ($\chi^2 = 11$ on $df = 2$), resulted in the same problems for variance estimation. These are not strictly mathematical problems, because the parameters are certainly identified in theory, but these are common statistical problems in these kinds of data.

Finally, we fit a *two-part spline* model (26.3d) by defining the knot-point at $\tau = 75$. A variety of additional knot points were investigated, and an optimal knot point

was found at $\tau = 73.2$ (using NLMIXED), but age 75 yielded almost as good a fit so it was retained here. The results of table (3d) give the estimates for these two separate age segments: (a) The intercepts at age 75 have a mean and variance ($\mu_0 = 60.4$ with $\sigma_0^2 = 170.5$), (b) the early age slopes, from the youngest ages up to age 75, exhibit a large (negative) mean and variance ($\mu_1 = -6.9$ with $\sigma_1^2 = 71.4$), (c) the later age slopes, from age 75 to the oldest ages, exhibit an even larger negative mean and positive variance ($\mu_2 = -9.5$ with $\sigma_2^2 = 94.7$), and (d) the fit is a clear improvement over the linear growth model ($\chi^2 = 53$ on $df = 3$). From this result, it appears a nonlinear age change model should include both variance components of cognitive decline between ages 65 and 75 (-7 per cent) but possibly different components with even more cognitive decline between ages 75 and 85 (-10 per cent). The trajectory plot of Figure 26.5 shows the informative results of this turning point model.

CHALLENGE 4: INVARIANCE OF MEASUREMENT OVER TIME

Another challenge raised in longitudinal data analysis is the important question of: 'Have we measured the same constructs at all occasions?' It is typically assumed that if we are measuring exactly the same variables ($Y[t]$) under exactly the same conditions and use the same scoring system on all occasions, then we have. However, this raises the useful questions of factorial invariance over time (Nesselroade, 1990; McArdle, 2007). When we can form a test of these questions as a measurement hypothesis, we can guide the longitudinal research along a sturdier path.

To start these kinds of measurement analyses we first select a set of data that only represent one occasion of measurement.

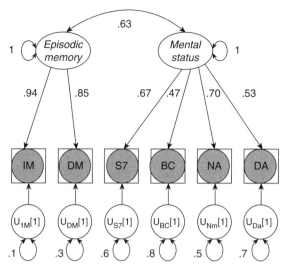

Figure 26.5   Two cognitive factors are well measured by the current HRS measures.

Under standard assumptions is usually the first occasion or the occasion with the most measures. We typically remove the means and start with deviation scores and consider a measurement model

$$Y[1] = \Lambda[1] f[1] + u[1] \qquad (26.6)$$

where each separate variable $Y[1]$ is represented by the same underlying common factor score ($f[1]$) based on a multiplicative factor loading ($\lambda[1]$) plus a unique factor score ($u[1]$). At this point, this kind of common factor model only needs to apply to the model *within each occasion*.

The HRS cognitive score is formed from several different sub-scales (for details see McArdle et al., 2007). For illustrative purposes here, we fit these kinds of common factor models to data from eight of these sub-scales. Table 26.4 lists the numerical results of goodness-of-fit for different common factor models fitted to the cognitive data sub-scales of the HRS. One of the most obvious results found here is that the one common factor model does

not fit these data very well (i.e., RMSEA $\varepsilon_a = .136$). In contrast, the two common factor model fits much better ($\varepsilon_a = .048$), and the three common factor model is nearly perfect ($\varepsilon_a = .022$).

Although we do have prior hypotheses about these cognitive sub-scales (see Horn and McArdle, 2007), we carried an exploratory rotation (using oblique Promax) of the two and three factor solutions, and the resolution of the three common factors is listed in Table 26.5. These results show strongest loadings for the first two variables, indicating a common factor termed Eposidic Memory (EM), a second factor including the next four variables, indicating a different common factor termed Mental Status (MS), and a third common factor indicated by the last two variables and termed Crystallized Knowledge (Gc; for details, see Horn and McArdle, 2007). Since the final two sub-scales (SI and VO) are not measured at all occasion in the HRS, we eliminate these from our consideration and form a final within-occasion model of two common factors drawn as the path diagram in Figure 26.6.

Table 26.5 Results for a three common factor model (MLE with Promax; $\rho_{12} = .23$, $\rho_{13} = .22$, $\rho_{23} = .50$, $\varepsilon_a = .022$)

Measure	Factor λ_1	Factor λ_2	Factor λ_3	Unique Ψ^2
IR[1]	.80	.10	−.01	.27
DR[1]	.92	.02	.02	.13
S7[1]	−.00	.61	.11	.54
BC[1]	−.06	.57	−.04	.73
NA[1]	.06	.64	.05	.52
DA[1]	.01	.59	−.10	.70
VO[1]	−.00	.21	.47	.63
SI[1]	.01	.01	.85	.26

Notes: IR = Immediate Word Recall (10 items);
DR = Delayed Recall (10 items); S7 = Serial 7s (5 trials);
BC = Backward Counting (2 trials); NA = Names (4 items);
DA = Dates (3 items); VO = Vocabulary (5 items);
SI = Similarities (5 items).

From the perspective of longitudinal measurement, this failure of the single factor model is highly informative. Although this is an exploratory analysis, and requires further validation, this implies the cognitive ability score used in the previous figures and latent curve models ($CA[t]$) is likely to represent an aggregate

of at least two or more different cognitive functions operating in different ways over time (see McArdle and Woodcock, 1997; Horn and McArdle, 2007; McArdle, 2007). This is not seen here as a failing of the latent curve models, because this was a measurement assumption that was not testable in the previous latent curve models. Nevertheless, our use of an aggregate that represents different constructs may have been the reason why some of the simpler models could not fit so well. Although many other measurement issues could be considered here (see McArdle et al., 2007) it is possible the use of an overaggregate and hence mislabeled score in a latent curve model can be one of the most confusing aspects of data analysis.

Two occasions of data provide the next opportunity to characterize some of the key longitudinal questions about the measurement of change. These data can come from the first and second occasions, or the first and last occasions, or the two most substantively meaningful occasions. In two-occasion longitudinal data where

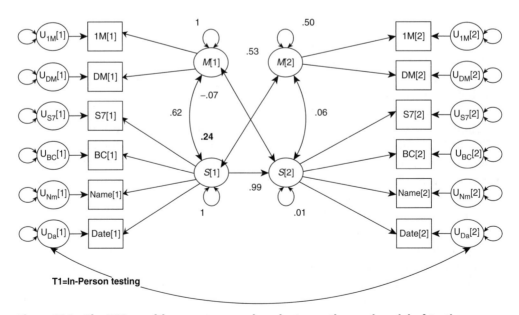

Figure 26.6 The HRS cognitive measures are invariant over time and model-of-testing.

the same variables ($Y[t]$) are repeatedly measured at a second occasion (over time, or over age, etc.), we can write

$$Y[1]^* = \Lambda[1] f[1] + u[1] \text{ and } Y[2]^*$$
$$= \Lambda[2] f[2] + u[2] \quad (26.7)$$

where each matrix now has a bracketed 1 or 2 designating the occasion of measurement. This kind of structural factor model applies to mode *within each occasion* and *between the two occasions* (see Meredith, 1964; Nesselroade, 1972; Horn and McArdle, 1992; McArdle and Nesselroade, 1994; Meredith and Horn, 2001).

This organization of the factor model permits a few key questions to be examined using specific model restrictions. The first question we can evaluate is whether or not the same number of factors are present at both occasions – 'Is the number of common factors $K[1] = K[2]$?' Assuming this leads to a reasonable fit, we can then ask questions about the invariance of the factor loadings $\Lambda[t]$ over time – 'Does $\Lambda[1] = \Lambda[2]$?' Another set of questions can be asked about the invariance of the factor score $f[t]$ over time – 'For all persons N, is $f[1]_n = f[2]_n$?' This last question is examined through the correlations over time – 'Does $\rho[1,2]=1$?' In a seminal series of papers, Meredith (1964) extended selection theorems to the common factor case (see Meredith and Horn, 2001). As it turns out, these *principles of factorial invariance for multiple groups also apply to multiple occasions.*

As many researchers have noted, these questions about the stability of the factor pattern and the stability of the factor scores raise both methodological and substantive issues. Most usefully, this use of multiple indicators allows us to clearly separate the stability due to (a) the *internal consistency reliability* of the factors and (b) the *test-retest correlation* of the factor scores. Each set of model restrictions of factor

invariance deals with a different question about *construct equivalence over time*. We can examine the evidence for these questions using the SEM and goodness-of-fit techniques (see McArdle, 2007).

These kinds of two-occasion models are fitted to the HRS data using the general framework of the path diagram of Figure 26.7. The six sub-scales that are repeated are considered to represent two different common factors ($EM[t]$ and $MS[t]$) at each of the first two occasions. Of key importance here is that the first occasion is typically carried out 'face-to-face' while the second occasion is often done over the 'telephone.' This means that the hypothesis of invariance applies to both time and 'modality.'

The numerical results of the goodness-of-fit of a series of models are listed in Table 26.6. These models fit with the most restricted model as a starting point – the one common factor model with factor loadings and uniquenesses constrained to be equal over time. As expected from the prior results, this model does not fit the HRS data very well ($L^2 = 8,600$ on $df = 69$, $\varepsilon_a = 0.087$). The relaxation of the factor loadings, so only the configuration of one factor is required, fits better ($L^2 = 8,579$ on $df = 64$) but is not considered a good fit relative to the increased number of parameters ($\varepsilon_a = 0.090$) or in the change in fit ($\chi^2 = 21$ on $df = 5$). When specific covariances are added to the original metric invariant model, following McArdle and Nesselroade (1994), the fit of the one factor model is still not within the acceptable limits (i.e., $\varepsilon_a = 0.066 > 0.050$). In contrast, the two-factor model drawn in Figure 26.5 represents a good fit to the two occasion data, no matter how it is constrained. This is true of the original metric invariant model ($\varepsilon_a = 0.050$) and, especially, the two-factor model with specific covariances ($\varepsilon_a = 0.023$). These longitudinal results strongly suggest we

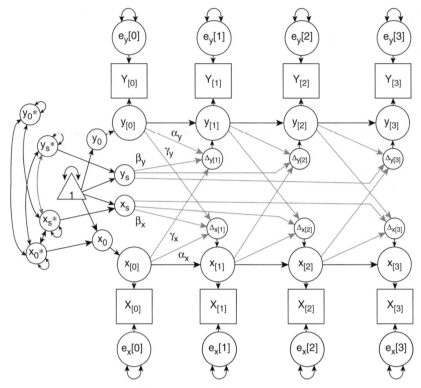

Figure 26.7   A bivariate latent difference score (LDS) model.

redo the prior latent curve analysis with two functions rather than one.

The path model of Figure 26.7 can now easily be extended to multiple time points

Table 26.6   Fit indices for 1 and 2 common factors based on six measures at two longitudinal occasions

6a: F = 1 models	χ^2	df	$D\chi^2/Ddf$	e_a
Invariant Λ, Ψ^2	8600	69	—	.087
Configural Λ	8579	64	21 / 5	.090
MI + Specifics	4534	63	4056 / 6	.066
Covariance				
6b : F = 2SS models				
Invariant Λ, Ψ^2	2579	63	—	.050
Configural Λ	2578	59	1 / 4	.051
MI + Specifics	423	57	2156 / 6	.023
Covariance				

Note: Model comparisons from likelihood-based goodness-of-fit indices.

(see McArdle et al., 2007), but it is not the only useful organization of these data. For example, we can rewrite a factor model with a simple set of *latent difference scores* ($\Delta f = f[2] - f[1]$) as depicted in Figure 26.3. This final model suggests the changes in the observed scores can be assessed in three parts: (a) the differences in the loadings over time ($\Lambda[2] - \Lambda[1]$) multiplied by the initial common factor score ($f[1]$), (b) the loadings at time 2 multiplied by the differences in the factor scores (Δf), and (c) the differences in the unique factors (Δu). It is most interesting that this difference score form does not alter the interpretation or statistical testing of factor invariance over time. If the factor loadings are invariant over time ($\Lambda[2] = \Lambda[1]$), then the first term in the model drops out and the result is simplified (i.e., ΔY

$= \Lambda\, \Delta f + \Delta u$). This result is practically useful – if the loadings are invariant over time, the factor pattern *between* occasions equals the factor pattern *within* occasions. When metric invariance is not a required result, the differences in the between and within factor loadings may be meaningful. This basic result for difference scores is consistent with previous multivariate work on this topic (e.g., 1970, Nesselroade and Cable, 1974).

CHALLENGE 5: OPPORTUNITIES FOR MODELING DYNAMIC INFLUENCES

A final challenge is raised here by common questions about longitudinal – 'What is the best change model for my data?' This is related to another challenging question – 'Do any of my constucts lead to changes in the other constructs?' This implies we can and should write and fit a set of equations with *changes in multiple variables* (McArdle et al., 2001). It is important to consider that these kinds of questions are very common in developmental theory, but answers are not yet very common in empirical practice.

The fundamental idea used here is that all change models have, as their basis, the change score as an outcome, and SEMs allow for some accounting for the errors-of measurement or unique components. Thus, some practical answers to these theoretical questions start with a more basic question – is there any reasonable way to relate the change score Equation 26.1 to the multilevel models [2] and [3]? A straightforward answer to this question comes from rewriting the first-level Equation 26.2 for two consecutive observations ($Y[t]$ and $Y[t+1]$) as

$$D\{t, t-1\} \qquad (26.8)$$
$$= Y[t]_n - Y[t-1]_n$$

$$= (g0_n + g1_nA[t] + e[t]_n)$$
$$\quad - (g0_n + g1_nA[t-1] + e[t-1]_n)$$
$$= (g0_n - g0_n) + (g1_nA[t] - g1_n$$
$$\quad \times A[t-1]) + (e[t]_n - e[t-1]_n)$$
$$= (0) + g1_n(A[t] - A[t-1])$$
$$\quad + (e[t]_n - e[t-1]_n)$$
$$= g1_n(D\{A[t, t-1]\}) + D\{e[t, t-1]_n\}$$

so it is clear that the difference between two time points is essentially two parts: (1) the individual slope ($g1$) multiplied by the group differences in the basis ($A[t] - A[t+1]$), and (2) the individual changes in the error terms. This also means that the changes in the non-error scores can be written as the prediction of the slopes (as in [26.3b]). It is worth noting that seminal statements made by some of the most important leaders in quantative methods strongly advocated that we need to avoid change scores (e.g., Cronbach and Furby, 1970; Lord, 1958). These statements focused primarily on the very real problems of measurement error in the change scores (the second component). In contrast, other researchers who investigated these statistical issues emphasized the benefits of using change scores (i.e., Allison, 1990; Nesselroade and Cable, 1974; Rogosa, 1979; Rogosa and Willett, 1983) because of the first terms. It is not surprising that the appropriate use of change scores remains a conundrum for many researchers, but it may be suprising that the multilevel model avoids this problem by focusing on the slope components ($g1$).

This simple latent variable difference score approach leads to a wide variety of possibilities we can consider under the term *dynamic-structural analysis* (see McArdle, 1988, 2001). On a formal basis, we first assume we have observed scores $Y[t]$ and $Y[t-1]$ measured over a defined interval of time (Δt), but we assume the latent variables are defined over an equal interval of time ($\Delta t = 1$). This definition of an equal interval latent time scale is non-trivial because it allows us to eliminate Δt from the rest of the equations. That is, in any model we can write

$$Y[t]_n = y[t]_n + e[t]_n \quad \text{and} \quad (26.9)$$

$$y[t]_n = y[t-1]_n + \Delta y[t]_n$$

with latent scores $y[t]$ and $y[t-1]$, residual scores $e[t]$, possibly representing measurement error, and *latent difference scores* $\Delta y[t]$. Even though this difference $\Delta y[t]$ is a theoretical score and not simply a fixed a linear combnation, we can write a structural model for *any latent change concept* without directly writing the resulting complex trajectory (as in McArdle and Nesselroade, 1994; McArdle, 2001; McArdle and Hamagami, 2001) as

$$Y[t]_n = g_{0,n} + (\Sigma_{i=1,t} \Delta y[t]_n) + u[t]_n$$
$$(26.10)$$

This simple algebraic device [26.10] allows us to generally define the trajectory equation based on a summation ($\Sigma_{i=1,t}$) or *accumulation of the latent changes* ($\Delta y[t]$) up to time t, and these structural expectations are automatically generated using any standard SEM software (e.g., LISREL, Mplus, Mx, etc.).

This approach makes it possible to consider any change model, including one where

$$\Delta y[t]_n = \alpha g_{1,n} + \beta y[t-1]_n + z[t]_n$$
$$(26.11)$$

where the g_1 is (as in Equation [26.2]) a latent slope score which is constant over time, and the α and β are coefficients describing the change. This *dual change model* combines an additive change parameter (α) with a multiplicative change parameter (β; see McArdle, 2001).

In general, these dynamic coefficients (α and β) are not all required to be invariant over time, and a family of more complex curves can result from fitting non-invariant coefficients ($\alpha[t]$ and/or $\beta[t]$) or adding stochastic disturbance terms ($z[t]$). However, if the residual components of the latent change are not included, the expectations describe a more restricted set of latent curves which are required to be deterministic and smooth over time. This deterministic approach will be used to compare groups in the analyses presented here.

The latent difference score approach is most useful when we start to examine time-dependent inter-relationships among multiple growth processes. As a final alternative model we use an expansion of our previous latent difference scores logic to write a *bivariate dynamic change score* model as

$$\Delta y[t]_n = \alpha_y y_{1,n} + \beta_y y[t-1]_n \quad (26.12)$$
$$+ \gamma_{yx} x[t-1]_n + z_y[t]_n,$$

and

$$\Delta x[t]_n = \alpha_x x_{1,n} + \beta_x x[t-1]_n \quad (26.13)$$
$$+ \gamma_{xy} y[t-1]_n + z_x[t]_n.$$

In this model each change is represented by dual changes (parameters α and β) but also include *coupling* parameters (γ). The coupling parameter (γ_{yx}) represents the time-dependent effect of latent $x[t]$ on $y[t]$, and the other coupling parameter (γ_{xy}) represents the time-dependent effect of latent $y[t]$ on $x[t]$.

This bivariate dynamic model is described in the path diagram of Figure 26.8. The key features of this model include the use of fixed unit values (unlabeled arrows) to define $\Delta y[t]$ and $\Delta x[t]$, and equality constraints within a variable (for the α, β, and

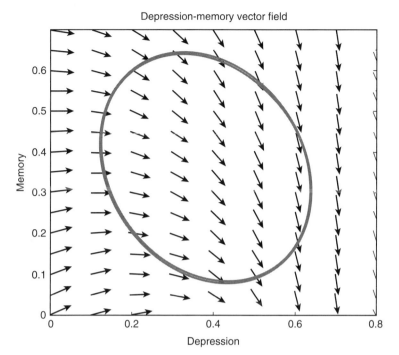

Figure 26.8   Bivariate change expectations (vector field) for directional dynamic where Depression → Memory (from McArdle, Hamagami, Fisher and Kadlec, 2009).

γ parameters) to simplify estimation and identification. These latent difference score models can lead to more complex nonlinear trajectory equations (e.g., non-homogeneous equations). These trajectories can be described by writing the implied basis coefficients $(A_j[t])$ as the linear accumulation of first differences for each variable $(\Sigma \Delta y[j], j = 0$ to $t)$. Additional unique covariances within occasions $(u_y[t]u_x[t])$ are possible, but these will be identifiable only when there are multiple $(M > 2)$ measured variables within each occasion.

As a practical example of this kind of dynamic model, let us consider testing some hypotheses about the joint impacts of memory loss and increases in depression in the elderly in the HRS. (Note: Depression in the HRS is measured by an abbreviated form of the CES-D, with higher scores

indicating more depression; see McArdle, Hamagami, Fisher and Kadlec, 2009.) In this specific case of the HRS data, we fit a model and we estimate the change equations of Table 26.7a. Of most interest here is the episodic memory factor $(EM[t])$ where the resulting equations are

$$\Delta memory[t]_n$$
$$= -0.27 \ slope\_memory_n$$
$$+ -0.77 memory[t-1]_n$$
$$- 1.54 \ depression[t-1]_n \quad (26.14)$$

and

$$\Delta depression[t]_n \quad\quad\quad (26.15)$$
$$= +0.83 \ slope\_depression_n$$
$$- 1.10 \ depression[t-1]_n$$
$$+ 0.13 \ memory[t-1] \quad (26.16)$$

Table 26.7   Results from alternative dynamic models applied to HRS data

7a: *Selected HRS bivariate dynamic results*

Dynamic equations for Memory-Status coupling

$$\Delta m[t] = +.01 - .49\, m[t-1] + .18\, s[t-1]$$

$$\Delta s[t] = -.01 - .16\, s[t-1] + .13\, m[t-1]$$

Dynamic equations for Status-Depression coupling

$$\Delta s[t] = -.01 - .03\, s[t-1] - .09\, d[t-1]$$

$$\Delta d[t] = +.01 + .04\, d[t-1] - .03\, s[t-1]$$

Dynamic equations for Memory-Depression coupling

$$\Delta m[t] = +.27 - .77\, m[t-1] - 1.54\, d[t-1]$$

$$\Delta d[t] = +.83 - 1.10\, d[t-1] + .13\, m[t-1]$$

7b: *Alternative model fits*	Likelihood (Deviance) L^2	Number of parameters	Difference $dL^2 \sim \chi^2$
Full BDCS model	−35831	20	–
Remove coupling from Depression → Status	−35786	19	45
Remove coupling from Status → Depression	−35832	19	1
No coupling	−35764	18	67

From a cursory look at these parameters it is clear that the coefficient of *depression* → $\Delta memory$ (−1.54) is large and negative while the coefficent of *memory*→ $\Delta depression$ is small (0.13). However, these parameters are highly dependent upon one another, as well as the different scales of measurement, so the appropriate way to check on the need for a dynamic influence is to try to eliminate it and check the loss in fit (as in McArdle et al., 2001). The results of this approach are listed in detail in Table 26.7b. Basically, when we fit a model without the influence of memory on depression, the model fits fairly well ($\chi^2 = 1$ on $df = 1$). But when we use the same procedure but eliminate the influence of depression on memory, the model does not fit well ($\chi 2 = 45$ on $df = 1$). The net result of this dynamic analysis is that we find that increases or decreases in *depression*[$t-1$]→ $\Delta memory$[1] and not the other way around.

The results of these Equations ([26.14] and [26.15]) cannot be expressed in terms of a simple set of univarate trajectories (as in Figure 26.1), but they can be expressed as a set of bivariate expectations, or a *vector field* (Boker and McArdle, 2005), and the expected values from these parameters are those that are displayed in Figure 26.8 (from Equations [26.14] and [26.15]). This plot is useful because it shows the expected direction of any pair of coordinates from any starting point ($y[t]$, $x[t]$), and the ellipse gives the symmetric 95 per cent confidence boundary around the actual data (at $t = 0$). The directional arrows are a way to display the expected pair of $\Delta t = 1$ visit changes (Δy, Δx) from this point. This figure shows an interesting dynamic property – *the change expectations of a dynamic model depend on the starting point*. From this perspective, we can also interpret the high level-level correlation, which describes the placement of the individuals in the vector field, and the negative slope-slope correlation, which describes the location of the subsequent change scores for individuals in the vector field. The resulting 'flow surface' for the shows the state of depression abilities has a tendency to impact score changes on the memory scores. Needless to say, these dynamic impacts are not easy to see in the typical comparison of changes in the means over time.

FUTURE STEPS

This chapter has dealt with some contemporary challenges for longitudinal data analysis. In all cases discussed here, the hope is that these challenges will be raised rather than ignored because there is a great deal of potential to learn from our longitudinal data. For example, in terms of the HRS longitudinal data we have learned:

(1) The mixed-effects multi-level latent curve model is a clear way to separate individual changes from group differences.
(2) The use of an age-basis rather than a time-basis may be useful with cognitive measures.
(3) The age-based curve is probably nonlinear, with more decline in cognition after age 75.
(4) The cognitive measures do not represent a single function, and at least two factors of cognition may be needed to measure the individual changes.
(5) The dynamic influences of variables such as depression have strong impacts on the decline of memory abilities. These fundamental observations about the longitudinal HRS data could not have been made before these specific challenges were considered. Of course, not all challenges have yet been met, but at least the basic issues are now clearer.

We have not fully focused on several basic measurement assumptions of all latent curve models – *longitudinal measurement equivalence* – i.e., the same unidimensional attribute is measured on the same persons, using exactly the same scale of measurement at every occasion. One key question: 'Is the scale of measurement the same at all levels of *Y*?' This is a non-trivial question that was raised at least as early as Stevens (1946), who suggested such an important property would only exist for interval (or ratio) level scales. The need for interval scales of measurement has plagued many other kinds of research (see Brand, 2007), so it is not surprising to find this problem emerge in the analysis of change. Cattell (1966) nicely illustrated this problem in his *tour-de-force* on scaling issues in multivariate analysis. 'This diagram shows the transformation between raw scores values in the upper row to what is known to be the true scale scores in the lower row. (A slight difference in the lower raw score means a lot, while equivalent differences at the top do not correspond to much real increase.) It will be seen that the rank order of three people in difference scores calculated in raw scores is exactly the opposite to that from scaled scores. Such complete reversal is, of course, an extreme instance (Cattell, 1966: 366). Of course, since the definition of true scores cannot be made without some manifest observations, it is not actually known how much these kinds of extreme difference scores do exist. A great deal of work in the history of psychometrics has been used to help develop improved scales to avoid these problems in an objective/empirical fashion. One outstanding and successful effort made about this problem comes from the work of Rasch (1960).

Factorial invariance, especially factor-loading invariance, was considered as a major requirement for any longitudinal analysis. As presented here, the goal of measurement invariance needs to be achieved before we can consider any SEMs of latent changes. Although only scale-level data are considered here, practical problems with measurement invariance at the scale level may indicate more basic measurement problems at the item level (McDonald, 1985). Using incomplete data principles, item invariance is possible even if the items are originally used in the context of different scales (Grimm et al., 2007; McArdle and Nesselroade 2003). There are many techniques for linkage across measurement scales with sparse longitudinal data, and invariant item-response models may be very useful for these purposes (McArdle et al., 2002; McArdle and Nesselroade, 2003).

New forms of multiple group and incomplete data approaches can be used with the dynamic models described here. By using a multilevel approach, we can also effectively analyze cases in which each person has different amounts of longitudinal data (i.e., unbalanced data or incomplete data), and some of the new SEM programs make this an easy task. These possibilities lead directly to the revival of practical experimental options based on incomplete data (e.g., McArdle and Woodcock, 1997). Incomplete data models have also been used to describe the potential benefits of a mixture of age- and time-based models, using only two time points of data collection – an accelerated longitudinal design (Duncan et al., 2006; McArdle and Bell, 2000; Raudenbush, 2001).

There are also many other elegant statistical models for longitudinal data. Several important breakthroughs in work on dynamic modeling of continuous time data have been made using SEM software (e.g., Boker 2001; Chow et al., 2007; Montfort et al., 2007; Oud and Jansen, 2000). These differential equation models offer many more dynamic possibilities, and this is increasingly important when large amounts of time points of data are collected ($T > N$). Other repeated-measures SEMs are based on the logic of partitioning variance components across multiple modalities (Kenny

and Zautra, 2001; Kroonenberg and Oort, 2003; Steyer et al., 2001). These models decompose factorial influences into orthogonal common and specific components, with an emphasis on separating trait factors from state factors. These models have interesting interpretations, and they may be useful when combined with other SEMs described here.

We have also not examined classic issues from the problems of scaling, group differences, lack of measurement the invariance of constructs, and the appropriate selection of an optimal timelag between changing longitudinal measurements. There are also many newer techniques that explore similar challenges (Hedecker and Gibbons, 2006; Muller and Stewart, 2006; Singer and Willett, 2003; Verbeke and Molenberghs, 2000; Walls and Schafer, 2006). The many good general references to the structural equation modeling approach (SEM; e.g., Kline, 2005; McDonald 1985) include several new books specifically about SEM for repeated measures (e.g., Bollen and Curran, 2006; Duncan et al., 2006). The general longitudinal approach has gained popularity, and for the most part, it nicely matches the scientific goals of longitudinal research (Nesselroade and Baltes, 1979).

So there is much to be learned from these and other longitudinal data analysis challenges. Researchers who attack any of these challenges are likely to come to different conclusions about their own longitudinal data, and this is as it should be. It is also certain that solving one of these problems is likely to create other problem, and more work will be needed. However, there is simply no reason to do the hard work of collecting longitudinal data if the longitudinal analysis does not match these efforts. Neither longitudinal data collection nor longitudinal data analysis should be thought of as simple or easy. The real challenge for longitudinal researchers is to try to deal these classic problems in measurement of change, so we can move on to newer and more informative problems.

ACKNOWLEDGMENT

This research was supported by grants from the *National Institute on Aging*; Number AG07137).

REFERENCES

Allison, P.D. (1990) 'Change scores as dependent variables in regression analysis', in C.C. Clogg (ed.) *Sociological Methodology 1990*. San Francisco, CA: Jossey-Bass. pp. 93–114.

Bock, R.D. (1975) *Multivariate Statistical Methods in Behavioral Research*, New York, NY: McGraw-Hill.

Bollen, K. and Curran, P.J. (2006) *Latent Curve Models: A Structural Equation Perspective*, New York, NY: Wiley.

Boker, S.M. (2001) 'Differential structural equation modeling of intra-individual variability', in L. Collins and A. Sayer (eds) *New Methods for the Analysis of Change*. Washington, DC: APA Press. pp. 3–28.

Browne, M. and Nesselroade, J.R. (2005) 'Representing psychological processes with dynamic factor models: Some promising uses and extensions of autoregressive moving average time series models', in A. Madeau and J.J. McArdle (eds) *Contemporary Advances in Psychometrics*. Mahwah, NJ: Lawrence Erlbaum Associates. pp. 415–452.

Chow, S-M., Ferrer, E. and Nesselroade, J.R. (2007) 'An unscented Kalman filter approach for the estimation of nonlinear dynamic systems models', *Multivariate Behavioral Research*, 42(2): 283–321.

Collins, L.M. (2006) 'Analysis of longitudinal data: The integration of theoretical model, temporal design, and statistical model', *Annual Review of Psychology*, 57: 505–528.

Collins, L. and Sayer, A. (2001)(eds) *New Methods for the Analysis of Change*. Washington, DC: APA Press.

Cronbach, L.J. and Furby, L. (1970) 'How we should measure change—or should we?' *Psychological Bulletin*, 74: 68–80.

Cudeck, R. and Harring, J.R. (2007) 'Analysis of nonlinear patterns of change with random coefficient models', *Annual Review of Psychology*, 58: 615–637.

Duncan, T.E., Duncan, S.C., Strycker, L.A. and Li, F. (2006) *An Introduction to Latent Variable Growth Curve Modeling: Concepts, Issues, and Applications: Second Edition*. Mahwah, NJ: Erlbaum.

Ferrer, E., Hamagami, F. and McArdle, J.J. (2004) 'Modeling latent growth curves with incomplete data using different types of structural equation modeling and multilevel software', *Structural Equation Modeling*, 11(3): 452–483.

Ferrer, E. and McArdle, J.J. (2004) 'An experimental analysis of dynamic hypotheses about cognitive abilities and achievement from childhood to early adulthood', *Developmental Psychology*, 40: 935–952.

Ferrer, E., McArdle, J.J., Shaywitz, B.A., Holahan, J.M., Marchione, K. and Shaywitz, S.E. (2007) 'Longitudinal models of developmental dynamics between reading and cognition from childhood to adolescence', *Developmental Psychology*, 43: 1460–1473.

Ghisletta, P. Bickel, J-F. and Lövdén, M. (2006) 'Does activity engagement protect against cognitive decline in old age? Methodological and analytical considerations', *Journal of Gerontology B Psychological Sciences*, 61: 253–261.

Ghisletta, P. and Lindenberger, U. (2003) 'Age-based structural dynamics between perceptual speed and knowledge in the Berlin Aging Study: Direct evidence for ability dedifferentiation in old age', *Psychology and Aging*, 18(4): 696–713.

Ghisletta, P. and Lindenberger, U. (2005) 'Exploring the structural dynamics of the link between sensory and cognitive functioning in old age: Longitudinal evidence from the Berlin Aging Study', *Intelligence*, 33: 555–587.

Ghisletta, P. and McArdle, J.J. (2001) 'Latent growth curve analyses of the development of height', *Structural Equation Modeling*, 8(4): 531–555.

Gollob, H.F. and Reichardt, C.S. (1987) 'Taking account of time lags in causal models', *Child Development*, 58: 80–92.

Grimm, K.J., Hamagami, F. and McArdle, J.J. (2007) 'Nonlinear growth models in research on cognitive aging', in K. v. Montfort, H. Oud and A. Satorra (eds) *Longitudinal models in the behavioural and related sciences*. Mahwah, NJ: Erlbaum. pp. 267–294.

Grimm, K.J. and McArdle, J.J. (2005) 'A note on the computer generation of mean and covariance expectations in latent growth curve analysis', in F. Dansereau and F.J. Yammarino (eds) *Multi-level issues in strategy and Methods*. New York, NY: Elsevier. pp. 335–364.

Hamagami, F. and McArdle, J.J. (2000) 'Advanced studies of individual differences linear dynamic models for longitudinal data analysis', in G. Marcoulides and R. Schumacker (eds) *New Developments and Techniques in Structural Equations Modeling.* Mahwah, NJ: Erlbaum. pp. 203–246.

Hamagami, F. and McArdle, J.J. (2007) 'Dynamic extensions of latent difference score models', in S.M. Boker and M.L. Wegner (eds) *Quantitative Methods in Contemporary Psychology.* Mahwah, NJ: Erlbaum. pp. 47–85.

Hamagami, F., McArdle, J.J. and Cohen, P. (2000) 'Bivariate dynamic systems analyses based on a latent difference score approach for personality disorder ratings', in V.J. Molfese and D.L. Molfese (eds) *Temperament and Personality Development Across the Life Span.* Mahwah, NJ: Erlbaum.

Harris, C.W. (ed.) (1963) *Problems in Measuring Change.* Madison, WI: University of Wisconsin Press.

Hedecker, D. and Gibbons, R. (2006) *Longitudinal Data Analysis.* New York, NY: Wiley.

Hertzog, C., Lindenberger, U., Ghisletta, P. and Oertzen, T.V. (2006) 'On the power of multivariate latent growth curve models to detect correlated change', *Psychological Methods*, 11(3): 244–252.

Horn, J.L. (1972) 'State, trait, and change dimensions of intelligence', *The British Journal of Mathematical and Statistical Psychology*, 42(2): 159–185.

Horn, J.L. and McArdle, J.J. (1980) 'Perspectives on mathematical and statistical model building (MAS-MOB) in research on aging', in L. Poon (ed.) *Aging in the 1980's: Psychological Issues.* Washington, DC: American Psychological Association. pp. 503–541.

Hsiao, C. (2003) *Analysis of Panel Data: Second Edition.* Cambridge, UK: Cambridge University Press.

Jöreskog, K.G. (1973) 'Analysis of covariance structures', in A.S. Goldberger and O.D. Duncan (eds) *Structural Equation Models in the Social Sciences.* New York, NY: Seminar Press.

Jöreskog, K.G. and Sörbom, D. (1979) *Advances in Factor Analysis and Structural Equation Models.* Cambridge, MA: Abt Books.

Kenny, D.A. and Zautra, A. (2001) 'The trait-state model for longitudinal data', in L. Collins and A. Sayer (eds) *New Methods for the Analysis of Change.* Washington, DC: APA Press. pp. 241–264.

Kline, R. (2005) *Principles and Practices in Structural Equation Modeling.* New York, NY: Guilford Press.

Kroonenberg P.M. and Oort F.J. (2003) 'Three-mode analysis of multimode covariance matrices', *British Journal of Mathematical and Statistical Psychology*, 56(2): 305–335.

Little, R.J.A. and Rubin, D.J. (2002) *Statistical Analysis with Missing Data: Second Edition.* New York: Wiley.

Lord, F. (1958) 'Further problems in the measurement of growth', *Educational and Psychological Measurement*, 18: 437–454.

Lord, F. (1967) 'A paradox in the interpretation of group comparisons', *Psychological Bulletin*, 68(5): 304–305.

Lövdén, M., Ghisletta, P., and Lindenberger, U. (2005) 'Social participation attenuates decline in perceptual speed in old and very old age', *Psychology and Aging*, 20: 423–434.

McArdle, J.J. (1986) 'Latent variable growth within behavior genetic models', *Behavior Genetics*, 16(1): 163–200.

McArdle, J.J. (1989) 'Structural modeling experiments using multiple growth functions', in P. Ackerman, R. Kanfer and R. Cudeck (eds) *Learning and Individual Differences: Abilities, Motivation, and Methodology.* Hillsdale, NJ: Erlbaum. pp. 71–117.

McArdle, J.J. (2001) 'A latent difference score approach to longitudinal dynamic structural analyses', in R. Cudeck, S. du Toit, and D. Sorbom (eds) *Structural Equation Modeling: Present and Future.* Lincolnwood, IL: Scientific Software International. pp. 342–380.

McArdle, J.J. (2007a) 'Dynamic structural equation modeling in longitudinal experimental studies', in K.V. Montfort, H. Oud and A. Satorra et al. (eds) *Longitudinal Models in the Behavioural and Related Sciences.* Mahwah, NJ: Lawrence Erlbaum. pp. 159–188.

McArdle, J.J. (2007b) 'Five steps in the structural factor analysis of longitudinal data', in R. Cudeck and R. MacCallum (eds) *Factor Analysis at 100 Years.* Mahwah, NJ: Erlbaum Associates. pp. 99–130.

McArdle, J.J. (2008) 'Latent variable modeling of differences and changes', *Annual Review of Psychology*, 60.

McArdle, J.J. and Bell, R.Q. (2000) 'An introduction to latent growth curve models for developmental data analysis', in T.D. Little, K.U. Schnabel, and J. Baumert, (eds) *Modeling Longitudinal and Multiple-Group Data: Practical Issues, Applied Approaches, and Scientific Examples.* Mahwah, NJ: Erlbaum. pp. 69–107.

McArdle, J.J. and Hamagami, F. (2001) 'Linear dynamic analyses of incomplete longitudinal data', in L. Collins and A. Sayer (eds) *Methods for the Analysis of Change.* Washington, DC: APA Press. pp. 137–176.

McArdle, J.J. and Hamagami, F. (2003) 'Structural equation models for evaluating dynamic concepts within longitudinal twin analyses', *Behavior Genetics*, 33(2): 137–159.

McArdle, J.J., Hamagami, F., Jones, K., Jolesz, F., Kikinis, R., Spiro, A. and Albert, M.S. (2004) 'Structural modeling of dynamic changes in memory and brain structure using longitudinal data from the normative aging study', *Journal of Gerontology: Psychological Sciences*, 59B(6): P294–P304.

McArdle, J.J., Grimm, K., Hamagami, F., Bowles, R. and Meredith, W. (2002) 'A dynamic structural equation analysis of vocabulary abilities over the life-span'. Presented at the Annual meeting of the *Society of Multivariate Experimental Psychologists*, Charlottesville, VA, October 2002.

McArdle, J.J., Hamagami, F., Meredith, W. and Bradway, K.P. (2001) 'Modeling the dynamic hypotheses of Gf-Gc theory using longitudinal life-span data', *Learning and Individual Differences*, 12(2000): 53–79.

McArdle, J.J. and Nesselroade, J.R. (2003) 'Growth curve analyses in contemporary psychological research', in J. Schinka and W. Velicer (eds) *Comprehensive Handbook of Psychology, Volume Two: Research Methods in Psychology*. New York, NY: Pergamon Press. pp. 447–480.

McArdle, J.J. and Nesselroade, J.R. (1994) 'Structuring data to study development and change', in S.H. Cohen and H.W. Reese (eds) *Life-Span Developmental Psychology: Methodological Innovations*. Hillsdale, NJ: Erlbaum. pp. 223–267.

McArdle, J. J., Small, B.J., Backman, L. and Fratiglioni, L. (2005) 'Longitudinal models of growth and survival applied to the early detection of Alzheimer's Disease', *Journal of Geriatric Psychiatry and Neurology*, 18(4): 234–241.

McArdle, J.J. and Woodcock, J.R. (1997) 'Expanding test–rest designs to include developmental time-lag components', *Psychological Methods*, 2(4): 403–435.

McCall, R.B. and Applebaum, M.I. (1973) 'Bias in the analysis of repeated measures designs: Some alternative approaches', *Child Development*, 44: 401–415.

McDonald, R.P. (1999) *Factor Analysis and Related Methods*. Hillsdale, N.J.: Erlbaum.

Meredith, W. and Horn, J.L. (2001) 'The role of factorial invariance in measuring growth and change', in L. Collins and A. Sayer (eds) *New Methods for the Analysis of Change*. Washington, DC: APA. pp. 201–240.

Meredith, W. and Tisak, J. (1990) 'Latent curve analysis', *Psychometrika*, 55: 107–122.

Montfort, K., Oud, H. and Satorra, A. (2007)(eds) *Longitudinal Models in the Behavioural and Related Sciences*. Mahwah, NJ: Erlbaum.

Muller, K.E. and Stewart, P.W. (2006) *Linear Model Theory*. NY: Wiley.

Muthén, B.O.and Curran, P. (1997) 'General longitudinal modeling of individual differences in experimental designs: A latent variable framework for analysis and power estimation', *Psychological Methods*, 2: 371–402.

Muthén, L.K. and Muthén, B.O. (2002) *Mplus, the Comprehensive Modeling Program for Applied Researchers User'S Guide*. Los Angeles, CA: Muthen and Muthen.

Nesselroade, J.R. and Baltes, P.B. (1979)(eds) *Longitudinal Research in the Study of Behavior and Development*. New York, NY: Academic Press.

Nesselroade, J.R. and Cable, D.G. (1974) 'Sometimes it's okay to factor difference scores – The separation of state and trait anxiety', *Multivariate Behavioral Research*, 9: 273–282.

Nesselroade, J.J., McArdle, J.J., Aggen, S.H. and Meyers, J. (2001) 'Dynamic factor analysis models for multivariate time series analysis', in D.M. Moskowitz and S.L. Hershberger (eds) *Modeling Individual Variability with Repeated Measures Data: Advances and Techniques*. Mahwah, NJ: Erlbaum.

Nesselroade, J.R., Stigler, S.M. and Baltes, P.B. (1980) 'Regression toward the mean and the study of change', *Psychological Bulletin*, 88(3): 622–637.

O'Brien, R.G. and Kaiser, M.K. (1985) 'MANOVA method for analyzing repeated measures designs: An extensive primer', *Psychological Bulletin*, 97(2): 316–333.

Orth, U., Berking, M., Walker, N., Meier, L.L. and Znoj, H. (2008) 'Forgiveness and psychological adjustment following interpersonal transgressions: A longitudinal analysis', *Journal of Research in Personality*, 42: 365–385.

Oud, J.H.L. and Jansen, R.A.R.G. (2000) 'Continuous time state space modeling of panel data by means of SEM', *Psychometrika*, 65: 199–215.

Raudenbush, S.W. (2001) 'Comparing personal trajectories and drawing causal inferences from longitudinal data', *Annual Review of Psychology*, 52: 501–525.

Rogosa, D. (1979) 'Causal models in longitudinal research: Rationale, formulation, and interpretation', in J.R. Nesselroade and P.B. Baltes (eds) *Longitudinal Research in the Study of Behavior and Development*. New York, NY: Academic Press. pp. 263–302.

Rogosa, D. and Willett (1983) 'Demonstrating the reliability of the difference score in the measurement of change', *Journal of Educational Measurement*, 20(4): 335–343.

Shadish, W., Cook, T.D. and Campbell, D.T. (2002) *Experimental and Quasi-Experimental Design for Generalized Causal Inference*. Boston, MA: Houghton-Mifflin.

Singer, J.D. and Willett, J. (2003) *Applied Longitudinal Data Analysis*. New York, NY: Oxford University Press.

Steyer, R., Partchev, I. and Shanahan, M.J. (2001) 'Modeling true intraindividual change in structural equation models: The case of poverty and children's psychological adjustment', in T.D. Little, K.U. Schnabel and J. Baumert, (eds) *Modeling Longitudinal and Multiple-Group Data: Practical Issues, Applied Approaches,* *and Scientific Examples.* Mahwah, NJ: Erlbaum. pp. 109–127.

Verbeke, G. and Molenberghs, G. (2000) *Linear Mixed Models for Longitudinal Data.* New York, NY: Springer.

Walls, T.A. and Schafer, J.L. (2006) *Models of Intensive Longitudinal Data.* New York, NY: Oxford University Press.

27

Measuring the Dimensions of Social Capital in Developing Countries[1]

Veronica Nyhan Jones and
Michael Woolcock

PROLOGUE

In the life of every policy concept, it seems, the time eventually comes when the pressures and imperatives to 'measure' can no longer be resisted; sooner or later, a senior manager will invoke the business cliché that 'what gets measured is what gets done' and staff will be summoned to demonstrate the 'value added' of their idea. Given these pressures, one has to respond as carefully as possible: capitulating entirely can mean that concepts that are inherently ill-suited to quantitative measurement (like culture or empowerment) find themselves stripped of their capacity to actually make a distinctive contribution to policy debates; grimly resisting can mean being either consigned to irrelevance or watching helplessly as some other (more opportunistic) group steps in to fill the void.

In the late 1990s and early 2000s, the small team working on 'social capital' at the World Bank faced precisely this dilemma.[2] Social capital, defined as the norms and networks that enable people to act collectively (Woolcock and Narayan, 2000), was the term that had come to prominence in the newly created Social Development Department within the World Bank.[3] Anxious to show that it could articulate a distinctive vision of development yet also engage constructively with economists (the dominant disciplinary voice within the Bank), the department – in partnership with social scientists in other parts of the organization – found that the concept of social capital, indeed its very words, had the potential to speak to these concerns. A group of us working on social capital issues across different parts of the Bank – social development, poverty reduction, and development research – soon found that we had attained, for better or worse, a reasonably high profile in the global social capital debates, especially as they pertained to development issues: it was clear that we had the resources, capacity and opportunity to lead on the global measurement issue, and that others fully expected us to do so. Internally, the idea had progressed to become part of the discourse of the Bank's highest profile document, the annual World Development Report (World Bank, 2000), yet it still faced attendant pressures to verify its salience in terms that high modern bureaucracies (Scott, 1998) require – that is, to be able to empirically substantiate claims that 'social capital' is causally linked to outcomes the development business cares about (education, health, incomes, poverty reduction, etc.) and that the Bank (and its counterparts in national governments) presided over policy instruments that could plausibly influence social capital. Various staff members at the Bank had already begun to contribute to such discussions in these terms (e.g., Narayan and Pritchett, 1999), but the securing of a large trust fund[4] ramped up these pressures and expectations considerably.

In conjunction with parallel initiatives in OECD countries to find broadly comparable measures of social capital (OECD, 2002),[5] the possibility of both harnessing this broader group of expertise, and learning from the first round of individual efforts to assess social capital in developing countries, provided a fertile setting into which to craft a document outlining the collective wisdom on social capital measurement. Far from being the 'final word' on the subject of measurement, the approaches we explored are more of a 'second word' – that is, an attempt to integrate and build upon methods used by a first generation of social capital researchers working on various issues in developing countries. It

quickly became apparent that doing justice to these earlier efforts, and to the larger body of social capital theory more generally, would require preparing two companion documents, one on the quantitative and another on the qualitative aspects of social capital. As the notion of 'second word' implies, these documents aspired primarily to incorporate the lessons from a disparate first round of field research, and to serve as a clearinghouse of questions and topics for researchers just beginning their foray into social capital assessment – in particular, helping those otherwise unable to access the latest journal articles (such as those in developing countries) and those not wanting to start from scratch. Not surprisingly perhaps, these efforts were greatly appreciated in some quarters and scoffed at in others, but such is the vexed nature of the concept, the issues to which it is being applied, and the contention surrounding the organization presiding over it.

The material presented here provides a summary of the contents of the two source documents prepared by the World Bank to assess social capital in developing countries (Grootaert et al., 2004; Dudwick et al., 2006),[6] and an attempt to integrate their key components. Since one core methodological consideration to take into account in each measurement enterprise is the context within which measurement tools will be applied, an attempt is also made to show how these tools can be adapted for different contexts. Some aspects of the questions and thematic issues may also be useful in high income countries (indeed, we know they have been so used), but the questions presume that respondents are primarily poor villagers or slum dwellers who are engaged in occupations and live in communities most likely to be associated with low-income countries. We of course welcome efforts to revise and refine these tools as the 'third word' on social capital measurement emerges in due course.

INTRODUCTION

Since the emergence of 'development' as a formal field of scholarly inquiry and policy activity in the mid-1940s, the perceived importance of the social dimensions – local organizations, culture, identities, networks, class relations, exclusion – have oscillated between three poles: being regarded as part of the problem, to being seen as epiphenomenal or irrelevant, to being seen as part of the solution (Moore, 1997; Woolcock and Narayan, 2000). In the early- to mid-1990s, in the wake of the ambivalence accompanying the post-socialist transitions, the 'social dimension as solution' pole had a period during which it could assert its veracity. Through the high-profile work of Robert Putnam (1993) on the social foundations of institutional change, and the overt championing of social development issues by the World Bank's new president, James Wolfensohn, the concept of social capital became the discursive fulcrum for a lively debate about social issues and their role in shaping development outcomes. The early twin challenges were to forge a coherent theory of the relationship(s) between social capital and economic development (Woolcock, 1998) and to construct purpose-built empirical measures to assess the various hypotheses about this relationship that were emerging.

Though various definitions of social capital were put forward, most coalesced around assertions that social capital contributed to economic, social, and political development by enabling information-sharing, mitigating opportunistic behavior, and facilitating collective decision-making (Woolcock and Narayan, 2000). Empirically, the initial wave of studies seemed to show that residents of communities with cohesive internal bonds, extensive connections to broad demographic and professional networks, and cooperative links to people in positions of power (e.g., police, politicians) – in short, those communities endowed with abundant stocks of bonding, bridging and linking social capital – were more likely to be 'housed, healthy, hired and happy' (Woolcock, 2001: 12). Of course, the presence or absence of these ties needed to be located within their larger political and institutional context, but in fields ranging from public health and business management to urban studies and economic development, it was increasingly hard to refute the fact that social factors played a large independent role in shaping outcomes of broad public concern.

For researchers seeking to refine and consolidate the renewed public interest in the social dimensions of policy issues afforded by 'social capital', especially as they pertained to development, the most tractable strategic step seemed to be to upgrade the quality of the evidence base. For those within the World Bank, now in rare possession of both a high-profile concept and champion, the next step was to demonstrate empirically that 'social capital' mattered for mainstream development concerns.

It quickly became apparent, however, that both the letter and spirit of social capital theory[7] did not readily lend itself to an obvious single metric; various proxy indices could be (and were) constructed, but in the early stages these were inevitably a creative re-packaging of whatever secondary data happened to be available.[8] Moreover, a key element of social capital theory was its emphasis on the importance of local context for shaping economic outcomes, suggesting strongly that an important contribution could be made by incorporating qualitative research methods. Therein lay the motive and opportunity to developing both more issue-specific quantitative instruments and more context-specific strategies for eliciting the idiosyncratic features of those contexts.

Other aspects of the emergent theory of social capital also made measurement problematic. One of the earliest critiques leveled against social capital theory, for example, was its seemingly exclusive focus on the 'positive' outcomes associated with participation, with having access to diverse social networks, and living in communities with strong norms of reciprocity and cooperation. Such critiques properly pointed out that less desirable social outcomes – teen pregnancy, dropping out of school, joining gangs, vigilante justice – could also be a product of residing in places with strong social bonds. One resolution of this argument was to note that other forms of 'capital', such as education ('human capital'), could also be used for constructive (curing cancer) and destructive (building bombs) purposes, and that, as such, the purposes to which a resource could be deployed did not, in and of itself, make it any less of a resource. For measurement purposes, however, the response to this concern was more prosaic: to document the many and varied ways in which different types and combinations of social resources were associated with a range of development outcomes. To this end, the first step was to construct a set of instruments capable of discerning such types and combinations.

Although theoretical and conceptual debates properly continue to play out (even if they are unlikely to ever reach a clean resolution),[9] these have occurred alongside efforts to enhance the quality and scale of empirical data available to assess the claims (and counterclaims) made regarding the efficacy of social capital, especially in the field of international development. The range of data sources now spans the full gamut of social science, from national household surveys, historical records, and field experiments to case studies, key informant interviews, and ethnographic investigations; all have been deployed in an effort to better understand the nature and extent of social relations in particular communities, its trajectories over time, and its consequences for human welfare.

Most research conducted on social capital in developing (and, for that matter, developed) countries, however, has been conducted using a single methodological instrument (e.g., surveys or participant observation). With the notable exception of Anirudh Krishna (2002, 2007), researchers have worked predominantly with either quantitative or qualitative methods, a consequence being that opportunities for fruitful exchange between the approaches have been lost. Moreover, the actual content of the tools used to collect data on social capital – as opposed to the final results obtained from them – have rarely been disclosed or made available to other researchers to draw upon. Seeking to correct this gap, this chapter provides an integrated summary of the development of two instruments (or 'toolkits'), one qualitative and the other quantitative, that have been field-tested by various groups of researchers inside and outside the World Bank.

The ultimate goal is to work iteratively toward approaches to measurement that are increasingly more refined, valid, reliable and useful. Moreover, because the salience and manifestations of social capital are so context dependent, researchers working with the materials outlined here are strongly advised to undertake the hard work of judiciously adapting the various component elements to suit the questions and situation at hand; as such, these tools are inherently and perpetually a 'work in progress'. Using the qualitative and quantitative components together is one way to better understanding and accommodating the idiosyncrasies of particular contexts while iteratively refining the components themselves.

In the sections that follow, we frame the measurement issues around six dimensions of social capital: (1) groups and networks; (2) trust and solidarity; (3) collective action and cooperation; (4) social cohesion and inclusion; (5) information and communication; and (6) empowerment and political action. (The structure and rationale for each dimension are provided below.) We present first the qualitative approaches to assessing these six dimensions, and then the quantitative, though ideally both should be incorporated as necessary, whether sequentially or in parallel, given the type of research question being considered. In practice, however, the distinctive skill sets associated with each approach, plus limited time and resources, mean that only one approach to measurement tends to be adopted for a specific study. This practice is especially unfortunate in the rigorous measurement of concepts relevant to development studies, since the issues under investigation are typically complex and rarely map neatly or obviously onto a single discipline or methodology. Choices about how to operationalize a concept have consequences, and as such we have tried to be as explicit as possible regarding how and why we operationalized social capital across our six dimensions in the way we did.

In order to adequately understand development issues and establish a firm basis on which to draw project and policy recommendations, data that offers both context-specific 'depth' (usually obtained via qualitative methods) and potentially generalizable 'breadth' (usually obtained via quantitative methods) is required (Bamberger, 2000; Rao and Woolcock, 2003). 'Social capital' is one such complex issue that benefits from the coherent integration of qualitative and quantitative

approaches to operationalization. Researchers in the field are thus encouraged to adopt the combination of qualitative and quantitative methods that best correspond to the specific nature of the issues under investigation. There are numerous ways to go about this; one example might be to conduct qualitative focus group discussions to feed into the design and/or modification of a quantitative survey (Jha et al., 2007).[10] Similarly, working with community groups later in the process to map local assets such as public meeting places may help to triangulate and interpret some survey findings. In-depth data provides a context within which to analyze and interpret the data generated by measurement instruments. Ideally an iterative process including both qualitative and quantitative methods would be used, but when this is not feasible some infrequent, low-cost use of mixed methods can still add significant value to a measurement enterprise. Given the context- and resource-specific nature of designing a mixed methods approach to measurement, it is difficult, and probably unrealistic, to prescribe such sequencing options in this paper but other more general references exist to help in the design and implementation phases (e.g., Tashakkori and Teddlie, 1998; Rao and Woolcock, 2003).

MEASURING SOCIAL CAPITAL ACROSS SIX DIMENSIONS

Given the diverse views in the literature about the key features (even the ontological status) of 'social capital', we are only too aware of the equally contentious views regarding whether and how social capital can be measured (and the additional concerns raised by having any such ventures endorsed by the World Bank). Our view is that these differences about how best to conceptualize and measure social capital are best resolved through practice rather than isolated or abstract theoretical debate, and through making increasingly more informed choices about which approaches to use in a given context on the basis of the best information and resources available. The approach we have taken to organizing the vast empirical literature is to conceptualize social capital as a household or community-level (i.e., 'micro') variable with six non-exclusive, overlapping dimensions, as opposed to something that is a feature of, say, an entire nation (such as inequality or ethnic diversity).[11] This choice of a 'micro' unit of analysis is consistent, we believe, with the general consensus among social capital researchers and permits dialogue with a vast array of established and emerging datasets on social indicators.

Before proceeding to outline the component elements of the six dimensions in more detail, it is worth discussing the process by which they were arrived at. The task of assembling both quantitative and qualitative instruments for measuring social capital began in 2000, as it became clear that the otherwise admirable profusion of individual instruments attempting to assess social capital lacked coherence and were inadequately feeding into one another. Each team was reinventing its own wheel, with all the attendant heterogeneity one might expect regarding quality and scope. Lest this situation feed a growing scepticism in certain quarters regarding the scholarly rigor of social capital research, the World Bank team decided to convene a gathering of leading academic and policy researchers and survey professionals (e.g., senior members of government statistical agencies) to see if we could identify a battery of questions distilled from the existing surveys (and our individual experience) that met our collective standards of usefulness,

reliability and validity. Over two days, this advisory group of 15 to 20 senior researchers[12] sifted through the available questions, and having selected the 'best' ones sought to then arrange these into clusters. The number and names of the six cluster titles emerged inductively, as the group sought to identify the most coherent way in which to present the fruits of its labors, and to render those fruits accessible to potential users. All attendees were in agreement that the final product should emphasize its inherently 'interim' nature, and encourage subsequent research efforts to build on and extend its contents.

The discussions surrounding the production of the quantitative survey instrument led inexorably to a proposal that it should ideally be complemented by a similar qualitative instrument. Qualitative research on social capital, by its very nature, adheres to less uniform protocols, yields fewer methodological source documents and less readily lends itself to successive iterations of 'best practices' compared to its quantitative counterpart; even so, it was felt that preparation of a qualitative research guide was important to do justice to the full implications and potential of social capital theory. Building on the six dimensions of the quantitative survey tool, a team of experienced qualitative researchers within the World Bank compiled a qualitative research instrument (see Dudwick et al., 2006); as with all such products, it was peer reviewed by a team of internal and external researchers before its final publication.

The following passages bring together the key elements of the quantitative and qualitative instruments for assessing social capital across six dimensions. We provide here a brief summary of what each dimension covers, and then proceed to explore different approaches to assessing it, first qualitatively and then quantitatively. Schematically, the dimensions reflect the group membership characteristics and subjective perceptions of trust and norms that are most commonly associated with social capital (dimensions 1 and 2), the main ways in which social capital operates (dimensions 3 and 4), and the major areas of application or outcomes (dimensions 5 and 6). It bears repeating that these instruments are works-in-progress, and should be used as such in any attempt to formally apply them in actual empirical research. These six dimensions were the product of the collective wisdom of our original advisory group, and the subsequent accumulation of evidence and 'best practices' from field research efforts should modify the content and sequencing of these dimensions accordingly.

USING QUALITATIVE METHODS TO CONTEXTUALIZE THE MEASUREMENT OF SOCIAL CAPITAL

The case for qualitative research rests on the unique and important insights that it brings in its own right and, secondarily, on its capacity to address the weaknesses of quantitative approaches. Indeed, the respective strengths and weaknesses of qualitative and quantitative approaches to measurement are largely complementary – that is, the weaknesses of one approach can be compensated for by the strengths of the other. Qualitative tools can be used to explore issues of process and causality that cannot be inferred from quantitative measurement instruments alone. Qualitative methods also can inform the modification and validation of measurement, for instance by allowing unanticipated responses and issues to arise.

The tools summarized below are most closely associated with the qualitative tradition. While they can be used in their own right, ideally these tools should be part of a broader, integrated methodological strategy for researching social capital. The text that follows is not intended to provide 'how-to' guidance on the use of these tools. Rather, it seeks to give the reader a broad understanding of which qualitative tools are relevant to different aspects of refining an approach to the operationalization of social capital. Additional resources are cited that offer detailed, practical instructions on how to apply these tools. Use of these approaches can augment and support the generation, validation, and application of context appropriate measurement tools.

The first category of qualitative methods can be referred to as participatory approaches (Mikkelsen, 1995; Narayan, 1995; Robb, 2002). Introduced to scholars and practitioners largely through the work of Robert Chambers (see Chambers, 1997 and Kumar and Chambers, 2002), participatory techniques – such as Rapid Rural Appraisal (RRA) and Participatory Poverty Assessments (PPA) – help development agencies learn about local poverty and project impacts in cost-effective ways.

The Rapid Rural Appraisal is especially useful with illiterate respondents (not all of whom are poor), allowing researchers to learn about their lives using simple techniques such as wealth rankings, oral histories, role playing, games, small group discussions, transect walks (see following section), and village map drawings. These techniques permit respondents who are not trained in quantitative reasoning, or who have little education, to provide meaningful graphical representations of their lives in a manner that gives outside researchers a quick snapshot of certain aspects of their living conditions.

RRA can be said to involve *instrumental* participation through novel techniques that enable researchers to better understand their subjects. A related approach is to use *transformative* participation techniques, such as Participatory Rural Appraisal (PRA), the goal of which is to facilitate a dialogue (rather than extract information) that assists the poor and others to learn about themselves and thereby gain new insights that lead to social change ('empowerment').[13] In PRA exercises, a skilled facilitator helps communities generate tangible visual diagrams of the processes that lead to deprivation or illness, strategies that are used in times of crisis, and fluctuation of resource availability and prices across different seasons. Eliciting information in this format helps the poor to conceive of potentially more effective ways to respond to the economic, political, and social challenges in their lives in ways that are not obvious *ex ante*. The process and findings provide a potentially enduring foundation for community groups to discuss action and change beyond the scope of a specific research agenda.

Participatory methods are conducted in groups. It is essential, therefore, that participants include representatives from each of the major subgroups in a community. The idea is that if a group reaches consensus on a particular issue after some discussion, this consensus will then be representative of views in a given community, be it a village or slum neighborhood, because outlying views would have been set aside in the process of debate. For this technique to work, the discussion must be extremely well moderated. The moderator must be sufficiently dynamic while also deftly able to steer the discussion in a meaningful direction, to navigate his or her way around potential conflicts and, in the end, establish consensus. The moderator's role is thus key to ensuring that high-quality data is gathered from a group discussion – an inadequate or inexperienced moderator can affect the quality of the data in a manner that is much more acute than an equivalently inadequate interviewer working with a structured quantitative questionnaire.

Even with a skilled facilitator, pre-existing relationships between local parties can either enable or undermine productive discussions.

Another important qualitative tool is the key-informant interview, that is, an interview with someone who is a formal or informal community leader or who has a particular perspective relevant to the study, such as women or members of an ethnic minority. Such interviews may be recorded using notes or tape recorder. The researcher may find that it takes some time to establish rapport with the interviewee; some local greeting rituals may also need to be followed. Though some respondents may be intimated by recording technologies, some may find it cathartic to tell their story to someone from outside the community. Expectations and issues such as anonymity must be clearly addressed at the start. Life histories and open-ended personal interviews are additional tools that have long been used in qualitative research. Indeed, it can be illuminating to interview the same people over time, just as it is useful to repeat household surveys.

The qualitative investigator can also engage in varying degrees of 'participant observation' as an actual member (e.g., a biography of growing up in a slum), a perceived actual member (e.g., a spy or a police informant in a drug cartel), an invited long-term guest (e.g., an anthropologist), or a more distant and detached short-term observer of a specific community. A final qualitative approach is textual analysis. Historians, archeologists, linguists, and scholars in cultural studies use such techniques to analyze various forms of media, ranging from archived legal documents, newspapers, artifacts, and government records to contemporary photographs, films, music, websites, and television reports. This approach provides interesting insights into local culture and politics untainted by the presence of a researcher.

APPLYING QUALITATIVE AND QUANTITATIVE TOOLS TO OPERATIONALIZING THE SIX DIMENSIONS OF SOCIAL CAPITAL

Each of the qualitative tools described in the previous section can be used to research the effects of social capital in poor and non-poor communities alike. The subsections that follow provide analytical frameworks – that is, key questions for focus group discussions and interviews, as well as potentially useful group activities – for each of the six dimensions of social capital outlined in the introduction to this chapter. Because the six dimensions overlap in practice, different iterations of some questions appear under more than one dimension. By the same token, an inquiry regarding one dimension may shed light on the other dimensions. Naturally, not all questions and issues included in the analytical frameworks that follow will be appropriate in every case. The entries below are therefore not intended as direct questions to respondents, but to better focus the research team on relevant concerns. Effective (and ethical) data collection respects the valuable time of respondents, simplifies the analysis phase, and forces additional rigor on the conceptual design of research. It may also save money.

These six dimensions can also be assessed quantitatively, using some form of household survey.[14] The value of quantitative data is that it can be readily aggregated, allowing for broad generalizations to be drawn over time and space about large numbers of people; as such, they are especially useful for determining the impact of projects and policies. In certain respects, survey data can also be seen as more 'objective', since the household survey format ensures

that there is less scope for pressure from other community members to influence how questions are answered.

Examples of questions from each of the six dimensions are included below. Together, these questions constitute the 'core' list of 27 questions identified by the team members and advisory group for the quantitative component of the larger project. A full list of 95 questions is provided in the Social Capital Integrated Questionnaire (SC-IQ) (see Grootaert et al., 2004). The 27 'core' questions represent our best collective effort to reduce the list, if required, to its most essential components. This list of 27 questions was determined at the original meeting of the advisory group for the quantitative instrument: it was the unanimous view of the group that one of its tasks should be to discipline itself to prioritize the questions according to their usefulness and the extent to which they had withstood critical scrutiny in different contexts over an extended time period. We were very conscious that not all research teams would have the time, resources, or inclination to ask the full battery of 95 questions – on the quantitative instrument, for example, we felt that the most likely users of our instrument would be those wanting to accommodate a new but small module on social capital questions, in which case we wanted to be able to respond to this particular need with a list of questions we believed (on the basis of our collective experience) were best suited to that purpose, even as we also provided a longer list for those needing to canvass a broader array of issues.

In both the qualitative and quantitative instruments, the assessment of social capital is framed around six dimensions, as follows.

Dimension 1 – Groups and Networks: The questions here consider the nature and extent of a household member's participation in various types of social organizations, community activities and informal networks, and the range of contributions that one gives and receives from them. It also considers the diversity of a given group's membership, how its leadership is selected, and how one's involvement has changed over time.

Dimension 2 – Trust and Solidarity: In addition to the canonical trust question asked in a remarkable number of cross-national surveys over many years, this category seeks to procure data on trust toward neighbors, key service providers, and strangers, and how these perceptions have changed over time.

Dimension 3 – Collective Action and Cooperation: This category explores whether and how household members have worked with others in their community on joint projects and/or in response to a crisis. It also considers the consequences of violating community expectations regarding participation.

Dimension 4 – Information and Communication: This category of questions explores the ways and means by which poor households receive information regarding market conditions and public services, and the extent of their access to communications infrastructure.

Dimension 5 – Social Cohesion and Inclusion: 'Communities' are not single entities, but rather are characterized by various forms of division and difference that can lead to conflict. Questions in this category seek to identify the nature and extent of these differences, the mechanisms by which they are managed, and which groups are excluded from key public services. Questions pertaining to every-day forms of social interaction are also considered.

Dimension 6 – Empowerment and Political Action:Individuals are 'empowered' to the extent they have a measure of control over institutions and processes directly affecting their well-being (World Bank, 2002). The questions in this section explore household members' sense of happiness, personal efficacy, and capacity to influence both local events and broader political outcomes.

Dimension 1: groups and networks

The first dimension we sought to opertional-ize was groups and networks. Understanding the groups and networks that enable people to access resources and collaborate to achieve shared goals is an important part of the concept of social capital. Informal networks are manifested in spontaneous and unregulated exchanges of information and resources within communities, as well as efforts at cooperation, coordination, and mutual assistance that help maximize the utilization of available resources. Informal networks can be connected through horizontal and vertical relationships and are shaped by a variety of environmental factors, including the market, kinship, and friendship.

Another kind of network consists of associations, in which members are linked horizontally. Such networks often have clearly delineated structures, roles, and rules that govern how group members cooperate to achieve common goals. These networks also have the potential to nurture self-help, mutual help, solidarity, and cooperative efforts in a community. 'Linking' (vertical) social capital, on the other hand, includes relations and interactions between a community and its leaders and extends to wider relations between the village, the government, and the marketplace.

The questions listed below are intended to get at the nature and extent of peoples' participation in various types of social organizations and networks (formal and informal), and the range of transactions that take place within these networks.

The questions also consider the diversity of a given group's membership and how its leadership is selected.

- Focus on several formal and informal groups and summarize their explicit and implicit functions. How often are the groups activated? Are informal groups based on social occasions (e.g., weddings, births, or deaths)? What other triggers bring members of a group together?
- What is exchanged (e.g., goods, services, favors, information, moral support, etc.) in community groups or networks?
- What are the most important aims of the exchange (e.g., to meet basic needs, increase income, meet basic social obligations, maintain or expand potentially useful relationships, or some combination thereof)?
- What characteristics are most valued among network members (e.g., trustworthiness, reciprocity, cooperation, honesty, community respect, etc.)?
- Who are the most socially or economically isolated people in the community? How does this isolation correlate with the kind or extent of networks to which these people belong?
- Who plays a leadership or mobilizing role in the groups or networks? How are they selected?

Social capital, in its best forms, helps the dissemination of information, reduces opportunistic behavior, and facilitates collective decision-making. The effectiveness with which social capital, in the form of the associations and networks, fulfills this role depends upon many aspects of these groups, reflecting their structure, their membership, and the way they function. The SC-IQ makes it possible to describe organizations along three key dimensions – each relevant to measuring the social more generally – namely (1) the density of membership, (2) the diversity of membership, and (3) network characteristics.

(1) The level of measurement is a key consideration when generating or modifying a survey or scale. At the level of households, the *density of membership* is measured by the average number of memberships of each household in existing organizations (this can be normalized by household size). This basic indicator can be cross-tabulated by location (region, province, urban/rural) or socio-economic characteristics of the household (income group, age and gender of the head of household, religion, ethnic group) to capture the distribution of memberships. The indicator can also be broken down by type of organization. A functional classification focuses on the prime objective of the association (education, health, credit, etc.). Another useful classification refers to the scope of the group: whether groups operate only in the community, are affiliated with other groups (inside or outside the community), or are part of a federated structure. Groups with linkages often have better access to resources, especially from outside the community, such as from government or NGOs. Using information on memberships, organizations can also be classified as to whether they represent primarily bonding, bridging, or linking social capital (World Bank, 2000).

(2) The SC-IQ data make it possible to assess the internal *diversity of membership* according to nine criteria: kinship, religion, gender, age, ethnicity/linguistic group, occupation, education, political affiliation, and income level. Diversity information can be used separately or combined in an index. For example, a 'diversity score' can be calculated for each organization, ranging from 0 to 9. These scores can be averaged over all or weighted to emphasize the most important organizations to which households belong. It is not immediately obvious whether a high degree of internal diversity is a positive or negative factor from the point of view of social capital. One could argue, on the one hand, that an internally homogeneous association would make it easier for members to trust each other, to share information, and to reach decisions. On the other hand, these members may also have similar

information so that less would be gained from exchanging information. Furthermore, the coexistence of a series of associations that are each internally homogeneous but along different criteria could render the decision-making process at the community level more difficult. Analysis in several countries has suggested that internally diverse associations yield higher levels of benefits than others, although homogeneous associations make it easier to bring about collective action (Grootaert, 1999, 2001). In any event, measuring internal diversity within associations – that is, identifying the nature and extent of social divisions within groups – is a fruitful basis on which to discern whether and how collective decisions are reached.

(3) The SC-IQ seeks to operationalize the nature and extent of networks along a number of dimensions: the size of the network, its internal diversity, and the extent to which it would provide assistance in case of need. Because 'network' is a difficult concept to define concretely in the context of a household survey, a pragmatic approach has been taken: a network is seen as a circle of 'close friends' – that is, people one feels at ease with, can talk to about private matters, or call upon for help. The size of the network then is captured by the number of such close friends. The usefulness of the network is assessed by asking the respondents whether they could turn to the network in a series of hypothetical emergency situations. The answers to these questions can be aggregated to yield a 'mutual support score' for the network. Diversity is assessed in a simpler way than was the case for associations, by focusing only on whether the network consists of people with different economic status. This is a key feature to determine the network's ability to provide resources to the respondent in case of need, and thus the network's usefulness in the management of risk.

Sample survey questions

1   I would like to ask you about the groups or organizations, networks, and associations to which you (or any member of your household) belong. These could be formally organized groups or just groups of people who get together regularly to do an activity or talk about things. Of how many such groups are you or any one in your household a member?

2   Of all these groups to which you or members of your household belong, which one is the most important to your household?

3   Thinking about the members of this group, are most of them of the same....
    A   Religion
    B   Gender
    C   Ethnic or linguistic background/race/caste/tribe

4   Do members mostly have the same...
    A   Occupation
    B   Educational background or level

5   How frequently does this group work with or interact with groups outside the village/neighborhood?
    Never   Rarely   Occasionally   Frequently

6   About how many close friends do you have these days? These are people you feel at ease with, can talk to about private matters, or call on for help.

7   If you suddenly needed to borrow a small amount of money [RURAL: enough to pay for expenses for your household for one week; URBAN: equal to about one week's wages], are there people beyond your immediate household and close relatives to whom you could turn and who would be willing and able to provide this money?
    Definitely   Probably   Unsure   Probably not
    Definitely not

Dimension 2: trust and solidarity

The second dimension of social capital we sought to operationlize was trust and solidarity. This dimension of social capital refers to the extent to which people feel they can rely on relatives, neighbors, colleagues, acquaintances, key service providers, and even strangers, either to assist them or (at least) do them no harm.

Adequately defining 'trust' in a given social context is a prerequisite for understanding the complexities of human relationships. Sometimes trust is a choice; in other cases, it reflects a necessary dependency based on established contacts or familiar networks. Distinguishing between these two ends of the continuum is important for understanding the range of people's social relationships and the ability of these relationships to endure difficult or rapidly changing circumstances.

- How would you define trust? What are some examples?
- How long have people in a given neighborhood or community lived together? How well do they know one another?
- Have new groups recently entered the community (e.g., refugees or economic migrants)?
- To what institutions (formal or informal) do people turn when they have individual or family problems?
- On whom do people rely for different kinds of assistance (e.g., goods, labor, cash, finding employment, entering university, etc.)?
- How is trust distributed in the community (e.g., primarily within extended families or clans or through specific networks and/or localities)?
- Do patterns of mistrust and suspicion exist between households or among groups?

Measurement of the more 'cognitive' aspects of social capital in the SC-IQ is organized around the themes of trust and solidarity. Trust is an abstract concept that is difficult to measure in the context of a household questionnaire, in part because it may mean different things to different people. The SC-IQ approach therefore focuses on operationalizing both generalized trust (the extent to which one trusts people overall) and on the extent of trust in specific types of people. Trust is also viewed in the context of specific transactions, such as lending and borrowing. Because of the difficulties in measuring trust, the questions in this section have a degree of redundancy

to them. In part, this serves the purpose of cross-validating the responses to different questions. It is possible to tabulate the answers to each trust question against the usual spatial or socio-economic character-istics, but because of the complexity of the concept of trust, it is recommended to use factor analysis or principal component analysis to identify any underlying common factors across the different questions. This approach has been successfully used in empirical work. For example, a study on trust in Uganda found that from a series of questions on trust, three factors emerged which identified three different dimensions of trust: trust in agencies, trust in members of one's immediate environment, and trust in the business community (Narayan and Cassidy, 2001).

Sample survey questions

8 Generally speaking, would you say that most people can be trusted or that you can't be too careful in dealing with people?
   People can be trusted   You can't be too careful

9 In general, do you agree or disagree with the following statements?
   A Most people in this village/neighborhood are willing to help if you need it.
   B In this village/neighborhood, one has to be alert or someone is likely to take advantage of you.
   Agree strongly   Agree somewhat   Neither agree nor disagree
   Disagree somewhat   Disagree strongly

10 How much do you trust...
    A Local government officials?
    B Central government officials?
    To a very great extent To a great extent Neither great nor small extent To a small extent To a very small extent

11 If a community project does not directly benefit you but has benefits for many others in the village/neighborhood, would you contribute time or money to the project?
    Will not contribute time   Will not contribute money
    Will contribute time   Will contribute money

Dimension 3: collective action and cooperation

The third dimension of social capital we sought to operationlize is collective action and cooperation. Collective action and cooperation are closely related to the dimension of trust and solidarity; however, the former dimension explores in greater depth whether and how people work with others in their community on joint projects and/or in response to a problem or crisis. It also considers the consequences of violating community expectations regarding participation norms. To understand this dimension, interviews with formal and informal community leaders or leaders of NGOs, associations, unions, or other groups (key-respondent interviews) can prove very useful for triangulating data collected in focus group discussions.

- Describe recent examples of collective action that have taken place in the community (or a segment of the community). What was the course and outcome of these activities?
- Who initiated the activities? How were people mobilized?
- Do social, cultural, or legal constraints limit the participation of specific groups (e.g., women, young people, poor people, minorities, etc.)?
- Are some groups, neighborhoods, and/or households more likely than others to work together, and if so, why?
- Are some groups, neighborhoods, and/or households more likely to exclude themselves or be excluded from collective activity, and if so, why?
- What kinds of constraints limit peoples' ability or willingness to work together (e.g., lack of time, lack of trust or confidence in outcomes, suspicion toward the mobilizers, etc.)?
- What are the social sanctions for violating expected norms of collective action in the community?

Collective action is the third basic type of proxy indicator for measuring social capital. The usefulness of this indicator stems from the fact that in the vast majority of settings, collective action is possible only if a significant amount of social capital is available in the community. The major exception occurs in totalitarian societies where the government can force people to work together on infrastructure projects or other types of common activities. Thus, the validity of the collective action indicator as a measure of social capital needs to be evaluated against the political context of a society. Collective action is an important aspect of community life in many countries, although the purposes of the action may differ widely. In some countries, collective action consists primarily of community-organized activities for building and maintaining infrastructure and for providing related public services. In other countries, collective action is more politically oriented and used primarily to lobby elected officials to provide more services to the community. As with other aspects of social capital, the context of measurement shapes the meaning of the resultant data.

The collective action section of the SC-IQ aims to collect information on: the extent of collective action, the type of the activities undertaken collectively, and an overall assessment of the extent of willingness to cooperate and participate in collective action. Each of these variables can be cross-tabulated against the usual set of spatial and socio-economic variables to obtain a pattern of the incidence of collective action. More interestingly perhaps is the cross-tabulation of collective action variables against the other indicators of social capital discussed previously. This would reveal whether communities with a high density of organizations and/or high levels of trust also display higher levels of collective action. Any correlations revealed by such tabulations might fruitfully be the subject of further multivariate analysis.

12 In the past 12 months did you or any one in your household participate in any communal activities, in which people came together to do some work for the benefit of the community? Yes No (skip to question 14)

13 How many times in the past 12 months?

14 If there was a water supply problem in this community, how likely is it that people will cooperate to try to solve the problem? Very likely Somewhat likely Neither likely nor unlikely Somewhat unlikely Very unlikely

Dimension 4: information and communication

The fourth dimension of social capital we sought to operationlize is information and communication. Increasing access to information is frequently recognized as a central mechanism for helping poor communities strengthen their voice in matters that affect their well-being (World Bank, 2002). The questions below are designed with the intention of exploring the ways and means by which households receive and share information regarding such issues as the community at large, market conditions, and public services, as well as the extent of their access to communications infrastructure. The following questions can help with measuring this aspect of social capital:

- Inventory the existing communication sources, their actual and perceived reliability, veracity, availability, and the extent to which these sources are used in practice.
- What are the preferred local sources and channels of information?
- What informal sources of information exist in the community? Which members of the community are included or excluded from such sources?
- What information is available through different networks? To different households and/or groups? (i.e., is there differential distribution within the community?)
- What information is not available to different households and/or groups (i.e., what are the limits of differential distribution within the community)?

Module 4 of the SC-IQ has a simple structure: it is a list of sources of information and means of communication. Analysis of this information is equally straightforward. Each item can be cross-tabulated separately against spatial and socio-economic variables to identify whether certain areas or groups have better or worse access to information and communication. The identified pattern can be compared against the pattern of other social capital variables established on the basis of the previous modules. If areas of low social capital are found to have poor access to information and communication, a further inquiry into possible causality might be warranted.

The information from module 4 can also be aggregated, either at the household level or at the community level, to obtain a single score for information and communication access. Factor analysis or principal component analysis are suitable techniques to that effect. Additional questions enable an assessment of the relative importance of groups and networks as sources for important information compared to 'impersonal' sources such as newspapers or television. Information on government activities and markets is directly relevant for the generation of income and/or for non-monetary aspects of well-being, and can therefore be included as an explanatory variable in multivariate analysis of household well-being.

Sample survey questions

15 In the past month, how many times have you made or received a phone call?

16 What are your three main sources of information about what the government is doing (such as agricultural extension, workfare, family planning, etc.)? Relatives, friends and neighbors Community bulletin board Local market Community or

local newspaper National newspaper Radio Television Groups or associations Business or work associates Political associates Community leader An agent of the government NGOs Internet

Dimension 5: social cohesion and inclusion

The fifth dimension of social capital we sought to operationalize is social cohesion and inclusion. Social cohesion and inclusion are closely related to the previous four dimensions of social capital, but focus more specifically on the tenacity of social bonds and their dual potential to include or exclude members of community. Cohesion and inclusion can be demonstrated through community events, such as weddings and funerals, or through activities that increase solidarity, strengthen social cohesion, improve communication, provide learning for coordinated activities, promote civic-mindedness and altruistic behavior, and develop a sense of collective consciousness. The following questions operationalize cohesion and inclusion:

- Are there recurring disagreements in networks and groups, or even demonstrated conflict?
- What community patterns of differentiation and exclusion exist with respect to opportunities, markets, information, and services?
- What prevents public services and expenditures from reaching the poorest and most vulnerable groups? Are the reasons related to ethnicity, gender, a political agenda, or geographic isolation?
- What are the patterns of inclusion and/or exclusion in political participation?
- How often do people from different social groups intermarry?
- What are the triggers for everyday conflict among members of a network and/or group (e.g., resource competition, serious social cleavages, socio-economic inequities)?
- What kinds of mediation have taken place to help the community resolve conflicts? Have these worked? Why? For how long?

Module 5 of the SC-IQ brings together three related topics: inclusion, sociability, and conflict and violence. The section on inclusion ranges from general perceptions of social unity and togetherness of the community to specific experiences with exclusion. The respondent is first asked whether there are any divisions in the community and, if so, what characteristics cause it. The level of analysis is often one of the most crucial issues in the measurement of social capital. Questions on exclusion from services at the level of the community are followed by more direct questions, such as whether the respondent has ever been the victim of exclusion. In this instance, the most policy-relevant information will come from the detailed cross-tabulation of the presence of exclusion by type of service against the characteristics deemed to be the grounds for exclusion. This tabulation will reveal whether exclusion exists across the board, due to characteristics such as gender or ethnicity, or if the reasons for exclusion vary by type of service or activity. Such information has a high diagnostic value in identifying sources of social stress in the community. To compare the incidence of exclusion across communities, an 'exclusion score' can be constructed by adding up the answers from several questions.

One of the positive manifestations of a high level of social capital in the community is the occurrence of frequent every-day social interactions. The frequency and nature of social interactions are effective indicators of the presence of social capital. This 'sociability' can take the form of meetings with people in public places, visits to other people's homes or visits from others into one's own home, and participation in community events such as sports or ceremonies. The section on sociability in module 5 covers each of these situations. In order to distinguish whether these daily social interactions are of the bonding or bridging variety, questions are asked whether the people with whom one meets are of the same or a different ethnic or linguistic group, economic status, social status, or religious group. The diversity of social interactions can usefully be compared to the diversity of the membership of associations (covered in module 1). Put together, these two items of information on diversity give a good picture of the internal divisiveness or cohesiveness of a community and whether bonding or bridging social capital predominates.

The presence of conflict in a community or in a larger area is often an indicator of the lack of trust or the lack of appropriate structural social capital to resolve conflicts, or both. The SC-IQ seeks to measure three important items of information on conflict and violence: the extent and trajectory of violence, the contribution made by internal divisiveness in the community, and the feelings of insecurity stemming from fear of crime and violence. To match perceptions with fact, certain questions in this module ask about the household's recent experience of crime. Because social capital has a spatial configuration, when seeking to measure it, it is useful to tabulate this information both at the household level and the community level. It is quite likely that perceptions of violence as well as experiences of it differ between rich and poor households, old and young people, etc. Likewise, different communities can have vastly different experiences with conflict and violence, even if they are geographically close. The comparison of communities will be made easier if the different questions on conflict and violence in module 5 are aggregated, either directly or by means of factor analysis.

Sample survey questions

17 There are often differences in characteristics between people living in the same village/neighborhood. For example, differences in wealth, income, social status, ethnic or linguistic background/race/caste/tribe, etc. There can also be differences in religious or political beliefs, or there can be differences due to age or sex. To what extent do any such differences characterize your village/neighborhood? Use a five point scale where 1 means to a very great extent and 5 means to a very small extent.

18 Do any of these differences cause problems?
Yes No (go to question 21)

19 Which two differences most often cause problems?
Differences: in education in landholding in wealth/material possessions in social status between men and women between younger and older generations between long-term and recent residents in political party affiliations in religious beliefs in ethnic or linguistic background/race/caste/tribe Other differences

20 Have these problems ever led to violence?
Yes No

21 How many times in the past month have you got together with people to have food or drinks, either in their home or in a public place?

22 [IF NOT ZERO] Were any of these people of different... ethnic or linguistic background/race/caste/tribe? Economic status? Social status? Religious groups?

23 In general, how safe from crime and violence do you feel when you are alone at home?
Very safe Moderately safe Neither safe nor unsafe Moderately unsafe Very unsafe

Dimension 6: empowerment and political action

The sixth dimension we sought to operationlize was empowerment and political action. Individuals are empowered to the extent that they have a measure of control over the institutions and processes that directly affect their well-being (World

Bank, 2002). The social capital dimension of empowerment and political action explores the sense of satisfaction, personal efficacy, and capacity of network and group members to influence both local events and broader political outcomes. Empowerment and political action can occur within a small neighborhood association or at broader local, regional, or national levels. Each level has its own importance and should be considered separately, as well as in conjunction with the others. This dimension also seeks to capture social cleavages, whether related to gender, ethnicity, religion, regionalism, or other factors. Key-informant interviews with political and labor leaders, together with representatives of the judicial system and media, are also important for exploring and operationalizing this dimension.

- How do customary, informal laws constrain or facilitate the ability of citizens to exert influence over public institutions?
- How do formal laws constrain or facilitate the ability of citizens to exert influence over public institutions?
- To what extent can members of a community hold public institutions and officials accountable for their actions?
- What kinds of formal and informal mechanisms are available to individuals and groups to demand accountability of local leaders and officials?
- Which groups or segments of the community have the greatest influence over public institutions?
- What is the source of influence of these groups (e.g., group size, ability to mobilize members or expand member base, connections to power elite, economic importance, etc.)?
- Which groups have the least influence over public institutions and why?

The final section of the SC-IQ attempts to measure phenomena that transcend, but include aspects of social capital. Empowerment refers to the expansion of assets and capabilities of people to participate in, negotiate with, influence, control, and hold accountable institutions that affect their lives (World Bank, 2002). Empowerment is brought about by a wide range of actions, such as making state institutions more responsive to poor people, removing social barriers, and building social opportunity (World Bank, 2000). Empowerment is thus a broader concept than social capital, and political action is only one of many activities that can be undertaken to increase empowerment.

In the context of the SC-IQ, empowerment is defined more narrowly as the ability to make decisions that affect everyday activities and may change the course of one's life. Respondents are asked to assess this ability directly. As discussed earlier, political action is one venue to practice and possibly increase this ability. Module 6 considers a number of concrete political activities such as filing petitions, attending public meetings, interacting with politicians, participating in demonstrations and campaigns, and voting in elections. The analysis of this information can follow a pattern similar to that recommended for the previous module. The data can be aggregated both at the level of the household and the level of the community. Different households, depending upon their demographic, economic, and social characteristics, will feel differently empowered and will participate in political action to differing degrees for the purpose of mapping and measuring. It is useful to compare this pattern of empowerment with the patterns of access to information, fear of violence, sociability, and other dimensions of social capital derived from other modules. By the same token, earlier analysis will already have provided a community score of social cohesiveness and inclusion, and this information can usefully be complemented with a community score of empowerment and political action.

Sample survey questions

24   In general, how happy do you consider yourself to be?
      Very happy Moderately happy Neither happy nor unhappy Moderately unhappy Very unhappy

25   Do you feel that you have the power to make important decisions that change the course of your life? Rate yourself on a 1 to 5 scale, where 1 means being totally unable to change your life, and 5 means having full control over your life.

26   In the past 12 months, how often have people in this village/neighborhood got together to jointly petition government officials or political leaders for something benefiting the community?
      Never Once A few times (<5) Many times (>5)

27   Lots of people find it difficult to get out and vote. Did you vote on the last state/national/presidential election?
      Yes No

CONCLUSION: INTEGRATING QUALITATIVE AND QUANTITATIVE APPROACHES TO MEASURING SOCIAL CAPITAL

Increasing evidence shows that social cohesion is critical for societies to prosper economically and for development to be sustainable. Social capital is not just the sum of the institutions which underpin a society; it is the glue that holds them together. Social capital is a multi-dimensional concept, and a difficult one to measure. Given that it is most frequently defined in terms of groups, networks, norms of reciprocity, cooperation, and trust, attempts to operationlize on social capital must be able to capture this multi-dimensionality. In order to develop measurement instruments with the validity and reliability to make use of social capital findings to improve development processes and outcomes, it is also necessary to attempt to measure the dynamic nature of interpersonal and group relations in the context in which it is being studied. As such, social capital readily lends itself to a mixed-methods research approach to measurement. Employing both qualitative and quantitative methods allows researchers with an interest in measuring social capital to uncover the links between different dimensions of social capital and poverty, as well as to construct a more comprehensive picture of the structures, perceptions, and processes of social capital in a given locality. Similar to so many development studies related phenomena, efforts to create rigorous measurement instruments for social capital that are contextually relevant can benefit from a range of methodological resources.

Even if quantitative and qualitative approaches are construed as existing along a continuum (Bamberger, 2000), rather than being wholly distinctive, the fact remains that most individual researchers are trained in and hired to perform primarily only one approach. The organizational imperatives of large development agencies also tend to give higher priority to measurement efforts reliant solely on quantitative approaches, which provide the 'de-contextualized' (though putatively 'more objective') measures that enable such agencies to 'see' complex problems and diverse contexts in ways that comport with their particular capacity to respond to them (Scott, 1998). Using and/or integrating both methods requires a deliberate choice and sustained commitment on the part of researchers to measure social capital; informing and facilitating such choices is one of the primary goals of this chapter (and the broader project from which it draws).

Many researchers have stressed the limitations of different approaches and/or called for more methodological pluralism in development research. Indeed, starting with the work of Epstein (1962), many researchers have made important contributions to development research by working across methodological lines (Tashakkori and Teddlie, 1998; Bamberger, 2000; Gacitua-Mario and Wodon, 2001). Ideally, researchers should endeavor to understand the strengths and weaknesses of each approach and discern practical strategies for combining them on a more regular basis when assessing social capital (Kanbur, 2003; Rao, 2002).[15] In this situation, as in others, measurement choices have consequences. It is important to note, however, that because qualitative research enables discussion on processes and, implicitly or explicitly, power relations, it carries the risk of aggravating local conflict (Barron et al., forthcoming). Well-intentioned researchers attempting to measure the social capital bear responsibility for that risk. In fact, methodological approaches can both unearth delicate relationship issues and raise local expectations; therefore careful planning, management, and follow-through are essential to *do no harm*. At a minimum, researchers should plan to disseminate their findings to local stakeholders at various stages of the exploration and ideally would consider how local follow up can be integrated into on-going government, civil, or private sector initiatives.

In summary, combining qualitative and quantitative approaches to the measurement of social capital offers practitioners several advantages. First, they gain a clearer, more nuanced understanding of the context of the communities and/or regions for which they design, monitor, and evaluate development interventions. Second, the two methods in combination can provide baseline socio-economic information that can improve the design of both research tools (e.g., a living standards survey or poverty assessment survey) and development projects. Third, quantitative and qualitative approaches to researching and operationalizing a concept together yield better impact and evaluation

data, enabling teams to understand the full impact of projects on social capital (which can be positive, negative, or both), and conversely, whether areas with certain types and levels of social capital experience more successful project implementation than areas with other types and levels of social capital (Labonne and Chase, 2008). Finally, when analyzed and disseminated locally, integrated quantitative and qualitative approaches to measurement can be sources of empowerment, enabling better understanding of the present and potentially new visions of the future. In this spirit, the present chapter will have served its purpose if it helps realize such goals; indeed, it is precisely through such pragmatic processes that the otherwise more abstract conceptual and methodological debates that continue to surround the questions of how best to measure social capital should be informed.

NOTES

1 This paper is a substantial extension and revision of Nyhan Jones and Woolcock (2009). The views expressed here are those of the authors alone, and should not be attributed to the IFC, the World Bank, or the University of Manchester.

2 Similar pressures and imperatives now face those working on local justice reform issues, as they did for a previous generation concerned with raising the profile of human development (which culminated in the UN's Human Development Index), gender, and the environment.

3 The intellectual and political history of social capital as idea and practice at the World Bank is outlined in Bebbington et al. (2004).

4 The fruits of this work were published as Grootaert and van Bastelaer (2002a, 2002b).

5 The governments of Australia, Canada, Finland, Ireland, and the United Kingdom have been notable leaders on incorporating social capital measures into their national statistics. See the UK's Office of National Statistics publication (Hall et al., 2008) and the useful citations provided therein.

6 Those interested in the details of these respective methodological approaches are advised to consult the original source documents, which are freely available online. Our indebtedness to our respective colleagues on these projects is duly acknowledged.

7 Detailed discussions of the intellectual history of 'social capital' are provided by Farr (2004) and Woolcock (1998).

8 Lochner et al. (1999) were among the first to provide a formal guide to social capital assessment, though this was primarily in the field of public health in developed countries. Within the World Bank, Krishna and Shrader (1999) provided the first attempt at such a tool.

9 On this point see Szreter and Woolcock (2004).

10 Other qualitative strategies for improving survey design include the use of 'anchoring vignettes' (Salomon et al., 2004; King and Wand, 2007), which seek to enhance the external validity and cross-cultural comparability of specific survey questions (on, say, government effectiveness or self-rated health) by using everyday examples , or anecdotes, familiar to respondents.

11 For a 'macro' level assessment of social cohesion and its link to economic growth, see Easterly et al. (2006).

12 The names of the group members are provided (and their valuable contributions duly acknowledged) in the original source documents (i.e., in Grootaert et al., 2004 and Dudwick et al., 2006).

13 The Self-Employed Women's Association (SEWA) in India has used a related approach with great success, helping poor slum dwellers to compile basic data on themselves that they can then present to municipal governments for the purpose of obtaining resources to which they are legally entitled. Participatory approaches, however, have the potential for abuse – see Cooke and Kothari (2001) and Brock and McGee (2002).

14 Details on the methodological challenges of measuring social capital via a standard survey instrument are usefully outlined in Durlauf and Fafchamps (2004) and Fafchamps (2006). These challenges stem in part from the various ways in which social capital has been measured, and from efforts that flow from the selected definition to aggregate across different dimensions into 'indexes'. We are often asked whether it is possible or desirable to aggregate individual measures across our six dimensions into a single 'index' of social capital, and if so to offer some guidance on how this might be done. Our response is that the task of the source documents, and indeed this chapter, is simply to lay out various research instruments that we think represent the best current practices regarding the quantitative and qualitative assessment of social capital; aggregation of measures is a separate analytical and technical task. Were we to provide an aggregation mechanism, we suspect this would too often be adopted uncritically, and absolve users of the responsibility of undertaking the hard work necessary to identify the most appropriate context-specific manner in which to undertake any aggregation procedure. In this sense, the aggregation issue for social capital researchers is merely one manifestation of a more generic problem across the social sciences.

15 King et al. (1994) and Brady and Collier (2004) provide more academic treatments of the potential commonalities of quantitative and qualitative approaches.

REFERENCES

Bamberger, M. (2000) *Integrating Quantitative and Qualitative Research in Development Projects.* Washington, D.C.: World Bank.

Barron, P., Diprose, R. and Woolcock, M. (forthcoming) *Contesting Development: Participatory Projects and Local Conflict Dynamics in Indonesia.* New Haven: Yale University Press.

Bebbington, A., Guggenheim, S., Olson, E. and Woolcock, M. (2004) 'Exploring Social Capital Debates at the World Bank', *Journal of Development Studies*, 40(5): 33–64.

Bebbington, A., Guggenheim, S., Olson, E. and Woolcock, M. (eds) (2006) *The Search for Empowerment: Social Capital as Idea and Practice at the World Bank.* Bloomfield, CT: Kumarian Press.

Brady, H. and Collier, D. (eds) (2004) *Rethinking Social Inquiry: Diverse Tools, Shared Standards.* Lanham, MD: Rowman and Littlefield.

Brock, K. and McGee, R. (2002) *Knowing Poverty: Critical Reflections on Participatory Research and Policy.* London: Earthscan Publications.

Chambers, R. (1997) *Whose Reality Counts? Putting the First Last.* London: Intermediate Technology Publications.

Cooke, W. and Kothari, U. (2001) *Participation: The New Tyranny?* London: Zed Books.

Dudwick, N., Kuehnast, K., Nyhan Jones, V. and Woolcock, M. (2006) 'Analyzing Social Capital in Context: A Guide to Using Qualitative Methods and Data' World Bank Institute Working Paper No. 37260. Washington, D.C.: The World Bank. Available online at: http://siteresources.worldbank.org/WBI/Resources/Analyzing_Social_Capital_in_Context-FINAL.pdf

Durlauf, S. and Fafchamps, M. (2004) 'Social Capital' Working Paper No. 10485. Cambridge, MA: National Bureau of Economic Research.

Easterly, W., Ritzen, J. and Woolcock, M. (2006) 'Social Cohesion, Institutions and Growth', *Economics & Politics*, 18(2): 103–20.

Epstein, S. (1962) *Economic Development and Social Change in South India.* Manchester, UK: University of Manchester Press.

Fafchamps, M. (2006) 'Development and Social Capital', *Journal of Development Studies*, 42(7): 1180–98.

Farr, J. (2004) 'Social Capital: A Conceptual History', *Political Theory*, 32(1): 6–33.

Gacitua-Mario, E. and Wodon, Q. (eds) (2001) 'Measurement and Meaning: Combining Quantitative and Qualitative Methods for the Analysis of Poverty and Social Exclusion in Latin America', Technical Paper 518, Latin America and Caribbean Region, Washington, D.C.: World Bank.

Grootaert, C. (1999) 'Social Capital, Household Welfare, and Poverty in Indonesia', Policy Research Working Paper 2148. Washington, D.C.: World Bank.

Grootaert, C. (2001) 'Does Social Capital Help the Poor? A Synthesis of Findings from the Local Level Institutions Studies in Bolivia, Burkina Faso, and Indonesia', Local Level Institutions Working Paper No. 10, Washington, D.C.: World Bank, Social Development Department.

Grootaert, C. and van Bastelaer, T. (eds) (2002a) *The Role of Social Capital in Development: An Empirical Assessment.* New York: Cambridge University Press.

Grootaert, C. and van Bastelaer, T. (eds) (2002b) *Understanding and Measuring Social Capital: A Multidisciplinary Tool for Practitioners.* Washington, D.C.: The World Bank.

Grootaert, C., Narayan, D., Nyhan Jones, V. and Woolcock, M. (2004) 'Measuring Social Capital: An Integrated Questionnaire', World Bank Working Paper No. 18. Washington, D.C.: The World Bank. Available online at: http://poverty2.forumone.com/files/11998_WP18-Web.pdf

Hall, C., Rafferty, A. and Higgins, V. (2008) 'Social Capital: An Introductory Guide', London: Economic and Social Data Service, and Office of National Statistics. Available at http://www.esds.ac.uk/government/docs/soccapguide.pdf (Accessed 11 February 2009).

Jha, S., Rao, V. and Woolcock, M. (2007) 'Governance in the Gullies: Democratic Responsiveness and Community Leadership in Delhi's Slums', *World Development,* 35(2): 230–46.

Kanbur, R. (2003) *Q Squared: Qualitative and Quantitative Methods of Poverty Appraisal.* New Delhi: Permanent Black.

King, G., Keohane, R. and Verba, S. (1994) *Designing Social Inquiry: Scientific Inference in Qualitative Research.* Princeton, NJ: Princeton University Press.

King, G. and Wand, J. (2007) 'Comparing Incomparable Survey Responses: Evaluating and Selecting Anchoring Vignettes', *Political Analysis*, 15(1): 46–66.

Krishna, A. (2002) *Active Social Capital: Tracing the Roots of Development and Democracy.* New York: Columbia University.

Krishna, A. (2007) 'How Does Social Capital Grow? A Seven-Year Study of Villages in India', *Journal of Politics*, 69(4): 941–56.

Krishna, A. and Shrader, E. (1999) 'Social Capital Assessment Tool'. Mimeo, Paris: Social Development Department, World Bank.

Kumar, S., and Chambers, R. (2002) *Methods for Community Participation.* London: Intermediate Technology Publications.

Labonne, J. and Chase, R. (2008) 'Do Community-Driven Development Projects Enhance Social Capital? Evidence from the Philippines', Policy Research Working Paper No. 4678. Washington, D.C.: The World Bank.

Lochner, K., Kawachi, I. and Kennedy, B. (1999) 'Social Capital: A Guide to Measurement', *Health & Place*, 5(4): 259–70.

Mikkelsen, B. (1995) *Methods for Development Work and Research: A Guide for Practitioners.* New Delhi: Sage Publications.

Moore, M. (1997) 'Societies, Polities and Capitalists in Developing Countries: A Literature Survey', *Journal of Development Studies*, 33(3): 287–363.

Narayan, D. (1995) *Toward Participatory Research.* Washington, D.C.: The World Bank.

Narayan, D., and Cassidy, M. (2001) 'A Dimensional Approach to Measuring Social Capital: Development and Validation of Social Capital Inventory', *Current Sociology*, 49(2): 49–93.

Narayan, D. and Pritchett, L. (1999) 'Cents and Sociability: Household Income and Social Capital in Rural Tanzania', *Economic Development and Cultural Change*, 47(4): 871–97.

Nyhan Jones, V. and Woolcock, M. (2009) 'Mixed Methods Assessment', in Gunnar S. and Svendsen, G. (eds) *Handbook of Social Capital,* Northampton, MA: Edward Elgar. pp. 379–401.

Organization for Economic Cooperation and Development (OECD) (2002) 'Social Capital: The Challenge of International Measurement', Report of an International Conference, September 25–27. Mimeo, Paris: OECD.

Putnam, R. (1993) *Making Democracy Work: Civic Traditions in Modern Italy.* Princeton, NJ: Princeton University Press.

Rao, V. (2002) 'Experiments in 'Participatory Econometrics': Improving the Connection between Economic Analysis and the Real World', *Economic and Political Weekly,* (May 18): 1887–91.

Rao, V. and Woolcock, M. (2003) 'Integrating Qualitative and Quantitative Approaches in Program

Evaluation', in Bourguignon, Francois J. and da Silva, Luiz Pereira (eds) *The Impact of Economic Policies on Poverty and Income Distribution: Evaluation Techniques and Tools.* New York: Oxford University Press. pp. 165–90.

Robb, C. (2002) *Can the Poor Influence Policy? Participatory Poverty Assessments in the Developing World* (Rev. edition). Washington, D.C.: International Monetary Fund.

Salomon, J. A., Tandon, A. and Murray, C. L. (2004) 'Comparability of Self-Rated Health: Cross-Sectional Multi-Country Survey Using Anchoring Vignettes', *British Medical Journal*, 328: 258–61.

Scott, J. (1998) *Seeing Like a State: How Certain Schemes to Improve the Human Condition Have Failed.* New Haven: Yale University Press.

Szreter, S. and Woolcock, M. (2004) 'Health by Association? Social Capital, Social Theory and the Political Economy of Public Health', *International Journal of Epidemiology*, 33(4): 650–67.

Tashakkori, A. and Teddlie, C. (1998) *Mixed Methodology: Combining Qualitative and Quantitative Approaches.* Thousand Oaks, CA: Sage.

Woolcock, M. (1998) 'Social Capital and Economic Development: Toward a Theoretical Synthesis and Policy Framework', *Theory and Society*, 27(2): 151–208.

Woolcock, M. (2001) 'The Place of Social Capital in Understanding Social and Economic Outcomes', *Canadian Journal of Policy Research*, 2(1): 11–17.

Woolcock, M. and Narayan, D. (2000) 'Social Capital: Implications for Development Theory, Research, and Policy', *World Bank Research Observer*, 15(2): 225–50.

World Bank (2000) *World Development Report 2000/2001: Attacking Poverty.* New York: Oxford University Press.

World Bank (2002) *Empowerment and Poverty Reduction—A Sourcebook.* Washington, D.C.: World Bank.

28

The Use of Administrative Data to Answer Policy Questions: Secondary Data on Crime and the Problem with Homicide

Marc Riedel

INTRODUCTION

This chapter defines secondary data 'as the use of statistical material and information originally gathered for another purpose' (Riedel, 2000: 1). Most treatments of secondary analysis focus on access and statistical analysis (Hakim, 1982; Kiecolt and Nathan, 1985; Dale et al., 2008). Our interest in this chapter is somewhat different; we are interested in statistics, specifically statistics about homicide. Specifically, the major concern is with the social process that affects the collection of statistics. Best (2004: xii–xiii) states the general interest:

> … we tend to assume that statistics are facts, little nuggets of truth that we uncover, much as a rock collectors find stones. After all, we

think, a statistic is a number, and numbers seem to be solid, factual proof that someone must have actually counted something. But that's the point: people count. For every number we encounter, some person had to do the counting. Instead of imagining that statistics are like rocks, we'd do better to think of them as jewels. Gemstones may be found in nature, but people have to create jewels. Jewels must be selected, cut, polished, and placed in settings to be viewed from particular angles. In much the same way, people create statistics: they choose what to count, how to go about counting, which of the resulting numbers they share with others, and which words they use to describe and interpret these figures.

> Numbers do not exist independent of people; understanding numbers requires knowing who counted what, why they bothered counting and how they went about it.

There is no objective definition of crime; like gemstones in nature, there is no 'external, objective 'crime reality' waiting to be discovered' (Bottomley, 1979: 23). Crime statistics are products of the criminal justice system and the activities of people who work in it. Official statistics and records are the product of a social process dependent on the social definitions of law and interactions of offenders, researchers, members of the community (victims, witnesses) and representatives of the criminal justice system (Bottomley, 1979; Jupp, 1989; Kitsuse and Cicourel, 1963).

Overview

Applying that perspective to homicide data, the place to start is with the legal definition of homicide, what it means, and how it is implemented. The social consensus about the seriousness of taking the life of another is indicated by efforts at a complete enumeration, both locally and nationally, by two distinct data collection systems. But such efforts are embedded in organizations that have their own social processes that may or may not lead to what is expected. Beginning with a discussion of homicide law, this chapter describes the different data collection systems and changes in them. Because the major problem is missing data in homicide, much of the chapter will discuss the extent and consequences as well as steps taken to correct the problem.

Violent crime, especially homicide, is the most disruptive and destructive crime in a civil society. In his classic, *Leviathan*, Thomas Hobbes enumerated the disastrous disorder of the natural state of man 'and which is worst of all, continuall feare, and danger of violent death; And the life of man, solitary, poore, nasty, brutish, and short' (Hobbes, 1904: 84).

Central to maintaining the social contract is law; in this case, the law of homicide. Thus, in the following section, we examine the legal definition of homicide and the major subdivisions into justifiable and criminal homicide. Because the focus is on secondary data, we examine instances where acts should be counted as homicides when they are not and when they should be counted as homicides and are not.

As noted previously, because of its gravity, homicide is the only crime where there are two local and national reporting systems. Because it is a crime, police investigate and report the event; a subset of what is collected is forwarded to the FBI's Uniform Crime Reporting (UCR) program who issues a national report, *Crime in the United States*. Because there is a public health interest in causes of death and disease, homicide is also listed as a cause of death on death certificates. Details of the homicide are also forwarded by local agencies and published annually by the National Center for Health Statistics as *Vital Statistics of the United States* (Riedel, 1990, 1999a, b).

The focus in this chapter is on FBI reporting program. While the UCR has a long history, it has undergone a reorganization and is gradually being supplanted by the National Incident Reporting System (NIBRS). Because vital statistics also collect data on homicide, it can be used to compare the relative accuracy of the two data sources.

As will be discussed, the major problem with homicide data is missing data. This occurs in two ways: (1) agencies fail to report and (2) data reported are missing data on offenders and information that can be reported by offenders. In the first case, it must be remembered that the UCR program is a voluntary program (FBI, 2007a). Rather than relying on the cumbersome process of requesting thousands of individual law enforcement agencies to report, the UCR program helped to establish state agencies that serve as a repository and forward the required statistics to the FBI. According to Maltz (1999) there were 44 state agencies that provided data to the UCR. Of the 44 state programs, 35 had a statute establishing a state reporting agency, seven did not, and two were unknown. A large component of voluntary co-operation remains as only six of the state statutes included a penalty for non-compliance; there is no evidence that non-compliance has resulted in a sanction (Lynch and Jarvis, 2008).

With respect to offender data, by virtue of its nature, homicide data is susceptible to incomplete reporting. It is assumed that because of the presence of a dead body that counting homicides would be an unequivocal matter. While this is true, and victim-based reporting is more valid, there is a need to collect information about the offender and circumstances of the offense. But offenders have no interest in being caught, much less counted, so the major component of missing data at the case level is information about the offender and information that only the offender can provide such as motive or circumstances of the offense.

The latter is a serious shortcoming from the point of view of an effective criminal-justice system as well as research to improve the functioning of the police. According to FBI data, of the 16,929 homicides (murder and manslaughter) reported in 2007, 38.8 per cent of the offenders were not 'cleared' or arrested and held for prosecution (FBI, 2007b). Aside from the social consequences of homicide offenders not arrested, research using offender data is liable to be biased because of a selected sample. What makes matters worse is that the public is generally unaware of the problem of declining arrest clearances.

Related to the latter matter of clearances, this chapter discusses the consequences of the fact that homicide is a statistically rare event. In one year for example, there were only 16,929 homicides in a US population of 301,621,157. By comparison, there were 855,856 aggravated assaults which is the second most frequent violent offense; the latter is 50 times more frequent than homicide (FBI, 2007b).

The fact that homicide is a rarely occurring phenomenon has two consequences. First, because it is rare and impossible to observe in quantity, there is no plausible way of doing research without reliance on data provided by law enforcement and medical examiners/coroners (Swigert, 1989). Like many other types of secondary data, counting is done by representatives of organizations with their own counting rules and goals. Because the counting is limited to the latter organizations, homicides are what the police and medical examiners/coroners say they are.

Second, because it is the responsibility of law enforcement to investigate and arrest offenders, there are questions of whether some types of data are unavailable because they reflect negatively on departmental as well as individual police performance. In the traditional UCR, data on arrest clearances – the extent to which offenders are arrested and held for prosecution – was limited to the per cent cleared by department. It was not possible to link cleared and uncleared cases to characteristics of specific offenses. With the gradual extension of NIBRS to other departments, information about what kinds of homicides are cleared and uncleared is becoming slowly available, although detailed information about investigations remains unavailable.

In addition to the expansion of NIBRS, there is another reason to believe homicide data is getting better. In the final section of this chapter, there is a brief description of the National Violent Death Reporting System (NVDRS) which is maintained by the CDC. The NVDRS is a surveillance system of suicides and homicide that integrates available data from both public health and law enforcement sources on an incident-by-incident basis. Currently, the public use data is available on the internet for 16 states for the years, 2003 to 2005.

THE MEANING OF HOMICIDE

Homicide is 'the killing of one human being by another' (Garner, 2004: 751). Homicide is a neutral term; to illustrate the non-criminal and criminal types, I was asked recently whether a Mafia hit-man is a serial killer? I answered in the affirmative, but by the same definition, so are combat soldiers killing insurgents in Iraq. The reason the answer is in the affirmative is that serial killers are frequently defined by the number of killings within a time frame. Serial homicide is commonly defined as the commission of three or more murders over a period of time, with a 'cooling off' period or hiatus between each murder (Simpson, 2000; Jenkins, 1994; Hickey, 2002).

The difference is, of course, whether the homicide is prohibited and punishable by law. Criminal homicide (murder and manslaughter) 'is the act of purposely, knowingly, recklessly, or negligently causing the death of another' (Garner, 2004: 751). Homicide can also be justifiable and carry no criminal sanction; justifiable homicides include legal executions and self-defense. Hence, the Mafia hit-man activities can be sanctioned as criminal homicide (murder) while the combat soldier's killings are justifiable and, perhaps, laudable. Indeed, the training of a combat soldier is largely a matter of convincing him or her that the legal distinction is a moral one (Sanford and Comstock,

1971). Unless otherwise noted, because this chapter is primarily concerned with criminal homicide, I use the general term, 'homicide.'

Finally, because homicide is the most serious crime and the one about which there is the most public consensus, the expectation is that it is least likely to be unreported. Relative to the number of other crimes that go unreported, the number of homicides is likely to be more accurate. However, law enforcement and medical examiners/coroners cannot apply counting rules without difficulties.

If a fatal event is to be classified and reported as a homicide, then the circumstances have to show that the death occurred through the deliberate actions of another. In other words, the counting rules used have to be able to distinguish between homicides and, for example, accidents and suicides. Sometimes, circumstances surrounding the death make it impossible to distinguish. For example, suppose a dead body washes up to an ocean shore near an isolated pier. The autopsy indicates an extremely high level of alcohol which means the person was undoubtedly extremely drunk. How did he die? Was he staggering along the pier in the early hours of the morning, fell off, too drunk to help himself, and drowned? Or was he pushed? In the former case the event would be classified as an accident while in the latter it would be a homicide.

There are circumstances where homicides are reported when, in fact, it is a suicide. The best known example of these false positives are described as 'suicide by cop.' Suicide by cop refers to those individuals who wish to die and use the police to effect that goal. Kennedy and colleagues (1998: 1) provide an example.

> A terrified woman called police because her ex-boyfriend was breaking into her home. Upon arrival, police heard screams coming from the

basement. They stopped halfway down the stairs and found the ex-boyfriend pointing a rifle at the floor. Officers observed a strange look on the subject's face as he slowly raised the rifle in their direction. Both officers fired their weapons, killing the suspect. The rifle was not loaded.

Research by Hutson et al. (1998) of 437 officer-involved shootings investigated by the Los Angeles Sheriff's Department from 1987 to 1997 indicated between 11 and 13 per cent were suicide by cop. Fifty-four per cent of the victims sustained fatal gunshots. All deaths were classified as homicides rather than suicides by the coroner.

It is also possible there are cases classified as an event other than homicide that should have been listed as a homicide. The research indicates these false negatives are predominantly in the cases of children under the age of one (Ewigman et al., 1993; Herman-Giddens et al., 1999). Overpeck et al. (1999: 274) used linked birth and death certificates for all US births from 1983 to 1991. Based on the striking similarity between intentional deaths and suspicious deaths, the authors conclude, 'that estimates of infant homicide that incorporate deaths with undetermined (suspicious) intent on birth certificates could be almost 20% greater than reported rates of homicide.'

Making a decision as to whether the child was the victim of a homicide or an accident is not only a matter of applying counting rules, but also a decision that can have a devastating effect on others. Finkelhor (1997: 22) describes the problem:

It is difficult to distinguish young children who are dropped, pushed, or thrown from those who die from falls. Even in many so-called accidental deaths, such as falls or auto fatalities, there may be a major component of willful parental negligence that is difficult to establish.' On the other hand, imagine the effect on parents of a dead child being accused of killing their child when, in fact, the death was an accident!

Since a 1995 report on child abuse and neglect by the US Advisory Board on Child Abuse and Neglect, nearly all states have established Child Death Review Teams to reduce the number of misclassified child deaths. Child Death Review Teams review medical, social service, and law enforcement information on the death of every child to reach a consensus as to the cause of death.

SECONDARY DATA AND THE FBI CRIME REPORTING PROGAM

Three types of secondary data

There are three major types of secondary data on crime: surveys, official records, and official statistics. Depending on how each is stored, each may also be referred to as archival data. The largest archive for criminal justice data in the United States is the National Archive of Criminal Justice data which is part of the Inter-University Consortium for Political and Social Research (2007).

The discussion will focus primarily on *official statistics*, specifically the Uniform Crime Reporting (UCR) program and the National Incident Based Reporting System (NIBRS). We will also discuss the National Center for Health Statistics classification of homicide and compare it to law enforcement data. Before doing that, however, a *survey* that provides extensive data on crime, the National Crime Victimization Survey will be briefly discussed. Following there will be a discussion of *official records*: police department records.

The national crime victimization survey

Surveys generally refer to a statistically representative sample of a population under study. The National Crime Victimization Study (NCVS), for example, uses a multistate cluster sample of the population of the

Unites States to obtain information about victims of crime. Other types of crime-related surveys are described at http://www.ojp.usdoj.gov/bjs/.

The current victimization survey contacts 42,000 households and is carried out every six months by the Census Bureau. The crimes include rape, robbery, aggravated assault, simple assault, personal larceny such as purse snatching, burglary, motor vehicle theft, and/or property theft. The survey collects information of characteristics of victims and offenders, relationships between victims and offenders, time and location of the offenses, self-protective actions taken by victims, injury or property losses, offenders use of weapons, drugs, and alcohol, and whether the crimes were reported to the police (Rennison and Rand, 2007).

The unit of analysis is the household and the interview, now carried out primarily by Computer Aided Telephone Interviewing, consists of two steps. In the first stage, screening questions are asked to determine whether the respondent has been the victim of a crime in the past four months. If the respondent indicates that someone in the household has been a victim, then an individual victimization report is completed for each incident mentioned in response to the screen questions.

Homicide is not included. The usual reason given is that the victim is dead. However, since the unit of analysis is a household, it is reasonable to expect that someone would remember a death by homicide in the household occurring in the past few months. The reasons for excluding homicide is the cost of sampling and the fact that homicide victim information is collected by two other agencies.

Agency data: official records

Both official records and official statistics are collections of information made available in permanent form by organizations that frequently retain a proprietary interest in their use. The term 'official' should not connote more legitimacy or authority on official records or official statistics than warranted. As used here, it is similar to Weber's (1946) characterization of a bureaucratic office as based on written documents (the files).

Official records, as distinct from official statistics, are collections of statistical data that are generated as a byproduct of the organization's mission or goal. Examples of official records include information from police departments, treatment agencies, probation departments, courts, etc. There are several differences between official records and official statistics.

First, because official records describe organizational activity, they are not designed or maintained for public consumption or research. Official statistics, by contrast, are presented in formats that are more easily used by researchers. Second, unlike official statistics which are freely available, official records are primarily for internal purposes and are more difficult to access.

Third, for each record, the amount of detail is typically greater for official records than for official statistics. Official statistics are collected from many agencies and disseminated widely; therefore, they focus on a fewer data elements. Fourth, the unit of analysis for official records is the same as the target of the service delivery effort, typically a person. Official statistics, on the other hand, may be available only at higher levels of aggregation such as monthly or annual counts (Riedel, 2000).

Finally, Hakim (1983) has noted that in the collection of official records, the persons who originally completed the forms may be present in the agency and accessible to the researcher. This gives the researcher the opportunity to learn more about how the information was gathered.

By contrast, official statistics are gathered from many different agencies and persons who completed the forms are not available. In these instances, written descriptions in the form of codebooks must suffice (Riedel, 2000).

Internally, official records are useful to administrative staff to supervise and provide service delivery. The same records provide information to defend agency performance externally and compete for additional resources. While police departments are generally open to research requests to collect homicide data, they are unwilling to provide access to data that reflect negatively on the department, administrative leadership, or the officers.

There are a number of city-wide data sets on homicide collected from police department files and available in the University of Michigan archives. Probably the best known and most detailed is homicide data from 1965 through 1995 from Chicago Police Department files collected by Richard Block and Carolyn Rebecca Block (2006).

Official statistics and the FBI reporting program

Uniform crime reports

The International Association of Chiefs of Police (IACP) initiated the collection of national crime data in 1929 and the FBI assumed control of the program the following year. In developing the nationwide reporting system that is the UCR Program, the Committee on Uniform Crime Records of International Association of Chiefs of Police encountered a major counting issue: how to convert the disparate state laws and definitions into one standardized system, that is, how to make crime reports 'uniform.' For example, the Illinois Uniform Crime Report classifies both first and second degree murder as murder and non-negligent

manslaughter for UCR reporting purposes (Department of State Police, 2006). In its final format, they settled upon seven major standardized offense definitions: murder and non-negligent manslaughter, rape, robbery, aggravated assault, burglary, larceny, and motor vehicle theft (Barnett-Ryan, 2007; Maltz, 2007).

According to the FBI (2007c), 'murder and non-negligent manslaughter is the willful (non-negligent) killing of one human being by another.' The definition does not include deaths caused by negligence, suicide, or accident; and attempts to murder or assaults to murder which are scored as aggravated assaults. Data are also collected and tabulated separately for negligent manslaughter and justifiable homicide (Riedel, 1999a).

There are three important forms that are used to collect homicide data. *Return A – Crimes Known to the Police (Aggregated Monthly)*: This form contains information on monthly crimes reported or known; number of founded complaints; unfounded complaints; number of offenses cleared by arrest or exceptionally cleared; number of clearances for persons under 18.

Unfounded complaints are events that upon investigation turn out to be fake or baseless. The FBI also defines exceptional clearances which are included in the calculation of the overall clearance rate. An exceptional clearance occurs when law enforcement has gathered enough evidence to turn the offender over for prosecution and identified the offender's location, but has encountered a circumstance which prohibits the agency from making an arrest. For example, the police may have identified the offender, but, before he could be arrested, find that he has died or fled to a country for which we have no extradition treaty. Such cases are reviewed and cleared administratively by supervising officers (FBI, 2007d).

Because exceptional clearances are included in the calculation of clearances, very little is known about how the exceptional clearance category is used by police departments. They may be used to inflate clearance rates. In one of the few studies to look at this, Riedel and Boulahanis (2007) found that, for the years 1982 to 1995, a mean of ten per cent of the homicide cases in Chicago were refused prosecution and, subsequently, exceptionally cleared and included among the cleared cases. Cases refused prosecution occurred either in private indoor or public outdoor locations, involved older offenders, or domestic altercations. In interviews, no explanation was given by the prosecution. Using NIBRS data from 1996 to 2002 and offenders who died before prosecution, Jarvis and Regoeczi (2007) found that, in comparison to cases cleared by arrest, those exceptionally cleared were older white female offenders.

Age, Race, and Sex of Arrested Offenders (Aggregated Monthly): There are two forms, one for adults and the other for persons under 18. This form reports the number of offenders arrested for homicide for a given month by age, race, and sex. Race is defined as white, black, American Indian or Alaska Native, Asian or Pacific Islander. Classification of the victim and offender as Hispanic was begun in 1980 (FBI, 2004e; Barnett-Ryan, 2007).

Supplementary Homicide Reports SHR (Incident Reports): The SHR form provides information on each reported case of murder and non-negligent manslaughter. This is a victim-based form that includes a situation code indicating combinations of single or multiple victims and single, multiple, or unknown offenders. The SHR also records the age, race, and sex of all victims and offenders, weapons used, victim/offender relationships, and circumstances of the offense such as whether the homicide involved a robbery, domestic violence, argument, or other circumstances.

NIBRS

In 1982, a joint task force of the Bureau of Justice Statistics and the FBI completed a study to improve the crime reporting structure of the United States. A key recommendation was the development of a national incident-based reporting system (Poggio et al., 1985). After several years of testing and development, the first official release of NIBRS data occurred in 1996 (Faggiani, 2007).

The concept of incident is central to NIBRS. An incident for NIBRS reporting purposes means one or more offenses committed by the same offender, or a group of offenders acting in concert, at the same time and place. All of the offenders in an incident are considered to have committed all of the offenses in the incident (National Archive of Criminal Justice Data, 2008a).

NIBRS compiles data on 22 Group A offenses and 11 Group B offenses. The group A and group B offenses are given in Table 28.1. Group A offenses, but not group B, are general classifications which are refined to specific offenses. For example, homicide offenses are further divided into murder and non-negligent manslaughter, negligent manslaughter, and justifiable homicide.

For each group A offense, there is an incident report for between four and six records or segments. Administrative, offense, victim, and offender segments are required for each offense. Property and arrestee segments may also be used. For Group B offenses, only information on arrestees is collected. Table 28.1 summarizes the record or segment types.

Table 28.2 indicates the amount of data collected on each crime in an incident. An ID key is spread to all the records to hold the incident together. Except for ID key

Table 28.1   Group A and Group B NIBRS offenses*

Group A offenses	Group B offenses
Arson	Bad checks
Assault offenses	Curfew/loitering/Vagrancy violations
Bribery	Disorderly conduct
Burglary/breaking and entering	Driving under the influence
Counterfeiting/forgery	Drunkenness
Destruction/damage/ vandalism of property	Family offenses, non-violent
Drug/narcotic offenses	Liquor law violations
Embezzlement	Peeping Tom
Extortion/blackmail	Runaway
Fraud offenses	Trespass of real property
Gambling offenses	All other offenses
Homicide offenses	
Kidnaping/abduction	
Larceny/theft offenses	
Motor vehicle theft	
Pornography/obscene material	
Prostitution offenses	
Robbery	
Sex offenses, forcible	
Sex offenses, non-forcible	
Stolen property offenses	
Weapon law violations	

*Taken from National Archive of Criminal Justice Data (2008a)

and a few other variables, the terms in the bracket refer to specific classifications. The data reported in Table 28.2 can be combined in a variety of ways with the different group A crimes in Table 28.1 to analyze different crime situations (Maxfield, 1999).

Because it is an incident-based system, NIBRS has many advantages. Among the many advantages listed by the Justice Research and Statistics Association (2008) is the elimination of the hierarchy rule which has been the target of severe criticism of the UCR reaching back at least as far as 1966. The hierarchy rule was originally instituted to eliminate the double counting of offenses that were part of the same incident. The hierarchy of offenses as given

in the FBI handbook lists murder and non-negligent manslaughter as the most serious and arson as the least serious (FBI, 2004e). Only the most serious offenses is counted in the UCR. For example, if a convenience store robbery ends in the death of one of the employee, Return A and the SHR records it as one murder and non-negligent manslaughter because homicide is more serious than robbery. NIBRS counts both the homicide and the robbery while the UCR does not count the robbery (Maltz, 1999).

The most important question for data-based analysis is the quality of the data. Quality control for NIBRS begins at the local level. Prior to being certified to contribute data to NIBRS, the agency is required to submit data on magnetic media for testing. The FBI provides detail documentation for coding and submitting data. The FBI provides data element definitions, specification of valid data values, data submission schedules, and resubmission guidelines and controls, etc. When data submissions are received, an extensive number of data quality checks are run and an incident report prepared if errors are found (Justice Research and Statistics Association, 2008).

The conversion from the UCR system to NIBRS has been gradual. As of September 2007, 31 states have been certified to report NIBRS to the FBI, and four additional states and the District of Columbia have individual agencies submitting NIBRS data. While NIBRS covers only 25 per cent of the population and 26 per cent of reported crime, the 25 largest agencies range from Fairfax county, VA (980,586) to Norfolk, VA (241,267). This partial coverage suggests caution in generalizing beyond NIBRS agencies (Justice Research and Statistics Association, 2008; Addington, 2006; 2008a; b; Roberts, 2007; 2008). While NIBRS data does not yet include

Table 28.2   Summary of NIBRS record types*

Group A offenses
Administrative segment. (One per incident)

1. Reporting agency number [ID key spread to all records]
2. Incident number [ID key]
3. Incident date/hour
4. [Exceptional clearance codes and date]

Offense segment. (At least 1 per incident; maximum, 10 per incident.) Not all fields coded for all offenses

1. [ID key]
2. Offense code [see Table 2]
3. Attempted/completed
4. Suspected of using [alcohol, drugs, computer equipment]
5. Bias motivation [code type]
6. Type of location
7. N premises entered
8. Method premise entry
9. Criminal/gang activity [if applicable, code collateral criminal activity (drugs, counterfeiting, gambling)]
10. Type of weapon or force involved

Property segment. (Prepared only for offenses involving property; maximum of 10 per property loss offense)

1. [ID key]
2. Type of property loss
3. Property description
4. Value of property
5. Date recovered
6. Number of stolen motor vehicles
7. Number of recovered motor vehicles
8. [Fields for illegal drugs]

Victim segment. (At least 1 per incident; maximum, 999 per incident)

1. [ID key]
2. Victim sequence number
3. Link to offense code. Field to link each victim to relevant offense records
4. Type of victim [individual, business, financial institution, government, religious organization, society/ public, other]
5. [Age, sex, race, ethnicity]
6. Resident status [resident of reporting jurisdiction]
7. Aggravated assault/homicide circumstances [similar to SHR codes]
8. Type of injury
9. Link to offender. Field to link this victim record to a specific offender record (below); maximum of 10 offender links
10. Victim relationship to offender [keyed to offender link]. For example, victim is sibling to offender 1, and acquaintance to offender 2.

Offender segment. (At least 1 per incident; maximum, 99 per incident)

1. [ID key]
2. Offender sequence number [Code 00 if nothing known about offender]
3. [Age, sex, race]

(*continued*)

Table 28.2   Continued

Arrestee segment. (Submit only if one or more arrestees; maximum, 99 per incident)

1. [ID key]
2. Arrestee sequence number
3. [ID link to reporting agency-maintained arrest report]
4. Arrest date
5. Arrest type [onview, summons-based arrest, summons issued]
6. Link to offense code. Field to link each arrestee to relevant offense records
7. Armed with [weapon codes]
8. [Age, sex, race, ethnicity]
9. Resident status [resident of reporting jurisdiction]
10. Disposition if under 18 [released, turned over to other authority]

*Source: Maxfield 1999: 124

urban areas with over one million inhabitants, the available research shows remarkable consistency between SHR, NIBRS, and other nationally representative measures (Chilton and Jarvis 1999a, b).

NIBRS is a very rich data source and is generating important research. The *Journal of Quantitative Criminology* (volume 15, 1999) under the editorship of Michael Maltz and Michael Maxfield devoted an entire issue to research with NIBRS. More recently, *Justice Research and Policy* (volume 9, 2007) under the editorship of Donald Faggiani has also devoted an issue to NIBRS research.

Mortality data

Homicides, like accidents and suicides, are defined as a public health problem. Thus, as mentioned earlier, homicides are classified as deaths from an external cause and is collected locally and incorporated into a national report on vital statistics.

The legal authority for collecting mortality data in the United States resides with the 50 states, two cities (Washington, DC, and New York City), and five territories (Puerto Rico, the Virgin Islands, Guam, American Samoa, and the Commonwealth of the Northern Mariana Islands) (National Center for Health Statistics, 2007a). Information on homicide is collected through the use

of a standardized death certificate that was revised in 2003 (National Center for Health Statistics, 2007b). The relevant items include:

1. age, race, gender, and ethnicity of victims;
2. whether victims were in the armed forces and social security numbers;
3. birthplaces, marital statuses, occupations, education, residences, and places of death;
4. places and manner of disposition and whether autopsies were performed;
5. parents' names and addresses; and
6. times, places, and causes of death and whether they occurred at work.

Death certificates are completed and cause of death certified by a medical officer. All diseases, conditions, or injuries that led to the person's death are listed. Death certificates are given to funeral directors who, to obtain a burial permit, give them to local registrars who are usually county health officers; they verify the certificates' completeness and accuracy, make records of them, and forward copies to state registrars. Personnel at state vital statistics offices check death certificates for incomplete or inconsistent information, then send them to the National Center for Health Statistics (NCHS) who compiles and issues the data as annual reports. At NCHS, cases are classified according to categories in the *International Classification of Diseases* (ICD) and entered into a national mortality data.

The ICD is published by the World Health Organization, a body that supports a world-wide vital statistics reporting system. The classifications contained in this publication are revised approximately every 10 years in a meeting of participating nations. The first revison used in the United States began in 1900; the current revision is the tenth (Hetzel, 1997).

Homicides are defined as injuries inflicted by another person with intent to injure or kill, by any means. The homicide codes (Y85 to Y09.) are given in Table 28.3.

A third digit is added for additional information. For example, Y06 includes Y06.0, neglect and maltreatment by spouse

Table 28.3 ICD 10 codes and causes of death*

Codes	Causes of death
X85.	Drugs, medicaments and biological substances
X86.	Corrosive substances
X87.	Pesticides
X88.	Gases and vapours
X89.	Other specified chemicals and noxious substances
X90.	Unspecified chemical or noxious substance
X91.	Hanging, strangulation and suffocation
X92.	Drowning and submersion
X93.	Handgun discharge
X94.	Rifle, shotgun and larger firearm discharge
X95.	Other and unspecified firearm discharge
X96.	Explosive material
X97.	Smoke, fire, and flames
X98.	Steam, hot vapours and hot objects
X99.	Sharp object
Y00.	Blunt object
Y01.	Pushing from high places
Y02.	Pushing or placing victim before moving object
Y03.	Crashing of motor vehicle
Y04.	Bodily force
Y05.	Sexual assault by bodily force
Y06.	Neglect and abandonment
Y07.	Other maltreatment syndromes
Y08.	Other specified means
Y09.	Unspecified means

*World Health Organization (2006)

or partner; Y06.1 refers to neglect and maltreatment by parent, etc. Additional codes are requested for place of occurrence and activity.

The codes Y35 to Y36 are reserved for deaths due to legal intervention such as police shootings and acts of war. Finally, Y10 through Y34 codes are reserved for events of undetermined intent (World Health Organization, 2006). Codes (*U01 to *U02) have been added recently by the NCHS (2007c) to classify death by acts of terrorism if the event is defined as terrorism by the Federal Government. The NCHS assumes complete coverage since 1933; no estimates are used; and all published data is considered final and not subject to revision (Cantor and Cohen, 1980).

Mortality statistics on homicide have been used to study homicide rates in other countries (Gartner, 1990, 1991, 1993; Pampel and Gartner, 1995). What is some-times overlooked in official statistics is that the amount of coverage is determined by the political and legal stability of government and the technical capacity for collecting official data. For example, while the United States, Canada and France had 100 per cent estimated mortality data coverage in 2000, Zimbabwe had less than 50 per cent coverage in 1990 (World Health Organization, 2008). Thus, comparative research is going to be limited to more highly developed countries.

Comparisons have been done between mortality data and UCR counts of homicide by Cantor and Cohen (1980), Rokaw et al. (1990), and Wiersema et al. (2000). Recently, Loftin et al. (2008) compared 1987 to 1991 homicides reported on the SHR to NCHS homicides using a sample of 167 cities with a population over 100,000.

There is little exact agreement between the two data sources. In terms of the number of homicides, only 5 of the 167 cities agreed exactly; 118 cities reported more NCHS homicides than SHR; and 44 cities report more SHR homicides than NCHS. To adjust for the fact that small cities report fewer homicides than large ones, the authors use victim rates for NCHS and SHR. Seven of the eight Florida cities were among those with large differences in favor of reporting more NCHS than SHR homicides.

There are three problems that make comparisons difficult. First, SHR reports are sometimes missing from the files.

Twenty-one of the 167 cities in our sample have no homicides in the file for at least 1 reporting year ... More than half of the cities that failed to report (57%) are missing for 2 or more years, and all eight cities in Florida plus Chattanooga, Tennessee failed to report for 4 of the 5 years in the study period.' (Loftin et al., 2008: 8)

Second, there are differences in the service areas of law enforcement and reporting areas used by NCHS. For example, the service area for Las Vegas police includes the city plus the unincorporated portions of Clark County. The difference between NCHS reports (193) and SHR (349) is a consequence of different reporting areas.

A third difference is the counting rule used for associating homicide victims with a reporting city. For NCHS, the victim's place of residence is used while for SHR, the homicide is by the law enforcement agency which is typically the place of occurrence. While the authors have only 20 cities that are geographically coextensive with county units, there appear to be more homicide victims classified by place of occurrence than place of residence.

Generally, researchers find that NCHS data are more useful and accurate than SHR. There is much less of a problem with coverage and reporting, political boundaries are consistent with Census Bureau and other federal agency definitions, and the use of place of residence makes it possible to calculate residence rates. However, NCHS data does not provide any information about offenders or circumstances that are frequently of interest to researchers.

It is finally being recognized that the most useful way of collecting homicide data is making the incident, rather than the victim, the unit of analysis. What makes NIBRS data much more useful than the UCR is that data are collected by incident which incorporates type of homicide, victim and offender information, circumstances, and whether the offender was arrested.

MISSING DATA

While being a voluntary program makes the problem of missing data greater, this is a persistent feature of official statistics. As indicated earlier, it is possible to correct official records because they are collected in an office; official statistics, on the other hand, are collected from many different agencies and further contact is usually not possible. The famous statistician, R. A. Fisher, is reputed to give the best advice on what to do with missing data: 'The best solution to handle missing data is to have none' (Kenny, 2007: vii). Unfortunately, that may not be a choice for many users of official statistics.

While the amount of research is limited, missing data is not limited to crime data. An indication of the amount of missing data in another discipline is provided by McKnight et al. (2007: 3). One of the authors gathered information on the prevalence, type, and treatment of missing data from a prominent psychological journal. The data collection covered over 300 articles across a 3-year period.

Not only were missing data prevalent across studies (approximately 90% had missing data), but the average amount of missing data for studies in our sample exceeded 30%.

Additionally, few of the articles included explicit mention of missing data, and even fewer indicated that the authors attended to the missing data, either by performing statistical procedures or by making disclaimers regarding the studies and conclusions.'

In short, most researchers do little or nothing with missing data.

There are two ways of doing nothing with missing data: listwise and pairwise deletion. Table 28.4 is a hypothetical matrix of seven cases, one dependent variable (Y) and six independent variables (X_1 through X_6).

Listwise deletion is accomplished by deleting *any case completely* that has missing values on one or more variables, then applying statistical analysis. For many statistical packages, this is the default option. For example, if a multivariate procedure was used on the data in Table 28.4 that included all six independent variables, listwise deletion would mean there were no cases available for analysis. Examination of Table 28.4 indicates every variable has one missing value, albeit in a different case. It is possible that listwise deletion would not introduce bias, but the question turns on the relationship of the missing data to the observed data (Allison, 2002).

The second way of handling missing data is pairwise deletion. Pairwise deletion

Table 28.4   Data matrix*

Cases	Variables						
	Y	X_1	X_2	X_3	X_4	X_5	X_6
1	0	1	1	1	1	1	1
2	1	0	1	1	1	1	1
3	1	1	0	1	1	1	1
4	1	1	1	0	1	1	1
5	1	1	1	1	0	1	1
6	1	1	1	1	1	0	1
7	1	1	1	1	1	1	0

Y = Dependent variable
X = Independent variable
1 = Reported value 0 = Missing value
*Taken from Riedel (2000: 114)

is accomplished by deleting cases *only on the variables that are being analyzed.* This makes a critical difference in terms of missing cases. In a bivariate analysis where Y is compared to X_1 only two cases are dropped from the analysis because of missing values (see Table 28.4). The difficulty is that comparisons between Y and X_1 uses a different subset of data from comparing Y and X_2. The statistical question is whether the two data subsets are drawn from the same populations or do they come from overlapping populations? In addition, pairwise deletion can create statistical anomalies (Cohen and Cohen, 1983; Riedel, 2000).

The alternative to listwise and pairwise deletion is imputation of the missing data. There are two types of missing data applicable to the UCR Program: missing cases or unit non-response and missing values or item non-response.

Missing cases/unit non-responses: Return A, SHR, and NIBRS

Missing cases and Return A
This section looks at unit non-reponse on Return A which is usually an indication of the number of reporting agencies. Unit non-response is also a problem for age, race, and sex of arrested offenders, but will not be considered here.

Maltz (2007) reports that the per cent of population covered by the UCR hovered around 90 per cent from the mid-1950s to the end of the century; in 2003, it grew to 91 per cent. As impressive as this might sound, especially for a voluntary program, 'this is a count of the population by agencies that submitted *at least one monthly report* to the FBI.' (Italics in the original) (Maltz, 2007: 276).

To get some idea of how serious missing data was, the Bureau of Justice Statistics used crime data reported to the FBI by each

Table 28.5   Reporting behavior of 18,413 police agencies,1992–1994*

Reporting frequency	Police agencies	
	Number	%
Total	18,413	100
Full reporting (36 months)	11,700	64
Partial reporting (1–35 months)	3,197	17
No reports	3,516	19
Special agency	2,650	14
Regular agency	866	8

*Taken from Maltz (1999: 9)

police agency for the years 1992 to 1994. Table 28.5 gives the results.

Table 28.5 indicates that 64 per cent of the 18,413 agencies reported crime for the full 36 months of the study and 17 per cent reported between 1 and 35 months of data. Almost a fifth of the agencies (19 per cent) turned in no reports. What mitigates this percentage somewhat and may be a limitation of the research is that 14 per cent of the agencies with no reports were special agencies. Special agencies were those in which other agencies reported for them or were special police agencies such as transit police, fish-and-game police or park police.

The 5 per cent or 866 regular police agencies that reported no crime data for 36 months contained some major jurisdictions. They were: 'primary police agencies in 3 cities and counties with populations over 100,000; 17 cities with populations between 50,000 and 100,000; and almost 200 cities with populations over 10,000' (Maltz, 1999: 9).

What is done with Return A missing data is imputation. While the UCR imputation methods have been subject to criticism, they will be mentioned briefly here (Maltz, 1999, 2007; Addington, 2008). The first of two methods involves agencies who submit three or more months of acceptable data.

A mean is calculated for the months of acceptable data and this mean is substituted for the missing months.

The second method is used when an agency submits only one or two months of acceptable data. All data for that agency are discarded. Each reporting agency with complete data is grouped into strata defined by whether it belongs to a Metropolitan Statistical Area, other cities, rural areas. The non-reporting agency is placed in the appropriate stratum and the estimated crime volume for that stratum is used. The annual crime rate is calculated using the non-reporting agency's population. If no comparable agencies are available, the previous year's data for the non-reporting agency is used as an estimate (Lynch and Jarvis, 2008).

Missing cases and the SHR

In the UCR Program, the Supplementary Homicide Reports (SHR) are the only data source that provides detail on the crime incident. Perhaps given the seriousness and social visibility of homicide, under reporting is less of a problem. Snyder and colleagues (1996) state that between 1980 and 1994, the SHR included 92 per cent of all homicides reported in the United States.

The FBI does not impute SHR data, but the National Archive of Criminal Justice Data (NACJD) does impute the number of homicides. The UCR program files, including SHR data, are available and can be downloaded from the National Archives of Criminal Justice Data (National Archive of Criminal Justice Data, 2008b).

To impute the number of homicides, NACJD weights the SHR cases by the ratio of the number of homicides reported in *Crime in the United States* to the number reported in the UCR. To account for unit non-response for the states, NACJD weights the ratio of the number of homicides reported for a given state in *Crime in the*

United States by the number of homicides reported for that state in the SHR.

Missing cases and NIBRS

Like the UCR, NIBRS is a voluntary system and missing cases raises its ugly head once more. While no imputation was used for either missing cases or missing values, Addington (2008) examined the unit non-response bias in NIBRS with respect to estimates of violent crime. She compared NIBRS data on murder, rape, and aggravated assaults to UCR Return A data for 2002 and 2003. Comparisons were made using the 2000 census for eleven population groups ranging from cities greater than one million to suburban counties.

The response rate is the ratio of NIBRS/UCR agencies. While the overall response rate for the 2002 data was 0.46 (all agencies responding would be 1.0). The response rate for cities over 250,000 is 0.16, but gets larger as the population group gets smaller. The highest response rates are for cities under 10,000, suburban, and rural counties. The latter had response rates ranging from 0.37 to 0.47. This is consistent with the general concern that NIBRS over represents small agencies.

Also using 2002 data and focusing only on murder rates, the NIBRS/UCR ratio was 0.66 for cities between 500,000 and 999,999, then declined sharply to 0.34 for cities from 250,000 to 499,999. For cities less than 250,000, the NIBRS/UCR ratio was 0.66.

While the evidence for unit non-response seems to favor more agreement for smaller population groups than larger ones, there is a great deal of variation. As Addington (2007: 46) notes the results 'indicate that the amount of bias in NIBRS data is not so small as to be ignorable, especially for national estimates and larger population groups.' NIBRS does not currently use missing data imputation although Addington does

suggest that the development and use of weighting schemes would increase the utility of the data.

Missing values/item non-responses: SHR and NIBRS

Missing values and the SHR

What is a larger problem for the SHR are item non-responses, that is, missing data within records. Although victim information is present, the item non-responses are generally offender characteristics or related to offenders such as missing victim/offender relationships which occur because of the absence of arrested offenders. In the case of the NACJD files, there are three weights in the offender file of which one will be described. Since the SHR is a victim-based file, supposing there are 1,000 victims in a specific age/sex/race category and 800 are killed by unknown offenders, the weight would equal 1.25 because the unknown offenders are treated as if they have the same age/race/sex characteristics as known offenders. Thus, if 25 per cent of the victims were killed by black males aged 15 to 24, then 25 per cent of the unknown offenders were killed by black male offenders 15 to 24 (Maltz, 1999).

Missing values and NIBRS

Addington (2004) also examined item non-response. She compared 1999 NIBRS data to two groups of SHR cases, one includes all homicides while the other is a stratified sample to minimize small agency bias. Addington hypothesized that NIBRS would have less missing data than SHR because NIBRS required certification, provided many formal and informal instructions, had extensive data edits, and provided a capability for updating individual records.

The results indicated that NIBRS does, indeed, have less missing data for offender data. What remained unchanged with respect to missing data were victim characteristics such as age, race, and sex of the victim. NIBRS had more missing weapon data than the full SHR, but, once the small agency bias was taken into account, missing weapon data was unchanged between the two data sources. NIBRS had much less missing data with victim/offender relationship than the full SHR, but remained unchanged using the sample SHR.

The biggest differences between the two data sources were for unknown homicides and circumstances of the offense such as whether the murder involved a felony, was the result of an argument, etc. NIBRS had more unknowns than the SHR and less missing data for felony homicides. The differences may have been due to data edits where offenses would be coded more often as felony related in SHR and unknown in NIBRS. Addington found that updating was underutilized because NIBRS does not provide clear guidance and no data edits trigger an update.

Current approaches to imputation

While the imputation methods currently appear to be reasonable approximations, the nature of missing data is much better understood today than when the methods used in previous paragraphs were implemented. Rubin (1976, 1987, 1996) and Little and Rubin (2002) indicate there are three ways that missing data is related to observed data.

The first mechanism is missing completely at random or MCAR. MCAR occurs when the probability of missing data is unrelated to the dependent variable or any other variable. Maltz (2007) gives the example of a natural disaster as when the state of Kentucky was unable to report four years of crime data because of flood damaged computers.

When this assumption is met for all variables, individuals with complete data can be seen as a simple random subsample of the complete data set. MCAR does allow for the missing of one variable to be related to the missing of another. For example, suppose it appears that people who do not report their income are younger than people who do report their income. If a t-test of age comparing missing to observed data is not significant, the result provides evidence that the data are missing completely at random (Allison, 2002).

A second mechanism is missing at random or MAR. Data on the dependent variable, Y, are MAR if the missing data on Y is unrelated to Y after controlling for other variables in the analysis (Allison, 2002). For example, if the probability that recorded income varies according to the age of the respondent, but does not vary within an age group, then the data are MAR (Little and Rubin, 2002). There are models for imputing data that are MAR, but much needs to be known about the structure of the data.

The final mechanism is described by Maltz (2007) as missing not at random (MNAR). Data that are MNAR cannot be imputed in customary ways. Examples include coding errors, agencies with nothing to report, and agencies that have never reported.

While the work by Rubin and his colleagues is a major step forward in understanding missing data, there is no consensus on the kind of imputation models that are most appropriate. Issues related to imputation, including multiple imputation, are discussed in more detail in a special issue of *Homicide Studies* (Riedel and Regoeczi, 2004).

The UCR program represents an invaluable source of information about crime in the United States stretching over many decades. In short, if we want to know about crime in the past and use it to formulate future policies, the only national source, albeit limited, is the UCR program. For that reason there is good reason for attempting to develop as valid and reliable data series as possible.

A first step would seem to be an analysis of UCR data to better understand why and how the data are missing before a longitudinal imputation scheme can be developed. This step, cleaning the data, has been pursued by Maltz (2007) and has recently made the results of his efforts available: http://sociology.osu.edu/mdm/UCR1960-2004.zip. level data.

ARREST CLEARANCES

The most widely used definition of homicide arrest clearance is provided by the UCR. According to the FBI, a law enforcement agency clears or solves a particular offense when 'at least one person is arrested, charged with the commission of an offense, and turned over to the court for prosecution …' (FBI, 2007d).

There has been a linear decline of arrest clearances for homicide from 92 per cent in 1960 to 60.7 per cent in 2006. In 1960, there were 4,883 homicides of which 391 were uncleared; in 2006, there were 17,034 homicides of which 6,694 were uncleared (Riedel, 2008). Of course, 60.7 per cent cleared is a national average; while some jurisdictions are higher, many are lower. For example, the homicide clearance rate in California in 2006 was 52 per cent (Criminal Justice Statistics Center, 2007). With respect to cities, Phoenix had a clearance rate of 40 per cent in 2006 (McEwen, 2007; Riedel, 2008).

In many respects, the decline of arrest clearances is more important than variations in homicide rates because it refers to offenders who are beyond the grasp of the criminal justice system and available to commit other crimes. In addition to further traumatizing the victim's friends and family, the low clearance rate undermines the morale of police officers and departments. Lastly, of course, the selectiveness of data on offenders risks biasing research inquiry (Riedel and Jarvis, 1998).

There are two major problems in studying homicide clearances. First, it is clear there is little public awareness or attention given to the problem of declining arrest clearances for homicide. For example, in a 2006 Christian Science Monitor article on declining arrest clearances, Scott Christianson asks one leading police scholar, Professor David Bayley of the State University of New York, why the arrest clearance rate had dropped so much Professor Bayley replied 'I haven't a clue, I've been involved in the field for 40 years and best as can tell, nobody has even raised this stuff. Hearing about it now is like being hit by a bus' (Christianson, (2006) http://www.november.org/stayinfo/breaking06/ArrestStats.html).

Second, until the advent of NIBRS, research on arrest clearances was limited to a few city data sets that collected clearance data with other homicide variables such as the Chicago data set mentioned earlier. Prior to NIBRS, there was no way to connect clearance data reported on the aggregated data to incident level measures. The only observations on clearances are monthly totals of the number of homicide cleared reported on Return A. Using Return A data, it is possible to study increases and decreases of arrest clearances over time and compare changes in jurisdictions to census data. However, there is no way of connecting these totals with characteristics of homicide reported on the SHR. Homicides cleared one month may refer to SHR homicides for that month or any other previous month.

While NIBRS reports clearances with other variables, there is little information about how homicides are investigated which would be useful to determine what practices are most effective. Researchers, such as Punkett and Lundmann (2003) who requested permission to observe how homicide detectives work, were denied. The one exception has been the research by Wellford and Cronin (1999) that examines investigation variables. This research is discussed in detail in Riedel (2008).

NIBRS and arrest clearances

In using official data for research, it is not only a matter of what the researcher decides to study, it is a matter of how the object of research – the dependent variable – is defined. For example, the Bureau of Labor Statistics (2007) counts the unemployed as 'if they do not have a job, have actively looked for work in the prior 4 weeks, and are currently available for work.' People are counted as employed if they did any work at all for pay or profit during the week of the survey. On the other hand, people who have no job and are not looking for one are not counted.

Traditionally, as Riedel (2008) has noted, arrest clearances have been operationally defined as a dichotomy: either the homicide was cleared or it was not. The difficulty with that measure is that some homicides are very easy to clear by arrest while others are very difficult to clear or not cleared at all. In his observations of Baltimore homicide detectives Simon (1991: 40) states:

The vocabulary of the homicide unit recognizes two distinct categories of homicide: whodunits and dunkers. Whodunits are genuine mysteries; dunkers are cases accompanied by ample evidence and an obvious suspect. Whodunits are best typified by crime scenes where a detective is called to some godforsaken back alley to find a body and little more. Dunkers are best typified by scenes at the which the detective steps over the body to meet the unrepentant husband, who has not bothered to change his bloodied clothes and requires little prompting to admit that he stabbed the bitch and would do so again given the chance.

Because NIBRS provides date of incident and date of arrest, researchers can use a more sensitive measure of clearances, time to clearance, instead of the dichotomy of cleared or uncleared. Research results agree that homicides are cleared quickly or not at all. Regoeczi et al. (2008) found that for all homicide cases 17 days had passed before half the cases had been cleared. The drop-off after 17 days is tremendous. For example, nearly six months pass (173 days) before the number of cases remaining uncleared drops from 45 per cent to 40 per cent. Addington (2008) found that for seven variables, between 25 and 30 per cent were cleared the same day and at least 40 per cent were cleared within seven days. Between 15 and 24 per cent were cleared between 8 and 30 days or over 30 days. The remainder, ranging from 23 and 37 per cent were uncleared. The variables were victim sex, race, age, home location, more than one victim, victim/offender relationship, and weapon used.

Drawing on NIBRS results in Riedel (2008) review of the research literature, the following was found.

- Because of greater surveillance, homicides involving children are cleared more quickly than homicides involving old victims.
- Female victims of homicide are cleared more quickly than male victims.
- Although the results are not uniform, white victims are cleared more quickly than minority victims.
- Homicides occurring in private residences are cleared more quickly than homicides in public areas.
- Homicides involving family members or domestic violence are cleared more quickly than more distant relationships.

- Because of the presence of forensic evidence, homicides involving weapons other than firearms are cleared more quickly.
- Homicides involving concomitant felonies such as robberies or drugs show mixed results; some studies show higher clearances while others show lower clearances.

THE NATIONAL VIOLENT DEATH REPORTING SYSTEM (NVDRS)

There are three reporting systems on homicide: UCR, NIBRS, and mortality data from NCHS that provide different information. Because there is no identification number that joins the cases from different systems together, there is no certain way of using information from different data sources for the same cases. The goal of NVDRS is to provide an integrated surveillance system for both homicide and suicide.

In 1999, six private foundations pooled their resources to create a National Violent Death Statistics System. In 2000, a meeting of experts recommended that direct a publically funded surveillance system similar to the National Violent Death Statistics System. In 2002, Congress appropriated 1.5 million dollars to begin development and implementation of a population based active surveillance system of violent deaths. This system is called the National Violent Death Reporting System (Steenkamp et al., 2006).

According to the NVDRS, a death due to violence is a death resulting from the intentional use of physical force or power against oneself, another person, or against a group or community, which is the World Health Organization definition of violence. The definition includes suicides, homicides, deaths from legal intervention (legal executions and acts of war excluded), deaths from undetermined intent, and unintentional firearm fatalities.

NVDRS is an incident-based system that collects data on the violent incident, all deaths that part of the incident, injury leading to deaths, and characteristics of the victims and suspects involved in the violent incident. Victim/offender relationships are included as well as the relationships of each person to the injury leading to the death.

All data in NVDRS are collected from existing sources. The three primary data sources are the death certificates, medical examiner/coroner records, and police records. Additional data sources that can be consulted are crime lab data, Child Fatality Review Team data, SHR, hospital data, Alcohol, Tobacco, Firearms, and Explosives (ATF) firearams information, and input from trained state level personnel inputting the data (CDC, 2007a).

All available data are entered into the system resulting in approximately 600 data entry locations. For each data entry, data sources are ranked to identify what is likely the best available information. For example, sex of the victim is taken first from the death certificate, second from the coroner/medical examiner records, and finally the police (CDC, 2004). Thus, researchers can either accept the primacy code assigned, other codes, or study the relationship among them.

State health departments are the data collectors and lead organizations. Once a death certificate is filed, each state violent death reporting system establishes the details of the case by drawing from the state data sources listed in the previous paragraph. As cases become available the information is transmitted daily through special software to CDC (Steenkamp et al., 2006). As of 2005, for 16 states, there were 15,962 violent deaths of all kinds reported. The two leading causes of death were suicide (8,949) and homicide (4,721) (Karch et al., 2008).

There are two available data sets. The first is the Public Use Data (PUD) which is available for 2003 to 2005. For reasons of confidentiality, it is divided into three files per year, an incident data, suspect data, and victim data. Documentation is also available and the 2005 data can be downloaded from the Inter-University Consortium for Political and Social Research as study no. 04704 (http://www.icpsr.umich.edu/cocoon/ICPSR/STUDY/04704.xml).

There is also a Restricted Access Data set for the years 2003 to 2006 which contains a much larger amount of detail. The codebook is available and can be obtained from the internet (CDC, 2004). However, before data is made available and to a researcher, a research proposal must be submitted and approved by NVDRS that not only includes how the data will be used, but how sensitive data that may reveal individual identification is protected. The applicant must be a Ph.D. at an established institution, must describe how the data will be stored, confidentiality preserved, and unauthorized access prevented. In addition, a letter of approval is needed from a person in the home institution charged with ethical review and the protection of human subjects (CDC, 2007b).

CONCLUSION

The collection, access, and availability of homicide data has undergone enormous changes from the initial UCR program of the 1930s. The early versions of the UCR contained relatively little usable research information about homicides. The shortcomings stimulated a great deal of comment and criticism (Robison, 1966; Sellin, 1931, 1951; Beattie, 1960; Lejins, 1966; Wolfgang, 1963).

The development and implementation of NIBRS represents a successful response to many of the earlier criticisms of the UCR program. The major problem that remains is missing data. To some extent,

criticism of the FBI for missing data both in the traditional UCR program and NIBRS is misplaced. The failure of law enforcement agencies to respond is more a responsibility of state programs than federal law enforcement. While a few states have developed centralized reporting programs, penalties for failure to report are few and sanctions that are implemented do not exist.

While mortality statistics have been a frequently used response to non-reporting of homicides, NVDRS represents a major step forward in a national statistical system for homicide data. Because the death certificate represents a lynch pin in the system, there is a basis upon which to evaluate the completeness of other data sources, including law enforcement records.

A major impetus to the development and use of better homicide data has been sophisticated electronic technology that has only become widely available in the last few decades. Without the use of computers, for example, the analysis of a detailed data base is simply too labor-intensive to be done. Electronic technology has impacted on homicide statistics in two ways.

First, there is the omnipresent internet. The use of the internet makes it possible to input data from agencies, archive data, download data, communicate with persons responsible for maintaining the data system, and share analyses. For NVDRS, a major design goal was to use the internet and standardized software to administer and regulate the daily and weekly flow of data (Paulozzi et al., 2004). The use of standardized reporting software was essential to accommodate the large amount of data being reported.

Second, it is difficult to underestimate the effect of powerful personal computers on the analysis of research data. For example, rather than being limited to rectangular data sets with cases that are listed down the side and variables across the top, modern computers make it possible to analyze hierarchical data sets like NIBRS. Thus, for a single incident, there are levels for victims, offenders, arrestees which require computer processing that would be impossible to do manually.

In addition, the advent of personal computers has made available powerful statistical techniques. For example, the various types of logistic regression use a process called maximum likelihood estimation to generate a model that fits the observed data. The process of generating this model manually would simply be impossible.

What are the challenges? Given that existing law enforcement data on homicide and, probably, future data will still be hampered by non-reporting and missing data, imputation approaches will be essential. While it would seem that past efforts at estimation have been simplistic, without a great deal more knowledge as to the type of imputation techniques most appropriate, criticisms would be premature.

As data systems become more detailed, confidentiality becomes a more important issue. NVDRS is at the forefront of the problem by insisting on a number of important steps to protect sensitive information about participants in a suicide or homicide incident. Given the development of a wide variety of statistical systems about crime, it is time for professional associations to consider detailed guidelines for their members. Probably because earlier data systems were so limited, associations like the American Society of Criminology and the Academy of Criminal Justice Sciences have paid little attention to how members use and misuse official statistics.

Finally, NIBRS has made it possible to explore declining homicide arrest clearances in new and different ways, including using time to clearance rather than a simple dichotomy of cleared or uncleared. However, there is very little known about what is done by the police in a homicide investigation. As Puckett and Lundman (2003) have noted, the process of police investigations is generally closed to researchers. Except for data from a single study of four unidentified cities by Wellford and Cronin (1999), there is very little systematic information about homicide investigations. As this author (Riedel, 2008) has said elsewhere:

> ...there is no question that a 61% arrest clearance rate for homicides in the United States has an impact on public safety. The lack of transparency of tax supported organizations and the lack of access to information how homicides are investigated and arrests made is not acceptable. Imagine, if you would, a disease was spreading throughout the United States with a 39% fatality rate for those infected. The public would never tolerate medical organizations that refused access to researchers on how the disease was caused and victims treated. Why should law enforcement organizations be any different?

REFERENCES

Addington, L. A. (2004) 'The effect of NIBRS reporting on item missing data in murder cases', *Homicide Studies*, 8: 193–213.

Addington, L. A. (2006) 'Using National Incident-Based Reporting System murder data to evaluate clearances: A research note', *Homicide Studies*, 19: 140–52.

Addington, L. A. (2008a) 'Hot v. cold cases: Examining time to clearance for homicides using NIBRS data', *Justice Research and Policy*, 9: 87–112.

Addington, L. A. (2008b) 'Assessing the extent of nonresponse bias on NIBRS estimates of violent crime', *Journal of Contemporary Criminal Justice*, 24: 32–48.

Allison, P. D. (2002) *Missing data*. Thousand Oaks, CA: Sage Publications.

Barnett-Ryan, C. (2007) 'Introduction to the Uniform Crime Reporting Program.' in J. P. Lynch and L. A. Addington (eds), *Understanding Crime Statistics: Revisiting the Divergence between the NCVS and UCR*, Cambridge: Cambridge University Press. pp. 55–89.

Beattie, R. H. (1960) 'Criminal Statistics in the United States 1960', *Journal of Criminal Law, Criminology, and Police Science*, 51: 49–65.

Best, J. (2004) *More Damned Lies and Statistics*. Berkeley, CA: University of California Press.

Block, C. R., Block, R. L. and the Illinois Criminal Justice Information Authority (1998) Homicides in Chicago, 1965–1995 [Computer file]. ICPSR06399-v5. Chicago, IL: Illinois Criminal Justice Information Authority [producer], Ann Arbor, MI: Inter-university Consortium for Political and Social Research [distributor], 2005-07-06. doi:10.3886/ICPSR06399http://www.icpsr.umich.edu/cocoon/NACJD/STUDY/06399.xml

Bottomley, K. (1979) *Criminology in Focus: Past Trends and Future Prospects*. Oxford: Martin Robertson.

Bureau of Labor Statistics (2007) 'Frequently Asked Questions', Retrieved July, 2008, (http://www.bls.gov/cps/cps_faq.htm#Ques5).

Cantor, D. and Cohen, L. E. (1980) 'Comparing measures of homicide trends: Methodological and substantive differences in the Vital Statistics and Uniform Crime Report Time Series (1933–1975)', *Social Science Research*, 9: 121–45.

Criminal Justice Statistics Center (2007) 'Crime in California 2006', State of California, Sacramento.

Centers for Disease Control and Prevention (CDC) (2004) 'Coding Manual NVDRS Version 2-2004', Retrieved July, 2008, (http://www.docstoc.com/docs/544453/NVDRS-Coding-Manual-Full—National-Violent-Death-Reporting-System-Coding-Manual).

Centers for Disease Control and Prevention (CDC) (2007a) 'National Violent Death Reporting System', Retrieved July, 2008, (http://www.cdc.gov/ncipc/profiles/nvdrs/default.htm

Centers for Disease Control and Prevention (CDC) (2007b) 'National Violent Death Reporting System Restricted Access Database Questions and Answers', Retrieved July, 2008, (http://www.cdc.gov/ncipc/profiles/nvdrs/restricted_access_database.htm).

Christianson, S. (2006) Questioning US Arrest Statistics [Electronic Version]. *Christian Science Monitor*. Retrieved November, 2006 from http://www.november.org/stayinfo/breaking06/ArrestStats.html.

Chilton, R. and Jarvis, J. (1999a) 'Using National Incident-Based Reporting System (NIBRS) to test estimates of arrestee and offender characteristics', *Journal of Quantitative Criminology*, 15: 207–29.

Chilton, R. and Jarvis, J. (1999b) 'Victims and offenders in two crime statistics programs: A comparison of the National Incident-Based Reporting System (NIBRS) and the National Crime Survey (NCVS)', *Journal of Quantitative Criminology*, 15: 193–206.

Cohen, J. and Cohen, P. (1983) *Applied Multiple Regression/Correlation Analysis for the Behavioral Sciences*. Hillsdale, NJ: Lawrence Erlbaum Associates.

Dale, A., Wathan, J. and Higgins, V. (2008) 'Secondary analysis of quantitative data sources', in P. Alasuutari, L. Bickman and J. Brannen, (eds) *Sage Handbook of Social Research Methods*, London: Sage Publications. pp. 520–35.

Department of State Police (2006) 'Crime in Illinois 2006', (http://www.isp.state.il.us/crime/cii2006.cfm).

Ewigman, B., Kiviahan, C. and Land, G. (1993) 'The Missouri child fatality study: Underreporting of maltreatment fatalities among children younger than five years of age, 1983 through 1986', *Pediatrics*, 91: 330–7.

Faggiani, D. (2007) 'Introduction', *Justice Research and Policy*, 9: 1–7.

Federal Bureau of Investigation (FBI) (2007a) 'Frequently Asked Questions', Retrieved June 2008 (http://www.fbi.gov/ucr/ucrquest.htm).

Federal Bureau of Investigation (FBI) (2007b) 'Table 1 – Crime in the United States 2007', Retrieved June, 2008 (http://www.fbi.gov/ucr/cius2007/data/table_01.html).

Federal Bureau of Investigation (FBI) (2007c) 'Violent Crime – Crime in the United States 2007', Retrieved June, 2008 (http://www.fbi.gov/ucr/cius2007/offenses/violent_crime/murder_homicide.html).

Federal Bureau of Investigation (FBI) (2007d) 'Clearances – Crime in the United States 2007', Retrieved June, 2008 (http://www.fbi.gov/ucr/cius2007/offenses/clearances/index.html).

Federal Bureau of Investigation (FBI) (2007e) *Uniform Crime Reporting Handbook*. Washington, DC: U. S. Government Printing Office.

Finkelhor, D. (1997) 'The homicides of children and youth', in G. K. Kantor and L. J. Jasinski (eds), *Out of the darkness: Contemporary perspectives on family violence*, Thousand Oaks, CA: Sage. pp. 17–34.

Garner, B. A. (2004) 'Homicide', in *Black's Law Dictionary*. St. Paul, MN: Thomson West. p. 751.

Gartner, R. (1990) 'The victims of homicide: A temporal and cross-national comparison', *American Sociological Review*, 55: 92–106.

Gartner, R. (1991) 'Family structure, welfare spending, and child homicide in developed democracies', *Journal of Marriage and the Family*, 53: 231–40.

Gartner, R. (1993) 'Methodological issues in cross-cultural large-survey research on violence', *Violence and Victims*, 8: 199–215.

Hakim, C. (1982) *Secondary Analysis in Social Research: A Guide to Data Sources and Methods with Examples*. London: Unwin Hyman.

Hakim, C. (1983) 'Research based on administrative records', *Sociological Review*, 31: 489–519.

Herman-Giddens, M. E., Brown, G., Verbiest, S., Carlson, P. J., Hooten, E. G., Howell, E. and Butts, J. D. (1999) 'Underascertainment of child abuse mortality in the United States', *JAMA* 281: 463–7.

Hetzel, A. M. (1997) 'History and organization of the Vital Statistics System.' Washington, D.C.: National Center for Health Statistics. (PHS 97-1003).

Hickey, E. W. (2002) *Serial Murderers and Their Victims*. Belmont, CA: Wadsworth.

Hobbes, T. (1904) *Leviathan: Or, the Matter, Forme and Power of a Commonwealth, Ecclesiasticall and Civill*. Cambridge: Cambridge University Press.

Hutson, H. R., Anglin, D., Yarbrough, J., Hardaway, K., Russell, M., Strote, J., Canter, M. and Blum, B. (1998) 'Suicide by cop', *Annals of Emergency Medicine*, 32: 665–9.

Inter-university Consortium for Political and Social Research (2007) 'ICPSR', Retrieved July, 2008, (http://www.icpsr.umich.edu/).

Jarvis, J. P. and Regoeczi, W. C. (2007) 'Homicides cleared by arrest and exceptionally: Linking investigative and methodological practice.' Presentation at the annual meeting of *Homicide Research Working Group*. Minneapolis.

Jenkins, P. (1994) *Using Murder: The Social Construction of Serial Homicide*. New York: Aldine de Gruyter.

Jupp, V. (1989) *Methods of Criminological Research*. London: Unwin Hyman.

Justice Research and Statistics Association (2008) 'Advantages of incident-based reporting over summary reporting', Retrieved July, 2008, (http://www.jrsainfo.org/ibrrc/background-status/advantages.shtml).

Karch, D. L., Lubell, K. M., Friday, J., Patel, N. and Williams, D. D. (2008) 'Surveillance for violent deaths – National Violent Death Reporting System, 16 States, 2005', *Morbidity and Mortality Weekly Report*, 45: 1–43.

Kennedy, D. B., Homant, R. J. and Hupp, T. R. (1998) 'Suicide by cop', *FBI Law Enforcement Bulletin*, 67: 21–7.

Kenny, D. A. (2007) 'Series Editor's Note', in McKnight, P.E., McKnight, K.M., Sidani, S. and Figueredo.A.J. (eds), in *Missing Data: A Gentle Introduction*. New York: Guilford Press. pp. vii–viii.

Kiecolt, K. J. and Nathan, L. E. (1985) *Secondary Analysis of Survey Data*. Beverly Hills, CA: Sage Publications.

Kitsuse, J. I. and Cicourel, A. V. (1963) 'A note on the uses of official statistics', *Social Problems*, 11: 131–9.

Lejins, P. P. (1966) 'Uniform crime reports', *University of Michigan Law Review*, 64: 1011–30.

Little, R. J. A. and Rubin, D. B. (2002) *Statistical Analysis with Missing Data*. Second edition. New York: Wiley.

Loftin, C., McDowall, D. and Fetzer, M. D. (2008) 'A comparison of SHR and vital statistics homicide estimates for US cities', *Journal of Contemporary Criminal Justice*, 24: 4–17.

Lynch, J. P. and Jarvis, J. P. (2008) 'Missing data and imputation in the Uniform Crime Reports and the effects on national estimates', *Journal of Contemporary Criminal Justice*, 24: 69–85.

McEwen, T. (2007) 'Homicide clearance rates in Phoenix, Arizona', Annual meeting of the Homicide Research Working Group. Minneapolis.

McKnight, P. E., McKnight, K. M., Sidani, S. and Figueredo, A. J. (2007) *Missing data: A gentle introduction*. New York: Guilford Press.

Maltz, M. D. (1999) 'Bridging gaps in police crime data', Washington D.C. Bureau of Justice.

Maltz, M. D. (2007) 'Missing UCR data and divergence of the NCVS and UCR trends', in J. P. Lynch and L. A. Addington (eds), *Understanding Crime Statistics: Revisiting the Divergence of the NCVS and UCR*. Cambridge: Cambridge University Press. pp. 269–94.

Maxfield, M. G. (1999) 'The National Incident-Based Reporting System: Research and policy applications', *Journal of Quantitative Criminology*, 15: 119–49.

National Center for Health Statistics (2007a) 'National Vital Statistics System', Retrieved July, 2008, (http://www.cdc.gov/nchs/nvss.htm#reengineering).

National Center for Health Statistics (2007b) 'U. S. Standard Death Certificate, 2003 Revision', Retrieved July, 2008, (http://www.cdc.gov/nchs/deaths.htm).

National Center for Health Statistics (2007c) 'Classification of death and injury resulting from terrorism', Retrieved July, 2008, (http://www.cdc.gov/nchs/about/otheract/icd9/terrorism_code.htm).

National Archive of Criminal Justice Data (2008a) 'NIBRS Concepts', Retrieved July, 2008, (http://www.icpsr.umich.edu/NACJD/NIBRS/concepts.html).

National Archive of Criminal Justice Data (2008b) 'The Source for Crime and Justice Data', Retrieved July, 2008, (http://www.icpsr.umich.edu/NACJD/).

Overpeck, M. D., Brenner, R. A., Trumble, A. C., Smith, G. S., MacDoman, M. F. and Berendes, H. W. (1999) 'Infant injury deaths with unknown intent: What else do we know?' *Injury Prevention*, 5: 272–6.

Pampel, F. C. and Gartner, R. (1995) 'Age structure, socio-political institutions, and national homicide rates', *European Sociological Review*, 11: 243–60.

Paulozzi, L., Mercy, J. A., Frazier, L. and Annest, J. L. (2004) 'CDC's National Violent Death Reporting System: Background and methodology', *Injury Prevention*, 10: 47–52.

Poggio, E. C., Kennedy, S. D. Chaiken, J. M. and Carlson, K. M. (1985) 'Blueprint for the future of the Uniform

Crime Reporting Program: Final report of the UCR study', Boston, MA: Abt Associates.

Puckett, J. L. and Lundman, R. J. (2003) 'Factors affecting homicide clearances: Multivariate analysis of a more complete conceptual framework', *Journal of Research in Crime and Delinquency*, 40: 171–93.

Regoeczi, W. C., Jarvis, J. P. and Riedel, M. (2008) 'Clearing murders: Is it about time?' *Journal of Research in Crime and Delinquency*, 45: 142–62.

Rennison, C. M. and Rand, M. R. (2007) 'Introduction to the National Crime Victimization Survey', in J. P. Lynch and L. A. Addington, (eds), *Understanding Crime Statistics: Revisiting the Divergence of the NCVS and UCR*. New York: Cambridge University Press. pp. 17–54.

Riedel, M. (2000) *Research Strategies for secondary data: A Criminological Approach*. Thousand Oaks, CA: Sage Publications.

Riedel, M. (1990) 'Nationwide homicide datasets: An evaluation of UCR and NCHS data', in D. L. MacKenzie, P. J. Baunach, and R. R. Roberg, (eds), *Measuring Crime: Large-Scale, Long-Range Efforts*. Albany, NY: State University of New York Press. pp. 175–205.

Riedel, M. (1998) 'Counting stranger homicides: A case study of statistical prestidigitation', *Homicide Studies*, 2: 206–19.

Riedel, M. (1999a) 'Sources of homicide data: A review and comparison', in M. D. Smith, and M. A. Zahn, (eds) *Homicide: A Sourcebook of Social Research*. Newbury Park, CA: Sage Publications. pp. 75–95.

Riedel, M. (1999b) 'Sources of homicide data', in M. D. Smith, and M. A. Zahn, (eds), *Studying and Preventing Homicide: Issues and Challenges*. Thousand Oak, CA: Sage Publications. pp. 31–51.

Riedel, M. (2008) 'Homicide arrest clearance: A review of the literature', S*ociology Compass*, 2: 1145–64.

Riedel, M. and Jarvis, J. (1998) 'The decline of arrest clearances for criminal homicide: Causes, correlates, and third parties', *Criminal Justice Policy Review*, 9: 279–305.

Riedel, M. and Regoeczi, W. C. (2004) 'Missing data in homicide research', *Homicide Studies*, 8: 163–92.

Riedel, M. and Boulahanis, J. (2007) 'Homicides exceptionally cleared and cleared by arrest: An exploratory study of police/prosecutor outcomes', *Homicide Studies*, 11: 151–163.

Roberts, A. (2007) 'Predictors of homicide clearances by arrest: An event history analysis of NIBRS incidents', *Homicide Studies*, 11: 82–93.

Roberts, A. (2008) 'Explaining differences in homicide clearance rates between Japan and the United States', *Homicide Studies*, 12: 136–45.

Robison, S. M. (1966) 'A critical review of the Uniform Crime Reports', *University of Michigan Law Review*, 64: 1031–54.

Rokaw, W. M., Mercy, J. A. and Smith, J. C. (1990) 'Comparing death certificate data with FBI Crime Reporting Statistics on US homicides'. *Public Health Reports*, 105: 447–55.

Rubin, D. B. (1976) 'Inference and missing data', *Biometrika*, 63: 581–92.

Rubin, D. B. (1987) *Multiple Imputation for Nonresponse in Surveys*. New York: John Wiley and Sons.

Rubin, D. B. (1996) 'Multiple imputation after 18+ years', *Journal of the American Statistical Association*, 91: 473–89.

Sanford, N. and Comstock, C. (1971) *Sanctions for evil: Sources of social destructiveness*. San Francisco, CA: Jossey-Bass.

Sellin, T. (1931) 'The basis of a crime index', *Journal of the American Institute of Criminal Law and Criminology*, 22: 335–56.

Sellin, T. (1951) 'The significance of records of crime', *The Law Quarterly Review*, 67: 489–504.

Simon, D. (1991) *Homicide: A Year on the Killing Streets*. New York: Houghton Mifflin.

Simpson, P. (2000) 'Serial killers' *St James Encyclopedia of Popular Culture*, Retrieved June, 2008, (http://findarticles.com/p/articles/mi_g1epc/is_tov/i_2419101084/pg_1).

Snyder, H. N., Sickmund, M., and Poe-Yamagata, E. (1996) *Juvenile Offenders and Victims: 1996 Update on Violence*. Washington, DC: Office of Juvenile Justice and Delinquency Prevention.

Steenkamp, M., Frazier, L., Lipskiy, N. DeBerry, S., Barker, T. L. and Karch, D. (2006) 'The National Violent Death Reporting System: An exciting new tool for public surveillance', *Injury Prevention*, 12(suppl 2): ii3–ii5.

Swigert, V. (1989) 'The discipline as data: Resolving the theoretical crisis in criminology', in S. F. Messner, M. D. Krohn and A. Liska, (eds), *Theoretical integration in the study of deviance and crime: Problems and prospects*. Albany, NY: State University of New York Press. pp. 129–35.

U. S. Advisory Board on Child Abuse and Neglect (1995) 'A nation's shame: Fatal child abuse and neglect in the United States.' Washington, DC: Health and Human Services.

Weber, M. (1946) 'Bureaucracy', in H. H. Gerth, and C.W. Mills, (eds), *From Max Weber: Essays in Sociology*. New York: Oxford University Press. pp. 196–244.

Wellford, C. and Cronin, J. (1999) *An Analysis of Variables Affecting the Clearance of Homicides: A Multistate Study*. Washington, DC: Justice Research and Statistics Association.

Wiersema, B., Loftin, C. and McDowall, D. (2000) 'A comparison of supplementary homicide reports and National Vital Statistics System homicides estimates for U.S. counties', *Homicide Studies*, 4: 317–40.

Wolfgang, M. E. (1963) 'Uniform Crime Reports: A critical appraisal', *University of Pennsylvania Law Review*, 111: 708–38.

World Health Organization (2006) 'External Causes of Morbidity and Mortality', Retrieved July, 2008, (http://www.who.int/classifications/apps/icd/icd10online/?gx85.htm+x85).

World Health Organization (2008) 'Table 4: Estimated Coverage of Mortality Data for Latest Year', Retrieved July, 2008, (http://www.who.int/whosis/database/morttable4.cfm#).

29

Assessing Performance of School Systems: The Measurement and Assessment Challenges of NCLB

Sean Mulvenon

INTRODUCTION

During the last 60 years the US education system has progressed from providing an opportunity for most students, to requiring an opportunity for all students, regardless of their race or economic background to obtain an education (Ferguson, 1998). However, much concern has been raised about the equity of these educational opportunities, including questions about the quality of teachers, administrators, financing and building facilities (Ferguson, 1998; Jerald, 2000; Leithwood, 1992; Morton and Mulvenon, 2007). These concerns, and others, raise interesting questions about how you ensure equity in educational opportunities for all students. One approach attempted in the US has been to use educational outcomes as a proxy measure of educational opportunities, which is essentially the approach attempted through the implementation of 'No Child Left Behind' (NCLB). In theory, if all students are able to attain minimal levels of achievement, then it is inferred their school system provides equity in educational opportunities for all students.

The effectiveness of NCLB is a much debated topic among educational policy experts and educational stakeholders (Cawelti, 2006; Duffy et al., 2008). However, the implementation of NCLB in the US has created a plethora of interesting measurement and assessment challenges that have evolved from the more global goal of ensuring equitable educational opportunities for all students. Since NCLB was passed in 2002, I have been involved in evaluating or implementing measurement and assessment models for several state educational systems. Additionally, from December 2005 through June 2008, I worked as a senior policy advisor for the Deputy Secretary of the US Department of Education, evaluating and researching various state NCLB measurement models. The opportunity to work at both the state and national levels provided outstanding experience and knowledge on the measurement and assessment challenges each state addressed in meeting the guidelines imposed through NCLB. The success of NCLB as an accountability model is predicated on the efficiency and validity of the measurement and assessment methods employed in the models to assess school performance.

The measurement models, the statistical methods, and the testing components of NCLB have raised some interesting questions relative to these respective fields, including the use, appropriateness of the methods, and the latent goals of techniques employed. My hopes in writing this chapter are to provide insight as to how, where, and what measurement and statistical issues have evolved due to NCLB, as well as to provide an assessment of the approaches, methods, and the impact on the fields of measurement, statistics, and testing. The success or failure of NCLB may have a lasting impact on these fields. Identifying where NCLB has been effective, or ineffective, is important in growing our understanding of how measurement and assessment models can be used more effectively in evaluating the performance of school systems.

In February, 2006, I was invited to speak at the University of Maryland about my experiences with NCLB. In response to questions asked by those in attendance, I challenged some of the measurement and statistical approaches employed in NCLB. Based on this presentation, I was asked to give an expanded version of this talk to the graduate student association at the 2007 annual conference of the National Council on Measurement in Education (NCME). In my presentation to NCME, I described NCLB as a 'giant measurement model' and directed specific comments at methodologies, statistical methods, and the development of tests which may be impacting the overall integrity of the measurement and assessment aspects of NCLB. The development of the NCME presentation led me to wonder what would happen if NCLB is ultimately ineffective due to measurement and assessment issues? Additionally, if this does happen, and in some regards I believe this may already be occurring, whom or what is going to be blamed for these measurement and assessment problems within NCLB? As an educational statistician this question concerns me because it is my belief that the fields of measurement, statistics, and testing may inappropriately be assigned much of the blame. It is my goal in this chapter to outline many of the measurement and assessment lessons learned from my experiences with NCLB. Further, I will provide recommendations on how to address the numerous challenges in developing measurement and assessment models to evaluate educational outcomes through NCLB.

UNDERSTANDING NCLB

The current form of the Elementary and Secondary Education Act (ESEA) is more commonly known as 'No Child Left Behind' or NCLB. It was overwhelmingly approved by the US Congress in 2001 and signed into law by President Bush in January, 2002. It had become a common belief that too many students, especially minority students and students from poverty, were underperforming in the US educational system (Linn, 2002). Many educational stakeholders represent NCLB as an initiative of President Bush and a Republican Congress. However, key co-sponsors of this legislation included Democratic legislators Senator Ted Kennedy and Congressman George Miller, demonstrating the bi-partisan nature of NCLB.

A primary influence behind the enactment of NCLB can be attributed to the pressure of business communities that consistently lobbied Congress for greater oversight of the US school system. A major contention of US business was that the 'product' from our school systems, the high-school graduate, was under-prepared in basic reading, writing, and mathematics. This lack of preparation or even consistent level of preparation has resulted in significant costs to business to provide training for these high school graduates. US businesses were demanding that students who graduate had minimal skills they could rely on and that could be documented (Hoff, 2006). A second issue that had emerged was recognition that if under-represented groups were to prosper in the US economy, there needed to be greater equity among school systems and higher expectations for the performance of all students (Goldhaber, 1999). The intersection of these two forces resulted in the creation of 'No Child Left Behind.'

An explicitly stated goal of NCLB is to ensure that schools are held accountable for the performance of all students in an attempt to eliminate the possibility that any student(s) could be 'left behind.' I doubt anyone would argue against this goal, but the measurement, assessment, and policy in methods implemented to ensure this outcome have raised strong objections to NCLB. Many of the objections raised regarding the measurement and assessment methods have merit (Crocker, 2003; Porter et al., 2005), including:

- use of a single test to evaluate school performance;
- selecting performance targets;
- test validity;
- validation studies.

Since the beginning, an emphasis of NCLB has been on measurement and assessment: how to measure performance and the statistics of evaluating performance. This emphasis has contributed to numerous opportunities for the fields of educational statisticians and measurement to make significant contributions to the process of assessing performance of students and school systems in NCLB.

GENERAL OVERVIEW OF THE ASSESSMENT PROCESS IN NCLB

Each State Educational Agency (SEA) was required to comply with specific NCLB mandates regarding tested grades, subjects, the type of exam, and procedures for evaluating the performance of school systems. A US Department of Education (USDOE) handbook provided details that grades 3–8 must be tested in math and reading, criterion referenced tests (CRT) must be employed, and all students must attain a performance level of 'proficient' by the year 2014. A student is considered 'proficient' if they obtain a scaled score on the CRTs identified by the SEA as meeting the educational requirements for performance in math or reading for their grade. Additionally, each SEA was required to develop a method for evaluating the performance of school systems, using the CRTs, the annual performance goals, and their progress toward meeting the goal of 100 per cent of students proficient by 2014 (US Department of Education, 2009a).

The measurement models within NCLB used to assess school performance can be reduced to nine specific requirements that represent a simplified list of the steps required to assess school performance for NCLB.

(1) Develop CRTs in reading and math for grades 3–8 and one grade in high school. Additionally, these CRTs must be aligned with the grade-specific curriculum as outlined by the SEA.
(2) Identify a scaled score for the CRTs in reading and math that represents whether a student is proficient or performing at the appropriate grade level.
(3) Assign a performance category to every student based on their performance on the CRTs. The most common are:

a) below basic;
b) basic;
c) proficient;
d) advanced.

(4) Assess *all* students in the designated grades as appropriate for all school systems.
(5) Disaggregate the scores of students for reading and math for nine subgroups in the school system for all students who were present for the full academic year (referred to as non-mobile students):

a) all students;
b) students participating in the Federal Free and Reduced Lunch Program;
c) limited English proficient students;
d) students with disabilities;
e) Asian or Pacific Island students;
f) African-American students;
g) Hispanic students;
h) Native American students;
i) Caucasian students.

(6) Assess the performance of school systems for each subgroup across all grades within a school;

or by grade using the percentage of students proficient.
(7) Establish performance goals, or Annual Measurable Objectives (AMOs), that will provide for all schools to have 100 per cent of students proficient on the state CRT exams by the year 2014.
(8) Determine a minimum number of students in a subgroup for a score to be employed or representative of a school system's performance (referred to as minimum *N*).
(9) Develop and evaluate the composite measure of performance of each school system and develop an assessment model that can be used to assign a performance label to the school system.

Applying these nine steps, each SEA basically assigns a 'label' describing the school system's performance. The performance labels may range from 'Meeting Performance Goals' to 'Schools in Need of Improvement,' and are in theory designed to provide a global representation of the overall performance of the school system.

ASSESSMENT MODELS

The forms of assessment models approved by the USDOE to comply with NCLB can be reduced to three approaches: (1) status, (2) growth, and (3) index.

Status models

Status models compare the percentage of students proficient in each applicable subgroup (which met the minimum *N* requirements) against the AMO. If the percentage of students proficient for a subgroup exceeds the AMO, then a school is identified as meeting the AMO for that subgroup. This process is repeated for all subgroups. The status model represents a cross-sectional measure of the performance of the school systems and is arguably the most simplistic. A recurring theme in education is to develop 'simplistic' models which the status model represents. A problem with simplistic models is they typically have greater measurement error.

Growth models

Growth models assess the change in performance for students from previous years or through use of projection methods to determine if a student will attain the level of 'proficient' in three to four years. If a performance trajectory suggests a student is 'on-track' to be proficient within three to four years, the student is considered 'proficient' for current year performance of the school system. Some SEAs consider a student who is 'proficient' in the current year as 'meeting growth' regardless of the actual change in performance (US Department of Education, 2009b). The determination of a school meeting the AMO in growth is completed similar to the status models with the total number of students proficient, i.e., meeting growth, divided by the total number of students assessed. If this percentage exceeds the AMO for a subgroup, then this subgroup is considered to have met the NCLB requirements. The primary goal of the growth models is to evaluate the progress of students toward attaining proficiency, representing what many consider to be a more effective measure of the performance of a school system in NCLB (Gong, 2004). Additional measurement issues associated with growth models will be discussed later in this chapter.

Index models

With index models, a SEA assigns points to each student based on their performance category on their CRT. For example, students who are proficient or advanced

may be assigned a score of 100 points, with basic students assigned 50 points, and those below basic assigned 0 points. If the average score for a subgroup in a school system exceeds the AMO then the school is deemed to have met the AMO for that subgroup using an index model. The primary goal of index models is to provide partial credit to school systems for those students who are below proficient, with the understanding that an educational effect is present with students who are below proficient. One measurement aspect required by the USDOE as part of index models is points provided to proficient and advanced students cannot be compensatory, with higher performing students compensating for the performance of lower performing students.

Overall assessment

A natural question about these assessment models is 'do they work?' Are school systems that are underperforming identified as such? Are school systems that are performing well represented correctly? If a school system meets the AMO for all subgroups, they are deemed to be making adequate progress within NCLB. The three assessment models all have inherent strengths, weaknesses, and challenges in the way they have been implemented by the various SEAs. It seems obvious that many things could be done to improve the assessment process in NCLB, including standardizing tests for all students in the US, implementation of effective growth models, national performance goals, etc., but first it may be possible to improve how the current system works. More importantly, evaluate some of the measurement and assessment issues and how they impact the fields of measurement, statistics, and testing.

The implementation of NCLB and the accompanying development of the measurement and assessment models have contributed to a series of measurement issues surrounding what is statistically appropriate, or more specifically, what is 'statistically allowed'. The evolution of measurement issues within NCLB can be directly traced to SEAs, expert consultants, and special interest groups that have attempted to develop the most flexible assessment systems. Presently, a case can be made that the nature of some of the flexible assessment systems create a mechanism where the overall validity of the assigned NCLB status to a school system may be suspect.

EXAMPLES OF MEASUREMENT CHALLENGES

The important question from NCLB and the school's perspective is: 'Does a given school meet the NCLB performance goal?' Each of the aforementioned NCLB models answers this question differently. What follows is a brief explanation of how each model answers this question and the strengths and weaknesses of each. To demonstrate the different measurement challenges, a few examples using the ALL (all students in the school system) and Black students subgroups are provided (see Figure 29.1).

Status model

School A in 2007 serves students in kindergarten through grade five and must be measured as part of NCLB. A total of 100 students in Grades 3–5 attended School A in 2007. The performance goal for this school system is 50 per cent of students proficient. School A had 30 per cent or 30 students proficient in 2006 and 33 per cent or 33 students proficient in 2007.

Growth model

School A has 70 growth scores for students in Grades 3–5. In reality, growth scores only exist for Grades 4 and 5, with no pre-test for students in Grade 3. A total of 10 students were proficient in Grade 3 on the CRT. Additionally, 23 students were proficient on the CRT in Grades 4 and 5. Thus, a total of 33 students were proficient on the CRT and the SEA has deemed these students to have 'met growth,' and will conduct no additional evaluation of the performance of these students. I will refer to these students as X1. Next, the growth for the remaining 45 students is examined using a projection method that determines whether a student is 'on-track' to be proficient in four years. A total of 10 students are identified as 'on-track' and considered proficient for the 2007 NCLB computations. I will refer to this group of students as X2. A metric developed to assess growth models is to combine X1 and X2 (33 + 10) to obtain 43. This value is divided by 100 students to obtain 43 per cent of students proficient in the growth model.

Index model

School A has 100 students assessed in 2007 and 33 are proficient. For each one of these students School A receives 100 points. Additionally, School A has 40 students that are identified as performing at the basic level and receives 50 points for each student. The average score for the school is 53 [((33 * 100) + (40 * 50))/100 = 5300 / 100 = 53].

Figure 29.1 provides examples of how schools are being evaluated as part of NCLB and helps to provide a basis for discussing some of the measurement anomalies or questions that have evolved since the implementation of NCLB. School A has 33 of 100 students who are proficient in

School A has 100 students and has 33 students identified as proficient. A total of 40 students were identified as basic. For the 67 students who were not proficient, 10 were identified as making growth. The target AMO is 50 per cent or .50. School A has 30 per cent of students proficient in 2006.

Step	Action	Met NCLB requirements
1)	Is .33% ⊒.50% (Group A ÷ C) (Group A = 33 proficient students, Group C = 100 total students)	NO
2)	Apply 95% confidence interval Is .33 + 1.96(.047) = .422 ⊒ .50[1]	NO
3)	Apply safe harbor (Improvement from 30% to 33% proficient does not meet the goal of a 10% reduction in the number of student, below proficient, i.e., 70% to 63% or a performance of 37% proficient)	NO
4)	Apply safe harbor with confidence interval Is .03 + 1.96(0.066)[2] = .1585 The value of .1585 ⊒ .07	YES
5)	Apply growth model (10 students made growth) $(X1 + X2) ÷ 100 = (33 + 10) ÷ 100 = .43$ .43#.50	NO
6)	Index model $((33 * 100) + (40 * 50)) ÷ 100 = 53$ 53 ⊒50	YES

[1]A standard binomial equation used to generate the confidence interval:

$$\text{s.e.} = \sqrt{\frac{.33(1-.33)}{100}} = \sqrt{.0022} = .047$$

[2]A standard binomial equation is used to generate the confidence for the difference in two proportions:

$$\text{s.e.} = \sqrt{\frac{.33(1-.33)}{100} + \frac{.30(1-.30)}{100}} = \sqrt{.0022 + .0021} = .066$$

Figure 29.1   School A status, growth, and index models for 2007.

reading and officially has 10 students who are 'on-track' for growth, yet this school is identified as 'Meeting Standards' for NCLB. The examples in Figure 29.1 are representative of the models that have been approved by the USDOE. The target AMO is 50 per cent and only 33 per cent of students passed the CRT in reading, but the school effectively meets the AMO target for every method but those based on actual performance. These examples provide an appropriate foundation for discussing questions regarding the validity and reliability of the measurement models and techniques being employed as part of NCLB. The rest of this chapter will examine and evaluate:

a) validity;
b) use of confidence intervals;
c) safe harbor;
d) minimum *N* issues.

As they apply to the use of:

a) status models;
b) growth models;
c) index models.

Additionally, the inclusion of Limited English Proficient (LEP) and Students with Disabilities (SWD) subgroups will be examined.

MEASUREMENT AND ASESSMENT ISSUES IN NCLB

Issue of validity

An effective measurement model requires both internal and external validity. The measurement models developed by the SEAs and subsequently approved by the USDOE may be lacking in terms of their internal and external validity. How does this happen and what exactly did happen to create a system within NCLB that contributed to questions of validity? A personal theory is that too much flexibility was provided in terms of what was statistically allowed and this has contributed to the questions of both internal and external validity.

Internal validity in NCLB

Is the measurement model that has been designed to assess school performance differentiating between effective and ineffective school systems? This is an important question and goes directly towards the internal validity of a measurement model. For example, when a school is identified as meeting NCLB or as a School In Need of Improvement (SINI), this status should be consistent with the actual performance of the school system.

External validity in NCLB

If the outcomes from this measurement model were compared to other methods to assess school performance, would it provide consistent results? The ability to transport a school accountability system to other states and have the system be equally effective is essential. A consistent concern with SEAs developing their own measurement models is the relative performance of school systems under other SEA scoring models. In particular, if one SEA's measurement model is identified as more 'flexible' (i.e., more school systems meet their performance goals), it is anticipated that other SEAs will adopt elements of their model. For example, Georgia was the first SEA to obtain permission from the USDOE to use confidence intervals (discussed later). The key question here is: does the measurement model employed produce consistent results that would be cross-validated via the use of other methods? The same issue applies to the CRTs employed by SEAs. For example, a New York Times article provided incredible detail on the inconsistencies of student achievement on state CRTs versus performance on the National Assessment of Educational Progress (NAEP) exam (Dillon, 2005). It seems that across the US students are performing well on state CRTs, but on the NAEP are demonstrating anemic performance.

Criterion-referenced tests and NCLB

A major emphasis of NCLB has been for SEAs to develop CRTs aligned with their specific curriculum objectives. The use of CRTs represented a compromise between those who wanted national tests and standards and those who wanted to retain the current autonomy of SEAs. The administration of CRTs represents use of a common objective metric for students within the individual SEAs while limiting the reliance on more subjective measures that had limited comparability between school systems. It was a reasonable compromise. However, as a result, each SEA has developed a CRT or adopted augmented norm referenced tests (NRT) to serve as their primary assessment within NCLB. The development of CRTs for use as the primary NCLB assessment has raised some interesting questions regarding technical standards for these exams. More specifically, what are the necessary technical merits, guidelines, and expectations for developing appropriate CRT exams?

The Arkansas Benchmark Exam is an excellent example of interesting measurement problems that have been identified due to the use of CRTs as part of NCLB. Further, it raises some interesting questions about the psychometric properties employed to develop CRT exams. The field of testing, and the science on how to develop tests, has seen tremendous growth in the last 40 years. The issues and examples provided below were selected to illustrate concerns regarding what is appropriate in the development of CRT exams.

Length of the test

One such issue involves the appropriate length for a CRT. In Arkansas, an explicit goal of developing the benchmark exam was to create a shorter exam and minimize the amount of testing. As a result, many of the content strands employed as part of the Arkansas Benchmark Exam are under-parameterized, resulting in greater standard errors and less accuracy when attempting to determine a student's score for a content strand. If a student's knowledge of content strand on probability is measured using 10 items that have been selected through conventional psychometric and test development procedures, it can reasonably be concluded that when a student correctly answers 8 or more items they have demonstrated knowledge of probability. If only three items are used to assess a student's

knowledge of probability it will be more difficult to determine what a score of 1, 2, or 3 items correct really means in terms of the student's knowledge of probability.

Next, what is an appropriate number of items to measure a content strand? Using current test development procedures you can compute standard errors and identify an appropriate number of items to measure a student's knowledge on a content strand. However, this must also be scaled against the scoring model selected by the SEA. For example, in the original form for the Arkansas Benchmark Exam, scaled scores were to range from 0 to 400 with a score of 200 representing a score of 'proficient.' The math exam had 40 multiple choice questions and 40 points from the open-response items for a total of 80 possible points. To convert this to a scale of 0 to 400 you have natural gaps in the scaled scores and a score of 200 was not possible on the math exam. The standard deviation for the math exam was 90 points, which we expect (i.e., a large value), but the interval for a performance level of Basic was 150 to 200, or only 50 points. The math exam had an incredibly platykurtic distribution, wide variations, and volatility in the scores. In contrast, the literacy exam had a standard deviation of approximately 30 points. In 2004, the mean literacy score for 4th grade students was 196 with a standard deviation of 31 points. The standard deviation was 62 per cent of the width of the performance levels ($31 \div 50 = .62$). The performance level for proficient was 200–249; and for advanced it was 250 or higher. As previously stated, basic was 150–199. As a result, very few students were considered advanced (a score greater than 249) or below basic (a score below 150). The effort to make the test 'short' had the adverse effect of raising questions about the validity and accuracy of the exam.

Open-response items

The use of open-response items can be an effective tool in understanding the thought processes of students as they complete course work. More specifically, at the classroom level, they can help facilitate instruction. A question that has been raised is whether open-response items have the same effectiveness on large scale standardized tests. The Arkansas Benchmark Exam employed a CRT mathematics exam where 50 per cent of the total score came from use of open-response items. Turner (2000) demonstrated that no additional information was generated by the use of open-response items on this CRT. The costs associated with open-response items and the length of time to score may be counterproductive to the goal of inclusion of these items on CRTs.

Technical merits of CRTs

The selection of items, number of items, calculation of standard errors, and inclusion of open-response items are all part of the development of psychometrically sound exams (Hambleton and Jones, 1993). In my NCME presentation I raised the question of technical merits or industry standards in the development of standardized tests for use in NCLB. During this presentation some cited AERA and APA ethical guidelines for testing, but these guidelines do not address test development standards. It may have become time not for a national test, but for national standards regarding test development. I would champion that greater emphasis be placed on the development of some industry standards to ensure that 'loose' or widely variant tests are not employed in SEA assessment models.

Variances to NCLB assessment plans: 'Gaming the system'

The next section of this chapter outlines some interesting policy decisions, directly related to measurement of school performance, that have been implemented as part of NCLB. Some involve application of statistical theory, whereas others involve policy decisions as part of a scoring performance of schools in SEA NCLE models.

Banking of scores

A policy used in scoring models in several states is 'banking of scores.' Effectively, 'banking of scores' is the policy of using certain types of scores in performance calculations for more than one school (CCSSO, 2004). It was proposed and accepted that middle-school or junior-high algebra scores, for students who have an SEA mandated algebra exam, could have these scores 'banked' and used a second time in NCLB computations for their high schools.

To evaluate the effect of 'banking' scores, a series of analyses was completed in Arkansas for the K-12 system. Two concerns in regard to 'banking' scores were raised: (1) excusing high schools of the responsibility for teaching algebra to low performing students, and (2) an attempt to just remove low performing schools from Alert or School Improvement status. Additionally, it could give the impression that high school principals from school districts, with middle- and junior-high school systems, are not held to the same standard as principals in elementary and middle schools. For example, an elementary school is accountable for those students in attendance at their schools. Why does a high school get credit for a student's math score when that student may never actually be required to complete a math class at that school? The practice of 'banking' math scores for high schools is assessing a K-12 score and not assessing the effectiveness of this high school in teaching mathematics.

There are at least two scenarios where the policy of 'banking' scores will cause even greater problems within NCLB. The first is when a school is removed from school improvement because of the 'banking' of scores, masking ineffective instruction at the high school. The second is the possibility of middle school algebra and geometry scores, linked to a high school, placing the high school on Alert, for students who have never actually attended the high school. The major policy issue associated with 'banking' scores is schools should be responsible for those students who attend their systems.

Use of confidence intervals

Another means of evaluating school performance within NCLB is with the use of confidence intervals. Statisticians advocate for the use of confidence intervals to more formally assess the likelihood or precision of a computation. Three issues have arisen with regard to the use of confidence intervals within NCLB: a) generation, b) width, and c) application.

Generation

In traditional statistical models, confidence intervals are generated that represent the likelihood or probability of a parameter residing within the 'intervals.' The conventional interpretation of the confidence interval is that the 'true' score of a point estimate will reside within the interval of a specified percentage of time. If a 95 per cent confidence interval is selected, then the true score will fall within the confidence intervals 95 per cent of the time.

Width

Determination of the width of the confidence interval is a function of the parameter being estimated and the distributional properties of the estimator

being used. Additionally, in conventional research designs, confidence intervals are related to the probability of correctly rejecting a null hypothesis given the null hypothesis is false. What exactly is the goal with the use of confidence intervals in NCLB? More specifically, many SEAs elected to use 95 or 99 per cent confidence intervals. I suspect, given a true null hypothesis, if a school obtained a score that was within a 99 per cent confidence interval of the performance goal it is deemed to be meeting this goal. This application of confidence intervals seems too liberal and defies the basis for their use in conventional measurement or research studies.

Application

Where do you apply the confidence intervals? Traditionally, the confidence interval is applied to the point estimator, with the interval being symmetric about this value. Most SEAs claim use of one-tailed intervals, but review of their computations will reveal that two-tailed intervals are actually computed with the upper-bound applied. This provides a wider confidence interval and I suspect is something done by design to increase the likelihood a school system will be identified as meeting the performance goal.

Computation of confidence intervals

To address these issues, confidence intervals were computed for *Safe Harbor* using standard statistical methodology for computing these ranges. *Safe Harbor* is a metric where if a school increases the number of students proficient by 10 per cent they are considered to have made 'safe harbor' and therefore to have met NCLB requirements. Both two-sided and one-sided confidence intervals were computed using a 75 per cent confidence band.

Equation for both One-Tailed and Two-Tailed confidence intervals

The confidence intervals were calculated using the following formula:

$$.75\text{C.I.} = \hat{p} \pm (z\text{-value}) \cdot \hat{\sigma}_{s.e.} \quad (29.1)$$

with

$$\hat{\sigma}_{s.e.} = \sqrt{\frac{\hat{p} \cdot (1 - \hat{p})}{N}} \quad (29.2)$$

and a z-value of 1.15, $\hat{p}$ is the per cent of students proficient, and N is the sample size. For the one-tail confidence intervals, a z-value of .674 is used and the C.I. has the form

$$\hat{p} + (z\text{-value})\hat{\sigma}_{s.e.} \quad (29.3)$$

Traditional use of confidence intervals in growth models for safe harbor

To demonstrate the process of safe harbor and use of confidence intervals in this process a few examples are provided. School A has 40 students and obtained the scores of 19.0 per cent proficient for 2007 Literacy and 22.0 per cent proficient for 2008 Literacy, with an improvement of three per cent. The goal for growth is $(100 - 19.0)/10 = 8.1$, so the target for 2008 becomes $19.0 + 8.1 = 27.1$ per cent of students proficient. Thus, School A does not meet expected growth for 2007–2008. However, applying confidence intervals School A can meet this goal. The upper bounds for the confidence intervals are:

one-tailed: $.22 + (.674)(.0654) = .2640$ or 26.45 per cent proficient for growth
two-tailed: $.22 + (1.15)(.0654) = .2952$ or 29.52 per cent proficient for growth

The values demonstrate the statistical power issues associated with using two-tailed versus one-tailed confidence intervals. This application of confidence intervals to individual schools in growth computations seems equitable. The problem is the application and computation of confidence intervals for schools with different numbers of students, but the same performance. For example, suppose School B had 19 and 22 per cent of students proficient in 2002 and 2003, respectively. The performance goal is the same as School A. However, School B had 100 students complete the CRT exams. Thus, the one- and two-tailed upper bound values become:

one-tailed: $.22 + (.674)(.041) = .2476$ or 24.8 per cent proficient for growth
two-tailed: $.22 + (1.15)(.041) = .2672$ or 26.7 per cent proficient for growth

School A, based on the two-tailed upper bound confidence interval for growth would be determined to have MET adequate yearly growth expectations. In contrast, School B has the same change in performance, but would be determined NOT to have met adequate yearly growth.

Too often in statistics we assume methods should be implemented much as we are taught, or teach, in our courses. However, sometimes things have to be more formally evaluated to understand the policy challenges. In 2004 a decision on the application of confidence intervals with NCLB was being discussed using the aforementioned traditional approach. More research revealed that a total of 16 schools in Arkansas would have been identified as meeting *Safe Harbor* 'growth' expectations, though they actually had negative growth from 2003–2004. For example, School C has 39 per cent of students proficient in 2003 and needed to improve to 45.1 per cent of students proficient. However, for 2004, School C only had 38 per cent of students proficient. The upper bound of the growth confidence limit for School C, when considering their sample size of 40, was .4683 or 46.83 per cent ($38 + 8.83 = 46.83$). Thus, a negative 'growth,' but an upper bound for the confidence interval that includes the performance goal for growth.

Approach employed in Arkansas

To address issues of sample size in Arkansas, confidence intervals were applied to the 100 per cent growth goal. For example, a 15 per cent standard error in per cent growth was multiplied by 1.15 (the 75 per cent z-score value) to produce .1725 per cent. This value was subtracted from 100 per cent to produce a lower bound confidence interval for per cent growth of .8275 or 82.75 per cent. If a school obtained at least 82.75 per cent of their expected growth it was deemed to have met expectations. This method was applied unilaterally to all schools and thus produced a standardized, common approach to employing confidence intervals without bias due to sample size. The individual computation of confidence intervals based on a school system size created numerous measurement problems, and in some cases, some inequities. As part of NCLB 100 per cent of students are to be tested, but if School A and School B both test 100 per cent of their students, but School A has 40 students versus School B's 500 students, the advantage gained by School A through the use of confidence intervals is significant, especially given the argument that by testing 100 per cent of students confidence intervals are unnecessary. The statistical basis for this approach was the performance goal which was originally based on an estimate of average percentage of students proficient in the bottom 20 per cent of schools. Given the performance goal was originally an estimate, confidence intervals were applied to this performance goal. If a school met the lower bound, regardless of their sample size, they were determined to meet the NCLB performance goal.

Selection of 'N'

To address some of the measurement issues with NCLB and the use of the various subgroups, each SEA was to select a minimum N or the minimal number of students to be held accountable for a subgroup. The selection of a minimum N is also related to the goal to protect the anonymity of students and be in compliance with the Family Educational Rights and Privacy Act (FERPA). However, the determination of the appropriate sample size (N) has gone beyond selection of a value to comply with FERPA.

As statisticians, many of us completed the proof in graduate school to demonstrate how you can accurately represent a population with as few as 25 observations. Additionally, as researchers, many of us receive Institutional Review Board (IRB) permission for studies with as few as 10 subjects, with this deemed an appropriate number to protect anonymity of participants. Thus, it seems reasonable to expect the minimum N for NCLB could be 10 for any subgroup. Nationally, many state systems have and are attempting to have their minimum N be a value much larger than 10. As part of NCLB if a school has fewer than the minimum N of students in any of the subgroup populations, they are exempted from 'accountability' in NCLB for that subgroup. Thus, the higher the minimum N, the less likely a school system is to have lower performing subgroups included in accountability for NCLB. To demonstrate the result of a higher minimum N value, in 2004 we examined the impact of increasing the minimum N in Arkansas from 25 to 40. A total of 86 schools in Arkansas did not test at least 40 students in any subgroup population. These schools received 'NA' or 'Not Applicable' for all subgroup populations. Further, if you do not have enough students to meet the minimum N in the state assessment plan, you automatically receive a school performance of 'Meets Standards' for NCLB.

Comparing Tables 29.1 and 29.2, it is evident that for 2004 there were 13 schools in 'Alert' and 'School Improvement' using a minimum *N* of 40 versus 49 schools in 'Alert' and 'School Improvement' using a minimum *N* of 25. Thus, by increasing the requirements for minimum *N* SEAs are actually able to eliminate students from various subgroups from inclusion in NCLB requirements for evaluating school performance – ironically, a move that is contrary to the label 'No Child Left Behind.'

ADDITIONAL MEASUREMENT AND RESEARCH ISSUES

Type I versus type II error in NCLB determinations

The preceding sections have addressed many of the statistical, measurement, and policy issues associated with measuring and assessing a school's performance as part of NCLB. A common theme when these issues are raised is related to whether it is more important to make errors in attributing success to unsuccessful schools or identify successful schools as failing. Either way, misidentification of schools represents error in NCLB models. One way of referring to this error is to relate it to

Type I and II errors used in conventional research designs. A Type I error occurs in research when an important difference is identified when in fact no difference exists. A Type II error occurs when it is determined that an important difference does not exist when in fact an important difference does exist. A direct extension of the terms Type I and Type II error can be applied to NCLB, with Type I error representing when a school system is identified as meeting the performance goal when in fact it is not meeting the performance goal; and a Type II error occurring when a school system is identified as not meeting a performance goal when in fact it is meeting the performance goal.

Validity of 'Labels' in growth models

School A is identified as proficient, but what does this label represent and is it accurate? The answer to this question helps us understand the 'validity' of NCLB measurement models. Are the status models effective? Is the use of growth models effective? These questions are also related to the previous issue of Type I and Type II errors. In analysis of selected SEA data and use of the SchoolMatters website (http://www.schoolmatters.com) it is becoming clear that most schools identified as not meeting the performance goals are chronically low performing schools

Table 29.1   2004 NCLB status for schools who tested less than 40 students in 2004 using minimum *N* of 25

2003 NCLB status	2004 NCLB status					
			School improvement			
	N	*Meets standard*	*Alert*	*SI_MS*	*SI*	*NA*
Meets standards	44	**22**	4	–	–	18
Alert	19	**9**	–	6	–	5
School improvement	23	–	–	**8**	9	6

Note. SI_MS is School improvement: Meets standards. SI is School improvement. A school can be in Year 1, Year 2, or Year 3 of School improvement.

Table 29.2   2004 NCLB status for schools that tested less than 40 students in 2004 using minimum *N* of 40 for three year total

	2004 NCLB status					
			School improvement			
2003 NCLB status	N	Meets standard	Alert	SI_MS	SI	NA
Meets standards	44	**28**	12	–	–	4
Alert	19	**4**	–		15	–
School improvement	23	–	–	**1**	22	–

Note. SI_MS is School improvement: Meets standards. SI is School improvement. A school can be in Year 1, Year 2, or Year 3 of School improvement.

in a majority of subgroups. The use of confidence intervals and minimum *N* values has dramatically increased the likelihood of Type I error in NCLB. In contrast, Type II is less common and most likely to occur in schools with larger student populations. Any measurement or statistical system will have Type I and Type II errors. Currently, the USDOE seems intent on addressing both types of errors via changes in the use of confidence intervals and minimum *N* for Type I errors; and measures of 'differentiated accountability' for select schools that perform well in a majority of categories, but are labeled as schools not meeting standards. Differentiated accountability is a new pilot program from the USDOE where a school that is performing well on most NCLB measures, but missing on one or two, may be given special consideration. Basically, differentiated accountability has been implemented to address issues of Type II errors in NCLB.

Definition(s) of growth allowed for NCLB models

Growth models can be applied to any type of data structure with assessment of growth, positive or negative, as a function of the expectations for the model. For example, in education, the goal would be to identify positive growth as representing

increases in student achievement and performance. In contrast, for many medical models the same growth model could be applied with an expectation of negative growth, for example, lower cholesterol levels identified as the goal of a new drug treatment. The present use of growth models allows for the identification of both positive and negative growth as meeting 'growth,' or improvement predicated on some prescribed conditions. For example, if a student is performing at the 10th percentile and increases performance to the 30th percentile, this is identified as positive growth. In contrast, if a student is performing at the 90th percentile and regresses to performance at the 70th percentile, as long as this student remains above the assigned performance goal, this negative growth is considered as an acceptable example of 'growth.' This use of both positive and negative growth to represent the notion of improved student achievement is troubling. An example is provided in Figure 29.2 to help demonstrate the 'flexibility' of what has been approved in regard to 'growth' in NCLB.

Most SEAs, in adherence to one of the USDOE core principals of the Pilot Growth Model Program, indicated ALL students would be measured in their growth models. In reality, this only occurs in selected Growth models via the scoring method.

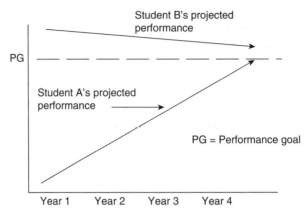

Student A is currently below proficient (year 1) but projected to be proficient in year 4. In this example of a growth model, student A would be considered proficient in year 1 for AYP determinations and in each of the succeeding years if he or she continues to be on this trajectory to proficiency. Additionally, though Student B is declining in performance, she/he would still be considered to have made adequate growth by remaining above the performance goal.

Figure 29.2   Growth scoring example.

In most SEAs, growth scores are computed for all students, thus implicitly meeting this core principle. However, they are only evaluated as part of the growth model if the students are not proficient or if they are projected to be below proficient in future years (US Department of Education, 2009b). This also contributes to issues of what constitutes 'growth' and adherence to the explicit intent of this program.

Two components of growth models in NCLB

Effectively, two components of growth models have evolved in NCLB. The first is the selection of a statistical method for measuring student growth. This is the identification of the most appropriate statistical method based on the type of test, quality of data, and the time frame the SEA is using to collect student achievement data. The second component is the transition of student achievement data from 'scores' on tests to values used in determination of an NCLB status for a school. This second component is an area where many SEAs demonstrated a willingness to be more creative in developing scoring procedures.

One interesting note was the number of SEAs that submitted a scoring system often referred to as a 'Status-Plus' model, which was developed by representatives of the Chief Council of State School Officers (CCSSO). This model was labeled a 'Status-Plus' model by the Arizona Department of Education (p. 4 of proposal) because it combined elements of the current 'Status' model with a growth component. In a status-plus model, a school determines the number of students proficient (X1), the number of students who were not proficient but made adequate growth (X2), and divides this total of X1 + X2 by the total number of students tested (X3). This new percentage [(X1 + X2) ÷ X3] is used as representing the students proficient in determining an NCLB status for a school (see Figure 29.1). The innovation in the status-plus scoring model aside, it is clear that this method does not really assess the overall impact of school systems in demonstrating growth.

OTHER AREAS OF CONCERN WITH NCLB MEASUREMENT MODELS

LEP students

The inclusion of Limited English Proficient (LEP) students has created some interesting measurement challenges in NCLB evaluation models. The classification of a student as LEP indicates that the student requires additional educational support services in order to receive instruction in English. The performance of LEP students is thus influenced by something 'outside' the traditional educational challenges of the other subgroups of NCLB and contributed to the use of alternative assessments.

Alternative assessments for LEP students

A provision in NCLB to provide *flexibility* was designed to allow for the use of alternative assessments for LEP students. Alternative assessments varied in scope and academic level predicated on the individual SEA, with SEAs allowed to develop and design their own assessments. However, are these alternative assessments parallel versions of the regular CRT exam administered to non-LEP students? More specifically, the content may be provided in a second language or accommodations allowed for administration of the regular CRT, but the overall assessment should be consistent with the academic and performance expectations of the regular CRT. In 2006, the USDOE denied many SEAs the use of their alternative assessments in NCLB determinations. The conventional wisdom was that these tests were inconsistent with the regular CRTs. Again, this is a test development issue that may require greater involvement by the testing community to identify appropriate technical standards.

An interesting policy issue with LEP students is the anticipation that effective LEP programs will in fact move students to a non-LEP status. Further, the influx of students into the LEP programs may be incredibly volatile, mitigating the ability of *status* or *index* models to be effectively applied to this subgroup in NCLB. For example, if I have 100 students in an LEP program and I graduate 50 to a non-LEP status, but I replace those 50 with 50 new LEP students, the scores on the *status* or *index* models are not assessing the actual performance of the LEP program. A major concern is this dynamic nature of LEP programs where it is expected that students will transition from the LEP program. The USDOE has allowed the performance of LEP graduates to be counted for their LEP programs for two additional years, which is a form of 'banking' scores for LEP.

Students with disabilities

The inclusion, or exclusion, of students with disabilities is a very contentious topic within NCLB. The educational structure in the US recognizes a category of students that require additional support due to physical and cognitive disabilities, or Students with Disabilities (SWD). The inclusion of SWD in NCLB, similar to LEP students, has created a number of interesting measurement and statistical questions about inclusion of these students.

Parallel forms of CRT exams

Similar to alternative assessments in LEP, an expectation of alternative assessments for SWD was that they would be parallel forms of the regularly administered CRT exams. As you may imagine, a plethora of professional test development companies were ready to meet the challenges associated with creating 'new' tests for SWDs to meet this requirement. The use of these alternative exams has also been questioned due to their technical quality.

Inclusion of SWD in NCLB

A strong case can be made that students with profound cognitive and physical disabilities should not be included in NCLB. To address this issue, the USDOE did provide the one and two per cent exemptions, which allow for the most extreme SWDs to be exempt from inclusion in NCLB models. The key concern of the policymakers is those students with lower ability, classified as SWD, but suffering no profound cognitive or physical disabilities. A case can be made that these students must be included in NCLB to avoid them 'being left behind.' However, this raises additional questions about the most appropriate methods to include these students. It is later recommended to include these students and assess them using both the SEA CRT exam and the alternative assessments. A combination of the two tests may be the best approach to address the issue of SWDs in NCLB.

Understanding the politics of NCLB

The impact of special interest groups, policy experts, lawyers, testing companies, and evaluation experts has contributed to many of the questions regarding the validity of measures associated with NCLB. To that point, the following are some of the demands or concerns raised by these groups regarding the many issues outlined in this chapter:

1) **Issue:** Lack of models that control for poverty or socioeconomic status of students.
   Problem: Students from poverty have traditionally lower performance levels.
   Desired outcome: Allow lower performance expectations for these students in NCLB.
2) **Issue:** Growth models that use an average schooling effect in their projections of student performance.

Problem: Control for the impact of school systems to improve accuracy of the projections of student performance in growth models.
Desired outcome: To allow projections to control for what has been the traditional performance of students in the school systems.

3) **Issue:** Use of 95 and 99 per cent confidence intervals.
   Problem: Measurement error in the assessment of school performance.
   Desired outcome: Provide maximum flexibility in the score a school uses for NCLB.
4) **Issue:** Increase in minimum N sample sizes for inclusion in NCLB models.
   Problem: Too many schools are being held accountable for more traditionally underperforming groups.
   Desired outcome: Increasing the minimum N values limits the inclusion of these subgroups in NCLB.
5) **Issue:** Partial points in index models for no demonstrated achievement.
   Problem: Provide partial credit for approaching Proficient.
   Desired outcome: Provide points for any level of attainment on the SEA CRT exams.
6) **Issue:** 'Banking' of scores in NCLB.
   Problem: The high performing 8th and 9th grade students are completing the required high school math courses prior to high school.
   Desired outcome: Allow the 8th and 9th grade student scores to be 'banked' and used in the high school computations for NCLB.
7) **Issue:** Inclusion of LEP and special education students.
   Problem: LEP and special education students have different educational issues that are contrary to regular education students.
   Desired outcome: Do not include these students in NCLB.
8) **Issue:** A lack of flexibility in NCLB measurement models.
   Problem: SEAs have schools in school improvement.
   Desired outcome: Let SEAs be more creative in how they evaluate school systems so more schools will not be in school improvement.

Each of these issues in its own way contributes to the measurement and validity problems associated with NCLB. The demands provided in (1)–(8) represent some of the more interesting measurement issues in NCLB. The issue of LEP and special education students represents a desire to address some legitimate measurement concerns, but simply goes too far. Finally, the issue of flexibility can be addressed by reviewing Figure 29.1. In the mythical School A, the only methods by which this school meets the AMO is through the use of confidence intervals or index models.

A common theme of all eight demands and concerns is that they are attempts to 'expand' the ability to identify schools as meeting NCLB and will ultimately increase Type I error rate. Further, to varying degrees all eight have been approved for use by the USDOE, and create mechanisms for 'leaving children behind.' In other words, the application of these eight issues and concerns ultimately creates a mechanism within NCLB to leave students behind. NCLB, given the demonstrated measurement and statistical anomalies, challenges, and use of suspect approaches is not lacking in flexibility, or is there rampant Type II error, as is propagated by many anti-NCLB groups. In fact, a case can be made that given the many NCLB scoring systems, use of confidence intervals, etc., there is actually rampant Type I error.

Measurement, statistical, and policy recommendations for NCLB

The goal of NCLB is to ensure that ALL children have access to equitable learning opportunities in their school systems. Any measurement system associated with NCLB must ensure that this goal is maintained. However, as identified in this Chapter, many things do need to be addressed. A series of recommendations are provided as possible remedies include the following:

1) Test ALL students in Grades 4, 8, and 12 using the National Assessment of Educational Progress (NAEP) exam. It would help to provide a common metric and identify those SEAs with consistently higher student achievement. It will also help to validate the individual CRTs employed by the various SEAs.

2) Require growth models for SEAs, but require retrospective computations of actual student performance. Require each student to act as their own control in the model and adjust the growth relative to the initial start values so more advanced students who have minor 'relative' gains can be evaluated on a standardized scale. Basically, all students are expected to attain at least a minimum level of growth for one-year improvement. Students below the desired minimal performance level will continue to be expected to make gains that allow them to attain the SEA performance goal in a five-year period.

3) Require LEP students to complete the SEA CRT exams and an English Language Acquisition (ELA) exam. If a student is making gains on both the CRT and ELA, they can be considered to have met growth. Similar to (2), there needs to be an expectation for performance where students will transition to a non-LEP status in three years.

4) Special education students should be assessed but not included in NCLB until appropriate tests with sound psychometric properties have been developed and made available to SEAs. Once the exams have been developed and appropriate growth models can be implemented, these students can be included in NCLB determinations for schools. Additionally, these students, even before inclusion in NCLB, should be administered the SEA CRT exams to document academic attainment and progress. It is reasonable that in SWD programs students should be making 'progress.'

5) Reduce the minimum N size to 20 students for all schools and subgroups.

6) Eliminate the use of confidence intervals! If a school is required to test 100 per cent of students and does so, why is the percentage of students proficient considered a sample and thus warrants use of a confidence interval? Further, why use a 95 or 99 per cent confidence interval?

If you must apply a correction for measurement error it would be more appropriate to apply that confidence interval to a student's score on the CRT.

7) Have a national panel of psychometric testing and measurement experts identify and develop appropriate technical standards for state CRTs and alternative assessments.

A common method used in measurement is to apply multiple methods of assessing performance, and the case can be made that use of status and growth, various scoring models, etc., is consistent with good practice in assessment. However, the complexity of including multiple methods for evaluating proficiency and growth may have actually increased the number of students that will be 'left behind.' Too often in statistics and research design a natural inclination is to increase the complexity of measurement models to address threats to validity of the assessments. The above suggestions may seem simplistic, but these seven steps will address the seminal measurement and assessment challenges within NCLB.

Success of NCLB

The success of NCLB will continue to be a much debated topic. The intent of NCLB was to 'leave no child behind' by holding schools accountable for the education of all students. However, the measurement models developed as part of NCLB have evolved into a quagmire of measures that raise serious questions about the validity of the 'labels' assigned to school systems. However, there has been some face, internal, and external validity of many of the measurement models approved and employed as part of NCLB.

Face validity of NCLB
The issue of face validity of NCLB is evident when you examine schools that

do and do not meet NCLB. A great public source for data on the achievement of school systems as part of NCLB is the SchoolMatters website. This website provides the performance data for school systems in the US, including whether they met the various requirements of NCLB. If you examine the per cent of students proficient, it becomes clear that schools that have a higher percentage of students proficient are identified as meeting the performance goals. Thus, some evidence of face validity of NCLB measurement models.

Internal validity of NCLB
The various SEAs developed their own CRTs and established performance goals. If you examine the performance of schools in California relative to schools in Florida, you obtain a different perspective in terms of what constitutes an effective school system. The performance goals in reading for California and Florida are 25 per cent and 71 per cent of students proficient, respectively. The performance goals and tests are different, so direct comparison of the performance of school systems is not appropriate. However, if you examine the relative performance of school systems within each SEA, it is clear that the 'lower' performing schools are the ones being identified as not meeting the performance goals in both states. Thus, some internal validity for NCLB is evident with lower performing schools in both systems assigned lower performance labels within NCLB.

External validity of NCLB
The external validity of NCLB is best measured by examining a common metric for all US students. The only common metric available for this comparison is through use of the NAEP exam scores for students in grades 4, 8 and 12. The performance of students has been increasing

on the NAEP exam in the US. It is important that more objective measures, including testing ALL students with NAEP in Grades 4, 8, and 12, be implemented by USDOE to help provide additional evidence of external validity of the impact of NCLB. Further, compare performance on the NAEP to performance on SEA CRTs, but do so by linking individual scores on both exams. Peterson and Hess (2008) have developed a state report card using NAEP and CRT scores, but to improve the measurement model this study should be completed by linking individual student scores, not by comparison of composite performance scores on the respective exams.

Overall interpretation of NCLB

It is clear when examining national and international studies that the performance of US students has declined over the last 40 years. It is also clear when examining fiscal models of money spent on education, the US system is the best funded in the world (Fletcher, 2007). According to Common Core Data (CCD) from the National Center for Education Statistics, approximately $500 billion was spent by SEAs on K-12 education in 2006. An additional $50 billion was provided by the USDOE to support NCLB and other educational programs. The CCD also provides information that there are approximately 55 million students in the US system in 2006. Thus, on average in the US we annually spend approximately $11,000 per student. It is a well funded educational system!

NCLB was implemented to address strong concerns of business in the US that the 'product' of education needed to improve. The goals of NCLB are laudable, reasonable, and certainly not unattainable. However, the once simplistic goal of ensuring 'No Child Left Behind' has been transformed into a measurement and assessment nightmare. With so many measurement, statistical, and testing 'sleights of hand' evident, the question of validity is troubling. This leads back to one of my original concerns regarding NCLB: what impact will any failures in assessing the performance of our school systems have on the fields of measurement, statistics, and testing. If NCLB is ultimately deemed as unsuccessful, it is my hope this lack of success will be correctly attributed to educational policy and not inappropriately attributed to measurement and assessment methods.

REFERENCES

Cawelti, G. (2006) 'The side effects of NCLB', *Educational Leadership*, 64(3): 64–8.

Crocker, L. (2003) 'Teaching for the test: Validity, fairness, and moral action', *Educational Measurement: Issues and Practice*, 22(3): 5–11.

Dillon, S. (2005) 'Students ace state tests, but earn D's from US', *The New York Times*, November 26.

Duffy, M., Giordano, V., Farrell, J., Paneque, O, and Crump, G (2008) 'No Child Left Behind: Values and research issues in high stakes assessments', *Counseling and Values*, 53(3).

Ferguson, R. F. (1998) 'Can schools narrow the Black-White test score gap', in C. Jencks and M. Phillips (eds) *The Black-White test score gap*. Washington, DC: Brookings Institution Press. pp. 318–75.

Fletcher, G. (2007) 'Curriculum-based reform. An eye on the future', *T.H.E. Journal*, 34(7): 26–7.

Gong, B. (2004) 'Models for Using Student Growth Measures in School Accountability', Presentation at the 'Brain Trust' on Value-added Models sponsored by the Chief Council of State School Officers, Washington, DC November 15–16.

Goldhaber, D. (1999) 'School Choice: An examination of the empirical evidence on achievement, parental decision making, and equity', *Educational Researcher*, 28(9):16–25.

Hambleton, R. and Jones, R. (1993) 'Comparison of Classical Test Theory and Item Response Theory and Their Applications to Test Development', [On-Line] Available: http://ncme.org/pubs/items/24.pdf

Hoff, D. (2006) Big Business Going to Bat for NCLB. [On-line] Available: http://www.edweek.org/ew/

articles/2006/10/18/08biz.h26.htmlandlevelId= 2100

Jerald, C. (2000) 'The state of the states', *Quality counts 2000: Who should teach?* [On-line]. Available: http://www.edweek.org/sreports/qc00/templates/ article.cfm?slug=sosintro.htm

Leithwood, K. (1992) 'Editor's conclusion: What have we learned and where to we go from here?' *School Effectiveness and School Improvement*, 3(2): 173–84.

Linn, R. (2002) 'Accountability systems: Implications of requirements of the no child left behind act of 2001', *Educational Researcher*, 31(6): 3–16.

Morton, K., and Mulvenon, S. (2007) *Highly qualified teachers and teacher examination passing scores.* Paper presented at the annual conference of the American Educational Research Association, Chicago, IL.

Peterson, P., and Hess, R. (2008) 'Few states set world class standards', *Education Next*, Summer: 70–73.

Porter, A., Linn, R. and Trimble, S. (2005) 'The effects of state decisions about NCLB adequate yearly progress targets', *Educational Measurement: Issues and Practices*, 24(4): 32–9.

US Department of Education (2009a) Standards and Assessment Group and Accountability Group. [On-line] Available: http://www.ed.gov/admins/lead/ account/saa.html

US Department of Education (2009b) Evaluation of the 2005–2006 Growth Model Pilot Program. [On-line] Available: http://ed.gov/admins/lead/ account/growthmodel/gmeval0109.doc

Author Index

General Index